P9-CST-681

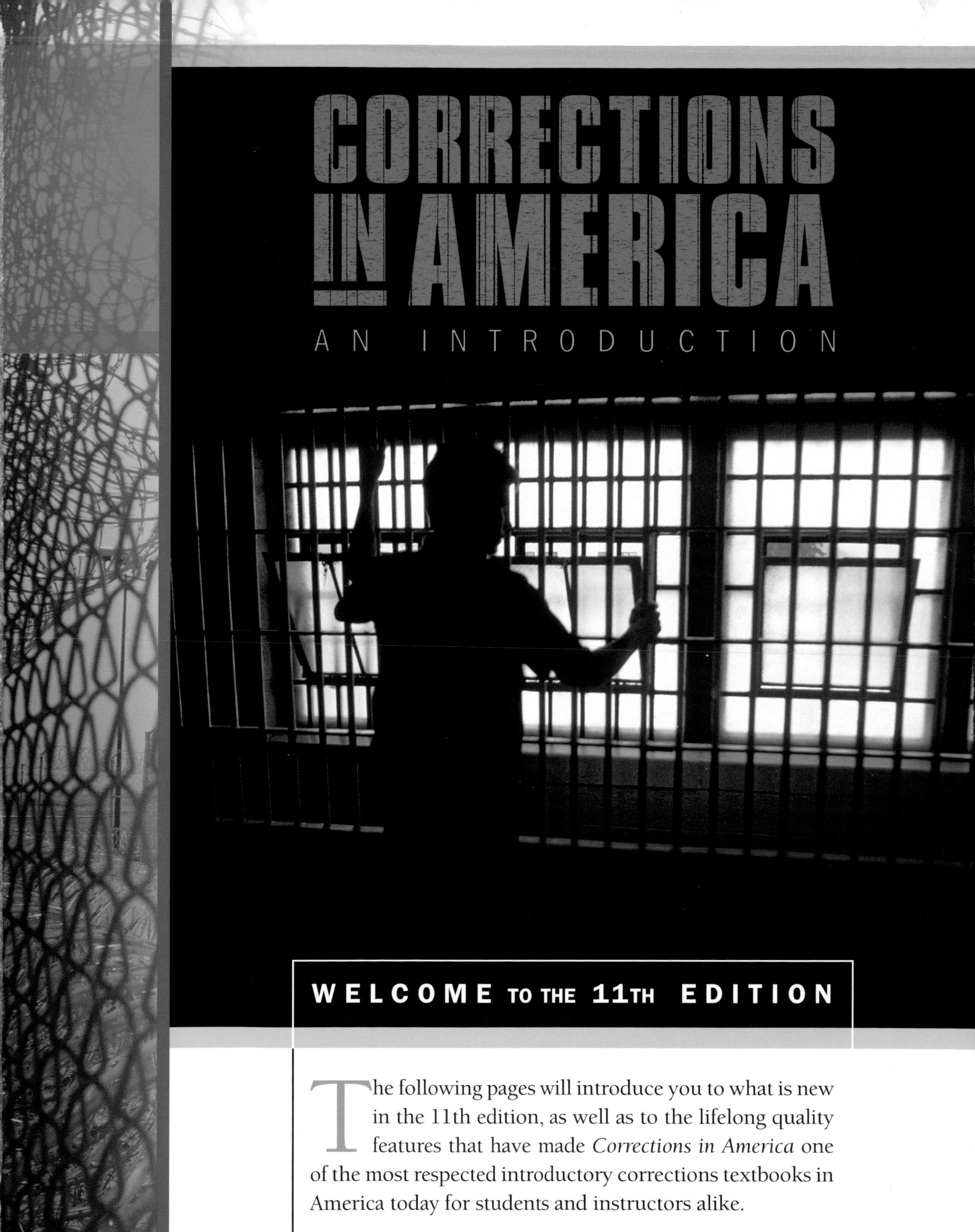

CORRECTIONS IN AMERICA

AN INTRODUCTION

WELCOME TO THE 11TH EDITION

The following pages will introduce you to what is new in the 11th edition, as well as to the lifelong quality features that have made *Corrections in America* one of the most respected introductory corrections textbooks in America today for students and instructors alike.

CONTEMPORARY TOPICS AND MAJOR ISSUES

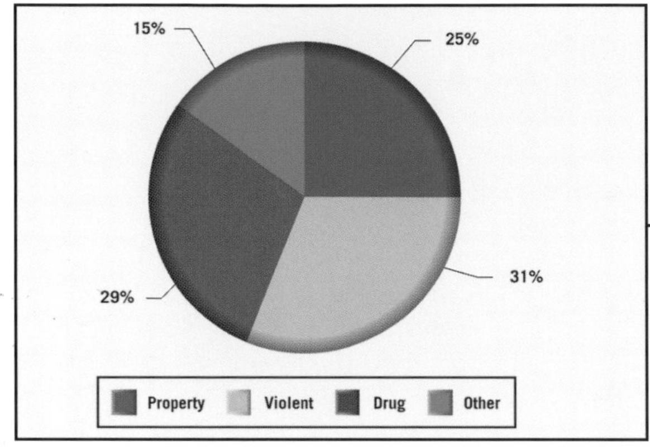

Current and Up-to-Date Information
The most recent data, statistics, and correctional information available

Expanded Coverage of Incarcerated Terrorists

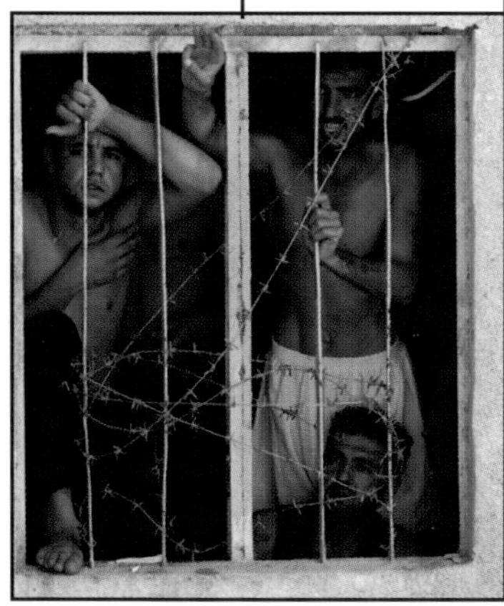

THE DEATH PENALTY AND TERRORISM

The federal government and the U.S Code of Military Justice have death penalty statutes that permit capital punishment for designated offenses. The accused would be tried in either a federal court or military tribunal, depending on the jurisdiction. If tried in federal court, the panoply of rights, immunities, and protections afforded under the U.S. Constitution would apply, including rules of procedure and evidence. The U.S. Code of Military Justice restricts many of the rights otherwise available to civilians. At the time of this writing, it is unclear which, if either, jurisdiction would be appropriate for terrorists.

By midyear 2005, a number of captured Taliban and al-Qaeda prisoners had been taken to military detention camp "X-ray" at Guantanamo Bay, Cuba. Detainees are believed to pose a threat to the United States or have intelligence value. Exactly how many detainees and their identities are unknown, although plans are to build 2,000 cells on this site and a permanent 200-bed military prison. Detainees may face a military trial, a trial in U.S. courts, prosecution in their homelands if returned, or trial in an international court. The first two of those options could result in the death penalty.

Expanded Coverage of Female Offenders

Expanded Coverage of Reentry

REENTRY: THE NEW CHALLENGE

The large number of incarcerated offenders in the United States has led to the inevitable result—numerous offenders will reenter society each year. In fact, reentry has become the new buzzword used by policy makers to describe the process by which offenders come back into the community. Some have argued that parole is essential to this process,[23] while others[24] believe that since a high percentage of offenders pose minimal risk to public safety, parole supervision should be eliminated or shortened to about six months. Given estimates that a significant percentage of offenders who will be returning to the community have a number of important needs,[25] little doubt remains that services and treatment in the community should be an important part of the reentry process. Indeed, several states have already created reentry programs designed to coordinate efforts and services between the institution, parole, and community correctional programs and treatment providers.

Expanded Coverage of Special Category Offenders

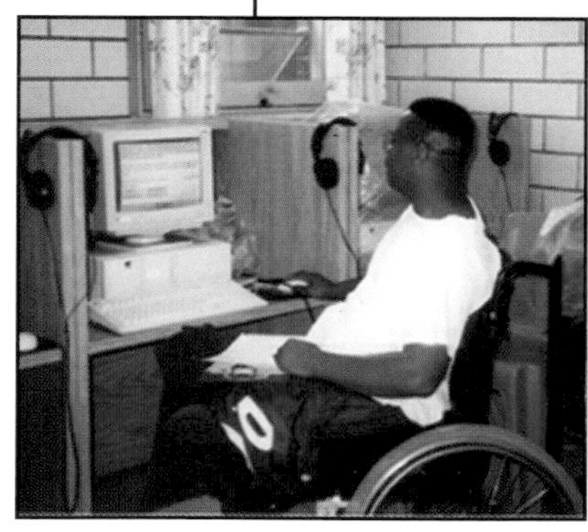

Student CD-ROM

An integrated multimedia learning tool that reinforces key information from the text; also includes video clips of the authors and leading criminologists discussing the issues facing today's world of corrections

Harry Allen

Edward Latessa

Francis Cullen

Deborah Wilson

PEARSON Prentice Hall

CORRECTIONS IN AMERICA AN INTRODUCTION ALLEN • LATESSA PONDER • SIMONSEN Eleventh Edition

Home | Select Chapter: TOC 1 2 3 4 5 6 7 8 9 10 11 12 13 14 15 more >> | Site Search: Go

Corrections in America: An Introduction

Eleventh Edition

Harry E. Allen
Edward J. Latessa
Bruce S. Ponder
Clifford E. Simonsen

Special thanks to Bruce Ponder for Web content development

Welcome to the World Wide Web online study guide for *Corrections in America: An Introduction, 11e*. This Companion Website supports the Allen/Latessa/Ponder/Simonsen *Corrections in America* textbook. New to this edition are Video Overviews by the authors that introduce each chapter. In addition to the Video Overviews, this valuable Companion Website consists of a glossary of terms, resource links for career information, research projects and essays, suggested reading for in-depth study of the major points in that chapter, a set of review questions that will focus your study and help prepare for exams, and much more. Let this exciting ancillary aid in the speed of your study and enrich your entire learning experience.

Please select a chapter above to begin this study guide.

Companion Website

Updated with links to current reports and articles in corrections and a plethora of study questions for review

UPDATED AND EXPANDED CHAPTER LEARNING TOOLS

Overview
Provides a brief explanation of the various topics covered in the chapter

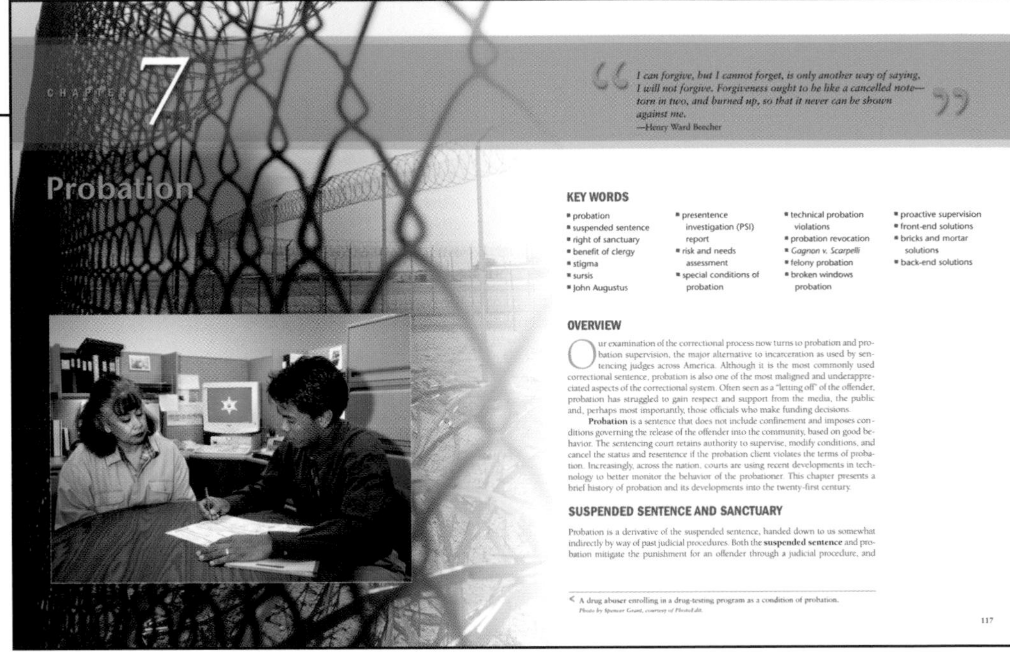

CHAPTER 7

Probation

I can forgive, but I cannot forget, is only another way of saying, I will not forgive. Forgiveness ought to be like a cancelled note—torn in two, and burned up, so that it never can be shown against me.
—Henry Ward Beecher

KEY WORDS

- probation
- suspended sentence
- right of sanctuary
- benefit of clergy
- stigma
- sursis
- John Augustus
- presentence investigation (PSI) report
- risk and needs assessment
- special conditions of probation
- technical probation violations
- probation revocation
- *Gagnon v. Scarpelli*
- felony probation
- broken windows probation
- proactive supervision
- front-end solutions
- bricks and mortar solutions
- back-end solutions

OVERVIEW

Our examination of the correctional process now turns to probation and probation supervision, the major alternative to incarceration as used by sentencing judges across America. Although it is the most commonly used correctional sentence, probation is also one of the most maligned and underappreciated aspects of the correctional system. Often seen as a "letting off" of the offender, probation has struggled to gain respect and support from the media, the public and, perhaps most importantly, those officials who make funding decisions.

Probation is a sentence that does not include confinement and imposes conditions governing the release of the offender into the community, based on good behavior. The sentencing court retains authority to supervise, modify conditions, and cancel the status and resentence if the probation client violates the terms of probation. Increasingly, across the nation, courts are using recent developments in technology to better monitor the behavior of the probationer. This chapter presents a brief history of probation and its developments into the twenty-first century.

SUSPENDED SENTENCE AND SANCTUARY

Probation is a derivative of the suspended sentence, handed down to us somewhat indirectly by way of past judicial procedures. Both the **suspended sentence** and probation mitigate the punishment for an offender through a judicial procedure, and

< A drug abuser enrolling in a drug-testing program as a condition of probation.

117

SIDEBARS

Plea Bargaining

Plea bargaining refers to the prosecutor's practice of permitting the defendant to plead to a lesser charge than the one he or she was arrested for, usually because the prosecutor does not feel the case is strong enough on the more serious charge or because the prosecutor hopes to persuade the defendant to provide information about other crimes or offenders. Plea bargaining may lead to the prosecutor agreeing to dismiss multiple charges, reduce charges, or recommend a light sentence. The gains that offenders are alleged to secure by plea bargaining may be less than anticipated, if not ephemeral, in many cases.

Sidebar
Includes expanded definitions and a fresh understanding of the latest correctional topics, legal issues, and controversial policies and practices

Correctional Brief
Short and intuitive vignettes on historical data, correctional facts, and articles discussing the current trends affecting today's world of corrections

Disparate Sentencing for Crack and Cocaine Use

In 1986, Congress created sentencing disparity for two of the most popular types of cocaine: powdered and crack (crystal). The sale of five grams of crack cocaine—barely a teaspoon full—results in a minimum of five years in federal prison for the violator. Sale of 100 times that amount of powdered cocaine—the type preferred by whites—is required to result in a comparable sentence. About 90 percent of those convicted of selling crack cocaine are black, and only 30 percent of those convicted of selling powdered cocaine are black. When the U.S. Sentencing Commission recommended changing the sentencing guidelines to equalize sentencing, both the U.S. House and Senate voted to block any change in the 100-to-1 ratio.

SOURCE: Michael Isikoff, "Crack, Coke, and Race," *Newsweek* (November 6, 1995): 77.

Correctional Profile
First-hand representations of key figures in the field of corrections or infamous criminal offenders and prisoners

Robert Stroud (1890–1963), named the "Birdman of Alcatraz," was possibly the most famous inmate in the federal prison at Alcatraz. He was a violent and murderous felon who killed a guard in front of 1,100 inmates. Later in life, he studied canaries and authored two books on canaries and their diseases. The special equipment to study canaries in his cell was used as a still for an alcoholic brew. He served fifty-four years in prison, forty-one of them in solitary confinement.

SUMMARY

At midyear 2005, 972 men and women had died by state execution since the day Gary Gilmore was shot through the heart in 1977. The U.S. Supreme Court has streamlined and expedited its procedures for appellate review and seems to have tackled the issue of capital punishment head-on. However, the death rows in thirty-eight states are packed, with over 3,500 convicted persons sentenced to die by hanging, electrocution, lethal injection, gas, or the firing squad.

After it showed clearly what provisions it was willing to accept with regard to the death penalty in *Gregg*, the Supreme Court has been relatively supportive of the states' implementing them. It is clear, however, that the limited circumstances acceptable for the ultimate punishment must be administered on a scrupulously equitable basis or the Supreme Court may hold that even such limited application of the sanction of death is unconstitutional. The matter of equity is the one that must be watched during the next few years, as the number of admissions to death row continues.

Finally, while the death penalty is a large chalkboard on which the basic rights of citizens are charted, only a small percentage of imprisoned offenders are on death row. Most will serve their sentences and be released to reenter society. We now turn to parole and inmate reentry.

Chapter Summary
Reinforces and details important concepts, major points, references, and the impact of each topic discussed

Corrections in America

ELEVENTH EDITION

Corrections in America

An Introduction

HARRY E. ALLEN, PH.D.
San Jose State University

EDWARD J. LATESSA, PH.D.
University of Cincinnati

BRUCE S. PONDER
Allen Ponder Associates

CLIFFORD E. SIMONSEN, PH.D.
Criminology Consultants International

UPPER SADDLE RIVER, NEW JERSEY 07458

Library of Congress Cataloging-in-Publication Data
Corrections in America: an introduction / Harry E. Allen . . . [et al.].—11th ed.
p. cm.
Rev. ed. of: Corrections in America / Harry E. Allen, Clifford E. Simonsen, Edward J. Latessa. 10th ed. c2004.
Includes bibliographical references and index.
ISBN 0-13-195085-1 (alk. paper)
1. Corrections—United States. I. Allen, Harry E. II. Allen, Harry E. Corrections in America.
HV9304.A63 2007
364.60973—dc22
2005025178

Executive Editor: Frank Mortimer, Jr.
Assistant Editor: Mayda Bosco
Marketing Manager: Adam Kloza
Editorial Assistant: Kelly Krug
Production Editor: Lori Dalberg, Carlisle Editorial Services
Production Liaison: Barbara Marttine Cappuccio
Director of Manufacturing and Production: Bruce Johnson
Managing Editor: Mary Carnis
Manufacturing Manager: Ilene Sanford
Manufacturing Buyer: Cathleen Petersen
Senior Design Coordinator: Mary Siener
Interior Design: Wanda España
Cover Designer: Jonathan Boylan
Cover Image: Dennis MacDonald/Photo Edit
Manager of Media Production: Amy Peltier
Media Production Project Manager: Lisa Rinaldi
Director, Image Resource Center: Melinda Reo
Manager, Rights and Permissions: Zina Arabia
Manager, Visual Research: Beth Brenzel
Manager, Cover Visual Research & Permissions: Karen Sanatar
Image Permission Coordinator: Richard Rodrigues
Photo Researcher: Elaine Soares
Formatting: Carlisle Publishing Services
Printing and Binding: Courier Kendallville

Pearson Education LTD.
Pearson Education Singapore, Pte. Ltd.
Pearson Education Canada, Ltd.
Pearson Education—Japan
Pearson Education Australia PTY. Limited
Pearson Education North Asia Ltd.
Pearson Educación de Mexico, S. A. de C.V.
Pearson Education Malaysia Pte. Ltd.

10 9 8 7 6 5 4 3 2 1
ISBN 0-13-195085-1
ISBN 0-13-172621-8

DEDICATION

To J. Hunter Allen, Sr., Jacquie, and the Allen family
Harry Allen

To the love of my life, Sally, and our four children:
Amy, Jennifer, Michael, and Allison
Edward Latessa

To Beverly, Fred, Marissa, and Steven
Bruce S. Ponder

To my dear wife Fran as well as to son Rick and his wife Cindy, to daughter Sheri and her partner Tracy, and to our two fine grandsons, Kris and Kori . . . I love you all
Clifford Simonsen

BRIEF CONTENTS

CONTENTS

ACKNOWLEDGMENTS

We would like to acknowledge the great assistance of people who merit special recognition in the eleventh edition of *Corrections in America*. Instructors, former students, and doctoral graduates were generous in pointing out the strengths and weaknesses of the tenth edition, and made considerable suggestions for improving the textbook. Fortunately, we took them seriously and have benefited from their inputs. Our formal reviewers heaped praise where there might be praise and uniformly agreed on subjects deserving more attention. We would like to thank these conscientious reviewers: Professor Kim Cattat, State University of New York, Brockport; Professor Ronald Iacovetta, Wichita State University, Wichita, Kansas; Professor Kathleen Nicolaides, University of North Carolina, Charlotte; and Professor Sonya Splane, Everest College, Phoenix, Arizona.

Frank Mortimer is a great editor with whom to work, keeping us uplifted by humor and gently prodded for performance. Mayda Bosco handled numerous details, taking many onerous duties off our shoulders while we rewrote, edited, amended, corrected, expanded, and repaired. Mary Carnis helped with fine suggestions about preparation of the manuscript, and encouraged us throughout production. Barbara Cappuccio was immensely helpful in the photograph and permissions areas. The media gurus of John Jordan, Amy Peltier, and Jody Small encouraged and stimulated us at every turn. Lori Dalberg labored with humor and diligence during her masterly effort to put the textbook together (and correct the authors' errors). To all, we say thank you!

Finally, we acknowledge our families who shouldered much absence from us, humored us, handled our human needs, bolstered us in despondency, and were there when we needed them. We could not have done it without you.

Harry E. Allen
Edward J. Latessa
Bruce S. Ponder
Clifford E. Simonsen

ABOUT THE AUTHORS

Harry E. Allen is Professor Emeritus in the Administration of Justice Department at San Jose State University, since 1997. Before joining San Jose State University in 1978, he served as Director of the Program for the Study of Crime and Delinquency at The Ohio State University. Previously, he served as Executive Secretary of the Governor's Task Force on Corrections for the State of Ohio, after teaching at Florida State University in the Department of Criminology and Corrections.

Professor Allen is the author or coauthor of numerous articles, chapters in books, essays, and textbooks, to include the first ten editions of *Corrections in America* with Clifford E. Simonsen, and the first three editions of *Corrections in the Community,* with Edward J. Latessa. He has been very active in professional associations and was the first criminologist to serve as President of both the American Society of Criminology and the Academy of Criminal Justice Sciences. He received the Herbert Block Award for service to the American Society of Criminology and the Founder's Award for contributions to the Academy of Criminal Justice Sciences. He is a Fellow in both the Western and American Societies of Criminology. He currently is designing and instructing online courses for the University of Louisville in the areas of ethics, computer applications, community corrections, terrorism, and alternatives to incarceration.

Edward J. Latessa is a Professor and Head of the Division of Criminal Justice at the University of Cincinnati. He received his Ph.D. in 1979 from The Ohio State University. Dr. Latessa has published more than seventy-five works in the area of criminal justice, corrections, and juvenile justice. He is coauthor of seven books including *Corrections in the Community,* which is now in its third edition. Professor Latessa has directed more than sixty-five funded research projects including, studies of day reporting centers, juvenile justice programs, drug courts, intensive supervision programs, halfway houses, and drug programs. He and his staff have also assessed more than 400 correctional programs throughout the United States. Dr. Latessa is a consultant with the National Institute of Corrections, and he has provided assistance and workshops in more than forty states. Dr. Latessa served as President of the Academy of Criminal Justice Sciences (1989–1990). He has also received several awards including the August Vollmer Award from the American Society of Criminology (2004), the Simon Dinitz Criminal Justice Research Award from the Ohio Department of Rehabilitation and Correction (2002), the Margaret Mead Award for dedicated service to the causes of social justice and humanitarian advancement by the International Community Corrections Association (2001), the Peter P. Lejins Award for Research from the American Correctional Association (1999); ACJS Fellow Award (1998); ACJS Founders Award (1992); and the Simon Dinitz award by the Ohio Community Corrections Organization. He and his wife Sally have four beautiful children.

Bruce S. Ponder grew up in part on the raj of the Maharaja of Dharbhanga and in Europe. He was a professional race car driver in the 1970s, winning major competitions including the "12-Hours of Sebring" (1972). He was formally trained in political science, and computer information systems and computer sciences. He has also studied terrorism extensively and team-taught in-service training programs on terrorism at the Southern Police Institute. Currently he is Internet coordinator and team instructor in a variety of courses in Justice Administration at the University of Louisville, particularly terrorism and corrections.

Clifford E. Simonsen has broad experience in correctional and security management (military and civilian) from jails to prisons and retail loss prevention, to premises, hospitals, and even nuclear weapons sites. He has a bachelor's degree in Law Enforcement and Corrections from the University of Nebraska at Omaha, a master's degree in Criminology and Corrections from Florida State University, and a master's degree and Ph.D. in Criminal Justice Administration from The Ohio State University with an emphasis in correctional administration. He was awarded the Certified Protection Professional (CPP) by the Professional Certification Board of the American Society for Industrial Security and lifetime membership by the International Society for Industrial Security for service to the profession. Dr. Simonsen commanded Criminal Investigation Detachments and conducted oversight of correctional facilities in Europe and Asia. A graduate of the Army Command and General Staff College, Industrial College of the Armed Forces (National Security), and the Army War College, he retired as a Colonel from the U.S. Army Military Police.

Dr. Simonsen has managed major high-security jails and correctional facilities that required constant monitoring of security systems and dealing with criminal and deviant behavior. He has authored or coauthored several textbooks on crime and criminal justice, to include ten editions of *Corrections in America,* with Harry Allen; *Private Security in America: An Introduction; Juvenile Justice in America: An Introduction;* and *Terrorism Today;* with Jeremy Spindlove, for Prentice Hall. As President of Criminology Consultants International, his consulting firm, he has testified (defense and plaintiff) as an expert witness in many cases involving negligent security and security operational issues and torts in correctional agencies and facilities. He has taught at several universities and is presently an adjunct at City University in Renton, Washington.

PART

1 Historical Perspectives

THE FOLLOWING CHAPTERS ARE COVERED IN PART 1:

OVERVIEW

A crucial question in corrections is "Who are offenders and what shall we do with them?" Part 1 deals with the process by which punishment originated as a private matter between an offending party and the victim but later came to be an official state function. Significant changes over time are examined, starting with 2000 B.C. and continuing through contemporary efforts to construct places of punishment and reform. Behind each of the four major answers to the crucial question lay assumptions about the nature of offenders and what to do with them. Part 1 details these perceptions, assumptions, and answers, as well as corresponding correctional practices and fads that have emerged during the last 4,000 years.

CHAPTER 1

Early History

(2000 B.C. to A.D. 1800)

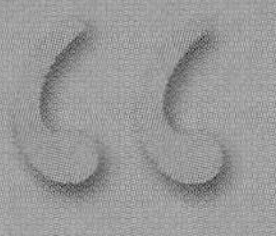

The descent to hell is easy. The gates stand open day and night. But to reclimb the slope and escape to the upper air: this is labor.

—Virgil, Aeneid, Book 6

KEY WORDS

- folkways
- mores
- laws
- retaliation
- blood feud
- vendetta
- *lex salica*
- *wergeld*
- *friedensgeld*
- outlaw
- *lex talionis*
- civil death
- "get right with God"
- Inquisition
- corporal punishment
- brank
- cat-o'-nine-tails
- *lex eterna*
- *lex naturalis*
- *lex humana*
- Mamertine Prison
- sanctuary
- Bridewell
- Age of Enlightenment
- Cesare Beccaria
- Classical School
- utilitarianism
- "hedonistic calculus"
- John Howard
- jail fever
- workhouse
- gaols
- banishment
- transportation
- hulks
- Maison de Force
- Hospice of San Michele
- William Penn
- Great Law
- penitentiary
- Walnut Street Jail
- Pennsylvania system

OVERVIEW

This textbook is not intended to be an in-depth history of corrections nor a dissertation on its legal aspects. It is helpful, however, to know at least a little of the fascinating historical background (legal and social) to gain an improved understanding of the concepts, practices, and operations that we will discuss later, and how we got to where corrections is today as we enter the twenty-first century. In describing this background, we avoid technical jargon to keep misunderstanding to a minimum. Where appropriate, specific individuals and events that have influenced the history of corrections are detailed in the profiles, sidebars, and briefs for easy reference and clarification.

It is important to study the growing field of corrections for a variety of reasons. This dynamic field is undergoing rapid, mind-boggling change. In the interest of reducing crime, protecting children, salvaging redeemable offenders, and increasing citizen and society safety, the nation has entered into an unprecedented prison construction program. Every two weeks, the nation needs to construct and open a 900-bed prison

< The only torture chamber that still exists intact. Johannes Kepler was a famous seventeenth century scientist in Germany. Kepler's mother was accused of being a witch. He saved her from the torture chamber by appealing to Emperor Mattias, Imperial Diet, Regensburg, Germany.

Photo by Erich Lessing, courtesy of Art Resource, New York.

and hire at least 150 new correctional officers! Corrections, as a major industry, needs to be able to find and hire competent, educated, and motivated persons.

Never have so many Americans been in the arms of the law and under correctional control; never has the percentage of the citizenry incarcerated been as high as at the end of the twentieth century. The size of this growing sector is rapidly increasing and—measured by the number of employees, offenders, and budgets—still undergoing significant growth.

Corrections impacts the lives of ordinary people almost daily. Employees of prisons (as well as probation and parole officers) are in immediate contact with frequently violent and aggressive offenders, much more so than the typical municipal police officer who, in a busy week, may interact once with such an offender. The populace in general, and students of corrections in particular, must understand the dynamics that affect all forms of correctional work. They also must understand criminal behavior, to better cope with the variety of offenders and to deal effectively with problematic clients. These factors are explored throughout this textbook and your instructor will help you gain the necessary knowledge to begin your journey into this fascinating field. We begin now by tracing the roots of corrections back to the early beginnings of civilization, as we know it.

BEHAVIOR AS A CONTINUUM

Behavior in social groups, whether they are primitive tribes or complex modern nations, can be looked on as points on a simple continuum, as shown in Figure 1.1. In all societies, certain acts or groups of acts have been universally discouraged, or proscribed. Such acts include murder, rape, kidnapping, and treason (or some form of rebellion against the group authority). By contrast, most societies have encouraged, or prescribed, such other behaviors as having children, marrying, hunting, growing food, and other actions that benefit the common welfare.

Folkways, Mores, and Laws

- Folkways are traditional social customs, including ways of thinking, feeling, or acting common to a group of people.
- Mores are the binding moral attitudes, habits, customs, and manners of a particular group of people.
- Laws are rules of conduct formally recognized as binding and are defined and enforced by a controlling authority.

Behavior that is situated toward the center of the continuum from either end is usually controlled by a set of social rules called **folkways.** These rules are enforced by means of mild discouragement (the raising of an eyebrow, staring, or a look of shock) or by mild encouragement (applause or a smile). Actions farther out on either end of the continuum, which serve either to perpetuate or to threaten the group's existence, are controlled by a stronger set of rules called **mores.** In the beginning, mores were enforced by means of strong social discouragement (verbal abuse, beatings, temporary ostracism, or even banishment) or strong encouragement (dowries, secure social or financial status, or fertility rites), and those informal controls still protect certain mores today. But as societies became more

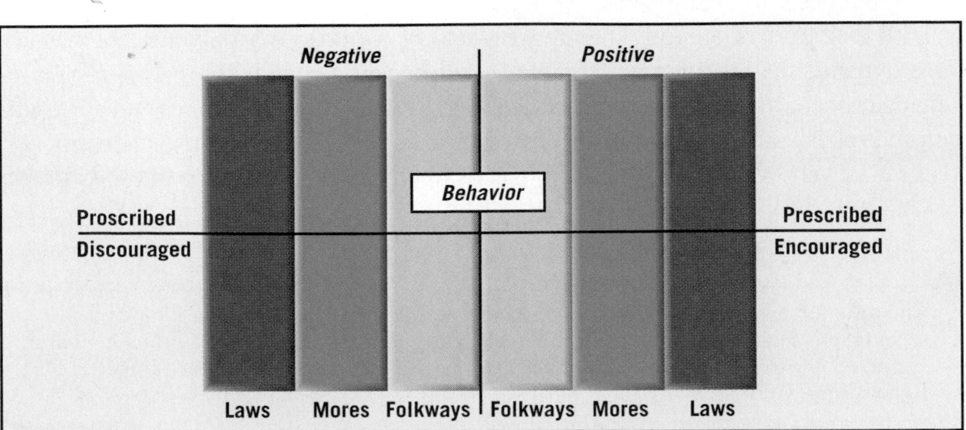

FIGURE 1.1

The Continuum of Behavior

complex, they devised more structured sanctions to prevent violation of the mores that were essential to the group's survival. These sanctions have been codified in the form of written rules, or **laws,** and the reward for obeying those laws is simply the ability to continue to function as a respected and productive member of society.

REDRESS OF WRONGS

Retaliation

The earliest remedy for wrongs done to one's person or property was simply to retaliate against the wrongdoer. In early primitive societies, personal **retaliation** was accepted and even encouraged by members of the tribal group. This ancient concept of personal revenge could hardly be considered "law." Yet it has influenced the development of most legal systems, especially English criminal law, from which most American criminal law derives.

The practice of personal retaliation was later augmented by the **blood feud,** in which the victim's family or tribe took revenge on the offender's family or tribe. Because this form of retaliation could easily escalate and result in an endless battle or **vendetta** between the injured factions, some method of control had to be devised to make blood feuds less costly and damaging.

The practice of retaliation usually begins to develop into a system of criminal law when it becomes customary for the victim of the wrongdoing to accept money or property in place of blood vengeance. This custom, when established, is usually dictated by tribal tradition and the relative positions of power between the injured party and the wrongdoer. Custom has always exerted great force among primitive societies. The acceptance of vengeance in the form of a payment (such as cattle, food, or personal services) was usually not compulsory, however, and victims were still free to take whatever vengeance they wished. Legal historians Albert Kocourek and John Wigmore described this pressure to retaliate:

> *It must not be forgotten that the right of personal revenge was also in many cases a duty. A man was bound by all the force of religion to avenge the death of his kinsman. This duty was by universal practice imposed upon the nearest male relative—the avenger of blood, as he is called in the Scripture accounts.*[1]

The custom of atonement for wrongs by payment to appease the victim's family or tribe became known as ***lex salica*** (or ***wergeld,*** in Europe). It is still in effect in many Middle Eastern and Far Eastern countries, with the amount of payment based on the injured person's rank and position in the social group.

SIDEBARS

Origins of Fines

Friedensgeld was the practice of paying restitution to the Crown, in addition to individuals, for crimes. It later replaced payment to individuals and became the system of fines paid to the state. With fines, the victim disappeared from the criminal justice system, becoming the ignored component of the crime.

Fines and Punishments

How did these simple, voluntary programs become part of an official system of fines and punishments? As tribal leaders, elders, and (later) kings came into power,[2] they began to exert their authority on the negotiations. Wrongdoers could choose to stay away from the proceedings; this was their right. But if they refused to abide by the imposed sentence, they were declared to be outside the law of the tribe (nation, family), or an **outlaw.** There is little doubt that outlawry, or exile, was the first punishment imposed by society,[3] and it heralded the beginning of criminal law as we now know it.

Criminal law, even primitive criminal law, requires an element of public action against the wrongdoer—as in a pronouncement of outlawry. Before this element of public action, the backgrounds of criminal law and sanctions seem to have

SIDEBARS

Two Ways to Pay for Homicide

Lex salica was the fine paid for homicide, and it varied according to the rank, sex, and age of the murdered person. In general, *lex salica* refers to a payment for death or injury. *Wergeld,* which means "man-money," originally referred to the death of an individual and the individual's supposed value to his or her family. It later referred to personal injury as well.

been parallel in most legal systems. The subsequent creation of legal codes and sanctions for different crimes either stressed or refined the vengeance factor, according to the particular society's values.

EARLY CODES

Babylonian and Sumerian Codes

Even primitive ethics demanded that a society express its vengeance within a system of regulations and rules. Moses was advised to follow the "eye for eye and tooth for tooth" doctrine stated in Exodus 21:24, but this concept of ***lex talionis*** is far older than the Bible; it appears in the Sumerian codes (1860 B.C.) and in the 1750 B.C. code of King Hammurabi of Babylon, compiled more than 500 years before the *Book of the Covenant* (1250 B.C.).

As early societies developed language and writing skills, they began attempting to record the laws of their nations. While most historians view the Hammurabic Code as the first comprehensive attempt at codifying social interaction, the Sumerian codes preceded it by about a century, and the principle of *lex talionis* was evident in both. The punishments handed out under these codes were harsh and based on vengeance (or *talion*), in many cases being inflicted by the injured party. In the Babylonian code, more than twenty-four offenses called for the penalty of death. Both codes also prescribed mutilation, whipping, or forced labor as punishments for numerous crimes.

The kinds of punishments applied to slaves and bonded servants have been cited by many scholars[4] as the origin of the punishments that in later law applied to all offenders. As stated by historian Gustav Radbruch:

> *Applied earlier almost exclusively to slaves, [the mutilating penalties] became used more and more on freemen during the Carolingian period [*A.D. *640–1012] and especially for offenses that betokened a base and servile mentality. Up to the end of the Carolingian era, punishments "to hide and hair" were overwhelmingly reserved for slaves. Even death penalties occurred as slave punishments and account for the growing popularity of such penalties in Carolingian times. The aggravated death penalties, combining corporal and capital punishments, have their roots in the penal law governing slaves.*[5]

The early punishments were considered synonymous with slavery; those punished even had their heads shaved, indicating the "mark of the slave."[6] In Roman days, the extensive use of penal servitude was spurred by the need for workers to perform hard labor in the great public works. The sentence to penal servitude was generally reserved for the lower classes; it usually meant life in chains, working in the mines or rowing in the galleys or ships, or building the public works planned by the government. The sentences carried with them the complete loss of citizenship and liberty until they died, and were classed, along with exile and death, as capital punishment. Penal servitude, or **civil death**, meant that the offender's property was confiscated in the name of the state and that his wife was declared a widow, eligible to remarry. To society, the criminal sentenced to penal servitude was, in effect, "dead."

Crime and Sin

Punishment of the individual in the name of the state also included the concept of superstitious revenge. Here crime was entangled with sin, and punishment in the form of *wergeld* (payment to the victim) or *friedensgeld* (payment to the state) was not sufficient. If society believed the crime might have offended a divinity, the accused had to undergo a long period of progressively harsher punishment to appease the gods. As time passed, the zone between church law and state law became more blurred, and the concept of personal responsibility for one's act was combined with the need to **"get right with God."**[7] The early codes, even the Ten Commandments, were designed to make the offender's punishment acceptable to both society and God.

Roman and Greek Codes

In the sixth century A.D., Emperor Justinian of Rome wrote his code of laws, one of the most ambitious early efforts to match a desirable amount of punishment with all possible crimes. Roman art of the period depicts the "scales of justice," a metaphor demanding that the punishment balance the crime. Justinian's effort, as might be expected, bogged down in the far-flung empire's morass of administrative details that were required to enforce it. The Code of Justinian did not survive the fall of the Roman Empire, but it left the foundation on which most of the Western world's legal codes were eventually built.

In Greece, the harsh Code of Draco provided the same penalties for both citizens and slaves, incorporating many of the concepts used in primitive societies (for example, vengeance, outlawry, and blood feuds). The Greeks were the first society to allow any of their citizens to prosecute an offender in the name of the injured party. This clearly illustrated that during that period the public interest and protection of the social order were becoming more important than individual injury and individual vengeance.

The Middle Ages

The Middle Ages was a long period of general social disorder. Vast changes in the social structure and the growing influence of the church on everyday life resulted in a divided system of justice. Reformation was viewed as a process of religious, not secular, redemption. As in early civilizations, the sinner had to pay two debts, one to society and another to God. The "ordeal" was the church's substitute for a trial by the leadership of the secular group, until the practice was abolished in A.D. 1215. In trials by ordeal, subjecting the accused to impossible, dangerous, or painful tests, in the belief that those who were truly innocent would emerge unscathed, whereas the guilty would suffer agonies and die, determined guilt or innocence. The brutality of most trials by ordeal ensured a very high percentage of convictions.

The church expanded the concept of crime to include some new areas, still reflected in modern codes. During the Middle Ages, sexual activity other than for the purpose of procreation was seen as especially sinful. Sexual offenses usually involved either public or "unnatural" acts, and they provoked horrible punishments, as did heresy and witchcraft. The church justified cruel reprisals as a means of saving the unfortunate sinner from the clutches of Satan. The zealous movement to stamp out heresy brought on the **Inquisition** and its use of the most vicious tortures imaginable to gain "confessions" and "repentance" from alleged heretics. Thousands upon thousands of persons died at the hands of the Inquisition in Spain and Holland, where these sometimes inhumane methods were the most extensively used. Punishment was not viewed as an end in itself, but as the offender's only hope of pacifying a wrathful God.

The main contribution of the medieval church to our study of corrections is the concept of free will. This idea assumes that individuals choose their actions,

SIDEBARS

The Inquisition

The Inquisition was a tribunal established by the Catholic Church in the Middle Ages with very wide powers for the suppression of heresy. The tribunal searched out heretics and other offenders rather than waiting for charges to be brought forward (somewhat in the manner of former Senator Joseph McCarthy, who rooted out so-called communists in the early 1950s). Emperor Frederick II made the Inquisition a formal institution in 1224, and it lasted until 1834.

good or bad, and thus can be held fully responsible for them. The religious doctrines of eternal punishment, atonement, and spiritual conversion rest on the assumption that individuals who commit sins could have acted differently if they had chosen to do so.

The early codes and their administration were usually based on the belief that punishment was necessary to avenge the victim, or to satisfy God. In early small tribal groups and less complex societies, direct compensation to the victim was used in place of revenge to prevent disintegration of the social structure through extended blood feuds. When those groups concentrated their power in a king or similar ruler with another title, the concept of crime as an offense against the victim gave way to the idea that crime (however lowly the victim) was an offense against the state and society in general. In the process, *wergeld* was replaced by *friedensgeld*, and the administration of punishment became the responsibility of the king. Concentrating that power also led to a tendency to ignore victims and their losses, while concentrating on the crime and the criminal.

PUNISHMENT

Capital and Corporal Punishment

The most common forms of state punishment over the centuries have been death, torture, mutilation, branding, public humiliation, fines, forfeits of property, banishment, imprisonment, and transportation.[8] These acts, and numerous variations on them, have always symbolized retribution for crimes. (Imprisonment and transportation are relatively modern penal practices and will be discussed in later chapters.)

The death penalty (killing the offender) was the most universal form of punishment among early societies. There was little knowledge of behavior modification and other modern techniques to control violent persons, and often the feared offenders were condemned to death by hanging, crucifixion, burning at the stake, drowning, being drawn and quartered, and any other cruel and unusual method the human mind could conceive. As technology advanced, methods for killing offenders became more sophisticated. In the belief that punishment, especially capital punishment, would act as a deterrent to others, societies carried out executions and lesser punishments in public.

Torture, mutilation, and branding fall in the general category of **corporal punishment** (any physical pain inflicted short of death). Many tortures were used to extract a "confession" from the accused, often resulting in the death penalty for an innocent person. Mutilation was often used in an attempt to match the crime with an "appropriate" punishment. (A liar's tongue was ripped out, a rapist's genitals were removed, and a thief's hands were cut off.) Branding was still practiced as late as the nineteenth century in many countries, including America. Corporal punishment was considered to be an example and a deterrent to other potential offenders.

The public humiliation of offenders was a popular practice in early America, utilizing such devices as the stocks, the pillory, ducking stools, the brank, and branding. The most significant aspect of those punishments was their public nature. Offenders were placed in the stocks (sitting down, hands and feet fastened into a locked frame) or in the pillory (standing, with head and hands fastened into a locked frame), and then flogged, spat upon, heaped with garbage, and reviled by passersby.

The ducking stool and the brank were used as common public punishments for gossips. The ducking stool was a chair or platform placed at the end of a long lever, allowing the operator on the bank of a stream to dunk the victim. The **brank** was a birdcage-like instrument placed over the offender's head, containing a plate

The pillory was a way to provide public humiliation.
Photo by Harry E. Allen

of iron with sharp spikes in it that extended into the subject's mouth. Any movement of the mouth or tongue would result in painful injury.

Flogging (or whipping) has been a common punishment in almost all Western civilizations. The method was used particularly to preserve discipline in domestic, military, and academic settings. It was usually administered by a short lash at the end of a solid handle about three feet long, or by a whip made of nine knotted wires, lines, or cords fastened to a handle (the famed **cat-o'-nine-tails**), sometimes with barbed wirespikes worked into the knots. Flogging was a popular method of inducing confessions at heresy trials, because few victims could stand up long under the tongue of the lash. Caning remains a legal punishment in countries such as Malaysia, Saudi Arabia, Singapore, and South Africa.[9]

Deterrence

The extensive use of capital and corporal punishment during the Middle Ages reflected, in part, a belief that public punishment would deter potential wrongdoers—a belief that the passing years have refuted: "It is plain that, however futile it may be, social revenge is the only honest, straightforward, and logical justification for punishing criminals. The claim for deterrence is belied by both history and logic."[10] No matter how society tried to "beat the devil" out of offenders, the only criminals who seemed to be deterred were the ones who had been tortured to *death*. Later, enlightened thinkers began to seek more rational deterrents for crime by investigating its cause.

Emergence of Secular Law

The problem of drawing up a set of laws that applied to the actions of men and women in earthly communities was compounded by Christian philosophers who insisted that law was made in heaven. In the fourth century A.D., St. Augustine recognized the need for justice, but only as decreed by God. The issue was somewhat clarified by Thomas Aquinas in the thirteenth century, when he distinguished among

The skull crusher was used for interrogations.
Photo by Harry E. Allen

three laws: eternal law ***(lex eterna),*** natural law ***(lex naturalis),*** and human law ***(lex humana),*** all intended for the common good.[11] The last was considered valid only if it did not conflict with the other two.

As time passed and the secular leaders (kings and other types of monarchs) became more powerful, they wanted to detach themselves from the divine legal order and its restrictions on their power. In the early fourteenth century, many scholars advocated the independence of the monarchy from the pope. England's lord chancellor, Sir Thomas More, opposed the forces advocating the unification of church and state and died on the executioner's block as a result. He refused to bend ecclesiastical law to suit the marital whims of his king, the fickle King Henry VIII. Sir Thomas More was out of step with his times in another sense as well. As an advocate of the seemingly radical theory that punishment could not prevent crime, he was one of the first to see that prevention might require a close look at the social conditions that gave rise to crime. In the sixteenth century, unfortunately, this line of thought was too far ahead of its time, but Sir Thomas More's ideas persisted and eventually contributed much to the foundation of modern theories in criminology and penology.

The early background of law and punishment points up the significance of social revenge as a justification for individual or societal punishment against an offender. This rationale allowed the development of penal slavery and civil death as retaliation for wrongs against the Crown. The idea of correcting an offender was entirely incidental to punishment. Imprisonment served purely for detention. Offenders who were condemned to the galleys or the sulfur mines suffered a form of social vengeance, often including the lash and other physical abuse, far more painful than was the loss of freedom alone. The offender was placed in dungeons, galleys, or mines to receive punishment, not as punishment.

The idea of punishment to repay society and expiate one's transgressions against God explains in part why most punishments remained cruel and barbarous. Presumably, the hardships of physical torture, social degradation, exile, or financial loss (the four fundamental types of punishment[12]) would be rewarded by eternal joy in heaven. Ironically, those punishments did little to halt the spread of crime:

"Even in the era when extremely severe punishment was imposed for crimes of minor importance, no evidence can be found to support the view that punitive measures materially curtailed the volume of crime."[13]

Early Prisons

What kinds of facilities for imprisonment existed during earlier ages? It is important to examine some aspects of the first institutions as they are related to later correctional practices. Some form of detention for offenders, whether temporary or permanent, has been a social institution from the earliest times. Offenders were, of course, always detained against their will, but the concept of imprisonment as a punishment in and of itself is a fairly recent thought. Formerly, imprisonment was primarily a means of holding the accused until the authorities had decided on his or her real punishment, chosen from the variety just described. Even those condemned to penal servitude in the Roman public works must surely have been kept in some special place at night, regardless of how primitive. Unfortunately, little is known about this form of imprisonment. Most places of confinement were basically cages. Later, stone quarries and similar places designed for other purposes were used to house prisoners. The only early Roman place of confinement we know much about is the **Mamertine Prison**, a vast system of primitive dungeons built under the main sewer of Rome in 64 B.C.[14]

In the Middle Ages, after the fall of Rome, fortresses, castles, bridge abutments, and town gates were strongly and securely built to defend against roving bands of raiders. With the advent of gunpowder, however, those fortress cities lost much of the deterrent power of their walls and towers. The massive structures were then used as places of confinement. Many became famous as places to house political prisoners.[15] It was not until the twelfth century that prison chambers were specifically included in castle plans.

The Christian church had followed the custom of **sanctuary** or asylum[16] since the time of Constantine, placing the wrongdoer in seclusion to create an atmosphere conducive to penitence. This form of imprisonment was modified into more formalized places of punishment within the walls of monasteries and abbeys. Long periods in solitary confinement for alleged transgressions against canon law were common. The prisons built during the Inquisition were similar in concept, if not in operation, to later cellular prisons in America.[17] The idea of reformation through isolation and prayer had some influence on our first penitentiaries, but in general, the impact of such practices in this respect remains hard to evaluate.

Workhouses

Bridewell, a workhouse, was created for the employment and housing of London's "riffraff" in 1557 and was based on the work ethic that followed the breakup of feudalism and the increased migration of the rural populations to urban areas. The workhouse was so successful that by 1576 Parliament required the construction of a Bridewell in every county in England. The same unsettled social conditions prevailed in Holland, and the Dutch began building workhouses in 1596 that were soon to be copied all over Europe.

Unfortunately, workhouses did not typify the places of confinement used for minor offenders and other prisoners in the seventeenth and eighteenth centuries. Most cities had to make prisons out of buildings erected for some other purpose. No attempt was made to keep the young from the old, the well from the sick, or even the males from the females. No food was provided for those without money, and sanitary conditions were usually deplorable. Exploitation of inmates by other inmates and jailers resulted in the most vicious acts of violence and degradation.

"Jail fever" (a common term for typhus), which was spread easily in such conditions, soon traveled to surrounding cities and became the main method of keeping the country's population down. By the beginning of the eighteenth century, workhouses, prisons, and houses of correction in England and the rest of Europe had deteriorated into shocking conditions. Forcing criminals to exist in such miserable prisons became perhaps the most ruthless—if abstract—social revenge of all the punishments thus far described. "Out of sight, out of mind" was the watchword of that period, with the public seldom being aware of what happened behind the walls (ironically, a condition not unknown at the beginning of the last millennium).

THE AGE OF ENLIGHTENMENT AND REFORM

As suggested, the underlying principle of public revenge for private wrongs invariably tipped the scales of justice in favor of the state. Corporal and capital punishment were the rule. Executioners in sixteenth- and seventeenth-century Europe had at least thirty different methods of death from which to choose. These ranged from hanging and burning at the stake to more creative forms such as stretching the prisoner to death on the rack. Public punishment and degradation were commonly prescribed for even minor offenses. Imprisonment served only as a preface to the imposition of some gory punishment, carried out in the name of justice. With over 200 crimes in England punishable by death, that nation witnessed some 800 public executions a year. As the seventeenth century drew to a close, the concept of retributive punishment by the state (with its implication that pity and justice are forever locked in opposition) was firmly entrenched in the laws of England and many other European countries.[18]

The events of the eighteenth century are especially important to the student of corrections. For it was during this period, later known as the **Age of Enlightenment,** that some of the most brilliant philosophers of our history recognized humanity's essential dignity and imperfection. Such giants as Charles Montesquieu, Voltaire, Cesare Beccaria, Jeremy Bentham, John Howard, and William Penn led the movement for reform. The impact of their work, though not confined to any one area, was particularly constructive with regard to the treatment of criminals. Let us consider the contribution made by each.

Charles Louis Secondat, Baron de la Brede et de Montesquieu (1689–1755)

was a French historian and philosopher who analyzed law as an expression of justice. He believed that harsh punishment would undermine morality and that appealing to moral sentiment was a better means of preventing crime.

Voltaire (François Marie Arouet) (1694–1778)

was the most versatile of the eighteenth-century philosophers, believing that the fear of shame was a deterrent to crime. He fought the legally sanctioned practice of torture, winning reversals—even after convicted felons had been executed—on convictions so obtained under the old code. He was imprisoned in the Bastille in 1726 and released on the condition that he leave France.

Montesquieu and Voltaire: The French Humanists

The French philosophical thinkers Montesquieu and Voltaire, along with Denis Diderot, epitomized the Age of Enlightenment's concern for the rights of humanity. In his essay *Persian Letters,*[19] Montesquieu used his mighty pen to bring the abuses of criminal law to public attention. Voltaire became involved in a number of trials that challenged the old ideas of legalized torture, criminal responsibility, and justice. The humanitarian efforts of those men paralleled the work of the most influential criminal law reformer of the era, **Cesare Beccaria,** founder of the **Classical School.** The best-known work of Beccaria is *An Essay on Crimes and Punishment,* a primary influence in the transition from punishment to corrections. It established the following principles:

1. The basis of all social action must be the utilitarian conception of the greatest happiness for the greatest number.
2. Crime must be considered an injury to society, and the only rational measure of crime is the extent of that injury.
3. Prevention of crime is more important than punishment for crimes; indeed punishment is justifiable only on the supposition that it helps to prevent

The "rack" was used for punishment.
Photo by Harry E. Allen

criminal conduct. In preventing crime it is necessary to improve and publish the laws, so that the nation can understand and support them; to reward virtue; and to improve the public's education both in regard to legislation and to life.

4. In criminal procedure secret accusations and torture should be abolished. There should be speedy trials. The accused should be treated humanely before trial and must have every right and facility to bring forward evidence on his or her behalf. Turning state's evidence should be done away with, as it amounts to no more than the public authorization of treachery.
5. The purpose of punishment is to deter persons from the commission of crime and not to provide social revenge. Not severity, but certainty and swiftness in punishment best secure this result. Punishment must be sure and swift and penalties determined strictly in accordance with the social damage wrought by the crime. Crimes against property should be punished solely by fines, or by imprisonment when the person is unable to pay the fine. Banishment is an excellent punishment for crimes against the state. There should be no capital punishment. Life imprisonment is a better deterrent. Capital punishment is irreparable and hence makes no provision for possible mistakes and the desirability of later rectification.
6. Imprisonment should be more widely employed but its mode of application should be greatly improved through providing better physical quarters and by separating and classifying the prisoners as to age, sex, and degree of criminality.[20]

Although Beccaria himself did not seek or receive great personal fame, his small volume[21] was praised as one of the most significant books produced during the Age of Enlightenment. Four of his newer ideas were incorporated into the French Code of Criminal Procedure in 1808 and into the French Penal Code of 1810:

1. An individual should be regarded as innocent until proven guilty.
2. An individual should not be forced to testify against himself or herself.

PROFILE

Denis Diderot (1713–1784)

was a French encyclopedist and philosopher who was thrown into prison in 1749 for his work *Lettre sur les Aveugles* ("Letter on the Blind"), a strong attack on orthodox religion. He worked for twenty years on his twenty-eight-volume encyclopedia, along with Voltaire, Montesquieu, and other great thinkers of the time. His encyclopedia became a force in the fight for change in the eighteenth century.

PROFILE

Cesare Bonesana, Marchase di Beccaria (1738–1794)

wrote *An Essay on Crimes and Punishment,* which was published anonymously in 1764. It was the most exciting essay on law of the eighteenth century. It proposed a reorientation of criminal law toward humanistic goals. Beccaria suggested that judges should not interpret the law, but that the law should be made more specific, because he believed the real measure of crime was its harm to society. He is regarded as the founder of the Classical School of criminology.

3. An individual should have the right to employ counsel and to cross-examine the state's witnesses.
4. An individual should have the right to a prompt and public trial and, in most cases, a trial by jury.

Among the philosophers inspired by Beccaria's ideas were the authors of the U.S. Constitution. It seems we owe a great deal to this shy Italian writer of the eighteenth century.[22]

Bentham and the Hedonistic Calculus

SIDEBARS

Utilitarianism

is a doctrine in which the aim of all action should be the greatest pleasure for the largest number of citizens. Hence, the law should be used to inflict enough pain on offenders that they will cease their criminal actions (the "good" to be achieved).

Jeremy Bentham was the leading reformer of the British criminal law system during the late eighteenth and early nineteenth centuries. He strongly advocated a system of graduated penalties to tie more closely the punishment to the crime. As political equality became a dominant philosophy, new penal policies were required to accommodate this change in emphasis. As Thorsten Sellin stated:

> *Older penal law had reflected the views dominant in societies where slavery or serfdom flourished, political inequality was the rule, and sovereignty was assumed to be resting in absolute monarchs. Now the most objectionable features of that law, which had favored the upper classes and had provided often arbitrary, brutal, and revolting corporal and capital punishments for the lower classes, were to be removed and equality before the law established. Judicial torture for the purpose of extracting evidence was to be abolished, other than penal measures used to control some conduct previously punished as crime, and punishments made only severe enough to outweigh the gains expected by the criminal from his crime. This meant a more humane law, no doubt, applied without discrimination to all citizens alike in harmony with the new democratic ideas.*[23]

PROFILE

Jeremy Bentham (1748–1832)

was the greatest leader in the reform of English criminal law. He believed that if punishments were designed to negate whatever pleasure or gain the criminal derived from crime, the crime rate would go down. He wrote prodigiously on all aspects of criminal justice. Something of a crackpot in his later years, he devised his ultimate prison: the Panopticon. This monstrosity was never constructed, but debate over it slowed progress in English penology.

Bentham believed that an individual's conduct could be influenced in a scientific manner. Asserting that the main objective of an intelligent person is to achieve the most pleasure while experiencing the least amount of pain, he developed his famous "**hedonistic calculus**,"[24] which he applied to his efforts to reform the criminal law. He, like Beccaria, believed punishment could act as a deterrent, but only if it were made appropriately relevant to the crime. This line of thought, adopted by active reformers Samuel Romilly and Robert Peel in the early nineteenth century, has been instrumental in the development of the modern prison.

John Howard

PROFILE

Sir Samuel Romilly (1757–1818),

a follower of Bentham, was an able lawyer and the most effective leader in direct and persistent agitation for reform of the English criminal code. He pressed for construction of the first modern English prison, Millbank, in 1816. His prison idea was taken up by Romilly's followers, Sir James Mackintosh (1765–1832) and Sir Thomas Fowell Buxton (1786–1845).

John Howard gave little thought to prisons or prison reform until he was appointed sheriff of Bedfordshire in 1773. The appointment opened his eyes to horrors he had never imagined. He was appalled by the conditions he found in the hulks and gaols and pressed for legislation to alleviate some of the abuses and improve sanitary conditions. He also traveled extensively on the European continent to examine prisons in other countries. He saw similarly deplorable conditions in most areas, but was most impressed by some of the institutions in France and Italy. In 1777, he described those conditions and suggested reforms in his *State of Prisons*. In 1779, Parliament passed the Penitentiary Act, providing four principles for reform: secure and sanitary structures, systematic inspection, abolition of fees, and a reformatory regime.[25]

The Penitentiary Act resulted in the first penitentiary, located at Wyndomham in Norfolk, England, and operated by Sir Thomas Beever, the sheriff of Wyndomham. As we will see later, the principles contained in the act, though lofty in concept, were hard to implement in the prevailing atmosphere of indifference. It is ironic that this great advocate for better prison conditions did himself die of **jail fever** (typhus) in the Russian Ukraine in 1790. John Howard's name has become synonymous with prison reform, and the John Howard Society has carried his ideas forward to this day.[26]

HOUSES OF CORRECTION, WORKHOUSES, AND GAOLS

The proliferation of Bridewell-style houses of correction in England was originally intended as a humanitarian move. As a result, in 1576, Parliament ordered that each county in England construct such an institution. They were not merely extensions of almshouses or poorhouses, but were actually penal institutions for all sorts of misdemeanants. Although the bloody penalties for major offenses were growing in number, not even the most callous would advocate harsh physical punishment for every offender. All sorts of rogues, from idlers to whores, were put into the Bridewells, where they were compelled to work under strict discipline at the direction of hard taskmasters. Today, the house of correction and the **workhouse** are regarded as synonymous. The workhouse, however, was not actually intended as a penal institution, but as a place for the training and care of the poor. In practice, however, the two soon became indistinguishable, first in England and later in America. Conditions and practices in such institutions were no better than those in the gaols (jails) by the turn of the eighteenth century.

The use of **gaols** to detain prisoners has a grim and unsavory history. As the eighteenth century began, gaol administration was usually left up to the whim of the gaoler, who was usually under the control of the sheriff. Gaols were often used to extort huge fines from those who had the means, by holding those people indefinitely in pretrial confinement until they gave in and paid. The lot of the common "gaolbird" was surely not a happy one. Many of the prisoners perished long before their trial dates. The squalid and unhealthy conditions gave rise to epidemics of jail fever (typhus) that spread to all levels of English life. John Howard claimed that more people died from this malady between 1773 and 1774 than were executed by the Crown.[27] Ironically, prisoners, not prison conditions, were blamed for the spread of the deadly disease, and even more sanguinary penalties for offenses were devised. Robert Caldwell describes the typical English gaol:

> *Devoid of privacy and restrictions, its contaminated air heavy with the stench of unwashed bodies, human excrement, and the discharge of loathsome sores, the gaol bred the basest thoughts and the foulest deeds. The inmates made their own rules, and the weak and the innocent were exposed to the tyranny of the strong and the vicious. Prostitutes plied their trade with ease, often with the connivance and support of the gaolers, who thus sought to supplement their fees. Even virtuous women sold themselves to obtain food and clothing, and frequently the worst elements of the town used the gaol as they would a brothel. Thus, idleness, vice, perversion, profligacy, shameless exploitation, and ruthless cruelty were compounded in hotbeds of infection and cesspools of corruption. These were the common gaols of England.*[28]

It is depressing to think that John Howard, shocked into humanitarian reform efforts when he found himself responsible for one of those human cesspools, was the only sheriff to undertake action against such institutions.

PROFILE

Sir Robert Peel (1788–1850)

was the leader in the English legislature for reform of the criminal code, pushing through programs devised by Bentham, Romilly, and others. He established the Irish constabulary, called the "Peelers" after the founder. In 1829, he started the London metropolitan police, known as "Bobbies," also after Sir Robert. He was active in all phases of criminal justice.

PROFILE

John Howard (1726–1790)

was captured by a French privateer and, as a prisoner of war, treated with great severity. When he gained his release and became high sheriff of Bedfordshire, he was shocked by the conditions he found in the English prison in 1773. He then devoted his life and fortune to prison reform. He abolished fees in his jail, improved sanitation, and required justices of the peace to visit his institution. His monumental study, *The State of Prisons in England and Wales* (1777), led Parliament to correct many abuses and was highly influential across western Europe and the colonies.

SIDEBARS

Gaols and Gaolbirds

Gaols (jails) were used primarily as places of detention. Some prisoners waited to be tried, others could not pay their fines, and still others awaited execution. No attempt was made to segregate prisoners by age, sex, or crime. Food was often sold by the sheriff at inflated prices, and those who could not pay or have food brought in starved. Early efforts of reformers like John Howard helped clean up the gaols, but even today jails are usually the worst disgrace of the criminal justice system. Gaolbird (jailbird) was coined because of the large, cage-like cells used to confine the prisoners in unsegregated bunches, like "birds in a cage."

TRANSPORTATION SYSTEMS

Deportation to the American Colonies and Australia

As the student has seen, one of the earliest forms of social vengeance was **banishment.** In primitive societies the offender was cast out into the wilderness, usually to be eaten by wild beasts or to succumb to the elements. As we have discovered, imprisonment and capital punishment were later substituted for banishment. Banishment to penal servitude was, in effect, civil death. Banishment to the gaols, however, more often than not ended in physical death.

The wandering and jobless lower classes, in the period following the breakup of feudalism, were concentrated mostly in high-crime slums in the major cities. As economic conditions worsened, the number of imprisonable crimes was increased to the point that the available prisons were filled. In England, from 1596 to 1776, the pressure was partially relieved by the deportation or **transportation** of malefactors to the colonies in America. Estimates vary greatly of how many original American settlers arrived in chains. Margaret Wilson estimates between 300 and 400 annually;[29] other authorities put the figure as high as 2,000 a year. The use of convict labor was widespread before the adoption of slavery in the colonies. And even though the entering flow of dangerous felons was somewhat slowed by the introduction of slavery, the poor and the misdemeanant continued to come in great numbers.

The American Revolution brought transportation to America to an abrupt halt in 1776; but England and Ireland[30] still needed somewhere to send the criminals overloading its crowded institutions. Captain James Cook had discovered Australia in 1770, and soon the system of transportation was transferred to that continent. It was planned that the criminals would help tame that new and wild land. More than 135,000 felons were sent to Australia between 1787 and 1875, when the British finally abandoned the system.

The ships in which felons were transported have been described as "floating hells," which is an understatement. The conditions below decks were worse than those of the gaols. Many died on the long voyages, but enough survived to make it a profitable venture for the ship owners, who fitted out ships specifically for that purpose.[31] Other nations turned to transportation in the nineteenth century, as we will see later.

CORRECTIONAL BRIEF

Transportation

Transportation ships were hired transports employed to convey convicts from England to New South Wales. Private business entrepreneurs carried offenders to another country for a fee, essentially making a pound off the backs of offenders. Contractors received between twenty and thirty pounds per head. The more convicts carried, the greater the profit would be; thus, overcrowding on the ships was the rule, not the exception. As a result of such a state of confinement, the most loathsome diseases were common and the death rate was extremely high: 158 of 502 who were placed on the *Neptune* in 1790 for conveyance to Australia died en route; and 95 of the 300 placed into the holds of the *Hillsborough* in 1799 died during the voyage. Those who did arrive were so near dead that they could not stand and it was necessary to sling them like goods and hoist them out of the ships, and when first landed they died at the rate of 10 to 12 a day. The government attempted in 1802 to correct these evils by sending convicts twice a year in ships specially fitted for the purpose that were under the direction of a transport board and commanded by naval officers. Although the transports continued to be crowded, health conditions apparently improved greatly because Sir T. B. Martin, head of the transport board, reported in 1819 that "within the past three years only 53 out of 6,409 convicts (a rate of 1 in 112) had died. Out of the 10 transports which had recently sailed only one or two had died."

CORRECTIONAL BRIEF

Convict Hulks

Convict hulks were among the earliest examples of imprisonment used as a method of dealing with criminals. The hulks, sometimes called "hell holes," were broken-down war vessels that were stripped and anchored on bays and rivers around England. They were unsanitary, full of vermin, and unventilated. Disease ran rampant and often wiped out the whole prisoner population, and sometimes the crew and neighboring citizens as well. The last European hulk was still maintained at Gibraltar as late as 1875.

Hulks: A Sordid Episode

From 1776 to 1875, even with limited transportation to Australia, the increased prisoner loads wreaked havoc in England's few available facilities. The immediate solution to that problem created one of the most odious episodes in the history of penology and corrections: the use of old **hulks**, abandoned or unusable transport ships anchored in rivers and harbors throughout the British Isles, to confine criminal offenders. The brutal and degrading conditions found in the gaols, houses of correction, and workhouses paled in comparison with the conditions found in those fetid and rotting human garbage dumps.

Those responsible for the hulks made no attempt to segregate young from old, hardened criminals from poor misdemeanants, or even men from women. Brutal flogging and degrading labor soon bred moral degeneration in both inmates and keepers. The hulks were originally intended only as a temporary solution to a problem, but they were not completely abandoned until 1858, eighty years later. (Hulks were used in California in the nineteenth century, and one state, Washington, considered the use of decommissioned U.S. Navy warships in 1976. New York used a floating jail for some time in the 1980s.) This episode in penal history becomes especially relevant when the problems of overcrowding in our maximum-security prisons are examined.

EARLY CELLULAR PRISONS

The Maison de Force at Ghent and the Hospice of San Michele

In his travels on the continent, John Howard was most impressed by Jean-Jacques Vilain's **Maison de Force** (stronghouse) at Ghent, Belgium, and by the Hospice (hospital) of San Michele in Rome. Although those institutions had developed along individually different lines, both made lasting impressions on Howard. Both served as workhouses, but otherwise they had little in common. Their differences were more important than their similarities.

Predecessors of the Belgian workhouses were those in neighboring Amsterdam, constructed around 1596. Most were intended to make a profit,[32] not to exemplify humanitarian ideals, and were seen as a place to put rogues and able-bodied beggars to work. The workhouses were modeled after the Bridewell institution in England and followed a similar pattern of hard work and cruel punishment. By the eighteenth century, Belgium, too, was faced with increasing numbers of beggars and

SIDEBARS

Hospice of San Michele

The Hospice of San Michele was built in 1704 by Pope Clement XI. The pope himself placed an inscription over the door that remains to this day: "It is insufficient to restrain the wicked by punishment unless you render them virtuous by corrective discipline."

vagrants, and the government called on administrator and disciplinarian Jean-Jacques Vilain for help. His solution—the Maison de Force built in Ghent in 1773—followed the basic workhouse pattern established in Holland and England, but in many respects it was far more just and humane.

Vilain's efforts at improving the administration of the workhouse earned him an honored place in penal history. He was one of the first to develop a system of classification to separate women and children from hardened criminals, and felons from minor offenders. Although he was a stern disciplinarian, he was opposed to life imprisonment and cruel punishment. Rather, he defined discipline by the rule, "If any man will not work, neither let him eat." Vilain's use of individual cells and a system of silence while working resembled the procedures observed at the Hospice of San Michele in Rome. His far-reaching concepts of fair and just treatment, when viewed against the harsh backdrop of that era, mark Vilain as a true visionary in the correctional field.

The **Hospice of San Michele** was designed for incorrigible boys and youths under age twenty. As such, it is generally recognized as one of the first institutions to handle juvenile offenders exclusively. Prisoners were administered massive doses of Scripture and hard work in hopes that this regimen would reform them. The rule of strict silence was enforced through the flogging of violators. (The use of separate cells for sleeping and a large central hall for working became the model for penal institutions in the nineteenth century.) This concept of expiation and penance, as applied to corrections, was new and exciting to John Howard, and his Puritan ethic enabled him to see the value of repentance and hard work as demonstrated by the program at San Michele. Under somewhat different policies, the Hospice of San Michele is still used today as a reformatory for delinquent boys.

The main concepts that carried over from the early cellular institutions were the monastic regimen of silence and expiation, the central community work area, and individual cells for sleeping. The philosophy of penitence and monastic contemplation of past wrongs espoused by those institutions was reflected in the Quakers' early prison efforts in America.

William Penn and the "Great Law"

The American colonies were governed by the British under codes established by the Duke of York in 1676 and part of the older Hampshire Code established in 1664. These codes were similar to those followed in England, and the use of capital and corporal punishment was the rule of the day. Branding, flogging, the stocks, the pillory, and the brank were also used extensively.

William Penn (1644–1718), an English Quaker, fought for religious freedom and individual rights. In 1681, he obtained a charter from King Charles II and founded the Quaker settlement of Pennsylvania.

William Penn, the founder of Pennsylvania and leader of the Quakers, brought the concept of more humanitarian treatment of offenders to America. The Quaker movement was the touchstone of penal reform not only in America, but also in Italy and England through its influence on such advocates as Beccaria and Howard. Compared with the other harsh colonial codes in force at the time, the **Great Law** of the Quakers was quite humane. This body of laws envisioned hard labor as a more effective punishment than death for serious crimes, and capital punishment was eliminated from the original codes. Later, in supplementary acts, murder and manslaughter were included as social crimes. Only premeditated murder was punishable by death, with other criminal acts treated according to the circumstances.

It is interesting to note that the Quakers' Great Law did away with most religious offenses and stuck to strictly secular criminal jurisprudence, a departure from the codes of other colonies and the earlier European codes. Under the Great Law, a "house of corrections" institution was established where most punishment was meted out in the form of hard labor. This was the first time that correctional confinement at hard labor was used as a punishment for serious crimes, and not merely as a preface to punishment scheduled for a later date.

The Quaker Code of 1682 was in force until 1718, when it was repealed, ironically, only one day after the death of William Penn. The English Anglican Code replaced the Great Law, and the mild Quaker philosophy gave way to harsh punishments. The new code was even worse than the previous codes of the Duke of York. Capital punishment was prescribed for thirteen offenses,[33] and mutilation, branding, and other corporal punishments were restored for many others.

The influence of Montesquieu, Voltaire, Beccaria, Bentham, Howard, and Penn was felt throughout colonial America. Much of the idealism embodied in the U.S. Constitution reflects the writings of those progressive eighteenth-century leaders. With their philosophies in mind, we can consider some of the major developments in correctional practice in that era of reform.

The Walnut Street Jail

As we have seen, the world of the eighteenth century had prisons, but they were generally used as places of detention for minor offenders and for pretrial confinement. One of the earliest American attempts to operate a state prison for felons was located in an abandoned copper mine in Simsbury, Connecticut.[34] This underground prison began operation in 1773 and quickly became the site of America's first prison riots, in 1774. Although some have called it the first state prison, it was really not much more than a throwback to the sulfur pits of ancient Rome, and it did nothing to advance the state of American corrections. The prisoners were housed in long mine shafts, and the administration buildings were placed near the entrances. Underground mine shaft prisons constituted one of several American attempts to provide a special place in which to house and work convicted felons. The establishment of such a special facility was finally accomplished in Pennsylvania in 1790.

It is hard to imagine a time when there were no long-term penitentiaries for felons, but before 1790 that was the case. Ironically, in that year, the first **penitentiary** in America, the prototype of the modern prison system, was born in the same city that spawned the fledgling United States as a nation. Philadelphia,

CORRECTIONAL BRIEF

The Walnut Street Jail

The Walnut Street Jail, until the innovation of solitary confinement for felons, was typical of colonial jails. They are described in David J. Rothman's *Discovery of the Asylum* (Boston: Little, Brown, 1971), p. 55. Jails in fact closely resembled the household in structure and routine. They lacked a distinct architecture and special procedures. When the Virginia burgess required that county prisons be "good, strong, and substantial," and explicitly recommended that they follow "after the form of Virginia housing," results were in keeping with these directions. The doors were perhaps somewhat sturdier, the locks slightly more impressive, but the general design of the jail was the same as for an ordinary residence. True to the household model, the keeper and his family resided in the jail, occupying one of its rooms; the prisoners lived several together in the other rooms, with little to differentiate the keeper's quarters from their own. They wore no special clothing or uniforms and usually neither cuffs nor chains restrained their movements. They walked—not marched—about the jail. The workhouse model was so irrelevant that nowhere were they required to perform the slightest labor.

Pennsylvania, the home of the Declaration of Independence, is also—thanks to the Quakers—the home of the **Walnut Street Jail**, the first true correctional institution in America.

Despite earlier efforts at prison reform, the Quakers had been thwarted in their humanistic goals by the repeal of Penn's Great Law in 1718. In 1776, the first American Penitentiary Act was passed, but its implementation was delayed because of the War of Independence. In 1790, with the Revolution behind them, the Quakers reasserted their concern with the treatment of convicted criminals.[35] After much prodding, they convinced the Pennsylvania legislature to declare a wing of the Walnut Street Jail a penitentiary house for all convicted felons except those sentenced to death.[36] Thus, although prisons, gaols, dungeons, and workhouses had been in existence for years, this wing was the first to be used exclusively for the correction of convicted felons.

Some of the concepts embodied in the Walnut Street Jail had their antecedents in the charter of William Penn in 1682. Those provisions, repressed by the harsh Anglican Code, were as follows:

1. All prisoners were to be bailable.
2. Those wrongfully imprisoned could recover double damages.
3. Prisons were to be free as to fees, food, and lodging.
4. The lands and goods of felons were to be liable for confiscation and double restitution to injured parties.
5. All counties were to provide houses to replace the pillory, stocks, and the like.[37]

Although not all of the idealistic reforms were adopted, the direction of change had been established. The system of prison discipline developed at the Walnut Street Jail became known as the **Pennsylvania system.** The Pennsylvania system was developed through the ideas and efforts of such reformers as Benjamin Franklin and Benjamin Rush, building on the humanitarian ideals of Howard, Bentham, Beccaria, and Montesquieu. Patriot and war hero William Bradford, who drafted the codes that implemented the system, praised the European reformers in the state legislature.

As originally conceived, the basic element of the Pennsylvania system called for solitary confinement without work. It was assumed that this method would result in quicker reformations. Offenders could reflect on their crimes all day and would soon repent so they might rejoin humanity. The terrible effects of such isolation—physical and psychological—soon became apparent. Some kind of work had to be provided, as well as moral and religious instruction, to maintain the prisoners' mental and bodily health. The work schedule thus was from eight to ten hours a day, and the prisoner worked in isolation, usually on piecework or handicrafts.

Increasingly more convicts were sent to the new state prison, and overcrowding shattered early hopes for its success. Even the original system of separate areas for women and children broke down with the flood of inmates. But despite the ultimate failure of the Walnut Street Jail program, it represented a major breakthrough for penology. New prisons were soon in demand throughout America, and the Walnut Street Jail was copied extensively, in at least ten states and many foreign countries.[38]

SIDEBARS

Penitentiary

Originally a place where offenders reflected on their crimes and repented (changed). Now a major adult facility where felons are incarcerated as punishment.

PROFILE

Benjamin Franklin (1706–1790)

founded the American Philosophical Society in Philadelphia in 1743. He served as Pennsylvania's appointed agent to England and a member of the second Continental Congress (1777) to draft the Declaration of Independence, which he signed. He was plenipotentiary to France and negotiated to obtain that country's help in the Revolution. He was also a statesman, scientist, and philosopher.

PROFILE

Benjamin Rush (1745–1813),

physician and political leader, was a member of both Continental Congresses (1776, 1777) and a signer of the Declaration of Independence. He established the first free dispensary in the United States (1786) and was an advocate of prison reform and humane treatment.

William Bradford (1721–1791),

the "Patriot Printer of 1776," was one of the early advocates of a Continental Congress. He was a member of the Sons of Liberty, a political rival of Benjamin Franklin, and an active reformer of the harsh British codes. As a major in the army, he became a hero of the Revolution.

SUMMARY

In this chapter, we initially observed the principle of punishment pass from an individual's response to a wrong, to a blood feud that involved the family, to an abstract action taken by some bureaucracy in the name of the state. The last approach to justice and punishment allowed the places of confinement to become human cesspools. It took the brilliant and dedicated reformers of the eighteenth century to establish the basis for modern penal philosophy.

As the eighteenth century drew to a close, a new feeling of vigor and energy sparked the move for prison reform. The decade after the opening of the Walnut Street Jail was full of hope for the concepts embodied there, however imperfectly. It would be an oversimplification to say that the Walnut Street Jail was the world's first real attempt at a prison for convicted felons. The eighteenth century produced many such attempts, both in Europe and in America. Some of the principles behind the Walnut Street Jail, however, had a permanent influence on the development of correctional institutions throughout the world. Connecticut's abortive attempt to establish a state prison at Simsbury failed because the mine shafts could not be made habitable and because there was little public enthusiasm for the project. The Quakers' compassionate efforts, though much more humane, were doomed to failure by the lack of public and political support, incompetent personnel, and enforced idleness. With the industrial age came overcrowded prisons, which forced the new administrators to consider much larger and more productive kinds of institutions. As America entered the nineteenth century, it also entered an age of expansion. The prison movement adopted this growth-oriented philosophy, and as we will see in the next chapter, the nineteenth and early twentieth centuries became the age of prisons.

REVIEW QUESTIONS

1. What are the differences among folkways, mores, and laws?
2. At what point in a society's development does retaliation begin to become criminal law?
3. What effect did the kings' increasing power have on punishment?
4. What was the first punishment imposed by society?
5. What is meant by civil death?
6. What is meant by free will?
7. What form of punishment has been most widely used?
8. What is meant by "deterrence as a result of punishment"?
9. What were some of the earliest forms of imprisonment?
10. From what does most American law derive?
11. What was Beccaria's main contribution to corrections?
12. What were John Howard's four principles for a penitentiary system?
13. Many reformers tried to improve prison conditions in the eighteenth century. Name at least three and describe their major contributions.
14. Why is it important to study corrections?

ENDNOTES

1. Albert Kocourek and John Wigmore, *Evolution of Law, Vol. 2, Punitive and Ancient Legal Institutions* (Boston: Little, Brown, 1915), p. 124. See also Jeffrie Murphy, "Two Cheers for Vindictiveness," *Punishment and Society* 2:2 (2000): 134–143.
2. Ronald Akers, "Toward a Comparative Definition of Criminal Law," *Journal of Criminal Law, Criminology and Police Science* (1965): 301–306.
3. Kocourek and Wigmore, *Evolution of Law,* Vol. 2, p. 126.
4. Thorsten Sellin, "A Look at Prison History," *Federal Probation* (September 1967): 18.
5. Gustav Radbruch, *Elegantiae Juris Criminalis,* 2nd ed. (Basel, Switzerland: Verlag fur Recht und Gesellschaft A. G., 1950), p. 5.
6. Slaves were also marked by branding on the forehead or by metal collars that could not be easily removed.
7. This religious requirement brought the two issues of sin and crime into the same arena and broadened the scope of the church courts. The offender was obligated to make retribution to both God and the state.
8. V. A. C. Catrell, *The Hanging Tree: Execution and the English People: 1770–1868* (New York: Oxford University Press, 1994). For an example of the American experience, see Robert Lilly, "Executing U.S. Soldiers in England, WW II," *British Journal of Criminology* 37:2 (1997): 262–288.
9. Editors, "Guards Get Jail and Cane for Prisoner's Death," *The Straits Times* (March 21, 1996): 2. See also Roger Mellem, "Government Violence in the War against Drugs," *International Journal of Comparative and Applied Criminal Justice* 18:1 (1994): 39–51.

10. Walter C. Reckless, *The Crime Problem,* 4th ed. (New York: Appleton-Century-Crofts, 1969), p. 497.
11. Harry Elmer Barnes and Negley K. Teeters, *New Horizons in Criminology,* 3rd ed. (Englewood Cliffs, NJ: Prentice-Hall, 1959), p. 286. For a more recent update on deterrence, see Stewart D'Alessio and Lisa Stolzenberg, "Crime, Arrests and Pretrial Jail Incarceration: A Test of the Deterrence Thesis," *Criminology* 36:4 (1998): 735–761.
12. Stephen Schafer, *Theories in Criminology* (New York: Random House, 1969), p. 25.
13. Edwin H. Sutherland, *Criminology* (Philadelphia: Lippincott, 1924), p. 317.
14. Reckless, *The Crime Problem,* p. 504. There is little evidence that increased use of incarceration will lead to lower levels of crime. See Rodney Hennington, W. Johnson, and T. Wells, "Supermax Prisons: Panacea or Desperation," *Corrections Management Quarterly* 3:2 (1999): 53–59; and Jesenia Pizarro and Vanja Stenius, "Supermax Prisons." *The Prison Journal* 84:2 (2004): 228–247.
15. Norman Johnston, *The Human Cage: A Brief History of Prison Architecture* (Washington, DC: American Foundation, 1973), p. 5. See also John Britton and E. Brayley, *Memoirs of the Tower of London* (Littleton, CO: Fred Rothman, 1994); and Dana Priest, "U.S. Preparing for Lifetime Jailing of Terror Suspects," *Seattle Times* (January 2, 2005), p. 3.
16. Johnston, *The Human Cage,* p. 6.
17. The practice of granting a criminal sanctuary from punishment was generally reserved for holy places. It was abandoned in England in the seventeenth century.
18. For an historical view of the development of Western criminal justice systems up to the eighteenth century, see Herbert Johnson and Nancy Wolfe, *History of Criminal Justice* (Cincinnati, OH: Anderson, 2003), pp. 24–109.
19. The *Persian Letters* was a satirical essay by Montesquieu on the abuses of current criminal law. The essay greatly influenced Beccaria. This, along with Voltaire's activities, led Beccaria to write his *An Essay on Crimes and Punishment.*
20. Barnes and Teeters, *New Horizons in Criminology,* p. 322.
21. Cesare Beccaria, *An Essay on Crimes and Punishment* (Philadelphia: P. H. Nicklin, 1819).
22. Beccaria's contributions to corrections as the father of modern criminology have been called into question in recent years. See Graeme Newman and Pietro Morongu, "Penological Reform and the Myth of Beccaria," *Criminology* 28 (1990): 325–346. Nonetheless, he remains the central figure in liberal penology.
23. Thorsten Sellin, "A Look at Prison History," *Federal Probation* 31:3 (1967): 20.
24. *Hedonistic calculus* was a term devised by Jeremy Bentham to describe the idea that "to achieve the most pleasure and the least pain is the main objective of an intelligent man."
25. Barnes and Teeters, New Horizons in Criminology, p. 335. See also John Freeman, *Prisons Past and Present* (London: Heinemann, 1978), for an excellent set of papers celebrating Howard's contributions to prison reform, and Jacques Petit et al., "The History of Incarceration in Penal Populations," *Criminologie* 28:1 (1995): 3–147 (in French).
26. The John Howard Society is a nonprofit organization supported by contributions. It provides casework service to inmates and their families, and it also works to promote community understanding of prison problems and offers technical assistance to correctional agencies (608 South Dearborn Street, Chicago, IL 60605). A biography of John Howard can be found at www.johnhoward.ca/bio.htm.
27. John Howard, *The State of Prisons* (New York: Dutton, 1929). For more background on Bridewells, see Leonard Roberts, "Bridewell: The World's First Attempt at Prisoner Rehabilitation Through Education," *Journal of Correctional Education* 35:3 (1984): 83–85. One example of Howard's influence can be found in the Wakefield Prison History, http://freepages.history.rootsweb.com/~wakefield/histpris.html (accessed January 9, 2005).
28. Robert G. Caldwell, *Criminology* (New York: Ronald Press, 1965), p. 494.
29. Margaret Wilson, *The Crime of Punishment* (New York: Harcourt, Brace and World, 1931), p. 224.
30. Bob Reece, *The Origins of Irish Convict Transportation to New South Wales* (New York: Palgrave, 2001).
31. Alexis Durham, "Origins of Interest in the Privatization of Punishment: The Nineteenth and Twentieth Century American Experience," *Criminology* 27 (1989): 107–139. See also the National Archives of Ireland, *Sources in the National Archives for Research into the Transportation of Irish Convicts to Australia (1791–1853): Introduction,* www.nationalarchives.ie/topics/transportation/transp1.htm (accessed January 9, 2005).
32. For a discussion of contemporary punishment for profit, see David Shichor, *Punishment for Profit: Private Prisons, Public Concerns* (Thousand Oaks, CA: Sage, 1995); and Colorado Criminal Justice Reform Coalition, "For Profit Incarceration," www.ccjrc.org/pdf/forprofit.pdf (accessed January 9, 2005).
33. Only larceny was exempt from capital punishment. All other major crimes were punishable by death. For a poignant view on contemporary flogging, see Azam Kamguian, *Why Islamic Law Should Be Opposed?*

www.secularislam.org/articles/opposed.htm (accessed January 9, 2005).

34. For a short history of this facility, see Charles W. Dean, "The Story of Newgate," *Federal Probation* (June 1977): 8–14. See also Alexis Durham, "Newgate of Connecticut: Origins and Early Days of an Early American Prison," *Justice Quarterly* 6 (1989): 89–116; and Judith Cook, *To Brave Every Danger* (London, UK: Macmillan, 1993).
35. Barnes and Teeters, New Horizons in Criminology, p. 336.
36. Negley K. Teeters, *The Cradle of the Penitentiary* (Philadelphia: Pennsylvania Prison Society, 1955).
37. Donald R. Taft, *Criminology,* 3rd ed. (New York: Macmillan, 1956), p. 478.
38. Harry E. Barnes, *The Story of Punishment,* 2nd ed. (Montclair, NJ: Patterson Smith, 1972), p. 136.

CHAPTER 2

Prisons
(1800 to the Present)

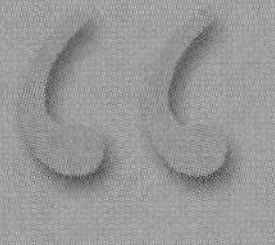

To the builders of this nitemare
Though you may never get to read these words I pity you;
For the cruelty of your minds have designed this Hell;
If men's buildings are a reflection of what they are,
This one portraits the ugliness of all humanity.
IF ONLY YOU HAD SOME COMPASSION
—On a prison wall

KEY WORDS

- Pennsylvania system
- outside cell
- Eastern Penitentiary
- inside cell
- Auburn system
- cell block
- congregate system
- penitentiary system
- disciplinarian
- silence
- lockstep formation
- prison stripes
- treadmill
- solitary confinement
- indeterminate sentence
- Irish system
- ticket-of-leave
- conditional liberty
- reformatory
- Zebulon Brockway
- industrial prison
- Hawes–Cooper Act
- Ashurst–Sumners Act
- Sanford Bates
- Alcatraz
- lock psychosis
- convict bogey
- ombudsman
- War on Drugs

OVERVIEW

The first chapter acquainted the student with how corrections has grown from individual to group punishment, then from group punishment to legal codes and punishment applied by the country or state. We saw how the concept of reform by penitence in the Walnut Street Jail grew to be a whole new concept—the penitentiary. In this chapter we examine how this simple concept grew into the vast network of prisons across America by exploring the first two competing concepts or systems of prison design and construction in the United States.

The student should remember that corrections must always ask the question "Who are offenders and what are we expected to do with them?" Offenders are (1) evil and must be destroyed, (2) out of touch with God and need to repent, (3) uneducated and ill trained to function in modern society, and (4) sick and in need of being cured. These answers are commonly known as the punishment, reform, education, and medical models of corrections. In the final part of this chapter, we explore the philosophical foundations on which these models were constructed and explain some of the rationales underlying current correctional developments. It is essential for the student to understand why this nation has entered into an age of massive change in public acceptance of crime and criminal and prison operations, what goals are being sought, and what might be the implications of the adoption of new programs, operations, and facilities. We begin with the two major competing concepts or systems that evolved and fought for prison designs and construction in the United States for the majority of the twentieth century.

< Iowa Men's Reformatory at Anamosa, deemed a masterpiece of architecture.
Photo by John Schultz, courtesy of American Correctional Association. Reprinted with permission.

THE PENNSYLVANIA SYSTEM

With the advent of the nineteenth century and the social upheaval produced by the Industrial Revolution, the citizens of Pennsylvania led the way in developing the penitentiary system. The Walnut Street Jail had been fairly effective for a decade, and the earlier **Pennsylvania system** was copied extensively in both architectural design and administration. But when the Philadelphia Society for the Alleviation of the Miseries of Public Prisons[1] observed the many emerging problems at the Walnut Street Jail, a radically new kind of prison was proposed for the state. It was suggested by some that solitary confinement without labor continue to be used as the sole reformatory process.

The Western Penitentiary at Pittsburgh, built in 1826, was based on the cellular isolation wing of the Walnut Street Jail. Essentially, the Western Penitentiary amounted to a poor imitation of Jeremy Bentham's proposed prison (Panopticon), an octagonal monstrosity that originally provided for solitary confinement and no labor. The legislature amended the program in 1829, maintaining solitary confinement but adding the provision that inmates perform some labor in their cells. In 1833, the small dark cells were torn down, and larger cells with enclosed exercise yards (**outside cells**)[2] were built. The efforts influenced the development of what became the Eastern Penitentiary, located in Philadelphia.

The **Eastern Penitentiary** became the model and primary exponent of the Pennsylvania, or "separate," system. This prison was built like a square wheel, with the cell blocks arranged like spokes around the hub, or central rotunda. The routine at Eastern was solitary confinement, silence, and labor in outside cells. This arrangement clearly stressed the maximum and continuous amount of separation of each inmate from all the others.

Although the Pennsylvania system aroused great international interest, it was adopted by only two other states. The New Jersey State Penitentiary in Trenton began operations in 1837, along the lines of the separate system. It was soon abandoned, however, in favor of that used at Auburn, New York. Rhode Island followed the same pattern as that of New Jersey. Its first prison, built in 1838 along the lines of the Eastern Penitentiary, had abandoned the separate system by 1852. By contrast, many European countries wholeheartedly adopted the Pennsylvania model.[3]

PROFILE

Louis Dwight (1793–1854)

organized the Prison Discipline Society of Boston. He was originally trained for the ministry but injured his lungs and could not preach. In 1824, he rode through the countryside distributing Bibles to prisoners. He was the most vocal advocate of the Auburn system and, as director of the Prison Discipline Society of Boston from 1825 to 1854, was the best source of information about that era of American prisons.

THE AUBURN SYSTEM

The major evils of the jails and other confinement facilities before 1800 were indiscriminate congregate confinement and enforced idleness. The rapid debasement of the prisoners when kept in filthy conditions, with men, women, and children thrown together under a regime of neglect and brutality, appalled the early reformers. The long-term prisons established in the last decade of the eighteenth century were not just a substitute for capital and corporal punishment; they were total administrative and custodial systems intended to remedy the evils of the old methods. In the first quarter of the nineteenth century, administrators experimented with many new systems. The leading contenders for the world's attention were the Eastern Penitentiary and the New York State Prison at Auburn, opened in 1819.

The Auburn prison administrators developed a system that was almost the opposite of that used at the Eastern Penitentiary. The building itself was based on a new **inside cell** design[4] and the cells were quite small when compared with those at Eastern. The small cells were designed to be used only for sleeping, not as a place for work. In addition, a new style of discipline was inaugurated at Auburn that became known as the **Auburn**, or "congregate," **system**.

In the early years of the Auburn prison, administrators tested the efficacy of the Pennsylvania system. They selected eighty of the most hardened convicts, placing them in solitary confinement and enforced idleness for two years, from Christmas 1821 through Christmas 1823. So many of those men succumbed to sickness and insanity that the experiment was discontinued long before the two-year mark. The Auburn administration thus claimed failure for solitary confinement when the method included idleness. Given the small inside cells in Auburn, their claim was no doubt a valid one. However, the Auburn experiment cannot be considered a fair comparison to the Pennsylvania system, because the latter system used large outside cells and provided for handicraft and other labor in the cells.[5]

Discipline at Auburn

An unfortunate by-product of the badly planned Auburn experiment was the use of solitary confinement as a means of punishment within the prison. The discipline regimen at Auburn also included congregate work in the shops during the day, separation of prisoners into small individual cells at night, silence at all times, lockstep marching formations, and a congregate meal at which the prisoners sat face-to-back.[6] There was great emphasis on silence. In the belief that verbal exchange between prisoners was contaminating, conversation was prevented by liberal use of the whip. An excellent description of the Auburn system in its early stages, drawn from a letter by Louis Dwight, as quoted by Harry Elmer Barnes, follows:

Harry Elmer Barnes (1889–1968)

was a great American educator and sociologist who coauthored many books on penology, punishment, and criminology.

> *At Auburn we have a more beautiful example still of what may be done by proper discipline, in a prison well constructed. It is not possible to describe the pleasure which we feel in contemplating this noble institution, after wading through the fraud, and the material and moral filth of many prisons. We regard it as a model worthy of the world's imitation. We do not mean that there is nothing in this institution which admits of improvement; for there have been a few cases of unjustifiable severity in punishments; but, upon the whole, the institution is immensely elevated above the old penitentiaries. The whole establishment, from the gate to the sewer, is a specimen of neatness. The unremitted industry, the entire subordination and subdued feelings of the convicts, has probably no parallel among an equal number of criminals. In their solitary cells they spend the night, with no other book but the Bible, and at sunrise they proceed, in military order, under the eye of the turnkeys, in solid columns, with the lock march, to their workshops; thence, in the same order at the hour of breakfast, to the common hall, where they partake of their wholesome and frugal meal in silence. Not even a whisper is heard; though the silence is such that a whisper might be heard through the whole apartment. The convicts are seated, in single file, at narrow tables, with their backs towards the center, so that there can be no interchange of signs. If one has more food than he wants, he raises his left hand; and if another has less, he raises his right hand, and the waiter changes it. When they have done eating, at the ringing of a little bell, of the softest sound, they rise from the table, form the solid columns, and return, under the eye of the turnkeys, to the workshops. From one end of the shops to the other, it is the testimony of many witnesses, that they have passed more than three hundred convicts, without seeing one leave his work, or turn his head to gaze at them. There is the most perfect attention to business from morning till night, interrupted only by the time necessary to dine, and never by the fact that the whole body of prisoners have done their tasks, and the time is now their own, and they can do as they please. At the close of the day, a little before sunset, the work is all laid*

> *aside at once, and the convicts return, in military order, to the solitary cells, where they partake of the frugal meal, which they were permitted to take from the kitchen, where it was furnished for them as they returned from the shops. After supper, they can, if they choose, read Scripture undisturbed and then reflect in silence on the errors of their lives. They must not disturb their fellow prisoners by even a whisper.*[7]

The Auburn system became the pattern for more than thirty state prisons in the next half century. Sing Sing Prison in New York followed the Auburn pattern in 1825. Wethersford Prison in Connecticut copied the Auburn system but used a more moderate form of their brutal punishments. Later prisons modeled their disciplinary systems after Wethersford.

Auburn's structural design, with inside cells and wings composed of two to four tiers of cells **(cell blocks)**, became the model for most prisons built in the following 150 years. Many variations and innovations on the Auburn concept were developed. The most popular of those types, first constructed in 1898 at Fresnes, France, became known as the "telephone pole" design. Regardless of the cell block arrangement, the inside cell design became the most common model in America.

One of the more important, but less noted, aspects of early prison architecture was the grand scale and sheer size of the institutions. "Bigger is better" (and more cost effective) was the watchword of early prison builders. Huge gothic-style structures achieved an effect similar to that of the medieval castles or cathedrals of Europe. They made the people inside seem small and insignificant. This feeling was further enhanced by the stern discipline employed in these huge castles of despair. Size is discussed again in later chapters, but we should note here that the size of the early prisons gave rise to a subtle pressure to keep them filled with society's castoffs.

PRISON COMPETITION

The main theme in both the Pennsylvania and Auburn prison systems was the belief that a regimen of silence and penitence would prevent cross infection and encourage improved behavior in the prisoner. Supporters of the Pennsylvania system claimed it was easier to control the prisoners, gave more consideration to their individual needs, prevented contamination by the complete separation of prisoners from one another, and provided more opportunity for meditation and penitence. Another advantage they cited was that prisoners could leave the Pennsylvania system with their background known only to a few administrators, because they did not come in contact with other prisoners.

On the other hand, supporters of the Auburn or congregate system argued that it was cheaper to construct and get started, offered better vocational training, and produced more money for the state.[8] The persuasive power of economics finally decided the battle, and the **congregate system** was adopted in almost all other American prisons, even in Pennsylvania. The Western Penitentiary was converted in 1869 and, finally in 1913, the Eastern Penitentiary changed its system. The capitulation of the Pennsylvania system followed many long years of fierce controversy between the two systems. "The only gratifying feature of the controversy was that both systems were so greatly superior to the unspeakable . . . system which they displaced that their competition inevitably worked for the betterment of penal conditions."[9]

RULES

As mentioned in Chapter 1, prisons can be viewed as yet another method to implement social vengeance for wrongs against society. Europeans examining the Auburn and Pennsylvania systems made a keen observation on the American society and its prisons:

> *It must be acknowledged that the* **penitentiary system** *in America is severe. While society in the United States gives the example of the most extended liberty, the prisons of the same country offer the spectacle of the most complete despotism.*[10]

In this context, the individual citizen's sense of guilt when he or she inflicts brutal or cruel punishment on another is diffused by the need for revenge on criminal offenders as a class and for the protection of society. The "out of sight, out of mind" principle was especially evident in the early nineteenth-century prisons. Most of them were located far out in the countryside, free from either interference or inspection by the communities that supplied the prisoners. It is not too hard to understand why rules and procedures emphasized the smooth and undisturbed operation of the prison rather than the modification of the individual prisoner's behavior. Administrators were usually judged by the prison's production record and the number of escapes, not by the number of successful rehabilitations. Because of this, rules were designed to keep prisoners under total control. It is those early and well-established prison practices that have been the most difficult to overcome in the emerging standards of good correctional practices.

Elam Lynds, warden of Auburn and later of Sing Sing (which he built), was one of the most influential persons in the development of early prison discipline in America. He is described as having been an extremely strict **disciplinarian** who believed that all convicts were cowards who could not be reformed until their spirit was broken. To this end he devised a system of brutal punishments and degrading procedures, many of which remained as accepted practice until very recent times.

The imposition of **silence** was seen as the most important part of the discipline program. The rule of absolute silence and noncommunication was maintained and enforced by the immediate use of the lash for the slightest infraction. Lynds advocated flogging as the most effective way to maintain order. He sometimes used a "cat" made of barbed wire strands, but more often a rawhide whip. The stereotype of the ex-con who is always talking out of the side of his mouth actually developed in the "silent" prisons to get around the silence rules.

Another bizarre form of discipline that was developed at Auburn was the **lockstep formation.** Prisoners were required to line up in close formation with their hands on the shoulders or under the arms of the prisoner in front. The line then moved rapidly toward its destination as the prisoners shuffled their feet in unison, without lifting them from the ground. Because this nonstop shuffle was "encouraged" by the use of the lash, any prisoner who fell out of lockstep risked a broken ankle or other serious injury from the steadily moving formation. Breaking the rule of silence during formation was considered especially objectionable and was punished viciously.

The use of degrading prison garb was also initiated at Auburn and Sing Sing. Early prisoners were allowed to wear the same clothing as the free society did. At Auburn and Sing Sing, different colors were used for the first-time offenders and for

A chain gang crew in 1933 Fulton County, Georgia, spends time in the infirmary in stripes.
Courtesy of AP/Wide World Photos.

SIDEBARS

Prison Stripes

A development of the various forms of attire used to degrade and identify prisoners. Wide, alternating black-and-white horizontal bands were placed on the loose-fitting heavy cotton garments. Stripes were still in use in the South as late as the 1940s and 1950s. They have been generally replaced in most security prisons by blue denims or whites.

SIDEBARS

The Treadmill

Treadmills were devised to provide an exercise outlet for prisoners in the workhouses in England. They were actually human-powered squirrel cages, and although sometimes used to power mills and factory tools, their primary function was to keep prisoners busy. The lack of activity in the Walnut Street Jail caused the treadmill to be introduced in the early 1800s. The term "on the treadmill" refers to motion without going anywhere, like the prisoners on the great wheels of the treadmills.

SIDEBARS

The Hole, or Solitary Confinement

Usually located in the lower levels of the prison, most solitary confinement cells were small four-by-eight cells with no light and solid walls and doors, usually painted black. Time in the hole was ordinarily accompanied by reduced rations and the loss of all privileges. Today solitary confinement is used for administrative or disciplinary segregation, commonly in cells similar to all others except for their single occupancy and loss of privileges such as television or radio.

repeaters. Bizarre outfits served to reveal the prisoners' classification at a glance, to institutionalize them further, and to facilitate identification of escapees. The famous **prison stripes** came into being in 1815 in New York. The stripes were abandoned in most prisons but they have since been returned by the Mississippi legislature in 1994 and by many other local jails and prisons.

The methods used to prevent conversation or communication during meals were also humiliating. As mentioned, prisoners were required to sit face-to-back. They were given their meager, and usually bland and unsavory, meal to eat in silence. If they wanted more food, they would raise one hand; if they had too much they raised the other. Any infraction of the rule of silence resulted in a flogging and the loss of a meal. This kind of entrenched procedure, very resistant to modern reforms, has been the source of many prison riots. Earlier prisons also had **treadmills** on which inmates labored, sometimes for exercise but frequently as a form of physical punishment.

One of the earliest and most well-known forms of prison discipline was the "prison-within-a-prison," or **solitary confinement**, used as punishment for violation of institutional rules. Although the early experiment with total solitary confinement at Auburn showed it could not serve as the basis of a permanent prison system, the administrators saw its possibilities as a punishment for infractions of prison rules. Most of the prisons designed along the Auburn model, therefore, had a block of cells somewhere inside the walls, often referred to as the "hole." Usually, a sentence to solitary confinement was accompanied by reduced rations as well, consisting often of only bread and water. Solitary confinement is frequently used to discipline prisoners even today, although under much more humane conditions.

The many new prisons that were constructed in the century after the Eastern Penitentiary and the Auburn Prison made few, if any, contributions to the development of penology or corrections. The two greatest innovations, which persist today, were prison industries and the massive structures that used the interior cell

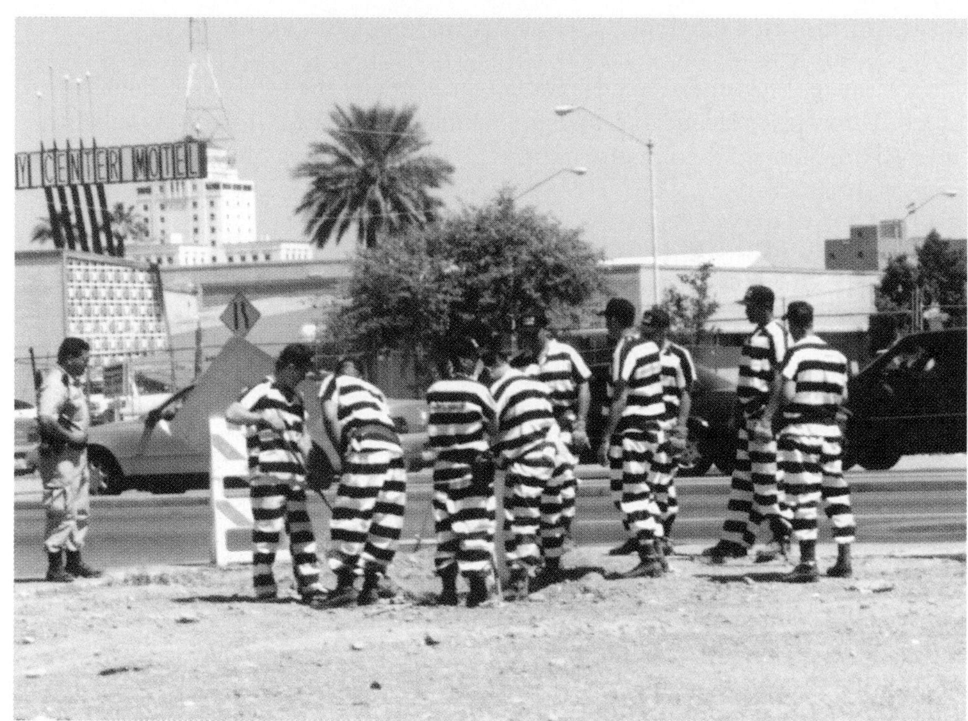

A modern chain gang crew helps with community cleanup in Phoenix, Arizona.

Photo by Jerri Edger, courtesy of Maricopa County Sheriff's Department.

block design. Enforced silence was finally seen as a failure and abandoned. Cruel and barbaric punishments, though publicly decried, are still sometimes used—largely because most prisons are isolated from society and its controls. The development of corrections between 1800 and 1870, using policies, procedures, and philosophies that were unjust, still produced better results than did the universally accepted capital and corporal punishment that preceded it. And in the following era the swing toward a more realistic and humanistic correctional approach began.

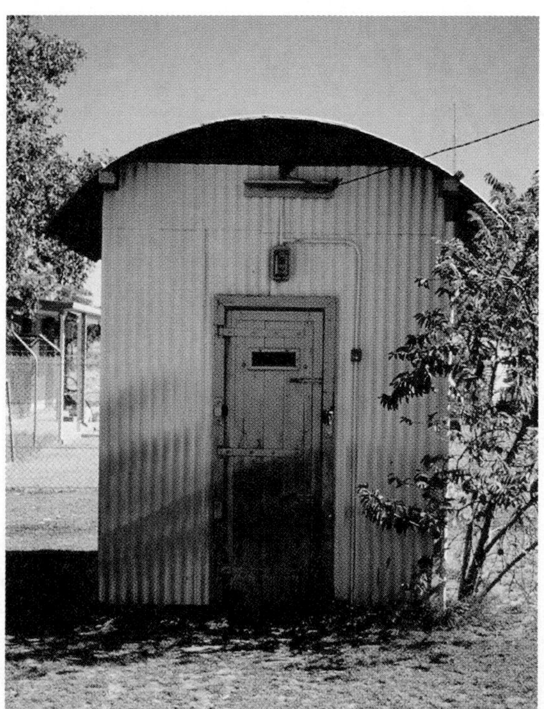

A "sweat box" punishment cell for solitary confinement.

Photo by Peter C. Unsinger, courtesy of American Correctional Association. Reprinted with permission.

Maconochie and Crofton: A New Approach

The reformatory system in America owes a great deal to the work of an Englishman, Captain Alexander Maconochie, and an Irishman, Sir Walter Crofton. Together they laid the foundation for reformative rather than purely punitive programs for the treatment of criminals.

Maconochie and the Indeterminate Sentence

In 1840, Captain Maconochie was put in charge of the British penal colony on Norfolk Island, about 800 miles east of Australia. To this island were sent the criminals who were "twice condemned": They had been shipped to Australia from England and then from Australia to Norfolk. Conditions were so bad at Norfolk that men reprieved from the death penalty wept, and those who were to die thanked God.[11] That was the kind of hell Maconochie inherited.

The first thing Maconochie did was to eliminate the flat sentence,[12] a system that had allowed no hope of release until the full time had been served. Then he developed a "mark system" whereby a convict could earn freedom by hard work and good behavior, thus creating the **indeterminate sentence.** This type of sentencing put the burden of release on the convict. As Maconochie said, "When a man keeps the key of his own prison, he is soon persuaded to fit it into the lock." The system had five principles:

1. Release should not be based on the completion of a sentence for a set period of time, but on the completion of a determined and specified quantity of labor. In brief, time sentences should be abolished, and task sentences substituted.
2. The quantity of labor a prisoner must perform should be expressed in a number of "marks," which he must earn, by improvement of conduct, frugality of living, and habits of industry, before he can be released.
3. While in prison he should earn everything he receives. All sustenance and indulgences should be added to his debt of marks.
4. When qualified by discipline to do so, he should work in association with a small number of other prisoners, forming a group of six or seven, and the whole group should be answerable for the conduct and labor of each member.
5. In the final stage, a prisoner, while still obliged to earn his daily tally of marks, should be given a proprietary interest in his own labor and be subject to a less rigorous discipline, to prepare him for release into society.[13]

It is a sad fact that Maconochie's visionary efforts toward rehabilitation were not appreciated or supported by the unenlightened bureaucrats above him. His results thus were disclaimed, and the colony fell back into its former brutalized routine almost as soon as he left it.

Crofton and the Irish System

Fortunately, Maconochie's ideas did reach beyond the shores of Norfolk Island. His successful use of the indeterminate sentence[14] showed that imprisonment could be used to prepare a convict for eventual return to the community. If this were true, then the length of sentence should not be an arbitrary period of time but should be related to the rehabilitation of the offender. Sir Walter Crofton of Ireland used that concept in developing what he called the "indeterminate system," which came to be known as the **Irish system.** He reasoned that if penitentiaries are places where offenders think about their crimes and can decide to stop their criminal misbehavior ("repent"), then there must be a mechanism to determine that this decision has in fact been made, as well as a mechanism for getting the inmate out when penitence has been done. The indeterminate sentence was believed to be the best mechanism.

The system Crofton devised, like Maconochie's, consisted of a series of stages, each bringing the convict closer to the free society. The first stage was solitary confinement and monotonous work. The second stage was assignment to public works and a progression through various grades, each grade shortening the length of stay. The last stage was assignment to an intermediate prison where the prisoner worked without supervision and moved in and out of the free community. If the prisoner's conduct continued to be good and if he or she were able to find employment, then the offender returned to the community on a conditional pardon or **ticket-of-leave.** This ticket could be revoked at any time within the span of the original fixed sentence if the prisoner's conduct was not up to standards established by those who supervised the conditional pardon. Crofton's plan was the first effort to establish a system of **conditional liberty** in the community, the system we know today as parole.

THE REFORMATORY ERA (1870 TO 1910)

Leaders in U.S. penology and prison administration met at the American Prison Congress of 1870[15] to discuss the direction that corrections practices should take. They were especially concerned about overcrowding, and they discussed what new kinds of prisons should be built to alleviate it. Many urged that Maconochie's and Crofton's plans be adopted in America. The members endorsed that idea, and the reformatory era in American corrections was born.

The first **reformatory** in America was built in 1876, in Elmira, New York, and became the model for all those that followed. **Zebulon Brockway**, the first superintendent, had introduced some new educational methods at the Detroit House of Corrections, and he expanded on that concept at Elmira. Elmira was originally built for adult felons, but it was used instead for youths from sixteen to thirty years of age who were serving their first term in prison. One observer cited the following characteristics as the standards for Elmira, and many of those reappeared in its imitators.

1. The material structural establishment itself. The general plan and arrangements should be those of the Auburn system, modified and modernized; and 10 percent of the cells might well be constructed like those of the Pennsylvania system. The whole should be supplied with suitable modern sanitary appliances and with abundance of natural and artificial light.
2. Clothing—not degradingly distinctive, but uniform, . . . fitly representing the respective grades or standing of the prisoners. . . . Scrupulous cleanliness should be maintained and the prisoners appropriately groomed.
3. A liberal prison diet designed to promote vigor. Deprivation of food, by a general regulation, is deprecated. . . .
4. All the modern appliances for scientific physical culture; a gymnasium completely equipped with baths and apparatus; and facilities for field athletics.
5. Facilities for manual training sufficient for about one-third of the population. . . . This special manual training covers, in addition to other exercises in other departments, mechanical and freehand drawing; sloyd [manual training] in wood and metals; cardboard constructive form work; clay modeling; cabinet making; clipping and filing; and iron molding.

PROFILE

Zebulon Reed Brockway (1827–1920),

along with Enoch C. Wines and Franklin Benjamin Sanborn, was the third member of the "big three" of penology in 1870. He served on many commissions to improve prisons and even founded the U.S. Army Disciplinary Barracks at Fort Leavenworth, Kansas. Later, he was the first superintendent at the Elmira Reformatory, where he used military organization and discipline to govern the prisoners. His book *Fifty Years of Prison Service* (1912) is a classic.

6. Trade instruction based on the needs and capacities of individual prisoners. (Where a thousand prisoners are involved, thirty-six trades may be usefully taught.)
7. A regimental military organization with a band of music, swords for officers, and dummy guns for the rank and file of prisoners.
8. School of letters with a curriculum that reaches from an adaptation of the kindergarten . . . up to the usual high school course; and, in addition, special classes in college subjects. . . .
9. A well-selected library for circulation, consultation, and for occasional semi-social use.
10. The weekly institutional newspaper, in lieu of all outside newspapers, edited and printed by the prisoners under due censorship.
11. Recreating and diverting entertainments for the mass of the population, provided in the great auditorium; not any vaudeville or minstrel shows, but entertainments of such a class as the middle cultured people of a community would enjoy. . . .
12. Religious opportunities . . . adapted to the hereditary [and] habitual . . . denominational predilection of the individual prisoners.
13. Definitely planned, carefully directed, emotional occasions; not summoned, primarily, for either instruction, diversion, nor, specifically, for a common religious impression, but, figuratively, for a kind of irrigation.[16]

The only real differences between the programs at Elmira and those at the adult prisons were the emphasis on reforming youth, increased academic education, and more extensive trade training. Two significant features were adopted for the reformatories, though: the indeterminate sentence and a grading system based on marks that could lead to parole.

Elmira was copied, in one form or another, by seventeen states between 1876 and 1913. Brockway's leadership produced the first attempt to offer programs of education and reformation to all inmates, adult or youth. Trade training, academic education, and the military type of discipline utilized at Elmira undoubtedly also influenced the programs of many of the older prisoners. Some aspects of the indeterminate sentence and parole concepts were finally extended to the state prisons. It is not surprising that in an era when public education was considered to be the answer to so many problems in the outside world, it was viewed as the answer to crime as well. But because the same physical environment and the same underpaid and poorly qualified personnel found in prisons were also found in reformatories, those institutions were soon reduced to junior prisons with the usual routine. The same old "prison discipline" was still the most dominant feature in any penal program.

Although the two main contributions of the reformatory era were the indeterminate sentence and parole, the seeds of education, vocational training, and individual rehabilitation had been sown. Even though such radical ideas could not flourish in the barren and hostile environment of that period, they took root and grew to fruition in later years.

POST–CIVIL WAR PRISONS

The sixteen states that built prisons between 1870 and 1900 were almost all in the northern or western part of the country. Their only claim to improvement was the introduction of plumbing and running water. All were of the Auburn type, and the only modifications in the older prison routine were the abandonment of the silent system and the use of the indeterminate sentence and parole.

In the South, devastated by the Civil War, the penitentiary system had been virtually wiped out. Some states attempted to solve their prison problems by leasing out their entire convict population to contractors.[17] Others took in contract work or devised combinations of both leasing out prisoners and taking in contracts. Yet another group of slaves thus replaced the freed blacks: the convicted felons. The South was unique in that many of its prisons ignored both the Auburn and reformatory systems. The South's agrarian economy made exploitation of cheap labor both easy and desirable. A large portion of the prison population in the South was composed of plantation blacks who had no influence or resources, and they were treated with no mercy.[18] Leasing was eventually replaced by prison farms in most southern states, but the practice was not completely erased until the mid-1920s. This sordid period in penal history, brought to light again in the 1960s in Arkansas,[19] simply confirms the depths to which even so-called civilized people can sink in the treatment of their castoffs. The correctional experience in the South made only a negative contribution in regard to both procedure and discipline.

THE TWENTIETH CENTURY AND THE INDUSTRIAL PRISON

The introduction of handicrafts into the solitary Eastern Penitentiary cells represented the origin of prison industries in America. In continental Europe and England, the infamous efforts to provide labor in the workhouses and Bridewells had resulted in such fruitless activities as the treadmill. The modern pressure to provide vocational training or earnings for inmates did not concern early American prison administrators; rather, they wanted to make the prisons self-sustaining. Toward this goal, the prison workshops were merely extensions of the early factory workshops. When the factory production system was introduced into prisons and they began to show actual profits from their output, legislators were quickly convinced that prison industries were a sound operation. The Auburn system held out over the less efficient Pennsylvania system because it paid better returns on the taxpayer's investment. By the 1860s, the system of absolute silence had begun to fall apart because of the necessity for communication in the industrial shops. Early prison industries, in effect, exploited the available free labor for the sole purpose of perpetuating the institution itself. Some leaders in the field, however, saw that a change in emphasis could make the industries an important factor in prisoner rehabilitation.

From the beginning of the twentieth century until 1940, the number of inmates in U.S. prisons increased by 174 percent.[20] Ten new Auburn-style prisons and even one based on Bentham's Panopticon were built during this period—often referred to as the industrial era for prisons in America, which finally reached its zenith in 1935. The new prisons were considered "as cold and hard and abnormal as the prisoners whom they were intended to persuade toward better things."[21]

The **industrial prison** can credit its origins to the profits turned by the first state prisons. Early in the nineteenth century, however, mechanics and cabinetmakers began to complain about the unfair competition they faced from the virtually free labor force available to prisons. The use of lease and contract systems aggravated the problem and led to a series of investigations that reached national prominence in 1886. The emergence of the labor union movement, coupled with abuses of the contract and lease systems of prison labor, eliminated those systems in the northern prisons by the end of the nineteenth century. They were replaced by piece-price[22] and state-account[23]

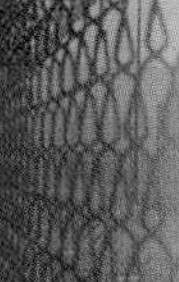

CORRECTIONAL BRIEF

Hawes–Cooper Act, Chap. 79. (1929)

Be it enacted by the Senate and House of Representatives of the United States of America in Congress assembled, That all goods, wares, and merchandise manufactured, produced, or mined, wholly or in part, by convicts or prisoners, except convicts or prisoners on parole or probation, or in any penal and/or reformatory institutions, except commodities manufactured in Federal penal and correctional institutions for use by the Federal Government, transported into any State or Territory of the United States and remaining therein for use, consumption, sale, or storage, shall upon arrival and delivery in such State or Territory be subject to the operation and effect of the laws of such State or Territory to the same extent and in the same manner as though such goods, wares, and merchandise had been manufactured, produced, or mined in such State or Territory, and shall not be exempt therefrom by reason of being introduced in the original package or otherwise.

SEC. 2 This act shall take effect five years after the date of its approval. Approved, January 19, 1929.

systems. Opposition to prison industries resulted in enforced idleness among the increasing inmate population. This forced the adult prisons to adopt reformatory methods in some measure but made self-sustaining institutions a thing of the past.

Because the story of prison industry's battle with organized labor is a history in itself, it is not covered here. The beginning of the end for large-scale prison industries, which kept inmates employed in some kind of work, was the enactment of two federal laws controlling the character of prison products. The **Hawes–Cooper Act**, passed in 1929, required that prison products be subject to the laws of any state to which they were shipped. The **Ashurst–Sumners Act**, passed in 1935, essentially stopped the interstate transport of prison products by requiring that all prison products shipped out of the state be labeled with the prison name and by prohibiting interstate shipment where state laws forbade it. In 1940, the Ashurst-Sumners Act was amended to prohibit fully the interstate shipment of prison products.

CORRECTIONAL BRIEF

Ashurst–Sumners Act, Chap. 412 (1935)

Be it enacted by the Senate and House of Representatives of the United States of America in Congress assembled, That it shall be unlawful for any person knowingly to transport or cause to be transported, in any manner or by any means whatsoever or aid or assist in obtaining transportation for or in transporting any goods, wares and merchandise manufactured, produced, or mined wholly or in part by convicts or prisoners [except convicts or prisoners on parole or probation], or in any penal or reformatory institution, from one State, Territory, Puerto Rico, Virgin islands, or District of the United States, or place noncontiguous but subject to the jurisdiction thereof, or from any foreign country, into any State, Territory, Puerto Rico, Virgin Islands, or District of the United States, or place noncontiguous but subject to the jurisdiction thereof, where said goods, wares, and merchandise are intended by any person interested therein to be received, possessed, sold, or in any manner used, either in the original package or otherwise in violation of any law of such State, Territory, Puerto Rico, Virgin Islands, or District of the United States, or place noncontiguous but subject to the jurisdiction thereof. Nothing herein shall apply to commodities manufactured in Federal penal and correctional institutions for use by the Federal Government.

SEC. 2 All packages containing any goods, wares, and merchandise manufactured, produced, or mined wholly or in part by convicts or prisoners, except convicts or prisoners on parole or probation, or in any penal or reformatory institution, when shipped or transported in interstate or foreign commerce shall be plainly and clearly marked, so that the name and address of the shipper, the name and address of the consignee, the nature of the contents, and the name and location of the penal or reformatory institution where produced wholly or in part may be readily ascertained on an inspection of the outside of such package.

The economic strains of the Great Depression, beginning with the Wall Street stock market crash in 1929 and which spanned the period from 1929 to 1940, led thirty-three states to pass laws that prohibited the sale of prison products on the open market. Those statutes tolled the death knell for the industrial prison. With the exception of a few license plate and state furniture shops, most state prisons took a giant step backward to their original purposes: punishment and custody. Fortunately, another model was emerging at the same time: the "new penology" of the 1930s and the U.S. Bureau of Prisons under the leadership of **Sanford Bates.**

PROFILE

Sanford Bates (1884–1972), a legendary figure in American corrections, was president of the American Correctional Association in 1926. He became the first superintendent of federal prisons in 1929 and the first director of the U.S. Bureau of Prisons in 1930. In 1937, he became the executive director of the Boys' Clubs of America. Later he served as commissioner of the New York State Board of Parole and commissioner of the New Jersey Department of Institutions and Agencies. He was also an active consultant and writer.

THE PERIOD OF TRANSITION (1935 TO 1960)

The quarter century between 1935 and 1960 was one of great turmoil in the prisons. Administrators, stuck with the huge fortresses of the previous century, were now deprived of the ability to provide meaningful work for inmates. The Depression and the criminal excesses of the 1920s and 1930s hardened the public's attitude toward convict rehabilitation at a time when behavioral scientists were just beginning to propose hopeful reforms in prisoner treatment. J. Edgar Hoover, director of the Federal Bureau of Investigation (FBI), led the battle against "hoity-toity professors" and the "cream-puff school of criminology." His war on crime helped give the world the supermaximum prison, **Alcatraz.** Located on an island in San Francisco Bay, Alcatraz was constructed to house the most hardened criminals confined in the federal prison system. When it was built in 1934, it was seen as the answer to the outrages of such desperate criminals as Al Capone, Robert Stroud ("Birdman of Alcatraz"), and Bonnie and Clyde. Eventually, the U.S. Bureau of Prisons abandoned this prison as too expensive to maintain.

PROFILE

Al Capone (1899–1947), U.S. gangster nicknamed "Scarface," joined gangs in his native Brooklyn and became the crime czar in Chicago in 1925. He ordered the execution of other gangsters, such as Bugs Moran's men who were machine-gunned in the St. Valentine's Day Massacre. Convicted of income tax evasion, he retired to Florida where he died of syphilis in 1947.

Such notables as Bernard Glueck at Sing Sing between 1915 and 1920, Edgar Doll and W. G. Ellis in New Jersey in 1925, and A. W. Stearns in Massachusetts in 1930 pioneered early efforts toward diagnostic classification and casework. Sanford Bates introduced procedures into the U.S. Bureau of Prisons in 1934. Although sometimes "borrowing" principles from states across the nation, the U.S. Bureau of Prisons gradually emerged as the national leader in corrections, introducing many new concepts that have been copied by state systems. Two major contributions were diagnosis and classification and the use of professional personnel such as psychiatrists and psychologists to help rehabilitate inmates. The federal system also led the way to more humane treatment and better living conditions (see Chapter 11). But no matter how they were cleaned up, prisons remained monuments to idleness, monotony, frustration, and repression. Despite attempts to tear down the massive walls around some prisons, the forces of **lock psychosis** continued to hold out. Prison inmates were feared as the **convict bogey,** which could be dealt with only by locking and relocking, counting and recounting.

PROFILE

Robert Stroud (1890–1963), named the "Birdman of Alcatraz," was possibly the most famous inmate in the federal prison at Alcatraz. He was a violent and murderous felon who killed a guard in front of 1,100 inmates. Later in life, he studied canaries and authored two books on canaries and their diseases. The special equipment to study canaries in his cell was used as a still for an alcoholic brew. He served fifty-four years in prison, forty-one of them in solitary confinement.

It is not too surprising that the long hours of idleness, forbidding architecture, growing populations, and unnecessarily repressive controls created unbearable tensions among the inmates. The first riots in this country, as noted earlier, were at the mine shaft prison in Simsbury, Connecticut. Riots at the Walnut Street Jail were reported in the early 1800s as well. The mid-nineteenth century, when prison industries provided extensive work for convicts, was a time of few riots. Presumably, either the inmates were too tired to riot or the control was too strict. As the prison industries died out, riots began to take place more regularly, adding evidence to the theory that enforced idleness causes restlessness and discontent among prisoners.

PROFILE

Bonnie Parker (1910–1934) and Clyde Barrow (1910–1934)

were the leaders of the Barrow gang, which terrorized the Midwest in 1933 and 1934. They were gunned down in a Ford V-8 during a famous ambush in 1934. Clyde's dead hands clutched a shotgun with seven notches on the stock, Bonnie's a pistol with three. Bonnie had sent a song, "The Story of Bonnie and Clyde," to a music publisher to be released after her death. It caught the imagination of the country and was a hit, making pseudo-heroes of these cheap killers (who were restored to fame again in the 1967 movie glorifying their exploits).

SIDEBARS

Lock Psychosis

The unreasonable fear by prison administrators that leads them to lock prisoners behind several layers of barred doors and other barricades. The huge ring of keys carried by most prison personnel is an outward manifestation of this psychosis. Counts are usually conducted several times a day to ensure that all prisoners are locked up. Modern correctional administrations use plastic wrist identifier bands for continuous inmate counting and location.

SIDEBARS

Convict Bogey

Society's exaggerated fear of the convict and ex-convict, which is usually far out of proportion to the real danger they present. The tough escaped convicts shown in the movies and on television are a contributing factor to the unreasonable fear of convicts as a group.

SIDEBARS

Prison Riot

A violent, tumultuous disturbance within a prison or other correctional institution involving seven or more inmates assembled together and acting in a common cause.

There was a wave of riots in the prisons between 1929 and 1932. During World War II there were few problems, but in 1946 there was even a riot in Alcatraz, the superprison.

Whether neglect of prisons and lack of meaningful activities finally bore bitter fruit or whether the rising prosperity of the 1950s simply presented too sharp a contrast with the bleak life on the inside, there was an explosion of prison discontent during the early part of that decade. More than 300 prison riots have occurred since 1774, and 90 percent of those have occurred in the last four decades.[24] The American Correctional Association investigated the 1950s riots and reported what appeared to be the main causes[25]:

1. Inadequate financial support and official and public indifference
2. Substandard personnel
3. Enforced idleness
4. Lack of professional leadership and professional programs
5. Excessive size and overcrowding of institutions
6. Political domination and motivation of management
7. Unwise sentencing and parole practices.

The explosion predicted from the conditions created by overcrowding, idleness, and lack of public concern erupted at Attica in the fall of 1971. The modern era became a period of seeking ways to prevent such events: Community-based corrections became the watchword for reform in corrections, and the "correctional filter" (discussed in Chapter 6) was supplied with more outlets for diverting inmates from seething, overcrowded prisons. Supreme Court decisions created further pressure for reform. The result, at least until the end of the 1970s, was a state of uneasy status quo. The status quo was broken in the beginning of the 1980s by riots at a New Mexico prison, which resulted in numerous brutal deaths and public outrage. Prison riots continued; in 1996, there were four prison riots over three days in federal prisons. In 2001, several inmates were injured in a California prison riot and, in 2004, there was a riot in a privately run correctional institution in Kentucky.[26]

It appears now that some of the programs designed to relieve the problems in the overcrowded fortress prisons have in fact contributed to many of the conditions and made them even riper for violence. The fortress prisons are still here, they are even more overcrowded, and their maximum-security clients are now the "bottom of the barrel" regarding behavioral problems. This has caused an abandonment of the medical model and steady movement toward a model emphasizing custody and control over everything else in a futile effort to keep peace in the institutions and "protect society." The problem of selecting a philosophy or ideology that is effective and reflective of society's mood is a problem administrators will have to confront in the next decade. To comprehend the current issues in corrections, we must examine the decision process and options available to the prosecution, judiciary, and releasing authorities.

THE MODERN ERA

The "modern era" of corrections is generally considered to have begun about 1960, and it was characterized by a pattern of change that was to highlight the next decade. The 1960s in the United States were noted for turbulent and violent confrontations at almost every level of activity affecting human rights. The forces for change at work in the overall society were also reflected in great pressures for change in corrections. The dramatic reinterpretations of criminal law, the civil rights movement, violent and nonviolent demonstrations in the streets, the assassinations of a popular president and two other important national figures, the continuation of the longest and most unpopular war in American history—all of these outside pressures were also felt inside the walls of the nation's prisons. Reaction took the form of periodic violent prison riots and disorders. The U.S. Supreme Court emerged as the primary external agent for the enforced recognition of the basic rights of those swept up in the criminal justice system. This external pressure was generated by a long series of significant judicial interpretations. In addition, leadership and funding by the federal government were given to correctional administrators and planners at the state and local levels, enabling them to create, implement, and evaluate new standards, policies, and practices. Unfortunately, aspiring politicians and the media have collectively generated and nurtured inaccurate stereotypes about offenders, blunting correctional gains and giving rise to more intractable problems.[27] The conservative movement in the political arena continues to cause a steady move to the right in corrections, wreaking havoc with the shrinking efforts at rehabilitation, which works. The turmoil continues.

INTERNALLY SOUGHT REFORM

Early prisons were less secure than modern ones, and escape was far more common. It was easier to "disappear" into early American society with a new name and a new start. Inmate security and control, improved in recent years, have made escape from prisons difficult; and systems of identification and control, including computer banks of data on each of us, have made escape into society almost impossible.

When the prisons became so secure that relief and escape were cut off, the inmates' frustration and agitation turned inward. Prisoners in this "total institution"[28] used disturbances and riots to express their desire for reforms and changes in rules and conditions. Disturbances also served to resolve power struggles between prison gangs[29] and inmate groups. The early disturbances were characterized by disorganization and rapid dispersion; inmates used those methods to settle old grudges, refusing to fall in line behind any kind of leadership. In the 1960s and 1970s, disturbances were commonplace in most large state systems, reflecting the usual grievances: crowded living conditions, harsh rules, poor food, excessive punishment, and guard brutality.[30] Even the highly respected federal prison system was rocked in 1987 by large-scale hostage taking by Cuban inmates who feared deportation. The growing awareness of individual rights on the outside that began in the 1960s led inmates to seek the same rights inside prisons.

Beginning about 1966, the nature of the demands changed from those involving basic conditions to those concerning basic rights. In that year, the Maryland Penitentiary in Baltimore was the scene of a riot involving over 1,000 inmates. The warden claimed the disturbance was caused by heat waves and overcrowding, but "the riot had to have social overtones," said Joseph Bullock, a member of the state house of delegates. "If they don't stop telling these people [blacks] about their rights," Bullock went on, "things will get worse."[31] Rioting and violence spilled over from the streets into the prisons of America. The

SIDEBARS

Ombudsman

An appointed official who receives and investigates inmates' complaints against correctional practices, reports findings, and recommends corrective action without the inmates' having to fear reprisal.

"political prisoner" label, particularly for blacks and Chicanos, offered a more acceptable way for minority groups to state their feelings of deprivation. They struck out at a system that they perceived gave them an unequal start in life and then jailed them for failing to live up to the rules of that system.[32] Clearly, outside social behavior and conditions do carry over into prison. Little that is new in society starts in prison.

Change, though often temporary, comes about as a result of prison riots. More often today, new voices can help shape prison policies, through an inmate council, grievance procedures, conflict resolution,[33] or inmates serving on regular prison committees, following a collaborative model. Some systems also use an **ombudsman** as a link between the prisoner and the establishment; this official receives and investigates complaints and sees that corrective action is taken. Correctional administrators have learned that the more diverse the correctional staff, the fewer the inmate assaults on other inmates and staff.[34]

The Prison Population Boom

From 1980 to 2005, at the time of this writing, the number of prison inmates in the nation increased more than 360 percent, from 320,000 to 1,470,000 prisoners. This population boom resulted from fear of crime[35] fueled by politicians, the **War on Drugs**, the media, and special interest groups. Yet crime declined significantly during this two-decade period. The level of violence also generally declined during the past few years, but the level of fear has remained steady. Fear of violence, drive-by shootings, juvenile gangs struggling to control the drug trade, drug use, and racism have combined to support a "get tough" environment.

The results, covered in more detail in later chapters, were rapid prison population expansion and an unprecedented growth in prison construction, increased prison overcrowding, reduction of early release mechanisms from prison, and massive jail populations and jail construction (see Figure 2.1). Alternatives to prison—probation, parole, and so-called intermediate punishments—also in-

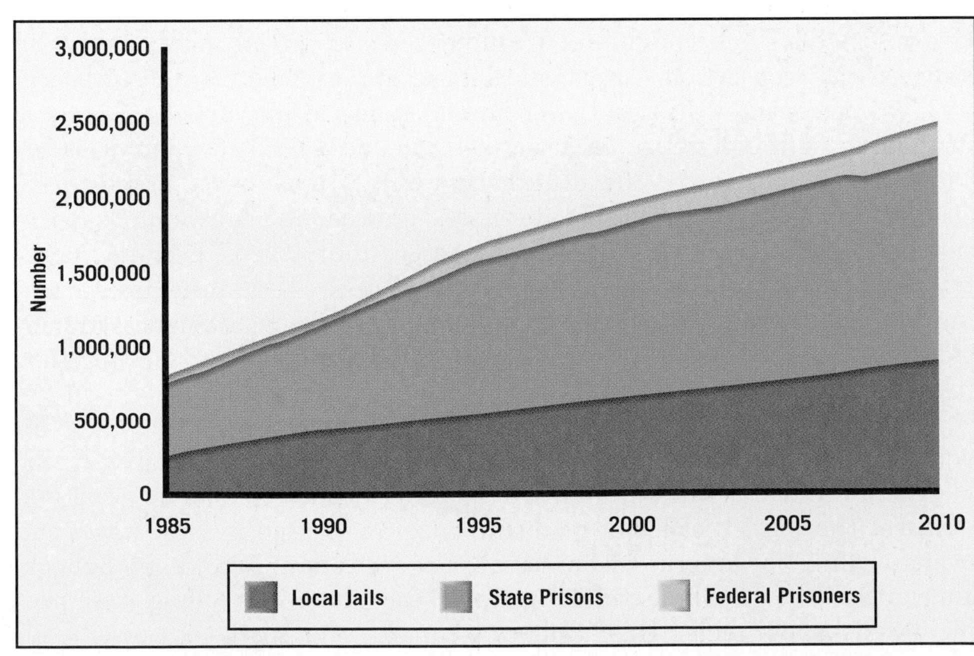

FIGURE 2.1

Number of Inmates in Custody, 1985–2010*

*Data extrapolated to 2010.

From Bureau of Justice Statistics, *Prisoners in 2003* (Washington, DC: BJS, 2004), p. 2.

creased during this time, but did not significantly reduce the pressure to build correctional facilities. Alternatives are needed not only to building of jails and prisons, but also for policies to buttress and expand corrections in the community. New ideas and programs are badly needed, as contemporary corrections appears to be running on empty.

SUMMARY

Now, in the first decade of the twenty-first century, corrections in America finds itself at a crossroads, a crisis unparalleled in the past 200 years. The remainder of this textbook will describe in detail current developments and practices in corrections, innovations, proposed solutions, and ways to ease the crisis and improve the effectiveness of the system. To understand those recent developments, we need to explore the correctional ideologies detailed in the next chapter.

REVIEW QUESTIONS

1. What effect did the Industrial Revolution have on prisons and prison discipline?
2. Which of the two early nineteenth-century prison systems won out in America? Why?
3. What were the major differences between prisons and reformatories?
4. Why have so many riots occurred in prisons?
5. How were American prison industries reduced in correctional importance?

ENDNOTES

1. The Philadelphia Society for the Alleviation of the Miseries of Public Prisons was originally formed by a group of concerned citizens in 1787. Because of their continued efforts, the law of 1790 was passed, and the Walnut Street Jail was remodeled to accommodate felons in solitary confinement. The society is now the Pennsylvania Prison Society [245 N. Broad Street, Suite 300, Philadelphia, PA 19107-1518; (215)564-6005; www.prisonsociety.org].
2. Outside cells were each about six feet wide, eight feet deep, and nine feet high, with a central corridor extending the length of the building in between. Some of them had individual yards added on the outside, with high walls between them.
3. That system, in modified form, is used to this day in Belgium, France, and West Germany. Additional international correctional material can be found under "Foreign Coverage" in each issue of *American Jails* and in the *International Journal of Comparative and Applied Criminal Justice*. See also Elmer Johnson, "Rule Violation of Japanese Inmates," *International Journal of Comparative and Applied Criminal Justice* 22:1 (1998): 17–30.
4. Inside cells are built back-to-back in tiers within a hollow building. Doors open onto galleries or runs that are eight to ten feet from the outside wall; cells are small and intended only for sleeping. The interior cellblock has become characteristic of American prisons.
5. The argument continues. See John Roberts, *Reform and Retribution: An Illustrated History of American Prisons* (Lanham, MD: American Correctional Association, 1997); and Norman Johnston, "The World's Most Influential Prison: Success or Failure?" *The Prison Journal* 84:4(S) (2004): 20S–40S.
6. Walter C. Reckless, *The Crime Problem*, 4th ed. (New York: Appleton-Century-Crofts, 1969), p. 548.
7. Harry Elmer Barnes, *The Story of Punishment*, 2nd ed. (Montclair, NJ: Patterson Smith, 1972), p. 136.
8. Robert G. Caldwell, *Criminology*, 2nd ed. (New York: Ronald Press, 1965), p. 506. See also George Goldman, M. McWilliams, and Vijay Pradhan, *The Economic Impact of Production in California Prison Industries* (Berkeley, CA: Department of Agriculture and Resource Economics, University of California, 1998). But see Corrections and Criminal Justice Coalition, "California Prison Industries Worth in Question," www.ccjc.org/id2.htm (accessed January 12, 2005).
9. Barnes, *The Story of Punishment*, p. 140.

10. G. de Beaumont and A. de Tocqueville, *On the Penitentiary System in the United States and Its Application in France* (Philadelphia: Francis Lieber, 1833).
11. Robert Waite, "From Penitentiary to Reformatory: The Road to Prison Reform," in Louis Knafler (ed.), *Criminal Justice History: An International Annual,* Vol. 12 (Westport, CT: Greenwood Press, 1993), pp. 85–106. See also Bob Reece, *The Origins of Irish Convict Transportation to New South Wales* (New York: Palgrave, 2001).
12. Flat sentence refers to a specific period of time (for example, five years, ten years) in confinement for an offense, with no time off for any reason.
13. Harry Elmer Barnes and Negley K. Teeters, *New Horizons in Criminology,* 3rd ed. (Englewood Cliffs, NJ: Prentice Hall, 1959), p. 419. See also Gilbert Geis, "Negley K. Teeters (1896–1971)", *The Prison Journal* 84:4S (2004): 5S–19S.
14. An indeterminate sentence usually has broad beginning and end figures (three to five years, one to ten years, and so on), instead of a certain fixed period. Prisoners are allowed to earn their freedom by means of good conduct. For the Irish experience, see Burke Carroll, *Colonial Discipline: The Making of the Irish Convict System* (Dublin: Four Courts Press, 2001).
15. Progressive penologists of the era met in Cincinnati, Ohio, on October 12, 1870, to plan the ideal prison system. Two earlier attempts to gather had failed, but this meeting of the American Prison Congress developed into the National Prison Association, later the American Correctional Association (4380 Forbes Avenue, Lanham, MD 20706-4322).
16. Barnes and Teeters, *New Horizons in Criminology,* p. 426.
17. Georgia, Florida, Mississippi, Louisiana, and Arkansas, in particular, followed this procedure. See Matthew Mancini, *One Dies, Get Another: Convict Leasing in the American South, 1866–1928* (Columbia, SC: University of South Carolina Press, 1996).
18. Harry E. Allen and Julie C. Abril, "The New Chain Gang: Corrections in the Next Century," *American Journal of Criminal Justice* 22:1 (1997): 1–12. See also Timothy Dodge, "State Convict Road Gangs in Alabama," *The Alabama Review* 53:4 (2000): 243–270.
19. Tom Murton and Joe Hyams, *Accomplices to the Crime: The Arkansas Prison Scandal* (New York: Grove Press, 1967).
20. Margaret Calahan, *Historical Corrections Statistics in the United States: 1850–1984* (Washington, DC: U.S. Department of Justice, 1986), p. 36.
21. Wayne Morse, *The Attorney General's Survey of Release Procedures* (Washington, DC: U.S. Government Printing Office, 1940).
22. Under the piece-price system, a variation of the contract system, the contractor supplied the raw material and paid a price for each delivered finished product. Thailand currently uses this system.
23. In the state-account or public-account system, all employment and activity are under the direction of the state, and products are sold on the open market. The prisoner receives a very small wage, and the profit goes to the state. Usually binder twine, rope, and hemp sacks were produced this way; it provided a lot of work for prisoners, but little training. See American Correctional Association, *A Study of Prison Industry: History, Components, and Goals* (Washington, DC: U.S. Department of Justice, 1986); and Queensland Criminal Justice Consortium, *Queensland Prison Industries 9* (Brisbane, Australia: QCJC, 2000).
24. See Mike Rolland, *Descent into Madness: An Inmate's Experience of the New Mexico State Prison Riot* (Cincinnati, OH: Anderson, 1997). See also Keith Carter, "The Casaurina Prison Riot," *Current Issues in Criminal Justice* 12:3 (2001): 363–375; and Lorna Rhodes, *Total Confinement* (Berkeley: University of California Press, 2004).
25. As cited in Barnes and Teeters, *New Horizons in Criminology,* p. 385.
26. Jennifer Harry, "Several Injured in California Prison Riot," *Corrections Today* 63:7 (2001): 12; and Deborah Yetter and Mark Pitsch, "Prison Riot Followed Increase in Inmates," www.courier-journal.com/localnews/2004/09/17ky/A1-prison0917-8527.html (accessed January 12, 2005).
27. Brent Staples, "Why Some Politicians Need Their Prisons to Stay Full," www.prisonersofthecensus.org/fact_27-12-2004.shtml (accessed January 12, 2005); and James Inciardi, "The Irrational Policy of American Drug Policy," *Ohio State Journal of Criminal Law* 1:1 (2003): 273–288.
28. Irving Goffman, "On the Characteristics of Total Institutions: Staff–Inmate Relations," in D. R. Cressey (ed.), *The Prison* (New York: Holt, Rinehart & Winston, 1966), pp. 16–22. This concept refers to the sum of conditions created by a large number of people living around the clock within a close space, with tightly scheduled sequences of activity coordinated by a central authority.
29. Reid Montgomery and G. Crews, *A History of Correctional Violence* (Lanham, MD: American Correctional Association, 1998). See also Arjen Boin and William Rattray, "Understanding Prison Riots," *Punishment and Society* 6:1 (2004): 47–65.
30. Ibid. See also John Conrad, "From Barbarism Toward Decency: Alabama's Long Road to Prison

Reform," *Journal of Research in Crime and Delinquency* 26 (1989): 307–328; and Barbara Belot and J. Marquardt, "The Political Community Model and Prisoner Litigation," *Prison Journal* 78:3 (1998): 299–329.

31. *New York Times* (July 9, 1966): 9. See also Christopher Stone, "Race, Crime and the Administration of Justice," *National Institute of Justice Journal* (April 1999): 26–32.
32. Phillip Kassel, "The Gang Crackdown in Massachusetts Prisons," *New England Journal on Criminal and Civil Confinement* 24:1 (1998): 37–63. See also Kalpana Patel and Alex Lord, "Ethnic Minority Sex Offenders' Experiences of Treatment," *Journal of Sexual Aggression* 7:1 (2001): 40–50.
33. Reginald Wilkinson and Tessa Unwin, "Intolerance in Prison," *Corrections Today* 61:3 (1999): 98–100.
34. Ibid.
35. John Hagan and Juleigh Coleman, "Returning Captives of the American War on Drugs," *Crime and Delinquency* 47:3 (2001): 352–367; and Ronald Weitzer and Charis Kubrin, "Breaking News," *Justice Quarterly* 21:3 (2004): 497–520.

CHAPTER 3

Correctional Ideologies: *The Pendulum Swings*

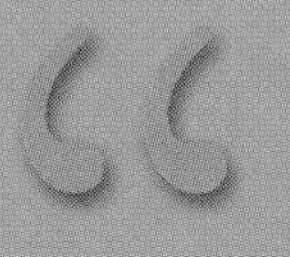

The massive prison construction represents a commitment by our nation to plan for social failure by spending billions of dollars to lock up hundreds of thousands of people while at the same time cutting billions of dollars from programs that would provide opportunity to young Americans.

—Steven Donziger, *The Real War on Crime*

KEY WORDS

- ideology
- correctional ideology
- punishment ideology
- treatment ideology
- prevention ideology
- deterrent effect
- stigma of conviction
- incapacitation
- theory of disablement
- selective incapacitation
- treatment model
- reformatory movement
- educational doctrine
- medical model
- reintegration model
- diversion
- "get tough" laws
- restorative justice

OVERVIEW

So far we have looked at the history and early development of corrections, outlining the major construction of prisons and facilities that reflected the thoughts of those years. An underlying policy question explored in the first two chapters of your textbook concerned the role of criminal law and offenders: Who are offenders and what shall we do with them? The answers identified thus far include the following: They are (1) evil and must be destroyed, (2) out of touch with God and need to repent, (3) poorly educated and ill trained to function in modern society, and (4) sick and in need of being cured—the punishment, reform, education, and medical models for corrections, respectively. In this chapter, we explore the philosophical underpinnings on which these models were built, and explain the rationales that underlie current correctional developments. We need to understand why the nation has entered into an age of massive change in attitudes and prison construction, what goals are being sought, and what the implications of the new programs and facilities might be. We begin with an understanding of what we refer to as ideologies.

CONFLICTING CORRECTIONAL IDEOLOGIES

To understand the current state of corrections, its problems and issues, and a possible future, we turn first to a discussion of ideologies. An **ideology**, according to *Webster's*, is "a systematic body of concepts, especially about human life or culture." A **correctional ideology**, then, refers to a body of ideas and practices that pertain to the processing of offenders, as determined by the law. Obviously, the actions of various correctional authorities and organizational units are shaped in large part by the

< Multiethnic group of teen boys marches at Los Angeles boot camp for juvenile offenders. *Photo by A. Ramey, courtesy of PhotoEdit.*

particular ideologies to which they subscribe or that are the will of the citizens they serve and protect. In the history of treatment and punishment of offenders, the ideologies of different societies have supplied both the basis and the rationalization for the broad range of efforts—draconian to semihumane—aimed at getting criminals off the streets. When a given effort becomes a clear failure, the ideology eventually will shift to justify a different approach.

In modern times, a strong belief in the efficacy of one correctional ideology or another has sometimes led administrators to commit vast sums of public treasure to an unproved approach or theory, thus shackling themselves to a possibly worthless plan for an indefinite period. By the same token, if the correctional administrator's ideology happens to conflict with the approach favored by the society he or she serves, the administrator may try to resolve the conflict in one of two ways: by working out a compromise to make it work better or by trying to sabotage the system to ensure its failure. If the superintendent of a juvenile institution believes society is trying to liberalize rules so rapidly that it threatens personal security, he or she may encourage or even trigger absconding and walk-aways from the targeted institution. In corrections, the backgrounds and ideologies of the keepers and the kept often diverge sharply, so it becomes difficult to convince both groups they can work toward a mutual goal.

Most of the ideologies applied to correctional actions over the years fall into one of three categories: **punishment, treatment,** or **prevention.** They often overlap, of course—punishment and treatment are usually justified as means to prevention, rather than as ends in themselves—but the division is useful for the purpose of this analysis.

THE PUNISHMENT IDEOLOGY

The idea that punishment can result in the offense being "paid" for and that its effect can be expanded from the specific criminal to the general public has been around from the earliest times. Most of the basic reasons for punishment can be placed in three general categories: retribution, deterrence, and incapacitation.

Retribution

Since the first system of laws was developed, punishment has been officially sanctioned as a means of regulating criminal behavior. The punishment ideology holds that the criminal is an enemy of society who deserves severe punishment, including banishment or death, for willfully breaking its rules. This philosophy has its roots in a societal need for retribution. As noted in Chapter 1, punishment once was administered in the form of immediate and personal retribution, by either the victim or the victim's family. Society's authorization of punishment can be traced to that individual need for retaliation and vengeance. Many theories try to explain the reason for the transfer of the vengeance motive from the individual to the state.

Philosophers have debated the reasons for this transfer to government of the victim's desire to strike back at the offender. Heinrich Oppenheimer lists several theories in *The Rationale of Punishment* (1913). Three of them are as follows:

1. In the *theological* view, retaliation fulfills a religious mission to punish the criminal.
2. In the *aesthetic* view, punishment resolves the social discord created by the offense and reestablishes a sense of harmony through requital.
3. In the *expiatory* view, guilt must be washed away through suffering.

CORRECTIONAL BRIEF

Retribution

Philosophically, this term generally means getting even with the perpetrator. The term *social revenge* suggests that individuals cannot exact punishment, but that the state will do so in their name.

Retribution assumes that the offenders willfully chose to commit the evil acts, are responsible for their own behavior, are likely to commit similar acts again, and should receive the punishment they richly deserve.

The "just deserts" movement in sentencing reflects the retribution philosophy. For many, it provides a justifiable rationale for support of the death penalty.

Many students of corrections, and penologists, have considerable difficulty with the concept of retribution, because it requires the state to make an offender suffer for the sake of suffering. To many, that idea runs counter to the Eighth Amendment's prohibition against cruel and unusual punishment. One respected criminologist has proposed that correctional punishments include electroshock in lieu of incarceration, because it can be calibrated, leaves less long-term emotional damage, is cheaper to administer, and would allow the victim the opportunity to witness the retribution. Is it possible that televising the electroshock sessions might act as a deterrent to other potential malefactors?

SOURCE: Graeme Newman, *Just and Painful: The Case for the Corporal Punishment of Criminals* (New York: Free Press, 1983).

Ledger Wood advances a fourth explanation, a *utilitarian theory*. Punishment is considered to be a means of achieving beneficial and social consequences through application of a specific form and degree of punishment deemed most appropriate to the particular offender after careful individualized study of the offender.[1]

Deterrence

Yet another reason for punishment of criminals is the belief that such actions have a **deterrent effect**, *specifically* on the offender or *generally* on others who might consider a similar act.[2] For punishment to serve as a deterrent, it must be swift, visible to others, closely linked to the forbidden action so that it discourages future recurrences of that crime, certain, and categorical (all persons committing a certain crime will receive the same punishment).[3] Furthermore, the state and its representatives must uphold superior values and conforming behavior to serve as irreproachable examples of good citizenship. Finally, after punishment, offenders must be allowed to resume their prior positions in society, without stigma or disability.

The failure of early penologists to recognize that uniform punishment was not as effective as selective and specialized punishment contributed to the failure of prisons based on the punishment ideology. Overpunishment has little deterrent effect as well, because when the compliance point has been passed and the punishment continues, the offender ceases to care about the crime. For example, even after an offender has successfully completed a punishment-oriented correctional process, the **stigma of conviction** and imprisonment is carried for the rest of the ex-offender's life.[4] Finding it almost impossible to get a job because of a criminal past, the ex-offender often decides, "If I'm going to have the name, I might as well play the game." At that point, neither the punishment nor the stigma is an effective deterrent, and the offender is likely to return to crime.[5]

SIDEBARS

Incapacitation

In terms of correctional strategy, to make an offender literally incapable of committing a crime by placing him or her in a facility and under the level of security that will prevent future crimes. Because some criminals commit multiple offenses, it is part of this theory that incapacitating those offenders will directly lower the rates of crime. Incapacitation as a crime control strategy requires accurate prediction. Unfortunately, the current level of technology and practice seldom provides valid predictions of criminal behavior.

Incapacitation

A third reason to punish the offender derives from the concept of **incapacitation**. This theory finds no hope for the individual as far as rehabilitation is concerned and

CORRECTIONAL BRIEF

Delaware's Infamous "Red Hannah"

The semiannual whipping and pillorying of criminals convicted at the present term of the court, of theft and other crimes, took place on Saturday. The attendance was small, probably not exceeding one hundred people, most of whom were boys. The following are the names of the "candidates," and the offenses for which they were sentenced:

- Joseph Derias, colored, horse stealing, 20 lashes, one hour in the pillory.
- Scott Wilson, larceny of clothing, 20 lashes.
- John Carpenter, colored, four cases of larceny (ice cream freezers, carriage reins, and a cow). He received 10 lashes in each case.
- John Conner, larceny of tomatoes, 5 lashes.
- John Smith, colored, house breaking, 20 lashes.
- John Brown, horse stealing, 20 lashes and one hour in the pillory.

—*Delawarean, May 27, 1876*

For centuries, the whipping post was a conspicuous part of Delaware's penal tradition. The first person to suffer the sanction was Robert Hutchinson, convicted of petty theft and sentenced to thirty-nine lashes on June 3, 1679. Each town and county had its own whipping post, but the one that earned a prominent place in the history of American corrections was the notorious "Red Hannah." As the *Wilmington Journal Every Evening* once described it:

> *In days gone by, the whipping post down in Kent County stood out brazenly in the open courtyard of the county jail not far from the old state house. It looked like an old-time octagonal pump without a bundle. It had a slit near the top of it in which the equally old-time pillory boards might be inserted when needed for punitive use. There also were iron shackles for holding the prisoners while they were being whipped. That whipping post was painted red from top to bottom. Negro residents bestowed upon it the name of "Red Hannah." Of any prisoner who had been whipped at the post it was said, "He has hugged Red Hannah!"*

Red Hannah was a survivor. Despite public and local congressional pressure to ban whipping in the state, during the second half of the twentieth century, almost 300 years after Robert Hutchinson received his thirty-nine lashes, old Red Hannah was still very much alive.

In 1963, the statutes that permitted whipping were challenged in the Delaware Supreme Court. The case was *State v. Cannon,* and the presiding judge held that the use of flogging to punish certain crimes did not violate either state or federal bans on cruel and unusual punishment. However, Red Hannah was ultimately laid to rest in 1973, when the statute authorizing the use of the lash was finally repealed by the Delaware legislature.

Old Red Hannah, Delaware's whipping post.

Photo by American Stock, courtesy of Getty Images, Inc./Hulton Archive Photos.

SOURCES: Robert G. Caldwell, *Red Hannah: Delaware's Whipping Post* (Philadelphia: University of Pennsylvania Press, 1947); *Delawarean* (May 27, 1876), p. 3; *Journal Every Evening* (August 2, 1938), p. 8; *State v. Cannon,* 55 Del. 587 (1963).

proposes that the only solution is temporarily to isolate, remove, or cripple such persons in some way. This approach is sometimes referred to as the **theory of disablement,** a euphemism for death, banishment, or mutilation. Ideally, the disablement should relate to the crime (for example, in some countries castration has been used to punish sex criminals). One variation of the isolation rationale of incapacitation is the **selective incapacitation** movement. Greenwood argued that prison overcrowding and the scarcity of beds in prisons require a policy of sending only repetitive or violent offenders to prison; he especially recommended prison for those who commit armed robbery.[6] Selective incapacitation[7] would thus result in better uses of correctional resources and more effective crime prevention, he believed.[8]

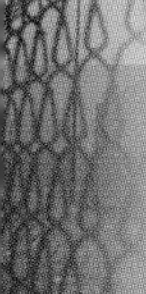

CORRECTIONAL BRIEF

Selective Incapacitation

This doctrine of isolating the offender, or causing "social disablement," proposes adopting a policy of incarcerating those whose criminal behavior is so damaging or probable that nothing short of isolation will prevent recidivism. This "nothing-else-works" approach would require correctly identifying those offenders who would be eligible for longer-term imprisonment and diverting others into correctional alternatives. Thus we would be able to make maximum effective use of prison cells, a scarce resource, to protect society from the depredations of such dangerous and repetitive offenders.

Current correctional technology, however, does not permit us to correctly identify those who require incapacitation. Rather, the evidence is that we would probably incarcerate numerous noneligibles (a "false-positive" problem) and release to lesser confinement many of those eligible (a "false-negative" problem). Whatever benefits might accrue to this sentencing doctrine have thus far eluded corrections. The difficulty is further spotlighted in the *Report to the Nation on Crime and Justice:*

Career criminals, though few in number, account for most crime. Even though chronic repeat offenders (those with five or more arrests by age 18) make up a relatively small proportion of all offenders, they commit a very high proportion of all crimes. The evidence includes data for juveniles and adults, males and females, and for urban and rural areas. In Wolfgang's Philadelphia study, chronic offenders accounted for 23 percent of all male offenders in the study, but they had committed 61 percent of all the crimes. Of all crimes by all members of the group studied, chronic offenders committed:

- *61 percent of all homicides*
- *76 percent of all rapes*
- *73 percent of all robberies*
- *65 percent of all aggravated assaults.*

SOURCES: Marianne W. Zowitz (ed.), *Report to the Nation on Crime and Justice* (Washington, DC: U.S. Department of Justice, Bureau of Justice Statistics, U.S. Government Printing Office, 1983), p. 35. Also Elmer Witekamp, Hans-Jurgen Kerner, and Volkard Schindler, "On the Dangerousness of Chronic/Habitual Offenders: A Reanalysis of the 1945 Philadelphia Birth Cohort Data," *Studies in Crime and Crime Prevention* 42:2 (1995): 157–175.

The Effect of Punishment

It is recognized that some punishment can be effective when applied in the right amounts and at the right time; and punishment may, in some cases, be a necessary predecessor to treatment. Few serious offenders readily seek or are amenable to treatment without some form of coercion or threat. When the ideology of punishment is applied in a correctional institution, however, the result is often negative for both the punished and the punisher. Correctional personnel tend to watch for minor rule infringements or nonconformism (horseplay, abusive language, skipping classes, etc.) so the punishment can be administered, and they overlook any positive actions by offenders.[9] Often the rules that are prepared for a punishment-oriented environment surround the offender with a wall of "do nots," leaving almost no leeway to "do" anything.

As evidenced by a high crime rate, punishment by the law does not seem to create much respect for the law, even in jurisdictions where punishment may actually be swift, harsh, and certain. Overuse of punishment in a society that claims to be open and free creates a situation in which the punished can characterize their punishers as persecutors of the poor and helpless. The accusation turns attention away from the crimes that put them there, and gives rise to the concept of the "political prisoner." Thus, minority group members are likely to blame their incarcerations on repression by the rich, on political persecution, or on attempted genocide. Punishments are then made more and more severe, in a desperate but hopeless effort to compensate for their ineffectiveness. Often such punishments motivate offenders to become more sophisticated criminals (rather than noncriminals) in the belief (no doubt valid) that the more skilled one is at a trade, the less

SIDEBARS

Prediction

When practitioners and researchers attempt to identify who would commit future crimes over a period of time (or a career), they basically predict that a person will or will not get into difficulty ("criminal" or "noncriminal"). If one predicts "criminal" and the subject does not get into trouble, we create a "false-positive" error. If the prediction is "noncriminal" and the subject commits a crime, the outcome is a "false-negative." It is hoped that one would be accurate in identifying and correctly classifying subjects into the correct categories.

Even using the most sophisticated prediction devices and schedules based on extensive life-history information, inmate psychological test scores, official records and institutional information, and inmate responses to questionnaires, errors of prediction abound. On occasion, predictors made more incorrect than correct predictions!

Three numbered prison cells with bed, sink, and writing table.
Photo by Bill Aron, courtesy of PhotoEdit.

likely one is to be caught. The offenders become hardened to the punishment, and the administrators learn to dole it out automatically as their only means of control.[10] Both parties are degraded in the process.

Both history and science refute the argument that the use of punishment can halt crime. The following factors contribute to make punishment the least effective means of reducing crime:

1. The use of punishment for deterrence must avoid the overseverity of application that arouses public sympathy for the offender.
2. Those persons most likely to be imprisoned are already accustomed to experiencing deprivations and frustration of personal goals routinely in daily life.
3. It is impossible to fashion a practical legal "slide rule" that will determine exact degrees of retribution appropriate for a list of crimes ranging from handkerchief theft to murder.
4. The simple application of naked coercion does not guarantee that the subjects of its force will alter their behavior to conform to new legal norms or to improve their conformity with norms previously violated.
5. The possibility of deterrence varies with the chances of keeping the particular type of crime secret and consequently of avoiding social reprobation.[11]

It must be understood that the significance of punishment as an ideology in correctional practice lies in the viewpoint of the punished offenders. If they see the punishment as an unjust imposition of the will and power of the establishment, and are reinforced in that belief by their peers (other offenders), their punishment will only encourage them to maintain negative attitudes and behavior patterns. By contrast, if offenders believe their punishment is both deserved and just, and their social group agrees, the punishment may have a startlingly different and more positive result. If a prosocial criminal (one who is not totally committed to a life of crime) is justly treated, that offender may abandon crime; but excessive punishment may push the offender over the edge and destroy every chance of reform. The punished and stigmatized offenders turn to those who are most like them for support and values. If they are embittered by the punishment they have received, they are likely to reject the very values the punishment was intended to reinforce.[12]

James Austin and Aaron McVey[13] examined the effects of recent political policies designed to increase punishment by increasing the probability of an offender's being arrested, convicted, and imprisoned, and serving longer sentences. We extend their predictions by noting that, if current punishment trends continue, the nation:

- Will have 1.5 million prison inmates by the year 2010.
- Will need to open a new 900-bed prison every other week for the next five years just to keep even with and accommodate prison growth.
- Will need to hire 4,000 new correctional officers for each of the next five years.
- Will have 100,000 elderly prisoners ("geriatric inmates") in prison by 2020.
- Will remain number one in the rate of incarceration per 100,000 residents.
- Have almost 8 million persons under correctional supervision.

Finally, the change in attitude has led to a painful search for alternatives to probation (regarded as too little punishment) and imprisonment (regarded as too expensive a form of punishment). The emerging alternatives—known as intermediate punishments—promise relief from the pressures of prison overcrowding. In addition, the new wave of punitiveness has contributed to selective incapacitation, an important and effective tool for correctional administrators, but only if it is designed to suit an individual offender and an individual situation (see Chapter 6). General and uniform punishment is still the rule rather than the exception, however, and the movement toward a **treatment model** is slow.

SIDEBARS

Determinate Sentencing

A fixed period of incarceration imposed on the offender by the sentencing court. The ideology underlying determinate sentencing is retribution, just deserts, or incapacitation. A presumptive sentence is a term of imprisonment suggested by a policy-setting governmental agency, such as the state legislature or a sentencing council. The sentencing judge is expected to impose the indicated sentence, unless certain circumstances proven in court would require a different (longer or shorter) period of imprisonment.

THE TREATMENT IDEOLOGY

A major trend in corrections is to approach the offender much as one would the mentally ill, the neglected, or the underprivileged. This more humane ideology, reflected in the treatment model, sees the criminal behavior as just another manifestation of pathology that can be handled by some form of therapeutic activity. Although the criminal may be referred to as "sick," the treatment ideology is not analogous to a medical approach. The closest comparison with physical illness lies in the need for offenders to recognize the danger and undesirability of their criminal behavior and then to make significant efforts to rid themselves of that behavior. The treatment model does not "remove" criminal behavior, as one might remove an infected limb; rather, the "patient" (inmate) is made to see the rewards of positive behavior and is encouraged and equipped to adopt it as a model.

SIDEBARS

Treatment

Treatment begins with a diagnosis of an offender's needs, the designing of a program plan to address that person's needs, the application of the intended program with periodic monitoring, and updating and modification of the plan to maximize effectiveness.

The treatment ideology does not encourage inmates to be coddled and allowed to do as they please within the institution. It is a fairly common belief among many elements of the criminal justice system that any program that is not punitive or restrictive is being "soft" or akin to "running a country club." In fact, some form of treatment ideology can be applied in even the most restrictive and security-oriented institutions. The main difference between the treatment and punishment ideologies is that in the former, offenders are assigned to the institution for a correctional program intended to prepare them for readjustment to or reintegration into the community, not just for punishment and confinement. There is room for

SIDEBARS

Positivism

A second major school in criminology which argues that most offenders do not exercise free will and that criminal actions result from social, biological, or psychological forces over which the person has no control. This school led to a search for causes of crime that lay within the offender or the social setting in which offenders lived, and forms the basis for the treatment and prevention ideologies.

SIDEBARS

Quakers

The Quakers are a religious group that has a strong pacifist and nonviolent ideology as part of their faith. Probably the two best-known Quakers in America were William Penn (after whom Pennsylvania was named) and Richard M. Nixon, the only American president of the United States to resign while serving in that office.

SIDEBARS

The Medical Model

This model in corrections implies that criminal behavior is comparable to a disease and, that if the disease (criminal behavior) can be diagnosed, it can be treated and the offender "cured." This model has been under attack from many points and has generally been replaced by individualized treatment to correct behavior instead of some underlying defect or disease.

punishment and security in the treatment approach, but little room for treatment in the punitive approach. The more humane treatment methods are intended to be used in conjunction with the employment of authority in a constructive and positive manner, but inmates must be allowed to try, even if they fail. Authoritarian procedures, used alone, only give the offender more ammunition to support a self-image as an oppressed and impotent pawn of the power structure.

The student should recall that the field of corrections, especially in its early history in America, underwent significant change as innovators again sought the answers to the question mentioned earlier: "Who are the offenders and what should we do with them?" The treatment ideology contains four separate answers to the question, commonly referred to as treatment doctrines.

The Quaker reform movement, arising in 1790, held that offenders were out of touch with God. The corresponding treatment approach was isolation. Prisoners were supplied with a Bible for reading and doing penitence. The doctrine for the Quakers was to help offenders find their way back to God; it was believed that once God was found, crime would cease.

The **reformatory movement** solutions, after 1890, provided somewhat different answers. Offenders were seen as disadvantaged, "unfortunate" persons whose education, training, and discipline had been inadequate. The **educational doctrine** answer was to provide education at a functional level, emphasis on vocational and occupational skills, and a regime of discipline that was aimed at the internalization of controls to prevent recurrence of criminal behavior when the prisoner was released.

The **medical model** that developed in the late 1920s and early 1930s, under the leadership of Sanford Bates and the U.S. Bureau of Prisons, saw the answers as lying within the individual. It then became necessary to diagnose the individual problem, develop a treatment program that might remedy it, and then apply treatment. When the "patient" was found to be well, he or she would be released to a program of aftercare in the community under the supervision of therapeutic parole officers who would continue casework therapy until the offender was "rehabilitated." The medical model offered hope of rehabilitation. It was the responsibility of corrections to "make the ill well." The "ill" would thus be passive recipients of beneficent therapy like patients in a hospital.

Underlying the treatment model is the indeterminate sentence and its assumptions of rehabilitation and early release, if the offender is treated and is reformed. The minimum and maximum periods (such as a one-to-five-year sentence) reflect the inability of the sentencing judge to know exactly when the prisoner would be reformed.

Before 1975, the federal system and all of the state systems had sentencing codes that were indeterminate, and boards of prison terms and parole, commonly called parole boards, were given broad discretion in determining when an inmate was ready for release under parole supervision. Since 1976, almost two-thirds of the states as well as the federal system have limited parole board discretion or abolished discretionary parole completely. In addition, the percentage of inmates released through parole board discretion declined from 72 percent to 39 percent at the end of 2003. Twenty-three states now use guidelines to structure their release decisions.

The fourth doctrine emerged in the late 1960s. It is acceptable to use either 1965 or 1969 as the date of origin but whichever date is used, this form of treatment was a significant trend throughout the 1980s. Known as the **reintegration model**, this form of treatment made differing assumptions about the cause and solutions to crime and the criminal. The community was seen as the basic etiological factor, and the offender was considered to be the product of a local community that excluded, failed to provide for, or discriminated against the offender. Because the basic cause is regarded as community related, proponents thought it best to address the problem by using community resources that correctional agencies would be able to marshal or develop. These would include reducing poverty rates, investing in children, urban revitalization, Head Start programs, and job training. The offender's role requires active participation in the effort to resolve the difficulty; correctional agencies then serve as brokers for services. Ideally, a community management approach is used, wherein several officers can specialize to maximize the delivery of opportunities to the offender, who is eager to reintegrate and become part of the community. The four doctrines require treatment and coexist in the correctional ideology called treatment, which we discuss in Chapter 14.

SIDEBARS

Indeterminate Sentencing

An indeterminate sentence is a sentence to incarceration pronounced by a judge that sets minimum and maximum periods of incarceration for the offender (such as "from one to five years"). The minimum term would establish the earliest release date (adjusted for certain time credits for, as an example, jail time during pretrial detention) or the date of first parole consideration to determine if the inmate should be released. At the maximum term, the inmate would have to be released.

THE PREVENTION IDEOLOGY

As mentioned, the problem of crime cannot be separated from the individual offender. In a sense, the problem can be temporarily removed from the community whenever the offender is sent off to prison. Almost all offenders are eventually released, however, and the problem returns unless it has been effectively treated while the offender was in the prison. Because of the perceived minimal success of present correctional programs (recidivism rates range from 40 to 70 percent),[14] many communities and governmental agencies are turning to crime prevention as a possible solution. Prevention methods have a dual focus: on the individual and on the environment in which he or she lives. Much crime prevention activity is designed to steer potential delinquents away from a life of trouble. Such programs generally begin at the school level, where truancy and dropping out are often the precursors of criminal activity. Those early programs, for the most part, attempt to identify the first signs of criminal behavior.

As Pogo Possum, the 1950s cartoon character of Walt Kelly, said: "Prediction is difficult, 'specially when it's about the future." Prediction is a complex process, even when it is carefully controlled.[15] The famous studies by Sheldon and Eleanor Glueck illustrate the problems inherent in most prediction efforts.[16] Prevention programs in schools today aim to treat problem children by providing specialized classes, vocational education, and counseling[17]; they do not aim to force juveniles out of the picture by expulsion from school. The prevention ideology recognizes that problem children must have supportive help, or they are very likely to use crime as an outlet for unhappiness and insecurity.

PROFILE

Sheldon (1896–1980) and Eleanor (1898–1972) Glueck

were a husband and wife team at Harvard University who worked together on a large number of privately funded research projects in an eclectic fashion. He held the Roscoe Pound Chair at Harvard Law School, and she was a trained social worker. Their work exerted great influence on the study of crime, especially juvenile delinquency. They authored 258 items in their forty years of work.

Those who advocate the prevention ideology are well aware that total prevention of crime is probably impossible. Emile Durkheim believed crime in some form was an inevitable accompaniment to human society and that if serious crime were prevented, authorities would focus their attention on minor offenses.[18] Essentially, the prevention ideology holds that crime may at least be reduced through an attack on the social and emotional problems that encourage a child's criminal inclinations.

PROFILE

Emile Durkheim (1853–1917)

an early sociological giant, was one of the first to talk about the impact of the social system on the individual. He studied suicide and developed his theory of *anomie*—a state of loneliness and isolation from the social group—and related it to those who chose to kill themselves.

The individual's environment is recognized as a crucial focus in the prevention of crime; the prevention ideology emphasizes the need to structure the environment so criminal opportunity is minimized. As an example, it has been said that the greatest crime prevention device ever invented was the streetlight. The movement toward crime prevention through environmental design has great promise for the future. The object of such an approach is not only to provide barriers to crime (such as window bars, fences, locks, and airport security checks),[19] but also to enhance the existing features that tend to discourage crime (for example, more lighting around homes and apartment buildings, more windows in dark hallways, and community projects aimed at getting people to know their neighbors). The conditions that produce a high or low crime rate in a given area are not all physical, however; the environment includes the people, activities, pressures, and ideas to which an individual is exposed every day. The prevention ideology advocates the maximum use of resources in areas that have special problems such as poverty and overcrowding—funds should be allocated for crime prevention rather than for prison construction.[20]

In community corrections, the prevention ideology is combined with treatment. The emphasis is on the identification and treatment of the problems that have caused past criminal behavior, to prevent its recurrence. Eventually, the emphasis may lead to a closer, more interdependent relationship between the agencies now involved in crime prevention and those that provide community services. As they presently operate, criminal justice agencies actually tend to create more problems for minor offenders, instead of treating the problems that got those people into trouble.[21] If schools, churches, service agencies, and similar organizations could become more involved, before persons become entangled in the criminal justice system, many criminal careers could be prevented before they start. **Diversion** and nonjudicial approaches to offenders are seen as potentially valuable alternatives to a more formal punishment-oriented reaction to the problem of crime.[22] A combination of prevention and treatment ideologies would be the most promising and humane organization of correctional beliefs and practices.

SIDEBARS

Community Corrections

This term describes sentences that provide alternatives to incarceration of offenders in prisons. These sentences often include participation in programs that are located in the same areas in which the offenders work and live. Community corrections sentences are designed to consider both the safety of the local residents and the treatment needs of offenders.

THE PENDULUM SWINGS

From 1976, when crime took a temporary downturn, to 1990, high crime rates caused the forces of society to turn again to the punishment ideology.[23] As the populations of the country's jails and prisons have grown to almost unmanageable proportions, administrators and legislatures become more willing to accept the turn backward in order to have at least some way to cope with the growing and more violent criminal populations. The following chapters discuss the problems faced by harried and chronically underfunded correctional administrators trying to deal with institutions that are so overcrowded that they are bursting at the seams. Budgets are stripped of so-called frills such as treatment and must be used to add beds, food, and custody staff to house and feed inmates while trying to protect society. The trend toward determinate sentences and **"get tough" laws** at all levels exacerbates the situation. At best, treatment is difficult to carry out in a security institution. At worst, treatment is all but impossible to find. That pessimistic situation formed a trend that began in the 1980s. The correctional "nonsystem" entered the first decade of the new century in a continuing state of indecision as to what to embrace as its core ideology.[24] The results were clear, however, and the hope for treatment that dominated in the 1960s and 1970s seems lost in the cry for "hard time" for offenders. Poor economic conditions in inner-city blighted areas and continued overcrowding exist at levels unprecedented in the short history of corrections in America.

Despite the increased reliance on punishment and the conservative backlash that has so negatively impacted corrections during the last two decades, there is growing support for both treatment and prevention among legislators[25] as well as the general public.[26] Perhaps that is why the best analogy is of the pendulum and its continuous path as it begins to swing from left to right. It will take major changes in the future for the pendulum of justice to begin a swing back toward the center, but necessity may require it to happen. The task ahead for today's students will be both important and difficult as they track the path of the pendulum.

RESTORATIVE JUSTICE

The debate over the future of the criminal justice system has historically been between proponents of a retributive, punitive philosophy and advocates of the traditional individual treatment mission. All of these approaches have failed to satisfy basic needs of individual crime victims, the community, and offenders. A new ideology is now being tried, mostly in the juvenile justice system, that seems to have some serious merit for consideration. The balanced and restorative justice (BARJ) model outlines an alternative philosophy, **restorative justice**, and a new mission, "the balanced approach."

The BARJ model requires criminal justice professionals to devote attention to enabling offenders to make amends to their victims and community, increasing offender competencies, and protecting the public through processes in which individual victims, the community, and offenders are all active participants.

The BARJ model responds to many issues raised by the victims' movement, including concerns that victims have had little opportunity for input into the resolution of their own cases, rarely feel heard, and often receive no restitution or expression of remorse from the offender. The balanced approach is based on an understanding of crime as an act against the victim and the community, which is an ancient idea common to tribal and religious traditions of many cultures. Practitioners have used techniques consistent with this approach for years; however, they have lacked a coherent philosophical framework that supports restorative practice and provides direction to guide all aspects of juvenile justice practice. The BARJ model provides an overarching vision and guidance for daily decisions.

Criminal justice professionals, including probation and parole officers, prosecutors, judges, case managers, and victim advocates, recognize the need for justice system reform. People who work on the front lines of the system are faced daily with the frustration of seeing growing numbers of young people and adults involved in criminal behavior. These offenders leave the system with little hope for real change; and, unfortunately, countless crime victims and community members are left out of the process. That frustration has inspired many of these professionals to work toward changing organizational culture, values, and programs to reflect a more balanced and restorative approach to juvenile justice.

The BARJ model is a vision for the future of corrections and criminal justice that builds on current innovative practices and is based on core values that have been part of most communities for centuries. It provides a framework for systemic reform and offers hope for preserving and revitalizing the juvenile justice system. Implementation must begin with consensus building among key stakeholders and testing with small pilot projects to develop the model. This evolutionary process can build on existing programs and practices that reflect restorative justice principles, such as victim–offender mediation, family group conferencing, community service, restitution, and work experience.

Balanced and Restorative Justice Philosophy

The foundation of restorative justice practice is a coherent set of values and principles, a guiding vision, and an action-oriented mission. The guiding principles of restorative justice are that crime is injury and crime hurts not only individual victims but also communities and offenders, and creates an obligation to make things right. All parties should be a part of the response to the crime, including the victim if he or she wishes, the community, and the offender. However, the victim's perspective is central to deciding how to repair (restore) the harm caused by the crime. Accountability for the offender means some accepting of responsibly to repair the harm done.

The community is ultimately responsible for the well-being of all its members, including both victim and offender, and all human beings have dignity and worth. Restoration means repairing the harm and rebuilding relationships in the community. It is the primary goal of restorative justice. Results are measured by how much repair was done rather than by how much punishment was inflicted. This ideology accepts that crime control cannot be achieved without the active involvement of the community.

The justice process is respectful of age, abilities, sexual orientation, family status, and diverse cultures and backgrounds (for example, racial, ethnic, geographic, religious, and economic backgrounds) and all are given equal protection and due process. The restorative justice vision needs to have support from the community, opportunity to define the harm experienced, and participation in decision making about steps for repair that result in increased victim recovery from the trauma of crime. It accepts that community involvement in preventing and controlling crime, improving neighborhoods, and strengthening the bonds among community members results in community protection.

Through understanding the human impact of their behavior, accepting responsibility, expressing remorse, taking action to repair the damage, and developing their own capacities, offenders become fully integrated and respected members of the community. Justice professionals, as community justice facilitators, organize and support processes in which individual crime victims, other community members, and juvenile offenders are involved in finding constructive resolutions to delinquency.

The Balanced Approach and Its Application

Transforming the current justice system into a more restorative model will and must require that professionals have the power to transform justice into a more balanced and restorative system. By developing new roles, setting new priorities, and redirecting resources, justice professionals can:

1. Make needed services available for victims of crime.
2. Give victims opportunities for involvement and input.
3. Actively involve community members, including individual crime victims and offenders, in making decisions and carrying out plans for resolving issues and restoring the community.
4. Build connections among community members.
5. Give offenders the opportunity and encouragement to take responsibility for their behavior.
6. Actively involve juvenile offenders in repairing the harm they caused.
7. Increase juvenile offenders' skills and abilities.

Although this approach is relatively new and requires additional research and application before it can be considered viable, it may turn the tide on the punishment and retribution ideologies that are now so much in favor of politicians and the public.[27]

CONTEMPORARY CORRECTIONS

The need for correctional reforms and structured plans to achieve them were documented by the President's Crime Commission, appointed by President Lyndon Johnson in the 1960s, by the President's Commission on Criminal Justice Standards and Goals, and by task forces in many states. The early 1960s emerged as a period of research that sought alternative methods, programs, treatment procedures, and designs for facilities. The most astonishing and significant findings included the following:

1. Long sentences are self-defeating with regard to rehabilitation.
2. Most offenders—perhaps as many as 85 percent—do not need to be incarcerated and could function better back in the community under supervision.
3. Most inmates derive maximum benefit from incarceration during their first two years; after that period, it becomes less and less likely that they could function as productive citizens if returned to society.
4. Community-based corrections are more realistic, less expensive, and at least as effective as incarceration.
5. Corrections, as a system, must encompass all aspects of rehabilitative service, including mental health, employment services, education, and social services.
6. Some offenders, because of their dangerousness, will require extensive incarceration and treatment programs especially designed and implemented in secure institutions. The staff in those institutions must be extensive and of high quality.
7. Most inmates are not mentally ill but suffer from a variety of educational, medical, psychological, maturational, economic, and interpersonal handicaps that are seldom reduced or resolved in contemporary correctional systems.
8. Inmates must be given the opportunity and capability to earn a living wage so as to compensate their victims and support their own families, keeping them off public assistance rolls.
9. The pay for currently incarcerated inmates is too low to be regarded as wages. Thus the rates of pay must be increased to at least the minimum wage on the outside for similar labor.
10. The private economic sector must be sought out and used to provide both training and work programs that will produce employable workers at the end of the corrections cycle.

Despite the evidence, four important developments in corrections have occurred during the last three decades of the twentieth century: (1) the abandonment of the ideological basis for postadjudication handling of convicted offenders, commonly referred to as the medical model; (2) the shift to determinate sentencing, which places limits on the judge's power to determine how long the offender might serve in prison; (3) a search for punishments that would be more effective than court-ordered probation and less severe than long-term incarceration, the so-called intermediate punishment; and (4) restorative justice.

By 2006, the majority of the states embraced determinate sentencing, abolishing discretionary parole release mechanisms in at least sixteen states and imposing mandatory add-on time for use of a gun in crimes, sale of narcotics,

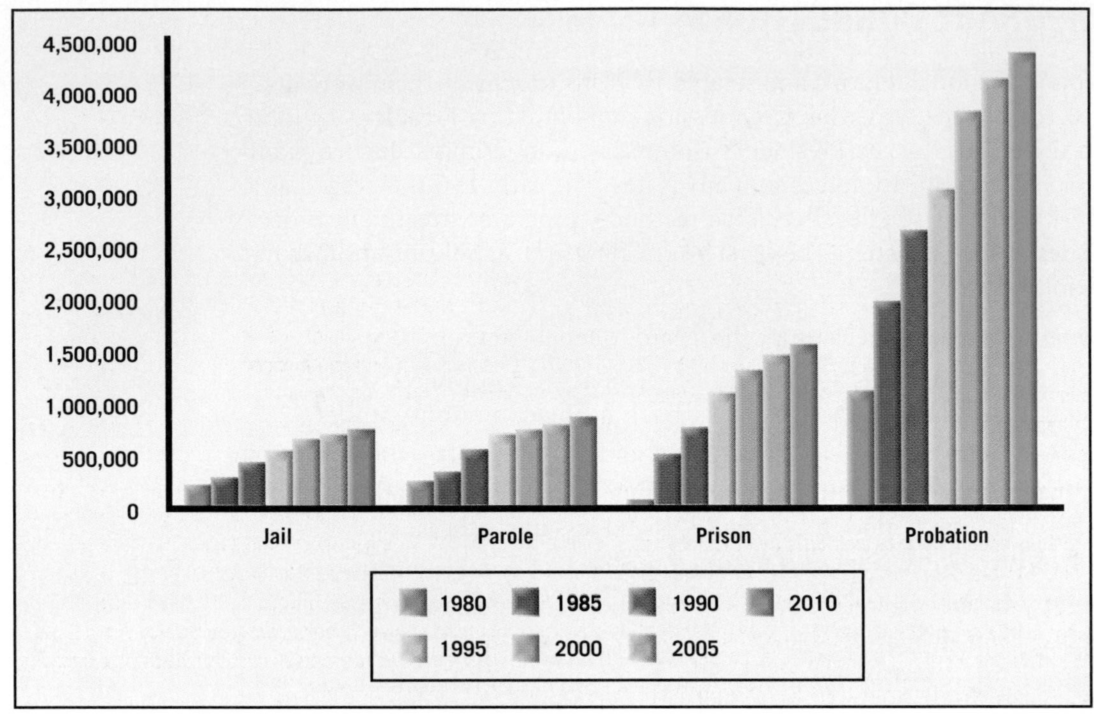

FIGURE 3.1

Adults Under Correctional Control: 1980–2010*

*Data for 2010 are estimated.

SOURCE: From Bureau of Justice Statistics (2002). Correctional Populations, 1980–2000 (www.ojp.udjoj.gov/bjs/glance/tables/corr2tab.htm).

and some especially brutal crimes. At least twenty-nine states and the District of Columbia have adopted the federal truth-in-sentencing standard that requires part I violent crime offenders to serve not less than 85 percent of their sentence in prison before becoming eligible for release. The reemergence of retribution in contemporary corrections has led in part to seriously overcrowded prisons, a deluge of lawsuits by prisoners seeking better conditions while incarcerated, and an intense search for new alternatives to imprisonment[28] that would still provide public safety and constitutionally viable conditions for prisoners.[29] As Latessa and Allen noted in 1999, "Ironically, for a movement begun by fiscal conservatives, the new get-tough policy has turned out to be the most costly approach to corrections yet attempted."[30]

By 2003, Americans under some form of correctional supervision swelled to previously unparalleled numbers: 7,650,000 adults. There were 2,110,137 adult men and women in the custody of state and federal prisons, another 691,300 were in local jails on a given day, 4,074,000 were on probation, and some 775,000 were on parole. In addition, 102,000 were in juvenile correctional facilities. Figure 3.1 provides a graphic of the growth curves, extended to 2010. The punishment ideology has contributed heavily to this growth, and has fueled the development of both the intermediate sanction and accreditation programs in the last four decades. These are explored in detail in Chapters 7 and 12.

CORRECTIONAL BRIEF

Some Effects of the War on Drugs

In the 1980s, a conservative crime prevention strategy commonly known as the "war on drugs" began in the United States. It adopts a narrow (and punitive) conception of the drug seller as a predatory offender willingly selling dangerous drugs to children and youths, amassing a fortune by corrupting innocent users and ruining their lives. A policy of criminalization and enforcement was adopted; little effort or resources were devoted to treatment and habilitation.

Law enforcement went on an "arrest binge," increasing the volume of persons arrested and creating massive problems for other components of the criminal justice system. Prosecutors, defenders, judges, jailers, and prison administrators spend much of their days trying to move their caseloads before the next wave of incoming arrests. Effects include transferring judges to criminal cases, creating faster plea bargaining, forging alternative control strategies (such as electronic monitoring and intensive supervision), shifting county inmates to state prisons by increasing the proportion of drug offenders committed to prisons, using temporary and makeshift holding facilities for inmates, forcing early release of sometimes dangerous inmates, and clogging both the courts and correctional systems.

Almost two-thirds of federal prison inmates are incarcerated for drug law violations; the national average for state systems is about 20 percent. One in eleven African American men ages 25 to 29 are incarcerated on any day.

The war on drugs has diverted attention from the causes of drug use and social problems, contributed to the abandonment of the lower class in terms of new services, expanded the power of the state in light of the rights of the individual, legitimized intrusion of American politics into Latin and South American governments, and not reduced the volume of crime or drug use. William Weir, an expert on gun control and drugs, argues that cynical politicians have manipulated the public to attain their own agenda and goals and, in so doing, created a "dope fiend" stereotype to generate votes. The "war" has increased violence and enhanced gangster roles for minority inner-city youth.

SOURCES: Christina Johns, *Power, Ideology and the War on Drugs* (Westport, CT: Praeger, 1992); John Klofas, "Drugs and Justice: The Impact of Drugs on Criminal Justice in a Metropolitan Community," *Crime and Delinquency* 39:2 (1993): 204–224; William Weir, *In the Shadow of the Dope Fiend: America's War on Drugs* (North Haven, CT: Archon Books, 1995); and Marc Mauer and Ryan King, *Schools and Prisons: Fifty Years After* Brown v. Board of Education (Washington, DC: The Sentencing Project, 2005).

SUMMARY

In this first decade of the new millennium, corrections in America stands at a crossroads, experiencing a major crisis unparalleled during the past 200 years. The remainder of this textbook describes current developments and practices in corrections, innovations, proposed solutions, and ways to ease the crisis and improve the effectiveness of the system. To understand those recent developments, we needed to explore the correctional ideologies detailed in this chapter.

It appears now that some of the programs designed to relieve the problems in the overcrowded fortress prisons have in fact contributed to many of the conditions and made them even more prone to violence. The fortress prisons are still here and they are even more overcrowded, and their maximum security clients are now the "bottom of the barrel" regarding behavioral problems.[31] This has caused an abandonment of the medical model and steady movement toward a model emphasizing custody and control over everything else in a futile effort to keep peace in the institutions and "protect society." The problem of selecting a philosophy or ideology that is effective yet also reflective of society's mood is a problem correctional administrators will have to confront in the next decade.

Only when American society decides which ideology or combination of ideologies most deserves its support will the problems facing the correctional administrator be properly addressed. It may be that some combination or blend will be the only practical or possible answer, given the vast variety of problems and offenders. Some offenders may respond only to a punitive ideology, at least until we are able to develop treatment techniques that offer greater potential for success and are constitutionally acceptable. The offender who can respond to treatment, however, must be given a chance to receive it, but without being totally free of some kind of control, because the protection of society remains the primary mission of corrections. The prevention ideology offers great promise, but it seems too idealistic to suffice in and of itself. As prison populations become increasingly large and unmanageable, it may become necessary to introduce ex-offenders into the prison environment, as leavening and change agents working with the correctional administration. This is becoming more acceptable in the fields of probation and parole. Those ideas will undoubtedly lead to the development of other alternatives to incarceration, and some possibilities are outlined in later chapters. To comprehend the current issues in corrections, we must examine the decision process and options available to the judiciary and releasing authorities. That process and its options are described in the next part.

REVIEW QUESTIONS

1. What basic ideologies have determined the handling of offenders over the years? Which is the oldest?
2. What criteria must be met if punishment is to act as a deterrent?
3. How does the treatment ideology differ from punishment? Are they necessarily exclusive of each other?
4. What are some of the changes currently taking place in the clientele of the correctional system?
5. How has the punishment ideology recently impacted on corrections?

ENDNOTES

1. As cited by Elmer H. Johnson, *Crime, Correction, and Society* (Homewood, IL: Dorsey Press, 1974), p. 173. See also Roger Hood, "Capital Punishment: A Global Perspective," *Punishment and Society* 3:3 (2001): 331–334.
2. Norman Carlson, "A More Balanced Correctional Philosophy," *FBI Law Enforcement Bulletin* 46 (January 1977): 22–25. See also John Cochran and Mitchell Chamblin, "Deterrence and Brutalization," *Justice Quarterly* 17:4 (2000): 685–706.
3. K. Blackman, R. Voas, R. Gullberg, et al., "Enforcement of Zero-Tolerance in the State of Washington," *Forensic Science Review* 13:2 (2001): 77–86.
4. John Irwin and James Austin, *It's About Time* (San Francisco: National Council on Crime and Delinquency, 1987), pp. 12–14. See also Hung Sung, "Rehabilitating Felony Drug Offenders Through Job Development," *Prison Journal* 81:2 (2001): 271–286.
5. Bradley Wright, A. Caspi, and T. Moffitt, "Does the Perceived Risk of Punishment Deter Criminally Prone Individuals?" *Journal of Research in Crime and Delinquency* 41:2 (2004): 180–213.
6. Peter B. Greenwood, *Selective Incapacitation* (Santa Monica, CA: Rand Corporation, 1983). But also see Simon Cole, "From the Sexual Psychopath to 'Megan's Law,' " *Journal of the History of Medicine and Allied Science* 55:3 (2000): 292–314.
7. Incapacitation remains a hotly debated topic in corrections. See Daniel Nagin, David Farrington, and Terrie Moffit, "Life Course Trajectories of Different Types of Offenders," *Criminology* 33:1 (1995): 111–139; and Mark Warr, "Life Course Trajectories and Desistance from Crime," *Criminology* 36:2 (1998): 183–216.
8. Hennessey Hayes and M. Geerken argue that it is possible to identify low rate offenders for early release. See H. Hayes and M. Geerken, "The Idea of Selective Release," *Justice Quarterly* 14:2 (1997): 353–370.
9. More than half of prison inmates will be charged with prison rule violations during their current sentences. See James Stephan, *Prison Rule Violations* (Washington, DC: Bureau of Justice Statistics, 1989). See also Stephen Schoenthaler, Stephen Amos, W. Doraz, et al., "The Effect of Randomized Vitamin-Mineral Supplementation on Violent and Non-Violent Antisocial Behavior Among Incarcerated Juveniles," *Journal of Nutritional and Environmental Medicine* 7:1 (1997): 343–352.
10. See the comments on the Alabama "dog house" by John Conrad, "From Barbarism Toward Decency: Alabama's Long Road to Prison Reform," *Journal of Research in Crime and Delinquency* 26 (November 1989): 307–328; Human Rights Watch, "No Escape: Male Rape in U.S. Prisons," www.hrw.org/reports/2001/prison.
11. Johnson, *Crime, Correction and Society,* pp. 361–365. A European view of punishment can be found in Pieter Spirenburg, *Man and Violence: Gender, Honor and Rituals in Modern Europe and America* (Columbus: Ohio State University Press, 1998).
12. There is a current rebirth of the punishment ideology, described in detail by Donald E. J. MacNamara, "The Medical Model in Corrections: Requiescat in Pace," *Criminology* 14 (February 1977): 439–448. See also Victor Hassine, *A Life Without Parole: Living in Prison Today,* 3rd ed. (Los Angeles: Roxbury, 2004).
13. James Austin and Aaron McVey, *The 1989 NCCD Prison Population Forecast: The Impact of the War on Drugs* (San Francisco: National Council on Crime and Delinquency, 1989), p. 13. See also Michael

Tonry, "Parochialism in the United States Sentencing Policy," *Crime and Delinquency* 45:1 (1999): 48–65; and Marc Mauer and Ryan King, *Schools and Prisons: Fifty Years After* Brown v. Board of Education (Washington, DC: The Sentencing Project, 2005).

14. Patrick Langan and David Levin, *Recidivism of Prisoners Released in 1994* (Washington, DC: Bureau of Justice Statistics, 2002). But see David Hartmann, J. Wolk, J. Johnston, et al., "Recidivism and Substance Abuse Outcomes in a Prison-Based Therapeutic Community," *Federal Probation* 61:4 (1997): 18–25; and Michael Pendergast, Elizabeth Hall, Harry Wexler, et al., "Amity Prison Based Therapeutic Community," *The Prison Journal* 84:1 (2004): 36–60.
15. For a discussion of prediction, see Anthony Petrosino and Caroline Petrosino, "The Public Safety Potential of Megan's Law in Massachusetts," *Crime and Delinquency* 45:1 (1999): 140–158.
16. See the discussion of the Gluecks' arguments in Melissa Johnson, "Youth, Violent Behavior and Exposure to Violence in Childhood," *Aggression and Violent Behavior* 3:2 (1998): 159–179.
17. See Linda Dahlberg, "Youth Violence in the United States: Major Trends, Risk Factors and Prevention Approaches," *American Journal of Preventive Medicine* 14:4 (1998): 259–272. See also American Academy of Child and Adolescent Psychiatry, "Children with Oppositional Defiant Disorder," www.aacap.org/publications/factsfam/72.htm (accessed January 20, 2005).
18. Emile Durkheim, *Division of Labor in Society,* trans. George Simpson (Glencoe, IL: Free Press, 1947). See also Dario Melossi, *The Sociology of Punishment* (Aldershot, UK: Dartmouth, 1998).
19. Carri Casteel, "Effectiveness of Crime Prevention Through Environmental Design in Reducing Robberies," *American Journal of Preventive Medicine* 18:4 (2000): 99–115; and City of Mesa, Arizona, "Crime Prevention Through Environmental Design," www.cityofmesa.org/police/literature/cpted.asp (accessed January 19, 2005).
20. Eric Fritsch, T. Caeti, and R. Taylor, "Gang Suppression Through Saturation Patrol, Aggressive Curfew and Truancy Enforcement," *Crime and Delinquency* 45:1 (1999): 122–139.
21. Daniel Nagin and J. Waldfogel, "The Effects of Conviction on Income Through Life," *International Review of Law and Economics* 18:1 (1998): 25–40.
22. David Shichor and D. Sechrest, "A Comparison of Medicated and Non-Medicated Offender Cases in California," *Juvenile and Family Court Journal* 49:2 (1998): 27–39; and Peggy Crown and John Parham, "*Can We Talk? Mediation in Juvenile Cases,*" www.lectlaw.com/files/cjs08.htm (accessed January 20, 2005).
23. That trend has stopped. The percentage of U.S. households victimized by violent crime or theft during 2003 remained at the lowest levels since 1994. Since 1994, property crimes have dropped 40 percent and violence by a stranger or burglary dropped 55 percent. Bureau of Justice Statistics, "Crime Victimization in U.S. Households Remains at Lowest Levels," www.ojp.usdoj.gov/bjs/pub/press/cnh03pr.htm (accessed January 19, 2005).
24. Harry E. Allen, Edward Latessa, and Gennaro Vito, "Corrections in the Year 2000," *Corrections Today* 49:2 (1987): 73–78.
25. T. Flanagan, E. McGarrell, and A. Lizotte, "Ideology and Crime Control Policy Positions in a State Legislature," *Journal of Criminal Justice* 17 (1989): 87–101; Marla Sandys and Edmund McGarrell, "Attitudes Toward Capital Punishment Among Indiana Legislators," *Justice Quarterly* 11:4 (1994): 651–677.
26. Francis Cullen, Bonnie Fisher, and Brandon Applegate, "Public Opinion About Punishment and Corrections," in Michael Tonry (ed.), *Crime and Justice* (Chicago: University of Chicago Press, 2000), pp. 1–79.
27. This material was extracted from Shay Bilchik, *Guide for Implementing the Restorative Justice Model (OJJDP)* (Washington, DC: U.S. Government Printing Office, December 1998). But see Sharon Levrant, F. Cullen, B. Fulton, and J. Wozniak, "Reconsidering Restorative Justice," *Crime and Delinquency* 45:1 (1999): 3–27; and Lening Zang and Sheldon Zang, "Reintegrative Shaming and Predatory Delinquency," *Journal of Research in Crime and Delinquency* 41:4 (2004): 433–453.
28. See William Spellman, "What Recent Studies Do (and Don't) Tell Us About Imprisonment and Crime," in Tonry, *Crime and Justice,* pp. 419–494.
29. Craig Hainey, "Mental Health Issues in Long-Term Solitary and 'Supermax' Confinement," *Crime and Delinquency* 49:1 (2003): 124–156; Michael Vaughn and Sue Collins, "Medical Malpractice in Correctional Facilities," *The Prison Journal* 84:4 (2004): 505–534; and Margaret Severson, "Mental Health Needs and Mental Health Care in Jails," *American Jails* 18:3 (2004): 9–18.
30. Edward Latessa and Harry Allen, *Corrections in the Community* (Cincinnati, OH: Anderson Publishing, 2004), p. 43.
31. Simon Fass and Chung-Ron Pi, "Getting Tough on Juvenile Crime: An Analysis of Costs and Benefits," *Journal of Research in Crime and Delinquency* 39:4 (2002): 363–399; and Jesenia Pizarro and Vanja Stenius, "Supermax Prisons," *The Prison Journal* 84:2 (2004): 248–264.

SUGGESTED READINGS: PART 1

Barnes, Harry Elmer. *The Story of Punishment,* 2nd ed. Montclair, NJ: Patterson Smith, 1972.

Barnes, Harry Elmer, and Negley K. Teeters. *New Horizons in Criminology,* 2nd ed. Englewood Cliffs, NJ: Prentice Hall, 1959.

Brockway, Zebulon Reed. *Fifty Years of Prison Service.* Montclair, NJ: Patterson Smith, 1969.

Donziger, Steven. *The Real War on Crime.* New York: HarperCollins, 1996.

Edwards, Todd. *The Aging Inmate Population.* Atlanta: Council on State Governments, 1998.

Hassine, Victor. *Life Without Parole: Living in Prison Today.* Los Angeles: Roxbury, 2004.

Irwin, John, and James Austin. *It's About Time.* San Francisco: National Council on Crime and Delinquency, 1997.

Kuhn, Andre. "Incarceration Rates." *Criminal Justice Abstracts* 30:2 (1998): 321–353.

Latessa, Edward, and Harry Allen. *Corrections in the Community.* Cincinnati, OH: Anderson, 2004.

Mauer, Marc, and Ryan King. *Schools and Prisons: Fifty Years After* Brown v. Board of Education. Washington, DC: The Sentencing Project, 2005.

Nagel, William. *The New Red Barn.* New York: Walker, 1973.

Roberts, John. *Reform and Retribution: An Illustrated History of American Prisons.* Lanham, MD: American Correctional Association, 1997.

Ross, Jeffrey, and Stephen Richards. *Behind Bars: Surviving Prisons.* Indianapolis, IN: Alpha, 2002.

Rothman, David J. *The Discovery of the Asylum.* Boston: Little, Brown, 1971.

PART

2

The Court Process

THE FOLLOWING CHAPTERS ARE COVERED IN PART 2:

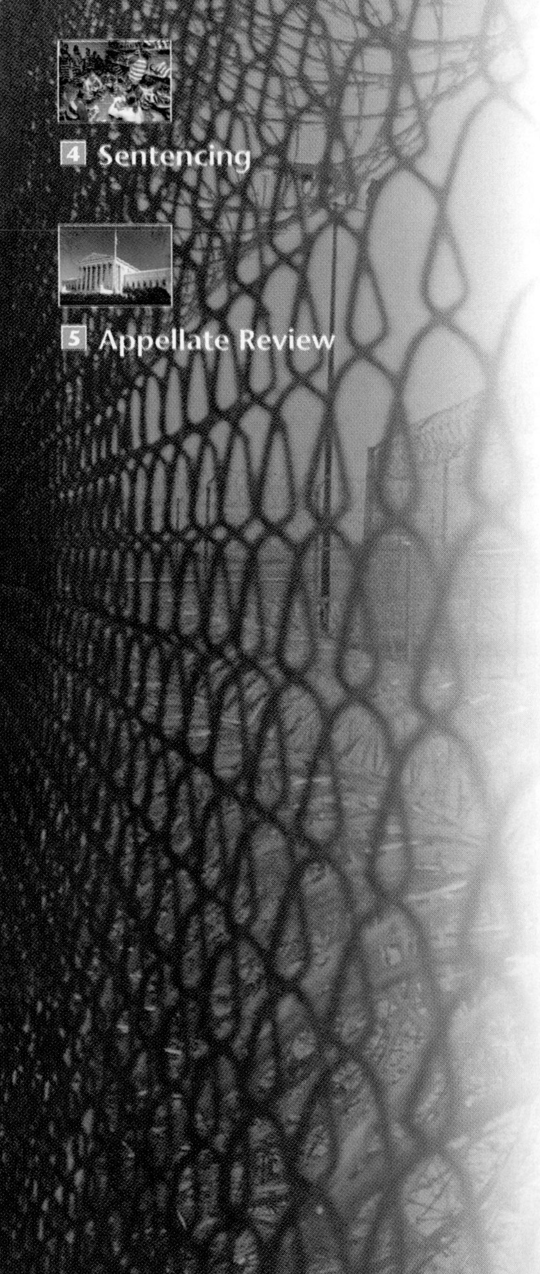

OVERVIEW

In Part 2, we examine issues that deal with sentencing criminal offenders. Students will also become acquainted with those processes by which offenders are placed in the major components of corrections and how sentencing practices influence correctional practices, programs, and facilities. Part 2 then discusses appellate review of convictions and sentencing. The correctional filter, by which offenders are placed, released, or diverted, is covered in depth. We begin our examination of this part with an inquiry into crime rates and find ourselves looking at a surprising outbreak in lawfulness in America as we begin the twenty-first century.

CHAPTER 4

Sentencing

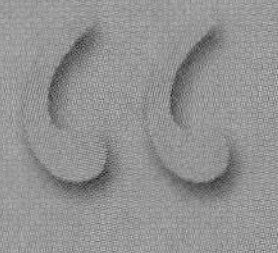

My object all sublime
I shall achieve in time—
To let the punishment fit the crime,
The punishment fit the crime.
—William S. Gilbert, *The Mikado*

KEY WORDS

- plea bargaining
- indeterminate sentencing
- sentencing disparity
- just deserts
- presentence report
- administrative sentencing
- determinate sentencing
- sentencing guidelines
- good-time policies
- presumptive sentencing
- deterrence by sentencing

OVERVIEW

Perhaps no part of the criminal justice system has had more criticism or controversy than the nation's courts as they struggle to make, as noted above, "the punishment fit the crime." This chapter will examine that critical decision and acquaint the student with the impact these decisions have on soaring prison populations and their impact in regard to the "correctional filter," as discussed next. Many criticize the court's efforts to apply "justice" while dealing with public opinion, jail and prison overcrowding, budget shortages, and legislative restrictions on the judge's discretion. Critics need a better understanding of the sentencing and appeals process, the latter of which is discussed in detail in Chapter 5. The student must keep in mind the incidences of crime and the sheer volume of cases when discussing the sentencing process and decisions made in America's courts. This issue will have a vital relationship to the material already covered and chapters yet to come. It will also prepare the student for understanding the complexities of the appellate process discussed in Chapter 5.

THE CORRECTIONAL FILTER

In our examination of the myriad dimensions and trends of corrections in America, we now come to the concept we call the *correctional filter,* representing the various sentencing options that sometimes confuse observers as to what is actually occurring in the criminal justice system. At every point of this filter, certain types of offenders and cases are shunted into alternative dispositions, the great bulk of which involve some type of correctional supervision other than jail or prison. Those offenders who

< Arraigned men await trial in a crowded holding cell, Maricopa County Jail, Arizona.
Photo by A. Ramey, courtesy of PhotoEdit.

FIGURE 4.1

Outcomes for Arrest for Type I Felony Crimes, 2003

SOURCE: From Federal Bureau of Investigation, "Crime in the United States 2003," www.Fbi.gov/ucr_cius_03/pdf/03sec4.pdf. Figure adapted from S. Silberman, *Criminal Violence, Criminal Justice* (New York: Random House, 1978), pp. 257-261.

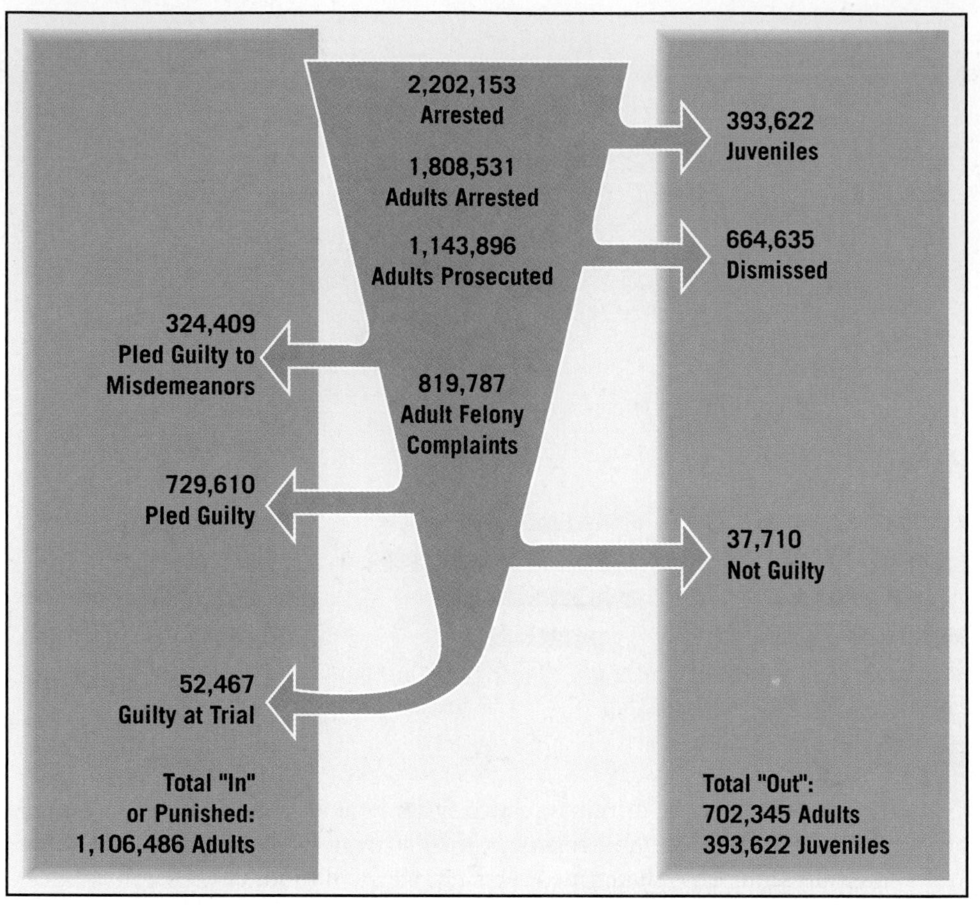

SIDEBARS

Misdemeanor

An offense usually punishable by incarceration in a local facility for a period of which the upper limit is prescribed by statute in a given jurisdiction, typically limited to a year or less.

SIDEBARS

Felony

A criminal offense punishable by death or by incarceration in a state or federal confinement facility for a period of which the lower limit is prescribed by statute in a given jurisdiction, typically one year or more.

SIDEBARS

Plea Bargaining

Plea bargaining refers to the prosecutor's practice of permitting the defendant to plead to a lesser charge than the one he or she was arrested for, usually because the prosecutor does not feel the case is strong enough on the more serious charge or because the prosecutor hopes to persuade the defendant to provide information about other crimes or offenders. Plea bargaining may lead to the prosecutor agreeing to dismiss multiple charges, reduce charges, or recommend a light sentence. The gains that offenders are alleged to secure by plea bargaining may be less than anticipated, if not ephemeral, in many cases.

are finally placed under custody and supervision in prisons are, for the most part, the worst of the worst. We now examine the processes, flows, and rationales of the correctional filter, as illustrated in Figure 4.1.

The Prosecutor's Decision

A major player in the correctional filter process is the prosecutor's office. It is here that prosecutors implement their broad discretionary power to dismiss charges or reduce them to charges for which the defendant will be more likely to plead guilty. Recent studies indicate that as many as 50 to 90 percent of the felony cases initiated by the police are bargained away by prosecutors; in 2002, this figure was 95 percent in large urban counties.[1] U.S. attorneys declined to prosecute 26 percent of the offenses investigated by federal law enforcement agencies in 2000; the comparable figure nationwide in 2002 was 27 percent.[2] A high percentage of charges not dismissed are reduced through **plea bargaining** to a less serious charge to which the defendant agrees to plead guilty. The most common explanation for this action of the correctional filter stems from high caseloads and limited resources, forcing harried prosecutors to dispense with much of their caseload as quickly as possible to avoid overwhelming their own offices, the courts, and overcrowded jails and prisons. The time factor does not explain, however, why some cases are prosecuted and others dismissed. Here, the wide discretionary power given to prosecutors becomes a crucial issue, and prosecutors consider such factors as the case's strength, evenhandedness, harm done to the victim, ethnicity, and the attorneys' personal attributes.[3]

CORRECTIONAL BRIEF

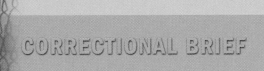

Disparate Sentencing for Crack and Cocaine Use

In 1986, Congress created sentencing disparity for two of the most popular types of cocaine: powdered and crack (crystal). The sale of five grams of crack cocaine—barely a teaspoon full—results in a minimum of five years in federal prison for the violator. Sale of 100 times that amount of powdered cocaine—the type preferred by whites—is required to result in a comparable sentence. About 90 percent of those convicted of selling crack cocaine are black, and only 30 percent of those convicted of selling powdered cocaine are black. When the U.S. Sentencing Commission recommended changing the sentencing guidelines to equalize sentencing, both the U.S. House and Senate voted to block any change in the 100-to-1 ratio.

SOURCE: Michael Isikoff, "Crack, Coke, and Race," *Newsweek* (November 6, 1995): 77.

THE SENTENCING DECISION

As suggested, defendants who reach the sentencing stage of criminal proceedings are those who have not yet completely evaded the correctional filter. They have either pled guilty to, or been found guilty of, a crime, either by a jury or bench trial.[4] The court must then decide in what fashion they will dispose of them. Making a sentencing decision is often the most complicated and difficult task for any judge. High rates of violent street crime, along with a large number of drug offenders and lengthier determinate sentences, make the sentencing decision more complex than it has ever been.

Rapid Change in Sentencing Processes

In 1930, most states and federal courts were operating under the **indeterminate sentencing** structure: The judge would impose a prison sentence with both a minimum and a maximum term in years, such as two years minimum to five years maximum, or five years minimum to twenty years maximum. The wide ranges of sentence lengths reflected the dominant rehabilitation goal of the correctional system and its belief that once the offender had been rehabilitated, the parole board would detect the change and then order the inmate's release. Parole boards would actually determine the length of the sentence served, using their authority of discretionary release. Following a long period of relative inactivity (1930 to 1974), American sentencing laws and practices began to undergo a rapid, fundamental restructuring of the sentencing process. The causes have been identified as follows[5]:

1. Prison uprisings (such as at Attica in New York, and others in New Mexico, Oklahoma, California, and Florida) indicated that inmates were particularly discontented with the rhetoric of rehabilitation and the reality of the prison environment.
2. The abuse of discretion caused concerns about individual rights, because prosecutors, judges, and parole boards were immune from review and some practiced arbitrary uses of discretion.
3. Court orders and decisions led to a movement that demanded accountability in official decision making and outcomes.

4. The rehabilitation ideal was challenged, both empirically and ideologically, which undermined the rationale of the indeterminate sentence's "parole after rehabilitation" corollary.
5. Experimental and statistical studies of judicial sentencing found substantial disparity and both racial and class discrimination.[6] Such inconsistencies and disparities fostered the conclusion that sentencing practices were unfair. (**Sentencing disparity** means that offenders committing the same crimes under the same circumstances are given different sentences by the same judge.)
6. Crime control and corrections became a political football,[7] useful for those seeking election to public office.

New Goals

Corrections by the 1970s generally functioned under the utilitarian goal of rehabilitation being possible. Dialogue and arguments from "hard-liners" brought other primary goals to the forefront in the 1980s. These included incapacitation of persons likely to commit future crimes and its variant of selective incapacitation, in which the highest-risk offenders would receive much longer sentences to prevent any more criminal activity.[8] From the mid-1990s on, such concepts as "three strikes and you're out" laws have become popular with the public and legislators. A dramatic rash of "headline crimes," especially heinous, combined with the perception of a growing level of violent crimes, has spurred on such movements since the early 1970s. The specific deterrence of sentenced offenders and the general deterrence of those contemplating committing a crime were legitimized as social policy goals. In addition, the retribution goal became attractive, inasmuch as it would impose deserved punishment. (Such a **just deserts** goal looks backward to the offender's personal culpability, focuses on the nature of the act, and considers the harm done.[9])

In total, twenty-five states and the federal government have enacted three-strikes legislation, increasing the length of sentences by a multiple of two, or setting minimum time to be served at twenty-five, thirty, or even forty years. Despite claims of prosecutors and legislators that such legislation was an essential crime-fighting tool, both for deterrence and incapacitation, it has not been applied extensively. There is little creditable evidence from investigations that enacting such laws has reduced crime. Instead, the evidence is that criminals are rarely concerned about being apprehended, that the laws target offenders beyond their peak ages of reoffending, that identifying high rate offenders early on before they perpetrate a high number of crimes is difficult and fraught with "false-positive" errors, and that other criminals simply replace any who would be incarcerated. Finally, eligible offenders have mostly experienced enhanced penalties prior to the imposition of such laws and the increased incarceration does not sufficiently increase the severity of punishment. There is some reason to suspect that such ineffective crime control measures serve to increase the geriatric populations in prison, creating a demand for nursing homes and other expensive medical treatments.[10]

Reform Options

As a result of the reform movement, sentencing practices were changed in the belief that the new practices would limit disparity and discretion and establish more detailed criteria for sentencing or new sentencing institutions. The resulting contradictory options include the following:

1. Abolishing plea bargaining
2. Establishing plea-bargaining rules and guidelines

3. Setting mandatory minimum sentences
4. Establishing statutory determinate sentencing
5. Setting voluntary or descriptive sentencing guidelines or presumptive or prescriptive sentencing guidelines
6. Creating sentencing councils
7. Requiring judges to provide reasons for their sentences
8. Setting parole guidelines to limit parole board discretion
9. Abolishing parole[11]
10. Adopting or modifying good-time procedures
11. Routinizing appellate review of sentences.[12]

These options represent only the principal steps designed to limit unbridled discretion, reduce discrimination, make sentencing fairer, and enhance justice.

SIDEBARS

Probation

Probation is a sentence imposed by the court that does not involve confinement, but does impose conditions to restrain the offender's actions in the community. The court retains authority to modify the conditions of sentence or to resentence the offender if he or she violates the conditions of the probation.

Reform Effects

In just a few decades, dramatic changes in sentencing structures and practices became evident. Release by a parole board was abolished in a large number of states, and mandatory sentencing guidelines were established in many others. In 1987, the U.S. Federal Sentencing Guidelines were promulgated. More than twenty states were using determinate sentencing (a sentence with a specific release date), and at least forty-eight states had established mandatory minimum sentences for at least one crime. Several states adopted statewide sentencing councils, and at least fifty jurisdictions drew up local sentencing guidelines. It is against that background of concern and change that we will look at the sentencing decision.

SIDEBARS

Parole

Release of an inmate from confinement prior to expiration of sentence on condition of good behavior and supervision in the community. This is also referred to as *post-incarceration supervision* or *aftercare*.

Predicting Behavior

If the sentencing procedure had no purpose but to punish the offender, as was the case until fairly recently, the judge's decision could be easily prescribed by statute. In modern times, however, the sentence is also expected to be the cornerstone for reintegration.

CORRECTIONAL BRIEF

Presumptive Sentencing

One alternative to limit sentencing disparity is the presumptive sentencing system, in which the state legislature sets minimum, average, and maximum terms, allowing the judge to select a term based on the characteristics of the offender and aggravating circumstances. The sentence imposed will be the time served, less any credits against the sentence that the offender earns (such as credit for time served in jail, good behavior in prison, program participation, and so on). California has a presumptive sentencing structure that provides three options to the sentencing judge, as seen here for the crime of burglary:

1. Aggravating circumstances—seven years
2. Presumptive (average) sentence—five years
3. Mitigating circumstances—three years.

Ordinarily, the judge would decide if the offender were to be placed on probation or sentenced to prison (the "in-out" decision). Assuming imprisonment to be the answer, the judge would impose the average sentence of five years, unless mitigating circumstances were present at the time of the offense (for example, if the offender were under the influence of a controlled substance or had a weak personality and was easily led into committing a crime for peer approval). If mitigating circumstances were proven, the judge would impose the least sentence (three years). However, if aggravating circumstances were proven, the judge must impose the highest sentence (seven years). Some examples of aggravating circumstances are gross bodily harm to victim, prior incarceration in prison, and vulnerability of victim (older than 60 years of age, blind, paraplegic, etc.).

Those broadly divergent objectives create a paradox that may force judges to choose between equally unwise alternatives based on the offense rather than the offender. The choice is often further complicated by subtle pressures from police, prosecutors, and the general public to incarcerate certain offenders for longer periods of time.

One of the main problems with the sentencing decision is that it requires judges to predict human behavior. As judges ask themselves if specific offenders will respond to prison positively or perhaps benefit more from psychiatric help while on probation, they have little factual information to guide them. In the final analysis, most judges must rely on a presentence investigation and their own intuition, experience, and imagination to produce the best decision.

The Presentence Investigation

Most of the states make a **presentence report** mandatory for offenses for which imprisonment can be more than one year. It is estimated that more than 85 percent of the states do prepare some kind of presentence report on felony cases, although there may be extreme variation in the report's usefulness and quality. The presentence report, if properly researched and prepared, can be an extremely valuable document for trial judges who are making sentencing decisions.

The presentence investigation report is usually prepared by the court's probation officer or by any available social workers. Privately commissioned presentence investigation reports prepared for the court,[13] as well as creation of local agencies to prepare individualized client-specific sentencing plans that stress nonincarceration sanctions[14] (such as in North Carolina), also serve to assist sentencing judges. The defense attorney usually reviews, and may challenge, points in the presentence report to help the judge make a sentencing decision based on information from all of the sources.[15] Walter C. Reckless pointed out the essential elements of a workable presentence investigation report. He said that, when written up and presented to the judge, this report should include in summary form the following information[16]:

1. Present offense (including the person's attitudes toward it and his or her role in it)
2. Previous criminal record, family situation (including tensions and discord and the factors affecting his or her happiness)
3. Neighborhood environment, school, and educational history
4. Employment history (especially the skills and the efficiency and stability as a worker)
5. Associates and participation
6. Habits (including alcohol, gambling, promiscuity, and so forth)
7. Physical and mental health (as reported by various sources and by special examinations)
8. Summary and recommendations.

Most presentence investigations will emphasize such objective facts in a case as age, grade reached in school, number of children, and so on. It is important also that the investigating officer capture as much subjective content as possible, especially how defendants look at their situation and the meaning of various plights and difficulties they face. The defendants' perspectives on life and the way they approach them, as well as their attitudes toward the objects and the relationships of their milieu, are the most crucial items in a presentence investigation, just as they are in more elaborate case studies. Subjective data, in short, give the more revealing clues as to what has shaped the destiny of the defendant so far and future possibilities.[17]

The presentence investigation report gives the judge a comprehensive and factual overview of the offender, the actual crime, and the offender's nature, history, habits, personality, problems, needs, and risks. It also usually contains a recommendation to the court of an appropriate disposition for the case. Judges tend to accept the presentence recommendation at a rate of about 83 percent for probation and 87 percent for imprisonment.

The presentence report serves many functions. Not only is it of immediate use in determining an appropriate sentence, but it also is used by correctional agencies or institutions for classification and program activities assignments. It will aid the probation officer in handling the case, should probation be the sentence imposed. It will also follow the offender to parole, at which time the parole officer will use it in planning and supervising the case. Appellate review courts use the document when considering an appeal of sentence, and the presentence investigation reports also offer a database from which to conduct research on convicted offenders, case flows, and court management.[18]

Judicial Versus Administrative Sentencing

Traditionally, the sentencing process has involved a judicial determination of the appropriate punishment for a specific crime. There have been extensive changes in judicial power in the last century, however, particularly during the last decade. In the early days, when a judge sentenced an offender to ten years in prison, it was almost a certainty that the offender would serve ten years to the day. As administrative forms of sentence shortening (involving such matters as good time, pardon, parole, and clemency) became more common, the correlation between the judge's sentence and the time the offender served largely disappeared. In practice, courts using indeterminate sentencing can establish minimum and maximum sentences within the sentencing statutes, but the actual length of the sentence is often left up

A court-appointed attorney argues for probation for his client.

Photo by Bob Daemmrich, courtesy of Stock Boston.

to the administrators of the correctional system, that is, to the executive rather than to the judicial branch of government. Therefore, those involved in **administrative sentencing** ultimately decide an offender's fate.

A comparison of the judicial and administrative styles of decision making in sentencing reveals some similar criteria:

1. A determination of how much time is right for the kind of crime at issue, with the decision maker's own sense of values and expectations usually (but not always) heavily influenced by the pressures of the local environment and perceived norms of colleagues[19]
2. Classification within that crime category of the offender's particular acts as mitigated, average, or aggravated
3. Offender's past criminal record (slight, average, or aggravated)
4. Offender's extent of repentance, attitude toward available treatment, and official prognosis of reformability
5. Anticipated public (usually meaning law enforcement) reaction to a proposed disposition.

Not all of these criteria are used or even relevant in every case, and many other variables may be raised because of the existence of particular facts (such as strong middle-class background and allegiance) or the peculiarities or hang-ups of an individual decision maker. Something approximating the given basic list, however, appears to comprise the critical factors in most sentence fixing. Presumably, very similar criteria are involved in prosecutorial sentence bargaining at the prearraignment stage.[20]

Practical Problems in Sentencing

As we have seen previously, the correctional filter of the criminal justice process reveals at every step an imbalance of input to output (number of arrests versus number of incarcerations). Many cases are winnowed out in the early stages, and it is a highly select group of prisoners who end up in prisons like Attica, Pelican Bay, and San Quentin. In a statistical sense, the negative selection process that admits the offender to prison may be considered more discriminating than the positive one that admits students to Ivy League colleges. But for the practical need to spread limited resources over an overwhelming number of cases, scores of additional offenders would join each of the relatively small proportion of offenders that end up in prison. The state and federal correctional systems are finite in size. The sentencing decision may be impacted by the decisions at the other end of the funnel process, which determine release rates. The system can become blocked if sentences do not approximately balance releases, resulting in dangerous overcrowding. At worst, prison overcrowding can contribute to judicial overuse of probation for offenders whose risk level is too high. This can result in overworked probation officers and unacceptably high probation failure rates by offenders who continue to commit serious crimes and whose probation is then revoked, requiring resentencing to imprisonment in state institutions. Sentencing, therefore, must take into account both the numbers of prisoners in the institutions and the limited resources for handling them.[21] Another source of pressure on the already overloaded correctional and court systems is the seemingly endless number of drug arrests that enter the juvenile and adult courts.

Charles Manson (1934–) was the cult leader of the Manson Family. Cult members brutally murdered Sharon Tate and her five friends in one event, and three others in separate events. Sentenced to death in California in 1971, their sentences were commuted to life imprisonment. Manson continues to be denied parole.

Problems in Setting Prison Terms

In the past, the determination of prison terms has been left largely to the courts. Decisions were made within the broad parameters of plea bargaining and statutory limitations. In the past two decades, however, control over the sentencing process has become more of a concern to state legislatures. Concerns about disparate sentences and other abuses or perceived abuses of the system have resulted in six basic strategies to formalize legislative control over the sentencing process:

1. **Determinate sentencing**—sentencing systems under which parole boards no longer may release prisoners before their sentences (minus good time) have expired
2. Mandatory prison terms—statutes through which legislatures require a prison term always to be imposed for convictions for certain offenses or offenders
3. **Sentencing guidelines**—procedures designed to structure sentencing decisions based on measures of offense severity and criminal history
4. Parole guidelines—procedures designed to structure parole release decisions based on measurable offender criteria
5. **Good-time policies**—statutes that allow for reducing a prison term based on an offender's behavior in prison
6. Emergency crowding provisions—policies that relieve prison crowding by systematically making inmates eligible for release sooner.

Prison populations are increasing in many states. Policies for setting prison terms influence the size of prison populations by both the number of people who are sentenced and the length of time that they stay in prison. As a result, many states have attempted to find ways to modify prison terms and reduce population pressures. Those methods include sentencing guidelines, such as those in Minnesota and Florida, that use available prison capacity as a consideration in setting the length of terms. Mechanisms also exist for accelerating good time and direct release of certain prisoners, usually those already close to their release date, under administrative provisions (such as emergency crowding laws, the use of commutation, sentence revisions, and early release programs).

The determinate sentencing states of California, Colorado, Connecticut, Illinois, Indiana, Maine, Minnesota, New Mexico, North Carolina, and Washington tend to give sentencing judges the least amount of discretion. Offenders usually receive fixed sentences and they are served in full, minus good-time credits. Generally in those states, parole boards continue to handle revocations and good-time decisions.

Such a sentencing structure limits "judicial imperialism" in sentencing, because the legislature heavily influences the sentence length. Whether there are unforeseen problems in **presumptive sentencing** remains to be proven, but California's prison population problems may well be due to a corollary of presumptive sentencing: abolition of parole board early-release authority that had been used in the past to control prison overcrowding.

Mandatory prison-term statutes exist in some form, for some crimes, in forty-eight states. Those statutes apply to certain crimes of violence and to habitual criminals, and the court's discretion in such cases (regarding, for example, probation, fines, and suspended sentences) has been eliminated by statute. In some states the imposition of a prison term is constrained by sentencing. A governor's commission, including a cross section of the state population, usually sets guidelines. As noted by a recent study:

> *A sentencing commission in each state monitors the use of the guidelines and departures from the recommended sentences by the judiciary. Written explanations are required from judges who depart from guideline ranges. The Minnesota Sentencing Guidelines Commission states that "while the sentencing guidelines are advisory to the sentencing judge, departures from the presumptive sentences*

SIDEBARS

Federal Truth-in-Sentencing Standard

This standard requires Part I violent offenders to serve no less than 85 percent of their sentence in prison before becoming eligible for release. These offenses include murder, nonnegligent manslaughter, rape, robbery, and aggravated assault. The District of Columbia and thirty-two states had adopted this standard by 2005.

CORRECTIONAL BRIEF

History of the Sentencing Guidelines

More than ten years ago Congress dramatically changed the federal sentencing system. The changes followed widespread discontent with the old sentencing system, and they ultimately led to the passage of the Federal Sentencing Guidelines in 1987. In the old system, judges determined criminal sentences. They considered the facts of each particular case—including the circumstances of the offense and the life history of the offender—and chose a sentence they considered fair. The only requirement was that the sentence be within a statutory range, and the ranges were often extremely broad. Statutes typically authorized sentences like "not more than five years," "not more than twenty years," or in some cases, "any term of years or life." Judges had authority to impose any sentence within the statutory range.

The imposition of the sentence was only the beginning. Once the person was in prison, the parole board determined the actual date of release. The parole board considered circumstances like the person's conduct in prison and efforts toward rehabilitation, and it released people to parole supervision when it thought they were ready—often after just half the sentence. If the person misbehaved after release, parole could be revoked and the person could be incarcerated for the remainder of the sentence.

In the 1970s, this practice fell into disfavor because it permitted too much disparity between cases. Different judges sentenced similar offenders differently, and parole boards became too powerful. If two identical offenders were each convicted of a crime carrying a sentence of "not more than twenty years," one might spend three years in custody and the other might spend fifteen. Evidence accumulated that the system led to arbitrary decision making and sometimes discrimination against poor people and minorities.

In 1984 Congress addressed these concerns by creating the United States Sentencing Commission and ordering the promulgation of the Federal Sentencing Guidelines. The new system sharply curtailed parole and confined judicially imposed sentences into narrow ranges. Congress enacted the guidelines into law in 1987 and in 1989 the Supreme Court held that the effort was constitutional. (See *Mistretta v. U.S.*).

Guidelines use standardized worksheets to calculate the sentence. In principle, the process is a lot like calculating income taxes with a federal 1040 form. The worksheet is complex and intricate, but in theory it guides everybody to the same conclusions. Guidelines operate by assigning an offense level to every crime—low offense levels for minor crimes and high levels for major crimes. At the same time, the guidelines direct the calculation of the criminal history of each defendant. A person with a clean record starts with zero criminal history points, and points are added for every subsequent offense.

The task of the judge is to look up on a grid the spot where the offense level intersects the criminal history. The grid assigns light sentences to people with low criminal histories who commit lesser crimes, and stiff sentences to people with long criminal histories who commit severe crimes. The judge then imposes a sentence in accordance with the sentencing guidelines grid unless there is a reason to depart.

The concept of the guidelines has been well received because it can lead to less sentencing disparity between judges and a more rational system overall. The federal system and roughly one-third of the states now use guideline sentencing systems. Different jurisdictions use different guidelines and have had different experiences with them. The general experience has been that guidelines represent an improvement over unfettered judicial discretion, but that they must be well structured and carefully conceived in order to succeed.

SOURCE: Coalition for Federal Sentencing Reform, "Guideline History," www.sentencing.org (revised July 2002).

established in the guidelines should be made only when substantial and compelling circumstances exist." Pennsylvania sentencing guidelines stipulate that court failure to explain sentences deviating from the recommendations "shall be grounds for vacating the sentence and resentencing the defendant." Furthermore, if the court does not consider the guidelines or inaccurately or inappropriately applies them, an imposed sentence may be vacated upon appeal to a higher court by either the defense or the prosecution.[22]

The range and particular format for sentencing guidelines can include such things as specifically worded statutes and grids with a range of judicial options. Parole guidelines are sometimes closely prescribed, and sometimes wide discretion is afforded to the parole board. The amount of flexibility in such decisions can directly enhance or detract from the efforts to relieve crowded prison conditions. Because most parole decisions are not based on time but on perceived "risk to the community," tighter and tighter criteria make it difficult to manage prison population size by such decisions. The Federal Sentencing Guidelines matrix is shown in Figure 4.2.

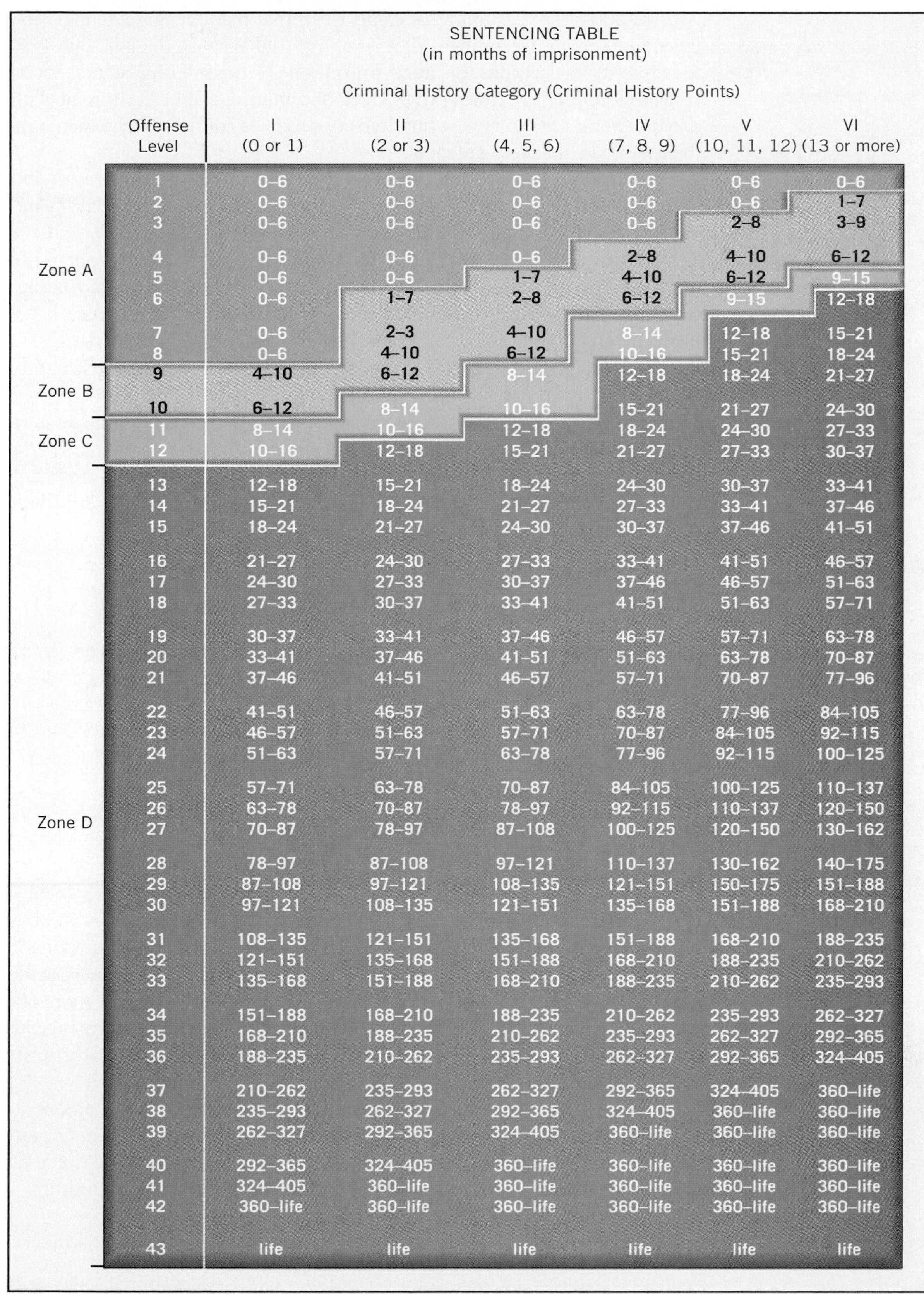

SENTENCING TABLE
(in months of imprisonment)

Zone	Offense Level	I (0 or 1)	II (2 or 3)	III (4, 5, 6)	IV (7, 8, 9)	V (10, 11, 12)	VI (13 or more)
		Criminal History Category (Criminal History Points)					
Zone A	1	0–6	0–6	0–6	0–6	0–6	0–6
	2	0–6	0–6	0–6	0–6	0–6	1–7
	3	0–6	0–6	0–6	0–6	2–8	3–9
	4	0–6	0–6	0–6	2–8	4–10	6–12
	5	0–6	0–6	1–7	4–10	6–12	9–15
	6	0–6	1–7	2–8	6–12	9–15	12–18
	7	0–6	2–3	4–10	8–14	12–18	15–21
	8	0–6	4–10	6–12	10–16	15–21	18–24
Zone B	9	4–10	6–12	8–14	12–18	18–24	21–27
	10	6–12	8–14	10–16	15–21	21–27	24–30
Zone C	11	8–14	10–16	12–18	18–24	24–30	27–33
	12	10–16	12–18	15–21	21–27	27–33	30–37
Zone D	13	12–18	15–21	18–24	24–30	30–37	33–41
	14	15–21	18–24	21–27	27–33	33–41	37–46
	15	18–24	21–27	24–30	30–37	37–46	41–51
	16	21–27	24–30	27–33	33–41	41–51	46–57
	17	24–30	27–33	30–37	37–46	46–57	51–63
	18	27–33	30–37	33–41	41–51	51–63	57–71
	19	30–37	33–41	37–46	46–57	57–71	63–78
	20	33–41	37–46	41–51	51–63	63–78	70–87
	21	37–46	41–51	46–57	57–71	70–87	77–96
	22	41–51	46–57	51–63	63–78	77–96	84–105
	23	46–57	51–63	57–71	70–87	84–105	92–115
	24	51–63	57–71	63–78	77–96	92–115	100–125
	25	57–71	63–78	70–87	84–105	100–125	110–137
	26	63–78	70–87	78–97	92–115	110–137	120–150
	27	70–87	78–97	87–108	100–125	120–150	130–162
	28	78–97	87–108	97–121	110–137	130–162	140–175
	29	87–108	97–121	108–135	121–151	150–175	151–188
	30	97–121	108–135	121–151	135–168	151–188	168–210
	31	108–135	121–151	135–168	151–188	168–210	188–235
	32	121–151	135–168	151–188	168–210	188–235	210–262
	33	135–168	151–188	168–210	188–235	210–262	235–293
	34	151–188	168–210	188–235	210–262	235–293	262–327
	35	168–210	188–235	210–262	235–293	262–327	292–365
	36	188–235	210–262	235–293	262–327	292–365	324–405
	37	210–262	235–293	262–327	292–365	324–405	360–life
	38	235–293	262–327	292–365	324–405	360–life	360–life
	39	262–327	292–365	324–405	360–life	360–life	360–life
	40	292–365	324–405	360–life	360–life	360–life	360–life
	41	324–405	360–life	360–life	360–life	360–life	360–life
	42	360–life	360–life	360–life	360–life	360–life	360–life
	43	life	life	life	life	life	life

FIGURE 4.2

Federal Sentencing Guidelines

SOURCE: Coalition for Federal Sentencing Reform, "History of the Guidelines," www.sentencing.org (accessed July 2, 2002).

SIDEBARS

Sixth Amendment

In all criminal prosecutions, the accused shall enjoy the right of a speedy and public trial, by an impartial jury of the State and district wherein the crime shall have been committed, which district shall have been previously ascertained by law, and to be informed of the nature and cause of the accusation; to be confronted with the witnesses against him; to have compulsory process for obtaining witnesses in his favor; and to have the Assistance of Counsel for his defense.

In 2005, the U.S. Supreme Court ruled that the federal guidelines violated a defendant's Sixth Amendment right to a jury trial because the guidelines required judges to make decisions that affect prison time by considering factors that had not come before the jury during trial. Later that month, the U.S. Supreme Court ordered lower courts to review hundreds of sentences of defendants then appealing their tainted enhanced sentence.

Good-time policies are another way to control behavior in correctional institutions and to control population pressures as well. The threat of losing up to one-third of their credits toward their sentences earned by good conduct serves as a control over some inmates' behavior. Our review of the changes in sentencing practices and their consequences in the last decade clearly shows the shifts that have taken place. Although discretion in determining sentence length has been somewhat removed from the sentencing judge and parole board, it was reduced by legislatures through their enactment of new sentencing structures, for reasons discussed earlier. In turn, in many jurisdictions, the prosecutor's discretion was increased. The prison populations will continue to climb as more and more offenders are committed and serve longer and longer sentences. American corrections appears to be on a collision course with a standard of human decency: the Eighth Amendment to the U.S. Constitution, which forbids cruel and unusual punishment.

Eighth Amendment

Excessive bail shall not be required, nor excessive fines imposed, nor cruel and unusual punishments inflicted.

FELONY SENTENCES IN STATE COURT, 2002

In 2002 (the last year for which there are national data), state courts convicted nearly 1,052,000 adults of a felony. Of convicted felons, 41 percent were sentenced to a state prison, and 28 percent were sentenced to a local jail (usually for a year or less). The remaining 31 percent were sentenced to probation. Of those convicted, some 95 percent pled guilty; the other 5 percent were found guilty either by a jury or by the judge in a bench trial.

Felons in state courts were convicted on drug offenses (32 percent), property offenses (34 percent), and violent offenses (19 percent). The rest were convicted of weapons offenses and other nonviolent crime.

The average sentence varied considerably. Those sentenced to local jail received seven months, on average. The average probation sentence was three years and two months. The average sentence length to prison was four and a half years, but offenders are more likely to serve more of that sentence before release than did a comparable group in 1990. If convicted and sentenced for two or more offenses, the mean sentence increased to 62 months. For rape, the prison sentence jumped from a mean of 83 months for one conviction offense to 123 months for two or more offenses.

Besides being sentenced to incarceration or probation, more than one-third of the convicted felons were ordered to pay a fine, pay victim restitution, receive treatment, perform community service, or comply with some other additional penalty, such as undergoing house arrest or appearing periodically for drug testing. A fine was imposed on at least 25 percent of convicted felons.

The likelihood of a felony arrest leading to a felony conviction increased in 2002, compared to 1994. This likelihood has generally risen for all crimes. Interestingly, the likelihood of felony conviction for drug trafficking exceeded that for all felony convictions, including murder (80 percent versus 70 percent).[23]

CORRECTIONAL BRIEF

The Role of Sentencing Commissions with Restorative Justice

When the purposes of sentencing commissions are presented in the literature, typically issues of fairness, equity, and consistency arise; sometimes the more systemic and prescriptive goals of increased retribution, more directed incapacitation for violent offenders, or cost effectiveness are offered. Research, evaluations, and other measurements of success are thus oriented around numbers and percentages incarcerated, length of incarceration, and comparison groups of offenders in other geographic or temporal venues.

This is not surprising, since the rhetoric of the day is so disposed, but even a slightly distant review of this situation reveals a glaring omission in policy, practice, and research—the victim. It is as if a collective decision was made to measure justice as punishment, with some small dissent to include rehabilitation, but every bit of it offender oriented.

A growing number of observers from inside and outside the criminal justice system are expressing their concern over this imbalance, and while it may not yet have reached the stage of a movement, there is enough activity that sentencing commissions would do well to anticipate the future and attempt to blend a victim focus into their agenda.

Generally referred to as *restorative justice,* this philosophy puts the victim and the community at the center. The primary concern is to right the wrong, using the offender as a vehicle where possible; to provide true involvement of the victim in the process—more than the allocution opportunity now sometimes extended to the victim.

Sentencing commissions can take five steps to improve focus on the victim:

1. Involve victims as commission members and in discussions. Involvement is the key to understanding the perspective and acknowledging the legitimacy of their role.
2. [Each Commission should] Include a goal of restoring the victim. [If this is not done], why should anyone expect victim restoration to be an aim of the criminal justice process?
3. Train and orient staff and the public to their responsibility. Training is paramount to many technical matters concerning calculation of guidelines, completion of forms, and impacts of commission rules. Shouldn't the effect on the primary victim be a centerpiece of concern rather than an afterthought, or worse, ignored?
4. Ensure policies and procedures are in place to allow victim involvement and restoration. The most obvious example is restitution. One of the most often-cited conditions of probation, few jurisdictions have in place any semblance of a professional system to identify, collect, track, and disburse restitution. The methods are available through the private sector if not other public agencies.
5. Measure success by identifying how victims and communities are restored, using measures such as restitution collected; community service hours; percentage of victims given the opportunity for a face-to-face dialogue with their offenders or to sit on an impact panel; and results of surveys. If we spend all our time collecting data on how we affect offenders, it sends a message that we don't care about the effect on victims.

As confounding as it already is to try to sort out commission responsibilities, broadening the role to include restorative justice may very well be a welcome diversion from the "how tough can we get" debate, and can create new allies for some beleaguered commissions. Victim advocates are a growing force on the justice scene and having them side by side with sentencing commissions is much preferable to having them head to head. In any case, as we strive toward the elusive goal of a fair and balanced justice delivery system, this is the right thing to do.

SOURCE: Thomas J. Quinn, *Sentencing Commission News,* April 1996, Issue 3.

DETERRENCE BY SENTENCING

A discussion of sentencing would be incomplete without mentioning the policy implications of the increasing demand for deterrence. Some writers now argue that those states that imprison more of the offender population (rather than use community corrections) would have lower crime rates if the proportion of persons sentenced to prison were to increase even more. Though **deterrence by sentencing** may appeal to conservatives who believe that the criminal justice system can affect the rates of crime and serve as a deterrent, the data on the effects of higher imprisonment rates do not bear out the presumed effects. In both the United States and Canada, the rates of crime do not go down with increased imprisonment.[24] Instead, the rates of crime go up when the proportion of offenders per 100,000 who are sentenced to prison is raised. Therefore, we may need to reevaluate our thinking about the continued use of imprisonment to deter others from committing crime, when studies show that it has just the opposite effect.[25]

SUMMARY

The past several decades represent a revolution in sentencing in the United States. Its many causes are discussed in this chapter. Among the changes imposed is the abolition of the parole board's authority to release offenders at its discretion and the adoption of sentencing guidelines for judges. Changes also include shifting to mandatory prison sentences for specified crimes, adoption of presumptive sentences, and other efforts to limit discretion and disparity in sentencing and length of time served in prison. So widespread have the changes been that only three states (North Dakota, Virginia, and Wyoming) have left their sentencing laws unchanged.

In addition to the sentencing law changes, sharp increases have occurred in the number of persons incarcerated. Never in the history of the United States have we had so many and such a large percentage per 100,000 of the population incarcerated in prisons. Reasons for the sudden increase are not exactly understood; it is obvious, however, that corrections is once again in crisis and on a collision course with the Eighth Amendment's prohibition against cruel and unusual punishment. The next chapter examines some legal issues, including appeals of sentences before and during incarceration.

REVIEW QUESTIONS

1. What is the principal reason for the judge's diminished sentencing power?
2. What aids are available to help the judge decide what sentence to impose?
3. What factors have led to the rapid changes in the sentencing structures in the United States?
4. Identify the basic policy goals of sentencing, and define each.
5. What roles can the presentence investigation report play in corrections?
6. Explain sentencing disparity.
7. In what ways can a prosecutor influence sentence length?
8. Why are prison populations increasing?
9. Cite the advantages and disadvantages of the indeterminate sentence.

ENDNOTES

1. Alaska abolished plea bargaining in 1975. In 1986, approximately 56 percent of all felony arrests were not prosecuted, and 7 percent of the felony arrests were reduced to misdemeanors. Alan Barnes, *Disparities Between Felony Charges at Time of Arrest and Those at Time of Prosecution* (Anchorage: Alaska Statistical Analysis Unit, 1988). California abolished plea bargaining at the superior (trial) court level in 1988, but numerous strategies were devised to avoid this restriction.
2. Bureau of Justice Statistics, *Federal Criminal Case Processing 2000* (Washington, DC: BJS, 2001), www.ojp.usdoj.gov/bjs/abstract/fccp00.htm.
3. John Wooldredge, "The Impact of Jurisdiction Size on Guilty Pleas in 569 State Courts," *Sociology and Social Research* 74:1(1989): 26–33; and David Baldus, George Woodworth, G. Young, et al., *The Disposition of Nebraska Capital and Non-Capital Homicide Cases: 1973–1999* (Lincoln: Nebraska Commission on Law Enforcement and Criminal Justice, 2001).
4. Matthew Durose and Patrick Langan, *Felony Sentencing in State Courts, 2002* (Washington, DC: U.S. Department of Justice, 2003), www.ojp.usdoj.gov/bjs/pub/pdf/fssc02/pdf. See also Gerard Rainville and Brian Reeves, *Felony Defendants in Large Urban Courts, 2000* (Washington, DC: Bureau of Justice Statistics, 2002), p. 45.
5. David Kopel, *Prison Blues: How America's Foolish Sentencing Policies Endanger Public Safety* (Washington, DC: Cato Institute, 1994); Michael Tonry, "Parochialism in United States Sentencing Policy," *Crime and Delinquency* 45:1 (1999): 48–65.

6. Nelson James, *Disparities in Processing Felony Arrests in New York State* (Albany: New York State Division of Criminal Justice, 1995). See also Robert Weidner and Richard Frase, "Legal and Extralegal Determinants of Intercounty Differences in Prison Use," *Criminal Justice Policy Review* 14:3 (2004): 173–195.
7. Steven Donziger, *The Real War on Crime* (New York: HarperCollins, 1996). See also Ted Gest, *Crime and Politics* (Oxford, UK: University of Oxford Press, 2001).
8. Franklin Zimring and Gordon Hawkins, *Incapacitation: Penal Confinement and the Restraint of Crime* (Oxford, UK: Oxford University Press, Studies in Crime and Public Policy, 1995). See also Alex Piquero and Paul Mazerolle, *Life-Course Criminology* (Belmont, CA: Wadsworth, 2001).
9. Michael Tony, *Sentencing Matters* (New York: Oxford University Press, 1996). See also Nancy Marion and Rick Farmer, "A Preliminary Examination of Presidential Anticrime Promises," *Criminal Justice Review* 29:1 (2004): 173–195.
10. Tomislav Kovandzic, John Sloan, and Lynne Vieraitis, "'Striking Out' as Crime Reduction Policy," *Justice Quarterly* 21:1 (2004): 207–239.
11. Pablo Martinez, B. Bryan, E. Benson, et al., *Abolishing Parole for Offenders Sentenced to Prison for Violent Offenses* (Austin: Texas Criminal Justice Policy Council, 1998).
12. Sandra Shane-Dubow, Alice Brown, and Erik Olsen, *Sentencing Reform in the United States: History, Content, and Effect* (Washington, DC: U.S. Department of Justice, 1985). See also Barry Krisberg, A. Breed, M. Wolfgang, et al., "Special Issue: NCCD 90th Anniversary," *Crime and Delinquency* 44:1 (1998): 5–177.
13. Thomson Kurz, T. Gitchoff, R. Holmes, et al. (eds.), "Private Presentence Investigations," *Journal of Contemporary Criminal Justice* 9:4 (1993): 298–374; and National Association of Sentencing Advocates, www.sentencingproject.org/nasa/index.html.
14. Laura Donnelly and Stevens Clarke, *North Carolina's Community Penalties Program: An Evaluation of Its Impact on Felony Sentencing in 1987–88* (Chapel Hill: University of North Carolina, 1990). See also Bruce Benson, *To Serve and Protect: Privatization and Community in Criminal Justice* (New York: New York University Press, 1998).
15. Elliott Atkins, "Post-Verdict Psychological Consultation in the Federal Court," *American Journal of Forensic Psychology* 14:3 (1996): 25–35.
16. Walter C. Reckless, *The Crime Problem*, 4th ed. (New York: Appleton-Century-Crofts, 1967), pp. 673–674. See also Jeanne Stinchcomb and Daryl Hippensteel, "Presentence Investigation Reports," *Criminal Justice Policy Review* 12:2 (2001): 164–177.
17. Loraine Geltsthorpe and Peta Raynor, "Organizational Effectiveness of Probation Officers' Reports to Sentencers," *British Journal of Criminology* 35:2 (1995): 188–200; Christopher Mumola and T. Bonczar, *Substance Abuse and Treatment of Adults on Probation* (Washington, DC: U.S. Department of Justice, 1998); and Missouri Bar Commission on Children and the Law, "Report to the President and Board of Directors of the Missouri Bar," *Juvenile and Family Court Journal* 49:3 (1998): 43–51.
18. Paul Wice, "Leadership," *Justice System Journal* 17:2 (1995): 271–372. See also Michael Cavadino, "Pre-Sentence Reports: The Effects of Legislation and National Standards," *British Journal of Criminology* 37:4 (1997): 529–548.
19. Peter Brimelow, "Judicial Imperialism," *Forbes* (June 1, 1987): 109–112. See in particular Gordon Bazemore and L. Feder, "Rehabilitation in the New Juvenile Court," *American Journal of Criminal Justice* 21:2 (1997): 181–212.
20. Mike McCorville and Chester Mirday, "Guilty Plea Courts: A Social Disciplinary Model of Criminal Justice," *Social Problems* 42:2 (1995): 216–234. But see Jon'a Meyer and Tara Gray, "Drunk Drivers in the Courts: Legal and Extra-Legal Factors Affecting Pleas and Sentences," *Journal of Criminal Justice* 25:2 (1997): 155–163.
21. Lisa Stolzenberg and S. D'Alessio, "The Impact of Prison Crowding on Male and Female Imprisonment Rates in Minnesota," *Justice Quarterly* 14:4 (1997): 793–809. See also Sean Nicholson-Crotty, "The Impact of Sentencing Guidelines on State-Level Sanctions," *Crime and Delinquency* 50:3 (2004): 395–411.
22. President's Commission on Law Enforcement and Administration of Justice, *The Challenge of Crime in a Free Society* (Washington, DC: U.S. Government Printing Office, 1967), p. 142. But see Barry Feld, "Race, Youth Violence and the Changing Jurisprudence of Waiver," *Behavioral Sciences and the Law* 19:1 (2001): 3–22.
23. Walter Durose and Patrick Langan, *Felony Sentences in State Courts, 2002* (Washington, DC: Bureau of Justice Statistics, 2004).
24. Conservatives are likely to argue that the decline in crime volume and rates that began in 1990 are a direct result of harsher punishment. Yet crime, as measured by the National Crime Victimization Survey, began to drop in 1971 and dropped about 27 percent since that time. The cause of a phenomenon has to precede the effect. The crime rates began to drop long before increases in sentence length and harsher laws began.
25. Charles Murray, Malcolm Davies, Andrew Rutherford, et al., *Does Prison Work?* (London: Institute of Economic Affairs, Health and Welfare, 1997).

CHAPTER 5

Appellate Review

Courts have held that prison officials have an affirmative duty to prevent inmates from acquiring and possessing dangerous instruments that could be used to assault other inmates. . . . Officials will continue to be liable when they possess knowledge of real risks to inmates and do not act reasonably to prevent assaults from occurring.

—Michael Vaughn and Rolando del Carmen

KEY WORDS

- railroading
- due process
- appeal
- affirm
- modify
- reverse
- remand
- collateral attack
- initial appearance
- recognizance
- preliminary hearing
- grand jury
- indictment
- information
- arraignment
- trial
- double jeopardy
- court of last resort
- court of appeals
- writ of habeas corpus
- civil rights
- writ of mandamus

OVERVIEW

Our examination of legal issues surrounding corrections for offenders and law violators would not be complete without integrating the path of appeals from the pretrial processes, convictions, penalties imposed, conditions of imprisonment, questions about civil rights violations, and the use of force. The prison walls can no more be a "concrete curtain" between offenders and prisoners under correctional control and those living in the free society. In the twenty-first century, offenders are still granted many of the same rights guaranteed by the U.S. Constitution. Prisoner rights are discussed in detail in Part 7. This chapter examines such items as motions to vacate sentences, habeas corpus, and civil rights. We begin with some of the basic tenets that apply to the justice system in America. The many types of legal cases involved with corrections are presented here in their most basic forms. Serious students of corrections, whether future academicians or practitioners, should become familiar with those key cases.

THE ISSUE OF DUE PROCESS

A basic tenet of the criminal justice process in America is that every defendant is presumed to be innocent until proven guilty. Not only does our system demand proof of guilt, but it also requires that the proof be obtained fairly and legally. The process of appellate review helps ensure that it will be just that. In effect, the appellate review

SIDEBARS

Railroaded

The term *railroaded* has become part of American slang. Its origins lie in the practice by early state prisons of having a train pick up prisoners at various points, jails, and counties along the way, and drop them at the prison. Sometimes local undesirables were put on the prison train to end up in prison under less than due process conditions.

< The United States Supreme Court building.
© Jeff Greenberg/Omni-Photo Communications, Inc.

SIDEBARS

Appeals

An ***appeal*** occurs when the defendant in a criminal case requests that a court with appellate jurisdiction rule on a decision that has been made at a trial court. In making its final disposition of the case, an appellate court may do one of the following:

- ***Affirm*** or uphold the lower court ruling;
- ***Modify*** the lower court ruling by changing it in part, but not totally reversing it;
- ***Reverse*** or set aside the lower court ruling and not require any further court action;
- Reverse and remand the case by overturning the lower court ruling that may range from conducting a new trial to entering a proper judgment; or
- ***Remand*** all or part of the case by sending it back to the lower court without overturning the lower court's ruling but with instructions for further proceedings that may range from conducting a new trial to entering a proper judgment.

SOURCE: Bureau of Justice Statistics, The Growth of Appeals (Washington, DC: U.S. Department of Justice, 1985), p. 3.

SIDEBARS

Fourteenth Amendment

All persons born and naturalized in the United States, and subject to the jurisdiction thereof, are citizens of the United States and of the State wherein they reside. No State shall make or enforce any law which shall abridge the privileges or immunities of citizens of the United States: nor shall any State deprive any person of life, liberty, or property, without due process of law, nor deny to any person within its jurisdiction the equal protection of the laws.

acts as a shield for the defendant caught up in the processes of criminal trial, incarceration, or supervision in the community. The state has considerable resources to prosecute those it considers offenders, and the Constitution protects us from the kind of government **railroading** that could deprive us of life, liberty, or property without the benefit of the due process of law.

Due process has been a constitutional right for all Americans under federal law since the passage of the Fourteenth Amendment in 1868. It was not until the "criminal law revolution" of the 1960s, however, that the due process clause of the Fourteenth Amendment was also made binding on all of the states through a series of Supreme Court decisions. In the field of corrections, like every other segment of criminal justice, those decisions created a climate of great challenge and rapid change. This chapter includes a brief examination of the appeal process and procedure, a glance at several significant cases, and an analysis of trends that appear to be emerging in appeals.[1]

One of the problems with "due process of law" is not that it is *due*—that is, something to which we are entitled—but rather the process of determining how *much* of it is due. Only a few decades ago, very few criminal cases were appealed. Since the U.S. Supreme Court case of *Gideon v. Wainwright* (1963), however, the picture has radically changed. The securing of the right to counsel for all defendants, stemming from that landmark decision, has opened the floodgates in the appellate courts across America. In some jurisdictions the rate of appeals is as high as 90 percent of all convictions.[2] **Collateral attack,**[3] or the filing of an appeal in the federal system while the state case is still undecided (almost unknown before the 1960s), is now routine in most state courts. The result of this massive overload in the appellate system was a monumental increase in the workload for state and federal judges. It has also created extended periods of litigation, often stretched out over several years, that have eroded any lingering belief that a conviction for a criminal offense must be considered final. The review procedure has as many as eleven steps in some state systems, and it is not unusual for a defendant to explore at least four or five. The eleven steps are as follows:

1. New trial motion filed in court where conviction was imposed
2. Appeal to state intermediate appellate court (in states where there is no intermediate appellate court this step would not be available)
3. Appeal to state supreme court
4. Petition to U.S. Supreme Court to review state court decision in appeal
5. Postconviction proceeding in state trial court
6. Appeal of postconviction proceeding to state intermediate appellate court
7. Appeal to state supreme court
8. Petition to U.S. Supreme Court to review state court decision on appeal from postconviction proceeding
9. Habeas corpus petition in federal district court
10. Appeal to U.S. Court of Appeals
11. Petition to U.S. Supreme Court to review court of appeals decision on habeas corpus petition.[4]

It is easy to see why the review process can take so long, especially when some steps may be used several times in a single appeal, with reviews of the same case taking place simultaneously in different court systems. Thus, due process may be a long

CORRECTIONAL BRIEF

The "Landmark Cases" of the 1960s and 1970s

Mapp v. Ohio The case of *Mapp v. Ohio* (exclusionary rule), 367 U.S. 643 (1960), opened a Pandora's box of Fourteenth Amendment rulings. A crack in the armor of state proceedings, it paved the way for the flood of cases heard by the Court during the next decade, in reference not only to illegally obtained evidence but also to all areas of individual rights.

Robinson v. California In the California case of *Robinson v. California* (cruel and unusual punishment), 370 U.S. 660 (1961), the Eighth Amendment's clause forbidding cruel and unusual punishment was made binding on state proceedings.

Gideon v. Wainwright In the crucial decision of *Gideon v. Wainwright* (right to counsel), 372 U.S. 335 (1963), the Court held that defendants in noncapital cases are entitled to assistance of counsel at trial as a matter of right. This right was extended to state proceedings, again under the provisions of the Fourteenth Amendment.

Miranda v. Arizona The application of the Fifth Amendment protections against self-incrimination was influenced by *Gideon v. Wainwright*, 372 U.S. 335 (1963). For the first time, in the 1966 decision of *Miranda v. Arizona*, 384 U.S. 436, a set of specific and detailed police warnings to the arrested person (and now the prison inmate) was required, through the due process clause, at specific and distinct points in the criminal process.

Johnson v. Avery A significant 1969 decision provided prisoners in state penal institutions with legal assistance in preparing habeas corpus proceedings. In *Johnson v. Avery*, 393 U.S. 483, the Court held that states not providing adequate legal assistance would have to put up with "jailhouse lawyers," prisoners determined to research and conduct their own and others' appeals.

Furman v. Georgia In *Furman v. Georgia*, 408 U.S. 238 (1972), the issue of cruel and unusual punishment as applied to the death penalty was raised in a petition by several states for clarification of that long-standing dilemma. In June 1972, the U.S. Supreme Court held that any statute that which permits a jury to demand the death penalty is unconstitutional.

and complicated procedure and, when appeal is part of the scheme, it can become a seemingly endless cycle.

THE PATH OF A CRIMINAL CASE

There are so many points in the criminal proceeding to which appellate actions can be directed that it is worthwhile to reexamine the steps in which the courts become participants. The first point at which most defendants come into contact with the criminal justice system is at the time of their arrest, usually by a police officer. Even at this early step, the potential for a later appeal is great. It is all too true that the "guilty often go free because the constable blundered." A suspect's Fourth and Fifth Amendment rights have been clearly established by decisions such as *Mapp v. Ohio* and *Miranda v. Arizona* (covered in a Correctional Brief later in this chapter). The failure of law enforcement officers to comply with the procedural safeguards established as a result of those landmark cases can mean an overturned conviction in a later review court.[5]

The next stage of the criminal justice process is usually the **initial appearance** before a judge. Often the court in which this appearance takes place may not actually have the jurisdiction to try the defendant, but the defendant has the right to state his or her case before a court as soon as possible after arrest.[6] This initial appearance is usually accompanied by the presentation of a complaint by the prosecution. The judge at the initial appearance has several tasks to perform, and the failure to perform them correctly can result—as with the arresting officer—in a successful appeal at a later time. Defendants must be made aware of the charges against them and warned against making any self-incriminating statements. If the accused is to be assigned an attorney at state expense, this procedure is initiated. When the initial court does not have the

SIDEBARS
Recognizance

Release on recognizance means the court accepts that the defendant will be available for trial and it does not need to exact a financial penalty (surety bond) for nonappearance. In a sense, it means "release on the defendant's word of honor."

jurisdiction to try a particular case, a decision must be made on the continued detention of the accused (in the case of dangerous persons), or some arrangement must be made for the accused's release prior to trial before the court of primary jurisdiction. The defendant can be released on his or her own **recognizance**[7] or may be required to post bail. In the first instance, the judge believes the defendants will appear in court as required because they have nothing to gain (and a reputation to lose) by running away. In the second, the defendant posts a certain sum of money that is forfeited if he or she fails to appear. In both cases, the object is to encourage the defendant's appearance at further proceedings on the case.

If the case does not fall under the initial court's jurisdiction, the defendant has the right to request a preliminary hearing, to examine the merits of binding the case over to a higher court. The **preliminary hearing** gives both defense and prosecution the opportunity to gather evidence and witnesses and present them informally. It constitutes a sort of preview of the case for both sides and for the judge. To the defendant, the preliminary hearing offers an informal evaluation of his or her chances in the later trial. It is at this point that many defendants decide to plead guilty to their charge or to negotiate a plea to a lesser charge.[8]

The next step is the filing of a formal criminal charge in the court that will try the case. If a federal crime punishable by death, imprisonment, hard labor, or loss of civil or political privileges has been committed, the filing of charges may be preceded by another review of the facts by a **grand jury.** If the grand jury agrees there is probable cause that the offense has occurred and the defendant might have done it, a document called an **indictment** is issued that constitutes the formal charging of the accused. A defendant has a right to participate in the preliminary hearing but is not usually allowed to appear before the grand jury unless special permission is obtained.

The federal government permits the waiver of a grand jury in noncapital cases; and the grand jury has been used less and less in recent years. (Watergate and Whitewater Gate were instances in which a grand jury was considered necessary.) If a grand jury inquiry is not required, the prosecutor simply files a document called an **information**, which contains the formal criminal charge. Many challenges are made in regard to this portion of the process. Some of the challenges must be made at this time, or they cannot be used as grounds for later appeal. In fact, the resolution of issues raised at this point—in regard to search and seizure, police interrogation techniques, and other questions as to the admissibility of evidence—may consume more court time than the actual trial.

The next critical point is the **arraignment,** the offender's first formal appearance before the trial court. At this point, the defendant is asked how he or she will plead. If the defendant chooses to stand mute, a plea of "not guilty" is entered automatically. It is when the defendant pleads guilty at this point (in about 90 percent of the cases) that the judge must be careful about procedural errors that might result in an appeal. The defendant who pleads guilty must understand the nature of the charges and the consequences of a guilty plea. The judge should have some basis for accepting the plea, usually evidence from the prosecutor that indicates or establishes guilt. Although there usually is little error on this last point, probably because those who plead guilty seldom appeal, it is another legal basis for appeals.

The **trial**, so memorably dramatized on television and in the movies, appears to be the main target for the appellate procedure. It is the trial that best illustrates the impact of our adversary system[9] on the process of criminal justice. Grounds for appeal abound in the trial, from the selection of the jury to the finding of guilt or innocence. The burden of proof of guilt, however, is on the prosecution throughout the trial. Many defense motions[10] are made only to establish grounds for later efforts at appeal. After a determination of guilt or innocence, the trial is completed.

The effect of most appeals is to require that a new trial be held—not to ensure an overturned conviction for the accused.

The last step in the court process is the *sentencing* by the court. The judge usually prescribes the sentence, but in some jurisdictions a jury can impose a sentence. In the case of a guilty plea, the sentencing usually follows the completion of a pretrial or presentencing investigation of the defendant, who has become the convicted offender. The sentencing process has not generated many appeal actions, probably because sentences are usually determined by specific statutes rather than by the judge's discretion. Excessive or cruel sentencing practices, as well as sentences outside sentencing guidelines, do come under appeal, however, and the indeterminate sentence has been attacked many times.

THE MECHANICS OF AN APPEAL

Now that we have seen the points at which appealable errors are most likely to occur, the effects of some of the major cases, and the potential of future appeals, it is important to know how one makes an appeal following a criminal conviction. The process is highly fragmented and cumbersome, but a basic scheme applies to most jurisdictions. Although there are many alternatives to this basic model, it covers most of the avenues for appeals.

The entire process stems, of course, from a conviction of guilt by some court system at the municipal, county, state, or federal level. In each case, the procedure for appeal is determined by the court of record for that case. Those appeals, known as postconviction remedies, are usually made by the defendant. The state is less likely to appeal a decision, regardless of the outcome. If the accused is convicted, that is the result the state was after, and if the accused is declared innocent, the state cannot appeal because the Constitution guarantees that someone who is found innocent cannot be placed in **double jeopardy**[11] (which is being subjected to a second trial, by the same jurisdiction, on the same facts). The effect of an appropriately introduced appeal is to grant a stay (delay) in the execution of the original sentence until the appeal has been decided. As soon as possible, if not immediately after the sentence is pronounced, the defendant's counsel must either move for a new trial or make an appeal on some reasonable grounds, because appellate courts usually dislike and make short work of "frivolous" appeals. But as long ago as 1933, the significance of the appeal process was firmly established:

> *Appellate courts do not reverse decisions simply because they disagree with them. Reversal must proceed from error of law and such error must be substantial. But if this account is to be veracious I must call attention to a fact familiar to every experienced lawyer, yet not apparent in the classical literature of the law, and probably not consciously admitted even to themselves by most appellate judges. Practically every decision of a lower court can be reversed. By that I mean practically every record contains some erroneous rulings [and] they can nearly always find some error if they want grounds for reversal.*[12]

Each state has an appellate tribunal that serves as the **court of last resort.** The titles vary, but no matter what the title, a pathway for appeal is open to all in the American judicial system.

The Courts of Appeal

The court level immediately above the trial court is usually called the **court of appeals.** In some states, and in the federal system, there is more than one level of appeal. In those cases, the highest level of appellate court is generally called the

Supreme Court. The Supreme Court of the United States is the court of last resort; cases decided there are considered final. The U.S. Supreme Court will usually hear cases from the state systems only after the defendant has exhausted all state remedies and the case has been finally adjudicated.[13]

In most state systems, the court of appeals reviews the trial court's decisions for judicial error. The facts in the case are not in question, and the trial court's decisions on that aspect of the case are generally binding on the appellate court. Because of that aspect of appellate review, evidence on the facts of the case is not presented to the court of appeals. Rather, the review is based only on the trial record. An appellate court cannot reverse the factual findings of the trial court unless they are totally erroneous. In states that have a second level of review, the trial record and the intermediary court's decision are examined. Usually, the refusal to hear an appeal over a lower appellate court's ruling is the same as upholding the decision, and the case stops there, unless an appeal is filed separately in a federal court of appeals on some constitutional issue.

The federal court system currently includes ninety-four trial courts (federal district courts) and thirteen intermediary review courts (courts of appeal) between the federal trial courts and the U.S. Supreme Court. The federal courts of appeal are spread across the country in "circuits" to facilitate servicing the ninety-four trial courts. Federal courts are restricted in their powers to cases arising under the Constitution, federal laws, or treaties; all cases affecting ambassadors, public ministers, and consuls; admiralty and maritime cases; and controversies where the United States is a party, controversies between states, between a state and a citizen of another state, between citizens of the same state claiming lands under grants from different states, and in cases between a state or citizens of a state and foreign states, citizens, or subjects.[14]

The federal courts of appeal are similar to the state courts of appeal in that they review for error the cases tried by the federal district courts. The Supreme Court is the ultimate interpreter of the Constitution and federal statutes. It reviews the decisions of the courts of appeal, and some direct appeals from district courts. The Supreme Court also reviews the decisions of state courts involving matters of federal

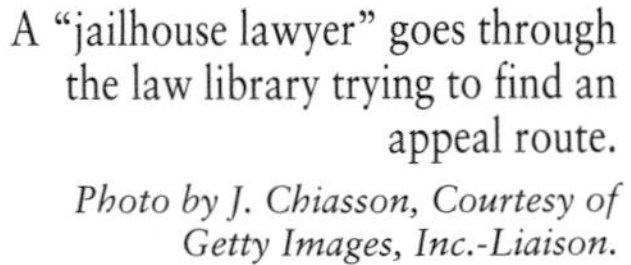

A "jailhouse lawyer" goes through the law library trying to find an appeal route.

Photo by J. Chiasson, Courtesy of Getty Images, Inc.-Liaison.

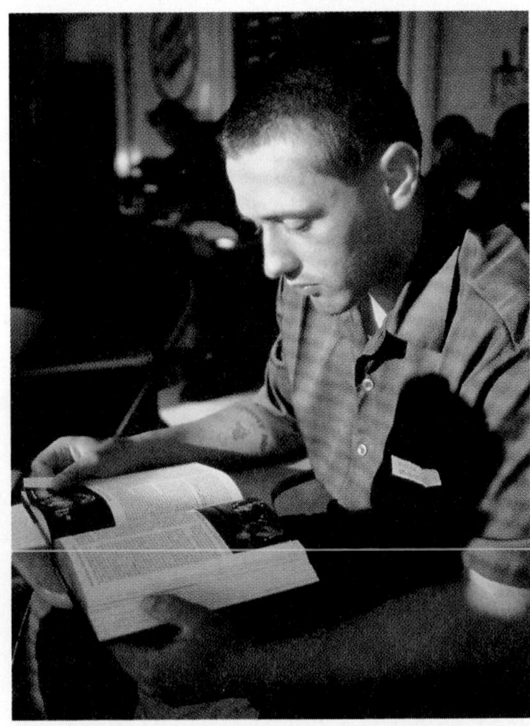

constitutional rights where the case has been finally adjudicated in the state court system. Besides its appellate function, the Court has original jurisdiction in suits where a state is a party and in controversies involving ambassadors, ministers, and consuls.[15]

APPEALS FROM BEHIND THE WALLS

In the early twentieth century, most appeals were based on the specific issues in the trial. In the 1960s, appeals began to move toward issues related to individual rights as stated and interpreted under the U.S. Constitution. Using the Fourteenth Amendment as a lever, the Supreme Court affirmed those rights to individuals in the separate states on a piecemeal basis. Under the "hands-off" doctrine established by chief justice Felix Frankfurter, the court had restricted its early decisions to the actions of judges. Later, abandoning the Frankfurter policy, the court began to impose procedural guidelines on law enforcement, corrections, and every other element of the criminal justice system. Constitutional rights of prisoners (discussed in Part 7) were more sharply defined by the appellate courts' decisions. Many of these appeals came from desperate people behind prison walls,[16] and those appeals continued to increase (civil rights appeals increased *389 percent* between 1977 and 1994, for example).[17]

SIDEBARS

Jailhouse Lawyers

Inmates claiming to have some legal knowledge, who counsel and assist other inmates in the preparation of legal documents such as habeas corpus, pleadings, and appeals to higher courts.

REFORM BY JUDICIAL DECREE

Corrections, as a social system, is above all a political unit established by an authorizing mandate, supported by tax revenues, and subject to political influences. It reflects both the system of justice and the overall sociocultural environment. The latter is the source of externally induced reform. In externally induced reform, individuals or groups outside the correctional system[18] effect changes.

At the state and local levels, correctional reform is usually accomplished through legislative or executive action. Examples of reform by legislation range from the complete revision of a state's criminal code to passage of simple amendments to bills, allowing such benefits as educational and home furloughs. The executive branch of government can also exert a direct effect on correctional reform through executive orders. Those orders can accomplish small but important changes, such as the abolition of mail censorship, the appointment of a task force of involved citizens to seek correctional reform, and the withholding of support for clearly unsound correctional programs.[19]

Between 1960 and 1972, American criminal law passed from a state of *evolution* to a state of *revolution*.[20] The step-by-step extension to the states of the various federal constitutional guarantees of individual rights was clearly the goal of the courts' quiet but effective revolution. The decisions of the much maligned—or revered—Warren Court are more readily understood when viewed from that perspective. During the 1960s, nearly all of the guarantees of the Fourth, Fifth, Sixth, and Eighth Amendments to the Constitution were made binding on the states, although the Rehnquist Court attempted to undo some of these advances. As previously mentioned, the Fourteenth Amendment (Due Process Clause) provided the primary leverage in the landmark decisions that impacted corrections. The extension of constitutional guarantees to all persons accused in state proceedings has produced dramatic and significant changes in criminal law and criminal procedures and important effects on corrections through appeals related to major landmark decisions.

It should be pointed out that in addition to these cases, from the 1960s and 1970s the Supreme Court also entertained cases concerning the civil rights of inmates, through interpretation of the Civil Rights Act of 1871. In the first decade of the twenty-first century, many prisons are under court orders or are facing constitutional challenges under Chapter 42, U.S. Code Section 1983.[21] Many states are

SIDEBARS

The Court-Appointed Master

A *court master* is a person knowledgeable in correctional administration and operations who has been appointed by the court to assist in the specific issues that arise in the case of a specific institution or system of institutions. The precise duties and powers depend on the terms of the court decree or settlement and include taking testimony, discovery of evidence, and monitoring implementation of court-ordered changes. The master is required to submit a "Report of Proceedings" for the court. Such reports may include suggestions for additional changes for the court to consider; the court may subsequently order correctional authorities to make such changes. Correctional administrators are generally leery of court masters, whose salaries and expenses they are frequently required to pay.

being sued, and federal masters have been appointed to oversee the conditions in state prisons.

Two major results of inmate litigation were the development of new mind-sets by correctional administrators and the development of nationwide standards to demonstrate to the courts that the level of practice in the institutions being sued was the best the industry could provide.[22] Although litigation is always a trying situation, it may well be the best way to effect change in correctional settings. The threat of federal court suits has brought about significant changes in practices, policies, and procedures.

COURT ORDERS AND COURT DECREES

Inmates in state and federal prisons increasingly petition the Court for relief under a variety of statutes. All functions and services of correctional institutions have been examined. These include use of force, indifference to medical needs, cruel and unusual punishment, food services, overcrowding, religious issues, lack of psychological services, right to treatment, and conditions of confinement, to mention only a few. It seems that there are few things done in prisons that inmates will not take action against. In mid-2003, the entire prison systems of ten states, and another thirty-three individual prisons, were under court order or had court-ordered consent decrees to make changes. See Figure 5.1. A total of ninety-three institutions were involved and court-appointed masters were assigned to oversee the court orders.

In the juvenile justice systems, in the same time frame, juvenile correctional systems continued to show improvement. Only four entire juvenile systems were under court order in 2003, down from fifteen states in 1995. In most cases the court orders were intended generally to improve conditions of confinement, reduce overcrowding, and improve services (especially medical services). Thirty-one institutions in the juvenile justice systems of only six states were under court order in 2003.

In summary, the student can now understand how external pressure from the courts, especially the U.S. Supreme Court, has modified and clarified the criminal law and offered basic constitutional guarantees to all persons, including those in-

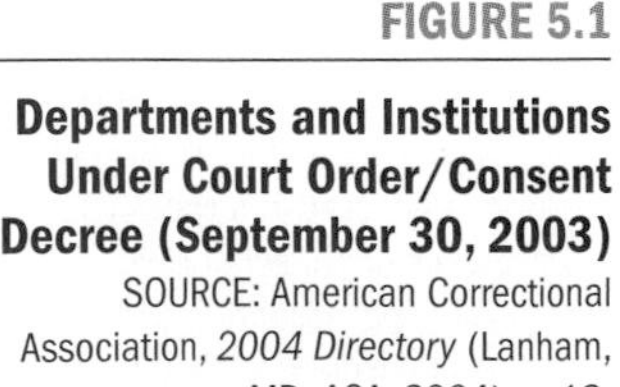

FIGURE 5.1

Departments and Institutions Under Court Order/Consent Decree (September 30, 2003)

SOURCE: American Correctional Association, *2004 Directory* (Lanham, MD: ACA, 2004), p. 18.

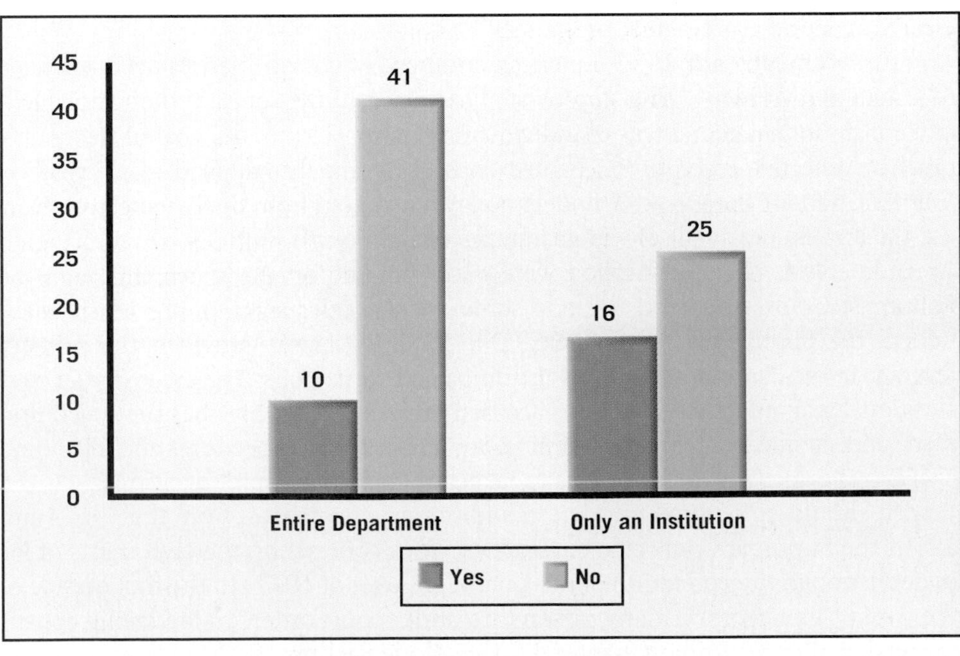

carcerated in state and federal prisons. Such pressures can be expected to continue, marching under the banner of the Fourteenth Amendment until all other federal constitutional protection provisions are also imposed on the states.[23]

APPEALS FLOOD THE COURTS

A flood of appeals made with the help of court-appointed lawyers and jailhouse lawyers filled the dockets of the appeals courts beginning in the 1960s and accelerating through the mid-1990s. As rights were established in the obvious areas outside prison walls (arrest, search and seizure, privacy and intrusion, cruel and unusual punishment), they were eventually tested with regard to events inside the walls as well. The autonomous and discretionary control over inmates was finally lifted, as the right to counsel moved into the prison as well as the courtroom. A milestone case was decided in the 1967–1968 Supreme Court term, when *Mempa v. Rhay* extended the right to counsel to state probation revocation hearings, previously considered an essentially administrative action. The Court held that the application of a deferred sentence was a "critical point" in the proceeding.

SIDEBARS

***Mempa v. Rhay*, 389 U.S. 128, 2d Cir. 3023 (1968)**

A petitioner filed a habeas corpus claiming a denial of the right to counsel at the probation revocation and sentencing proceedings. The Supreme Court of the state of Washington denied the petition. The U.S. Supreme Court reversed the previous decision, asserting the necessity that counsel be present at such a hearing.

Types of Prisoner Petitions

The three types of suits filed by prison inmates in federal district court are habeas corpus, civil rights, and mandamus. In brief, habeas corpus suits by prisoners challenge the constitutionality of their imprisonment, civil rights suits seek redress of civil rights violations by government officials, and mandamus suits seek to compel a government official to perform a duty owed.[24]

The basic principle of the **writ of habeas corpus** is that the government is accountable to the courts for a person's imprisonment. If the government cannot show that the person's imprisonment conforms to the fundamental principles of law, that person is entitled to immediate release. The most frequently cited reason for habeas corpus petitions by state inmates is "ineffective assistance of counsel" (25 percent). Other commonly cited reasons include errors by the trial court (15 percent), due process violations (14 percent), and self-incrimination (12 percent). For federal inmates, habeas corpus petitions generally challenge the constitutionality of imprisonment or constitute motions to vacate a sentence.

The foundation for **civil rights** petitions originates in the Fourteenth Amendment of the U.S. Constitution. It prohibits the states from "depriving any person of life, liberty, or property without due process of law." Petitions by state prisoners most frequently challenge physical security (21 percent), inadequate medical treatment (17 percent), and due process (13 percent).

The **writ of mandamus** ("we command") is an extraordinary remedy based on common law that is used when the plaintiff has no other adequate means to attain the desired relief. The mandamus petition is filed when the inmate seeks to compel a government official to perform a duty owed to the inmate (ministerial or nondiscretionary duties). The petitions are infrequent, varied in nature, and more typically specific to individual circumstances.

Legislative Initiatives to Reduce Prisoner Litigation

In 1980, the Civil Rights of Institutionalized Persons Act (CRIPA) was enacted by Congress to reduce the number of civil rights petitions filed in the federal courts. This act requires inmates to exhaust state-level administrative remedies before filing their petitions in the federal courts. Congress obviously intended to reserve the federal courts for more serious civil rights violations or other significant constitutional issues.

Despite the intent of Congress, the number of civil rights cases filed in federal court have increased more than threefold from the 1980s and 1990s. This increase was primarily caused by the huge increase in the number of state prisoners. The rate of petitions per 1,000 inmates remained stable.

During 1996, two additional legislative enactments sought to further limit prisoners' ability to file petitions in the federal courts. One was the Prison Litigation Reform Act (PLRA), seeking to reduce the number of petitions filed by inmates claiming civil rights violations. The three major changes were requiring inmates to exhaust all administrative remedies before filing in federal court, requiring inmates to pay applicable filing fees and court costs even if filing *in forma pauperis* ("I am a pauper"), and forbidding inmates from filing *in forma pauperis* if they have had prior petitions dismissed as being frivolous or malicious.

The second act (Antiterrorism and Effective Death Penalty Act, or AEDPA) requires inmates to exhaust direct appeals at the state level before filing a petition in federal court, establishes a one-year statute of limitations from the time their conviction becomes final (after all direct appeals of the conviction and/or the sentence have been exhausted), and requires that a panel of the appeals court approve successive petitions being filed in district court.

After the PLRA was enacted, both the rate and number of civil rights petitions decreased dramatically, as was the intent of Congress. After AEDPA, both the filing rate and the number of habeas corpus petitions by state inmates increased, primarily as a consequence of the increasing size of the prison population.

By either measure (the rate per 1,000 prisoners or volume of petitions filed), prisoner petitions filed in U.S. district courts (1980 to 2003) decreased. This pattern is graphically displayed in Figure 5.2.

Some state appellate courts have responded to caseload growth in a variety of other ways. Those coping strategies include adding judgeships, creating new or expanding existing appellate courts, deciding cases without published opinions or writing memo opinions, temporarily assigning judges from the retired

FIGURE 5.2

Petitions Filed in U.S. District Courts by State and Federal Prisoners

SOURCE: Sourcebook of Criminal Justice Statistics Online, "Petitions Filed in U.S. District Courts by Federal and State Prisoners," www.albany.edu/sourcebook/pdf/t565.pdf (accessed February 13, 2005).

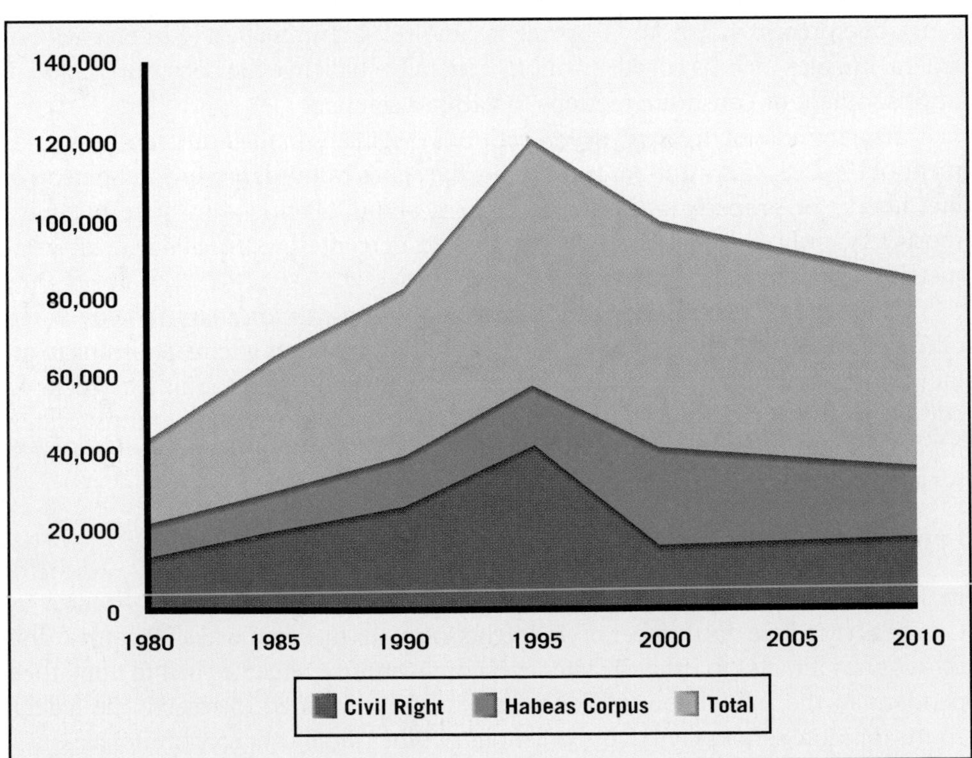

ranks or from lower courts, and reducing panel sizes. Expediting hearings, limiting oral arguments, and setting time limits on arguments and briefs are other mechanisms. The reduction of protections of cherished constitutional rights in the name of expediency to meet a crisis or facilitate vague political goals in the name of a war on drugs (regardless of the nobility of the espoused goals) poses some serious and unacceptable threats to every citizen, convicted criminal or not.

SUMMARY

Appeals will continue until inmates behind prison walls are permitted the same constitutionally guaranteed protections accorded to their counterparts in the free world, except those obviously denied by incarceration such as the right to privacy, to choose one's associates, and freedom of movement. When appeals do fail, however, convicted and sentenced offenders must pay a debt to society in the correctional process, the subject we take up in Part 3.

REVIEW QUESTIONS

1. Explain the difference between a court of appeals and a Supreme Court.
2. Why is there such a logjam in the appellate system? What are some suggestions for easing the pressure?
3. What rights does an inmate have? What rights does an inmate not have?
4. Explain why the rights of inmates began to be extensively defined in the 1960s.
5. What are appeals, and what options are available to appeal courts when a decision is made?
6. What might be done to cut down on frivolous appeals?
7. How can appeal courts manage caseloads more efficiently?
8. What steps has Congress taken to reduce the number of appeals in federal courts?
9. What innovations have states taken to reduce the backlog of appeals in state courts?
10. What are the areas of civil rights violations state prisoners are raising in federal courts?

ENDNOTES

1. Editors, "Supreme Court Review," *Journal of Criminal Law and Criminology* 83:4 (1993): 693–717. But see John Capone, "Facilitating Fairness: The Judge's Role in the Sixth Amendment Right to Effective Counsel," *Journal of Criminal Law and Criminology* 93:4 (2004): 881–912.
2. Because plea bargaining reduces the offender's ability to appeal, it is not surprising that most appeals arise from trials. Trials typically involve crimes against the person and sentences of five years or less. Defendants are not particularly successful; offenders win about 20 percent of the time and have their convictions overturned in only about 10 percent of their appeals. See Jimmy Williams, "Role of Appellants, Sentencing Guidelines, Decision Making in Criminal Appeals," *Journal of Criminal Justice* 23:1 (1995): 83–91. Some 16 percent of offenders convicted in federal courts appealed in 1999. Bureau of Justice Statistics, *Federal Criminal Case Processing, 2002* (Washington, DC: BJS, 2005).
3. For an excellent review of legal trends and issues in corrections, see Rolando del Carmen, S. Ritter, and B. Witt, *Briefs of Leading Cases in Corrections* (Cincinnati, OH: Anderson Publishing, 2002).
4. National Advisory Commission on Criminal Justice Standards and Goals, *Corrections* (Washington, DC: U.S. Government Printing Office, 1973), p. 113.
5. Rudolph Alexander, "The *Mapp*, *Escobedo*, and *Miranda* Decisions: Do They Serve a Liberal or Conservative Agenda?" *Criminal Justice Policy Review* 4:1 (1990): 39–52. See also Vernon McKay, L. Raifman, S. Greenberg, et al., "Forensic Pretrial Police Interviews of Deaf Subjects: Avoiding Legal Pitfalls," *International Journal of Law and Psychiatry* 24:1 (2001): 43–59.
6. This is what is generally called the *right to habeas corpus*. Ronald Allen, J. Brody, M. Costigan, et al.,

"Supreme Court Review," *Journal of Criminal Law and Criminology* 87:3 (1997): 633–1065.

7. Bureau of Justice Statistics, *Felony Defendants in Large Urban Courts, 1998* (Washington, DC: BJS, 2001).
8. This is a classic example of plea bargaining. See also Gail Kellough and Scot Worley, "Remand for Plea: Bail Decisions and Plea Bargaining as Commensurate Decisions," *The British Journal of Criminology* 42:1 (2002): 186–210.
9. The adversary system refers to the battle between the prosecution and defense attorneys during a trial when each cross-examines and attacks the witnesses and facts presented by the other. Shari Seibman-Diamond, J. Casper, C. Herbert, et al., "Juror Reactions to Attorneys at Trial," *Journal of Criminal Law and Criminology* 87:1 (1997): 17–47.
10. Such motions usually concern the admissibility of evidence and are aimed at suppressing the presentation of evidence that might hurt the defense attorney's case. See Beth Dwerman, "The Supreme Court's Prohibition of Gender-based Preemptory Challenges," *Journal of Criminal Law and Criminology* 85:4 (1995): 1028–1061.
11. David Chu, "The Substitution of Words for Analysis and Other Judicial Pitfalls: Why David Sattazahn Should Have Received Double Jeopardy Protection," *Journal of Criminal Law and Criminology* 94:3 (2004): 587–623.
12. Joseph N. Ulman, *The Judge Takes the Stand* (New York: Knopf, 1933), pp. 265–266.
13. Appeals in federal courts have been reduced in number by congressional initiatives to reduce prisoner litigation.
14. U.S. Constitution, Article III, Section 2. See Singer Hausser, *The State of Corrections: Tennessee's Prisons Before and After Court Intervention* (Nashville, TN: The Comptroller of the Treasury, 1998).
15. John Palmer, *Constitutional Rights of Prisoners* (Cincinnati, OH: Anderson, 1999), p. 12.
16. Prison jailhouse lawyers can resist controls and conditions placed on them by correctional institutions by assisting in filing lawsuits, and have been described as "primitive rebels." See Hawkeye Gross, *Tales from the Joint* (Boulder, CO: Palladin Press, 1995); and Dragan Milovanovic, "Jailhouse Lawyers and Jailhouse Lawyering," *International Journal of the Sociology of the Law* 16:4 (1998): 455–475.
17. Gross, *Tales from the Joint*. See also Michael Vaughn and Linda Smith, "Questioning Authorized Truth," *Justice Quarterly* 16:4 (1999): 907–918.
18. John Conrad, "The Rights of Wrongdoers," *Criminal Justice Research Bulletin* 3:1 (1987): 18–24. See also Christopher Smith, "The Prison Reform Litigation Era," *The Prison Journal* 83:3 (2003): 337–358.
19. Such as prison farming.
20. Editors of *Criminal Law Reporter, The Criminal Law Revolution and Its Aftermath, 1960–71* (Washington, DC: BNA Books, 1972).
21. Richard Ball, "Prison Conditions at the Extreme," *Journal of Contemporary Criminal Justice* 13:1 (1997): 55–72.
22. Malcolm Feeley and E. Rubin, *Judicial Policy Making and the Modern State* (New York: Cambridge University Press, 1998); John Fliter, *Prisoners' Rights: The Supreme Court and Evolving Standards of Decency* (Westport, CT: Greenwood Press, 2001).
23. National Advisory Commission on Criminal Justice Standards and Goals, *Courts* (Washington, DC: U.S. Government Printing Office, 1972), p. 20.
24. This section was drawn primarily from the Bureau of Justice Statistics, *Prisoner Petitions Filed in U.S. District Courts, 2000, with Trends 1980–2000* (Washington, DC: BJS, 2002). See also Bureau of Justice Statistics, *Federal Criminal Cases Processing 2002, with Trends 1982–2002* (Washington, DC: BJS, 2005).

SUGGESTED READINGS: PART 2

Bureau of Justice Statistics. *Felony Sentences in State Courts, 2002*. Washington, DC: BJS, 2005.

Bureau of Justice Statistics. *Prison and Jail Inmates at Midyear 2003*. Washington, DC: BJS, 2004.

Clear, Todd, Dina Rose, and J. Ryder. "Incarceration and the Community: The Problem of Removing and Returning Offenders." *Crime and Delinquency* 47:3 (2001): 335–351.

Currie, Elliott. *Crime and Punishment in America; Why the Solutions to America's Most Stubborn Social Crises Have Not Worked–And What Will*. New York: Metropolitan Books, 1998.

Donziger, Steven. *The Real War on Crime*. New York: HarperCollins, 1996.

Gest, Ted. *Crime and Politics*. Oxford, UK: Oxford University Press, 2001.

Munos, Ed, and B. McMorris, "Misdemeanor Sentencing Decisions: The Cost of Being Native American," *Justice Professional* 15:3 (2002): 239–259.

Stith, Kate, and J. Cabranes. *Fear of Judging: Sentencing Guidelines in Federal Courts*. Chicago: University of Chicago Press, 1998.

PART

3

Alternatives to Imprisonment

THE FOLLOWING CHAPTERS ARE COVERED IN PART 3:

OVERVIEW

Part 3 is concerned with those processes, facilities, and programs that deal with clients on the "front end" of the corrections system, before offenders are committed to prison for their law-violating behavior. We examine jails and detention facilities and processes, as well as probation and other court sanctions for controlling offenders that fall short of imprisonment: intermediate sanctions. Corrections handles more offenders on the front end than can be found at any other portion of the system, and Part 3 identifies the strengths, challenges, and outcomes of alternatives to imprisonment.

CHAPTER 6

Jails and Detention Facilities

. . . more than 11 million people a year are booked into local jails and another 11 million are released from the jails, which is almost comparable to the entire population of Ohio and Illinois.

—Ken Kerle

KEY WORDS

- jail
- jail inmates
- presumption of innocence
- new generation jail
- podular/direct supervision
- "holdback" jail inmates
- fee system
- price-tag justice
- weekender
- pretrial alternatives
- pretrial jail incarceration
- criminal history data
- mental health issues

OVERVIEW

Now that the student has explored the overall history, ideologies, and legal processes for dealing with misdemeanants and felons in America, it is time to examine those processes, facilities, and programs designed to deal with them at the "front end" of the corrections system. The vast majority of offenders begin their journey through the correctional system in a **jail** or detention facility. For some, this is the last stop, whereas for others, it is only the beginning.

This chapter provides an overview of the period immediately after apprehension of a defendant to the eventual disposition of the offender: return to society or transfer to prison. Clearly our nation has developed many different processes and

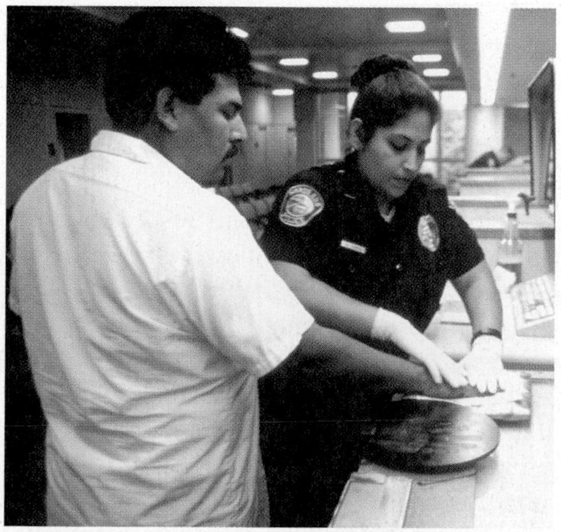

Hispanic policewoman booking Hispanic man at jail takes his palm print.

Photo by Spencer Grant, courtesy of PhotoEdit.

< Jail inmates playing cards and throwing gang signs in their dorm facility.

Photo by Dennis Anderson, courtesy of AP/Wide World Photos.

FIGURE 6.1

Number of Jails by Their Rated Capacity

SOURCE: Bureau of Justice Statistics, "Census of Jails, 1999," www.ojp.usdoj.gov/bjs/pub/pdf/cj99.pdf, 2001, p. 3.

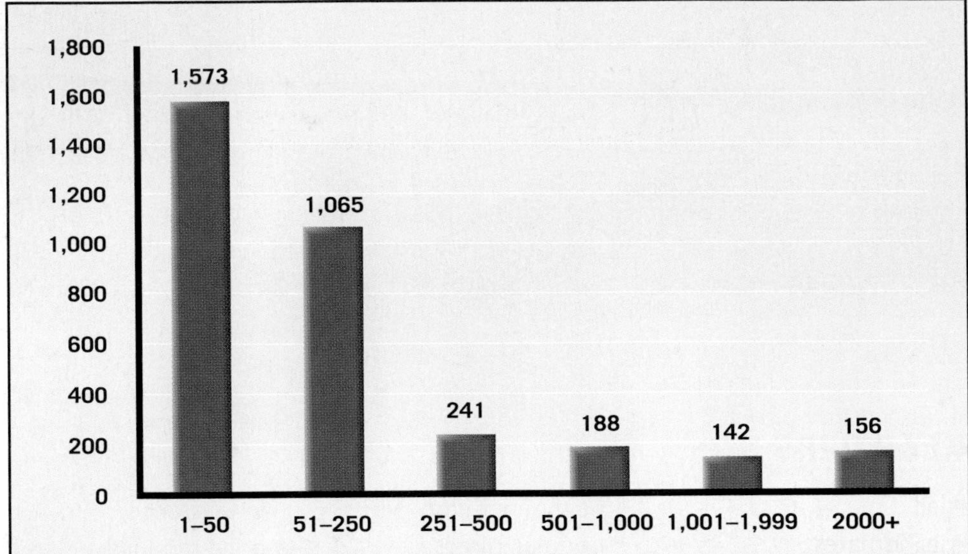

SIDEBARS

Jails

- receive individuals pending arraignment and hold them awaiting trial, conviction, or sentencing.
- readmit probation, parole, and bail-bond violators and absconders.
- temporarily detain juveniles pending transfer to juvenile authorities.
- hold persons pending their movement to appropriate mental health facilities.
- hold individuals for the military, for protective custody, for contempt, and for the courts as witnesses.
- release convicted inmates to the community upon completion of their sentences.
- transfer inmates to federal, state, or other authorities.
- house inmates for federal, state, or other authorities to help relieve crowded facilities.
- relinquish custody of temporary detainees to juvenile and medical authorities.
- sometimes operate community-based programs as alternatives to incarceration.
- hold inmates sentenced to short terms (generally under one year).

SOURCE: Paige Harrison and Jennifer Karberg, Prison and Jail Inmates at Midyear 2003 *(Washington, DC: Bureau of Justice Statistics, 2004), p. 7.*

institutions to meet the primary mission of corrections, that is, to protect society. This chapter takes an in-depth look at local jails and detention centers as the very first step in an often long and winding road, taken in the name of justice. That path will eventually result in most of the offenders returning to society, having paid a debt for crimes committed, large or small. The "scales of justice" attempt to balance the crime and the appropriate punishment, and this process starts with apprehension by the police and booking at a local facility.

As the student will discover, of all the institutions through which offenders pass on their way through the correctional funnel, none has a more diverse population (or a more sordid past) than the jails. Jails are confinement facilities usually operated by a local law enforcement agency, for holding detained persons pending adjudication and/or persons committed after adjudication for less than one year. The jail is the first institutional contact within the criminal justice system that most accused adult males and females (and many juveniles) experience. Most jails are small, although some are huge. See Figure 6.1. Whether large or small, however, jails are predominantly city, county, or regional facilities, funding for which can be erratic and unpredictable.

JAILS: A GRIM HISTORY

The housing of offenders and suspected criminals in local detention facilities is a practice as old as the definition of crime. The processes and practices at the local gaol, lockup, workhouse, stockade, hulk,[1] or detention center changed little over the centuries, until about the mid-1900s. Only recently has any serious attempt been made to provide programs or treatment for jail inmates, and even those efforts must be carefully monitored or officials are likely to abandon them.[2] Originally devised as a place to lock up and restrain all classes of misfits, the jail has a long and sordid history. As discussed in Chapter 1, John Howard was made keenly aware of the appalling gaol conditions in eighteenth-century England when he found himself the proprietor of one of its worst. His effort to reform the practices and improve the conditions in the gaols and prisons of England and the rest of Europe parallels the periodic attempts by American reformers to clean up our jails. As recently as the early 1970s, little had changed with regard to the jails of America, some of which were almost a century old.

The early jails in America were similar to those in Europe. Most were composed of small rooms in which as many as twenty to thirty prisoners were jammed together. The purpose of jails, as originally conceived by Henry II of England when he ordered the construction of the first official English jail at the Assize of Clarendon in 1166, was to detain suspected or accused offenders until they could be brought before a court. Seldom were the jails adequately heated or ventilated, and food was either sold by the jailer or brought in by family or friends. Conditions within the early jails defy description, and the problems of overcrowding and poor sanitation continue to plague some jails today. Many are exemplary, but at best a few are warehouses for the misdemeanant, vagrant, petty offender, and common drunk. At worst, they are overcrowded, understaffed, underfunded "festering sores," as described by a former director of the Law Enforcement Assistance Administration. The jail, perhaps more than any other segment of the correctional system, has been difficult to change and tends to deteriorate more quickly than it can be improved. Undoubtedly, some of this is because jails are funded through local taxes. Traditionally jails have not been high on the priority list for support from local politicians. Thus, jails have been called the "cloacal region of corrections."[3]

SIDEBARS

John Howard Association

Named after the jail reformer, this association was formed in 1901 and is devoted to prison and jail reform and the prevention and control of crime and delinquency. It provides professional consultation and survey services in crime and delinquency and publishes a bimonthly newsletter.

Felons, misdemeanants, and some nonviolent juveniles in both of these categories make up the major population of jails. However, additional categories of **jail inmates** include persons with mental illnesses for whom there are no other facilities, parolees and probationers awaiting hearings, federal prisoners awaiting pickup by marshals, and offenders sentenced to departments of corrections for whom there is not yet space but who cannot be released. In some states, felons serving relatively short sentences can also be housed in local jails to complete their sentences.

The jail has been at the end of the line for receiving public and governmental support since the days when John Howard inherited the abomination of a gaol at Bedfordshire, England, in 1773. Though public attention turns to jails from time to time when politicians or the media expose a particularly appalling situation, the jails seem to revert quickly back to their original deplorable state. In the last few

Jessamine County (Kentucky) Jail annex, attached about 1930, a first-generation small-town jail.
Photo by Harry E. Allen.

years, a number of new facilities based on new management concepts have been constructed to provide better conditions and programs for the misdemeanant prisoners and felony detainees, but these new facilities are still too few, and many jurisdictions still operate antiquated facilities from another era. While community programs and facilities are sometimes used to provide work and educational programs for short-term sentenced prisoners, there are too few of these programs to alleviate the boredom and poor conditions of many jails.

Of all the problems that plague the criminal justice system, none is more confused and irrational than the question of what should be done with the offender in the period before trial (see Figure 6.2). In the United States, the concept of "innocent until proven guilty" creates many problems for the local jail. Pretrial detention and procedures for pretrial liberty have been the subject of hot debate among personnel in the criminal justice system for many decades.[4] The **presumption of innocence** is difficult to maintain once the defendant has been arrested and detained in jail. The police find that presumption difficult to accept if they have acted on probable cause (high probability of guilt) in first making the arrest or have caught the individual in the act. Several projects studying the effects of pretrial decisions on sentencing offer evidence that this period is critical to later correctional efforts.[5]

FIGURE 6.2

General Processing Path in Jails

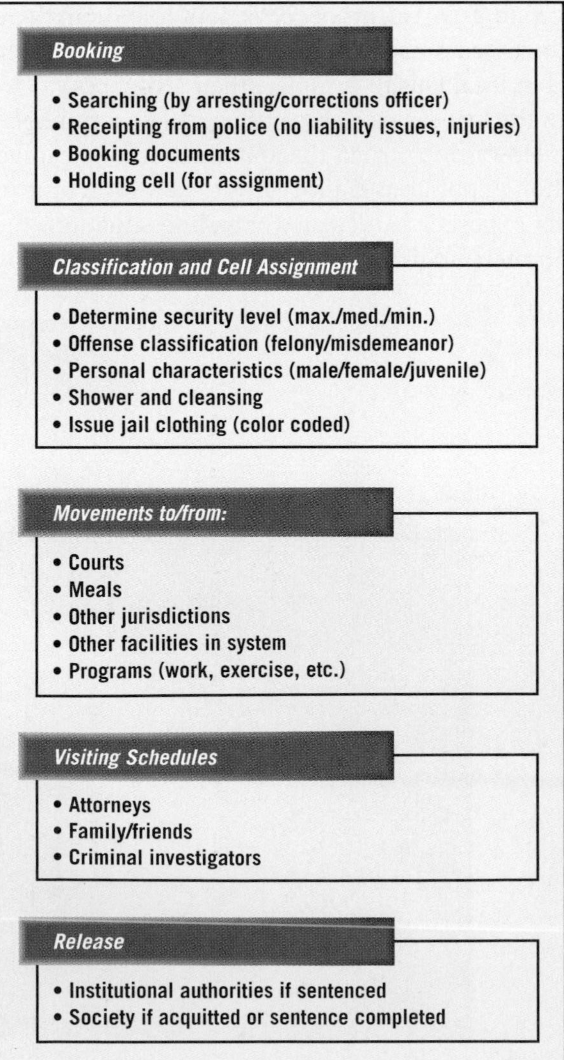

It is even more difficult for the public to realize that "not guilty" does not necessarily mean that the offender is "innocent." Not guilty simply means that it was not possible to establish guilt "beyond a reasonable doubt" for the offense for which the defendant was charged and tried.

The problem of pretrial release is clear when we consider that the Sixth Amendment to the Constitution guarantees a "speedy and public trial" (see the Chapter 4 sidebar titled "Sixth Amendment"). This presents a problem for the innocent person being held, because he or she looks guiltier with each passing day in confinement. A 2002 study found that the median time from arrest to adjudication for felony defendants was about six months. Some 59 percent of all convicted offenders in this study received sentences to incarceration.[6]

SIDEBARS

Detention

The legally authorized confinement of a person subject to criminal or juvenile court proceedings until commitment to a correctional facility or release. Detention describes the custodial status (reason for custody) of persons held in confinement after arrest or while awaiting the completion of judicial proceedings. Release from detention can occur either prior to or after trial or adjudication, as a dismissal of the case, an acquittal, or sentencing disposition that does not require confinement.

JAILS TODAY

Urban dwellers in America have responded to the need for local lockups and correctional facilities in a number of ways. The most common confinement facility is the lockup, but the size and quality of those facilities vary greatly. There is quite a difference between the one-cell lockup of a small town and the gigantic facilities of New York City and Los Angeles, which have capacity ratings of 24,400 and 20,793, respectively. The counterpart of the city lockup is the county jail, but jails, lockups, detention facilities, workhouses, and a number of other units are all commonly referred to as jails. (We refer to all of these facilities as city or county jails, except when it is more relevant to refer to them by another designation.) Policies and programs vary greatly among cities and counties, but some general descriptions and suggestions can be made for small, medium, and large systems. Twenty-five percent of U.S. jails hold fewer than 50 up to 249 inmates, yet the twenty-five largest jail systems hold almost one in every three jail inmates.

SIDEBARS

Jails Near 100% of Rated Capacity

- On June 30, 2003, an estimated 691,301 persons were held in local jails, up from 621,149 at midyear 2000.
- Between 1990 and 2003, the number of inmates held in jail increased 71 percent—from 405,320 to 691,301, or about 5 percent per year.
- In the year ending June 30, 2003, the capacity of the nation's jails rose by 22,572 beds. Jails were operating at 94 percent of their rated capacity.
- At midyear 2003, 238 of every 100,000 U.S. residents were held in local jails, up from 163 per 100,000 in 1990.

SOURCE: Paige Harrison and Jennifer Karberg, Prison and Jail Inmates at Midyear 2003 *(Washington, DC: Bureau of Justice Statistics, 2004).*

JAIL POPULATIONS AND CHARACTERISTICS

The felon and the misdemeanant, the first-time and the repeat offender, the adult (male and female) and the juvenile, the accused and the convicted, not to mention the guilty and the innocent, are housed in America's jails. Jails house individuals pending arraignment as well as those awaiting trial, conviction, and sentencing; probation, parole, and bail-bond violators and absconders; juveniles pending transfer to juvenile facilities; persons with mental illnesses awaiting transfer to appropriate facilities in the mental health system; chronic alcoholics; and drug abusers.[7] Individuals in jail also include persons being held for the military or in protective custody; material witnesses; persons found in contempt of court; persons awaiting transfer to state, federal, or other local authorities; and temporarily detained persons. More than one-half of the persons jailed are there pretrial, about 10 percent have been found guilty but are as yet not sentenced, and the remainder are actually serving sentences. (This latter category is rising as local jurisdictions crack down on those who drive while intoxicated[8] and on domestic disturbance[9] crimes.) Each of these categories represents a challenge to jail administrators and managers.

Because jails are so scattered and varied in operations and record keeping, it is always difficult to develop accurate data regarding jails and jail populations. However, the most recent study of jail inmates available from the U.S. Department of Justice provides reasonably current and reliable information.[10]

Data sources available for analysis indicated an average daily population of 691,301 persons held in locally operated jails in mid-2003, an increase of 36 percent over the 1995 total, and nearly 70 percent greater than that of 1990 (see Figure 6.3).

FIGURE 6.3

Number of Jail Inmates, 1985–2010

SOURCE: Paige Harrison and Jennifer Karberg, *Prison and Jail Inmates at Midyear 2003* (Washington, DC: Bureau of Justice Statistics, 2004). Data extrapolated for 2005 and 2010.

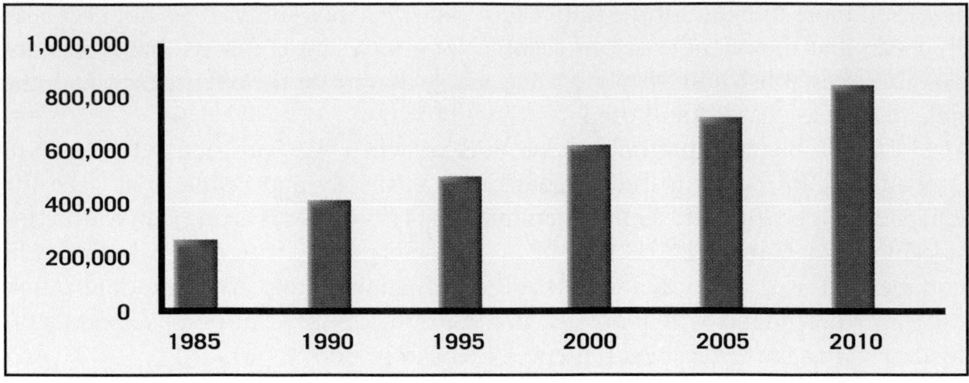

The latest profile of jail inmates reflected the traditional twofold function of a jail: a place for the temporary detention of pretrial defendants and a confinement facility where many convicted persons, predominantly misdemeanants, serve out their sentences, usually for less than one year. To further complicate the situation, many pretrial inmates may be kept in a jail for several months or longer before they can get a trial date. Slightly more than half of all jail inmates have not been convicted of a crime.

In 2003, 56 percent of the jail inmates were pretrial, accused but not convicted of a crime. Court-appointed lawyers, public defenders, or legal aid attorneys were representing most of those who had counsel. A large percentage of all pretrial inmates remained in jail, even though the authorities had set bail for them.

For those persons held in the nation's jails in midyear 2003, there were 10 percent more whites than blacks, but blacks were still disproportionately represented. Relative to the number of black U.S. residents, blacks were some five times more likely than whites to have been held in a local jail in midyear 2003. Hispanics were the fastest growing segment of the jail population, which is consistent with their rising number in the U.S. population (see Figure 6.4).[11]

The 2001 adult jail population consisted predominantly of males at 88 percent, 2 percentage points lower than 1990. Most jail inmates were young men in

FIGURE 6.4

Ethnicity of Jail Inmates, 2003

SOURCE: Paige Harrison and Jennifer Karberg, *Prison and Jail Inmates at Midyear 2003* (Washington, DC: Bureau of Justice Statistics, 2004), p. 8.

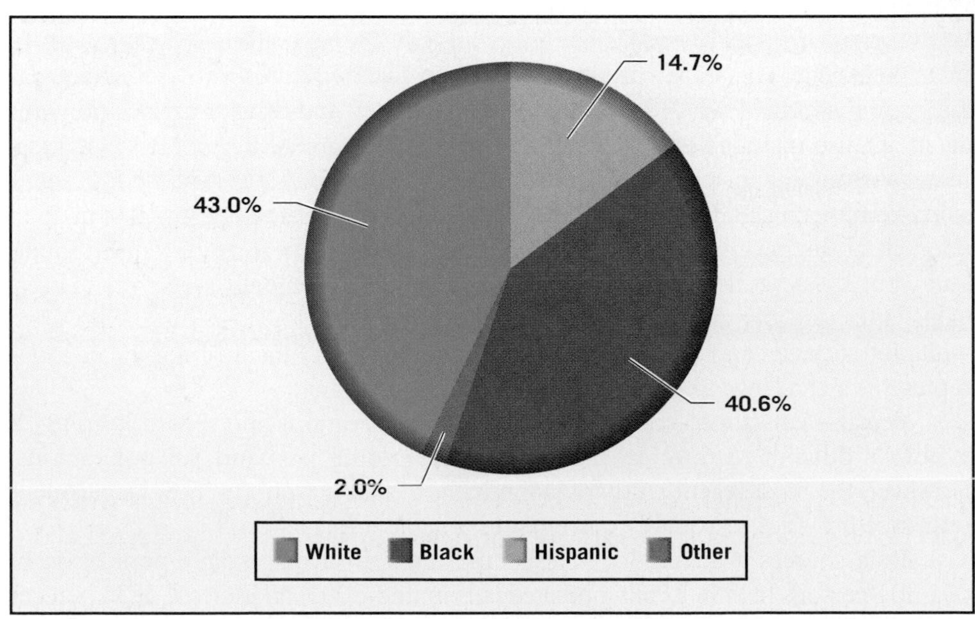

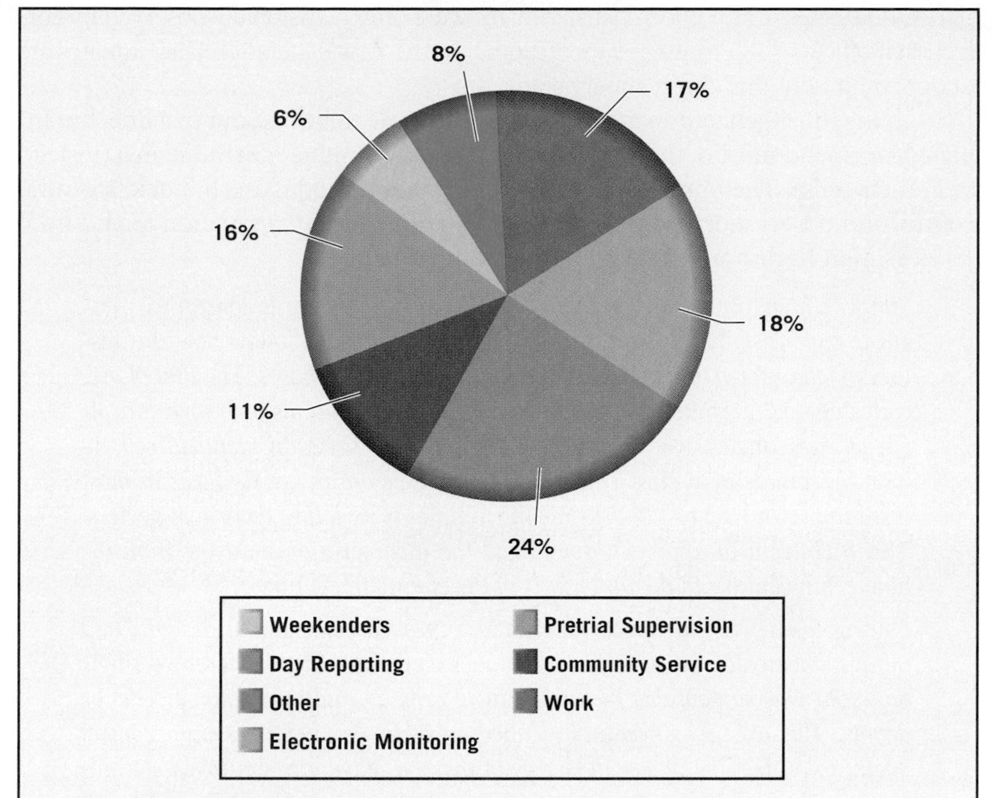

FIGURE 6.5

Persons Supervised Outside Jail Facilities, Midyear 2003

SOURCE: Paige Harrison and Jennifer Karberg, *Prison and Jail Inmates at Midyear 2003* (Washington, DC: Bureau of Justice Statistics, 2004), p. 7.

their twenties. The largest twenty-five jails in the United States housed 31 percent of all inmates in the nation's jails; the remaining 69 percent were housed in the remaining approximately 3,247 facilities of every size and description.

In addition to the pretrial and convicted offenders who are serving short sentences (usually less than a year) that typify city and county jails, some states (such as Texas) operate state jails. Texas has sixteen adult detention facilities (jails) housing nonviolent third-degree felony offenders or Class A misdemeanants. Punishment for this group of offenders could be up to two years incarceration in a state jail facility and a fine not to exceed $10,000, with possible community supervision following release from the state jail. In 2004, the state jail facilities in Texas housed more than 18,000 offenders.

The most effective way to deal with nondangerous persons or to protect the innocent is either to keep them out of jail or to release them as soon as possible. Pretrial diversion, electronic monitoring, weekend confinement, community work orders, increased use of bail and personal recognizance, more extensive use of fines (including day fines and time payments), and various forms of work and study release all are viable alternatives to the destructive and expensive enforced idleness of most jails.[12] In many jurisdictions, jail crowding has forced many public officials to seek creative ways to handle offenders. Figure 6.5 illustrates programs that jails are using to supervise offenders outside of the jail facility.

THE NEW GENERATION JAIL

Jail design was essentially unchanged until the 1970s when we began to see a new type of jail facility now referred to as the **new generation jail.** This jail is a radical departure from the traditional jail in its architecture, interior design, and design philosophy. The new generation jail is a facility designed for maximum interaction between the staff and inmates. In traditional jails, inmates were only occasionally observed by correctional officers ("intermittent supervision"). In the new generation jails, inmates are under continuous and direct supervision.

In the third-generation new jails, cells continue to be laid out in a line, but inmates can spend most of their waking hours in a communal dayroom area (instead of in their cells). The fourth-generation jail contains a podular cell block, a central control and observation room, and a dayroom corridor for circulation to and from services. Ken Kerle aptly describes these podular jails:

> *Simply stated, direct supervision in a jail means an officer is constantly present to supervise the inmates. Jail architecture historians follow how this history of jail architecture evolved through three different phases. The first phase, called linear/intermittent surveillance, spawned institutions with corridors often at right angles, where an officer walked by a series of identical cells to monitor inmate activities. This was usually done on an hourly basis in most institutions and the rest of the time the inmates were left to their own devices. This architectural approach dominated the incarceration industry from the nineteenth century to the latter part of the twentieth century.*
>
> *During the 1970s, architects submitted improved correctional designs, and more sophisticated construction techniques were introduced whereby a single dayroom was surrounded by either single cells or multi-occupancy cells, or dorms. This area was eventually called a "pod." A vandal resistant control booth, to protect the officer in charge of the pod, gave him improved surveillance and the opportunity to monitor inmate activities on a constant basis. This second development was called podular/remote surveillance.*
>
> *Note that the word supervision does not appear in either of these concepts. In the first instance, an officer walking by a cell block has little time to actively supervise unless something untoward occurs. In the second instance, the officer is locked in the control booth to keep the inmates out. While the officer has communication with the inmates through a speaker system, he is not in the position to actively supervise them. A jail administrator summarized the problems with this approach:*
>
> - *If a problem occurred in a pod, the officer had to call "out front" for assistance. Inmates did not recognize the officer as the authority; rather, he appeared to them as a "puppet master" inside the booth, which they referred to as a "fishbowl."*
> - *From a staff point of view, the flow of information between officers and inmates was drastically reduced.*
> - *When an incident occurred, staff frequently didn't know to what they were responding.*
> - *If there was violence and many staff members responded, the inmates often ended up going through the disciplinary process. Chances of working out compromises were minimized.*
> - *Staff on duty in the "fishbowl" would frequently overlook minor infractions. They believed it just wasn't worth the trouble to operations elsewhere by calling for assistance.*
> - *Staff lacked knowledge of individual inmates and could not give accurate information on inmate behavior. They had to second guess stress levels when trouble emanated in the pod. In both the linear/intermittent and the podular/remote designs, the vandal-proof furnishings graced the inside of*

> *the cells and dayrooms. Architects and contractors, jail and staff all assumed from past experience that the inmates would try to tear the place up, and so the stainless steel picnic tables were bolted to the floor, stainless steel combination toilets/washbasins were installed in the cells, and all doors were solid steel with maximum security locking devices.*

The **podular/direct supervision** *model began in 1974 in the Federal Bureau of Prisons' three metropolitan correctional centers in New York City, San Diego, and Chicago. Instead of the vandal-proof fixtures, this jail had commercial grade chairs, tables, and vitreous china toilets and sinks. Soft furnishings and carpeting helped to reduce the noise caused by steel and concrete. Much to the surprise of everyone, the more normalized physical environment survived and the predicted destruction did not occur. The twenty-two beds in segregation units did not fill up and there was no locking down of any of the housing units.*

Local jails were slow to emulate this new approach, whereby a correctional officer stayed inside the pod with the inmates for the entire shift. It was not until 1981 that the first local facility opened as a direct supervision jail in Contra Costa County, California. Still, many people who worked in jails could not believe that this new approach would work. Some assumed erroneously that federal inmates weren't as tough as local inmates. These local inmates, they believed would tear up the jail and assault the single officer inside the pod, which held from thirty to fifty inmates. Of course, some resented the idea of commercial grade furnishings that produced a more humanized environment and made it more livable. These inconsiderate individuals conveniently forget that the staffs who manage and supervise the inmates spend their working days in the jail environment. Pleasant surroundings and reduced noise levels can help inhibit stress. Despite the initial reluctance at the local government level, there was a substantial increase in the number of new jails adopting the direct supervision model. By the time AJA had published its 2nd edition of

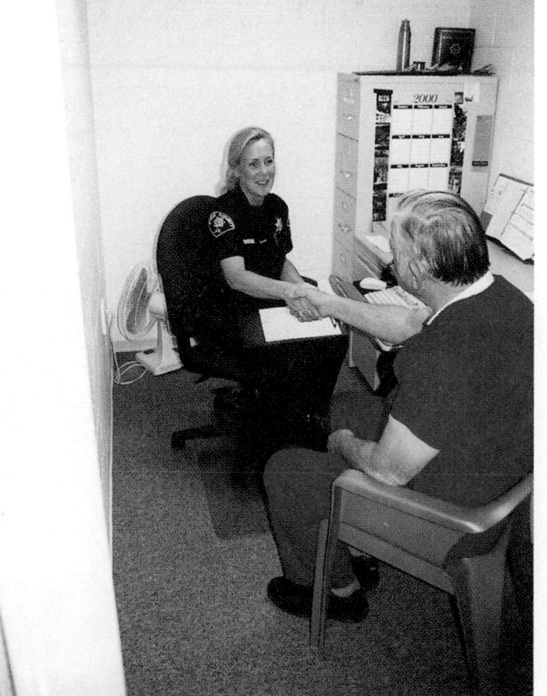

Classification and counseling can be done right inside the pod in new facilities.

Photo by Clifford E. Simonsen, courtesy of King County Department of Adult Detention.

Who's Who in Jail Management 1994, *it listed 114 jails that had switched to direct supervision (pp. 401–405). The following year, the NIC Jails Division published* Podular Direct Supervision 1995, *which showed a considerable increase in direct supervision jails. The direct supervision strategy is believed to reduce inmate violation of and formal processing for contraband possession, destruction of property, escapes, insolence, suicides, and violence problems.*[13]

THE JAIL IN CONTEXT

The Problem with Overcrowding

Mandatory sentences, get-tough polices, and increased pressure from state correctional systems to reduce institutional populations is rapidly changing the makeup of America's jails (and probationers), with serious offenders being housed together with local drunks and misdemeanants. Already overcrowded and difficult to control, many jails have become dumping grounds where little is accomplished other than locking up and feeding the population.

Although there have been improvements, in many physical facilities these have been set back by overcrowding and by the more violent populations.[14] More than one in four of the largest jails is under court order to limit population and to improve specific conditions of confinement (food service, medical services, fire hazards, inmate classification, segregation policies, etc.).

Who are the "rabble" that the jail accepts at entry to the justice system and will probably discharge after a brief stay? Are they dangerous predators? Or are they just marginal people who pose some threat to the community and must be controlled? The answer may be both. We turn first to an examination of the makeup of these residents of the nation's jails. About one in every eight jail inmates is being held for other correctional authorities, about 12 percent of the total inmates, a consistent pattern for the past several years. They are being held back for state and federal prison systems, as well as other local correctional agencies. Almost all of the **"holdback" jail inmates** were being delayed due to overcrowding in adult prisons for felony offenders. A small percentage was federal prisoners being held for trans-

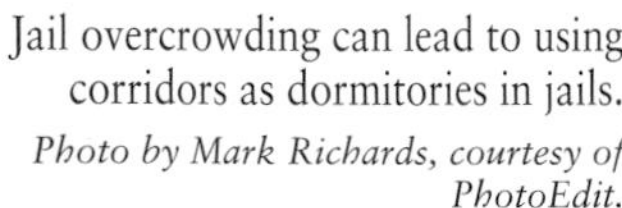

Jail overcrowding can lead to using corridors as dormitories in jails.
Photo by Mark Richards, courtesy of PhotoEdit.

fer to U.S. Bureau of Prisons institutions. The Bureau of Prisons has recently developed jail facilities in their own system and therefore reduced their population of holdbacks drastically. Holdbacks are found at about half of all jails. Most jails charge fees for holding inmates for other jurisdictions. Those holdbacks, while helpful to the jail's budget, can contribute to jail overcrowding in many local jail jurisdictions.

A large percentage of jail inmates have used alcohol and drugs sometime in their lives, and more than four of ten had been drinking just before their offense, almost half being drunk or very drunk at the time of their offense. This pattern of substance abuse is even more pronounced among convicted jail inmates. More than half were under the influence of drugs or alcohol (or both) at the time of their current offense. About a quarter of the jail inmates had participated in a drug treatment program and nearly a sixth in an alcohol abuse treatment program.

As noted earlier, the twenty-five largest jails in the United States house 31 percent of the nation's total jail inmates, with 36 percent exceeding their capacity. Most jail administrators acknowledge that all flexibility in a jail, with regard to classification and housing, is lost when the jail is at 90 percent of capacity. The largest jails in 2003 were at 90 percent of capacity. Those jails with unused capacity were between 68 and 99 percent of capacity being used.[15] A major cause of overcrowding in facilities is the pressure to close other facilities that do not meet acceptable standards.[16] Between 1972 and 2003, the number of jails available to house adult prisoners dropped from 3,921 to 3,365. That number of jail facilities will most likely continue to decline into this century. Rated capacities (total beds) for jails have risen sharply to 736,471 (well over 100 percent) in the same time period. The explanation for this trend is due largely to the fact that most new jails that replace the older, smaller facilities are built to hold many more beds. Although most of the old, decrepit jails probably deserved to be closed, the expanding jail populations and related problems have created management and control problems within the system. Overcrowding and idleness have thus become typical of those jails that have not expanded programs along with the "brick and mortar" approach to jail crowding.

Growing populations have made vast and varied jails—including tents.

Photo by Clifford E. Simonsen, courtesy of Maricopa County Sheriff's Department.

Some efforts to find solutions to reduce overcrowding include conversion of an abandoned motel to a jail annex, purchase of manufactured housing units (modular units that can be interconnected), construction of a canvas tent–based housing community, leasing bed space from other jurisdictions, house arrest for work release prisoners, electronic monitoring of defendants not otherwise eligible for pretrial release, double-bunking at an existing facility, and contracting with community residential programs for alcohol- and drug-dependent inmates in need of such services.[17]

Problems with Personnel

The structures used to house our jails reflect the multitude of problems connected with those facilities. Certainly, the lack of adequate personnel is a crucial factor. Most jails are operated by the law enforcement agency that has jurisdiction in the particular area, although in at least one state, Kentucky, "jailers" are elected by the public. Many sheriff's deputies begin their service with a mandatory two-year tour of duty as a jailer, which many feel is not the role for which they were hired and trained. Because many of the full-time jail personnel are county police officers, dedicated to putting offenders into jail, the primary emphasis is on custodial convenience rather than correctional services. The philosophy behind that includes an almost fanatical concern with security, leaving the responsibility for the jails' internal operation to the inmates themselves. It is that situation which has produced the most reprehensible conditions in many of the large municipal jails. When jail personnel are not sworn officers but lower-paid custodial individuals, the conditions can become still worse. The need for preservice and inservice training of jailers and other jail personnel has been clearly perceived by jail inspectors. The immediate requirement is not an influx of professional staff, but extensive training aimed at breaking the habitual work patterns of uninterested, politically appointed, and unqualified jail personnel. Low pay, high turnover, and poor working conditions contribute significantly to the personnel problems faced by many jail facilities.

One problem with upgrading personnel and facilities has its roots in the long history of the jail's separate **fee system,** which stems from a practice in early England. The office of sheriff in those days was an important political position of pomp and prestige (the sheriff was the king's executive officer at the local government level), but the sheriff did very little work in the jail. The distasteful duty of caring for the jail and its inmates was usually sold as a concession to a keeper, or gaoler. Fees for maintaining the inmates were extracted from their families, friends, or estates. Under that system, the greater the number of inmates and the longer they were kept, the more income would accrue to the jailer. To increase his profit, the jailer cut his expenses to a minimum and operated the jail as cheaply as possible.

The fee system was used in America for many years, until it was largely replaced by a variation. The inmates themselves are no longer required to pay the fees for their upkeep (although in some jurisdictions inmates housed in jail are now being required to pay for their keep, or at a minimum an "intake fee"). In many states, a per diem fee for each prisoner's upkeep is paid by the state or by federal agencies with which the jail has a contract. Leasing bed space from other jurisdictions is a more current example. Some states (such as California) pay their counties to incarcerate state-sentenced offenders with short sentences. Not surprisingly, sheriffs will often exploit a system that pays the sheriff to arrest and jail as many persons as possible. In other states it is the local county that pays for the keep of offenders housed in jail. In rural counties it is not unheard of for a judge to send someone to prison to save the county the cost of housing the offender.

Jail Standards

The standards for jails have been a matter of concern for many years. Many argue that given the diversity of size and function, not to mention funding disparity, it is difficult to implement standard criteria. However, at least twenty-one states report having some jail standards, with all but four mandatory. Maine was the first to report the establishment of some standards in 1951, followed by Michigan in 1953 and California with full standards in 1963.[18] In addition, professional organizations, such as the American Jail Association and the American Correctional Association, have developed standards and accreditation processes, and the National Institute of Corrections has provided technical assistance to numerous jails across the country. Despite the challenges, there has been an increasing movement to upgrade and improve the jails operating in America. Making jails more humane is a worthy goal; however, for many public officials, the most persuasive reason for adapting jail standards is to avoid costly litigation and lawsuits. It is clear that upgrading jails is as critical a need as any other in the criminal justice system.[19]

American Jail Association (AJA)

The AJA Mission Statement reads as follows:
The purposes of the Association, as stated in its certificate of incorporation, are:

- To band together all those concerned with or interested in the custody and care of persons awaiting trial, serving sentences, or otherwise locally confined; to improve the conditions and systems in which such persons are detained.
- To advance professionalism through training, information exchange, technical assistance, publications, and conferences.
- To provide leadership in the development of professional standards, pertinent legislation, management practices, programs, and services.
- To present and advance the interests, needs, concerns, and proficiency of the profession as deemed appropriate by the membership and their representatives.

Health Care in Jails

No discussion of jail conditions would be adequate without addressing health conditions. During the last two decades, the health care of jail inmates has been the subject of endless litigation,[20] included in civil rights mandates, addressed through court orders, and mandated through state regulation. It is clear that provision of adequate inmate health and mental health care[21] is no longer an option but is compulsory. Across the nation, jail managers are taking steps to meet these mandates, including the following:

1. Determining the real costs of and identifying existing community medical service providers; adopting health maintenance organization (HMO) models
2. Resolving security issues for transporting inmates to hospitals and medical care appointments
3. Innovating scheduling for medical staff
4. Providing special housing (for geriatrics, tuberculosis patients, early-stage HIV inmates, pregnant inmates, etc.)

Male inmates talk on phones in the recreation room at Maricopa County Jail, Arizona.

Photo by A. Ramey, courtesy of PhotoEdit.

CORRECTIONAL BRIEF

Jail Provides Mental Health and Substance Abuse Services

"I would like to invite you to come visit my neighborhood. It has a higher concentration of substance abusers and chronically mentally ill people than any other area of the city."

Several years ago, Sheriff James H. Dunning of Alexandria, Virginia, gave this invitation to city council members and various department heads at the council's annual budget meeting. At first, people were taken aback that a distinguished politician could have such a "neighborhood"—until he identified it as the city's adult detention center.

Sheriff Dunning went on to say that a high percentage of the nearly 500 residents of his neighborhood was sure to move into the council members' neighborhoods once released from jail. That night Sheriff Dunning brought home to the city's decision makers the very real message that a jail is not an institution that can be ostracized from the natural flow of city resources. Members of his neighborhood, he said, are citizens of Alexandria and therefore have every right to the same services—particularly mental health and substance abuse services—available to other citizens.

Jail officials work closely with the Alexandria Department of Mental Health, Mental Retardation and Substance Abuse to provide services to inmates in need of mental health treatment. Through a cost-sharing approach, 7.5 full-time staff members from the mental health and substance abuse department are assigned to the detention center. In addition, a host of specialists from the department provide a variety of services such as case management, training, and research when needed.

Central to the success of the jail's mental health and substance abuse programming is the effective use of jail staff. The jail has designated "special management deputies" and unit counselors who receive ongoing mental health training. These individuals provide most of the first-line psychological intervention and triage, leaving only high-priority cases for evaluation and treatment by the mental health department specialists.

The jail also has a behavior management team composed of deputies, mental health, medical and classification staff that meets weekly. Team members must distinguish between inmates with traditional behavior problems and those who may be mentally ill, and then develop a coordinated adjustment plan among the various disciplines.

SOURCE: Connie Fortin, "Jail Provides Mental Health and Substance Abuse Services," *Corrections Today* 55:6 (1993): 105–106.

SIDEBARS

Detoxification Center

A public or private facility for the short-term treatment of either acutely intoxicated persons or drug or alcohol abusers. Such a center functions as an alternative to jail for persons in an intoxicated condition who have been taken into custody.

5. Seeking accreditation (sometimes as a defense against litigation and claims of deliberate indifference)
6. Planning for future problems.[22]

Demands of this nature will require jail managers to find ways to creatively adopt proven techniques and implement innovations that would permit continued quality health care while curtailing costs of services.[23]

ALTERNATIVES TO JAIL

Extended confinement of presumed innocent persons, as with pretrial detention of the nonadjudicated felon later found not guilty, is a serious problem. The defendant who is truly innocent, but is exposed through long pretrial confinement to the conditions of even the finest jail, will soon build up considerable resentment and animosity toward the criminal justice system and to corrections in particular. The convicted offender eventually sent to a correctional institution also will have negative feelings about the inequities of a system that appears to choose arbitrarily to confine some defendants before trial while releasing others.

Fines

The confusion in defining and enforcing misdemeanor statutes is reflected in the absence of uniform techniques and systems for dealing with misdemeanants. Although different states vary greatly in their approaches, and jurisdictions within states may also be inconsistent, some patterns are fairly constant. As mentioned, the bulk of the misdemeanor cases are disposed of through confinement or probation, but alternatives for disposition exist, the most prevalent being the use of fines.

Cynical inmates often refer to fines as **price-tag justice.** In the case of misdemeanor offenses, the fine is in many cases offered as an alternative to a period of confinement, meaning the offender who cannot pay is confined, in effect, for being "poor" rather than for being "guilty." The sheer number of misdemeanor cases the lower courts must hear forces the judges to be able to provide only the most cursory kind of justice. Some lower courts may hear more than 100 misdemeanor cases in a single morning. It is difficult, under such circumstances, to conduct any kind of in-depth diagnosis of the offender, the offense, or the offender's ability to pay a fine. The amount of fine for a particular crime is virtually standardized, and paying it is like paying forfeited bail or a parking ticket. For the individual unable to pay, a term in the lockup is often seen as the only alternative. In some cases, however, fines can be paid on the installment plan. That procedure gives offenders a chance to keep their jobs or seek work to pay the fine. Combined with weekend confinement and community work orders, the installment plan has greatly improved misdemeanor justice.

As part of the increased enthusiasm for intermediate punishments and search for a graduated progression of intermediate sanctions (see Chapter 8), courts have increasingly begun to use fines and day fines (a sliding dollar amount determined by the offender's daily wages). The Vera Institute of Justice implemented a project to demonstrate and then evaluate the efficacy of using day fines in Staten Island, New York. The project demonstrated the following:

1. The day-fine concept could be implemented in a typical American court of limited jurisdiction.
2. Day fines could substitute for fixed fines ("the same or similar amount to be imposed on all defendants convicted of similar offenses").
3. Fine amounts were higher for more affluent offenders under the day-fine system.
4. Overall revenues increased.
5. High rates of collection could be sustained despite the higher average day-fine amounts.
6. The deep skepticism among criminal justice professionals about the court's ability to enforce and collect such fines was unfounded.[24]

Both fines and day fines are likely to be used more extensively by courts to achieve a graduated progression of penalties for less serious crimes as well as enhancing the programs and efforts aimed at reducing jail overcrowding.

Weekend Confinement

To lessen the negative impacts of short-term incarceration and allow offenders to retain current employment, some jurisdictions permit sentences to be served during nonworking weekends. Many refer to it as "doing time on the installment plan." Such weekend confinement generally requires a guilty misdemeanant to check into the jail on Friday after work and leave Sunday morning, sometimes early enough to permit church attendance. A **weekender** serving his or her sentence over a number of months would generally be credited with three days of confinement per weekend. Minimum security facilities (not the maximum security jails) are appropriate for such offenders.

Community Work Orders

Sentencing judges sometimes order misdemeanants to perform a period of service to the community as a substitute for, or in partial satisfaction of, a fine. This disposition is generally a condition of a suspended (or partially suspended) sentence or of probation. It can be used in a variety of ways: a sentence in itself, work in lieu of cash fine, a condition of suspended sentence, or a condition of probation.[25]

The offender "volunteers" his or her services to a community agency for a certain number of hours per week over a specified period of time. The total number of hours, often assessed as the legal minimum wage, is often determined by the amount of the fine that would have been imposed or by the portion of the fine that is suspended.

Other alternatives for the misdemeanant are probation without adjudication and the suspended sentence. Both are variations on the same theme: holding formal disposition over the head of the offender for a period of time, often under specified conditions, and then nullifying the conviction. In probation without adjudication (also known as deferred prosecution), offenders can forego prosecution as long as they meet certain established conditions, usually for a specific period of time. The suspended sentence is used whenever offenders obviously do not require supervision to ensure their good behavior. This alternative is primarily used for first offenders considered to be so impressed with their arrest and conviction that further sanctions against them would be of little positive value.

The extent to which these alternatives are employed is not really known, because little research has been conducted in this area; at midyear 2003, at least 10 percent of jail inmates were outside the facility on confinement alternatives.[26] It is apparent that the misdemeanants, like adult felons, often fall out of the correctional funnel before it narrows. If they did not, the jails of the country simply could not hold them.

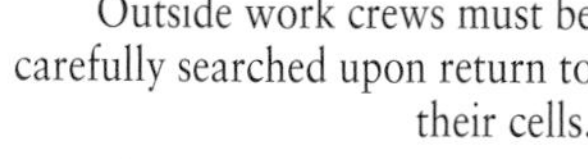

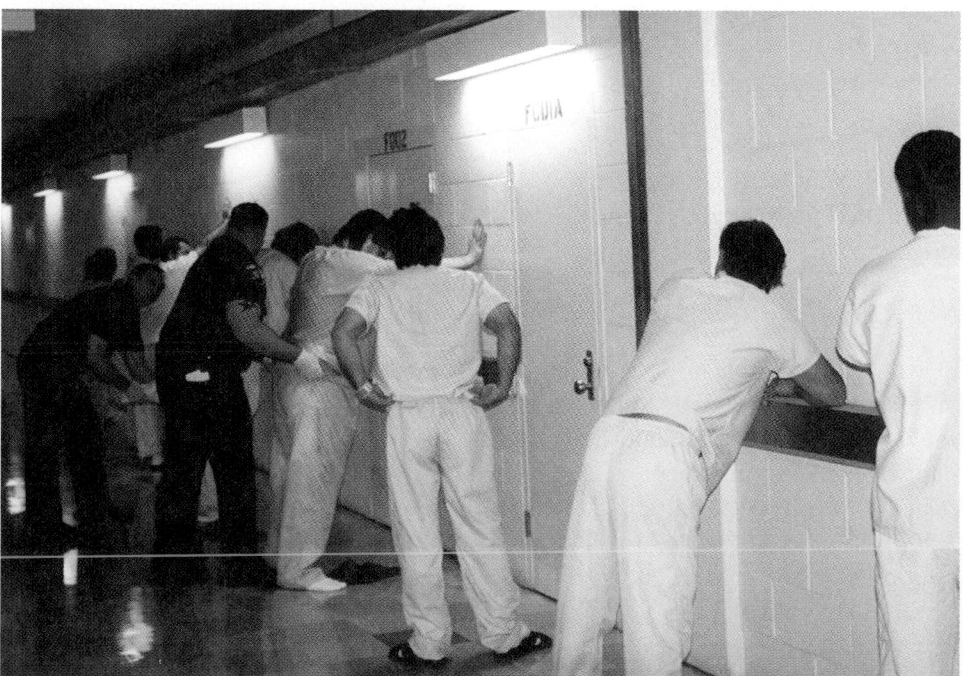

Outside work crews must be carefully searched upon return to their cells.
Photo by Clifford E. Simonsen, courtesy of King County Department of Adult Detention.

ALTERNATIVES TO JAIL AT THE PRETRIAL STAGE

Incarceration is one of the most severe punishments meted out by the American criminal justice system. Yet more than one-half of all persons in local jails are awaiting trial. In effect, we are using our most severe sanction against many individuals who have not yet been convicted of a crime. If detention were necessary and if there were no reasonable alternatives to the jailing of suspects, that situation would be understandable; but experience with alternatives to jail has indicated that many (but not all) people now incarcerated could probably be released safely and economically, pending disposition of the charges against them. Most of them would appear in court as required without being held in jail.

Some tentative conclusions can be drawn from the experience of existing programs:

1. Pretrial alternatives generally cost much less than jail incarceration.
2. Persons released before trial seem to fare better in court than do those who are incarcerated.
3. Pretrial release alternatives appear to be as effective as jail in preventing recidivism and can reduce the size of criminal justice agency workloads.
4. Alternative programs can reduce jail populations and eliminate the need for expansion or new construction.

Pretrial alternatives to detention run along a continuum of increasing controls or sanctions. Any community wishing to maximize the use of alternatives will provide a series of options that offer varying levels of supervision and services. Such a process will permit the release of more persons with less waste of expensive resources. The least interventionary and least costly options are used for low-risk cases. More expensive options and options involving greater interference in the life of the individual, such as house arrest and electronic monitoring, are reserved for cases in which those are the only alternatives to the even more costly option of jail incarceration.

Although jails keep alleged offenders off the streets, they also keep those same individuals away from their work, family, friends, and business (even if crime might be their business). Already tenuous ties to the community may be further strained by the jail experience. Moreover, other disreputable members of society (derelicts, drug abusers, hustlers, drunks, etc.) may vandalize and/or burglarize their residence, which may have been left unattended and unguarded for even the brief time of jail detention. The average length of stay in jails nationwide (both pretrial and sentenced) is about a combined average of almost ninety days. Finally, jails are important because of what happens to the inmates there. The shock of incarceration, loss of control over their environment, danger from violent inmates, absence of meaningful activity, and dead time weigh heavily on the minds of new inmates. Psychological problems already affecting behavior may be exacerbated; self-mutilation[27] and suicide[28]occasionally occur. Sometimes it is difficult to rebut those who argue that the purpose of **pretrial jail incarceration** is punishment.

Less than one-half of all jail inmates grew up in a household with both parents present; almost four in ten have lived in a single-parent household. More than a third have family members (usually a brother or sister) who have also been incarcerated. More than a fourth have a parent or guardian who abused alcohol while the inmate was growing up. One in six male inmates reported sexual or physical abuse (or both) by an adult before the current incarceration, and one in eight had taken medication prescribed by a psychiatrist or other doctor for an emotional or mental problem.

Characteristics of female jail inmates are explored in greater detail in Chapter 15, and the patterns just described are generally more egregious for female than male jail inmates. Self-reports on drug abuse by jail inmates, sometimes known for their self-serving and deceptive purposes, are in part verified through urinalysis testing conducted at jail sites across the nation. Results for arrestees and across different charges at arrest indicate even more extensive drug use than previously self-reported, particularly by robbery and burglary arrestees.

As for their criminal activities, usually almost one in four has been arrested for a crime of violence and another three of four have been arrested for crimes against property. A large percentage of criminals are charged with drug violations. A bit less than one-half have been previously sentenced to incarceration or probation prior to their instant offense. The proportion of inmates with mental illness is high.

Those sociodemographic and **criminal history data** suggest a marginal group of mostly male offenders who have had a lengthy but not necessarily serious involvement in criminal activity. They could best be seen as a group of high-need disadvantaged urban dwellers whose needs have not been adequately addressed by the social services agencies in their local communities. The number of inmates of the largest jails who died further describes their needs. Of the 919 inmates who died in jails at year-end 1999, more than one in three died at their own hands (suicide). Almost 42 percent died of natural causes (excluding AIDS). The fact that one of eleven inmate deaths in jails was attributed to causes related to AIDS suggests that compassionate release of the fatally ill is a concept that has still to be fully embraced by local correctional facilities.

SUMMARY

We have covered the somewhat disconnected jail system and its operational problems, innovations, and future directions. This chapter provides a snapshot and characteristics overview of the kinds of people and their behaviors who make up the clients of the nation's jails. The data, as difficult as they are to gather, suggest that these "clients" are a group of the American society's so-called losers. The best way to solve the long-term problems of the millions of residents who rotate through America's jails is to address the underlying problems faced by jail inmates. The jail system, which deals with problems ranging from drunk drivers and petty theft to aggravated murder, evokes terror in some involuntary residents of these facilities and a "business as usual" attitude in others who have experienced it before. These residents are trying to cope with drug and alcohol abuse, unemployment, domestic problems, medical and **mental health issues** and needs, inadequate education and illiteracy, and failure to adapt to an urban environment. Students interested in making an impact on corrections and finding creative solutions to persistent problems can fulfill that desire by beginning their career with the local jails and community corrections.

What becomes of this varied population of offenders passing through the jails of America? Most are convicted and become labeled as "offenders," then move on to the many options discussed in later chapters. The four categories of persons who move on to other venues of the correctional system are male offenders, female offenders, juvenile offenders, and a particular set of clients known as "special category offenders." In later chapters, we examine each of these categories and discuss their impact and special characteristics as applied to corrections. As mentioned at the beginning of this chapter, these discussions deal with developing a better understanding of the people in the system and using such knowledge to improve the ways to deal with them in the various systems of corrections.

Although improving jail facilities and upgrading jail personnel takes a great deal of time and money, many other helpful procedures can be initiated more simply. The National Jail Committee of the American Correctional Association recommended some in 1937. The fact that so many of those suggestions would still benefit jails today, almost seventy years later, reflects most of local jail systems' general resistance to change. The accreditation process has significantly improved jail practices in many jurisdictions, as have standards, both developed by the American Correctional Association in the 1990s. Jail administrators have an obligation to society to seek methods that can work in their own communities. Administrators are the practitioners who, with community involvement, must break the tradition of neglect and indifference that is the jail's legacy. Unless vigorous and imaginative leadership is exhibited, even revitalized jails will soon regress to their squalid past.

The best policy is to search for ways to keep people out of jail, yet still protect the citizenry. Providing security and staff training and meeting the standards suggested by the professional associations that oversee the staff can meet both goals.

The student must be constantly aware that it is the fine people who keep the jails of America moving ahead, against tremendous problems, that keep them from slipping back into the horrors of the past. We now move on to a look at one of the major alternatives for going from jail to a prison after conviction—probation. In times of overcrowding, probation has become a major player in correctional supervision and will probably expand further in the coming decade.

REVIEW QUESTIONS

1. Why has the fee system been such a detriment to jail progress?
2. Do you think offenders housed in jail should be made to pay for their upkeep? Their medical care?
3. What is the area of greatest weakness in the jails? Would more personnel be the answer? Why or why not?
4. What are the major alternatives to pretrial confinement?
5. Describe the operation of a new generation jail.
6. What medical problems must jails address?
7. Draft a plan for reducing jail overcrowding.
8. Why is the jail so important to the correctional system?
9. What is meant when we describe the jail population as "rabble"?
10. Identify five major problems that jail inmates bring to the institution.
11. Why are so many prison-bound inmates held back in jails?
12. Describe the diversity of the jail inmate population.
13. What special problems do inmates bring to the jail setting?
14. Identify three trends in jail facilities.

ENDNOTES

1. Norval Morris and David Rothman (eds.), *The Oxford Dictionary of the Prison: The Practice of Punishment in Western Society* (Oxford, UK: Oxford University Press, 1995).
2. For an excellent overview of involving the community in jail administration, see William Wood, "A Practical Guide to Community Relations," *American Jails* 6:5 (1992): 14–17; and Taylor Dueker, "Visitation Boom in Omaha," *American Jails* 18:5 (2004): 65–67.
3. Hans Mattick and Alexander Aidman, "The Cloacal Region of Corrections," *The Annals* 381:1 (January 1969): 109–118. See also Karol Lucken, "The Dynamics of Penal Reform," *Crime, Law and Social Change* 26:4 (1997): 367–384. Yet jails are deluged with mentally ill people. See Lois Ventura, C. Cassel, J. Jacoby, et al., "Case Management and Recidivism of Mentally Ill Persons Released from Jail," *Psychiatric Services* 49:10 (1998): 1330–1337.
4. Thomas Bak, *Defendants Who Avoid Detention: A Good Risk?* (Washington, DC: Administrative Office of the U.S. Courts, 1994).
5. Marian Williams, "The Effect of Pretrial Detention on Imprisonment Decisions," *Criminal Justice Review* 28:2 (2003): 299–316.
6. William Durose and Patrick Langan, *State Court Sentencing of Convicted Felons, 2002* (Washington, DC: Bureau of Justice Statistics, 2004), p. 1.
7. Paige Harrison and Jennifer Karberg, *Prison and Jail Inmates at Midyear 2003* (Washington, DC: US Department of Justice, 2004), p. 7.
8. David DeYoung, "An Evaluation of the Effectiveness of Alcohol Treatment Driver License Actions and Jail Terms in Reducing Drunk Driving in California," *Addiction* 92:8 (1997): 989–997; and Arthur Pratt, "The Results of Substance Abuse Treatment Programs in Five County Jails," *American Jails* 12:5 (1998): 59–61. See also Allen Rodgers, "Effect of

Minnesota's License Plate Impoundment on Recidivism of Multiple DWI Violators," *Alcohol, Drugs and Driving* 10:2 (1995): 127–134; and Robert Langworthy and Edward Latessa, "Treatment of Chronic Drunk Drivers: The Turning Point Project Five Years Later," *Journal of Criminal Justice* 24:3 (1996): 273–281.

9. Amy Thistlewaite, J. Wooldredge, and D. Gibbs, "Severity of Dispositions and Domestic Violence Recidivism," *Crime and Delinquency* 44:3 (1998): 388–398; and Edward Gondolf, *The Impact of Mandatory Court Review on Batterer Program Compliance* (Harrisburg, PA: Pennsylvania Commission on Crime and Delinquency, 1997).
10. Harrison and Karberg, *Prison and Jail Inmates at Midyear 2003*.
11. Although blacks are disproportionately involved in the criminal justice system, a long-standing criminological taboo exists against discussing the relationship between crime and race. There is no "black criminology" to tease out the data or theoretically interpret the observed overinvolvement. The three basic arguments are that there are more black offenders per 100,000 population, or that certain black offenders tend to commit very large numbers of crime, or that criminal justice system personnel decision makers are biased against blacks in decision making. See the excellent critique by Kathleen Russell, "Development of a Black Criminology and the Role of the Black Criminologist," *Justice Quarterly* 9:4 (1992): 667–683; and Shawn Gabiddon, Helen Greene, and Kideste Wilder, "Still Excluded?" *Journal of Research in Crime and Delinquency* 41:4 (2004): 384–406. For an examination of the juvenile justice system issues, see Christina DeJong and K. Jackson, "Putting Race into Context: Race, Juvenile Justice Processing, and Urbanization," *Justice Quarterly* 15:3 (1998): 487–504.
12. John Clark and H. Alan, *The Pretrial Release Decision Making Process* (Washington, DC: Pretrial Services Resource Center, 1996); and Brian Paine and Randy Gainey, "The Electronic Monitoring of Offenders Released from Jail or Prison," *The Prison Journal* 84:4 (2004): 413–435.
13. Ken Kerle, *American Jails* (New York: Butterworth-Heinemann, 1998), pp. 190–191. See also Jeffrey Senese, Joe Wilson, Arthur Evans, et al., "Evaluating Jail Reform: Inmate Infraction and Disciplinary Response in a Traditional and a Podular/Direct Supervision Jail," *American Jails* 6:4 (1992): 14–24. See also James Skidmore, "Tarrant County Sheriff's Metropolitan Confinement Bureau," *American Jails* 13:5 (1998): 80–81.
14. Virginia Hutchinson, K. Teller and T. Reid, "Inmate Behavior Management," *American Jails* 19:2 (2005): 9–14.
15. Harrison and Karberg, *Prison and Jail Inmates at Midyear 2003*, p. 8.
16. Wayne Welsh, *Counties in Court: Jail Overcrowding and Court-Ordered Reform* (Philadelphia: Temple University Press, 1995). See also Ernest Cowles, R. Schmitz, and B. Bass, *An Implementation Evaluation of the Pretrial and Drug Intervention Programs in Illinois' Macon and Peoria Counties* (Chicago: Illinois Criminal Justice Information Agency, 1998).
17. National Center of Addiction and Substance Abuse at Columbia University, *Behind Bars: Substance Abuse and American Prison Population* (New York: NCASACU, 1998).
18. Mike Howerton, "Jail Standards in 2001: Results of a 21-State Survey," *American Jails* 15:5 (2001): 9–11.
19. A review of the first two decades of new generation jails can be found in Raymond Harris and David Russell, "Podular Direct Supervision: The First Twenty Years," *American Jails* 9:3 (1995): 11–12. See also Gerald Bayens, J. Williams, and J. Ortiz, "Jail Type and Inmate Behavior," *Federal Probation* 61:3 (1997): 54–62.
20. Frederick Bennett, "After the Litigation: Part I," *American Jails* 6:3 (1992): 81–84; "After the Litigation: Part II," *American Jails* 6:4 (1992): 30–36; Matthew Lopes, "The Role of the Masters in Correctional Litigation," *American Jails* 6:4 (1993): 27–29; Daniel Pollack, "How to Find a Good Lawyer," *Corrections Today* 54:8 (1992): 114–118; and Heidi M. Murphy, "Supreme Court Ruling Changes the Standard on Inmate Abuse," *Corrections Today* 54:1 (1992): 195.
21. Patrick Kinkade, M. Leone, and S. Semond, "The Consequences of Jail Crowding," *Crime and Delinquency* 41:1 (1995): 150–161. See also Richard Lamb and L. Weinberger, "Persons with Severe Mental Illness in Jails and Prisons," *Psychiatric Services* 49:4 (1998): 483–492; and the special issue "Mental Health Issues in Corrections," *Corrections Today* 67:1 (2005): 22–53.
22. James Tesoriero and Malcom McCullough, "Correctional Health Care Now and Into the Twenty-First Century," in *Vision for Change* (New York: Prentice Hall, 1996), pp. 215–236.
23. Patricia Satterfield, "Creating Strategies for Controlling Health Care Costs," *Corrections Today* 54:2 (1992): 190–194. See also Frank Cousins, "The Business Side of Health Care in the Corrections Industry," *American Jails* 18:3 (2004): 56–60.

24. Linda Winterfield and Sally Hillsman, *The Staten Island Day-Fine Project* (Washington, DC: US Department of Justice, 1993). See also the policy statement of the National Council on Crime and Delinquency, *Criminal Justice Policy Statement* (San Francisco: NCCD, 1992); and Judith Greene, *The Maricopa County FARE Probation Experiment* (New York: Vera Institute of Justice, 1996).
25. Paul Hudson, *The State Jail System Today* (Austin: Texas Criminal Justice Policy Council, 1998).
26. Harrison and Karberg, *Prison and Jail Inmates at Midyear 2003*, p. 8.
27. Janet Haines et al., "The Psycho-Physiology of Self-Mutilation," *Journal of Abnormal Psychology* 104:3 (1995): 471–489.
28. Lindsay Haines and Eric Blauw (eds.), "Prison Suicide," *Crises* 18:4 (1997): 146–189; and Alan Felthouse and A. Tomkins (eds.), "Mental Health Issues in Correctional Settings," *Behavior Sciences and the Law* 15:4 (1997): 379–523.

CHAPTER 7

Probation

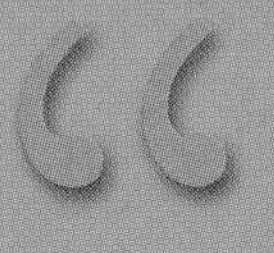

I can forgive, but I cannot forget, is only another way of saying, I will not forgive. Forgiveness ought to be like a cancelled note—torn in two, and burned up, so that it never can be shown against me.

—Henry Ward Beecher

KEY WORDS

- probation
- suspended sentence
- right of sanctuary
- benefit of clergy
- stigma
- sursis
- John Augustus
- presentence investigation (PSI) report
- risk and needs assessment
- special conditions of probation
- technical probation violations
- probation revocation
- *Gagnon v. Scarpelli*
- felony probation
- broken windows probation
- proactive supervision
- front-end solutions
- bricks and mortar solutions
- back-end solutions

OVERVIEW

Our examination of the correctional process now turns to probation and probation supervision, the major alternative to incarceration as used by sentencing judges across America. Although it is the most commonly used correctional sentence, probation is also one of the most maligned and underappreciated aspects of the correctional system. Often seen as a "letting off" of the offender, probation has struggled to gain respect and support from the media, the public and, perhaps most importantly, those officials who make funding decisions.

Probation is a sentence that does not include confinement and imposes conditions governing the release of the offender into the community, based on good behavior. The sentencing court retains authority to supervise, modify conditions, and cancel the status and resentence if the probation client violates the terms of probation. Increasingly, across the nation, courts are using recent developments in technology to better monitor the behavior of the probationer. This chapter presents a brief history of probation and its developments into the twenty-first century.

SUSPENDED SENTENCE AND SANCTUARY

Probation is a derivative of the suspended sentence, handed down to us somewhat indirectly by way of past judicial procedures. Both the **suspended sentence** and probation mitigate the punishment for an offender through a judicial procedure, and

< A drug abuser enrolling in a drug-testing program as a condition of probation.
Photo by Spencer Grant, courtesy of PhotoEdit.

their earliest antecedent is found in the right of sanctuary,[1] frequently cited in the Bible. In many cultures, holy places and certain cities were traditionally set aside as places for sanctuary.

The **right of sanctuary** was written into Mosaic law.[2] To escape the blood vengeance of a victim's family, a killer could go to certain specified cities and find refuge. During the Middle Ages, many churches offered sanctuary for those hiding from harsh secular law. The practice of sanctuary disappeared in England in the seventeenth century and was replaced with **benefit of clergy.** This practice, originally reserved for clerics, was eventually extended to those who could pass the Psalm 51 test—a test of the offender's ability to read the verse that begins "Have mercy upon me." Since anyone who could read (such as the clergy) was eligible to be tried under Church law and thus escape the death penalty, this became known as the "neck verse," meaning they could not be hung by the neck until dead. The result was a form of suspended sentence that allowed the offender to move about in society.

SIDEBARS

Stigma

A mark of shame and disgrace assigned to an offender by virtue of his or her having committed an offense. Stigma also means the person is devalued (from a previous status), and the social reaction is generally to avoid, punish, or isolate the devalued person. Societal reaction is believed to create additional difficulties for ex-offenders who desire to become nonoffenders or to "go straight."

The suspended sentence differs from probation, though the terms are sometimes used interchangeably. The suspended sentence does not require supervision and usually does not prescribe a specified set of goals for the offender to work toward. It is merely a form of quasi-freedom that can be revoked, with a prison sentence imposed at the instruction of the court. Sentence can be suspended in two ways:

1. The sentence is imposed, but its execution is suspended.
2. Both the imposition and execution of the sentence are suspended.

Of the two, the second is the more desirable because of the reduced **stigma;** however, the practice of suspending sentences, like sanctuary, has generally been replaced in America with supervised probation. Sentences may be vacated by the sentencing judge, and the offender may be placed at liberty in the community, but that is a relatively infrequent occurrence.

Under the European model of suspended sentence, or **sursis** (surcease), the offender has satisfactorily fulfilled the conditions if no further offense is committed during the established period. Little control or supervision is provided, with the result that most offenders with suspended sentences are denied the specialized or therapeutic services needed to prevent further criminal involvement.[3]

THE HISTORY OF PROBATION

Probation has undergone a number of changes since its informal beginnings in the nineteenth century. Let us take a brief look at how the concept was born. **John Augustus,**[4] a Boston shoemaker, is credited with being the father of probation. He liked to spend his spare moments observing what took place in the courts, and he was disturbed that minor offenders and common drunks were often forced to remain in jail because they had no money to pay their fines. He convinced the authorities to allow him to pay their fines and offered them friendly supervision. Between 1841 and 1858, Augustus bailed out almost 2,000 men, women, and children.

PROFILE

John Augustus (1785–1859),

called the father of probation, was a Boston shoemaker interested particularly in the temperance crusade in the 1840s. As a member of the Washington Total Abstinence Society, he worked at getting men to give up alcohol. Part of his voluntary service in Boston was to visit courts and request temporary suspensions or postponements of sentences.

His method was to bail the offender after conviction, to utilize this favor as an entering wedge into the convict's confidence and friendship, and through such evidence of friendliness as helping the offender to obtain a job and aiding his or her family in various ways, to drive the wedge home. When the defendant was later brought into court for sentencing, Augustus would report on his progress toward reformation, and the judge would usually fine the convict one cent and costs, instead of committing him or her to an institution.[5]

A juvenile court judge counsels a probationer.
Photo by Billy Barnes, courtesy of PhotoEdit.

Augustus's efforts encouraged his home state of Massachusetts to pass the first probation statute in 1878. Four more states had followed suit by 1900.[6] Probation was thus established as a legitimate alternative to incarceration, and a strong impetus to employ it—the need to supervise young offenders and keep them out of adult prisons—came with the creation of the first juvenile court[7] in Cook County, Illinois, in 1899.

THE SPREAD OF PROBATION

Juvenile probation service developed with the growing movement for creation of juvenile courts. By 1910, thirty-seven states and the District of Columbia had passed a children's court act, and forty had established some kind of probation service for juveniles. Every state had enacted juvenile probation service in some measure by 1927, as the practice became firmly entrenched.

Not until 1956, however, was probation available for adult offenders in every state. The variations in the organization and operation of probation services make it difficult to compare them by state, but the growth in the number of registered probation officers attests to the rapid acceptance of this area of corrections. In 1907, the first directory of probation officers identified 795 volunteers, welfare workers, court personnel, and part-time personnel serving as officers. Most of them were in the juvenile system. By 1937, the figure had grown to more than 3,800, of which 80 percent were in full-time service. By 2002, it was estimated that probation officers numbered over 88,000.[8]

The enabling legislation eventually passed at state and federal levels not only enacted statutes that permitted probation, but eventually defined specific categories of offenses for which probation could not be granted. The latter could include crimes of violence, assaultive behavior that inflicted gross bodily harm on the victim, rape or other sex offenses, capital offenses, train robbing, livestock rustling, certain habitual offenders, and related offenses. Despite these restrictions imposed by legislatures, granting probation is a highly personalized process that focuses not only on the offender but also on the victim. Restorative justice is an example of a contemporary thrust that maximizes focus on the offender, victim, and community.[9]

TABLE 7.1 Imposition of Probation by Crime of Conviction

CRIME OF CONVICTION	PERCENT OF CONVICTED FELONS RECEIVING PROBATION SENTENCES
Homicide	5
Rape	11
Robbery	14
Burglary	28
Aggravated assult	29
Drug trafficking	32
Larceny	33

SOURCE: Matthew Durose and Patrick Langan, *Felony Sentences in State Courts, 2002* (Washington, DC: Bureau of Justice Statistics, 2004), p. 2.

It is clear that the legislators enacting probation statutes intended juvenile offenders and misdemeanants to be its beneficiaries, not hard-core criminal offenders. This was in keeping with the child-saving and progressive agenda that intended to reclaim offenders before they became antisocial and professional offenders committed to criminal careers. As we shall see later, probation is also a sentencing option for adult felons and, depending on the criminal circumstaces, an occasional violent offender. Table 7.1 provides an overview of the frequency

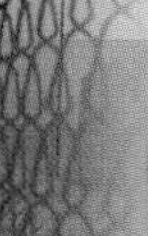

CORRECTIONAL BRIEF

Position Statement on Probation

Purpose The purpose of probation is to assist in reducing the incidence and impact of crime by probationers in the community. The core services of probation are to provide investigation and reports to the court, to help develop appropriate court dispositions for adult offenders and juvenile delinquents, and to supervise those persons placed on probation. Probation departments in fulfilling their purpose may also provide a broad range of services including, but not limited to, crime and delinquency prevention, victim restitution programs, and intern/volunteer programs.

Position The mission of probation is to protect the public interest and safety by reducing the incidence and impact of crime by probationers. This role is accomplished by:

- Assisting the courts in decision making through the probation report and in the enforcement of court orders;
- Providing services and programs that afford opportunities for offenders to become more law-abiding;
- Providing and cooperating in programs and activities for the prevention of crime and delinquency; and
- Furthering the administration of fair and individualized justice.

Probation is premised upon the following beliefs:

- Society has a right to be protected from persons who cause its members harm, regardless of the reasons for such harm.
- Offenders have rights deserving of protection.
- Victims of crime have rights deserving of protection.
- Human beings are capable of change.
- Not all offenders have the same capacity or willingness to benefit from measures designed to produce law-abiding citizens.
- Intervention in an offender's life should be the minimal amount needed to protect society and promote law-abiding behavior.
- Probation does not recognize the concept of retributive justice.
- Incarceration may be destructive and should be imposed only when necessary.
- When public safety is not compromised, society and offenders are best served through community correctional programs.

SOURCE: American Probation and Parole Association, *APPA Position Statement on Probation*, APPA website at www.appa-net.org/about%20appa/probatio.htm (accessed March 8, 2005).

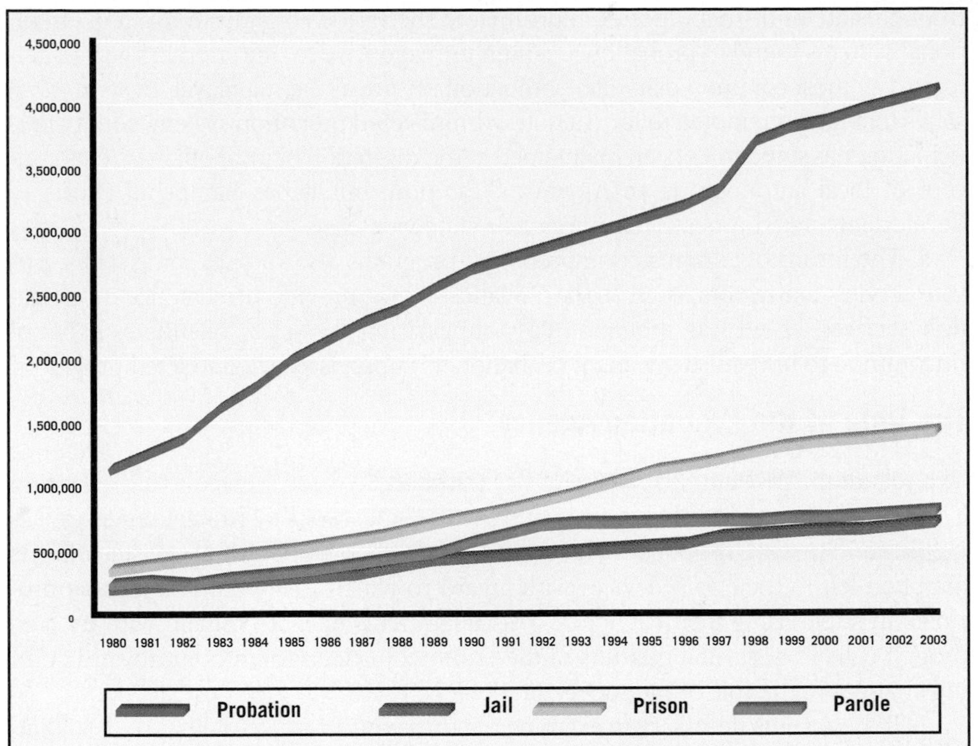

FIGURE 7.1

Adult Correctional Populations

SOURCE: *Bureau of Justice Statistics Correctional Surveys, 1980–2003,* www.ojp.usdoj.gov/bjs/glance/corr2.htm (accessed March 8, 2005).

with which probation is imposed, by crime of conviction. As these figures illustrate, probation is used for a wide range of offenses, but property crimes are the most dominant.

The American Probation and Parole Association policy statement given in the accompanying Correctional Brief identifies the purpose and mission of probation. Judges and corrections and justice advocates have identified the advantages of probation, which can be summarized as follows:

- Uses existing community resources to assist offenders to address their personal and individual problems.
- Saves fiscal resources over the cost of imprisonment.
- Avoids prisonization, a process that tends to exacerbate the underlying causes of criminal behavior in an artificial setting that lessens the ability of the prisoner to function when released to society.
- Keeps offenders' families and dependents off local welfare rolls.
- Provides restitution for and reconciliation with victims.
- Allows selective incapacitation, permitting the use of scarce prison cells to isolate and control aggressive and assaultive offenders.[10]

Thus, it should be of little surprise that the majority of offenders are under sentence to probation (see Figure 7.1).

ORGANIZATION AND ADMINISTRATION OF PROBATION

The problems associated with a lack of organization in the criminal justice system are exemplified in probation services. Under the original concept, the judges themselves were to administer the probation services. For many jurisdictions this is still the way in which probation is managed, whereas in other states probation is administered

SIDEBARS

Selective Incapacitation

The doctrine of isolating the offender, or "social disablement," proposes adopting a policy of incarcerating those whose criminal behavior is so damaging or probable that nothing short of isolation will prevent recidivism. Nothing else would work.

through state or district offices. Unfortunately, the various organizational and operational systems found in probation are often unresponsive to one another's goals or efforts. The most common plan offers probation service at the state level. Even in those states that have attempted to form a state-administered probation system, county participation has sometimes been maintained at the discretion of local officials. This concept of local autonomy is an American tradition, but it has hampered efforts to develop integrated probation services on a statewide basis.

The means of administering probation programs also vary. In some states, private service contractors, such as the Salvation Army, provide presentence investigation services, as well as probation case supervision for select offenders. It is not uncommon to have misdemeanant probationers supervised by contracted providers.

The Role of the Probation Agency

The role of the probation department has traditionally been viewed as a dichotomy. The supervision role involves maintaining surveillance (societal protection) as well as helping and treating the offender (counseling and rehabilitation). Supervising officers are often left to their own devices with regard to which role would be most appropriate in supervising their caseloads. This dilemma is likely to remain with us even though calls from several quarters of the criminal justice system point toward coming changes in the role of the supervising officer.[11]

To begin, it is necessary to examine the duties and responsibilities of probation agencies. First and foremost, they provide supervision of offenders in the community. The basic question remains: What is the purpose of supervision? To some, the function of supervision, drawn from the social work field, is based on the casework model. Supervision is the basis of a treatment program. The officer uses all information available about the offender to diagnose that person's needs and to design a treatment plan. Yet, providing treatment is only one aspect of supervision. In addition, the probation officer is expected to maintain surveillance of those offenders who make up the caseload. Surveillance can take many forms, ranging from office

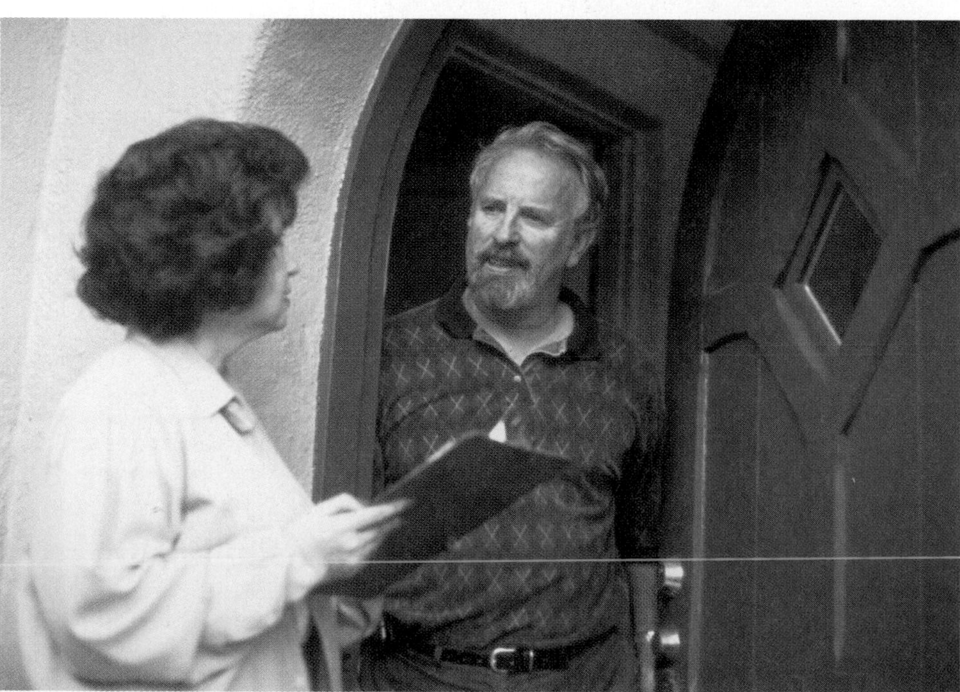

Probation officers often visit probationers at home.
Photo by M. K. Denny, courtesy of PhotoEdit.

and field contacts, to drug testing, to electronic monitoring. Although some believe that the treatment and surveillance responsibilities of the probation department are almost diametrically opposed, the reality is that probation has two missions: to rehabilitate the offenders who are amenable to treatment, while simultaneously protecting society from those who prove to be dangerous. The agency that can adequately balance these goals can best meet the challenges of probation in the twenty-first century.

The Decision to Grant Probation

The decision to grant probation is a complicated process, one further impacted by the plea bargaining process. Recall that plea bargaining is usually undertaken by the prosecutor and defense counsel and can include a reduction in the severity of the charge, the number of counts to which the offender would plead guilty, probation versus incarceration, the length of sentence to be imposed, and whether sentences are to be served concurrently or consecutively. More recently, with the passage of sentence enhancement, habitual offender, and third-strike statutes, defendants might also negotiate on pleading to a misdemeanor versus a felony charge to avoid the first strike necessary for the imposition of sentence enhancement, particularly third-strike sentences. In California, for example, an offender with two previous felony convictions who is facing conviction for a third felony could receive a sentence of twenty-five years to life, whichever is higher, and must serve a minimum of twenty-five years.[12]

The judiciary tends to acquiesce to the negotiated plea outcomes but, in many cases, can decide the sentencing outcome or refuse to accept the proposed agreement ("bust the deal"). This is a crucial point inasmuch as some 90 percent of felony arrestees may have pled guilty for preferential consideration. Such a plea usually vitiates collateral appeal, sharply reducing the legal bases for initiating appellate court review.

When the crime for which someone is convicted falls within the legally permissible range of offenses for which probation may be imposed, or where mandated by state law, a presentence investigation will be ordered, although

A public defender works with a jail inmate on getting him probation.
Photo by Michael Newman, courtesy of PhotoEdit.

some states permit the offender to waive the presentence investigation. The basic function of the presentence report is to provide information permitting the most appropriate sentence to be imposed. It can also serve as a background document for the supervising probation officer and the prison classification committee, as well as any later parole supervision officer, should the offender be imprisoned. The presentence report also provides a wealth of information permitting process and outcome evaluations, as well as developing sentencing guidelines, probation supervision strategies, and specific programs designed to meet emerging challenges for probation agencies (such as identifying offenders with high drug relapse potential and instituting drug treatment programs particularly designed for high-risk cases).

The Presentence Investigation Report

One of the primary responsibilities of the probation agency is investigation. Other responsibilities include, supervision, program advocacy, restitution management, victim–offender reconciliation, brokerage, enforcement of probation conditions, and community safety. Investigation includes gathering facts and information about the offense and arrest, offender background, technical violations, and, more immediately, preparing the presentence investigation report.

The **presentence investigation (PSI) report** is the document that results from an investigation undertaken by a court-authorized officer or agency. Under the direction of the criminal court, it evaluates the background, past criminal behavior, offense situation, personal and family circumstances, personality, need, and level of risk of the offender convicted of the crime, in order to assist the court in making an informed disposition decision and, hence, determining the most appropriate sentence.

In addition to such facts about the offender as educational and employment histories, residential stability, financial circumstances, marital and parental responsibilities, and military history, the report also must provide certain subjective data that are useful to the court. These data would include an assessment of the offender's personality and character, needs and risks, and attitude of remorse and contrition. Most reports conclude with a sound recommendation for sentence disposition and relevant conditions to be imposed if the disposition were to be probation. Both reliability and accuracy are essential, because the court tends to closely follow the recommendation of the investigator. The latter needs are so crucial that the PSI report (minus any specific details that might permit identification of sources who might fear retribution) is generally shared with defense counsel and can be challenged or refuted in a sentencing hearing.

Private Presentence Investigation Reports

Some private sector providers develop defense-based disposition reports, also called private presentence investigation reports, that recommend specific treatment programs and goals that the court might consider in sentencing. Macallair found that such recommended probation alternatives and adjuncts consistently lowered commitments to state correctional facilities.[13] In general, private PSIs are expensive and not widely commissioned.

A final note about the PSI report. No report is complete without a plan of supervision developed by the investigator and presented to the court. Not only would the report include such traditional supervision options as fines, restitution, community service orders, day reporting, and probation, but increasingly it also gives

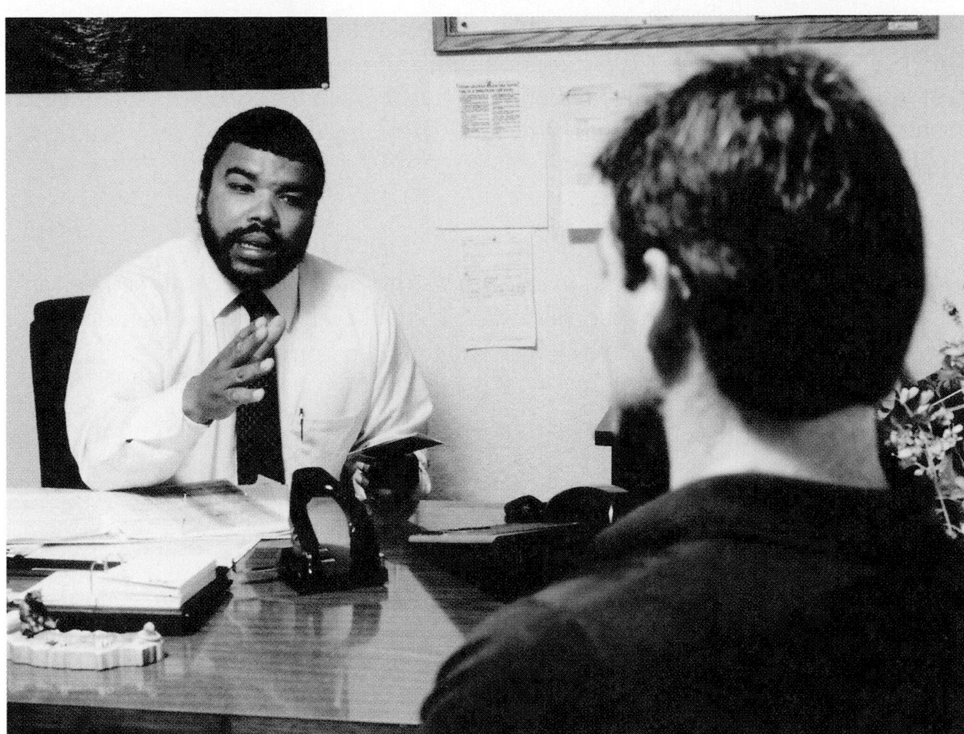

A probation officer works with a probationer on his plan.
Courtesy of California Department of Corrections.

attention to the victim by allowing a victim impact statement and, on occasion, the victim's recommendation for sentence outcome. Surprisingly, some victims are willing to propose constructive responses and solutions in addition to the self-serving request for restitution and compensation.[14]

The Sentencing Hearing

Most criminal courts conduct sentencing hearings independent of the determination of guilt. At such a hearing, the court would consider the PSI report's contents and recommendations, statements by prosecution and defense counsel, statements from victims, privately commissioned presentence reports, and other evidence that might be germane and relevant to the deliberations.

There are no clear-cut factors that heavily influence the outcome of the sentencing hearing, although it is clear that the presentence investigation report plays a central role. If the offender has prior convictions, has inflicted bodily harm, used a weapon in the commission of the crime, is unknown to the victim or has committed a stranger-to-stranger crime, has previously been imprisoned in a correctional institution, has indicators of mental illness, or appears to be engaged in a career of crime, the more likely recommendation would be incarceration in an institution for adult offenders (prison). Judges tend to concur with such recommendations about 85 percent of the time.

If the bulk of the evidence before the court is that the offender displays most of the following, then the sentencing judge is more likely to impose probation:

- Basically a prosocial offender who has committed a first crime
- Good education and work histories
- Married with dependents
- Underlying need to address a personal problem such as drug or alcohol abuse
- Low-risk score.

Offenders, of course, seldom fall into the two extreme examples. For this reason, probation departments have adopted **risk and needs assessment** instruments that provide good to excellent prediction of future offender behavior. Such instruments tend to classify clients into risk level (high, medium, low) and need level (high, medium, and low).

Risk Assessment

The latest generation of classification instruments has successfully combined risk and needs and is relatively easy to use. For example, the Level of Service Inventory—Revised (LSI-R)[15] assesses offender risk by examining ten domains:

- Criminal history
- Financial
- Companions
- Accommodations
- Alcohol and drug problems
- Education and employment
- Leisure and recreation activities
- Family/marital
- Emotional problems
- Attitudes and orientation.

SIDEBARS

Split Sentences

Often a judge will combine some jail time with probation. This is called a split sentence. Other variations include combining probation with weekend confinement, boot camps, and residential programming.

Figure 7.2 shows recidivism rates as they correspond to LSI-R scores; in general, the higher the level of services inventory score, the more likely the offender group to reoffend. Assessments such as the LSI-R help judges and probation departments make better decisions about who to place on probation, whether to increase conditions and supervision levels, and what range and type of services are needed.

TARGETING RISK FACTORS: CHALLENGE FOR PROBATION

Before addressing the conditions of probation that could be imposed by the sentencing court, it is necessary to explore some of the dimensions and problems that probationers face and that cause offenders many problems, and contribute to the

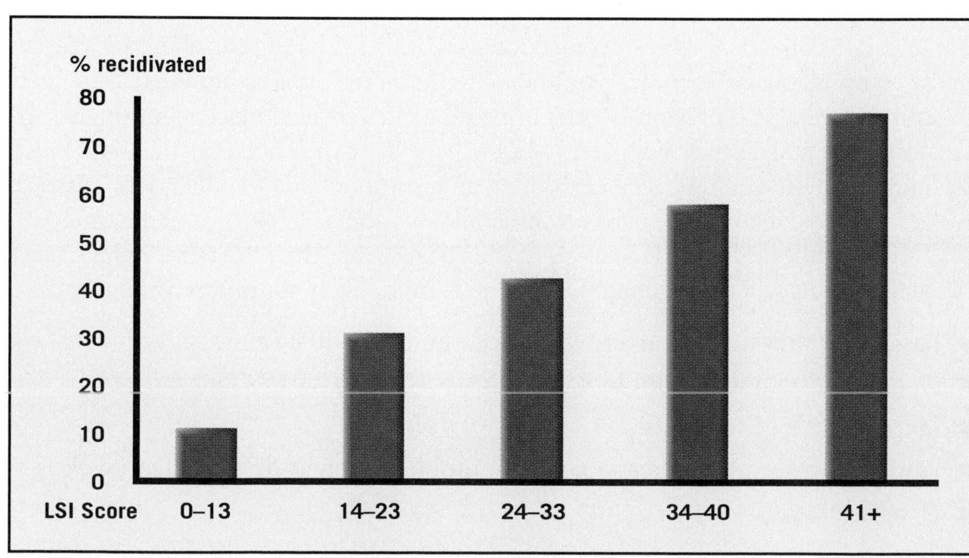

FIGURE 7.2

The Level of Services—Revised and Recidivism

SOURCE: Don Andrews and James Bonta, *"LSI-R": The Level of Service Inventory–Revised* (Toronto: Multi-Health Systems, Inc., 1995).

commission of crime. These figures will help you understand the serious and complicated issues with which sentencing courts and supervising probation officers must deal in the corrections process. Although recent national figures are not available, a 2005 study of community corrections in Ohio examined more than 17,000 offenders under community control. This study found that 84 percent of offenders in the community had a history of drug use, 69 percent prior alcohol abuse, 70 percent had not completed high school, 62 percent were unemployed at the time of arrest, and the vast majority had a prior criminal record.[16] There is no reason to believe that these rates are not similar across the country. In addition to substance abuse problems and a lack of employment and education, probationers also have a number of other problems and risk factors that must be addressed. These include a lack of self-control, bad companions, antisocial attitudes, emotional problems, family conflict, and mental illness.

Fortunately, studies have demonstrated that recidivism can be significantly diminished if offenders on probation or in detention receive treatment and services specific to their risk and need factors, and if they complete the treatment program.[17] Post-treatment reductions of criminal activities are especially pronounced when certain principles are adhered to. Known as the principles of effective correctional intervention, they form the basis of what has become referred to as the "what works" research.[18] The accompanying Correctional Brief provides more information on the "what works" research.

It should be evident that probationers as a group tend to have a wide range of risk and need factors, and that treatment and services should play a large part in supervision. It also requires the sentencing court to impose specific treatment conditions, and for supervising officers to direct the implementation of that treatment.

CONDITIONS OF PROBATION

Courts may impose any reasonable condition on the offender, as long as the condition is related to some identifiable correctional objective. The probation officer is expected to monitor the probationer's adherence to these conditions. General conditions imposed on all offenders would include reporting regularly to the supervising officer, obeying laws, submitting to searches, not being in possession of firearms or using drugs, avoiding excessive use of alcohol, not associating with known criminals, not leaving the jurisdiction of the court without prior approval, notifying the officer of any change of job or residence, paying probation fees, and so on.

Specific conditions, not capriciously imposed, can be required of the probationer, such as participating in methadone maintenance, taking Antibuse, attending Alcoholics Anonymous meetings, urine testing, obtaining psychological or psychiatric treatment, attending a day attendance center or halfway house, restitution or victim compensation, house arrest, electronic monitoring, weekend confinement in jail or residential center, vocational training, or other court-ordered requirements. Such specific conditions are individually designed to assist the probationer in successful completion of court requirements and expectations, as well as reintegration. The proportion of probationers who successfully complete probation range from about 60 percent to some 85 percent (see accompanying Correctional Brief).

Being on "Paper"

Offenders call being on probation being on "paper." Being on "wet paper" means that they are not allowed to drink while under supervision.

Specific conditions are frequently imposed as part of the original court order for probation, but could also be imposed by the court later if the probation client is not abiding by the conditions of probation or poses a danger for failure of probation (see Table 7.2). Probation officers sometimes ask the court to impose more than one special condition after probation begins, especially if the client ignores the orders or deliberately refuses to participate in a program. Urine tests that reveal continued drug abuse or excessive use of alcohol, or irregular employment attendance, may result in

CORRECTIONAL BRIEF

What Works in Reducing Recidivism?

"What works" is not a program or an intervention, but a body of knowledge based on more than thirty years of research that has been conducted by numerous scholars in North America and Europe. Also referred to as evidence-based practice, the "what works" movement demonstrates empirically that theoretically sound, well-designed programs that meet certain conditions can appreciably reduce recidivism rates for offenders. Through the review and analysis of hundreds of studies, researchers have identified a set of principles that should guide correctional programs.

The first is the risk principle, or the "who" to target—those offenders who pose the higher risk of continued criminal conduct. This principle states that our most intensive correctional treatment and intervention programs should be reserved for higher-risk offenders. *Risk* in this context refers to those offenders with a higher probability of recidivating. Why waste our programs on offenders who do not need them? This is a waste of resources and, more importantly, research has clearly demonstrated that when we place lower-risk offenders in our more structured programs, we often increase their failure rates (and thus reduce the overall effectiveness of the program). This occurs for several reasons.

First, placing low-risk offenders in with higher-risk offenders only serves to increase the chances of failure for the low-risk offender. For example, let's say that your teenage son or daughter did not use drugs, but got into some trouble with the law. Would you want them in a program or group with heavy drug users? Of course you wouldn't, since it is more likely that the higher-risk youth would influence your child more than the other way around.

Second, placing low-risk offenders in these programs also tends to disrupt their prosocial networks; in other words, the very attributes that make them low risk become interrupted, such as school, employment, family, and so forth. Remember, if they do not have these attributes it is unlikely they are low risk to begin with. The risk principle can best be seen from a recent study of offenders in Ohio who were placed in a halfway house or community-based correctional facility (CBCF). The study found that the recidivism rate for higher risk offenders who were placed in a halfway house or CBCF was reduced, while the recidivism rates for the low-risk offenders who were placed in the programs actually increased.

The second principle is referred to as the need principle, or the "what" to target—criminogenic factors that are highly correlated with criminal conduct. The need principle states that programs should target crime-producing needs, such as antisocial attitudes, values, and beliefs, antisocial peer associations, substance abuse, lack of problem-solving and self-control skills, and other factors that are highly correlated with criminal conduct. Furthermore, programs need to ensure that the vast majority of their interventions are focused on these factors. Noncriminogenic factors such as self-esteem, physical conditioning, understanding one's culture or history, and creative abilities will not have much effect on recidivism rates. An example of a program that tends to target noncriminogenic factors can be seen in offender-based military-style boot camps. These programs tend to focus on noncriminogenic factors, such as drill and ceremony, physical conditioning, discipline, self-esteem, and bonding offenders together. Because they tend to focus on non-crime-producing needs, most studies show that boot camps have little impact on future criminal behavior.

The third principle is the treatment principle, or the "how"—the ways in which correctional programs should target risk and need factors. This principle states that the most effective programs are behavioral in nature. Behavioral programs have several attributes. First, they are centered on the *present* circumstances and risk factors that are responsible for the offender's behavior. Second, they are *action* oriented rather than talk oriented. In other words, offenders do something about their difficulties rather than just talk about them. Third, they teach offenders new, prosocial skills to replace the antisocial ones (e.g., stealing, cheating, lying) through modeling, practice, and reinforcement. Examples of behavioral programs would include structured social learning programs where new skills are taught and behaviors and attitudes are consistently reinforced; cognitive behavioral programs that target attitudes, values, peers, substance abuse, anger, and so on; and family-based interventions that train family on appropriate behavioral techniques. Interventions based on these approaches are very structured and emphasize the importance of modeling and behavioral rehearsal techniques that engender self-efficacy, challenge of cognitive distortions, and assist offenders in developing good problem-solving and self-control skills. These strategies have been demonstrated to be effective in reducing recidivism. Nonbehavioral interventions that are often used in programs would include drug and alcohol education, fear tactics and other emotional appeals, talk therapy, nondirective client-centered approaches, having them read books, lectures, milieu therapy, and self-help. There is little empirical evidence that these approaches will lead to long-term reductions in recidivism.

Finally, a host of other considerations will increase correctional program effectiveness. These include targeting responsivity factors such as a lack of motivation or other barriers that can influence someone's participation in a program; making sure that you have well-trained and interpersonally sensitive staff; providing close monitoring of offenders' whereabouts and associates; assisting with other needs that offenders might have; ensuring the program is delivered as designed through quality assurance processes; and providing structured aftercare. These program attributes all enhance correctional program effectiveness.

If we put it all together we have the "who, what, and how" of correctional intervention, also known as "what works."

SOURCE: Edward J. Latessa, "From Theory to Practice: What Works in Reducing Recidivism?" In *State of Crime and Justice in Ohio* (Columbus, OH: Ohio Office of Criminal Justice Services, 2004).

CORRECTIONAL BRIEF

National Survey of Adults on Probation

The first national survey of adults on probation revealed that probationers account for the largest share of adults under correctional supervision (57% of all offenders, including those held in jails, prisons, or on parole). Major findings included the following:

- Drug trafficking (15%) and possession (13%) were the most common offenses among felons; driving while intoxicated (35%) and assault (11%) among misdemeanants.
- Half of all probationers had a prior sentence to probation or incarceration: 30% to jail and 42% to probation.
- Drug or alcohol treatment was a sentence condition for 41% of adults on probation; 37% had received treatment. Drug testing was required of a third of the probationers.
- About three-quarters of the felons and two-thirds of the misdemeanants had been contacted by a probation officer in the last month.
- Since entering probation, nearly one in five had had a formal disciplinary hearing. Of these, 38% had been arrested or convicted for a new offense, 41% had failed to report or absconded, and 38% had failed to pay a fine or make restitution.
- The court had tightened the conditions of confinement to compel adherence to court-ordered sanctions ("tourniquet sentencing"): 42% were allowed to continue their probation but with the imposition of additional conditions, and 29% served jail or prison time.
- Unemployed probationers were more likely to have the disciplinary hearing than those who were employed.

Approximately 62% of those placed on probation will successfully complete their sentences, serving on average of 26 months under supervision.

SOURCES: Thomas Bonczar, *Characteristics of Adults on Probation, 1995* (Washington, DC: U.S. Department of Justice, 1997); C. Camp and G. Camp, *The Correctional Yearbook 1998* (Middletown, CT: Criminal Justice Institute, 1998).

tourniquet sentencing, which happens when the court increases the conditions of supervision to enforce participation in programs until the client agrees to conform his or her behavior to expectations.

The most frequently imposed **special conditions of probation** include intermediate sanctions, which are discussed in more detail in Chapter 8. Some of these are house arrest, day attendance centers, electronic monitoring, intensive supervision,

TABLE 7.2 Special Conditions Imposed on Probationers

CONDITION OF SENTENCE	PERCENTAGE OF PROBATIONERS
Supervision fees	61%
Fines	56
Court costs	55
Employment	35
Mandatory drug testing	33
Restitution to victim	30
Alcohol abuse treatment	29
Community service	26
Drug abuse treatment	23
At least one condition	99

SOURCE: Thomas Bonczar, *Characteristics of Adults on Probation* (Washington, DC: Bureau of Justice Statistics, 1997), p. 7.

CORRECTIONAL BRIEF

Federal Offenders on Probation

The number of federal offenders on probation declined slightly in 2002 (−0.7%) and at the beginning of 2002 included 31,562 offenders. Offenders required to comply with at least one special condition of supervision increased from 67% to 92% from 1996 to 2002.

Between 1987 and 1996 the success rates (offenders terminating supervision successfully) were high:

- 85% of those on probation were successes.
- 66% of supervised releases were successes.

SOURCES: Lauren Glaze and Seri Palla, *Probation and Parole in the United States, 2002* (Washington, DC: U.S. Department of Justice, 2004); and William Adams and Jeffrey Roth, *Federal Offenders Under Community Supervision, 1987–96* (Washington, DC: U.S. Department of Justice, 1998), p. 5.

halfway house residency, boot camp programs, and split sentences (jail time followed by probation or by weekend jail time). The point here is that probation supervision can be strengthened by a variety of alternative sanctions that can be imposed to maximize the benefits of probation, avoid criminal reoffending, protect the local community, and assist clients to address their basic and underlying crime causative needs. See Table 7.3. The alternative programs are explored in more detail in the following chapter.

TABLE 7.3 Prior Abuse of Probationers and Other Correctional Populations, by Sex (in Percent)

	TOTAL	MALE	FEMALE
Ever Abused before Admission:			
Probationers	15.7%	9.3%	40.4%
Jail inmates	16.4	12.9	47.6
State prison inmates	18.7	16.1	57.2
Federal prison inmates	9.5	7.2	39.9
Physically Abused:			
Probationers	12.8%	7.4%	33.5%
Jail inmates	13.3	10.7	37.3
State prison inmates	15.4	13.4	46.5
Federal prison inmates	7.9	6.0	32.3
Sexually Abused:			
Probationers	8.4%	4.1%	25.2%
Jail inmates	8.8	5.6	37.2
State prison inmates	7.9	5.8	39.0
Federal prison inmates	3.7	2.2	22.8

SOURCE: Caroline Wolf Harlow, *Prior Abuse Reported by Inmates and Probationers* (Washington, DC: U.S. Department of Justice, 1999), p. 1.

CORRECTIONAL BRIEF

Probationers Who Have Been Abused

A study of correctional populations published in 1999 indicates that probationers have frequently been the target of physical and sexual abuse. Abuse was by far more frequently reported by female than male offenders, but both populations appear to have been maltreated. About one in eleven male and four in ten female probationers reported either physical or sexual abuse, or both. One in three female and one in twelve male probationers reported physical abuse. One in four female and one in twenty-five male probationers indicated sexual abuse. Incarcerated offenders had consistently higher rates of abuse. Among all respondents:

- A third of women in state prisons, a sixth in federal prisons, and a quarter in jails said they had been raped before their sentence.
- Over half the abused women said they were hurt by spouses or boyfriends, and less than a third, by parents or guardians.
- Over half the abused men in correctional populations identified parents or guardians as abusers.
- Abused state prisoners were more likely than those not abused to be serving a sentence for a violent crime (61% of abused men and 34% of the abused women).
- Illegal drug use and regular drinking were more common among abused offenders than among those who said they were not abused.

SOURCE: Caroline Wolf Harlow, *Prior Abuse Reported by Inmates and Probationers* (Washington, DC: U.S. Department of Justice, 1999), pp. 1–3.

PROBATION REVOCATION

Once placed on probation, clients are supervised and assisted by probation officers who increasingly use community resources and programs to assist in the reintegration effort to meet the individual's needs. If the probationer addresses these, secures assistance from community resources, and resolves underlying problems, the probation officer may request the court to dismiss the offender from supervision by closing the case. Some jurisdictions permit the issuance of "certificates of rehabilitation" for offenders who have been successful on probation. Other offenders do not pursue official recognition, and are never seen in the criminal justice system again.

Offenders vary in their ability to conform their behavior to expectations (see Table 7.4). Some are indifferent or hostile, being unwilling or unable to cooperate

CORRECTIONAL BRIEF

Caseload Management in Probation

A national assessment of probation (and parole) agency directors found that caseload management led the list of their workload problems. In particular they pointed out that

- 92 percent indicated they needed more field officers to handle the increased caseloads that they attributed to the increase in substance abuse cases;
- 87 percent were concerned about the need for substance abuse treatment programs in their jurisdictions;
- 81 percent said that these programs needed to be improved;
- 63 percent reported substance monitoring programs were available in their jurisdictions; and
- 82 percent said that their clients needed better access to mental health professionals.

SOURCE: Bureau of Justice Statistics, *Survey of Probation and Parole Agency Directors* (Washington, DC: U.S. Department of Justice, 1995), pp. 1–2.

TABLE 7.4 Reasons for Disciplinary Hearings of Adult Probationers, by Severity of Most Serious Offense, 1995

REASON FOR DISCIPLINARY HEARING[a]	TOTAL	FELONY	MISDEMEANOR
Absconded/failed to maintain contact	41.1%	43.3%	37.6%
New offense	38.4%	43.2%	31.0%
Arrested	30.4	34.9	23.5
Convicted	13.9	15.8	10.5
Failure to pay fines or restitution	37.9%	34.1%	43.0%
Drug/alcohol violation			
Failure to attend/complete treatment program	22.5%	17.5%	33.0%
Positive drug test	11.2	14.3	5.6
Alcohol abuse	2.7	2.9	2.7
Violation of confinement restrictions			
Failure to do jail time/return from furlough	2.5%	2.5%	2.8%
Violation of home confinement	1.3	1.6	.6
Other violations			
Failure to complete community service	8.5%	9.5%	6.7%
Other	6.8	6.9	6.7
Number of probationers[b]	457,279	297,481	144,550

[a]Detail adds to more than total because some probationers had more than one disciplinary hearing, while others had a single hearing with more than one reason.

[b]Excludes probationers who never had a disciplinary hearing or for whom information on disciplinary hearings was not reported.

SOURCE: Thomas Bonczar, *Characteristics of Adults on Probation, 1995* (Washington, DC: U.S. Department of Justice, 1997), p. 10.

with their supervising officer or the court. Some are too immature emotionally to comply with directions. A few face unrealistic conditions with which compliance is not possible, such as extensive victim restitution or employment in an economically depressed period or area. Still others drift toward further criminal behavior by violating the conditions of their probation (particularly the alcohol and drug abuse requirements) that might not be illegal per se, but are interpreted as indicators of future illegal behavior. In these circumstances, the supervising probation officer must deal with **technical probation violations.**

In such circumstances, supervising officers must act to issue stern warnings or arrest their clients. Probationers are taken back to court with requests that court-ordered conditions be tightened (or relaxed, if they are inappropriate). The judge typically warns the probationer, and may increase conditions or frequency of supervision. The conditions imposed on probationers can be found in Table 7.2. Frequently these warnings and official actions are sufficient to coerce client conformity but, if not, or if the client repetitively violates conditions of probation or is arrested by law enforcement officers for an alleged new crime, a hearing may be held to determine if probation should be revoked (a process called **probation revocation**) and a different sentencing alternative imposed (such as a jail sentence or imprisonment). If the probationer is not in jail, a warrant may be issued for the arrest of the probationer.

The probation hearing is a serious event, because it poses a potential for "grievous loss of liberty" for the offender. The hearing is governed by the U.S. Supreme Court decision known as ***Gagnon v. Scarpelli.*** In brief, this case held that probation is a privilege not a right but, once granted, the probationer has an interest in remaining on probation (an "entitlement"). The Court ruled that probation cannot be withdrawn or be revoked without observing the following elements of due process:

- The probationer must be informed in writing of the charge against him or her.
- The written notice must be given to the probationer in advance of the revocation hearing.
- The probationer has the right to attend the hearing and to present evidence on his or her own behalf.
- The probationer has the right to challenge those testifying against him or her.
- The probationer has the right to confront and cross-examine witnesses.
- The probationer has the right to have legal counsel present if the charges are sufficiently complicated or the case is so complex that an ordinary person would not be able to comprehend the legal issues.

States may provide more rights than those just listed, but cannot provide less.

The revocation hearing can lead to several outcomes:

- The supervision level of the case may be increased.
- The offender is warned and admonished, then returned to probation supervision.
- The court can impose additional conditions, then return the offender to community supervision.
- The court can revoke probation and resentence the offender to an incarceration setting, such as jail or prison.
- The court can consider the legal competence of the offender and order a mental health examination, the outcome of which could be commitment to a mental health service or transfer of the case to a probate court for proceedings under the jurisdiction's health and welfare code, or commitment to a state mental facility.
- A bench warrant can be issued for offenders who cannot be found or who have left the jurisdiction of the court.

Of those probationers who experienced a disciplinary hearing in 1995 (the most current national study), the most frequent reason for the hearing was absconding or failure to contact a probation officer. This was followed by arrest or conviction on a new offense (38 percent). See Table 7.4 for the national data on both misdemeanor and felony offender hearings.

Among persons under probation supervision who had experienced one or more disciplinary hearings in 1995, 42 percent were permitted to continue their sentence but only with the imposition of additional conditions. Almost three in ten were incarcerated in jail or prison; and 29 percent had their supervision reinstated without any new conditions.

Probationers work in all kinds of settings.

Photo by Bob Daemmrich, courtesy of The Image Works.

FELONY PROBATION

The rapid growth of serious and violent crime in America during the 1980s contributed to prison over crowding and spurred a movement toward the increase in the use of **felony probation.** Probation, as we have seen, had traditionally been for misdemeanors and low-level nonviolent crime. But prison overcrowding and bulging jails forced the correctional administrators to take a close look at some other categories of felons for relief of an overtaxed system. Because incarceration costs (see Table 7.5) and building costs have become so high, and the institutions so crowded, felony probation has become quite common. We need only look at the dismal results from incarceration to agree that it may be possible to increase this option when combined with a thorough and complete presentencing investigation report and consideration of risk. Programs combined with probation services to protect the community are explored in more detail in the next chapter.

TABLE 7.5 Daily Cost of Correctional Programs per Client, 2002

PROGRAM	COST
Probation	$4.18
Prison	62.22
Parole	6.94

SOURCE: C. Camp and G. Camp, *The Corrections Yearbook 2002* (Middletown, CT: Criminal Justice Institute, 2003).

THE BROKEN WINDOWS APPROACH

Recently, some leaders of the probation and parole approaches have called for a dramatic change in the way in which community supervision achieves public safety.[19] This new model is called the "broken windows" approach. Borrowing heavily from community policing, the application of **broken windows probation** in probation and parole calls for a new partnership with the community. With this approach, the probation officer is asked to collaborate with the community and victim, hold the offender accountable, and improve and expand the leadership of probation. The key strategies outlined with this model include the following[20]:

- Placing public safety first
- Working in the community
- Developing partners in the community
- Rationally allocating scarce resources
- Enforcing conditions and penalizing violations
- Emphasizing performance-based initiatives
- Encouraging strong and steady leadership

Although the goals of the broken windows approach are lofty, the model is not without its critics. Taxman and Bryne[21] argue that the model is filled with rhetoric, is unrealistic, and is based on a flawed approach. Furthermore, they contend that it ignores the significant body of research indicating that the most effective way to achieve public safety is through well-designed and implemented treatment. Table 7.6 illustrates the differences between what Taxman and Bryne call the **proactive supervision** model and the broken windows model. The Maryland Department of Public Safety and Correctional Services recently initiated the proactive approach to community supervision. Moving away from traditional supervision this approach advocates a much more prescriptive strategy that includes more fieldwork combined with evidenced-based practices. The accompanying Correctional Brief describes this strategy. The debate about how to make probation more effective will continue, and it remains to be seen if the broken windows model can live up to its promises.

PROBATION AND ITS ROLE IN CORRECTIONS

Because of the prison population crisis across the nation, states are exploring many strategies to reduce the overcrowding. The basic three strategies can be described as front-end solutions, bricks and mortar, and back-end solutions. Probation is one of the most popular of the three types.

Front-end solutions are alternative sentences such as probation and intermediate punishments that include house arrest, deferred prosecution, electronic monitoring, shock probation, intensive supervised probation, intermittent jail incarceration, and other programs (see Chapter 8).

Bricks and mortar solutions refer to attempts to construct new or renovate existing facilities to expand available beds. Even though there are literally billions of dollars in construction, renovation, expansion, and ongoing retrofitting, no one with any understanding of the comprehensive nature of the problem holds much hope that the nation can build enough prisons to accommodate the influx of inmates (see Chapter 9).

TABLE 7.6 Fixing Broken Windows Probation: A Comparison of Two Strategies

	THE BROKEN WINDOWS MODEL	THE PROACTIVE SUPERVISION MODEL
Definition of the Public Safety Problem	Probation should be held responsible for the level of public safety in each community, including crime rates, fear of crime, school safety, and quality of life.	Probation should be held responsible for the supervision and control of all offenders under their direct supervision.
The Duties of Probation Officers	Probation officers, should be involved not only in offender surveillance and control, but also in crime prevention efforts and various forms of advocacy and community change.	Probation officers should focus their efforts on the direct supervision of offenders while the responsibility for resource development and coordination should be completed by creating a new "resource specialist" position within probation.
The Location of Probation Officers	Probation officers should supervise offenders exclusively in the community rather than in the office. Supervision should be place-based rather than offender-based.	Probation officers should utilize a combination of office and field visits, but the purpose of the contact is always the supervision of the offender, not the place.
The Role of the Probation Officers	The probation officer should be a "generalist" with the ability to supervise a wide range of offenders (e.g., drug offenders, alcohol offenders, nonviolent offenders, sex offenders, mentally ill offenders), utilizing a classic brokerage model.	Probation officers should be hired and trained with the skills to handle a specialized caseload (e.g., drug offenders, alcohol offenders, non-violent offenders, sex offenders, mentally ill offenders) including assessment procedures, counseling techniques and a comprehensive knowledge of the treatment network (in-patient and out-patient).
The Acquisition and Allocation of Probation Resources	Probation departments need to develop improved strategies for the rational allocation of existing resources, focusing on two primary agency needs: (1) better assessment of offender "risk" to public safety (e.g., sex offenders, gang members, drug dealers) (2) the assignment of field staff to areas with greatest public safety needs.	Probation departments need to "make the case" for increased resources for offender treatment and supervision, by proposing legislation that mandates minimum levels of probation (e.g., case load size services) and allows agents to use sanctions as a tool to improve public safety.
Enforcement of Probation Conditions	Probation officers utilize a range of field surveillance techniques to identify offender noncompliance and quickly respond to violations. A structured hierarchy of sanctions will be used for initial violations with revocation and (return to) prison/jail for repeat "offenders."	Probation departments develop strategies (in conjunction with local judiciary) to reduce the number of conditions established and to enforce the conditions set, using a structured hierarchy of non-incarcerative sanctions.
Location of Absconders	Probation departments establish separate probation absconder location and apprehension units to better protect the community.	Probation departments develop a task force to better understand the nature (and impact) of the absconder problem. Utilizing a problem-oriented probation strategy, probation officers will be required directly to focus on addressing the cause(s) of the problem, rather than the consequences.
Partnerships in the Community	A wide range of probation-community partnerships will be developed, including both crime prevention and community betterment activities.	Probation departments will focus on improving the treatment networks in their community and on those related activities that will enhance the supervision function.

SOURCE: Faye Taxman and James Bryne, "Fixing Broken Windows Probation," *Perspectives* 25:2 (2001): 23–29.

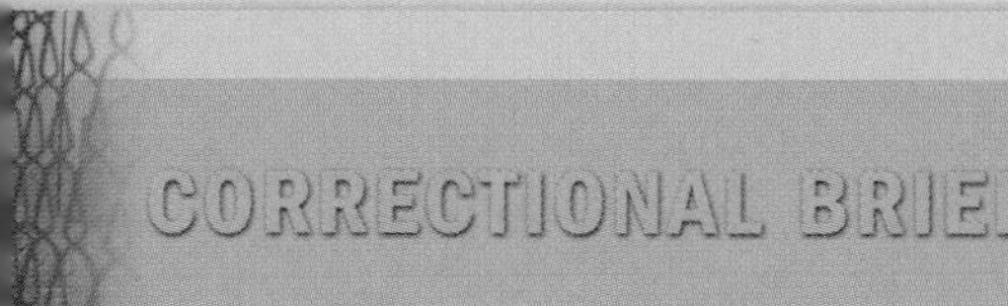

Being Proactive with Offenders in the Community

Proactive community supervision (PCS) improves community supervision by improving offenders' lives and fully restoring them as productive participants to the community. To accomplish this task, agents are active in the communities in which they serve. The PCS model emphasizes offender management tools such as motivational interviewing, risk and needs assessment, quality contact standards, and implementation of "what works" principles that improve an offender's ability to succeed in the community. By using these tools, the role of the agent is changed: Agents become role models of helpful and prosocial behavior for the offenders and the community.

By working with the community, supervision can accomplish the following:

- Protect public safety,
- Hold offenders accountable to victims and the community, and
- Help offenders become responsible and productive.

Under the PCS model:

- Agents' caseloads are reduced to appropriate levels so that agents can spend more time in neighborhoods working one-on-one with offenders;
- Agents and supervisors receive training on how to motivate offenders, identify critical risk factors, and create practical supervision plans; and
- Agents and supervisors receive suitable technological tools such as laptop computers to help them perform their jobs while working outside the office in the community.

The community can expect agents to:

- Spend their days near where parolees and probationers call home;
- Work with parolees and probationers to help them beat the drug and alcohol addictions that can lead them back to crime and violence;
- Help parolees and probationers get basic education and job skills so they can become contributing citizens;
- Build relationships with offenders' families, friends and neighbors—people who can alert agents before trouble arises;
- Intervene before an offender commits a new crime; and
- Respond quickly when an offender's behavior necessitates removal from the community.

SOURCE: Maryland Department of Public Safety and Correctional Services, www.dpscs.state.md.us/rehabservs/ (accessed March 8, 2005).

Back-end solutions refer to ways used to reduce prison populations after the offender arrives in prison. They can be viewed as "early-out" or "extended limits" options: parole, shock parole, emergency release (usually court ordered), expanded good-time credits to count against the minimum sentence, work and educational furlough, prerelease to halfway houses (used extensively by the U.S. Bureau of Prisons, the federal prison system), and other programs. These are explained in Chapter 21.

Probation has established itself as a major component of corrections. It appears the emphasis on probation as the preferred disposition will keep it in the forefront of correctional reform. If the costs of probation and prison are compared, as shown earlier in Table 7.5, daily costs of $4.18 per day as opposed to an average of $62.22 per day in prison, the taxpayer will rule in favor of probation. As the population grows, the number of offenders and variations on probation strategies will surely increase as well. Students of probation concur that the practice is approximately 60 percent effective on a national basis. An alternative to imprisonment that is about one-eighth as costly (and at least as effective) has great appeal and clearly answers the need for a sound and economical approach to corrections.

SUMMARY

Across the nation, probation is administered by hundreds of separate agencies, with a wide variety of rules and structures seen among the states. Whereas one agency may be required to serve juvenile, misdemeanant, and felony offenders, another agency may handle only one type of offender. The term *probation* has various meanings within the multiple areas of corrections. More than 1.35 percent of the nation's adults are on probation on a given day. African Americans, who comprise about 13 percent of the nation's population, represented about a third of the probationers in 2003; Hispanics comprised another 12 percent.[22]

The set of functions, activities, and services that probation performs for its administrative agency and the offender is the probation *process*. The process model for probation service is usually seen as a series of interlinking activities among the courts, the offender, and the offender's community and its resources. The process includes the offender's *reporting* regularly to a probation officer; the *servicing* of the offender's needs through treatment, counseling, and so on; and the officer's *supervision* of the probationer to ensure that the rules of the probation order are observed. Hence, probation today is a process that gives the judge an alternative disposition, which results in an improved status for the offender within a subsystem of the criminal justice system.

REVIEW QUESTIONS

1. Explain the purpose of probation, and describe the methods by which it is usually administered.
2. How do probation officers enforce the conditions ordered by the court?
3. What are some of the restrictions often applied to probation? What kinds of offenders are usually denied probation?
4. Do you think a conflict exists between surveillance and treatment?
5. Identify and define five front-end solutions to prison overcrowding.
6. What are the national trends in probation?
7. Why should probation be the sentence of choice?
8. What are special conditions of probation? Give three examples and explain why they might be imposed.
9. What is the relation of alcohol abuse to criminal behavior?
10. Does drug abuse treatment work? Under what circumstances?
11. Explain the general process of probation revocation.
12. Why would an LSI-R be useful in probation supervision?

ENDNOTES

1. Norman Johnston, *The Human Cage: A Brief History of Prison Architecture* (New York: Walker, 1973), p. 8. See also Herman Bianchi, *Justice as Sanctuary* (Bloomington: Indiana University Press, 1994).
2. See Numbers 35:6 and Joshua 20:2–6.
3. David Fogel, "Nordic Approaches to Crime and Justice," *CJ International* 3:1 (1987): 8–21. See also D. Farabee, M. Pendergast, and D. Anglin, "The Effectiveness of Coerced Treatment for Drug-Abusing Offenders," *Federal Probation* 62:1 (1998): 3–10.
4. Alexander Smith and Louis Berlin, *Introduction to Probation and Parole* (St. Paul, MN: West, 1976), pp. 76–78. See also Edward Latessa and Harry Allen, *Corrections in the Community* (Cincinnati, OH: Anderson Publishing, 2004), pp. 105–106.
5. Harry Elmer Barnes and Negley K. Teeters, *New Horizons in Criminology*, 3rd ed. (Englewood Cliffs, NJ: Prentice Hall, 1959), p. 554.
6. Missouri (1897), Rhode Island (1899), New Jersey (1900), and Vermont (1900).
7. Cook County (Chicago), Illinois.
8. Camille Camp and George Camp, *The Corrections Yearbook 2002* (South Salem, NY: Criminal Justice Institute, 2003), p. 7. For an examination of probationer work groups, see G. Bayens, M. Manske, and J. Smykla, "The Attitudes of Criminal Justice Workgroups Toward Intensive Supervised Probation," *American Journal of Criminal Justice* 22:2 (1998): 189–206.
9. Dennis Sullivan, L. Tifft, and P. Cordella (eds.), "Special Issue: The Phenomenon of Restorative Justice," *Contemporary Justice Review* 1:1 (1998): 1–166.
10. Latessa and Allen, *Corrections in the Community*, pp. 165–166.
11. See F. Taxman and J. Bryne, "Fixing Broken Windows Probation," *Perspectives* 25:2 (2001): 23–29.

12. Harry E. Allen and Julie C. Abril, "Fanning the Flames of Fear Revisited: Three Strikes in California." Paper presented at the Annual Meeting of the American Society of Criminology, Washington, DC, November 11, 1998. See also Eric Lotke, Jason Coburn, and Vincent Schiraldi, "Three Strikes and You're Out," www.justicepolicy.org/ (accessed March 8, 2005).
13. Dan Macallair, "Disposition Case Advocacy in San Francisco's Juvenile Justice System," *Crime and Delinquency* 40:1 (1994): 84–95.
14. See also Mark Umbreit and W. Bradshaw, "Victim Experience of Meeting Adult and Juvenile Offenders," *Federal Probation* 61:4 (1998): 33–39; and David Karp, Gordon Bazemore, and J. D. Chesire, "The Role and Attitudes of Restorative Board Members," *Crime and Delinquency* 50:4 (2004): 487–515.
15. D. Andrews and J. Bonta, *LSI-R, The Level of Service Inventory—Revised* (Toronto: Multi-Health Systems, Inc., 1995).
16. Christopher Lowenkamp, and Edward J. Latessa. *Evaluation of Ohio's CCA Funded Programs* (Cincinnati, OH: Division of Criminal Justice, University of Cincinnati, 2005).
17. Annette Jolin and Brian Stipak, "Drug Treatment and Electronically Monitored Home Confinement," *Crime and Delinquency* 38:2 (1992): 158–170.
18. Paul Gendreau. "The Principles of Effective Interventions with Offenders," in A. T. Harland (ed.), *Choosing Correctional Options That Work: Defining Demand and Evaluating the Supply* (Thousand Oaks, CA: Sage, 1996), pp. 117–130.
19. T. Arola and R. Lawrence, "Broken Windows Probation," *Perspectives* 24:1 (2000): 27–33.
20. The Reinventing Probation Council that drafted the initial report on broken windows and probation included Ronald Corbett, Dan Beto, John DiIulio, J. Richard Faulkner, Bernard Fitzgerald, Irwin Gregg, Norman Helber, Gerald Hinzman, Robert Malvestuto, Mario Paparozzi, Rocco Pozzi, and Edward Rhine. See Reinventing Probation Council, *Transforming Probation through Leadership: The Broken Windows Model,* www.manhattaninstitute.org/html/broken_windows.htm (accessed 2001).
21. Taxman and Bryne, "Fixing Broken Windows Probation."
22. Lauren Glaze and Seri Palla, *Probation and Parole in the United States, 2003* (Washington, DC: U.S. Department of Justice, 2004), p. 4.

CHAPTER 8

Diversion and Intermediate Sanctions

The manifold implications of the concept of community corrections pivot around a profound idea: official reactions to the convicted offender should be related to the community forces which contribute to criminality, which are involved in the definition of crime as a social problem, and which largely determine whether or not rehabilitation programs will produce his integration within the control system regulating the behavior of non-criminals.

—Elmer H. Johnson

KEY WORDS

- diversion
- pretrial intervention programs
- community corrections acts (CCAs)
- intermediate sanctions
- day attendance center
- restitution orders
- house arrest
- electronic monitoring
- risk management
- desistance
- restitution
- intensive supervised probation (ISP)
- tourniquet sentencing
- drug court
- community work order
- home detention
- electronic parole
- community residential treatment center
- day reporting center
- shock probation
- boot camp

OVERVIEW

Our investigation of the correctional process has focused thus far on jails as the entry point of the overall process and on probation as the major non-incarceration sanction arrow in the quiver of the sentencing judges. Although probation is by far the most widely used correctional sanction, it is but one aspect of community corrections. In this chapter we explore some diversion options along with the growing use of intermediate sanctions, which are the various new correctional options used as adjuncts to and part of probation. Note, however, that some jurisdictions use these sanctions not as part of probation but standing on their own.

DIVERSION: KEEPING THE OFFENDER OUT OF THE SYSTEM

Some jurisdictions have established policies to minimize assignment of certain non-dangerous or problematic offenders to the justice system, particularly the mentally disordered,[1] drug abusers,[2] and alcohol abusers.[3] **Diversion** from the criminal justice system has taken place in one form or another since social controls were first established. In most cases, informal diversions merely indicate an official's exercise of discretion at some point in the criminal process.

SIDEBARS

Diversion

The official halting (or suspension) of any legally prescribed processing point after a recorded justice system entry, or formal criminal justice proceedings against an alleged offender, and referral of that person to a treatment or care program administered by a nonjustice or private agency, or no referral.

Officials apply electronic monitoring device to offender's leg.
Photo by Tony Freeman, courtesy of PhotoEdit.

More formal diversions include suspension of the criminal process in favor of some noncriminal disposition. Fewer than 25 percent of reported offenses in America result in an arrest, and only about one-third of those arrests result in a criminal conviction. This is the correctional funnel at work and an indication that preconviction diversion is not uncommon.

Diversion may occur at a number of points in the criminal justice system. The primary points are prior to police contact, prior to official police processing, and prior to official court processing. Three basic models emerge to determine which agency might be responsible for diversion: community-based diversion programs, police-based diversion programs, and court-based diversion programs. Although each of the models usually involves more than one agency or group, programs will generally be grouped according to who initiates the action and what agency will have primary responsibility for its implementation.

Most diversion programs now in effect constitute informal responses to the ambiguities of existing legislation. The value of such programs is difficult if not impossible to estimate. Again, one must try to measure an event that was prevented: What did not happen as a result of diversion? Their goals and procedures must be clearly articulated and integrated into the rest of the criminal justice system.

Community-Based Diversion Programs

Diversion projects are most effective when integrated into a community-based correctional system with many levels of supervision and custody. The currently informal options on an accountable basis must be formalized without making the process too rigid. If community-based programs are too restricted, they will become mere institutions without walls. Diversion is seen as the first threshold of the community corrections system, designed to remove as many offenders as possible from the process before their conviction and labeling as a criminal.

Although programs that aim toward a total or partial alternative to incarceration are improvements, they do not always eliminate the stigma of a criminal record. Diversion programs tied to treatment and services in the community, however, both avoid the problems of incarceration and remove the criminal label. Those programs are seen not as a substitute for probation services but as a method of filling the gap between offenders eligible for probation and cases in which the charges can be dropped. Diversion should be accompanied by a formalized agreement with offenders as to what they are to do in return for the elimination of their arrest records. A set of alternative treatment services and residential reinforcements may be needed to help diverted individuals handle their problems. The diverted individuals should have the advantages available to all other categories of offenders and ex-inmates who are being treated in the local network.

Police-Based Diversion Programs

Police agencies have practiced diversion, informally, by using their power of discretion at the time of an offender's arrest. Several programs have been established to encourage more diversions on a formal basis. Police have been reluctant in the past to formalize their practice of discretion because of public opinion criticizing their actions as being too soft. Most formalized programs are aimed at youthful offenders in an effort to keep them from beginning a career of crime.

Another example of diversionary tactics at the police level is the family crisis intervention approach. This approach, which has been used in several large cities, is especially important as domestic violence laws across the country become more tough and are enforced more often. Laws often now result in the arrest of both parties until the question as to who initiated the violence is resolved. There are indications that the police, by identifying conflict situations at an early stage of development, can prevent the escalation of violence. A general model involves the use of officers specially trained for effective family crisis intervention to respond to family disturbances. The officers attempt to resolve the conflict on the scene. If they cannot, the antagonists are arrested[4] and, in some jurisdictions, referred to a community agency instead of jail.

Court-Based Diversion Programs

The courts are involved with diversion in several ways. One method is to use civil commitment for individuals who presumably can be treated more efficiently in a hospital situation. A more common and reasonable use of diversion by the courts is found in **pretrial intervention programs,** which have been funded extensively by the U.S. Department of Labor. The general pattern of such actions, at the end of the prescribed period of the continuance, is to allow:

1. Dismissal of pending charges based on satisfactory project participation and demonstrated self-improvement
2. Extension of the continuance to allow the program staff more time to work with the person (usually for an additional thirty to ninety days)
3. Return of the defendant to normal court processing, without prejudice, because of unsatisfactory performance in the program.

Diversion is especially appropriate for the public drunk and the first-time drug abuser, a major thrust behind the drug court movement. The current alternative to incarceration for public drunks is to send them to a detoxification center. Voluntary attendance at detoxification centers demonstrates the willingness of many problem drinkers to accept treatment, if only for free room and board.

The severity of criminal sanctions and public reaction to most drug offenses makes the diversion of drug abuse cases a sensitive area. With the country awash in illegal drugs, and drug use by the general population quite high, the wave of enforcement activity has made it difficult to divert all but the least violent of users, leaving the hard cases to sweat it out in institutions that seldom provide meaningful programs. Most diversion programs for drug users are concentrated on juveniles and are aimed at first-time arrestees, although drug courts address all age groups.

The spectrum of diversionary programs is geared toward the same goal: provision of a reasonable alternative to incarceration in large, overcrowded, and punitive prisons.[5] Again, as in the development of many other aspects of correctional services, such programs often begin as independent actions by concerned professionals and community groups. As a result of earlier efforts, **community corrections acts (CCAs)** have been authorized as a statutory medium for including citizens and bringing funding to local governments and county agencies to plan, develop, and deliver correctional services and sanctions at the local level.[6] At least twenty-two states have passed such enabling legislation, encouraging intermediate sanctions, advocacy for juveniles, local community organization involvement, victim–offender reconciliation, victim restitution, employment services, and county residential facilities, among many others. Some private state contracts with prison agencies for county programs offer to leave control at the community level. Subsidiaries can be provided, or a super agency can be structured to meet the needs of all offenders throughout the state. The best implemented CCAs are in Colorado and Florida, which offer model programs that could be copied by other jurisdictions.

BETWEEN PROBATION AND PRISONS

The dominant characteristic of intermediate sanctions is the use of increased surveillance and tighter controls over nonincarcerated offenders. In this context intermediate sanctions are referred to as "punishing smarter," since the sanction is thought to be tough enough to impress upon the offender the seriousness of the act, without the costs associated with longer-term incarceration. Advocates for the offender object on the basis that these efforts use increased punishment as a rationale and tighter controls are not needed. Others argue that prison construction is too expensive for most jurisdictions and intermediate sanctions save the costs of constructing, staffing, and maintaining incarceration facilities. Still other proponents see intermediate sanctions as a way to push for more treatment and services, which are thought to be more readily available (and more effective) in the community. These advocates note the reintegrative aspects of intermediate sanctions and point to reduced recidivism among offenders assigned to such programs. Some intermediate sanctions are less expensive and more effective than incarceration, while others are clearly intended to "get tough" with offenders. Although not yet fully integrated into the coordinated system of community corrections, these intermediate sanctions are rapidly being adopted across the nation into a wide system of local, county, state, and federal correctional systems. We first review the use of intermediate sanctions as an adjunct to probation.

As we saw in the previous chapter, probation has become the backbone of contemporary corrections and is used to treat offenders and provide protection to the community through supervising probationers. In the last two decades, prompted by crowding of jails and prisons as well as a shift in the philosophical assumptions about controlling offenders,[7] a broad range of different treatments and innovative technologies has been developed. These innovative programs and control schemes are generally called **intermediate sanctions.**[8] A study of intermediate sanctions must start with a look at the overcrowding issue.

CORRECTIONAL BRIEF

Intermediate Sanctions

Intermediate sanctions, ranging in severity from day fines to so-called boot camps, are interventions that are beginning to fill the sentencing gap between prison at one extreme and probation at the other. Lengthy prison terms may be inappropriate for some offenders; for others, probation may be too inconsequential and may not provide the degree of public supervision necessary to ensure public safety.

By expanding sentencing options, intermediate sanctions enable the criminal justice system to tailor punishment more closely to the nature of the crime and the criminal. An appropriate range of punishments makes it possible for the system to hold offenders strictly accountable for their actions.

Intermediate sanctions provide economic disincentives for criminal behavior, permit effective and efficient use of limited criminal justice resources, strengthen the credibility of the court, and provide revenue to offset not only program cost but also victim loss.

SOURCES: Voncile Gowdy, *Intermediate Sanctions* (Washington, DC: U.S. Department of Justice, 1993), p. 1; Office of Justice Programs, *How to Use Structured Fines (Day Fines) as an Intermediate Sanction* (Washington, DC: U.S. Department of Justice, 1996); and K. Cartwright, B. Applegate, R. Mutchnick, et al. "Interventions with DWIs and Drug Offenders using Electronic Monitoring," *Federal Probation* 61:3 (1997): 19–22.

OVERCROWDING

The impetus for the development and expansion of community corrections and intermediate sanctions has been the overcrowding of our jails and prisons. Most repeat offenders receive increasingly severe punishments,[9] including sentences to jail and prison. In the United States, the lag between onset of offending and eventual confinement as an adult is approximately ten years. In other words, *persistent* offenders are more likely to have been subject to other correctional control (fines, **day attendance centers, restitution orders, house arrest,** and even **electronic monitoring**) while in the community prior to their first incarceration.

The processing of offenders in the justice system has become a **risk management** strategy, and persistent offenders are usually given increasingly restrictive alternatives while corrections tries to stop their criminal behavior (that is, encourage **desistance**). Many offenders are given a number of such opportunities and assistance before a sentencing judge resorts to incarceration, the most punitive weapon in the armory of corrections.

Before the 1970s, many if not most offenders were placed on probation, to achieve the ideal of rehabilitation.[10] Individualized treatment during that relatively progressive era became subject to strong attack by conservatives, researchers, and liberals of many stripes. The arguments were that prison and parole officials were abusing their discretion, rehabilitation did not work, strict law and order should be used to capture the streets, and offenders richly deserved punishment. This was seen as the only way to protect law-abiding citizens as well as to retain the social fabric. This philosophy was particularly evident in the nation's War on Drugs program, a war that has clearly not been won.[11]

Coupled with the demise of the medical model, politicians at both local and national levels used the issue of crime as a vehicle to demonstrate how getting tough would solve the problem.[12] Seeking reelection on the hard-line bandwagon may have served narrow political ends. However, it also led to the enactment of a series of stringent policies ranging from a shift to determinate punishment, to mandatory minimum sentences to prison, and to the building of more supermax prisons.[13]

These events coincided with the 1945 to 1976 "baby boom" population bulge, whose members entered the "high commitment" years of ages twenty-nine to thirty-nine between 1975 and 1985. These four major forces—a larger number of persons at risk to commit crime and be incarcerated, the shift to conservative beliefs about how to deal with offenders and crime, the War on Drugs,[14] and enactment of more stringent punishments—contributed to an ever-increasing stream of offenders being committed to prison (up from 448,264 in 1975 to over 2.1 million in 2004).[15] By 1998, the combined number of prisoners in the nation and in jails exceeded any previous total. "America the Free" has become the free world's leader in rate of incarceration, exceeding even the Russian Republic of the former Soviet Union. Prisons bulge, and the nation continues its building binge, trying to construct sufficient numbers of jail and prison cells to accommodate the massive increase of incarcerated offenders. When it earlier became evident that the bricks and mortar approach could not be met, correctional innovators turned to developing alternative punishment programs, variously known as intermediate sanctions or intermediate punishments. A study in 2004 showed comparisons of rates of incarceration among the United States, South Africa, the Russian Republic, and other nations[16] (see Figure 8.1). What is interesting in this study is the comparison with the rest of the world's industrialized nations.

FIGURE 8.1

Rate of Incarceration in Selected Nations

SOURCE: The Sentencing Project, *New Incarceration Figures: Rising Population Despite Falling Crime Rates* (Washington, DC: TSP, 2004), p. 6.

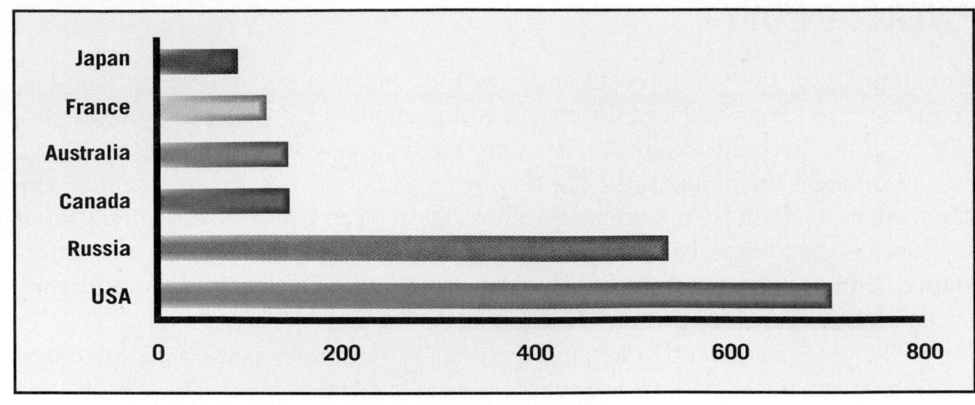

SIDEBARS

Attractiveness of Intermediate Sanctions

Intermediate sanctions are attractive for the following five reasons:

1. Channeling offenders into community-based corrections is believed to be able to reduce or delay prison overcrowding.
2. Intermediate punishments are designed for offenders believed to pose too much risk for probation services but not enough risk to be sent to prison.
3. They are generally less expensive than incarceration in either jail or prison.
4. They are believed to offer more rehabilitation and reintegration potential than does incarceration.
5. It is believed that expansion and fine-tuning of alternative sanctions will eventually lead to a valid continuum of sentencing alternatives.

SOURCE: Peter Wood and H. Grasmick, "Toward the Development of Punishment Equivalencies," Justice Quarterly *16:1 (1999): 19–50.*

SIDEBARS

Restitution

A court-ordered condition of probation that requires the offender to repair the financial, emotional, or physical damage done (a reparative sentence) by making financial payment of money to the victim or, alternatively, to a fund to provide services to victims. In addition, restitution programs are frequently ordered in the absence of a sentence to probation.

INTERMEDIATE SANCTIONS

Intermediate sanctions provide midrange dispositions that better reflect the severity of the offense than do probation or imprisonment. While many if not most offenders can best be served by reintegration programming, some are thought to be too dangerous to be released to traditional probation supervision with infrequent face-to-face contacts. Thus, a continuum of sanctions ranging from probation to imprisonment has been developed: restitution, fines, day fines, community service, intensive supervised probation, house arrest, electronic monitoring, and shock incarceration. The latter includes shock probation and shock parole, as well as boot camps. Figure 8.2 depicts the range of sentencing options. We begin our more detailed examination of these programs with restitution.

Restitution Programs

A common condition for probation is the requirement that victims be compensated for their losses or injury as a form of **restitution.** The emphasis given to the study of victimology in the last few years has resulted in some state compensation of crime victims by payment of medical costs and other financial reimbursement. Through the system of probation, however, the offender often repays the victim. It is important that probation authorities link the amount of payment to the offender's ability to pay. Paying on installments is usually the most realistic approach. In some cases a partial restitution may be all that is reasonably possible (for example, in the case of an arsonist who burns down a multimillion-dollar building).

Many reasons are offered to support restitution programs. Obviously, restitution offsets the victim's loss when property is stolen; restitution can even be ordered for the deductible amount an insurance company might require an insured victim to pay before the insurance coverage would become effective. Time lost from work while being a witness in court and being hospitalized are subject to offender restitution. It appears that restitution may be ordered for any injury caused by the offense for which the offender was convicted. Other rationales are that restitution forces the offender to accept personal responsibility for the crime; restitution can lead to reconciliation of offender and victim[17]; and, finally, it provides one way the victim can overcome the otherwise impersonal processing of victims within the justice system. Although more than 30 percent of all adults on probation in 1995 and 12 percent of offenders on felony probation in 2002 were ordered to make restitution,[18] it appears that restitution programs are more numerous in the juvenile justice systems than they are in the adult system.[19] Although almost every state has restitution programs in operation, Georgia, Texas, Florida, Minnesota, and Michigan appear to be leaders in program development.

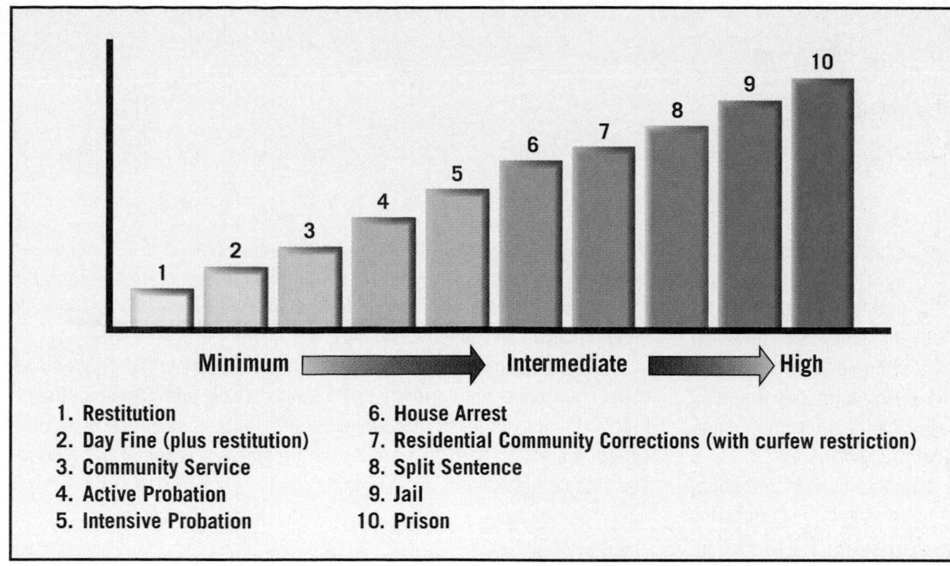

FIGURE 8.2

A Range of Sentencing Options, Ranked by the Level of Punishment

SOURCE: James Byrne, "The Future of Intensive Probation Supervision," *Crime and Delinquency* 36:1 (1990): 3–34.

(Restitution programs also have been extensively implemented and evaluated in Great Britain, Austria, Germany, and Australia.) In Minnesota, parolees may also be required to reside in a residential restitution center and pay part of their wages to victims. Other jurisdictions require victim–offender conferences to establish the amount of financial compensation due the victim.

SIDEBARS

Restitution Center

Residential facility to which offenders who fall behind on their restitution payments are sent to live until they catch up on payments.

Intensive Supervised Probation

Another alternative sanction program is **intensive supervised probation (ISP)**, which is designed to provide increased surveillance of offenders deemed to be too serious for "routine" probation. The program is a management strategy for probation services that need to increase the level of surveillance for individuals who do not adjust to regular probation requirements. ISP is a program frequently found in **tourniquet sentencing.**

Georgia is believed to have been the first jurisdiction to impose a statewide system of ISP (starting in 1974) and, by 1990, every state had at least one jurisdiction—city, county, or state—with the program. There is no generic ISP. It is a form of release that emphasizes close monitoring of convicted offenders and requires rigorous conditions on that release. Most ISP programs call for the following[20]:

- Some combination of multiple weekly contacts with a supervising officer
- Random and unannounced drug testing
- Stringent enforcement of probation or parole conditions
- Required participation in relevant treatment programs, employment, and perhaps community service.

Current issues largely revolve around the effectiveness of intensive supervision. Yet, measures of success vary depending on the stated goals and objectives each program sets out to address.[21] For instance, the goals of a treatment-oriented program differ from the goals of a program that places emphasis on offender punishment and control. However, it is possible to isolate two overriding themes of recent intensive supervision programs that raise several issues. First, "intensive probation supervision is expected to divert offenders from incarceration in order to alleviate prison overcrowding, avoid the exorbitant costs of building and sustaining prisons, and prevent the stultifying and stigmatizing effects of imprisonment." Second, ISP is expected to

SIDEBARS

Tourniquet Sentencing

James Byrne has identified the major sanction options that sentencing might impose, and ranked them by levels of punishment inherent in each. Restitution, for example, is seen as less punitive than community service; house arrest is a lower level of punishment than jail incarceration. You should remember that judges can and frequently do impose several sanctions simultaneously and retain authority to initiate tourniquet sentencing, a process that increases and tightens the numbers and conditions of punishments until the probationer is brought under the most effective control.

SOURCE: James Byrne, "The Future of Intensive Probation Supervision," Crime and Delinquency *36:1 (1990): 3–34; Edward Latessa and Harry Allen,* Corrections in the Community *(Cincinnati, OH: Anderson Publishing, 2003).*

CORRECTIONAL BRIEF

Types of ISPS

ISPs are usually classified as prison diversion, enhanced probation, and enhanced parole. Each has a different goal.

Diversion is commonly referred to as a "front door" program because its goal is to limit the number of offenders entering prison. Prison diversion programs generally identify incoming lower-risk inmates to participate in an ISP in the community as a substitute for a prison term. Day reporting centers are usually programs to divert drug-abusing offenders from criminal court processing and possible commitment to prison.

Enhancement programs generally select already sentenced probationers and parolees and subject them to closer supervision in the community than would regular probation or parole. People placed in ISP-enhanced probation or enhanced parole programs show evidence of failure under routine supervision or have committed offenses deemed to be too serious for supervision on routine caseloads.

Treatment and service components in the ISPs included drug and alcohol counseling, employment, community service, and payment of restitution. On many of these measures, ISP offenders participated more than control members; participation in such programs was found to be correlated with a reduction in recidivism.

SOURCE: Joan Petersilia and Susan Turner, *Evaluating Intensive Supervision of Probation/Parole: Results of a Nationwide Experiment* (Washington, DC: U.S. Department of Justice, 1993), pp. 2, 7; Ernest Cowles, R. Schmidtz and B. Bass. *An Implementation of Pretrial and Drug Intervention Program in Illinois Macon and Peoria Counties* (Chicago, IL: Illinois Criminal Justice Information Authority, 1998).

promote public safety through surveillance strategies, while promoting a sense of responsibility and accountability through probation fees, restitution, and community service activities.[22] These goals generate issues regarding the ability of ISP programs to reduce recidivism, divert offenders from prison, and ensure public safety.

In a study summarizing the state of ISP, Fulton, Latessa, Stichman, and Travis[23] summarize the findings concerning ISP:

- ISPs have failed to alleviate prison crowding.
- Most ISP studies have found no significant differences between recidivism rates of ISP offenders and offenders with comparison groups.
- There appears to be a relationship between greater participation in treatment and employment programs and lower recidivism rates.
- ISPs appear to be more effective than regular supervision or prison in meeting offenders' needs.
- ISPs that reflect certain principles of effective intervention are associated with lower rates of recidivism.
- ISP does provide an intermediate punishment.
- Although ISPs are less expensive than prison, they are more expensive than originally thought.

The debate over control versus treatment has raged for many years. Recently, there has been a new movement, initiated by the American Probation and Parole Association, to develop a more balanced approach to ISP supervision.[24] This approach continues to support strict conditions and supervision practices, but within the context of more services and higher-quality treatment.

Drug and Other Problem-Solving Courts

In recent years, many judges have become disillusioned with the revolving door of jail and prison for offenders who suffered from addictions and mental disorders. As a result there has been an explosion of so-called therapeutic courts,

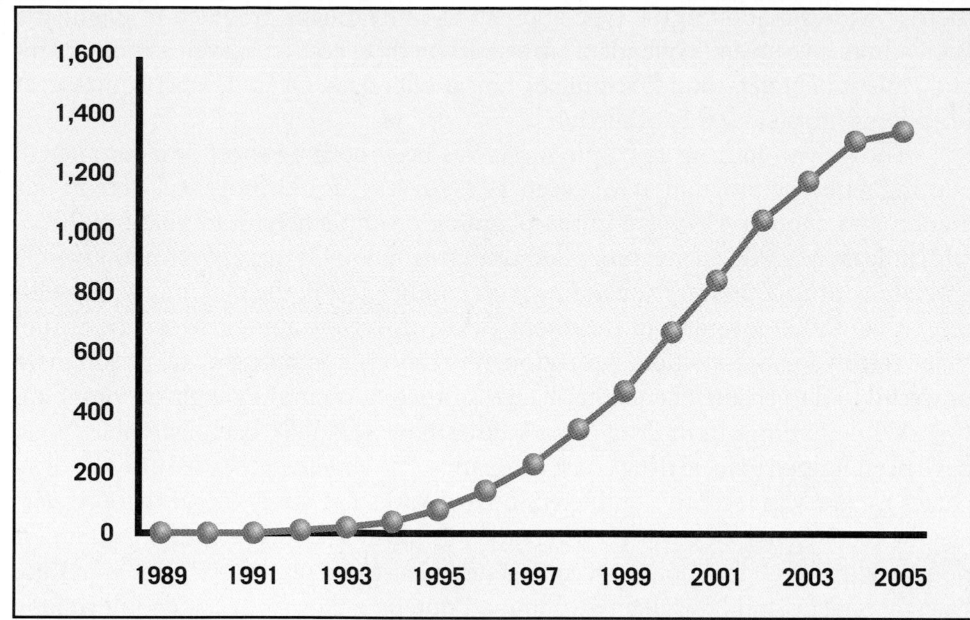

FIGURE 8.3

Operational Drug Courts in the United States, 2005

SOURCE: National Drug Institute, "Drug Courts: A National Phenomenon," www.ndci.org/courtfacts.htm (accessed April 29, 2005). Data for 2004 and 2005 are extrapolated.

ranging from mental health to domestic violence. Figure 8.3 shows the number of problem-solving courts throughout the United States. The greatest number of these specialty courts has been for drug offenders. **Drug courts** divert drug-abusing offenders to intensively monitored treatment instead of incarceration. The main purpose of drug court programs is to use the authority of the court to reduce crime by changing defendants' drug-using behavior. Under this concept, in exchange for the possibility of dismissed charges or reduced sentences, defendants are diverted to drug court programs in various ways and at various stages of the judicial process, depending on the circumstances. Judges preside over drug court proceedings; monitor the progress of defendants through frequent status hearings; and prescribe sanctions and rewards as appropriate in collaboration with prosecutors, defense attorneys, treatment providers, and others. Basic elements of a drug court include the following[25]:

- A single drug court judge and staff who provide both focus and leadership
- Expedited adjudication through early identification and referral of appropriate program participants, initiating treatment as soon as possible after arrest
- Both intensive treatment and aftercare for drug-abusing defendants
- Comprehensive, in-depth, and coordinated supervision of drug defendants in regular (sometimes daily) status hearings that monitor both treatment progress and offender compliance
- Enhanced and increasing defendant accountability under a graduated series of rewards and punishments appropriate to conforming or violative behavior
- Mandatory and frequent drug (and alcohol) testing
- Supervised and individual case monitoring.

Drug court programs are highly diverse in approach, characteristics, and completion and retention rates, as discussed later. Some programs report that they deferred prosecuting offenders who would enter the program; others allowed offenders to enter the program after their case had been adjudicated; and still others allowed offenders to enter their program on a trial basis after entering a plea. Yet all programs have a treatment component as part of their overall program, although there is wide variation in the type and extent of treatment provided to offenders. Both adults and juvenile offenders are served by drug courts, as well as nonviolent and violent offenders, and first-time or repeat offenders. Overall, most courts treat offenders with a substance addiction.

The growth in drug court programs has been nothing short of phenomenal. Starting with one program in Miami in 1989, at least 1,183 programs were in operation and another 414 were in the planning or implementation phase in 2003, with at least 229,000 clients processed or in treatment. Of these, over 380 juvenile and family drug courts were operating with another 162 in the planning stage, with more than 9,000 juveniles in treatment.[26] The threat of immediate sanctions (jail time, return for prosecution, probation revocation, commitment to prison) is a powerful tool to ensure client compliance and retention in the treatment program.

While findings from drug court studies have generally been favorable, most have been limited to local drug court programs. The largest statewide study on drug courts to date was recently conducted in New York. The study found that on average the reconviction rate was 29 percent lower for drug court participants than for nonparticipants.[27] In another recent statewide study of drug courts in Ohio, Latessa, Shaffer, and Lowenkamp examined outcome data from both adult (felony and misdemeanants) and juvenile drug court programs.[28] The results from this study are illustrated in Figure 8.4. The data show some variation in the results across drug courts, but overall participants in drug courts reported 15 percent lower rearrest rates than those drug offenders who did not participate in a drug court program.

In addition to reducing recidivism, drug courts have been found to be cost effective. A study done by the Washington State Institute for Public Policy estimated that the average drug court participant produces $6,779 in benefits.[29] In New York researchers estimate that $254 million in incarceration costs were saved by diverting 18,000 offenders to drug court. Finally, California researchers concluded that drug courts in that state save $18 million per year.[30]

Compared to jail and prison, drug courts appear to be cost effective and to reduce criminal conduct. While similar data are not yet available on mental health court and other problem-solving court programs, drug courts are galvanizing if not revolutionizing the criminal justice system response to drug abuse.[31]

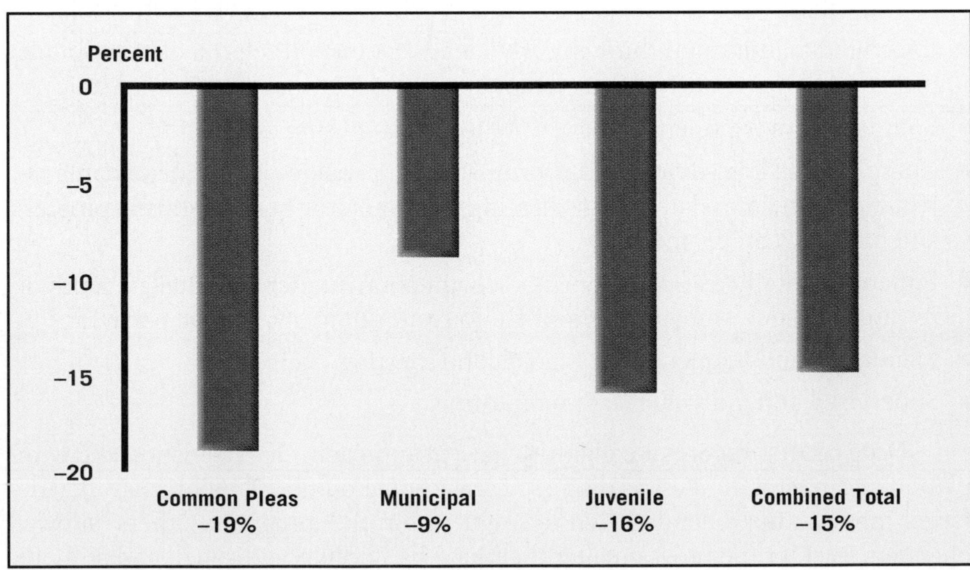

FIGURE 8.4

Reductions in Rearrest Rates Between Drug Courts and Comparison Groups Across All Drug Court Groups

SOURCE: Edward Latessa, D. Shaffer, and C. Lowenkamp, *Outcome Evaluation of Ohio's Drug Court Efforts* (Cincinnati, OH; Center for Criminal Justice Research, University of Cincinnati, 2002), p. 7.

Community Service Programs

Community service or work order programs represent court-ordered unpaid work for a specific number of hours that offenders must perform, usually in the form of free labor to some charitable organization or in public service such as serving as a volunteer hospital orderly, doing street cleaning, performing maintenance or repair of public housing, or providing service to indigent groups. Some examples of the latter would be sentencing a dentist to perform 100 hours of free dental service for welfare recipients or a physician to provide 50 hours of free medical attention to jail inmates on Saturdays.

SIDEBARS

Community Service

A program of compensation for injury to society by offender performance of service in the community, without pay.

Both **community work orders** and restitution programs have their critics.[32] Some argue that offenders committing crimes of violence should not be allowed a penalty less than incarceration for their offenses, and that the physical and psychological costs to victims of crimes of violence are almost impossible to calculate. There also seems to be some uncertainty over whether an offender sentenced to perform community work or restitution ought to be resentenced to incarceration for noncompliance. Despite the criticism, there appears to be consensus that offenders should repay their victims for losses, even if the repayment is as symbolic as community work. A recent study of a community service program designed as an alternative to incarceration for adult misdemeanor offenders found a 66 percent completion rate.[33]

Home Detention

In the United States, house arrest usually conjures up images of political control and fascist repression,[34] but it is actually court-ordered **home detention**, the confining of offenders to their households for the duration of their sentence. Introduced in 1984, in Florida, home detention rapidly spread throughout a nation searching for punitive, safe, and secure alternatives to incarceration.[35] The sentence is usually imposed in conjunction with probation but may be imposed by the court as a separate punishment (as it is in Florida). Florida's Community Control Program (FCCP) was

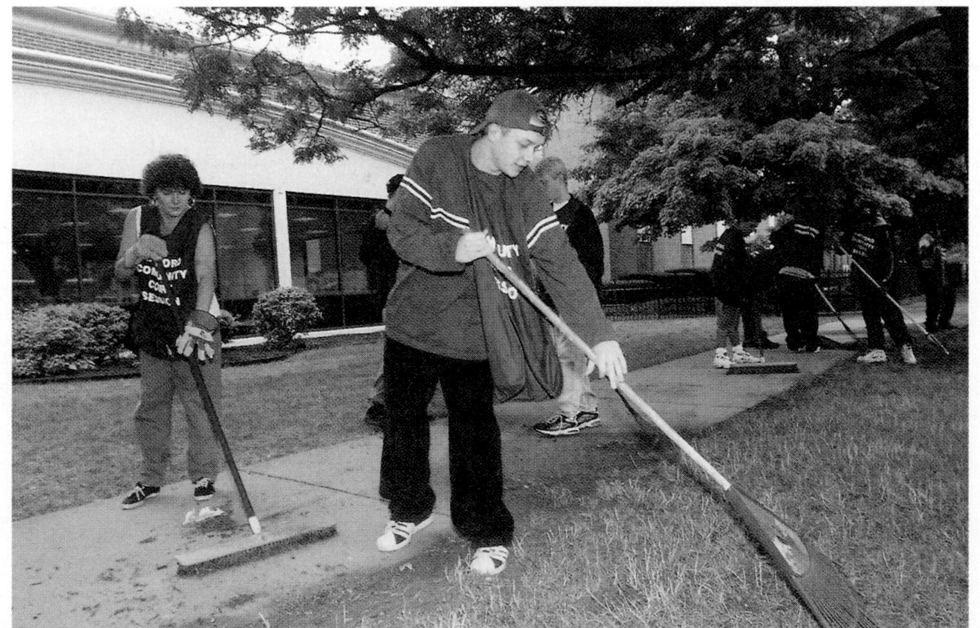

Community service is a major option to incarceration.
Courtesy of AP/Wide World Photos.

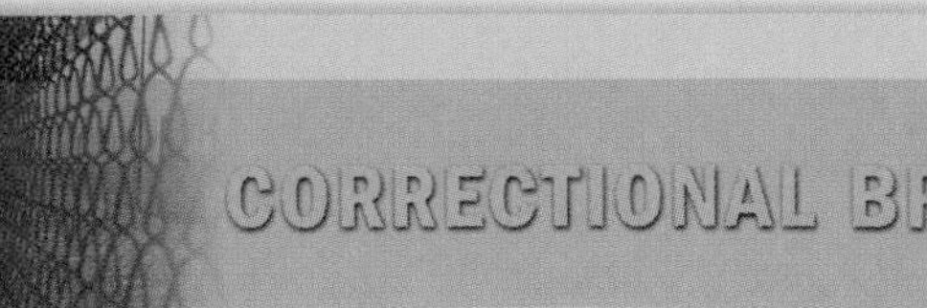

Florida Community Control Program (FCCP)

FCCP is in no way soft treatment for those sentenced to it. Although based in the community rather than behind bars, it is punishment oriented, with stringent safeguards for the public's safety. Those offenders not actually undertaking an approved activity such as drug treatment are often under house arrest. Supervising officers visit them a minimum of 28 times a month, and the state's sentencing guidelines list a term on community control as just below prison—and ahead of jail—in severity.

The National Council on Crime and Delinquency [evaluation] found that not only has the program helped alleviate prison crowding, the offenders who complete the program demonstrate a lower new offense rate than those released from a prison term for similar offenses.

SOURCE: Charles DeWitt, in Dennis Wagner and Christopher Baird (eds.), *Evaluation of the Florida Community Control Program* (Washington, DC: U.S. Department of Justice, 1993), p. 2.

designed to provide a safe diversion alternative and to help address the problem of prison population escalation and associated high costs.[36]

Participants may be required to make victim compensation, perform community work service, pay probation fees, undergo drug and alcohol testing, and, in some instances, wear electronic monitoring equipment to verify their presence in the residence. (In some jurisdictions, house arrest is used on a pretrial basis, as an isolated sentence, in conjunction with probation or parole, or with a prerelease status such as education or work furlough.) House arrest allows the offender to leave his or her residence only for specific purposes and hours approved by the court or supervising officer. Being absent without leave is a technical violation of conditions that may result in resentencing to jail or prison.[37] Home detention is a punitive sentence and was designed in most cases to relieve institutional overcrowding. For many offenders it is their last chance to escape from being committed to prison. In addition to surveillance of the offender, home detention is viewed as a cost avoidance program, a front-end solution to prison overcrowding, and a flexible alternative for certain offenders (such as a pregnant offender until time of delivery). The use of telemonitoring devices, discussed later, can significantly increase the correctional surveillance of offenders.

The most significant critical argument against home detention is that, by making a nonincarcerative control mechanism available to corrections, many petty offenders are brought under correctional control who would best be handled by diversion, fines, or mental health services. In general, such inclusive actions are viewed as "net widening," which occurs when offenders are sentenced to community control who might otherwise have received a lesser or even no sentence.[38]

The National Council on Crime and Delinquency conducted an evaluation of the FCCP and concluded that the impact on prison crowding, offender behavior, and state correctional costs has been positive. With an estimated prison diversion rate of 54 percent, community control is cost effective despite the combined effect of net widening and the punishments imposed on almost 10 percent of FCCP participants for technical violations. Furthermore, the new offense rate for community control offenders is lower than that for similar offenders sentenced to prison and released without supervision. For every 100 cases diverted from prison, Florida saved more than $250,000.[39] Home detention is expected to receive increased endorsement in this millennium and may become the sentence of choice for many nonviolent offenders in lieu of jail, prison, or even formal probation.[40]

Electronic Monitoring

Home detention has a long history as a criminal penalty, but its new popularity with correctional authorities is due to the advent of electronic monitoring, a technological link that is thought to make the sanction both practical and affordable. The concept of electronic monitoring is not new, and was proposed in 1964 by Schwitzgebel as **electronic parole.** It was initially used to monitor the location of mental patients.[41] One of the first studies of home detention enforced by electronic monitoring began in 1986 and, by early 1998, it was estimated that there were 1,500 electronic programs and 95,000 monitoring units in use.[42]

Electronic monitoring can be active or passive. In active monitoring, a transmitter attached to the offender's wrist or ankle sends signals relayed by a home telephone to the supervising office during the hours the offender is required to be at home. Under passive monitoring, a computer program is used to call the offender randomly during the hours designated for home confinement. The offender inserts the wristlet or anklet into a verifier to confirm his or her presence in the residence. There does not appear to be any difference in recidivism between those on passive or active systems. (Only about one in three offenders on home detention wear monitoring devices, although there were 19,000 probation and parole cases under electronic monitoring in 1998.)[43]

SIDEBARS

Electronic Monitoring

A surveillance program that utilizes computer technology and devices that monitor the presence of offenders under home detention. It can also be used to detect alcohol and drug use, as well as the exact location of the offender outside of the dwelling (global positioning system).

National surveys indicate that electronic monitoring was initially (1987) used for property offenders on probation, but a much broader range of offenders is being monitored now than in the past. Monitoring has been expanded to include probationers but also to follow up on persons after incarceration, to control those sentenced to community corrections, and to monitor persons before trial or sentencing. Studies of telemonitoring of offenders noted certain findings:

- Most jurisdictions using electronic monitoring tested some offenders for drug use, and many routinely tested all. Some sites charged for the testing; more than 66 percent charged offenders for at least part of the cost of leasing the monitoring equipment.
- The average monitoring term in 1989 was 79 days. The longer the period of monitoring, the higher the odds of success. The chances of termination do not

CORRECTIONAL BRIEF

Electronically Monitored House Arrest

One study of the use of electronically monitored home detention focused not on persons already convicted but on defendants awaiting trial. The research site was Marion County (Indianapolis), Indiana, and only defendants who did not qualify for release on recognizance, could not raise bail, and could not secure a bondsman were considered for pretrial home detention. The pretrial program's goal was to ensure the defendant's presence in court while relieving jail congestion. Fewer than 25 percent of referred detainees passed screening; most failed the "suitable residence with telephone" criterion for inclusion in the project. Alleged crimes among defendants accepted for home pretrial detention included theft, DUI, forgery, habitual traffic offenses, disorderly conduct, and drug law violations.

Home detention with electronic monitoring was successful for 73 percent of participants. Defendants most likely to complete home detention successfully lived with a spouse or opposite-gender roommate. Of the 27 percent failures, 13 percent were technical violators, and 14 percent were absconders. Those most likely to abscond were eventually sentenced to jail or prison. In the United Kingdom, some 82 percent successfully completed their supervision.

SOURCES: Voncile Gowdy, *Intermediate Sanctions* (Washington, DC: U.S. Department of Justice, 1993), p. 6; and Ed Mortimer and C. May, *Electronic Monitoring in Practice* (London: U.K. Home Office, 1997).

vary by type of offense, except that those committing major traffic violations committed fewer technical violations and new offenses.

- There were no significant differences in successful terminations among probationers, offenders on parole, or those in community corrections. All had successful termination rates ranging between 74 and 86 percent.
- Rule violations resulted in reincarceration, brief confinement at a residential facility, intensified office reporting requirements, stricter curfews, or additional community service.[44]
- The experience of other countries using electronic monitoring indicates an uneven value as a reintegration program.[45]

Recent evaluations of electronic monitoring in Los Angeles and Lake County, Illinois, and in the states of Oklahoma, Florida, and Texas, and England and Wales[46] have shown mixed results. While the technology no doubt will be improved and expanded in the coming decade, many unanswered questions remain about the effectiveness of electronic monitoring.

Community Residential Treatment Centers

SIDEBARS

Community Corrections

Community corrections is a general term used to refer to various types of noninstitutional correctional programs for criminal offenders. These programs, including diversion, pretrial release, probation, restitution and community service, temporary release, halfway houses, and parole, form a continuum of options for dealing with offenders in the community. Although each program offers different services and serves different groups of offenders, their similarities outweigh their differences.

Formerly known as halfway houses, **community residential treatment centers** are a valuable adjunct to community control and treatment services. Originally designed as residences for homeless men, they are now seen as the possible nuclei of community-based correctional networks of residential centers, drug-free and alcohol-free living spaces, prerelease guidance centers, and private sector involvement with multiple-problem offenders in need of intensive services. They also serve as noninstitutional residence facilities for a number of different classes of offenders, most of whom are high-need offenders and pose a medium to high risk to community corrections.

University of Cincinnati investigators headed by Edward Latessa have conducted much of the contemporary evaluative work in the area of community residential centers. A synopsis of a program evaluation will suffice to suggest how community residential centers fit into intermediate sanctions. In evaluating a treatment program for adult offenders sentenced to probation, Latessa and Travis found that, in comparison with other similarly situated offenders, members of their study group had less formal education and were far less likely to have married. They exhibited more prior involvement in alcohol and drug treatment, and suffered from more psychiatric problems. Hence, the study group was higher need, higher risk, and more likely to recidivate. The center's clients received more services and treatment in almost every area examined. Even though prior criminal histories would have predicted higher failure rates, the center's clients did as well as the comparison group in terms of reoffending. Employment services and enrolling in an educational program reduced recidivism.[47]

SIDEBARS

Community Residential Treatment Center

A nonconfining residential facility for adjudicated adults or juveniles or those subject to criminal or juvenile proceedings, intended as an alternative to confinement for persons not suited for probation or needing a period of readjustment to the community after confinement.

In the largest studies of residential correctional programs ever conducted, University of Cincinnati researchers examined nearly 14,000 offenders served by over forty-five residential programs in Ohio. Overall figures indicated that the residential programs resulted in slightly reduced recidivism rates. However, when the risk level of the offenders was factored in, the results showed that most of the programs had a significant impact with high-risk offenders, but actually increased the failure rates for lower-risk offenders.[48] This finding was not unexpected, since other studies have also shown detrimental effects with low-risk offenders.[49] Figures 8.5 and 8.6 show the results from this study.

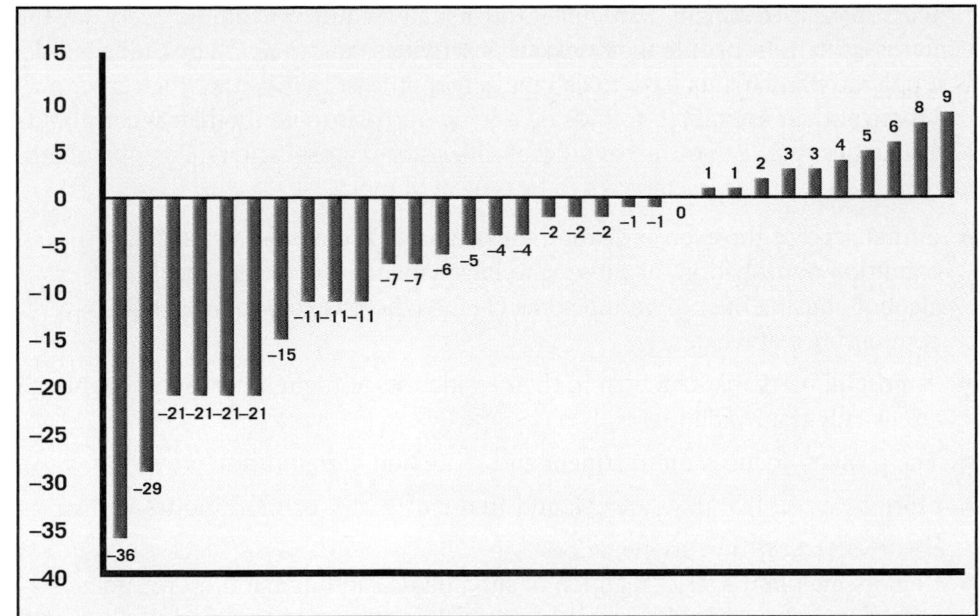

FIGURE 8.5

Treatment Effects for Low-Risk Offenders

- Numbers represent difference in predicted recidivism rates between the comparison and treatment groups.
- Negative numbers indicate a difference favoring the comparison group.
- Each column represents a different program in the study.

SOURCE: C. Lowenkamp and E. Latessa, *Evaluation of Ohio's Halfway House and Community Based Correctional Facilities* (Cincinnati, OH: University of Cincinnati, 2002).

Clearly, for high-risk offenders, residential centers that provide specific client-needed services can be valuable assets in offender control and outcome,[50] particularly for community control clients whose technical violations are a result of high needs otherwise unaddressed within the community.

Day Reporting Centers

The **day reporting center** (called the *attendance center* in Australia) is an intermediate punishment option usually associated with probation but which also can accept parolees, parole violators, furloughees from prison, and persons on pretrial release or early release from jail. The center provides a variety of treatment and referral programs, along with extensive supervision and surveillance.

Most centers operate in late afternoon and evening hours and are staffed by probation officers, treatment specialists, vocational counselors, and volunteers; the

SIDEBARS

Day Reporting Center

Facility to which offenders are sent for scheduling and monitoring of their activities. The centers also accommodate potentially failing probationers as well as probation violators who attend day-long treatment and intervention programs.

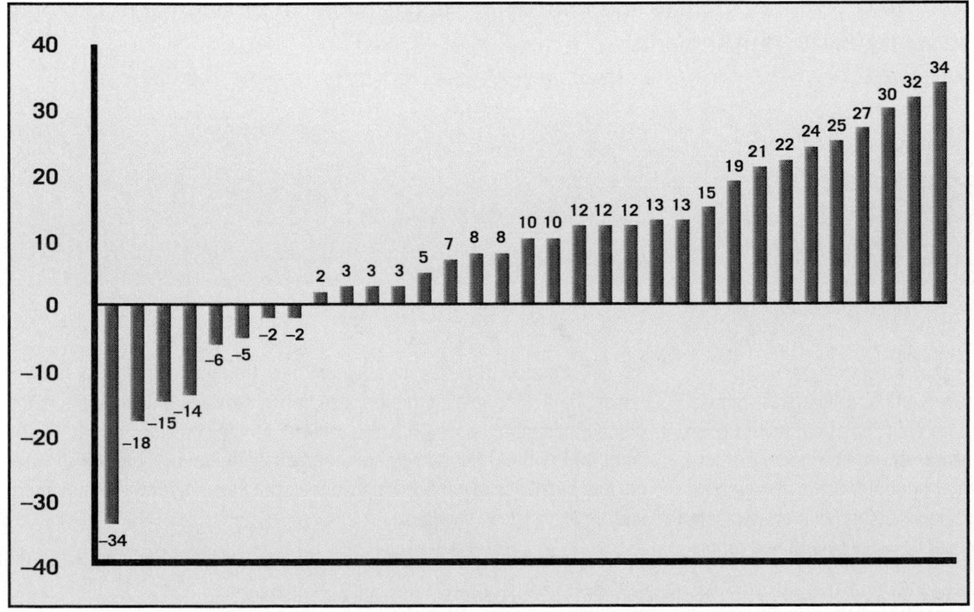

FIGURE 8.6

Treatment Effects for High-Risk Offenders

- Numbers represent difference in predicted recidivism rates between the comparison and treatment groups.
- Negative numbers indicate a difference favoring the comparison group.
- Each column represents a different program in the study.

SOURCE: C. Lowenkamp and E. Latessa, *Evaluation of Ohio's Halfway House and Community Based Correctional Facilities* (Cincinnati, OH: University of Cincinnati, 2002).

primary focus is treatment. Participants are usually required to attend every day the center is open, to schedule their next day's activities, and to abide by the schedule. Not only do participants have to call the center at least twice a day, the center may call them at their appointed rounds on a frequent basis to verify their whereabouts and activities. While there are significant differences across centers, Parent and others[51] found certain characteristics to be typical of most:

- Centers accept those on probation, those ordered to attend as a special condition of probation, or those who have violated probation; drug- and alcohol-abusing offenders; and some clients who pose low risk to their communities of residence.
- Almost all participants return to their residences at night, because day centers are usually nonresidential.
- The primary focus is on treatment and reduction of institution crowding.
- Most are open five days a week and frequently fifty or more hours within the week.
- Centers maintain a strict regimen of surveillance and demand more contact with clients than would be available even through intensive supervised probation.
- Centers direct clients through several phases of control, tapering off in the latter phase by providing about seventy hours per week of surveillance.
- Centers test clients for drug use at least once a week during the initial and most intensive phases.
- Centers offer several services on site that would address clients' unemployment, counseling, education, and life-skill needs, while also referring offenders to off-site drug abuse treatment, attendance at which is required.
- Centers demand clients fulfill community service orders.
- Centers collect program fees from each client.

This nonresidential punishment is designed to ensure a high level of community safety and client participation. Clients are forced to accept responsibility for their own behavior and change. Service provision audits indicate that centers are providing the required services and referrals.[52] Such centers have a definite role to play in intermediate punishments.

CORRECTIONAL BRIEF

Federal Pretrial Services

While federal pretrial services officers are charged with supervising each defendant released to their custody, not every offender is actively supervised. Some defendants—primarily those the court has determined pose no flight risk or danger to the community—are released only under the condition that they do not commit any offense. Other defendants are released under more restrictive release conditions. These defendants are typically required to report to a pretrial services officer on a predetermined reporting schedule or to reside in a community treatment facility or halfway house. During the release period, the pretrial services officer monitors the defendant's compliance with the release conditions and reports to the court and to the U.S. attorney any violations. Additionally, pretrial services officers might assist released individuals with securing employment, medical, legal, or social services.

SOURCE: John Scalia, *Federal Pretrial Release and Detention, 1996* (Washington, DC: U.S. Department of Justice, 1999), p. 8.

Shock Incarceration

The intermediate sanctions already discussed assume the offender can be contained and treated within existing community programs and technologies, and that tourniquet sentencing will serve to control behavior and prevent new crime. Intermediate punishments, however, also include two major alternatives for nonpredatory offenders who are, in addition, not career criminals. We discuss two here: **shock probation** and **boot camps.** We begin with shock probation.

SIDEBARS

Shock incarceration

A short period of jail or prison incarceration (the "shock"), followed by sentence reduction and early release.

Shock Probation In 1965, the Ohio legislature passed a law permitting sentencing judges to incarcerate offenders in state prisons for short periods of time, and then recall the inmate to probation within the community. The assumption was that a short period of incarceration (90 to 130 days), followed by a period of probation, would "shock" the offender into abandoning criminal activity and into pursuit of law-abiding behavior. Clearly, this program was based on a specific deterrence model, and was designed for a segment of the offender population for whom probation was insufficient punishment but long-term imprisonment was not necessary. The method would not be used for first-time offenders but for persons not yet committed to giving up predatory behavior.

This option, rapidly adopted by at least fourteen states,[53] puts decision making squarely in the hands of the judiciary. The sentencing judge is allowed to reconsider the original sentence to prison and, upon motion, to recall the inmate and place him or her on probation, under conditions deemed appropriate.

Evaluations of the effectiveness of shock probation in preventing recidivism and cost avoidance have focused on Ohio, Texas, and Kentucky. Vito has conducted the most sophisticated evaluations and concluded the following[54]:

1. The shock experience should not be limited to first-time offenders; eligibility should properly include those with prior records, as deemed eligible by the judge.
2. The length of incarceration necessary to secure the deterrent effect could be much shorter, probably thirty days or less.
3. Reincarceration rates have never exceeded 26 percent and, in Ohio, have been as low as 10 percent. The level of these rates clearly indicates that the program has potential for reintegration.
4. Shock probation has considerable potential to reduce the institutional overcrowding characteristic of contemporary corrections.[55]

Shock probation can be seen as an alternative disposition for sentencing judges who wish to control probationer behavior through deterrence and tourniquet sentencing. It is one of the last ditch programs of prison avoidance available to judges faced with the difficult decision of how best to protect the public while maximizing offender reintegration.

Boot Camp Programs Boot camps first appeared in Georgia (1983) and Oklahoma (1984). The concept spread quickly, and it is now estimated that there are fifty-two boot camp prisons in thirty-nine state correctional jurisdictions, in addition to fifteen jail programs and thirty-two probation and parole camps. It is estimated that in 2001, over 16,150 offenders were placed in adult boot camps.[56]

SIDEBARS

Boot Camp

A demanding program of intense, military-type discipline and conditioning, employing physical exercise, basic education, life- and work-skill development, and substance abuse treatment. Designed for juvenile and youthful offenders.

While labeled a recent innovation, the basic elements of boot camp were present in the Elmira Reformatory in 1876, designed by Zebulon Reed Brockway. In its form, boot camp combines elements of basic military training and traditional correctional philosophy, particularly rehabilitation. Although there is no generic boot

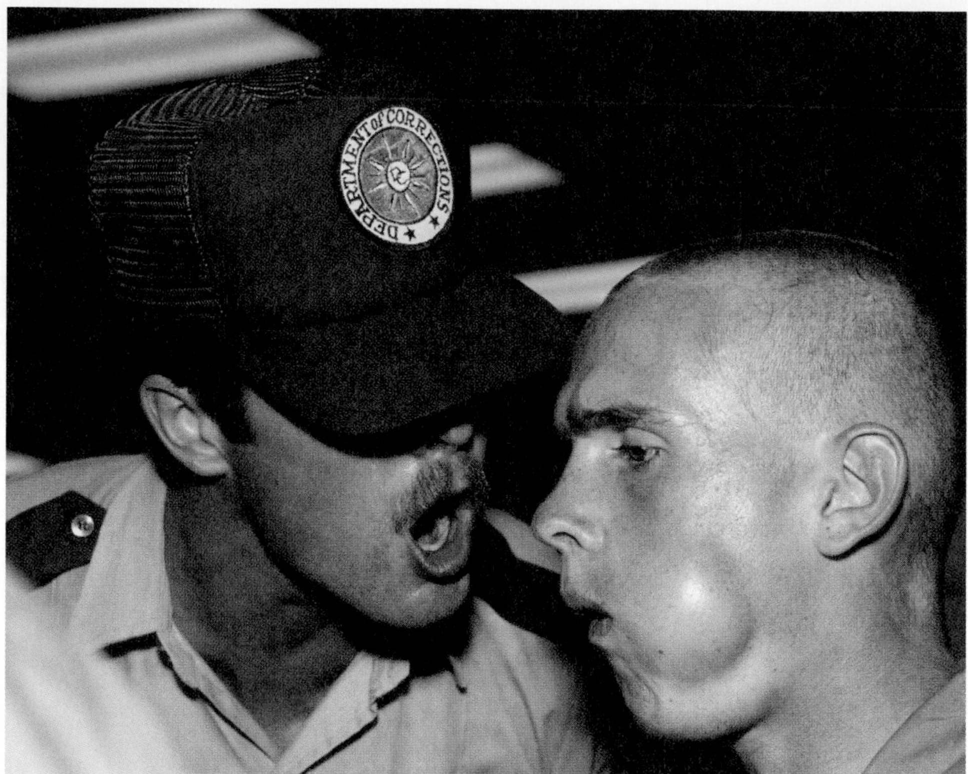

Corrections officer shouting at inmate.
Courtesy of Bettmann/CORBIS.

camp because individual programs vary in form and objectives, the typical boot camp is targeted at young nonviolent offenders.[57] Once in the camp, the participant is subjected to a regimen of the following:

- Military drills and discipline
- Physical exercise
- Hard physical labor
- Specialized education and training
- Counseling and treatment for substance abuse and addiction.

Most boot camp programs require the inmates to enter as volunteers,[58] offering as an incentive an incarceration period of a few months, compared to the much longer periods they would have spent in prison or on probation. Generally, a state boot camp graduate is released to parole, intensive supervision, home confinement, or some type of community corrections.

The philosophy behind the prison boot camps is simple. Offenders who can be turned around before they commit a major crime should be able to improve their opportunities for living a successful life free of incarceration. Traditional prisons generally have not been viewed as successful in rehabilitating offenders. According to boot camp advocates, the population at greatest risk of entering prison are the poorly educated, young adult offenders. They come from a low-income background, have not had proper role models or discipline, have few or no work skills, and are subjected to an environment where drug use and trafficking are common. Because many misdirected young persons have become productive citizens after exposure to military training, the boot camp endeavors to provide this same discipline and direction to persons who still have a chance of being diverted from a life of crime and incarceration.

Although boot camps are popular with judges, the public, and politicians, results from studies of the effectiveness of boot camp programs in reducing recidi-

Probationers in Programs

At some time since entering probation supervision, more than 60 percent of all 2.5 million probationers had participated in some type of special supervision or other program. The most common was alcohol or drug treatment/counseling: 33 percent of felons and 42 percent of misdemeanants had received such treatment while under their current sentence to probation.

Nearly one-third had been tested for drugs at least once since entering probation. Some 15 percent of felony probationers had participated in intensive probation supervision, and another 10 percent received psychiatric or psychological counseling.

Participation in other programs:

Day reporting program	5.3% (132,500 probationers!)
Residential program	4.9
Electronic monitoring	3.5
Sex offender program	2.7

SOURCE: Thomas Bonczar, *Characteristics of Adults on Probation, 1995* (Washington, DC: U.S. Department of Justice, 1997), p. 9.

vism have not been positive. An outcome study conducted in Texas[59] compared the rearrest rates of four different types of community facilities for adult offenders: boot camps, treatment centers, intermediate sanction facilities (used for probation violators), and substance abuse treatment facilities. The results are presented in Figure 8.7. The boot camp reported rearrest rates nearly double the other programs. Note also that when risk and need scores from a standardized assessment tool were compared for offenders in all four programs, the only difference was in the need scores, with the boot camp residents reporting fewer higher need offenders than the other options. Finally, a study conducted by researchers in Washington State found that, on average, juvenile boot camps increased recidivism rates about 11 percent.[60] Findings from boot camp evaluations make the following conclusions:

- Low- or moderate-risk juvenile and adult offenders who are subjected to a high level of supervision (boot camps) actually do worse than those left on traditional probation.[61]
- High percentages of minority youth are served by boot camps. The conclusion is that the boot camp model fails to connect with this population.
- Some evidence shows that the rate of recidivism declined in boot camp programs for adults where offenders spent 3 hours or more per day in therapeutic activity and had some type of aftercare.[62]

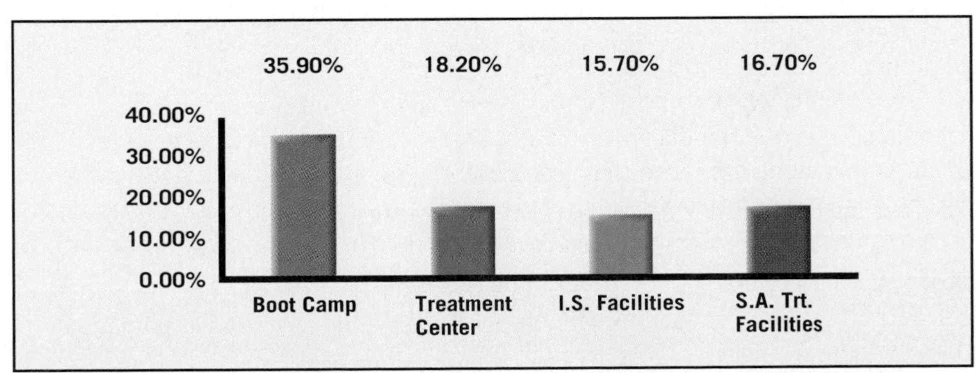

FIGURE 8.7

Rearrest Rates for Residents Discharged from Community Correctional Facilities in Texas: Two-Year Follow-Up (in percent)

SOURCE: *Community Corrections Facilities Outcome Study*, Texas Department of Criminal Justice, January 1999.

- In general, studies have found similar recidivism rates for those who completed boot camps and comparable offenders who spent long periods of time in prison.

There are several reasons why boot camps are not producing the desired reductions in recidivism.[63] Boot camps tend to:

- Bond delinquent and criminal groups together.
- Target non–crime-producing needs such as physical conditioning, drill and ceremony, and self-esteem.
- Mix low-, medium-, and high-risk offenders together.
- Model aggressive behavior.

Despite these findings, the boot camp concept still appeals to diverse elements of the justice system. Offenders generally will be returned to the community in a much shorter period without the stigma of having been in prison. For the judge, it is a sentencing option that provides sanctions more restrictive than probation but less restrictive than a conventional prison. For the correctional system, it allows the placement of individuals outside the traditional prison environment and reduces costs and crowding by moving the persons through the system in less time.

As a result of the research, some boot camp programs have abandoned the military-style training and incorporated education, substance abuse treatment, aftercare, job corps, and industrial components. Only future research will tell if these efforts have been successful.

SUMMARY

Corrections is undergoing rapid change as innovators search for programs, technologies, strategies, and policies for coping with the increasing number and diversity of jail and prison populations, as well as the crush of overcrowding. Not only are institutions crowded, but probation, parole, and community corrections are also impacted by the waves of offenders caught in the arms of the law.

Our review of diversion and intermediate sanctions provides insight into the reasons for the volume of clients and also describes promising programs and strategies for managing the risks posed by different types of offenders who need differing treatments and supervision. Change will continue. This is an exciting time for corrections as a field and for students wishing to have an impact on the futures of clients and the safety of communities.

In the next chapters we examine the use of incarceration, as those who make it through the correctional filter finally end up in the prisons of the nation. Well over 1 million people have been placed into incarceration and the number grows every day. What is imprisonment and what is it like? The next chapter will seek some answers to these questions.

REVIEW QUESTIONS

1. Explain several ways in which offenders can be diverted from the correctional system.
2. Differentiate between shock probation and boot camp shock incarceration.
3. What roles do community residential treatment centers play in corrections?
4. Did Florida's Community Control Program achieve its objectives?
5. Describe a boot camp program.
6. Describe the day reporting center and its purposes.
7. Define a drug court and describe its operations.

8. Explain the effectiveness of drug courts and of day reporting centers.
9. What are some other types of specialty courts that are emerging in the United States?
10. Why haven't boot camps been effective in reducing recidivism?
11. What types of offenders should be placed in residential correctional facilities?

ENDNOTES

1. Maryland Governor's Office, *Administration Report to the State/Local Criminal Justice/Mental Health Task Force* (Baltimore, MD: MGO, 1995); James Byrne and F. Taxman, "Crime Control Policy and Community Corrections Practice," *Evaluation and Program Planning* 17:2 (1994): 221–233; Richard Lamb and L. Weinberger, "Persons with Severe Mental Illnesses in Jails and Prisons," *Psychiatric Services* 49:4 (1998): 483–492; and the special focus issue "Mental Health Issues in Corrections" *Corrections Today* 67:1 (2005).
2. A. Barthwell, P. Bokos, and J. Bailey, "Interventions/Wilmer: A Continuum of Care for Substance Abusers in the Criminal Justice System," *Journal of Psychoactive Drugs* 27:1 (1995): 39–47; and Michael Finigan, *An Outcome Program Evaluation of the Multnomah County S.T.O.P. Drug Diversion Program* (West Linn, OR: Northwest Professional Consortium, 1998). Note that stereotypes of drug users are generally erroneous, particularly the ideas that most drug users are burned out and disconnected from mainstream society. Some seven in ten drug users work full time and are not poor. Laura Meckler, "7 in 10 Drug Users Work Full-Time," America Online, September 8, 1999.
3. Robert Langworthy and E. Latessa, "Treatment of Chronic Drunk Drivers," *Journal of Criminal Justice* 24:3 (1996): 273–281. See also K. Blackmun, R. Voas, R. Gulberg, et al., "Enforcement of Zero Tolerance in the State of Washington," *Forensic Science Review* 13:2 (2001): 77–86.
4. Richard Tolman and A. Weisz, "Coordinated Community Incarceration for Domestic Violence: The Effects of Arrests and Prosecutions on Recidivism of Women Abuser Perspectives," *Crime and Delinquency* 41:4 (1995): 401–495; Christopher Calson and F. Nidey, "Mandatory Penalties, Victim Compensation, and the Judicial Processing of Domestic Abuse Assault Cases," *Crime and Delinquency* 41:1 (1995): 132–149; and Carole Chancy and G. Saltzstein, "Democratic Control and Bureaucratic Responsiveness: The Police and Domestic Violence," *American Journal of Political Science* 42:3 (1998): 745–768.
5. Harry E. Allen, R. Seiter, E. Carlson, et al., *Halfway House: Program Models* (Washington, DC: U.S. Department of Justice, 1979). See also Bobbie Huskey, "Community Residential Centers," *Corrections Today* 54:8 (1992): 70–73; and Rhonda Reeves, "Future Forecast: Examining Community Corrections' Role in the Justice System," *Corrections Today* 54:8 (1992): 74–79.
6. Edward Latessa, L. Travis, and A. Holsinger, *Evaluation of Ohio's Community Corrections Acts Programs in Community-Based Correctional Facilities* (Cincinnati, OH: Division of Criminal Justice, University of Cincinnati, 1997).
7. Malcolm M. Feeley and Jonathan Simon, "The New Penology: Notes on the Emerging Strategy of Corrections and Its Implications," *Criminology* 30:4 (1992): 449–474. See also Steven Donziger, *The Real War on Crime* (New York: HarperCollins, 1996), pp. 55–62; and Michael Tonry, "Parochialism in U.S. Sentencing Policy," *Crime and Delinquency* 45:1 (1999): 48–65.
8. Voncile Gowdy, *Intermediate Sanctions* (Washington, DC: U.S. Department of Justice, 1993). See also the theme issue of *Corrections Today* 57:1 (1995); and Jeffrey Ulmer, "Intermediate Sanctions," *Sociological Inquiry* 71:2 (2001): 164–193.
9. Daniel Nagin and David Farrington, "The Onset and Persistence of Offending," *Criminology* 30:4 (1992): 501–524; Mark Cohen, "The Monetary Value of Saving a High-Risk Youth," *Journal of Quantitative Criminology* 14:1 (1998): 5–33; and Shadd Maruna, *Making Good: How Ex-Convicts Reform and Rebuild Their Lives* (Washington, DC: American Psychological Association, 2001).
10. Francis Cullen, Edward Latessa, Velmer Burton, and Lucien Lombardo, "The Correctional Orientation of Prison Wardens: Is the Rehabilitative Ideal Supported?" *Criminology* 31:1 (1993): 69–92; and Jody Sundt and F. Cullen, "The Role of the Contemporary Prison Chaplain," *Prison Journal* 78:3 (1998): 271–298.
11. John Hagan and Juleigh Coleman, "Returning Captives of the American War on Drugs," *Crime and Delinquency* 47:3 (1001): 352–367.
12. Editors, "Alternatives to Prison: Cheaper Is Better," *The Economist* (November 19, 1994): 33; Steven Barkan and S. Cohn, "Racial Prejudice and Support by Whites for Police Use of Force," *Justice Quarterly* 15:4 (1998): 743–753.
13. Michael Tonry, "Racial Politics, Racial Disparities, and the War on Crime," *Crime and Delinquency* 40:4 (1994): 475–494. See also Christiana DeLong and K. Jackson, "Putting Race into Context: Race, Juvenile

Justice Processing, and Urbanization," *Justice Quarterly* 15:3 (1998): 448–504.

14. Bruce Benson, D. Rasmussen, and I. Kim, "Deterrence and Public Policy," *International Review of Law and Economics* 18:1 (1998): 77–100.
15. Paige M. Harrison and Allen J. Beck, *Prisoners in 2001* (Washington, DC: U.S. Department of Justice, 2002), p. 1.
16. Marc Mauer, "Comparative International Rates of Incarceration." (Washington, DC: The Sentencing Project, 2003).
17. William Bradshaw and M. Umbreit, "Crime Victims Meet Juvenile Offenders," *Juvenile and Family Court Journal* 49:3 (1998): 17–25; and Audrey Evje and Robert Cushman, *A Summary of the Reconciliation Programs* (Sacramento, CA: Judicial Council of California, 2000).
18. Thomas Bonczar, *Characteristics of Adults on Probation, 1995* (Washington, DC: U.S. Department of Justice, 1997), p. 7; and Matthew DuRose and Patrick Langan, *Felony Sentences in State Courts, 2002* (Washington, DC: Bureau of Justice Statistics, 2004), p. 10.
19. Roy Sudipto, "Juvenile Restitution and Recidivism in a Midwestern County," *Federal Probation* 59:1 (1995): 55–62. See also Karen Suter, *Delinquency Prevention in Texas* (Austin, TX: Texas Juvenile Probation Commission, 1997).
20. Joan Petersilia and Susan Turner, *Evaluating Intensive Supervised Probation/Parole: Results of a Nationwide Experiment* (Washington, DC: U.S. Department of Justice, 1993). See also Angela Robertson, P. Grimes, and K. Rogers, "A Short-Run Cost Benefit Analysis of Community-Based Interventions for Juvenile Offenders," *Crime and Delinquency* 47:2 (2001): 265–284.
21. B. Fulton, S. Stone, and P. Gendreau, *Restructuring Intensive Supervision Programs: Applying "What Works"* (Lexington, KY: American Probation and Parole Association, 1994). See also F. Cullen and P. Gendreau, "From Nothing Works to What Works," *The Prison Journal* 81:3 (2000): 313–338.
22. J. Byrne, A. Lurigio, and C. Baird, "The Effectiveness of the New Intensive Supervision Programs," *Research in Corrections* 2:1 (1989): 1–48.
23. B. Fulton, E. Latessa, A. Stichman, and L. F. Travis, "The State of ISP: Research and Policy Implications," *Federal Probation* 61:4 (1997): 65–75.
24. B. Fulton, P. Gendreau, and M. Paparozzi, "APPA's Prototypical Intensive Supervision Program: ISP As It Was Meant to Be," *Perspectives* 19:2 (1996): 25–41. See also B. Fulton et al., *Restructuring Intensive Supervision Programs.*
25. West Huddleston, "Drug Court and Jail-Based Treatment," *Corrections Today* 60:6 (1998): 98. See also Paul Stageberg, B. Wilson, and R. Moore, *Final Report of the Polk County Adult Drug Court* (Des Moines, IA: Iowa Division of Criminal Justice Policy, 2001).
26. American University Drug Court Clearinghouse and Technical Assistance Project. *Summary of Drug Court Activity by State and County* (Washington, DC: AUDCCTAP, 2003).
27. M. Rempel, D. Fox-Kralstein, A. Cissner, et al., *The New York State Adult Drug Court Evaluation: Policies, Participants and Impacts* (New York: Center for Court Innovation, 2003).
28. Edward Latessa, Deborah Shaffer, and Christopher Lowenkamp, *Outcome Evaluation of Ohio's Drug Court Efforts* (Cincinnati, OH: Center for Criminal Justice Research, University of Cincinnati, 2002).
29. Washington State Institute for Public Policy, *Drug Courts for Adult Defendants: Outcome Evaluation and Cost Benefit Analysis* (Olympia, WA: WSIPP, 2003).
30. NPC Research, Inc., and Administrative Office of the Courts, Judicial Council of California, *California Drug Courts: A Methodology for Determining Costs and Avoided Costs: Phase I: Building the Methodology: Final Report.* (Portland, OR: Authors, October 2002).
31. James Brown, "Drug Courts: Are They Needed and Will They Succeed in Breaking the Cycle of Drug-Related Crime? *New England Journal on Civil and Criminal Confinement* 23:1 (1997): 63–99.
32. Julie Martin, "Community Services: Are the Goals of This Alternative Sentencing Tool Being Met?" *Court Review* 28:4 (1991): 5–11. But see Wade Myers, P. Burton, Paula Sanders, et al., "Project 'Back-on-Track' at One Year," *Journal of the American Academy of Clinical and Adolescent Psychiatry* 39:9 (2000): 1127–1134.
33. Gail Caputo, D. Young, and R. Porter, *Community Services for Repeat Misdemeanants in New York City* (New York: Vera Institute, 1998).
34. Michael Maxfield and Terry Baumer, "Home Detention with Electronic Monitoring: Comparing Pretrial and Postconviction Programs," *Crime and Delinquency* 36:4 (1990): 521–536; and Ann Farrell, "Mothers Offending Against Their Role: An Australian Experience," *Women and Criminal Justice* 9:4 (1998): 47–67.
35. Leonard Flynn, "House Arrest," *Corrections Today* 48:5 (1986): 64–68.
36. K. Courtright, B. Berg, and R. Mutchnick, "The Cost Effectiveness of Using House Arrest with Electronic Monitoring for Drunk Drivers," *Federal Probation* 61:3 (1997): 19–22.
37. Government Accounting Office, *Intermediate Sanctions* (Washington, DC: GAO, 1990). Evaluations of the home detention program in Great Britain found a 5 percent "recall to prison" rate for prison inmates released onto home detention. Kath Dodgson, P. Goodwin, H. Philip, et al., *Electronic Monitoring of*

Released Prisoners (London: U.K. Home Office, 2001).

38. James Kammer, K. Minor, and J. Wells, "An Outcome Study of the Diversion Plus Program for Juvenile Offenders," *Federal Probation* 61:2 (1997): 51–56; and M. Cusson, "Intermediate Punishments, Electronic Monitoring and Abolitionism," *Revue Internationale de Criminologie et de Police Technique Scientifique* 51:1 (1998): 34–45.
39. Dennis Wagner and Christopher Baird, *Evaluation of the Florida Community Control Program* (Washington, DC: U.S. Department of Justice, 1993), p. 5. It is possible to have cost savings and similar outcomes. See Elizabeth Deschenes and P. Greenwood, "Alternative Placements for Juvenile Offenders," *Journal of Research in Crime and Delinquency* 35:3 (1998): 267–294.
40. See Alison Church and S. Dunston, *Home Detention: The Evaluation of the Home Detention Pilot Programme, 1995–1997* (Wellington: New Zealand Ministry of Justice, 1997).
41. R. K. Schwitzgebel, R. L. Schwitzgebel, W. N. Pahnke, and W. S. Hurd, "A Program of Research in Behavioral Electronics," *Behavioral Scientist* 9:3 (1964): 233–238. See also Michael Vitello, "Three Strikes: Can We Return to Rationality?" *Journal of Criminal Law and Criminology* 87:2 (1997): 395–481.
42. Scott Vollum and Chris Hale, "Electronic Monitoring: Research Review," *Corrections Compendium* (July 2002): 1.
43. Joan Petersilia, *Expanding Options for Criminal Sentencing* (Santa Monica, CA: Rand, 1987), p. 37; C. Camp and G. Camp, *The Corrections Yearbook 1998* (Middletown, CT: Criminal Justice Institute, 1998), p. 124. See also Editors, "Florida to Mandate GP [Global Positioning] Devices for Sex Offenders" *Correctional News* 11:3 (2005), p. 1.
44. Government Accounting Office, *Intermediate Sanctions*, pp. 6–7.
45. Church and Dunston, *Home Detention;* and Mike Nellis, "The Electronic Monitoring of Offenders in England and Wales," *British Journal of Criminology* 31:2 (1991): 165–185.
46. J. R. Lilly, "Tagging Revisited," *The Howard Journal* 29:4 (1990): 229–245; National Association for the Care of Offenders and the Prevention of Crime, *The Electronic Monitoring of Offenders* (London: NACOPC, 1989); and Michael Brown and Preston Elrod, "Electronic House Arrest: An Examination of Citizen Attitudes," *Crime and Delinquency* 41:3 (1995): 332–346.
47. Edward J. Latessa and Lawrence F. Travis, "Halfway Houses or Probation: A Comparison of Alternative Dispositions," *Journal of Crime and Justice* 14:1 (1991): 53–75; and Edward Latessa, L. Travis, and A. Holsinger, *Evaluation of Ohio's Community-Based Correctional Facilities: Final Report* (Cincinnati, OH: Division of Criminal Justice, University of Cincinnati, 1997).
48. Christopher Lowenkamp and Edward J. Latessa, *Evaluation of Ohio's Residential Correctional Programs* (Cincinnati, OH: Center for Criminal Justice Research, University of Cincinnati, 2002). See also Christopher Lowenkamp and Edward Latessa, "Increasing the Effectiveness of Correctional Programming Through the Risk Principle: Identifying Offenders for Residential Placement," *Criminology and Public Policy* 4:2 (2005): 501–528.
49. J. Stephen Wormith and Mark E. Oliver, "Offender Treatment Attrition and Its Relationship with Risk, Responsivity, and Recidivism," *Criminal Justice and Behavior* 29:4 (2002): 447–471.
50. Latessa and Travis, "Halfway Houses or Probation"; and Joseph Callahan and K. Koenning, "The Comprehensive Sanctions Center in the Northern District of Ohio," *Federal Probation* 59:3 (1995): 52–57.
51. Dale Parent, J. Byrne, V. Tsarfaty, et al., *Day Reporting Center* (Washington, DC: U.S. Department of Justice, 1995).
52. Stan Orchowsky, L. Jodie, and T. Bogle, *Evaluation of the Richmond Day Reporting Center* (Richmond, VA: Virginia Criminal Justice Research Center, 1995); and Jack McDevitt, M. Domino, and K. Baum, *Metropolitan Day Reporting Center: An Evaluation* (Boston: Center for Criminal Justice Policy Research, Northeastern University, 1997).
53. Gennaro Vito and Harry Allen, "Shock Probation in Ohio: A Comparison of Outcomes," *International Journal of Offender Therapy and Comparative Criminology* 25:1 (1981): 7.
54. Gennaro Vito, "Developments in Shock Probation: A Review of Research Findings and Policy Implications," *Federal Probation* 50:1 (1985): 22–27.
55. See also Michael Vaughn, "Listening to the Experts: A National Study of Correctional Administrators' Responses to Prison Overcrowding," *Criminal Justice Review* 18:1 (1993): 12–25.
56. *Ibid.*, pp. 23–25. But also see Bruce Mendelsohn, *The Challenge of Prison Crowding* (Frederick, MD: Aspen, 1996). See also Camp and Camp, *The Corrections Yearbook Adult Corrections 2002*.
57. See also Blair Bourque et al., *Boot Camps for Juvenile Offenders* (Washington, DC: U.S. Department of Justice, 1996).
58. The bulk of the following section is drawn from the U.S. Government Accounting Office, *Prison Boot Camps* (Washington, DC: U.S. Department of Justice, 1993).
59. Texas Department of Criminal Justice, *Community Corrections Facilities Outcome Study* (Austin, TX: Texas Department of Criminal Justice, 1999).

60. Steve Aos, P. Phipps, R. Barnoski, and R. Lieb, *The Comparative Costs and Benefits of Programs to Reduce Crime: A Review of the National Research Findings with Implications for Washington State* (Olympia, WA: Washington State Institute for Public Policy, 1999).
61. David Altschuler and Troy Armstrong, *Intensive Aftercare for High-Risk Juveniles: A Community Care Model: Program Summary* (Washington, DC: Office of Juvenile Justice and Delinquency Prevention, Office of Justice Programs, U.S. Department of Justice, 1994).
62. Doris MacKenzie and Sam Souryal, *Multisite Evaluation of Shock Incarceration* (Washington, DC: National Institute of Justice, Office of Justice Programs, U.S. Department of Justice, 1994).
63. Dale Colledge and J. Gerber, "Rethinking the Assumption About Boot Camps," *Journal of Offender Rehabilitation* 28:1 (1998): 71–87. See Kay Harris, "Key Differences Among Community Corrections Acts in the United States: An Overview," *Prison Journal* 76:2 (1996): 192–238.

SUGGESTED READINGS: PART 3

Bonta, James, S. Wallace-Capretta, and J. Rooney. "Can Electronic Monitoring Make a Difference?" *Crime and Delinquency* 46:1 (2000): 61–75.

Gendreau, Paul, Shelia A. French, and Angela Taylor. *What Works (What Doesn't Work)—Revised 2002: The Principles of Effective Correctional Treatment.* Monograph Series. LaCrosse, WI: International Community Corrections Association, 2002.

Latessa, Edward, and H. Allen. *Corrections in the Community,* 3rd ed. Cincinnati, OH: Anderson Publishing, 2003.

Latessa, Edward, Francis T. Cullen, and Paul Gendreau. "Beyond Correctional Quackery: Professionalism and the Possibility of Effective Treatment," *Federal Probation* 66:1 (2002): 43–44.

Lowenkamp, Christopher, and Edward Latessa. *Evaluation of Ohio's CCA Funded Programs Final Report.* Cincinnati, OH: Center for Criminal Justice Research, University of Cincinnati, 2005.

Lowenkamp, Christopher, and Edward Latessa. "Increasing the Effectiveness of Correctional Programming Through the Risk Principle: Identifying Offenders for Residential Placement." *Criminology and Public Policy* 4:2 (2005): 501–528.

Lutze, Faith, and D. Brody. "Mental Abuse as Cruel and Unusual Punishment: Do Boot Camp Prisons Violate the Eighth Amendment?" *Crime and Delinquency* 45:2 (1999): 242–255.

MacKenzie, Doris, K. Browning, S. Skroban, and D. Smith. "The Impact of Probation on the Criminal Activities of Offenders," *Journal of Research in Crime and Delinquency* 36:4 (1999): 423–453.

Marciniak, Liz. "The Use of Day Reporting as an Intermediate Sanction," *The Prison Journal* 79:2 (1999): 205–225.

Taxman, Faye, D. Soule, and A. Gelb. "Graduated Sanctions," *The Prison Journal* 79:2 (1999): 182–204.

PART

4 Correctional Systems

THE FOLLOWING CHAPTERS ARE COVERED IN PART 4:

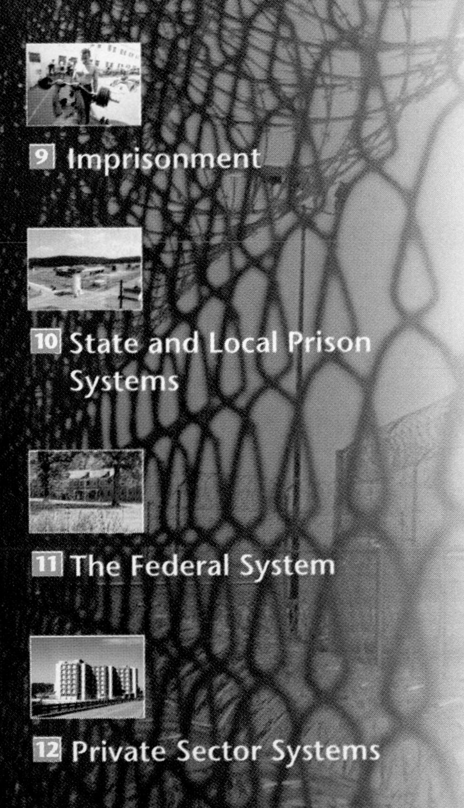

OVERVIEW

Part 4 explains imprisonment in federal, state, and local correctional systems, and explores the roles and contributions of the private sector to the correctional process. Correctional systems at all levels achieve basic functions of security, public protection, and inmate custody and treatment. Yet much controversy surrounds imprisonment, especially if done for private gain. Part 4 identifies and details the basic issues and proposes solutions.

CHAPTER 9

Imprisonment

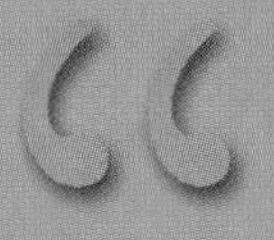

The mere fact that the individual's movements are restricted, however, is far less serious than the fact that imprisonment means that the inmate is cut off from family, relatives and friends, not in self-isolation of the hermit or misanthrope, but in the involuntary seclusion of the outlaw.

—Gresham M. Sykes

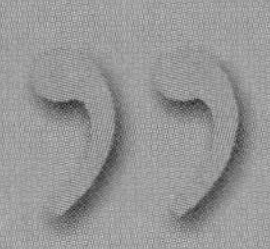

KEY WORDS

- "get tough" legislation
- War on Crime
- overcrowding
- baby boom
- classification
- maximum security
- Gothic-style monoliths
- prisonization
- supermax
- special housing unit (SHU)
- medium security
- minimum security
- open institutions

OVERVIEW

The student has seen that the use of imprisonment to punish and reform grew from solitary penitence in a small wing of the Walnut Street Jail in 1790 to over 1,700 prisons (106 federal and 1,612 state) today.[1] Despite this growth in the use of imprisonment in hopes of reducing crime and recidivism, many institutions continue to lag behind demand for cells and thus remain overcrowded. Since 1990, prison population housed as a "percentage of rated capacity" has averaged well over capacity at the state level and 139 percent at the federal level.[2] This chapter examines the ideological rationale, conditions, effects, and some impacts flowing from the imprisonment of more than 1,400,000 persons in those prisons, reformatories, and correctional centers across the United States. We provide the student with a glimpse into the daily life of prisoners and its impact on them and society. It is easy to dwell on statistics and forget that each and every number represents a human being, each of whom has hopes, fears, and emotions, the same as any other person.

More than thirty years ago, Peter Garabedian wrote a classic article[3] on social roles and socialization in a prison, which dealt with attitudes toward self, others, and philosophy of life. He asked the prisoners to score the statements listed below from low to high, on a scale from 1 (low) to 10 (high).

1. You've got to have confidence in yourself if you're going to be successful.
2. I generally feel guilty whenever I do wrong.

< Imprisonment and lots of "dead time" lead to "buffing up" with weights by inmates.
Photo by Donna DeCesare, courtesy of Impact Visuals Photo and Graphics, Inc.

3. "Might is right" and "every man for himself" are the main rules of living, regardless of what people say.
4. The biggest criminals are protected by society and rarely get to prison.
5. I worry a lot about unimportant matters.
6. There's a little larceny in everybody, if you're really honest about it.
7. The only criminals I really know are the ones here in the institution.
8. You have to take care of yourself because nobody else is going to take care of you.
9. Inmates can trust me to be honest and loyal in my dealings with them.
10. I am very nervous much of the time.
11. Who you know is more important than what you know, and brains are more important than brawn.
12. Most people try to be law abiding and true.
13. It makes me sore to have people tell me what to do.
14. Police, judges, prosecutors, and politicians are just as crooked as most of the people they send to prison.
15. Most people are not very friendly toward me.

Prison

A state, federal, or local confinement facility having custodial authority and control over adult felons convicted and sentenced to confinement for more than one year.

Each of these items was assumed by researchers to reflect a component of the attitudinal organization of a given prisoner role type: "right guys" (obey the inmate code and oppose both staff and institutional roles); "toughs" (overly aggressive inmates who rely on physical violence or force in dealing with others); "rats" (inmate informants who squeal on illegal inmate activities and betray other inmates); "wolves" (aggressive inmates who prey on weaker inmates), and so on.

In the ensuing years the results from this classification effort fell out of use and the emphasis in prisons has been on a constant pendulum between all the ideologies explored in Chapter 3. Our examination of the correctional process to this point has now covered jails and detention facilities, explored probation, and looked at numerous intermediate sanctions used to control and supervise offenders short of long-term incarceration in a state, local, or federal prison. That option, the last arrow in the quiver of options that no longer allows some retention of the offender in a community setting, is the most extreme and punitive process in corrections. Imprisonment is for offenders who are believed to be so violent or unreliable that they must be placed in one of the more than 1,700 varied prison facilities that have been built to protect society from such offenders.

No matter how attractively built and modern prisons may be, they will never rank high as desirable places in which to live. They can be dangerous for inmates and staff (see Figure 9.1). In addition to incapacitating inhabitants from committing more crimes while incarcerated behind the bars, walls, and fences, prisons are also places where offenders must serve out the punishment directed by the courts. During the last decades of the twentieth century, in large part due to the War on Drugs, use of prisons dramatically increased, with the vague hope of keeping abreast of the huge surge of offenders sentenced to prisons. In this chapter we explore the levels of prison processes, the growth in prison populations, and the building binge that has come about as a result. We begin with an examination of the phenomenon of prison population growth, with the student always keeping in mind the human side of the equation.

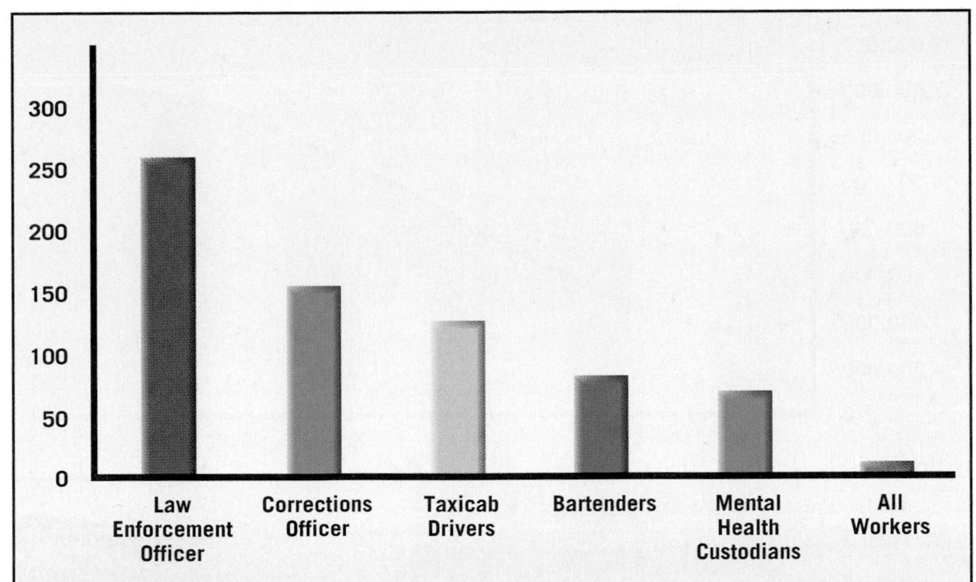

FIGURE 9.1

Violent Incidents per 1,000 Workers

SOURCE: Bureau of Justice Statistics, *Law Enforcement Officers Most at Risk for Workplace Violence: 2001*, www. ojp. usdoj.gov/bjs/pub/press/vw99pr.htm.

PRISON POPULATIONS CONTINUE TO CLIMB

Since 1980, the United States has experienced the most unprecedented expansion of the building of prisons in its history, perhaps in the history of the free world. This increase is attributed to a number of factors to be explained here, including the increasing fear of crime and criminals by citizens, a perception of being victimized, increased media attention and coverage of "**get tough" legislation**, selective prosecution of violent offenders, the impact of the so-called **War on Crime**, and increased severity and length of new sentencing initiatives (see Figure 9.2). More recent evidence suggests that violent offenders contributed 55 percent of the population increase, and that incarceration of drug offenders accounted for another 21 percent.

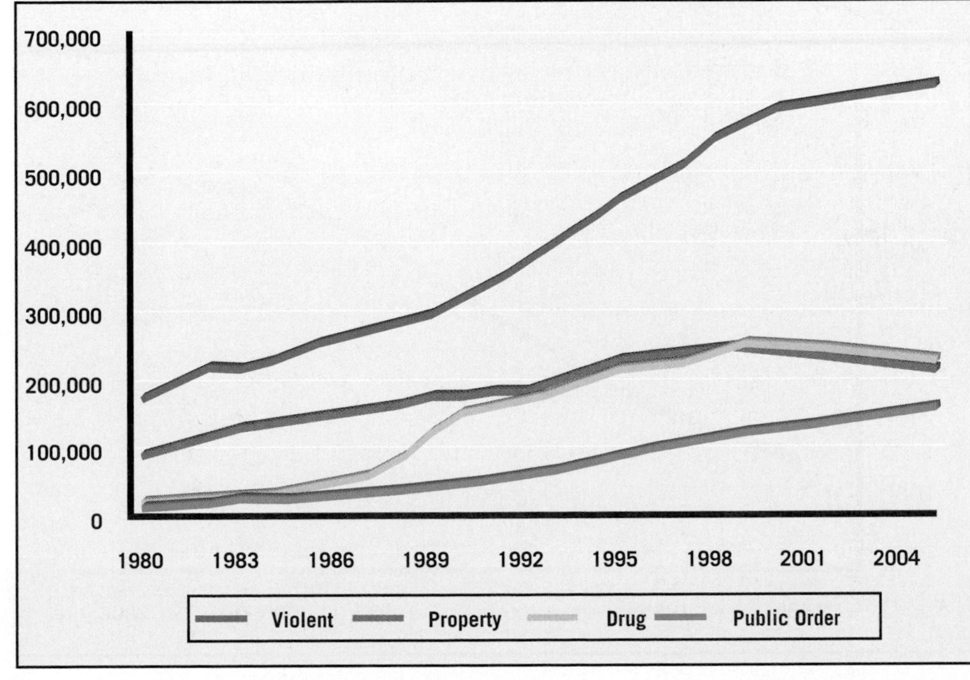

FIGURE 9.2

State Prison Population by Offense Type, 1980–2005*

*Data for 2002–2005 are extrapolated.

SOURCE: Bureau of Justice Statistics, *State Inmates by Most Serious Offense*, www.ojp.usdoj.gov/bjs/glances/tables/corrtyptab.htm.

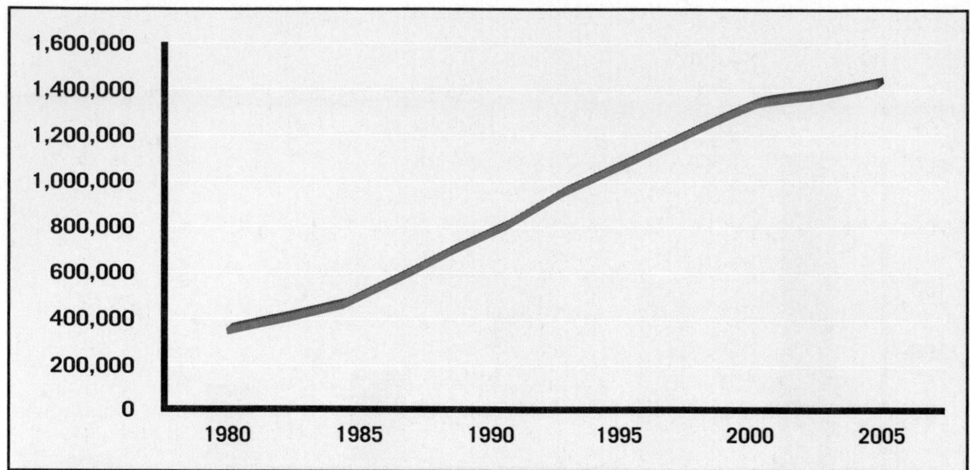

FIGURE 9.3

State and Federal Prisoners, 1980–2005*

*Data for 2004 and 2005 are extrapolated.

SOURCE: Bureau of Justice Statistics, *Prisoners in 2003* (Washington, DC: BJS, 2004), p. 2.

Property and public order offenses contributed the remaining 24 percent of the increase.[4] Since 1990, the number of prisoners in the federal Bureau of Prisons has increased by more than 147 percent, and in state prisons by 73 percent! Hundreds of billions of dollars have been invested in building literally hundreds of prisons. Over 2.1 million adult Americans were behind the bars of jails and prisons in the United States at year-end 2003. Over 4.8 million offenders were under supervision of probation or parole at year-end 2003 (see Chapter 7). This totals to 6.9 million Americans who have been tried, convicted, and are now under some form of correctional supervision.[5]

The number of state and federal prisoners from 1980 to 2005 (estimated) can be found in Figure 9.3. The incarceration rate per 100,000 population from 1980 to 2005 can be found in Figure 9.4.

It is sad to report that one in thirty-two adults and one in twenty adult men are today under some form of correctional supervision in the United States; one in eight black men age 25 to 29 is in prison. In total, black men are imprisoned at a rate greater than seven times that of white men (3,405 to 465 per 100,000, respectively), arguably because blacks are arrested at higher rates than whites, are arrested

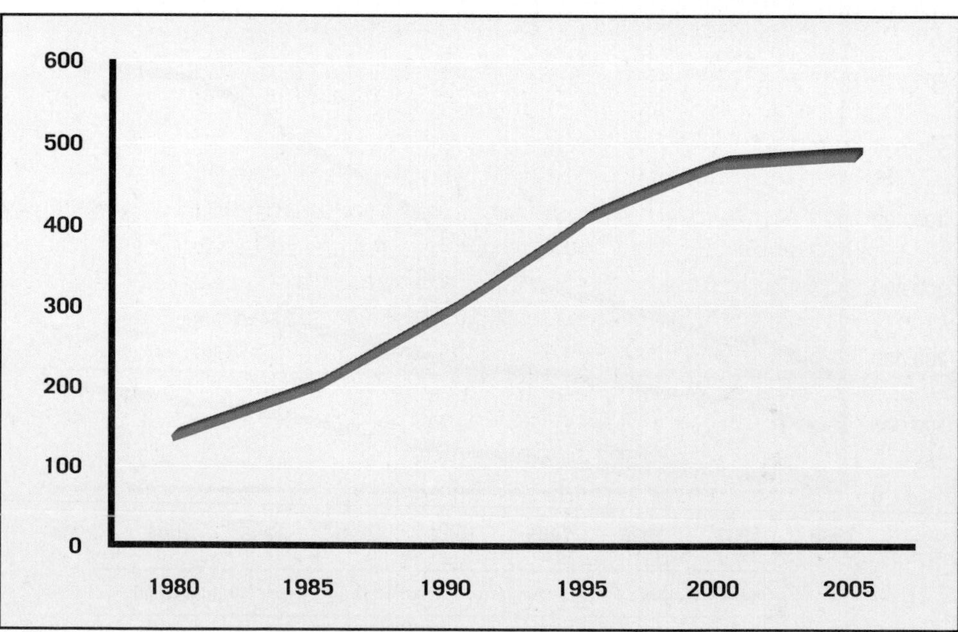

FIGURE 9.4

Incarceration Rate, 1980–2005*

*Data for 2005 are extrapolated.

SOURCE: Bureau of Justice Statistics, *Sentenced Inmates per 100,000 Population*, www.ojp.usdoj.gov/bjs/glance/tables/inccrttab.htm.

for crimes that are differentially punished, and are processed more severely by the criminal justice system.[6]

Marc Mauer and Ryan Scott King addressed the racial imbalance of African American males in prison and note that there now are more incarcerated black men in their twenties than the total number of all incarcerated African Americans in 1984 (201,300 versus 98,000).[7] Based on current trends, almost one in three (32%) black males born today can expect to go to prison in their lifetime.

Causal factors that Mauer and King identified were:

1. Blacks have higher rates of involvement in some crimes (for example, blacks accounted for 38 percent of all arrests for violent offenses, yet are only 12 percent of the total population).
2. Imprisonment rates in the nation are, in general, rising, primarily fueled by the "get tough" policies that demand harsher sentencing practices.
3. The War on Drugs that has affected black communities disproportionately. In wealthier communities, drug abuse is handled as a public health problem; in poorer ones, such problems are more likely to be addressed through the criminal justice system.
4. Harsher punishment of crack cocaine offenders has a detrimental effect on the African American community. Persons convicted of selling 500 grams of powder cocaine would be sentenced to a mandatory five years of imprisonment. The same penalty is triggered for sale of only 5 grams of crack, the cheaper drug predominantly sold in black communities.
5. "School zone" drug laws carry an enhanced sentence if the sale occurs within about 1,000 to 1,500 feet of a school campus, even between consenting adults at 3:00 A.M. Since African Americans disproportionately live in urban areas, any such crime would produce the enhanced penalty.
6. Habitual offender and three-strike laws have a disproportionate impact on African Americans. In California, blacks represent about 6 percent of the state's population but comprise 29 percent of the prison population. They represent almost 48 percent of the persons serving three-strike sentences that carry a minimum of twenty-five years to life imprisonment, with no time credits for good behavior or program participation.

The authors argue that such differences may be a function of racism in action or could be simply a by-product of even-handed justice. They conclude that imposing crime policies with such profound racial dynamics flies in the face of the nation's commitment to a free and democratic society.

Looking at statistics does not allow the student to grasp that there are human beings involved in the prison situation on both sides of the bars of the old and new monolithic structures built to house, feed, and secure a prisoner population the size of San Diego and San Francisco combined. These growth rates, should they remain constant, translate into a nationwide need for over 2,500 prison (and 2,100 jail) bed spaces and almost 500 new correctional officer positions per month, to accommodate the surge in population. On average, each bed will cost $70,909 for construction and $22,650 per inmate per year.[8] See Table 9.1.

The trends of the past decade indicate that we are willing and ready to build more and more prisons and incarcerate an even larger percentage of the population. Efforts for prison improvement fly in the face of "get tough" legislation, the population's epidemic fear of crime, and sentencing laws and procedures that put even more persons behind bars. Some of the ambivalence of the American public

TABLE 9.1 Costs of Prison Services

SERVICE	NATIONAL AVERAGE COST PER INMATE YEAR
Imprisonment	$22,650
Medical care	2,525
Food	955
Utilities	1,217
Cost per taxpayer (year)	100

SOURCE: Editors, "Minnesota DOC Says Prison Crisis Looms," *Correctional News* 10:7 (2004): 6.

regarding prisons and imprisonment relates to a lack of clear understanding and mutual acceptance of the purpose for confinement.[9]

The consequent **overcrowding** of the system means that offenders are doubled up in cells meant for one; packed into makeshift dormitories; and bunked in the basements, corridors, converted hospital facilities, tents, trailers, warehouses, and program activity areas of the nation's prisons. There are currently 482 Americans (and 915 adult males) in prison for every 100,000 citizens—the highest known rate for any industrialized nation. If present trends continue, almost 1.6 million Americans were expected to be in prisons by the year 2007.[10] Prisons remain crowded despite the building binge.

The incidence of colds, infectious diseases, hepatitis, drug-resistant tuberculosis, sexually communicable diseases, psychological disturbances, and psychiatric crises also is related to overcrowding. The more overcrowded the institution, the higher the incidence of medical problems. Paradoxically, American prisoners are the only U.S. residents who have a constitutional right to receive free medical care because they are otherwise prevented from securing such care on their own.[11]

Overcrowded maximum-security prisons appear to be most likely to have the worst impact on prisoner health and safety. Correctional administrators and elected officials must plan to reduce the negative impacts of imprisonment on offenders for parole consideration. Since 1996, many state legislatures have mandated that in-

CORRECTIONAL BRIEF

Effects of Prison Overcrowding

Despite the fact that the nation has opened or expanded almost 300 prisons in less than ten years, the average prison space available for inmates has dropped by over 10 percent. Prison overcrowding has gotten worse, especially as crime has become more violent, and drug-related crimes have more often resulted in confinement.

What effects does prison crowding have? One is that fewer programs can be made available for inmates on a relative basis; another is that recreational opportunities are fewer. But it is in the health and safety areas that the impact is felt most.

The rates of death, suicide, homicide, inmate assault, and disturbance increase as prison population density increases (population density is measured by square feet of floor space per inmate). This finding holds regardless of whether a prisoner is confined in maximum, medium, or minimum security. Such data are further exacerbated by the increasingly more violent persons being imprisoned.

mates will serve at least 85 percent of their original sentence in prison before release. The policy makers continue to ignore the evidence that an increased use of imprisonment is positively correlated with higher, rather than lower, levels of crime.[12] Public safety is not enhanced by greater use of imprisonment.[13]

Another factor contributing to the increase of the prison population as a whole was the growth of the general population in the nineteen- to twenty-nine-year-old age group. This is seen as the population at risk, because crime is usually a young man's activity. That group is a direct result of the **baby boom** that followed World War II, which clogged the school systems of America in the 1950s and 1960s and has now affected yet another area—urban crime. That group is also the one with the highest unemployment rate and, in a time of general underemployment, will continue to commit crime out of proportion to its size.[14]

CLASSIFICATION: A BASIC ELEMENT OF CORRECTIONS

The demoralizing influence of the early maximum-security prisons and the enforced idleness they produced resulted in two major movements in corrections over the last half of the twentieth century. One course of action has been to continually upgrade living conditions and humanitarian treatment within the security prisons. The second action has introduced **classification,** a concept borrowed from psychology, into the imprisonment process. Classification in prison usually refers to one of two actions:

1. A differentiation of the prisoner population into custodial or security groups, thus permitting a degree of planned custodial flexibility not previously possible.
2. Opening of the prisons to the teacher, psychologist, social worker, psychiatrist, and others.[15]

The advent of classification in the post–World War II era marked a substantial shift for imprisonment from punishment to correction and rehabilitation as its goal. These events were timely because, as noted in Chapter 2, unionism and federal legislation of the 1930s severely restricted prison industries. The idleness that followed the restrictive federal laws would have been even more troublesome were it not for the Prison Industries Reorganization Administration. Operating between 1935 and 1940, that agency developed programs of constructive activities for prisons, contributing to the development of rehabilitation programs employed by prisons between 1940 and 1973.

Correctional treatment is generally assumed to begin with the classification process. Classification procedures are conducted in reception units located within the prisons or at special reception and classification centers at another location. Classification committees, reception-diagnostic centers, or community classification teams sometimes perform these procedures. The purpose of classification varies among institutions, but basically it is expected to help with inmate management or treatment planning efforts.[16]

Although behavior management categories are valuable tools for the correctional administrator, it is most difficult when prisons are at or over their capacity. A general rule of thumb in flexibility for assigning prisoners to appropriate housing to their management categories is that 90 percent of capacity leaves no flexibility. It is also essential that continuing status evaluation and reclassification be done. If treatment in the correctional setting is to be effective, the inmate must be reclassified and different treatments designed and applied from time to time by classification workers. Unfortunately, many a well-conceived treatment plan has failed because of inaccurate or nonexistent reclassification.

The usual purpose for classification, from the viewpoint of the staff, is to create a plan that will "correct" the prisoners and send them back to society as changed people. The prisoners, on the other hand, look on the classification process as yet another way to get out. They try to determine what they are supposed to do to prove they are ready for release and then do it. Because the emphasis on what they must do tends to shift in accordance with the convenience of the administration or the composition of the treatment staff or "suggestions for improvement," this is not an easy task. An inmate may be classified as deficient in education, for example, and so he or she begins day classes; but because the inmate is a skilled baker, he or she is needed in the kitchen and must shift to that role to earn a "good attitude" rating for potential release. In the complex organization of the prison, institutional needs must be met first, even at the expense of correcting the offenders.

Classification was hailed as a revolution in corrections, moving the focus from the mass production tactics of the past to the use of individualized treatment. The failure of classification and advanced social work techniques lies partly in the fact that the prison establishment is resistant to change and partly to the poor environment for change provided in the prisons themselves. Several states have abandoned classification reception-diagnostic centers as counterproductive, because the centers raised inmate and staff expectations above the level of possible achievement. The treatment model has a place somewhere in corrections, but not, it seems, in high-security prisons.

After classification, the offender may be sent to one of seven security levels of institutions: maximum, high/close, multiple, medium, minimum, intake, or community/other facilities. We start with the approximately 135,000 male and 3,500 female offenders housed in the nation's maximum-security institutions.

MAXIMUM-SECURITY PRISONS

The purposes of confinement are punishment, deterrence, incapacitation, rehabilitation, and, more recently, reintegration back into the community. The specific goals and the settings for their achievement are dictated by the particular society's dominant orientation, whether toward individual rights or collective security. Because both orientations command a strong following in America, neither one has entirely super-

CORRECTIONAL BRIEF

The Rise in Imprisonment

Two trends are responsible for the present rise in confinement. First, longer sentences are being imposed for such nonviolent felonies as larceny, theft, and motor vehicle theft. In 1992, according to the Uniform Crime Report, these crimes accounted for 66 percent of crime in America. As James Q. Wilson, who has not in the past been averse to imprisonment, recently wrote: "Very large increases in the prison population can produce only very modest reductions in crime rates. . . . Judges," he observes, "already send the most serious offenders with the longest records to prison," and "the most serious offenders typically get the longest sentences."

Second, everyone who works in the criminal justice system recognizes that drugs have become its driving force. According to the Bureau of Justice Statistics (1992), more than half of all violent offenders in state prisons said they were under the influence of alcohol or drugs at the time of their offense.

SOURCE: Jerome H. Skolnick, "What Not to Do About Crime: The American Society of Criminology 1994 Presidential Address," *Criminology* 33:1 (1995): 9.

seded the other. The scales have tipped in favor of security more often than equity, however, but the battle continues. Championed by politicians and the media, the trend has swung toward using incarceration primarily for purposes of punishment and deterrence.

Prisons were originally built as places that stressed **maximum security** above all other concerns. Typically, they were surrounded by a wall, usually thirty to fifty feet high and several feet thick, topped with razor wire, and equipped with towers staffed by armed guards trained and prepared to prevent possible escapes or riots. Modern structures are more likely to be surrounded by chain-link fence, lit by floodlights after dark, and sometimes bounded by electrified wire fences to further discourage escape attempts. These fortresses are usually placed far out in the countryside, away from the mainstream of American life.

Maximum-Security Prison

A facility designed, built, and managed so as to minimize escape, disturbance, and violence while maximizing control over the inmate population. Custody and security are the primary concerns in a maximum-security prison.

The walled prison was so popular that it was not until 1926 that the first prison without a massive wall appeared in the United States, at the District of Columbia Reformatory in Lorton, Virginia. This facility was finally closed in 1998 by court order because of the conditions there. In the past, it was clear when one approached a typical maximum-security prison that it was designed for control and punishment. The fearsome and forbidding atmosphere of the Auburn style of prison exemplifies the penal philosophy that prisoners must not only do time for their misdeeds but also do so in an environment that emphasizes rejection, doubt, guilt, inferiority, diffusion, self-absorption, apathy, and despair. It is small wonder that these kinds of prisons often released inmates who were less stable emotionally than they were when they entered.

The huge, **Gothic-style monoliths** had been built in the belief that that kind of architecture, as part of the total prison system, would aid in the restoration of prisoners. Gothic architecture was designed to overwhelm the person who entered such structures, just as Notre Dame and the other great gothic churches of Europe made people feel small and insignificant. The idea was discredited by the beginning of the twentieth century, however, and both American and European penologists began to concentrate on treatment strategies. But because America was left with almost sixty of those monstrosities, built before 1900 with only economy, security, and isolation in

Razor wire is ubiquitous in all types of correctional facilities today.

Photo by C. Simonsen, courtesy of Washington State Department of Corrections.

CORRECTIONAL BRIEF

Prison Workloads

A national survey of wardens and state commissioners of corrections revealed considerable agreement on prison workload problems:

- More than half reported that their facilities were full, primarily because of drug offenders serving long sentences who occupied 75 percent of available cells.
- Identifying gang members and gang activities were major problems, and there was a need to develop programs that would discourage gang activities in prison.
- Three of four wardens indicated a need for more program staff, particularly to deal with alcohol and drug substance abuse as well as sex offenders.

One warden noted: "Lines for everything are longer: inmate canteen, inmate meds, meals. Sentence length and distant parole eligibility (if at all) build a central core population. This core population will probably quadruple in the next seven years."

SOURCE: National Institute of Justice, *NJ Survey of Wardens and State Commissioners of Corrections* (Washington, DC: U.S. Department of Justice, 1995), pp. 1–2.

mind, the new programs had to be designed to fit the existing structures. Of course, it should have been the other way around—the physical plants should have been built to fit the programs—and correctional philosophy has changed drastically in the past century. America is no longer tied to the approaches of nearly two centuries ago by the outmoded architecture of most maximum-security prisons.

Inside the Walls

After classification, offenders may be transported to another institution. If they are fortunate, prisoners will be placed in one of the smaller institutions; if not, they will enter one of the giant walled cities. The offenders will pass through a double fence or stone wall surrounded by manned guard towers. As the large steel main gate slams shut behind them, the process of **prisonization** begins. Donald Clemmer, the originator of this term,[17] describes it best:

> *Every man who enters the penitentiary undergoes prisonization to some extent. The first and most obvious integrative step concerns his status. He becomes at once an anonymous figure in a subordinate group. A number replaces a name. He wears the clothes of the other members of the subordinate group. He is questioned and admonished. He soon learns that the warden is all-powerful. He soon learns the ranks, titles, and authority of various officials. And whether he uses the prison slang and argot or not, he comes to know their meanings. Even though a new man may hold himself aloof from other inmates and remain a solitary figure, he finds himself within a few months referring to or thinking of keepers as "screws," the physician as the "croaker," and using the local nicknames to designate persons. He follows the examples already set in wearing his cap. He learns to eat in haste and in obtaining food he imitates the tricks of those near him.*
>
> *After the new arrival recovers from the effects of the swallowing-up process, he assigns a new meaning to conditions he had previously taken for granted. The fact that food, shelter, clothing, and a work activity had been given him originally made no special impression. It is only after some weeks or months that there comes to him a new interpretation of these necessities of life. This new conception results from mingling with other men and it places emphasis*

An inmate peers through a slot in the door of his cell in old Folsom Prison in California.

Photo by Rich Pedroncelli, courtesy of AP/Wide World Photos.

on the fact that the environment should administer to him. This point is intangible and difficult to describe insofar as it is only a subtle and minute change in attitude from the taken-for-granted perception. Exhaustive questioning of hundreds of men reveals that this slight change in attitude is a fundamental step in the process we are calling prisonization.

The effort to depersonalize and routinize is seemingly without respite. The maximum-security prison is geared to supervision, control, and surveillance of the inmate's every move. Every other human consideration is weighed against its possible effect on security.

The pragmatic penal leaders in the last half of the nineteenth century began to accept imprisonment as a valid end in itself, rather than as a means to reform. This attitude turned prisons into a dumping ground for America's poor and "different" masses. Immigrants, blacks, and people who did not fit the all-American image were likely candidates for such remote asylums. The reformers' rhetoric spoke of rehabilitation, but the actions of corrections administrators belied that emphasis. Prisons were built to keep the prisoners in, but also to keep the public out. To justify the imprisonment of such a heterogeneous group of offenders under such rigid control required a theory of uniform treatment and uniform punishment, without regard to individual differences.

The tendency in the nineteenth century to incarcerate minorities out of proportion to their numbers in society remained with us at the end of the twentieth century. By 2003, adult black males in America were more than seven times more likely to be in prison than were adult white males. For females, the ratio is almost five to one. The reasons for the disparity are hotly debated.

New inmates are reminded of that principle as they are processed into the prison. The buildings, policies, rules, regulations, and control procedures are designed to eliminate all prisoner control over the environment. No privacy is allowed in their windowless and open cells. Even the toilets are open to view, and showers are taken under close visual observation. Every consideration is given by

SIDEBARS

Prisonization

The process by which the inmate learns, through socialization, the rules and regulations of the penal institution, as well as the informal values, rules, and customs of the penitentiary culture. Once these values have been inculcated, the inmate becomes generally inoculated against conventional values. Thus, prisonization can be seen as a criminalization process whereby a criminal novice is transformed from basically a prosocial errant to a committed predatory criminal.

It is important to remember that correctional staff can be prisonized as well, although the degree and extent of socialization is not as extensive, nor long lasting. Prisonization for the officer generally reflects the necessity of managing and interacting with inmates; the officer has to know and manipulate the inmate system to attain individual and institutional goals.

Inmates pass string to send notes across cells in maximum security, Holman unit, Alabama.
Photo by A. Ramey, courtesy of PhotoEdit.

the designers and operators to prevent intrusion or contact from the outside. Visits are usually closely supervised, and a visitor's contacts with the inmates are sometimes possible only by special communication devices[18] that allow conversation but no physical contact. A body search of the inmate, including visual inspection of all body cavities, is invariably conducted if contact has been made. Everything is locked, and all movements require short trips between locked doors.[19]

This description offers only a rough idea of a maximum-security prison on the inside. Nothing can substitute for an actual visit to or confinement in one of these monuments to society's triumph of external control over internal reform. Although some of these human cages are more than 180 years old, others are relatively new; but the differences involve only minor physical refinements, not basic philosophical changes. Such prisons form the backbone of corrections because they house well over 135,000 inmates and because they are durable.[20]

Prisons vary so greatly from state to state that generalizations are dangerous, and the comments of Alexis de Tocqueville in that regard, though made over a century and a half ago, are still valid today.[21] He wrote in 1833 that "aside from common interests, the several states preserve their individual independence, and each

A shank is a makeshift weapon used by inmates to settle scores as they occur.
Courtesy of Dupont Advanced Fibers Systems.

of them is sovereign master to rule itself according to its own pleasure. By the side of one state, the penitentiaries of which might serve as a model, we find another whose prisons present the example of everything which ought to be avoided."[22]

Supermax: The Next Notch Up on Security

In the 1990s, violent, seriously disruptive, assaultive, and escape-prone inmates, including gang activists, posed immense challenges to prison security and custody. Challenges included threats to the safety of staff and inmates, danger to the security of an institution, and the collapse of protective custody. The super-maximum prison (or **supermax**) is a response to the need to manage and securely control inmates exhibiting continuous violent or seriously disruptive behavior while incarcerated. Is this the trend of the future? What litigation issues can be anticipated?

Supermax housing is a free-standing facility, or a distinct unit within a facility, that provides for the management and secure control of inmates who have been officially designated as exhibiting violent or seriously disruptive behavior while incarcerated. Such inmates have been determined to be a threat to safety and security in even the traditional high-security facilities, and only separation, restricted movement, and limited direct access to staff and other inmates can control their behavior.

Supermax housing does not include maximum or close custody facilities or units that are designated for routine housing of inmates with high custody needs, inmates in disciplinary segregation or protective custody, or other inmates requiring segregation or separation for other routine purposes. A common definition of supermax housing is difficult to pin down. It is clear that what is "supermax" in one jurisdiction may not be so in another. It is evident that some jurisdictions' supermax facilities or units house only those inmates who cannot be controlled in traditional segregation or administrative confinement conditions. Others are, essentially, an extension or expansion of traditional segregation or administrative confinement and may house protective custody or disciplinary segregation inmates or both.

In some jurisdictions, mentally ill inmates are specifically excluded from the supermax population, while in others this level of control is viewed as necessary because of the paucity of mental health resources. Some supermax facilities or units have transitional beds that provide an opportunity for inmates to earn privileges that are similar to those in the maximum-security general population. In the case of a supermax unit within a high-custody facility, the supermax bed count does not usually include transitional beds to the same extent as in a free-standing supermax facility.

The Special Housing Unit: A Jail Within a Maximum-Security Prison

What do you do with an inmate who is housed in a supermax institution and commits a violent or illegal act while in residence there? If the inmate is already in the highest custody category, there has to be some way to control that person, but how? The answer in most systems is to have a **special housing unit (SHU)**. This alternative to the austere conditions in supermax is the last stage of inmate control within a high-security institution. The way in which a SHU is designed and utilized depends on the facility and conformation of the construction. Reserved for the "baddest of the bad," this austere setting is often accompanied by the use of such restraints as handcuffs, leg irons, and belly chains until the inmate is under control and begins to conform to behavioral rules. This modern version of "the hole" differs in many ways from the old solitary confinement, although handled through a wide range of procedures.

The SHU has become the object of a great deal of litigation and it will be some time before all the "cans and cannots" will be firmed up because conditions and procedures for dealing with this penultimate group of offenders are being examined and approved by courts in every state employing these programs. The use of restraints and the employment of tactical teams to deal with these offenders have been pretty well established, but the litigation continues. Medical staff to detect the signs of mental[23] or physical deterioration and treat such effects that often arise from isolation and restricted movement must carefully monitor those who spend long periods of time in these extremely secure and barren settings. As more and more serious offenders spend the rest of their lives in confinement, it is clear that something like the SHUs will evolve and become standardized to provide that extra level of security that will provide protection for inmates and staff against violence and injury on the part of already violent persons.

SIDEBARS

Medium- and Minimum-Security Prisons

Medium-security institutions are prisons designed, built, and operated to prevent escape, disturbances, and violence. Double fences topped with barbed or razor wire usually enclose such institutions. However, they have fewer restrictions on the movement and activities of prison inmates than those found in maximum-security institutions. Minimum-security prisons allow maximum inmate movement, freedom, and self-determination, while still following methods to avoid escape, violence, and disturbances. Most inmates prefer less secure settings, but usually such environments are viewed as privileges for inmates who are felt to be trustworthy or who have proven their ability to conform in less structured environments. Regular reclassification reviews will improve the match between lesser security and inmate trustworthiness.

MEDIUM-SECURITY INSTITUTIONS

In the twentieth century, various experimental alternatives to the maximum-security approach were launched. Much of the construction in corrections during the past half century has been for **medium-security** institutions, in which four in ten of all state prisoners are now housed. Early medium-security prisons were hard to distinguish from maximum-security institutions; control was still the dominant concern. Even though security may be almost as tight in a medium-security prison, the prisoners are not made so aware that they are being watched. Medium-security prisons also are usually smaller, without the overwhelming impersonality of the maximum-security monoliths. There are more inmate programs and the offender's routine is somewhat less regimented.

Some of the most recent medium-security prisons are patterned after the so-called community college campus design, including attractive residence areas with single rooms (not cells) and dormitories for inmates. External fences and subtle features installed within buildings to maintain security and protect the inmates from

Even in a tent facility the guards must always look for contraband and drugs.

Photo by Jerri Edgar, courtesy of Maricopa County Sheriff's Department.

one another are the only obvious signs that the prisoners are under constant observation. Sophisticated electronic and other surveillance equipment is used, but unobtrusively. Assisting in the effective design of these new correctional facilities are such organizations as the National Clearinghouse for Correctional Programming and Architecture.[24] Because it seems that the United States will continue to use imprisonment as its primary response to criminal behavior, the new medium-security systems may well represent the first wave of the future for correctional prisons in America.

NEW PRISONS: 1989 TO 2004

Since 1989, the prison construction boom has begun to slow (see Figure 9.5). More than 400 new prison facilities were added (excluding renovations, expansions, and extensions of existing prisons, as well as prison camps, community work release units, facilities for offenders convicted of driving under the influence of alcohol and drugs, etc.). Any new prison built in the twenty-first century is most likely to be a medium-security facility.

A newer trend to emerge from overreliance on prisons for correcting offenders is the bricks and mortar solution to prison overcrowding, in which states basically attempt to solve a policy problem by constructing new buildings or renovating older facilities (see Chapter 6). Ordinarily, construction is time consuming, and prisons are "handcrafted" on site; the expected time from the decision to build to committing the first inmate to prison is almost five years. Innovations in prison construction, aimed at cost effectiveness and quicker completion times, have taken place in Oklahoma, Florida, Arizona, California, and Ohio. These newer options in construction and financing have allowed corrections to avoid more costly and time-consuming construction approaches and have somewhat, but not totally, eased prison overcrowding. In addition, some states use private sector prisons as an additional strategy to avoid prison overcrowding. At the end of 2003, thirty states and the federal prison system reported a total of 95,500 prisoners held in privately operated facilities.[25]

Two other kinds of correctional institutions are prisons in name, but not in their operations today. These are **minimum-security** and **open institutions,** designed to serve the needs of rural farm areas and public works rather than those of

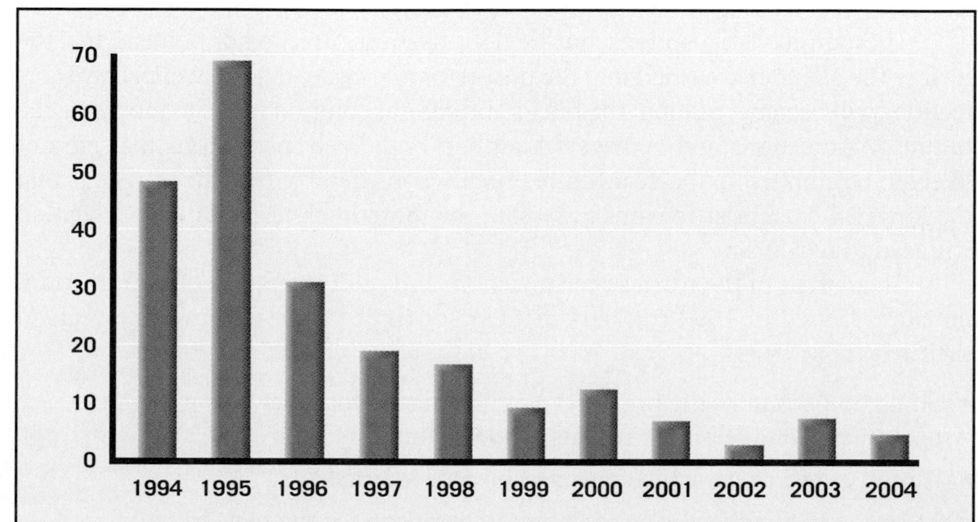

FIGURE 9.5

New Institutions Opened, 1994–2004

SOURCE: American Correctional Association, *2004 Directory* (Lanham, MD: ACA, 2004).

the offender. Prisoners with good security classifications are assigned to such programs, which range from plantation-style prison farms to small forestry, forest fire fighting, and road camps.

In many ways, the minimum-security and open facilities are beneficial. They rescue relatively stable inmates from the oppressive rigors of confinement and from personal danger in the large stifling prisons. As long as we continue to give long prison terms to offenders who are little threat to themselves or the public, the open facilities are preferable to traditional prisons. On the other hand, if we develop more programs of education, work, vocational training, and treatment within the maximum- and medium-security institutions, inmates in the minimum-security work-oriented camps may miss those opportunities.[26] Also, as intermediate punishments and community-based corrections programs continue to drain off the least dangerous and more treatable offenders, the open facilities will lose their value—they are not suited to the hard-core offenders who will remain. Professionals in the corrections field will have to resist efforts to place offenders into minimum-security or open facilities for economic reasons, rather than placing them into community-based programs for correctional treatment reasons.

The minimum-security institution is a logical compromise between the medium-security prison and community-based corrections. The abandonment of the fortress-style prisons of a bygone era is a necessary step in that direction, because a few very small maximum-security facilities could be built or renovated to house the estimated 15 to 25 percent of the incarcerated felons who need that kind of protection and surveillance.

ALTERNATIVES TO PRISON OVERCROWDING

Of the three basic correctional options for reducing prison populations and overcrowding, the student has encountered two: the bricks and mortar building program and the front-end, or prison-avoidance, programming. The latter includes restitution programs, intensive supervised probation, house arrest, electronic monitoring, shock probation, boot camps,[27] intermittent imprisonment, and other innovative programs of intermediate sanctions (see Chapter 8). In the next chapter, which deals with state and local systems, we discuss the back-end alternatives: early release, parole, increased good-time credits, home arrest under parole, halfway houses, prerelease centers, and other alternatives to prison overcrowding.

They are all viable options, but we need to stress three major points. First, the further the offender is carried into the prison–parole cycle, the more expensive corrections will become. Second, the bricks and mortar solution tends to mortgage the future of corrections and taxpayers, saddling both with institutions that are not likely to be emptied in the near future. Finally, considerable evidence suggests that the longer the offender remains in prison, the more likely it is that incapacitation will lead to recidivism.

An analysis of the rearrest, reconviction, and reincarceration of over 250,000 inmates released in 1994 tracked offenders for three years. Within three years of their release in 1994:

- Some 68 percent of the prisoners were rearrested for a new offense, almost exclusively for a felony or serious misdemeanor.
- Almost 47 percent were reconvicted for a new crime.
- More than 25 percent were resentenced to prison for the new crime.

- More than 50 percent were back in prison, either serving time for a new prison sentence or a technical violation of their release, such as failing drug tests, missing appointments with a parole officer, or being arrested for a new crime.

Those released prisoners with the highest rearrest rates were motor vehicle thieves (79 percent), sellers of stolen property (77 percent), larcenists (75 percent), burglars (74 percent), or robbers or those formerly in prison for possessing, using, or selling illegal weapons (70 percent each).[28] Prisons that are overcrowded and serve as warehouses do little to lower the recidivism rate.

THE FUTURE OF IMPRISONMENT

It has frequently been shown that the large adult prisons operated by the state provide the least effective means to rehabilitate and reintegrate offenders. Despite findings to that effect, in the 1920s,[29] 1930s,[30] 1960s,[31] 1970s,[32] 1980s,[33] and 1990s,[34] the building and filling of prisons continued. The advent, and relative success, of community-based treatment of criminal offenders has begun to dent the armor of the diehards who advocate punitive prison as the ultimate correctional solution. It is the threat that those new programs pose to the old-line institutional staff that must be overcome before the present system, which exists primarily to perpetuate itself, can undergo any real change.

In the last five years, the rate of increase in the number of prisoners has slowed, in part due to selective incapacitation, the baby boomers passing through the high-crime-rate years, diversion of drug-abusing offenders and drug-addicted parolees, and increased use of technology in parole supervision. All are positive signs of more effective correctional policy and management as corrections enters the twenty-first century.

SUMMARY

The opening of new institutions reached a new peak in 1995, but had slowed by mid-2005. Because of the new sentencing structures, drug-related crime, and unacceptable levels of violence, it seems that the realities of prison population increases will create a need to open 2,500 new beds for inmates per month in America, which is a difficult goal to attain in the foreseeable future. In the next three chapters the student will examine the various correctional systems that have appeared in the United States to provide the programs and institutions to handle adult prisoners.

REVIEW QUESTIONS

1. What are the main purposes of confinement?
2. Differentiate between classification for management and for treatment.
3. Describe a typical maximum-security prison. Explain the main differences among maximum-, medium-, and minimum-security institutions.
4. What are the front-end solutions to prison overcrowding? The bricks and mortar solution?
5. What are the impacts of prison overcrowding?
6. Develop an argument against imprisonment of offenders from the recidivism perspective.
7. Why is the nation's prison population so high?
8. Why have prison populations grown so rapidly?
9. Describe a typical supermax prison.
10. Debate: The high imprisonment rate for African American men is due to racism in the justice system.

ENDNOTES

1. American Correctional Association, *2004 Directory* (Lanham, MD: ACA, 2004), p. 30.
2. Paige Harrison and Allen Beck, *Prisoners in 2003* (Washington, DC: U.S. Department of Justice, 2004), p. 7.
3. Peter Garabedian, "Social Roles in Prison," in Leon Radzinowicz and M. Wolfgang (eds.), *The Criminal in Confinement* (New York: Basic Books, 1971), pp. 116–117.
4. Bureau of Justice Statistics, *Prisoners in 2001* (Washington, DC: BJS, 2002), pp. 12–13.
5. Lauren Glaze and Seri Palla, *Probation and Parole in the United States, 2003* (Washington, DC: Bureau of Justice Statistics, 2004), p. 9.
6. Harrison and Beck, *Prisoners in 2003*, p. 9. See also Marc Mauer and Ryan King, *Schools and Prisons Fifty Years After* Brown v. Board of Education (Washington, DC: The Sentencing Project, 2004).
7. Mauer and King, *Schools and Prisons.*
8. Editors, "Minnesota DOC Says Prison Crisis Looms," *Correctional News* 10:7 (2004): 6.
9. Michael Tonry, "Mandatory Penalties," in *Crime and Justice: A Review of the Research*, Vol. 16 (Chicago: University of Chicago Press, 1993), pp. 243–273.
10. Harrison and Beck, *Prisoners in 2003*, p. 4; and Harry Allen, "The American Dream and Crime in the Twenty-First Century," *Justice Quarterly* 12:3 (1995): 427–445.
11. Joan Petersilia, "Hard Time," *Corrections Today* 67:2 (2005), p. 66.
12. The news on recidivism from the prison front—absent meaningful programs responsibly delivered and continued assistance once released—is abysmal. Recent studies found releasees who had earlier committed robberies had a 70 percent rearrest rate for new crimes. Bureau of Justice Statistics, *Recidivism of Prisoners Released in 1994*, www.ojp.usdoj.gov/bjs/pub/pdf/rpr94.pdf. A study of Canadian male releasees found a 53 percent return rate: Philip Firestone, J. Bradford, M. McCoy, et al., "Recidivism in Convicted Rapists," *Journal of the American Academy of Psychiatry and the Law* 26:2 (1998): 185–200.
13. Petersilia, "Hard Time," p. 67.
14. Lance Hannon and J. DeFranzo, "Welfare and Property Crime," *Justice Quarterly* 15:2 (1998): 273–288; and Anna Campbell, S. Muncer, and D. Bibel, "Female–Female Criminal Involvement," *Journal of Research in Crime and Delinquency* 35:4 (1998): 413–428.
15. Randy Borum, "Managing At-Risk Juvenile Offenders in the Community," *Journal of Contemporary Criminal Justice* 19:1 (2003): 114–137; and Christopher Lowenkamp and Edward Latessa, "Developing Successful Reentry Programs," *Corrections Today* 67:2 (2005): 72–77.
16. United Nations Department of Economic and Social Affairs, *Standard Minimum Rules for the Treatment of Prisoners and Related Recommendations* (New York: United Nations, 1958), p. B-16.
17. Donald Clemmer, "The Process of Prisonization," in Radzinowicz and Wolfgang, *The Criminal in Confinement*, pp. 92–93. See also Brent Paterline and D. Petersen, "Structural and Social Psychological Determinants of Prisonization," *Journal of Contemporary Justice* 27:5 (1999): 427–441.
18. Special devices for communicating include telephones on either side of bulletproof glass and booths with wire screen between inmates and visitors. See Taylor Duecker, "Video Visitation a Boon in Omaha," *American Jails* 18:5 (2004): 65–67.
19. For discussion of architecture, construction, design, and innovations in jails and prisons, see the special theme issue of *Corrections Today* 59:2 (1997): 70–108. See also Gail Elias and K. Ricci, *Women in Jail: Facilities Planning Issues* (Washington, DC: National Institute of Corrections, 1997).
20. ACA, *2004 Directory*, p. 46.
21. Alexis de Tocqueville was one of the French commissioners who visited America in 1833. He wrote a treatise on what he observed in the American penitentiary system.
22. Gustave de Beaumont and Alexis de Tocqueville, *On the Penitentiary System in the United States and Its Application in France* (Carbondale: Southern Illinois University Press, 1964), p. 48.
23. Jensenia Pizarro and Vanja Stenius, "Supermax Prisons," *The Prison Journal* 84:2 (2004): 248–264.
24. Dale Sechrest and Shelley Price, *Correctional Facility Design and Construction Management* (Washington, DC: U.S. Department of Justice, 1985). See also the special themes issues of *Corrections Today* 51 (April 1989), 52 (April 1990), 55 (April 1993), and 59 (April 1997).
25. Harrison and Beck, *Prisoners in 2003*, p. 5.
26. Frank Porporino and David Robinson, *Can Educating Adult Offenders Counteract Recidivism?* (Ontario: Correctional Service of Canada, 1992); Kaye McLarren, *Reducing Reoffending: What Works Now* (Wellington: Penal Division, New Zealand Department of Justice, 1992); and Faith Lutze, "Are Shock Incarceration Programs More Rehabilitative Than the Traditional Prisons?" *Justice Quarterly* 15:3 (1998): 547–566. But see Jim Croyne, *The Repugnant Warehouse* (Clifton Park, NY: Elysium Publishing, 1996).
27. J. Burns and G. Vito, "An Impact Analysis of the Alabama Boot Camp Program," *Federal Probation* 59:1

(1995): 63–67. But see Dale Colledge and J. Gerber, "Rethinking the Assumptions About Boot Camps," *Federal Probation* 62:1 (1998): 54–67; and Vanessa St. Gerard, "Federal Prisons to Eliminate Boot Camps," *Corrections Today* 67:2 (2005): 13.

28. Bureau of Justice Statistics, *Recidivism of Prisoners Released in 1994*.
29. National Commission on Law Observance and Enforcement (Wickersham Commission), *Report on Prisons* (Washington, DC: U.S. Government Printing Office, 1929).
30. *Attorney General's Survey of Release Procedures* (Washington, DC: U.S. Government Printing Office, 1939).
31. President's Commission on Law Enforcement and Administration of Justice, *Corrections* (Washington, DC: U.S. Government Printing Office, 1967).
32. National Advisory Commission on Criminal Justice Standards and Goals, *Corrections* (Washington, DC: U.S. Government Printing Office, 1973).
33. Marilyn McShane and Frank Williams, "Running on Empty: Creativity and the Correctional Agenda," *Crime and Delinquency* 35:4 (1989): 562–576.
34. Joan Petersilia, "A Crime Control Rationale for Reinventing Community Corrections," *Spectrum* (Summer 1995): 16–27.

CHAPTER 10

State and Local Prison Systems

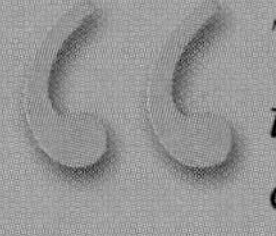

The endurance of these monolithic structures is surpassed only by the tenacity of the assumptions and attitudes on which they were founded: the cause of crime is located in the individual offender; he should be punished for his acts; behavior is modifiable; and isolated institutions are appropriate settings in which to modify an individual's behavior. America had created a theory, reformation by confinement, and the system has been unwilling to abandon it although it has proved unworkable.

—William G. Nagel, *The New Red Barn*

KEY WORDS

- alternative to death
- agricultural prison
- work camps
- classification process
- institutional needs
- security threat group (STG)
- supermax prison

OVERVIEW

In past chapters we have examined the philosophies, the clients, and the functions and tasks of the operators of jails, probation, and America's prisons. We have seen the male–female and racial allocations to the facilities that make up systems that cost the taxpayers almost $43 billion to operate each year. (See Figure 10.1 for a breakout of these system costs.) This chapter takes you into the basic

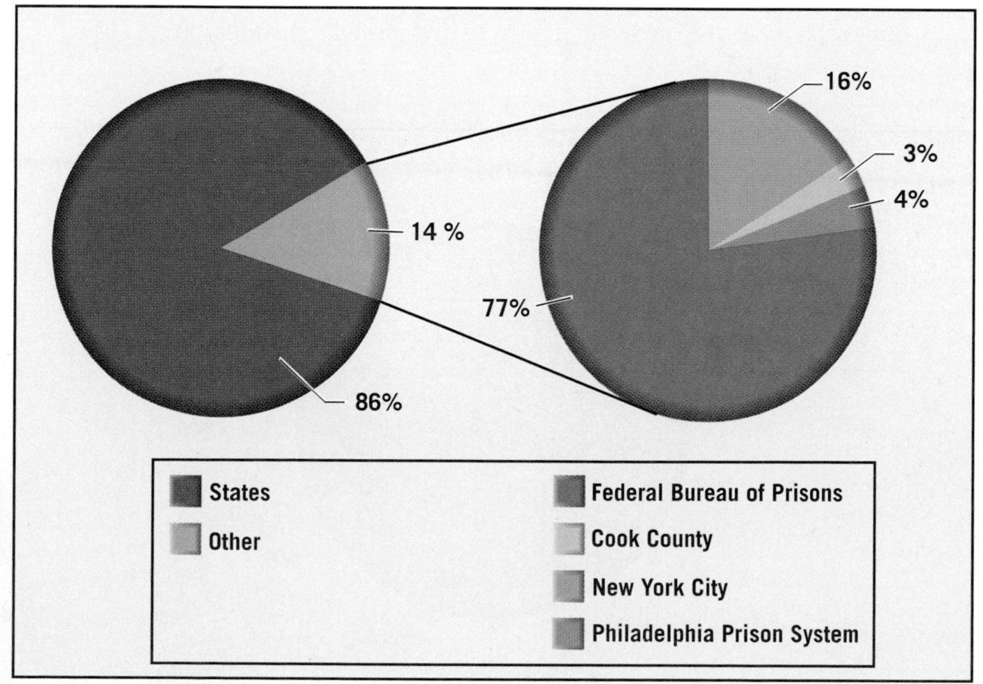

FIGURE 10.1

Annual Costs of Prisons in the United States, 2003: $42,939,742,000

SOURCE: American Correctional Association, *2004 Directory* (Lanham, MD: ACA, 2004), p. 20.

< Hays Prison in Georgia, a modern high-security prison.
Photo by Point de Vue, courtesy of Gamma Press USA, Inc.

functions and characteristics of the state prisons, using male adult offenders, who constitute 93 percent of the population, as our vehicle.[1] Women inmates are discussed in Chapter 15. Because they are not an insignificant part of daily state and local adult prison activity, the male inmate and institution are used here as a demonstration of how most of the systems operate.

STATE CORRECTIONAL INSTITUTIONS: THE CORE OF THE SYSTEM

This chapter explores the state systems for housing the well over 1,410,000 adult sentenced male and female offenders in more than 1,600 adult state and local prisons in America[2] as of 2004. Juvenile institutions, detention centers, jails, workhouses, and other facilities for misdemeanants and minor offenders are not included. The major correctional institutions contained in the state systems are maximum close, medium-, and minimum-security prisons (see Figure 10.2), many of which are modeled after the nineteenth-century concepts in the Auburn penitentiary.

Those institutions form the core of most state correctional programs charged with the simultaneous, and often conflicting, functions of punishment and reform. Most are short on money and personnel, but they are still expected to prevent their graduates from returning to crime. Security and custody are the primary emphases in these prisons, and their environments are isolated both physically and philosophically from the mainstream of life. James V. Bennett, a former director of the federal Bureau of Prisons, described the ironic situation thirty years ago:

> *Even our modern prison system is proceeding on a rather uncertain course because its administration is necessarily a series of compromises. On the one hand, prisons are expected to punish; on the other, they are supposed to reform. They are expected to discipline rigorously at the same time that they teach self-reliance. They are built to be operated like vast impersonal machines, yet they are expected to fit men to live normal community lives. They*

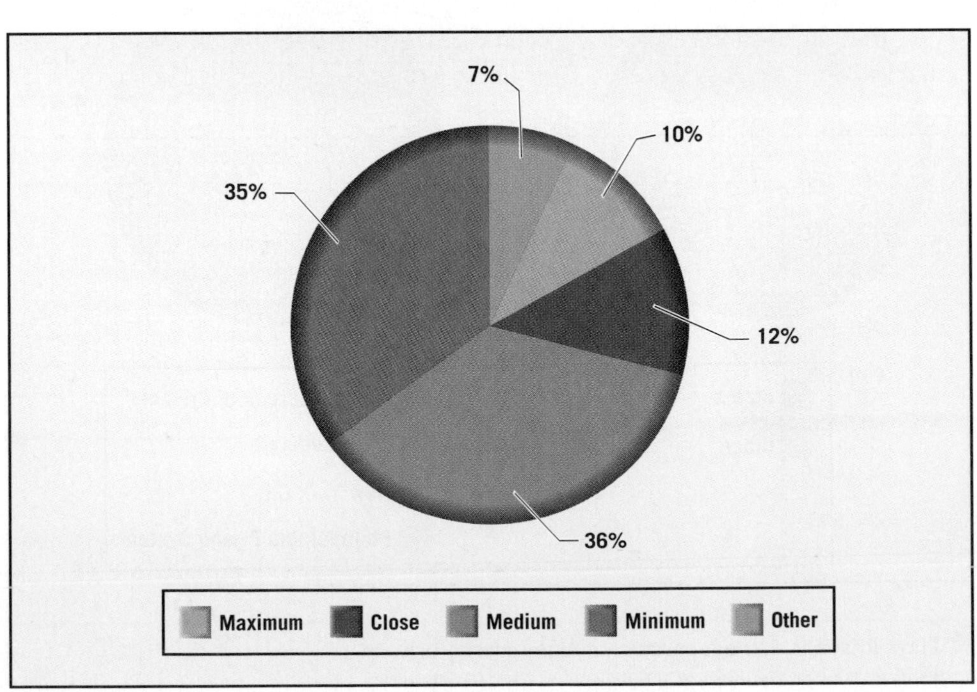

FIGURE 10.2

Percentage of Male Inmates in Security Levels, 2003

SOURCE: American Correctional Association, *2004 Directory* (Lanham, MD: ACA, 2003), p. 56.

operate in accordance with a fixed autocratic routine, yet they are expected to develop individual initiative. All too frequently restrictive laws force prisoners into idleness despite the fact that one of their primary objectives is to teach men how to earn an honest living. They refuse a prisoner a voice in self-government, but they expect him to become a thinking citizen in a democratic society. To some, prisons are nothing but "country clubs" catering to the whims and fancies of the inmates. To others the prison atmosphere seems charged only with bitterness, rancor, and an all-pervading sense of defeat. And so the whole paradoxical scheme continues, because our ideas and views regarding the function of correctional institutions in our society are confused, fuzzy, and nebulous.[3]

Correctional institutions are both a blessing and a curse. Reflecting a positive and humane movement away from the cruel punishments of the eighteenth century, they provided an **alternative to death** and flogging; but in terms of reforming inmates so they can lead a noncriminal life in the free world, prisons have mostly failed. Still, the public's perceived need to feel safe and secure and the prison's effectiveness in isolating offenders from society have unfortunately made this system the primary response to criminal behavior. The 1,410,000 male and female inmates confined in state correctional institutions for adults at mid-year 2004 were distributed among maximum, close medium, minimum, and other security institutions.[4] We project that by the year 2010, prison populations (state and local city systems) will have grown to over 1.3 million Americans (see Figure 10.3), and with the federal inmates calculated in, to approximately 1.6 million prisoners.

Organization of State Systems

Of all the thousands of various types of correctional facilities in America—public and private, adult and juvenile, community and city, and others—only 16 percent of them are under the control of state agencies. It is not surprising that the correctional "system" in most states is not really systematized at all. Organizational rigidity and huge investments in bricks and mortar have handicapped meaningful revision and modernization of corrections. Rehabilitation and reintegration require that organizational structures be concerned with more than just institutional programs. In at least six states, that organizational need has been met by exercising control over all correctional activities at the state level. Hawaii, for example, has a unified jail and prison

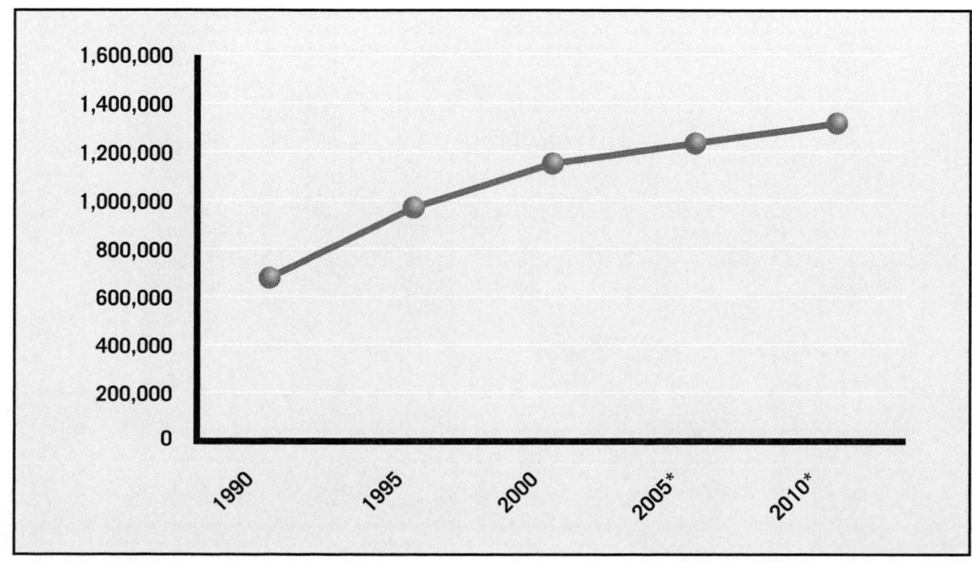

FIGURE 10.3

Inmates in State Prisons: 1990–2010*

*Data for 2005 and 2010 are extrapolated.

SOURCE: Paige Harrison and Allen Beck, *Prisoners in 2003* (Washington, DC: Bureau of Justice Statistics, 2004), p. 2.

SIDEBARS

Pennsylvania Prison Society

The Pennsylvania Prison Society is the modern version of the Philadelphia Society for Alleviating the Miseries of Public Prisons, founded by Dr. Benjamin Rush in 1787. The "new" name was adopted in 1887. For over two centuries, the society has worked as an advocate for prisoners, prison reform, and humane treatment. The society sponsors the *Prison Journal*, a refereed journal currently edited at the Indiana University of Pennsylvania.

PROFILE

Sir Thomas Beever (1726–1814)

designed and operated the Gaol at Wymondham, in Norfolk, England. Though little known by most correctional students, the Philadelphia Society for Alleviating the Miseries of Public Prisons noted his work at the gaol in a 1790 pamphlet. This resulted in the Pennsylvania Act of April 5, 1790, which created the first penitentiary in the United States at the Walnut Street Jail.

system. In Canada, all offenders sentenced to two years or less of imprisonment are incarcerated at a provincial ("state-level") prison, whereas those serving longer sentences are committed to the federal prison system.

Corrections at the state level generally is organized into a separate department of corrections (with a cabinet-level secretary or director appointed by the governor) or a division within a larger state department. Most correctional administrators consider the separate department to be more effective, and having the director at the cabinet level adds great flexibility and prestige to the correctional operation. Without an intermediate level of organization, the director of a separate department has the ability to move more freely at the policy-making level. An autonomous department is able to control the allocation of personnel and fiscal resources, using economy-of-scale purchasing and operating with minimum competition from other divisions within the same department. Centralized control also has the advantage of providing effective administrative functions that are unique to correctional problems.

The corrections process must include a system of multilevel programs and facilities to provide the spectrum of services required to make a statewide program work. Most state correctional systems are concerned only with the principal institutions and parole services, leaving the majority of correctional problems in the state to units of local government.

Development of State Systems

Each type of state correctional system has developed as a matter of historical accident as much as in response to a state's particular needs. As might be expected, the large industrial prisons of the northeast United States are more in evidence in the major industrial states, generally in the area between Illinois and New York. Most of those institutions were built early in the prison movement and were designed to take advantage of the cheap labor force inmates represented. They were the hardest hit by the restrictions the government later placed on prison industries in the 1930s.

At present, the industry allowed in the giant institutions does not provide full employment for large inmate populations.[5] In an effort to spread the few jobs

An example of a modern maximum-security prison.
Photo by Renato Rotolo, courtesy of Getty Images, Inc.-Liaison.

San Quentin State Prison.
Courtesy State of California Department of Corrections.

among the many inmates, supervisors try to slow production and make the work last as long as possible. Those procedures are not likely to provide the inmate with a very good model for job success on the outside. The general picture of activity in the one-time industrial prisons is one of idleness and boredom. Despite even the most dedicated attempts by the staff inside and outside the institutions, there are just not enough meaningful jobs or other programs to help the thousands crowded into the likes of the Raifords (Florida), Atticas (New York), and San Quentins (California) of the country, although some exceptional programs exist.

The **agricultural prison** was begun in the southern states. Prison farms became very profitable ventures for those states and thus have been slow to change. Prisoners who served on public works and state farms replaced the pre–Civil War slave labor in many states, not only in the South.[6] Here again, authorities may have rationalized that the training received from farm work and mines[7] helped prepare offenders for return to a basically agrarian southern economy, but the real intent was to use free labor to produce farm products. Cheap prison labor was often leased out to farm owners at a great profit to both the farmer and the state that collected the fee. The use of prison farms has become less profitable, however, with the advent of highly mechanized farming methods in most agricultural states.

Other regions of the country have designated certain institutions as farm oriented. The food produced in those institutions has been used to feed the rest of the institutions in the state. Many states have now begun to abandon that practice as the realization has hit that farming experience is of little value to the primarily urban inmate found to be a large majority in most contemporary prisons. Another problem with prison farms has been the negative reaction from farm organizations, whose members argue that competition from the state is unfair, much the same argument as union workers protested about prison manufacturing industries in the early part of the twentieth century.[8]

Many states have chosen to set up **work camps** and other forms of prisoner activity appropriate to their particular needs. Lumber camps have been used, as have road prisons or camps to construct and maintain roads. Recent versions of the work camp have been geared to provide a combination of hard work in the outdoors and programmed treatment aimed at preparing the offender for release. It is

PROFILE

Jeremy Bentham (1748–1832)

was the creator of the "panopticon" plan for prisons, consisting of a huge structure covered by a glass roof. A central cupola with cell blocks radiating out like spokes of a wheel allowed the guards to see into the cells. The U.S. government built several of these monsters. The first was at Richmond, Virginia, in 1800, and the last was Statesville Prison in Illinois in 1919. Bentham believed that more light would help control inmates, long before the electric light bulb was invented.

considered more beneficial for offenders to do time in the relatively healthful atmosphere of a small work camp than to languish in the idleness and boredom of the large prisons.

Classification and Assignment in State Prisons

Most state codes provide for the separation or classification of prisoners, their division into different grades with promotion or demotion according to merit or demerit, their employment and instruction in industrial pursuits, and their education. Most also stipulate that reformation of prisoners is a primary goal, although certain exceptions apply. California, for example, now advocates punishment.

In most systems, the initial classification determines the institution to which an inmate will be assigned. The receiving institution then determines whether the individual shall remain in maximum security or be transferred to a medium- or minimum-security penitentiary. (Each state in the United States has at least one maximum-security institution.) Most states base their transfer decisions on a perception of the individual's ability to handle the next lowest level of security. Also important is an evaluation of the individual's ability to adjust to a program geared primarily to work, to academic or vocational training, or to the needs of the growing number of older offenders. A classification committee usually participates in making those decisions.

The **classification process** continues at the institutional level. Although each receiving institution emphasizes different programs, each has some version of education, counseling, and the other ingredients of a total program. Theoretically, individuals are assigned according to their needs but, realistically, assignments are too often made to conform to institutional needs. For example, an inmate may genuinely want to learn welding. If the welding class is filled, as it often might be, but there is a vacancy in the furniture shop, the inmate may be assigned to the furniture shop, and no effort would be made to offer additional welding instruction. Also, inmates will often be assigned to a maintenance operation, such as food service or janitorial work, that is unlikely to conform to their own vocational plans or ambitions. An essential element of effective classification is a periodic review of the inmate's progress through the recommended program. All institutions allow for this reevaluation, usually called *reclassification*. The purpose is to adjust the program in accordance with the inmate's progress and needs. Realistically, however, decisions are all too frequently made on the basis of the available vacancies and **institutional needs.**

In 2005, the U.S. Supreme Court determined that new or recently transferred inmates may not be segregated by race in the classification process. Prison administrators would argue that such segregation serves institutional interests and has legitimate correctional functions, lowering the volume of conflicts between security threat groups ("gangs") and inmates who bear grudges against other inmates or groups.[9]

Institution personnel may genuinely wish to provide the recommended program for an inmate. However, the need to keep the institution running smoothly inevitably shapes these decisions. Personnel may rationalize maintenance assignments on the basis that many, if not most, inmates need the experience of accepting supervision, developing regular work habits, learning to relate to coworkers, and other such skills. All of that may be true, but the treatment staff members are no less frustrated than the inmates when their recommended and prescribed programs are ignored. The classification and assignment process just described is only a composite of what the more effective programs provide.

TABLE 10.1 Number of Sentenced Male Prisoners Under State or Federal Jurisdiction, 2003, by Race and Age

AGE	TOTAL	WHITE	BLACK	HISPANIC
18–19	26,300	7,500	13,100	5,100
20–24	219,400	63,800	104,100	48,500
25–29	245,300	68,700	116,700	57,300
30–34	238,200	77,500	106,500	51,000
35–39	228,200	82,700	99,200	41,000
40–44	197,900	78,500	83,900	30,400
45–54	190,800	80,200	78,600	26,600
55 or older	60,300	33,300	17,900	7,500
Total	1,409,280	493,400	621,300	268,100

SOURCE: Paige Harrison and Allen Beck, *Prisoners in 2003* (Washington, DC: Bureau of Justice Statistics, 2004), p. 9.

INMATES IN STATE PRISONS

In 1983, the U.S. Department of Justice conducted a national survey of inmates in state correctional facilities in the United States and found an estimated 381,955 offenders under the jurisdiction of state government.[10] Since that study was conducted, the population of state prisons has skyrocketed to almost 1.5 million, an increase of over 284 percent (see Table 10.1).

An overwhelming majority of the inmates (93 percent) are males and, relative to the numbers of men and women in the U.S. resident population, their incarceration rate is about 15 times higher (915 males to 62 females) per 100,000 populations. The number of white male to black male inmates has been increasing at the state level, and is now 35 and 44 percent, respectively.[11] All other minority males (Hispanics and others) now total 12 percent of the state prison populations. Hispanics are the fastest growing group in state prisons.[12] The average age is about thirty-three years; and over 9 percent of the total population was at least age fifty, reflecting the graying of America's general population as well as populations of inmates. Imprisonment rates for adult males by race can be found in Figure 10.4.

SIDEBARS

Criminal Justice Status

At the time of their current arrest, almost half of the male inmates in state prisons had some prior criminal justice status. One in four were on parole, and one in five were on probation. Almost 1 percent had escaped from confinement.

SIDEBARS

Criminal History

In 1997, at the time of the last national survey of male inmates in state prisons, almost half (48 percent) were violent recidivists. Another three in ten were nonviolent recidivists. Less than one in four had no previous sentence.

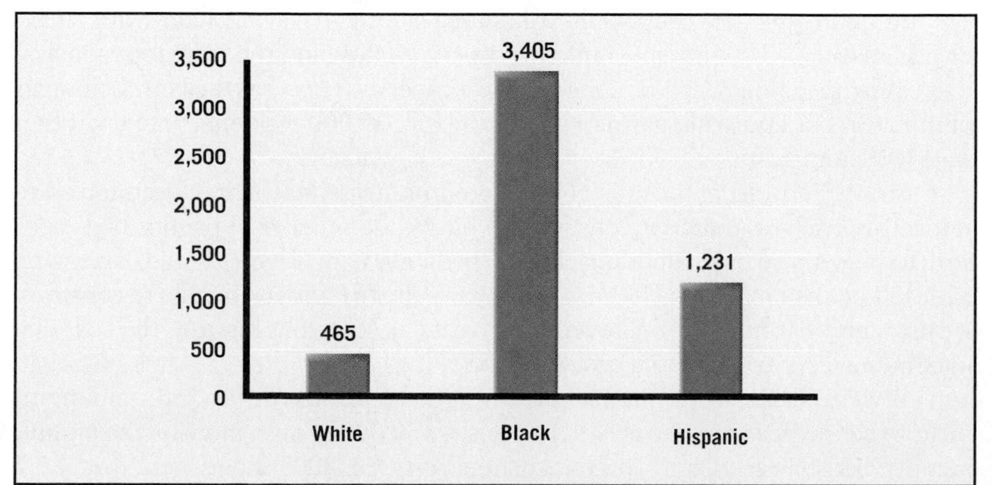

FIGURE 10.4

Incarceration Rates of Male Prisoners by Group, 2003*

*Rate per 100,000 residents of each group.

SOURCE: Paige Harrison and Allen Beck, *Prisoners in 2003* (Washington, DC: Bureau of Justice Statistics, 2004), p. 9.

FIGURE 10.5

Current Offenses of Male Inmates

SOURCE: Bureau of Justice Statistics, *Surveys of State and Federal Inmates, 1997* (Washington, DC: BJS, 2002), p. 51.

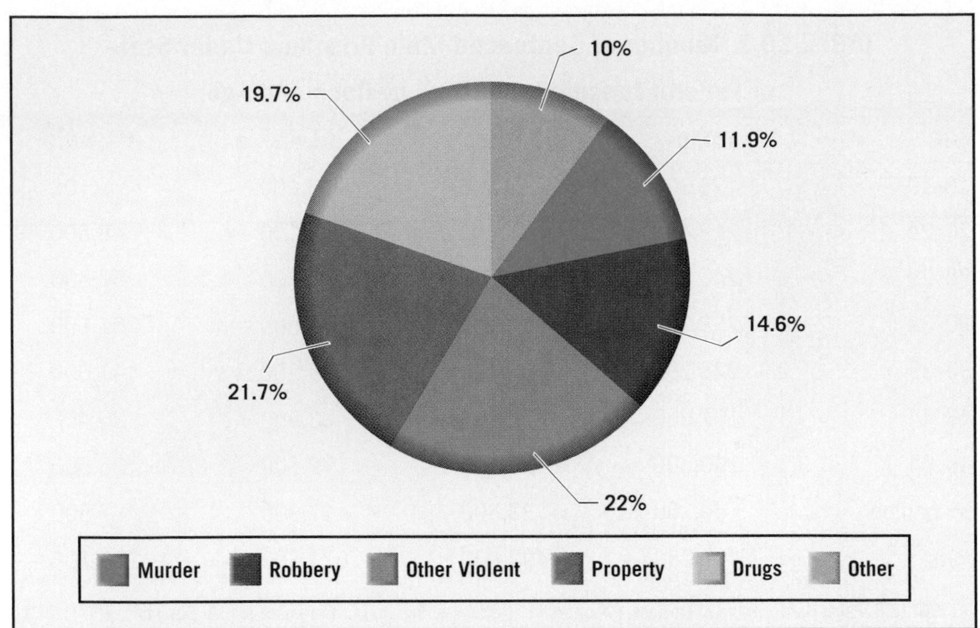

SIDEBARS

Educational Attainment

Almost four in ten male inmates in state prison did not graduate from high school. Another three in ten had attained GED education, and one in three had at least graduated from high school and may have had some college education.

SIDEBARS

Marital Status

About one in six male inmates in state prison was married at the time of the last national survey of state prisoners (1997). Almost six in ten had never married, and the other 25 percent were separated, divorced, or widowed.

SIDEBARS

Drug Abuse

More than eight in ten male inmates in state prisons report that they had used illegal drugs in their lives, and almost one in three inmates reported using drugs at the time of the offense for which he was currently incarcerated.

SIDEBARS

Alcohol Abuse

Alcohol abuse is widespread among male inmates in prison; more than eight in ten reported they consumed alcohol. Four in ten report consuming at least a fifth of liquor in a single day ("binge drinking") and more than one in three reported they were under the influence of alcohol at the time of their offense. Most had previously participated in alcohol/drug programs while under correctional supervision.

Minorities, particularly African American males, are incarcerated at a much higher rate than are white males.[13]

The offenses for which state prisoners are currently incarcerated are shown in Figure 10.5. In sum, almost five in ten inmates in state prisons were convicted of crimes of violence, including murder, manslaughter, rape, sexual assault, robbery, and assault. About one in five was incarcerated for a drug offense, usually drug trafficking. Less than one in three were in prison for property and all other crimes (see Figure 10.5).

As a group, state prison inmates were much less educated than their counterparts in the civilian population. At least 70 percent of the inmates had not received a high school diploma or GED, in contrast with 36 percent of the general population eighteen years of age or older who had not.

In terms of their criminal offenses, almost half (49 percent) were classified as violent in 2003. The average sentence length imposed was more than eight years,[14] although 9 percent of the prisoners were incarcerated under life sentences. One in three had incurred at least one other sentence, in addition to the instant offense, and one in four had previously served time as a juvenile offender.

In 2003, the 1,116,000 adult male inmates were in state facilities with an average capacity of 100 percent (full). Twenty-two states (and the federal prison system) were operating at or above their highest capacity. Texas has the largest number of inmates, but Louisiana has more inmates per 100,000 residents than any other state (801 inmates).

To keep abreast of the crush of new commitments, states have been forced to resort to a bricks and mortar construction binge; the number of prisons beds constructed each year is astounding. Prison beds are expensive to build, averaging $74,000 per bed in 2000.[15] If the state borrows funds ("floats a bond") to construct a prison and pays the loan off over thirty years at 4 percent interest, the cost of a maximum-security bed could cost $160,000.

In general, the lower the security level, the less the cost per bed; minimum-security beds cost an average of $29,311 versus $80,000 or even more for maximum-security beds. The prison bed construction costs for 2003 alone were over $6.7

Vocational training helps build a new facility.

Photo by Spencer Tirey, courtesy of Getty Images, Inc.-Liaison.

billion. The per diem cost of incarceration for adults averages $62.05 per inmate, or $88 million a day to house, feed, control, and care for the nation's adult male state inmates. Despite the construction, remodeling, redesigning, and renovations, American prisons remain overcrowded. The U.S. Supreme Court may have to examine again the realities of imprisonment in the first decade of the 2000s and also the Eighth Amendment, possibly forcing changes in corrections. Clearly, the escalating problems for harried correctional administrators are only beginning. Fortunately, some of those problems are being addressed in actions in the U.S. Supreme Court.

LOCAL ADULT CITY-OPERATED PRISONS

In calculating the numbers of inmates in adult prisons, one must not forget the "Big Four," a group of local institutions that are even larger than most states' prison systems:

1. Cook County Department of Corrections
2. New York City Department of Corrections
3. Washington, D.C., Department of Corrections
4. Philadelphia Prison System.

These four large systems consist of 110 adult prisons and a large number of other institutions and programs, and were reported as holding well over 30,000 adult offenders in 2003. One seldom thinks of cities as needing their own correctional systems, but these four cities have chosen to have them. Their operations are similar to the state prisons, but they allow inmates to be housed nearer to home. It may be that some of the other large U.S. cities may get into their own corrections game as well, but most have shown little interest. Many local jail systems are already so overcrowded that most do not have the time to plan that far ahead. The trends of the Big Four should be followed carefully.

Two other groups of jurisdictions that operate prison systems are the five U.S. military branches and correctional authorities in the U.S. territories and

FIGURE 10.6

Prisoners Under Military Jurisdiction and Branch of Service, 2003

SOURCE: Harrison Paige and Allen Beck, *Prisoners in 2003* (Washington, DC: Bureau of Justice Statistics, 2004), p. 8.

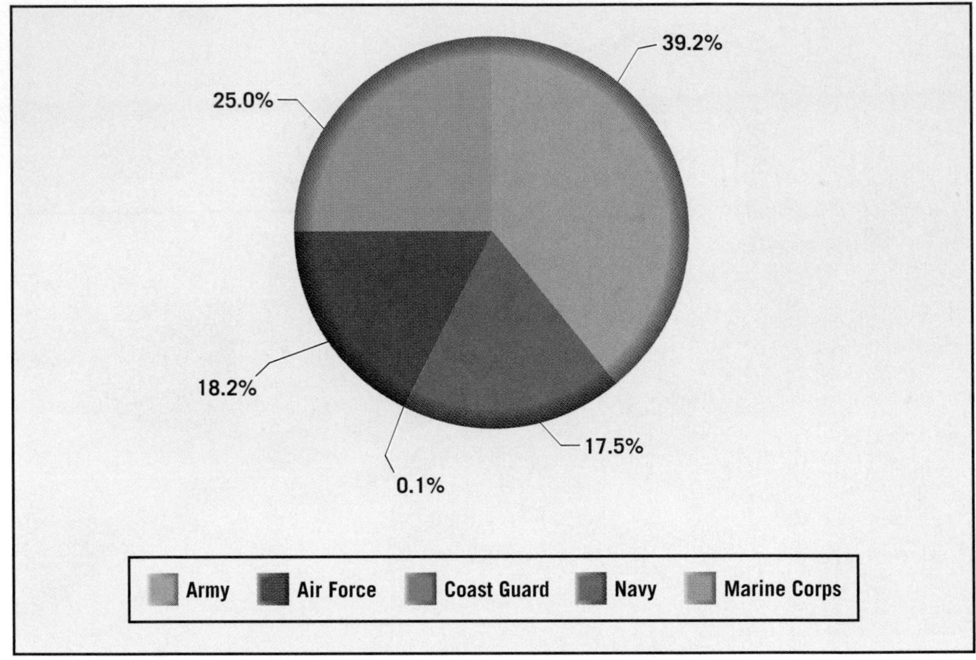

commonwealths. Information on these correctional authorities is detailed in the accompanying Correctional Brief and in Figure 10.6.

ARE PRISONS "CRUEL AND UNUSUAL PUNISHMENT"?

Whether prisons are state or local, or house males or females, the problems of institutionalization are ever present in our prisons. Understaffing, underbudgeting, and lack of citizen interest or involvement often become excuses for allowing conditions to deteriorate and sink to the lowest levels. Beginning in the 1970s, both state and federal courts were asked to examine the operations and policies of correctional facilities and personnel to ensure compliance with the Eighth Amendment's prohibition against cruel and unusual punishment. By February 1983, the courts had declared unconstitutional the entire prison systems of Alabama, Florida, Louisiana, Mississippi, Oklahoma, Rhode Island, Tennessee, Texas, and all the male penal institutions of Michigan. In addition, at least one or more facilities in another twenty-one states were operating under either a court order or a consent decree (permission to continue to operate until a fix has been completed within a specific time frame) as a result of inmate crowding and/or the conditions of confinement. Yet another seven states were involved in ongoing litigation relating to overcrowding and/or the conditions of release from prison. Finally, in eight states, the courts had appointed receivers or masters to operate the state prison system or facility, had ordered the emergency release of inmates because of crowding, or had designated specific prisons to be closed.[16] The courts took those actions only as a last resort when it had become clear that the states involved had relinquished their responsibility to protect the constitutional rights of the inmates under their custody and care. Correctional construction began in earnest as a response to prison overcrowding. Between 1987 and 2003, more than 600 new prisons were built and added to correctional systems.[17]

SIDEBARS

Privacy

The issue of privacy in prison is almost an oxymoron, but it raises many legal, social, and administrative concerns. Privacy was recognized as a right as early as 1890, and its importance to human dignity is self-evident. Privacy was one of the major human rights that came under full attack in the "total institution." Overcrowding of prisons exacerbates the loss of privacy, and prison administrators must work hard to avoid costly and time-consuming litigation efforts in regard to privacy.

The states, understandably, have reacted with great indignation over the Supreme Court's intruding into the domain of the executive branch at the state

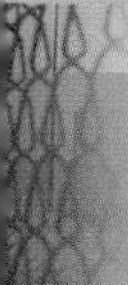

CORRECTIONAL BRIEF

Prisoners in Custody of Correctional Authorities in the U.S. Territories, 2003

The U.S. territories and commonwealths—American Samoa, Guam, Northern Mariana Islands, Puerto Rico, and Virgin Islands—reported 16,494 inmates under the jurisdiction of their prison systems at yearend 2003, slightly more than in 2002.

Relative to the resident populations of the territories, the rate of incarceration was 292 prisoners per 100,000 residents—nearly two-thirds of the combined rate of the fifty states and the District of Columbia.

Puerto Rico, the largest of the territories, had the most sentenced prisoners (15,046 at yearend 2003). Twenty-five states and the District of Columbia had fewer sentenced inmates than Puerto Rico; twelve states had lower incarceration rates.

Prisoners in Custody, Year-end 2001

Territory	Number	Rate of Incarceration per 100,000 Residents
American Samoa	174	247
Guam	579	169
Mariana Islands	136	101
Puerto Rico	15,046	301
U.S. Virgin Islands	559	338
Total	16,494	292

SOURCE: Paige Harrison and Allen Beck, *Prisoners in 2003* (Washington, DC: Bureau of Justice Statistics, 2004), p. 2.

level. Where does the Court get the right to intervene in such matters? The Civil Rights Law of 1871 provides for the principal method of allowing such inmate complaints into the federal courts. That statute provides that citizens denied constitutional rights by the state may sue in the federal court. Originally designed to protect the newly freed slaves in the post–Civil War era, the statute was generally forgotten until a landmark case in 1964 (*Cooper v. Pate*). In that case, the Court finally ruled in favor of a prisoner's seeking relief in federal court by way of the 1871 act.

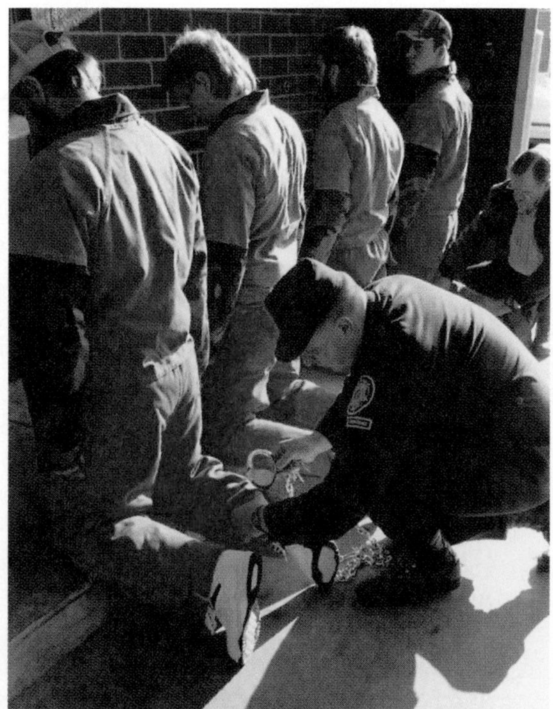

Prisoners are shackled to do volunteer work picking up trash on the highway.

Photo by Michael Mercier, courtesy of AP/Wide World Photos.

The procedure has been tentative and careful, each step breaking new ground for prisoners' rights:

> *These decisions provided almost all of the legal groundwork necessary for "conditions suits." They all came while Earl Warren was chief justice. But under Warren Burger, the Supreme Court has shown even more interest in prison cases. In some areas, it has extended prisoners' rights; in others it has held the line. But it has held fast to one principle: no one must interfere with the right of inmates to take their complaints to federal courts.*
>
> *With these sketchy guidelines, federal district judges have been feeling their way. In the first cases dealing with specific prison practices, the judges would balance the constitutional rights of the prisoners against the prison officials' legitimate interests in security, rehabilitation, and order. If the officials' defense were not sufficient, then the practice would be ordered changed. If such a ruling was upheld on appeal by one of the eleven U.S. Circuit Courts of Appeal, then it became a binding precedent within that circuit and was available to guide judges in other circuits. Only if the U.S. Supreme Court issues a ruling on a case is the precedent binding across the nation, although approval can be implied when the Court declines to hear an appeal. The Supreme Court has declined appeals on all the broad conditions suits that have been brought before it. District court judges have generally built upon each other's decisions in these areas. This judicial activism has not taken place in a vacuum, of course. In most areas of constitutional law inmates have ridden on the coattails of more popular causes such as school desegregation and voting rights for minorities. The extension of the class-action suit has made broad-based challenges to prison conditions possible. Increased activism among lawyers and the growth of legal aid programs was an important factor.*[18]

The states are not giving up easily, however, and have appealed these decisions. Each case is different, of course, but they have all been slowed in their immediate impact by the issuance of a decision of the Fifth Circuit Court of Appeals, written in regard to the Alabama order:

> *This seemingly inexorable march toward greater judicial activism was slowed when the Fifth Circuit Court of Appeals issued its ruling on the state's appeal of the Alabama order. In an opinion by a three-judge panel, written by Judge J. P. Coleman, a former governor of Mississippi, the appeals court affirmed the basic finding of unconstitutionality, but it reduced the scope of Johnson's original order. The court ordered a new hearing on the judge's requirement of 60 square feet of space per inmate in new construction. It dissolved the Human Rights Committee and dismissed the hired consultant, although it said the judge could appoint a single monitor for each prison* "to observe, and to report his observations to the court, with no authority to intervene in daily prison operations" *[emphasis in original]. The court also overturned Judge Johnson's order forbidding the state to require women visitors to prisons to stand over a mirror and drop their underwear as part of a routine search for contraband.*
>
> *The most significant part of Judge Johnson's order, that dealing with idleness, was also cut back. Rehabilitation programs, the court said, could not be required. Because the order that each inmate be assigned to a job "should not impose any real burden" on prison officials, it let that part stand. But it ruled that it could not be used as a precedent in future cases. "If the state furnishes its prisoners with reasonably adequate food, clothing, shelter, sanitation, medical care,*

CORRECTIONAL BRIEF

The Supermax Prison

Violent, seriously disruptive, assaultive, and escape-prone inmates, including gang activists, pose immense challenges to prison security and custody. Challenges include threats to the safety of staff and other inmates, danger to the security of the institution, and inmates who require protective custody. The super-maximum prison ("supermax") is a response to the need to manage and securely control inmates exhibiting violent or seriously disruptive behavior while incarcerated.

A supermax prison is a freestanding facility (or distinct unit within a facility) that provides for the management and secure control of inmates who have been officially designated as exhibiting violent or seriously disruptive behavior while incarcerated.

The first super-maximum prison was Alcatraz; the earliest supermax housing opened in 1954 in Mississippi. At present there are at least fifty-seven supermax facilities or units nationwide, providing about 20,000 beds, or about 2 percent of those serving sentences of at least a year.

Within the supermax can usually be found a special housing unit (SHU) for the most difficult to handle offenders, sometimes called the "worst of the worst." The SHU enforces the strictest discipline and isolation, reinforced by physical means. There, inmates are typically held in their cells twenty-three hours a day and eat in their cells. There are few interactions between staff and inmate, and almost none between inmates.

When a SHU inmate leaves the cell, that prisoner is typically cuffed and leg-shackled; two or three officers escort each unit inmate. Recreation is solitary, typically for thirty minutes, perhaps three times a week, in a bare cell with no equipment.

Controversy abounds over the operations of a SHU. First is the question of how inmates are selected for SHU isolation; one sufficient criterion is gang membership. How does a gang member earn release from a SHU? By renouncing the gang and providing intelligence to correctional officers? What are the implications of this snitch behavior for a "blood-in, blood-out" prison gang and would this lead to shortened life expectancy?

Second is the cost penalty, because SHUs are labor intensive; multiple escorts are required for each inmate leaving the cell. Third is the surge of litigation over sensory deprivation, classification, access to law libraries and attorneys, quality of mental health services, and excessive use of force (*Madrid v. Gomez,* 889 F. Supp. 1146, 1995). This Pelican Bay, California, lawsuit determined that holding mentally ill inmates in a SHU where there was extremely limited mental health services and in isolation (which can accelerate mental health deterioration) was cruel and unusual punishment, a violation of the Eighth Amendment. [The current practices and effects of supermax prisons are discussed by Jesenia Pizarro and Vanja Stenius, "The Supermax Prison," *The Prison Journal* 84:1 (2004): 248–264.]

On the other hand, using the supermax prison can dramatically cut down on prison violence, assaults, and murders of prison officers and other inmates. What would you do if you were managing an institution operating at 83 percent over its maximum capacity, with several gangs and a high concentration of severely violent and aggressive inmates present?

SOURCE: LIS, Inc., *Supermax Housing: A Survey of Current Practice* (Langmont, CO: National Institute of Corrections, 1997), pp. 1-6.

and personal safety, so as to avoid the imposition of cruel and unusual punishment, that ends its obligations under Amendment Eight," the decision stated.[19]

Eighth Amendment lawsuits over prison conditions continue (*Madrid v. Gomez,* for example).[20]

Realistically, we must acknowledge that the prison has little control over who will be committed. Nor does it exercise much control over sentence length, parole eligibility, minimal sentence proportion to be served, or legislative allocations. The current prison situation is a result in part of the high-risk age category (sixteen to twenty-nine) that the baby boom has brought about, the more conservative response to crime, the public's fear of crime and criminals, increased sentence lengths, and the higher failure rates of parolees who must then be returned to prison. Yet the cruel and unusual punishment conditions continue.

Prior to the mid-1970s, the inmate social system was controlled internally by "old hand" inmates whose exemplary behavior had won them the grudging respect of the inmate body. Challenges to their status and the prison routine desired by the old hands would be met with the necessary force to remove the challenger through murder or, where necessary, institutional riot. When the War on

SIDEBARS

Mixed Gender Staffing and Observation

Many prison facilities continue to allow observation of inmates' genitalia and bodily functions by correctional officers and other prison staff of the opposite gender. This is usually explained away as necessary for security purposes, and that this is a professional duty akin to female nurses and male patients. A few states have prohibited the practice as a final invasion of privacy of the prisoner.

Drugs began, members of street gangs and "crazies" were committed to prison, where they challenged the former social system. The old hands lost control of the institutions and prison gangs emerged as a segment of the social structure in institutions, in part as a defense mechanism against the super-violent and aggressive acts of the crazies and other gangs.[21] Correctional administrators, faced with violent acts and correctional officer casualties, began to create supermaximum prisons to isolate the most dangerous and violent, as well as gangs (**security threat groups** or **STGs**). **Supermax prisons** were greeted with an explosion of lawsuits that continues today.[22] Corrections administrators face emerging challenges!

One other response by corrections was to add more correctional personnel. More than 405,000 persons were employed in state correctional facilities in 2003, an increase of 209 percent over the number in 1985. The staff-to-inmate ratio rose to almost six overall. On September 30, 2003, there were more than 248,000 custodial staff employees, 23 percent of whom were female.[23]

Correctional opportunities will continue to increase, and students will be sought who have the skills and willingness to work in the prisons of tomorrow. There is clearly a need for active citizen support for corrections, especially at the state level, and for active monitoring of our prison conditions.

CORRECTIONAL BRIEF

Security Threat Groups ("Prison Gangs")

The prison security threat group (STG) was defined by the American Correctional Association as "two or more inmates, acting together, who pose a threat to the security or safety of staff/inmates, and/or are disruptive to programs and/or to the orderly management of the facility/system." Members engage in such activities as planning, organizing, and committing unlawful acts (selling drugs, murder) and threatening, soliciting, or financing unlawful acts or other acts that would violate the institution's or department's policies, rules, or regulations. Unlike street gangs, with which many are affiliated, STGs are more sophisticated, organized, and calculating. They seek to control their environment by threats and intimidation of staff and other inmates.

Frequently organized along racial and ethnic lines, members adhere to a strict code of behavior, silence, and lifelong membership. They have a hierarchical order and are frequently organized along such clearly defined goals and objectives as contract murder, homosexual prostitution, drug trafficking, and gambling. Group cohesion and behavior are enforced by brutal and violent means that include beatings, maiming, and murder. Most STGs are not only anti-authority, they are also characterized by both racist hate and distrust of other gangs. Vendettas between gangs within an institution can wreak havoc with order and create inmate fear, staff anxiety, and avalanches of request from inmates for administrative segregation.

Dealing with the escalating growth of STGs requires intelligence, the systematic gathering of information on individuals and groups, and the marshalling of that information into useful data that can be used to combat prison gangs. Prison administrators can sensitize staff to be vigilant for gang signs (colors, tattoos, interactions between individuals, hand signs, etc.). After gangs and their members have been identified, gang isolation inside and between institutions can reduce the threat potential and STG activities. In the long run, combating gang activities by attacking a gang's line of authority and internal organization are not enough. Facilities must also provide programs and activities for nongang inmates. Small STG prisons that isolate members of a specific gang and that have both low inmate-to-staff ratios and direct supervision are a start. Supermax prisons are mandatory for control of the gang leaders, once STGs are entrenched.

These proactive strategies and efforts are not sufficient to manage this set of problems. Nonaffiliated inmates must be protected from the unlawful activities and enforced recruitment into gangs. Institutional programs must be developed and emphasized that range from educational and vocational training through industrial and recreational programs. Options include developing a continuum of lessened security levels to which nongang members might aspire, and this must be developed as part of the modern correctional system. While this discussion does not exhaust the list of possible policies that can be used to contain gang threat, it serves as an exploration of the challenge of corrections in the current century.

SOURCES: American Correctional Association, *Gangs in Correctional Facilities* (Laurel, MD: ACA, 1993). See also Reginald Wilkinson, M. Meyer, and T. Unwin, *Ohio Prison Gangs: A Counterfeit Family* (Columbus, OH: Ohio Department of Rehabilitation and Correction, 1996); and Security Threat Group Intelligence Unit, Florida Department of Corrections, *Major Prison Gangs*, www.dc.state.fl.us/security_reports_gangs_prison/html (accessed April 20, 2005).

Jail inmates stand in the doorway of their dorm in the Los Angeles County Jail, part of the 20,000 inmates in a system built for half that number.
Courtesy of AP/Wide World Photos.

SIDEBARS

Inmates Pay into Fund for Crime Victims

More than $518,000 was collected from the wages of working inmates over a period of two years in Minnesota to fund services for crime victims.

The Minnesota Department of Corrections deducts between 5 and 10 percent from the pay inmates earn working in correctional industry jobs. All inmates whose biweekly gross wages are over $50 are subject to the deduction.

Funds are used for a variety of programs that assist crime victims and witnesses throughout the state.

The surcharge began in 1985 in accordance with state law authorizing the withholding policy. A recent law requiring that other mandated deductions be made first, such as court-ordered victim restitution and child support payments, may impact the amount collected through this surcharge in future years.

TRAINING IN STATE SYSTEMS

One other way to improve the ability of state systems to react to a rapidly changing environment is to improve the requirements for entry-level staff, and then to improve the training of staff who are already in the system. The federal system has always had the advantage of high entry standards and excellent training programs for staff. Most state systems require only the following:

1. High school diploma or GED
2. No record of prior felony convictions
3. Minimum age of twenty-one (some states accept eighteen)
4. Valid driver's license (of that state).

These seem to be minimal requirements for a job that commands so much influence over the lives and rights of inmates. Some of the more progressive states are beginning to raise these standards. California and Florida require extensive background investigations. California estimates it will need about 3,000 new corrections officers a year for the next few years to staff prison expansion and officer turnover. Florida has a correctional officer training program, taught in conjunction with community colleges, that amounts to over 500 hours, which must be completed before the employees can pass their probation periods.

The general rule is for employees to have at least eighty hours of training within their probationary period, usually six months. Some jurisdictions get around that requirement by making most of the training on-the-job activity. Most states try to provide at least some training. Before the efforts of the 1970s and subsequent lawsuits, most training amounted to the employee being handed a set of keys, a walkthrough, and told to go to work. Some states, as is done in Florida, now work closely with their community colleges to provide preservice and postservice training, especially in the social sciences. Others have built state training academies that provide basic and ongoing training.

The need to have better trained staff has caused many private and nonprofit agencies to start training academies for preemployment programs for corrections officers. Such programs have concentrated on finding interested minorities and women, and have done quite well. Others have tried the same approach, but lacking rigid standards, careful screening, and close association with the correctional agencies, they have failed.

Many administrators of correctional programs at the state level would like to raise entry-level standards to require, as a minimum, a two-year degree and promotional qualifications in line with that base point (for example, a bachelor's degree for captains, master's degree for superintendents). They have a long battle ahead. Those already in the system are usually afraid of the proposed requirements and oppose the raising of such standards. These negative attitudes are enhanced by union standards for promotion that are primarily based on seniority, not training. It seems that some progress could be made if the nondegreed incumbents were given a more liberal opportunity to be "grandfathered" in to the new programs. Training in the future high-tech prisons is essential; it is an area to watch carefully in the future.

SUMMARY

The state and local adult correctional systems in America are as diverse as the states and cities themselves. We have provided but an overview of problems facing correctional administrators when they try to model a unified and coordinated system of corrections within the framework of fragmented and antiquated institutions, poorly trained and low-paid officers, and often antiquated procedures. The prison remains the core of most state correctional systems, despite its clear failure as a means of rehabilitation and reintegration of offenders (currently the two major goals of corrections). Classification of inmates and subsequent assignment and reassignment are still based more on the institution's needs and security than on individual needs.

Movements to absorb all correctional programs under the state's supervision and control encounter almost insurmountable political and practical obstacles at every step. The massive overcrowding in state institutions, causing funding to go for bricks and mortar rather than for managerial or administrative improvements, also hampers new concepts. Capacities of institutions also reflect the continuing problems created by overcrowding and growth. Obviously all of the major systems are extremely and critically overcrowded.

Longer sentences and stiffer enforcement measures have filled existing beds faster than they can be built. Alternatives to confinement have been used for all but the very few, and those few are not generally the individuals the public wants out on the streets. Although the new institutions are being constructed, in the majority of cases, to constitutional standards with regard to square footage and other considerations, there seems to be little doubt that the single cells will soon become double-bunked. Taxpayers are beginning to rethink the allocation of funds to build more and more prisons, often at a total cost of up to $200,000 per bed.

State correctional systems have inherited the legacy of a sometimes well-intentioned but often inhumane past. The purposes for which many of the crumbling old institutions were built and the procedures for operating those facilities are no longer in tune with society or behavioral science. The cry to tear down the monuments is a valid one, but practicalities dictate that the flood of inmates must be kept somewhere, and public safety takes precedence over innovative solutions. Many new programs outside the prisons are being constructed, including intermediate sanctions. Much progress is being made, sometimes at the prodding of citizens' groups. In the next chapter we examine a truly centralized and integrated correctional system: the federal Bureau of Prisons.

REVIEW QUESTIONS

1. Characterize the current state inmate population in the nation.
2. How much time does a state inmate generally spend in prison?
3. How would you decide that a prison was "cruel and unusual" punishment?
4. Why are alternatives to incarceration beginning to be so necessary for correctional administrators?
5. What impact does overcrowding have on the reform of institutional programs in state systems?
6. How are inmates classified?
7. Has the institutional inmate-to-staff ratio gone up or down? Why?
8. What three trends are likely to surface in state correctional facilities during the next ten years?
9. Why did the supermax prison arise?
10. What can be done to reduce the challenge of prison gangs?

ENDNOTES

1. Paige Harrison and Allen Beck, *Prisoners in 2004* (Washington, DC: Bureau of Justice Statistics, 2005), p. 4.
2. American Correctional Association, *2004 Directory* (Lanham, MD: ACA, 2004), p. 26.
3. Quoted in Harry Elmer Barnes and Negley J. Teeters, *New Horizons in Criminology,* 3rd ed. (Englewood Cliffs, NJ: Prentice Hall, 1959), pp. 461–462.
4. Harrison and Beck, *Prisoners in 2003,* p. 1.
5. Steven Garvey, "Freeing Prisoners' Labor," *Stanford Law Review* 50:2 (1998): 339–398. Camp and Camp report that 64 percent of adults in prison were employed in a prison industry, on a prison farm, or in other prison work in 2000. Camille Camp and George Camp, *The Corrections Yearbook 2000: Adult Corrections* (Middletown, CT: Criminal Justice Institute, 2000), pp. 96–97.
6. Harry E. Allen and Julie C. Abril, "The New Chain Gang: Corrections in the Next Century," *American Journal of Criminal Justice* 22:1 (1997): 1–12. See also David Oshinsky, *Worse Than Slavery: Parchman Farms and the Ordeal of Jim Crow Justice* (New York: Free Press, 1996); and Rebukah Chu, Craig Rivera, and Colin Loftin, "Herding and Homicide," *Social Forces* 78:3 (2000): 971–978.
7. Karen Shapiro, *The New South Rebellion: Tennessee Coalfields, 1971–1986* (Chapel Hill: University of North Carolina Press, 1998); and Mary Curtin, *Black Prisoners and Their World* (Charlottesville, VA: University Press of Virginia, 2000).
8. James Vardalis and Fred Becker, "Legislative Opinions Concerning the Private Operations of State Prisons," *Criminal Justice Policy Review* 11:2 (2000): 136–148.
9. Linda Greenhouse, "Justices Tighten Review of California Prison Segregation," *New York Times* (February 24, 2005): 16.
10. Bureau of Justice Statistics, *Prisoners in 1983* (Washington, DC: BJS, 1984).
11. Harrison and Beck, *Prisoners in 2003,* p. 4.
12. Ibid, p. 9.
13. Disproportionate minority confinement is a heated controversy in corrections, particularly in secure juvenile facilities. See Patricia Devine, K. Coolbaugh, and S. Jenkins, *Disproportionate Minority Confinement: Lessons Learned from Five States* (Washington, DC: Office of Justice Programs, 1998). See also Leadership Conference on Civil Rights, *Justice on Trial: Racial Disparities in the American Criminal Justice System* (Washington, DC: LCCR, 2000).
14. Bureau of Justice Statistics, *Trends in State Parole, 1990–2000* (Washington, DC: BJS, 2001), p. 6
15. Extrapolated from Camp and Camp, *The 2000 Corrections Yearbook,* p. 73.
16. Bureau of Justice Statistics, *Report to the Nation on Crime and Justice* (Washington, DC: U.S. Department of Justice, 1983), p. 80.
17. ACA, *2004 Directory.*
18. S. Gettinger, "Cruel and Unusual Prisons," *Corrections Magazine* 3 (December 1977): 3–16.
19. Ibid, p. 10.
20. 889 F. Supp. 1146 (1995). See also Nadine Curran, "Blue Hair in the Bighouse," *New England Journal on Criminal and Civil Confinement* 26:2 (2000): 225–264.
21. Victor Hassine, *Life Without Parole: Living in Prison Today* (Los Angeles: Roxbury, 2002).
22. To learn more about supermax prisons, see also David Ward, "A Corrections Dilemma: How to Evaluate Super-Max Regimes," *Corrections Today* 57:5 (1997): 108; and Rodney Henningsen, W. Johnson, and T. Wells, "Supermax Prisons: Panacea or Desperation?" *Corrections Management Quarterly* 3:2 (1999): 53–59.
23. ACA, *2004 Directory,* p. 46.

CHAPTER 11

The Federal System

That there is hereby established in the Department of Justice a Bureau of Prisons . . . responsible for the safekeeping, care, protection, instruction, and discipline of all persons charged with or convicted of offenses against the United States.

—Public Law No. 218, approved by President Herbert Hoover, May 14, 1930

KEY WORDS

- Justice Department
- U.S. penitentiary
- Alderson
- Federal Bureau of Prisons
- Sanford Bates
- regional offices
- minimum-security level
- low-security level
- medium-security level
- high-security level
- administrative-security level
- UNICOR

OVERVIEW

With this proclamation, the federal government went into the business of corrections in a big way. The history of incarcerating offenders for violations of federal law is long and interesting. With the power of the federal government (and the federal purse) behind it, the federal Bureau of Prisons has become an innovator and leader in correctional management and operations. The Bureau of Prisons (BOP) is a system entirely separate from state and local correctional agencies. It is designed and intended to deal primarily with those who have violated federal laws. Based on a 1997 federal law, the BOP is also responsible for incarcerating the District of Columbia's sentenced felon inmate population. Because the federal system, like the juvenile system discussed in Chapter 17, slowly developed as an independent entity, a review of its background and history is necessary and useful for understanding where this system originated, what it is doing, and where it might be going.[1]

THE USE OF STATE FACILITIES

In the late 1700s and for most of the 1800s, federal prisoners were sent to state and local institutions to serve their sentences. One of the first acts of Congress was to pass a bill (An Act to Establish the Judicial Courts of the United States) encouraging the states to pass laws providing for the incarceration of federal law violators in state institutions. Most of the states did pass such laws, and all federal offenders sentenced to one year or more served their sentences in state facilities. Offenders who were sentenced to terms of less than one year or those being held in detention awaiting trial were usually confined in local jails, a practice that continues today on a limited scale.

< Federal Prison for Women, Alderson, West Virginia ("Camp Cupcake").
Photo by Jeff Greenberg, courtesy of The Image Works.

Inmate workers help build USP Atlanta, circa 1900.
Courtesy of Federal Bureau of Prisons.

In 1870, Congress established the **Justice Department.** A general agent was established in the Department of Justice and was placed in charge of all federal prisoners in state and local institutions. Later, the "general agent" became the superintendent of prisons, responsible to an assistant attorney general for the care and custody of all federal prisoners.

State prisons became seriously overcrowded in the period that followed the Civil War. With increased numbers of both state and federal prisoners, many states became reluctant to take federal prisoners when they could not even care properly for their own. Consequently, in some states only federal prisoners from that specific state were accepted. In states where neither suitable nor adequate facilities were available, transporting federal inmates to appropriate facilities involved lengthy travel and high costs. In 1885, there were 1,027 federal prisoners in state prisons and approximately 10,000 in county jails. By 1895, those numbers had risen to 2,516 federal prisoners in state prisons and approximately 15,000 in county jails.

On March 3, 1891, the U.S. Congress passed a bill (An Act for the Erection of United States Prisons and for the Imprisonment of United States Prisoners, and for Other Purposes) authorizing the construction of three penitentiaries, although their funding was not approved until later. The establishment of federal prison facilities was considered necessary because of the rapidly increasing number of federal inmates, the states' growing reluctance to house federal prisoners, and the exclusion of federal prisoners from contract labor.

EARLY FEDERAL PRISON FACILITIES

Until 1895, all military prisoners not in state prisons were confined at Fort Leavenworth in eastern Kansas. But the War Department then decided to house its prisoners in several different military installations. Consequently, the Department of Justice acquired the surplus military prison at Fort Leavenworth. For the first time, federal prisoners, including those transferred from state institutions as well as new commitments, were confined in a federal facility. In short order the Department of Justice realized the prison, adapted from former quartermaster warehouses, was inadequate. Therefore, on July 10, 1896, Congress appropriated funds for the construction of one of the previously authorized penitentiaries. It would be capable of holding 1,200 inmates and was to be built on the Fort Leavenworth military reservation three miles from the existing prison. Because the penitentiary was built by convict labor, construction took many years. The Leavenworth Penitentiary opened in 1906, but was not finally completed until 1928.

A second penitentiary at McNeil Island, Washington, was constructed between 1872 and 1875. The federal government designated it as a **U.S. penitentiary** in 1909.[2] Construction on a third penitentiary at Atlanta, Georgia, began in 1899 and it opened in 1902. The Auburn style of architecture, characterized by multitiered cell blocks and a fortress-like appearance, was adopted for all three penitentiaries.

Between 1900 and 1935, American prisons, including federal institutions, were primarily custodial, punitive, and industrial. Overcrowding at the federal prisons during this period left few resources for anything but custodial care. Nevertheless, significant developments during the early 1900s affected the operation of federal institutions, including passage of the following acts:

- White Slave Act in 1910 (interstate commerce of prostitution)
- Harrison Narcotic Act in 1914 (records must be kept and taxes paid on controlled substances)
- Volsteadt Act in 1918 (prohibit the sale and consumption of alcohol)
- Dyer Act of 1919 (interstate transportation of stolen vehicles)

Together, these acts brought a large number of people under federal criminal jurisdiction. The number of offenders incarcerated under those statutes swelled the federal prison population beyond the available physical capacity. Largely because of the population increase in federal prisons, Congress authorized in 1925 a reformatory for "male persons between the ages of seventeen and thirty," which was constructed in Chillicothe, Ohio.[3]

By the 1920s, growth in the number of female prisoners being housed in state facilities warranted the building of special federal facilities for women. In 1927, a new 500-bed female institution opened at **Alderson,** West Virginia. In 1929, when overcrowding reached a critical stage in the New York City area, the state and local authorities ordered all federal prisoners removed from the Tombs and the Raymond Street Jail. Responding to this crisis, a federal detention center was built in a newly constructed three-story garage and called the Federal Detention Headquarters (also known as the West Street Jail).

PROFILE

Mary Belle Harris (1874–1957)

had a lengthy career in corrections and pioneered the development of evaluation and classification systems for inmates. She was the first superintendent for the new women's federal prison at Alderson, West Virginia, which opened in 1925. Her management style underscored the following thoughts:

1. Too many staff members utilize lack of information as an excuse for doing nothing.
2. For the average run of problems, the less attention paid to peculiarities, the better.
3. Employment of parolees serves as a model to others being asked to do so.
4. No work should be used as punishment because it degrades the positive concept of labor.
5. Judges should visit facilities to which they send individuals.
6. Inmates should be given tasks they can attain to know success and achievement.

THE BUREAU OF PRISONS IS BORN

In 1929, Congress created the House Special Committee on Federal Penal and Reformatory Institutions. After extensive deliberations it offered the following recommendations:

- Establishment of a centralized administration of federal prisons at the bureau level
- Increased expenditure for federal probation officers, to be appointed by federal judges and exempt from civil service regulations
- Establishment of a full-time parole board

PROFILE

Sanford Bates (1884–1972) was the first director of the U.S. Bureau of Prisons. He also held the top executive positions in three state systems and had a long and distinguished career in prison administration, education, and the legal profession. He is widely considered the father of modern penology and believed that "a prison system so contrived as to aid in the reformation of its inmates offers ultimately the best protection for society." A short list of his accomplishments and contributions to corrections includes the presidency of the American Prison Association (now the ACA) in 1926, appointment to the American Crime Study Commission (1928–1930), sole U.S. commissioner to the International Prison Commission (1932), president of the Washington Council of Social Agencies (1934–1935), president of the American Parole Association (1940–1943), and member of the United Nations Commission on Crime Prevention (1951–1955).

- Provision of facilities by the District of Columbia for its prisoners
- Transfer of all military prisoners held in civil prisons to Fort Leavenworth military barracks
- Removal of the minimum age of prisoners at the U.S. Industrial Reformatory at Chillicothe, Ohio
- Expeditious establishment of the two narcotic treatment farms previously authorized
- Passage of H.R. 11285 authorizing road camps for federal offenders
- Provision of additional employment opportunities for federal offenders
- Employment of an adequate number of nonfederal jail inspectors and linking payments for those facilities to conditions and programs found in them
- Construction of institutions to include two additional penitentiaries, a hospital for the care of the criminally insane, and a system of federal jails and workhouses in the more congested parts of the country.

Legislation was drafted, passed, and signed into law by President Herbert Hoover on May 14, 1930, creating the **Federal Bureau of Prisons** within the Department of Justice. **Sanford Bates,** an experienced warden, was appointed by President Hoover to be the first director of the Bureau of Prisons. The selection of Bates signified that the attitude toward penal administration in the federal government had shifted from political patronage to professional qualifications.

Early Growth of the Federal Bureau of Prisons

It was soon obvious that three penitentiaries, a reformatory for young men and one for women, a jail, and eight camps did not meet the growing needs of the federal prison system. Federal prisoners with sentences of a year or less could not be legally

Sanford Bates.
Courtesy of Federal Bureau of Prisons.

confined in the penitentiaries, and many were unsuitable for open camps. The Department of Justice decided to build new structures or remodel existing structures to serve as regional jails.

In the early 1930s, the old New Orleans Mint was modified for use as a jail. A new regional jail was opened in La Tuna, Texas, primarily to house the influx of immigration violators. A similar institution was opened in Milan, Michigan (near Detroit). Another penitentiary was added in Lewisburg, Pennsylvania, and a men's reformatory was constructed west of the Mississippi River in El Reno, Oklahoma. A hospital for mentally ill prisoners (and for those with chronic medical ailments) was opened in Springfield, Missouri. The crime wave of the 1930s, combined with the expanding role of the federal government in crime control, brought the old military prison on Alcatraz Island in California under the control of the Department of Justice in 1934.

Recent Developments

Public attitudes toward criminals and the appropriate societal response to them were influenced by many factors during the 1980s. Chief among those were increasing crime rates and the growing problems in administering prisons. Inmate disruptions at Attica and other institutions provided opportunities for the public to reexamine the goals of prisons.[4]

In the early 1970s, the courts began to intervene more often in prison issues. Then-Director Norman A. Carlson realized the direction the court system was taking. He saw to it that some significant changes were made in inmate management in the BOP, including (1) enhancements to due process in disciplinary procedures, (2) an administrative remedy process (allowing inmates to express concerns and gain relief from prison administrators before burdening the courts), and (3) an enhanced equal employment opportunity program that increased recruitment of minorities for staff positions.

Director Carlson (who served from 1970 to 1987) believed that the bureau should cooperate with and assist state and local correctional systems. In 1972, the National Institute of Corrections was established within the bureau as an entity to provide assistance and training to state and local correctional and detention facilities. In 1974, the bureau was divided into five regions, each region being managed by a regional director. Also that year, Mr. Carlson formed an executive staff of the agency's assistant directors and regional directors. In the mid-1970s, bureau institutions began to seek accreditation from the American Correctional Association, the country's premier professional organization for corrections.

Mr. Carlson' s insistence on the importance of staff training resulted in the establishment of several small staff training facilities and later the consolidation of training at the Federal Law Enforcement Training Center (FLETC) in Glynco, Georgia, in 1982. The mainstay of the bureau's Staff Training Academy at FLETC is a three-week introduction to basic correctional techniques course for all new employees.

A significant development during the 1970s and 1980s was the assignment of responsibility for the planning and management of inmate programs to treatment teams under the concept of unit management. Although the staff makeup of the teams varied among institutions, they usually included a caseworker and a correctional counselor. Unit management gives inmates direct daily contact with the staff who make most of the decisions about their daily lives. Most of these staff members have offices in inmate living units. This results in improved

PROFILE

James V. Bennett (1894–1978)

was another leading penal reformer who led the federal Bureau of Prisons for almost three decades (1937-1964). He personally led a sweeping reorganization of the federal system and implemented several innovations in prison administration and programming that brought an international reputation to this outspoken advocate of "individualized treatment" for the rehabilitation of offenders. His report in 1928 called for the establishment of a "coordinated system of federal correctional institutions"—a centralized bureau that would manage and operate federal prisons. His reputation as an advocate of rehabilitation was matched by his ability as a shrewd administrator. His rehabilitation approach became known as the "medical model" for corrections.

PROFILE

Myrl E. Alexander (1909–1993)

was director of the federal Bureau of Prisons from 1964 to 1970, after a rich and interesting career that began as a junior warden's assistant in 1931 at the U.S. Penitentiary in Atlanta. He became one of the youngest wardens, at thirty-four years of age, at the Federal Correctional Institution in Danbury, Connecticut. At the end of World War II, he accompanied then-Director Bennett to Germany, where he remained to de-Nazify the German prison system until June 1946. He was known for his humane and decent attitude toward prisoners and staff.

The federal penitentiary at Atlanta burns as a result of a Cuban prisoner uprising in 1987.
Photo by Rich Feld, courtesy of AP/Wide World Photos.

inmate access to staff and greater staff access to inmates, providing staff with an awareness of significant inmate concerns and potential problems. The unit staff is directly responsible for the program involvement of inmates in the unit. Unit staff receive input from other employees involved in an inmate's progress (such as work supervisors, teachers, and psychologists) and meet with the inmate on a regular basis to develop, review, and discuss the work assignment and programs in which the inmate should be involved, as well as any other needs or concerns. These regularly scheduled meetings do not preclude inmates from approaching a member of the unit team or any other appropriate staff member at any time to discuss their particular issues. The BOP considers its staff to be the most important part of inmate management. Constructive interaction and frequent communication between staff and inmates help to ensure accountability, security, and positive inmate behavior. The bureau encourages staff to talk with and be available to inmates and to be receptive to inmate concerns.

The bureau's rehabilitation programs and their increasing sophistication were challenged in the mid-1970s by academicians, researchers, and practitioners

CORRECTIONAL BRIEF

Correctional Workers First

Regardless of the specific discipline in which a staff member works, all employees in the Bureau of Prisons are considered to be "correctional workers first." This means that everyone is responsible for the security and good order of the institution. All staff members are expected to be vigilant and attentive to inmate accountability and security issues, to respond to emergencies, and to maintain a proficiency in custodial and security matters, as well as in their particular job specialty.

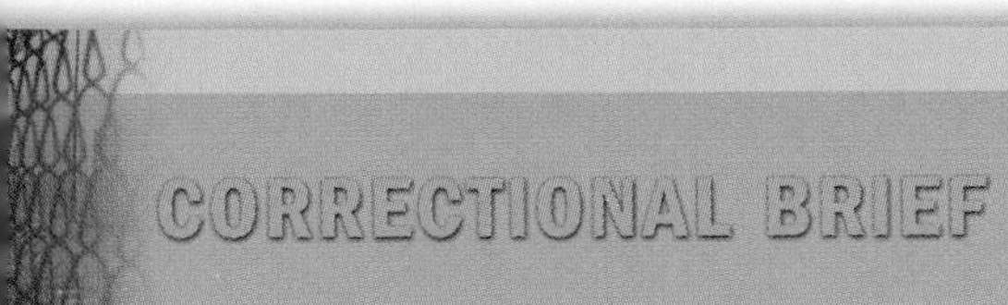

Career Service Orientation

One core value of the Bureau of Prisons is its career service orientation. This cultural anchor describes the BOP as a "career-oriented service, which has enjoyed a consistent management philosophy and a continuity of leadership, enabling it to evolve as a stable, professional leader in the field of corrections." The bureau has had only seven directors in its more than seventy-year history: Sanford Bates (1930–1937), James V. Bennett (1937–1964), Myrl E. Alexander (1964–1970), Norman A. Carlson (1970–1987), J. Michael Quinlan (1987–1992), Kathleen Hawk Sawyer (2003); and Harley Lappin (2004–present).

who pointed out that little documentation supported the existing traditional rehabilitation programming.[5] The bureau had relied on the medical model, which viewed crime as a "sickness" and inmates as "treatable." In 1976, the bureau formally de-emphasized the medical model and adopted a more balanced approach, recognizing that rehabilitation, retribution, incapacitation, and deterrence were legitimate objectives of corrections. Within the balanced model, the bureau continued to provide a variety of work and literacy programs, as well as educational, vocational training, counseling, and self-improvement programs.

The 1970s found the Bureau of Prisons with more new facilities than it had at any time since the 1930s. A steady increase in inmate population during the first five years of the decade dictated the acquisition of additional and modernized facilities to reduce overcrowding, create more humane and safe living conditions, and possibly close the first three old penitentiaries at McNeil Island, Washington; Atlanta, Georgia; and Leavenworth, Kansas.[6]

The Bureau of Prisons experienced as much change in the 1970s as it did at any other time in its history, yet many of the bureau's fundamental activities remained unchanged. This apparent contradiction can be explained as the result of contradictory input from Congress, public professional corrections personnel, and others who, on the one hand, wish prisons to be secure and protective of the public and, on the other, wish in some way to reform or change the individual.

ORGANIZATION AND ADMINISTRATION

The federal Bureau of Prisons provides administration at the central office in Washington, D.C., and from six **regional offices.** The central office consists of the director's office and eight divisions that are responsible for establishing national policy, developing and reviewing programs, providing training and technical assistance to the field, and coordinating agency operations in the various disciplines. The bureau has divided responsibility for overseeing day-to-day operations of federal prisons in six regions. An assistant director heads each division; an Office of General Counsel and an Office of Inspections report to the director. The six regions are headed by regional directors and are located in Atlanta, Dallas, Philadelphia, Kansas City, Dublin (near San Francisco), and Annapolis Junction (in Maryland).

The regional offices and the central office provide administrative oversight and support to federal prisons and community corrections offices. Institution wardens are responsible for managing the prisons, and report to a regional director. Community corrections offices oversee community-based programs such as halfway houses and home confinement.

INMATE POPULATIONS EXPLODE

The inmate population of the Bureau of Prisons numbered more than 182,000 in mid-2005 (approximately 154,000 of these inmates were confined in bureau-operated correctional institutions or detention centers). This is 139 percent of highest capacity.[7] The rest were confined through agreements with state and local governments and through contracts with privately operated community corrections centers, detention centers, prisons, and juvenile facilities. Inmate prison population increases are due to federal court sentencing of offenders to longer terms of confinement for serious crimes and the effort to combat organized crime, drug trafficking, and illegal immigration. As of March 2005, the percentage of inmates serving sentences for drug law violations was 54 percent. The Bureau of Prisons has opened eight new correctional facilities since the year 2000.

COMMUNITY-BASED PROGRAMS AND CONTRACT FACILITIES

Prison space is a scarce and costly resource, to be used in situations when the interests of society must be protected. Because of the continuing record-high prison population growth in the federal system, the use of alternatives to incarceration for nonviolent offenders is essential. A large number of prisoners are confined in the bureau's contract facilities. Approximately 75 percent of eligible offenders released to the community are regularly released through community treatment centers. Those centers are used for offenders near release as a transition back to home, job, and community. Time is used to find a job, locate a place to live, and reestablish family ties. Some adult inmates sentenced to less than six months are confined in halfway houses or local jails.

All persons adjudicated under the Juvenile Justice and Delinquency Prevention Act are placed under contract in local and state facilities as well as in such facilities as boys' ranches, group homes, or foster homes. Most adult inmates sentenced to serve less than six months are confined in local jails.

With the rapid growth of the federal inmate population, the bureau has contracted for private corrections beds to complement the facilities constructed and operated by the agency. The bureau's utilization of private sources for secure bed space began in the mid-1980s and has grown significantly in the recent past. The bureau had approximately 17,700 inmates in secure adult correctional and detention facilities being provided by private corrections firms in mid-year 2005. The bureau contracts for housing federal offenders when that arrangement is cost effective, complements its operations and programs, and provides some flexibility to avoid extreme overcrowding. The bureau has had success in contracting with the private sector for the confinement of minimum-security and low-security inmates.

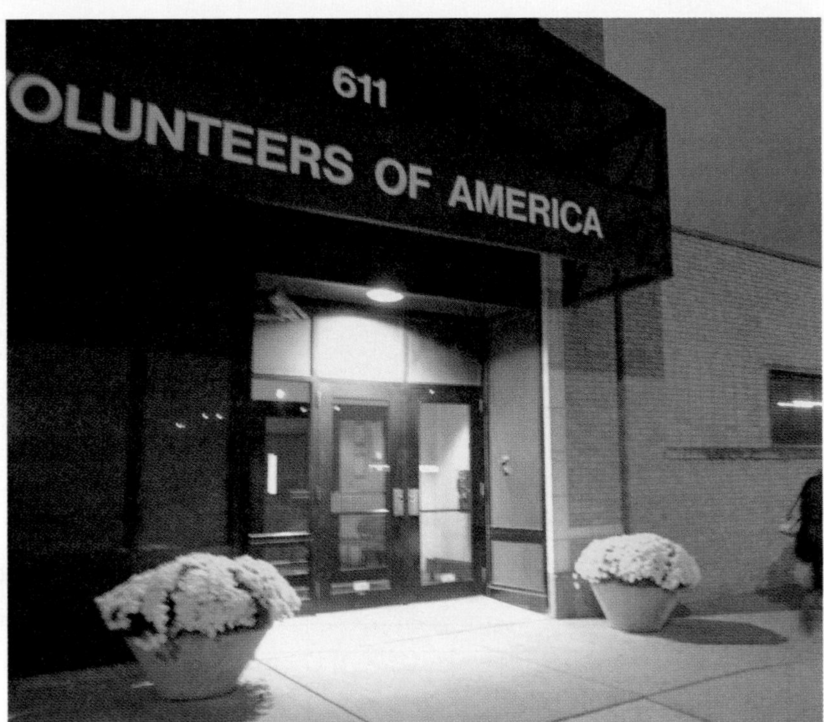

Community corrections center under contract to the Bureau of Prisons.
Courtesy of AP/WideWorld Photos.

A MODEL INMATE CLASSIFICATION SYSTEM

The BOP's latest formal inmate classification system has been in effect since April 1979. Variables such as severity of offense, history of escapes or violence, expected length of incarceration, and type of prior commitments are used to determine an inmate's security level. The federal system groups the 102 institutions into five security levels: minimum, low, medium, high, and administrative as follows:

1. **Minimum-security level** institutions, also known as federal prison camps, have dormitory housing, a relatively low staff-to-inmate ratio, and limited or no perimeter fences. These institutions are work and program oriented, and many are located adjacent to larger institutions or on military bases, where inmates help to serve the labor needs of the institution or base.
2. **Low-security level** federal correctional institutions (FCIs) have double-fenced perimeters, mostly dormitory housing, and strong work and program components. The staff-to-inmate ratio in these institutions is higher than in minimum-security facilities.
3. **Medium-security level** FCIs have strengthened perimeters (often double fences with electronic detection systems), mostly cell-type housing, a wide variety of work and treatment programs, and an even higher staff-to-inmate ratio than low-security institutions, providing even greater internal controls.
4. **High-security level** institutions, also known as U.S. penitentiaries (USPs) have high-security perimeters (either walled or double fenced), multiple- and single-occupant cell housing, close staff supervision, and close control of inmate movement.

FIGURE 11.1

Inmates by Security Classification, 2005

SOURCE: Federal Bureau of Prisons, *Quick Facts About the Federal Bureau of Prisons*, www.bop.gov/about/facts.jsp (accessed April 25, 2005).

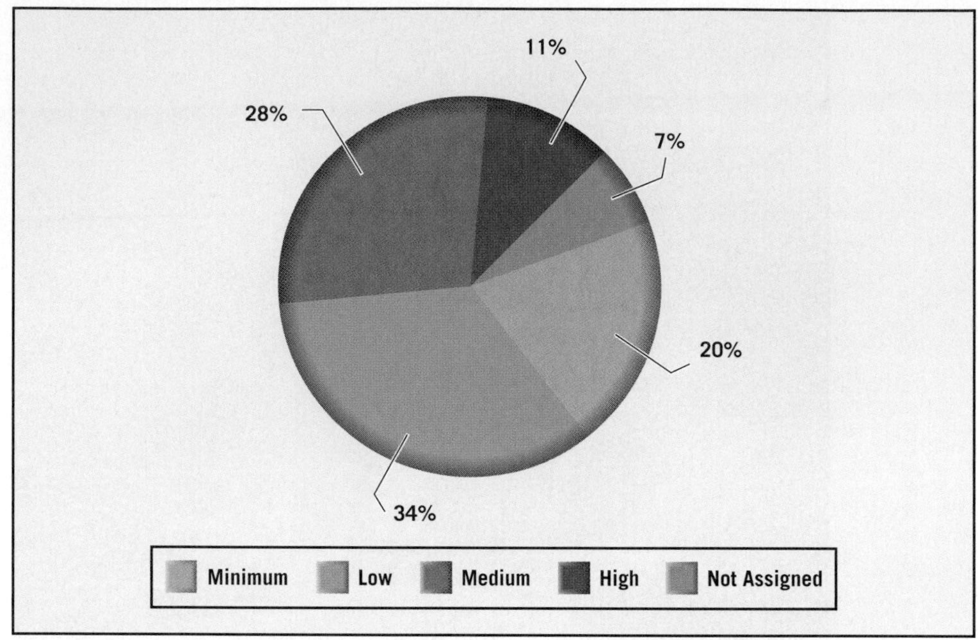

5. **Administrative-security level** facilities are institutions with special missions, such as the detention of pretrial offenders, the treatment of inmates with serious or chronic medical problems, or the containment of extremely dangerous, violent, or escape-prone inmates. Administrative facilities are capable of holding inmates in all security categories.[8]

Data on inmates of the BOP by inmate security level are presented in Figure 11.1.

The Bureau of Prisons is responsible for carrying out the judgments of federal courts when a period of confinement is ordered. All sentenced offenders

CORRECTIONAL BRIEF

Allegations of Sexual Misconduct

The Bureau of Prisons takes very seriously all allegations of sexual misconduct within our nation's federal correctional facilities. Every allegation is reviewed and, where warranted, referred for criminal prosecution. We have a "zero-tolerance" standard for sexual abuse of inmates.

Over the past decade the BOP has taken additional steps to eliminate sexual abuse in its facilities, by training all staff on how to prevent it, by conveying the severity of the consequences for engaging in it, and by informing inmates on how to report it.

In April 1997, the bureau approved a new plan to prevent sexual abuse and assaults of inmates. In January 1998, it revised its policy to include procedures for recognizing, preventing, and confidentially reporting the sexual abuse of inmates by staff. By the end of Spring 1998, all bureau institution employees had received initial training to recognize, prevent, and report sexual abuse of inmates. Bureau staff will continue to receive annual specialized training regarding implementation of the BOP's national policy standard regarding sexual abuse/assault prevention and intervention. In addition, the bureau has developed an inmate awareness program, including procedures for reporting sexual abuse by staff.

SOURCE: Federal BOP Office of Public Information, www.bop.gov (accessed April 2005).

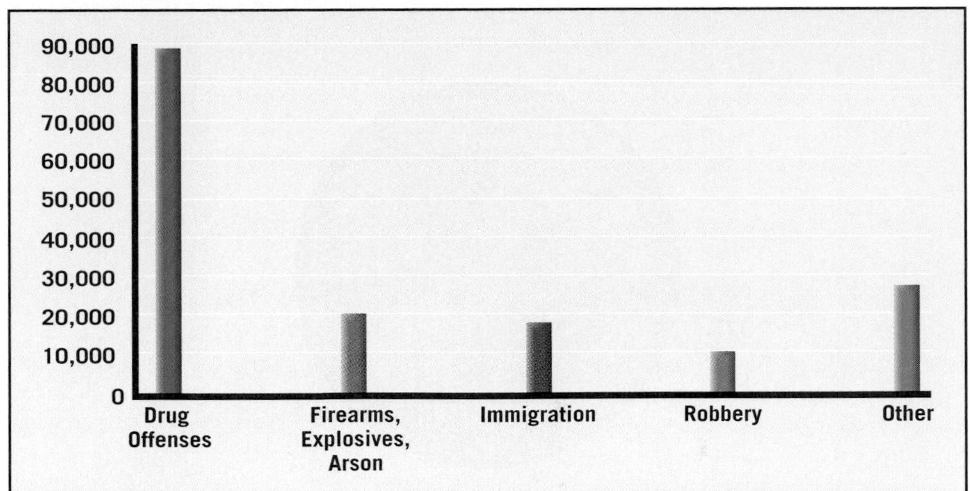

FIGURE 11.2

Types of Offenses Committed by BOP Inmates, 2005

SOURCE: Federal Bureau of Prisons, *Quick Facts About the Bureau of Prisons*, www.bop.gov/about/facts.jsp (accessed April 25, 2005).

who are medically able are required to complete a regular daily work assignment. In addition, all offenders have opportunities to participate in educational, vocational training, work, religious, and counseling programs. In their major institutions, ranging from minimum to high security, more than 34,500 employees were at work in April 2005. They were 72 percent male and 28 percent female. Addressing its growth projections, the bureau had 102 facilities on line at mid-year 2005, in hopes of providing for continued growth in the federal prison population. The types of offenses committed by BOP inmates are shown in Figure 11.2.

The classification system, designed to place offenders in the least restrictive institution possible that is closest to their homes, has been effective. Moving as many inmates as possible into open institutions such as prison camps results in higher-security level institutions becoming more humane through reduced crowding. Characteristics of federal prisoners in mid-2002 are shown in the Figures 11.3 and 11.4.

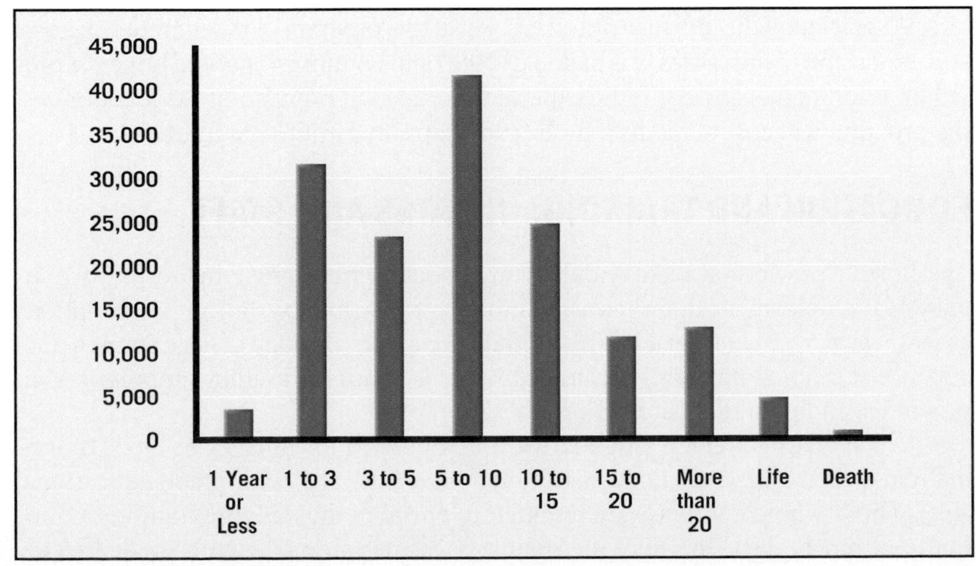

FIGURE 11.3

Length of Sentences Imposed, 2005

SOURCE: Federal Bureau of Prisons, *Quick Facts About the Bureau of Prisons*, www.bop.gov/about/facts.jsp (accessed April 25, 2005).

FIGURE 11.4

Citizenship of Inmates, 2005

SOURCE: Federal Bureau of Prisons, *Quick Facts About the Bureau of Prisons*, www.bop.gov/about/facts.jsp (accessed April 25, 2005).

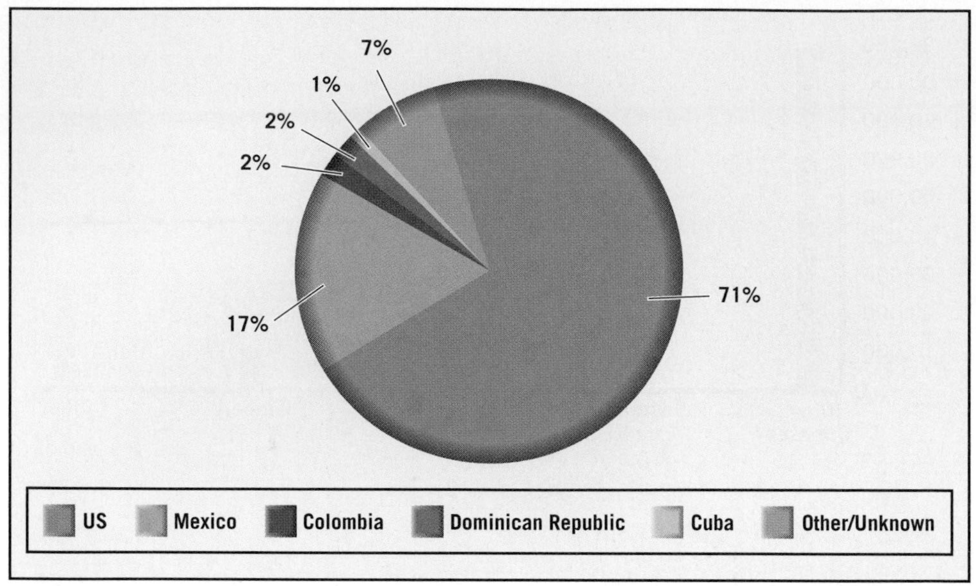

UNICOR: FEDERAL PRISON INDUSTRIES, INC.

Federal Prison Industries, Inc., with the corporate trade name **UNICOR,** is a wholly owned government corporation that sells its products and services to other federal agencies. UNICOR's mission is to support the Bureau of Prisons through the gainful employment of inmates in diversified work programs.

Approximately 25 percent of eligible inmates confined in the federal prison system are employed by UNICOR. The industrial operations located in most federal institutions constructively employ inmates and assist in preparing them for employment opportunities upon release. Occupational training is also offered through UNICOR (as well as through institutional education programs) and includes on-the-job training, vocational education, and apprenticeship programs. Hundreds of formal training programs in various trades are offered by federal institutions. Vocational training, apprenticeship programs, and occupational education programs exist in at least 90 percent of the federal institutions. An active program of plant modernization and expansion of industries was begun in 1983 and continues apace in hopes of providing meaningful activity for the expected increases in population. As it continues, the program will ensure modern production capacity far into the future.

EDUCATION AND TRAINING: INMATES AND STAFF

The bureau provides academic and occupational training programs to prepare inmates for employment upon release. Enrollment is voluntary, but program options are extensive, ranging from adult basic education (ABE) through college courses. Occupational training programs include accredited vocational training, apprenticeship programs, and preindustrial training.

A mandatory literacy program was implemented for inmates in 1983. It originally required all federal inmates to function at least at a sixth-grade educational level. Those who could not were required to enroll in the ABE program for a minimum of ninety days. In 1986, the standard was raised to an eighth-grade literacy level, the nationally accepted functional literacy level. In 1991, the Crime Control

Act of 1990 (P.L. 101-647) directed the federal Bureau of Prisons to have a mandatory functional literacy program for all mentally capable inmates in place. The bureau voluntarily raised the standard to twelfth grade and required participation for a minimum of 240 hours or until they obtain the GED. All promotions in federal prison industries and in institution work assignments were made contingent on the inmate's achieving literacy. The Violent Crime Control and Law Enforcement Act of 1994 and the Prison Litigation Reform Act of 1995 link good-time credits to participation in the GED program.

The ABE program has been quite successful. Certificates for completion of the GED program have been awarded to tens of thousands of inmates (at least 6,000 a year). English as a second language (ESL) is also provided for all who need it. Other vocational training programs provide job training in such fields as computer sciences, business, diesel mechanics, construction and building trades, drafting and blueprints, and culinary arts.

Staff training provides every bureau employee with the knowledge, skills, and abilities required to ensure high standards of employee performance and conduct. The staff training network consists of the Staff Training Academy at the Federal Law Enforcement Training Center in Glynco, Georgia, and the Management and Specialty Training Center in Denver, Colorado. Administrators in the Human Resource Management Division in Washington, D.C., oversee the program. All new employees are required to undergo three weeks of formal training during their first sixty days with the Bureau of Prisons, as well as an institution familiarization program at their worksite.

PROFILE

Linda Allen

in 1978, became the first woman correctional officer at the U.S. penitentiary at McNeil Island, Washington (now a Washington State correctional facility), breaking the barrier to female officers at a high-security institution. Now that this is commonplace at state and federal prisons, there are issues to consider in the recruitment, placement, and retention of these highly qualified females.

FEDERAL FEMALE OFFENDERS

The Bureau of Prisons continues to focus on improving programs and services for female offenders. It operates a number of all-female facilities. These facilities include stand-alone secure institutions and many prison camps adjacent to secure institutions.

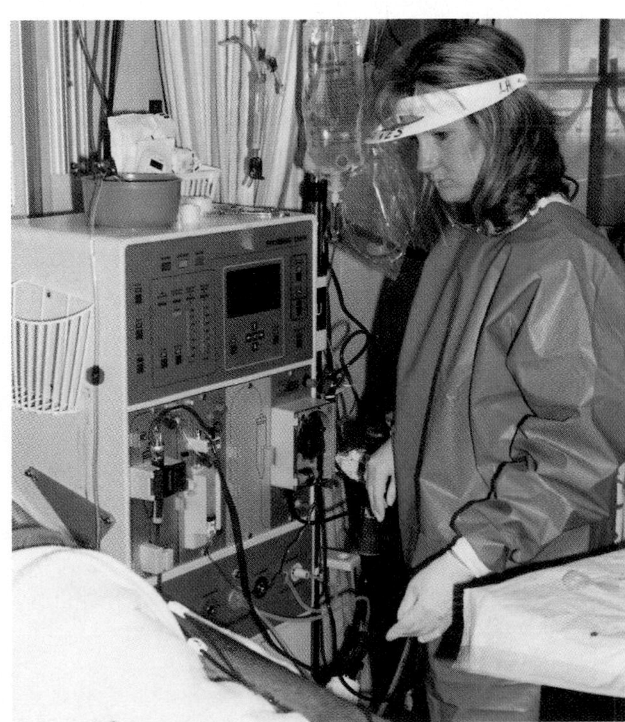

Dialysis nurse provides kidney dialysis in prison infirmary.
Courtesy of Federal Bureau of Prisons, Springfield.

The number of female offenders in the bureau's inmate population continues to increase. Recognizing that women offenders have different social, psychological, educational, family, and health care needs, the bureau continues to design and implement special programs for women offenders. Programs include teaching women how to reduce stress; how to prevent, identify, obtain, and manage treatment for medical problems; and how to improve their personal relationships, how to be a better parent, and how to grieve over lost relationships. Several facilities also operate intensive treatment programs that focus on helping women who have histories of chronic sexual, emotional, or physical abuse by teaching them how to handle their victimization and learn ways to seek positive relationships. Federal facilities housed over 12,300 female offenders in mid-2005, about 7 percent of the total population of federal inmates.[9]

COMMUNITY CORRECTIONS IN THE FEDERAL SYSTEM

Community corrections is an integral component of the bureau's correctional programs. The bureau contracts with community corrections centers (also known as halfway houses) to provide assistance to inmates who are nearing release from prison. Community corrections centers provide a structured, supervised environment and support in job placement, counseling, and other services. Community corrections centers allow prerelease inmates to gradually rebuild their ties to the community, and they allow correctional staff to supervise offenders' activities during this readjustment phase. An important component of the community corrections center program is transitional drug abuse treatment for inmates who have completed residential substance abuse treatment while confined in a bureau institution.

Some federal inmates are placed on home confinement for a brief period at the end of their prison terms. They serve this portion of their sentences at home under strict schedules and curfew requirements. Some community corrections centers enhance the accountability of inmates on home confinement through electronic monitoring.

Approximately 45 percent of federal offenders in community-based programs are housed in comprehensive sanctions centers. Comprehensive sanctions centers are similar to community corrections centers, but they have a more structured sys-

CORRECTIONAL BRIEF

Correctional Complexes

The Bureau of Prisons has been involved in a major program of correctional facility construction for almost two decades in response to a significant increase in the prison population. One result of that construction program is the development of correctional complexes. Correctional complexes, which the bureau began constructing in the late 1980s, consist of several institutions with different missions and security levels located in proximity to one another.

Correctional complexes increase efficiency through the sharing of services, enable staff to gain experience at institutions with varying security levels, and enhance emergency preparedness by having additional resources close by.

Federal community corrections center in Houston.
Courtesy of Federal Bureau of Prisons.

tem for granting offenders gradual access to the community. They also require inmates to participate in more programs and they formally involve the U.S. Probation Office in the release planning process.

Through the community corrections program, the bureau has developed agreements with state and local governments and contracts with privately operated facilities for the confinement of juvenile offenders and for the detention or secure confinement of some federal inmates.

The bureau's community corrections program is administered by the staff in its central office, community corrections regional administrators, and regional management teams in each of the bureau's six regional offices, and the employees of twenty-nine community corrections management field offices throughout the United States.

CHANGING POPULATION OF FEDERAL INSTITUTIONS

A former governor of Georgia, Lester Maddox, is credited with saying (when asked how to improve that state's correctional system) "What we need here is a better class of prisoner." The Bureau of Prisons was looked on for years as dealing with just the "cream of criminals." Whether true or apocryphal, times have changed, and the federal system has to deal with some real problem inmates today. The BOP is now experiencing some of the challenges associated with crowding and management of inmates with significant histories of violence and gang-related activities. In 1984, Congress passed a law that abolished federal parole, limited good time, established a number of determinate sentences, and created the US. Sentencing Commission as an independent body, located in the judicial branch of the government. The commission began its work in 1985 and submitted new guidelines that have dramatically altered sentencing practices in the federal criminal justice system. Federal prison populations grew markedly by 2000, more as a result of the Anti-Drug Abuse Act of 1986 and the career offender provision of the Comprehensive Crime Control Act of 1984 than as a result of the guidelines. A summary of their impacts follows[10]:

1. "Straight" probationary sentences (i.e., sentences that require no form of confinement) were reduced significantly.
2. For especially serious crimes, such as drug offenses and crimes against persons, probationary sentences were no longer available.
3. For other crimes, such as property offenses, the proportion of sentences involving some form of probation did not change appreciably, although probation with a condition of confinement may have been substituted for straight probation.
4. Average time served for violent offenses increased substantially. For most property crimes, average time served remained largely unchanged. Exceptions include burglary and income tax fraud, for which average time served went up.

The changes have had a major impact on the correctional administrators in the Bureau of Prisons in the form of a massive increase in the numbers and types of inmates confined in federal institutions, which are already quite overcrowded.

SUMMARY

The Bureau of Prisons is a major correctional system that helps to meet society's goals of ensuring public safety and providing appropriate, efficient, safe, and humane correctional services and programs to federal offenders. The bureau has attacked some of the major issues head-on and has made notable progress; but there are no simple solutions to the long-festering problems of corrections, whether state or federal. Much hard work lies ahead for the bureau and for all other correctional agencies in the United States.

One of the bright spots on the horizon is the increasing use by the courts and corrections of community-based treatment as a less-structured alternative to incarceration for selected offenders. A substantial percentage of offenders, however, are not suitable for treatment in the relative freedom of community-based programs. Into that category fall many multiple offenders who have long histories of serious, often violent, crimes.

To achieve maximum correctional benefits for all offenders, the Bureau of Prisons has sought to develop a balanced approach, recognizing that no single all-purpose treatment method can be expected to produce effective results. One main challenge of the future undoubtedly will be to sustain the present level of public and legislative interest, which demands a concerted effort by the correctional community and by concerned citizens.

REVIEW QUESTIONS

1. Explain the various kinds of institutions in the federal prison system.
2. What forces led to the shift in philosophy of the federal Bureau of Prisons in the 1970s?
3. Outline the institutional security classification system.
4. Why does the bureau have such an advantage over state systems in generating programs?
5. Why has the prison population of the bureau increased during the last few years?
6. Characterize inmates in the BOP institutions.

ENDNOTES

1. With kind permission from the bureau, and many thanks for the extremely helpful assistance of Matthew Bronick at FBOP Headquarters for supplying historical and contemporary facts and helping to get our terminology correct in the prior edition. This chapter has drawn heavily from BOP annual reports and various other bureau publications. The authors appreciate the cooperation and assistance and especially the provision of historical and other photographs. For critical views, see Jim Coyne, *The Repugnant Warehouse: An Exposé of the Federal Prison System* (Clifton Park, NY: Elysium Publishing, 1995); and Daniel Rose Burton, D. Pens, P. Wright, et al., *The Celling of America: An Inside Look at the U.S. Prison Industry* (Monroe, ME: Common Courage Press, 1998).
2. The facility is now part of the prison system of the state of Washington.
3. This facility is currently an Ohio correctional institution.
4. Between November 21 and 23, 1987, eighty-nine federal prison staff were seized as hostages at the Atlanta Penitentiary and at the Alien Detention Center at Oakdale, Louisiana. The uprisings have been described as the most disruptive episodes in the history of the Bureau of Prisons. Hostages were eventually released after the attorney general agreed to review each case of the Marielitos, Cubans who arrived in the nation during the Mariel boatlift. See "After Atlanta and Oakdale," *Corrections Today* 50 (1988): 26, 64–65; Bert Useem, C. Camp, and G. Camp, *Resolution of Prison Riots* (South Salem, NY: Criminal Justice Institute, 1993); and Mike Rolland, *Descent into Madness* (Cincinnati, OH: Anderson Publishing, 1997).
5. See Harry Allen and Nick Gatz, "Abandoning the Medical Model in Corrections: Some Implications and Alternatives," *Prison Journal* 54 (Autumn 1974): 4–14; and Simon Dinitz, "Nothing Fails Like a Little Success," in Edward Sagarin (ed.), *Criminology: New Concerns* (Beverly Hills, CA: Sage, 1979), pp. 105–118. But see C. T. Lowenkamp and E. L. Latessa, "Developing Successful Reentry Programs," *Corrections Today* 76:2 (2005), 72–77.
6. Only McNeil Island has been closed, and has since been sold to the state of Washington to help solve some of its prison overcrowding. The institutions at Atlanta and Leavenworth still serve the overcrowded system.
7. Paige Harrison and Allen Beck, *Prisoners in 2003* (Washington, DC: Bureau of Justice Statistics, 2004), p. 7.
8. Federal Bureau of Prisons, *Quick Facts*, www.bop.gov/about/facts.jsp (accessed April 26, 2005).
9. Ibid.
10. National Institute of Justice, "The Impact of Federal Sentencing Guidelines," in NIJ Reports: ***Research in Action*** (Washington, DC: U.S. Department of Justice, 1987), p. 2. Data updated to 2002.

CHAPTER 12

Private Sector Prisons

Prison supply, especially at current prices, is unable to meet demand. The resultant overcrowding, combined with taxpayer reluctance to bear the costs of new construction and added operational expenses, creates a dilemma for penology. Commercial prisons, privately owned and operated under government contract, may offer at least a partial solution.
—Charles Logan and Christine Rausch

KEY WORDS

- self-insured
- slaves of the master
- employer model
- privatization
- technologies for surveillance
- growth industry
- electronic monitoring
- Corrections Corporation of America (CCA)
- U.S. Corrections Corporation (USCC)
- The GEO Group
- Esmor Correctional

OVERVIEW

The words quoted above, written a decade ago, foretold the continuing overcrowding problem that the student has seen as a constant issue throughout this text. The state, city, and federal correctional administrators wrestled with this issue when the population of their combined institutions was approximately one-third of what it is now. This chapter deals with what has become another major factor in trying to keep up with the tidal wave of populations under the supervision of criminal justice agencies: privatization of correctional services and facilities.

As will be shown, privatization of institutions is not a new idea. The major challenge for privatization is to provide for the incarceration of convicted felons in long-term, secure facilities by a private, for-profit company. The state of Tennessee was the first to consider the privatization of its entire adult prison system. One of the first and largest of the providers of privately operated adult correctional facilities made an offer to take over the complete management and operation of the beleaguered Tennessee system. For a number of reasons, that proposal was not accepted and Tennessee decided instead to pour millions into upgrading what it had. This chapter discusses the pros and cons of privatization and its vast growth in the last two decades. We have seen this issue grow from a single paragraph to an entire chapter in the past few editions of this text. It seems fitting that this chapter is the last in your overview of correctional systems, because it relates to almost every other topic in the text. Bear in mind that private sector *prisons* remain the fourth largest correctional system in the nation.

< A multilevel male/female Corrections Corporation of America–managed facility in Panama City, Florida.
Courtesy of Corrections Corporation of America.

THE PRIVATE SECTOR IN COMMUNITY CORRECTIONS

The idea of involving the private sector in providing management and operation of correctional facilities may come as a shock to many students, but the concept of having government services provided by contracting with the private sector was actually the primary method of obtaining those services for the first hundred or so years of the United States' existence. Transportation, fire protection, police, and even armies were often provided on contract. It was only in America's second century that services began to be provided through governmental bureaucratic agencies. In recent years, however, the cost of government-provided services has risen so high that many services are now moving "back to the future" to obtain correctional services being provided through the private sector.

The correctional field has experienced a number of privatization precedents: health care, food service, education, mental health, transportation, and training have been provided by private contractors to many systems. From the time of John Augustus, most juvenile and adult halfway houses and other services have been provided by private for-profit, private nonprofit, or charitable organizations. As the need for more community corrections has grown, primarily due to overcrowded jails and prisons, many entrepreneurs in the private and private nonprofit sectors have become involved in the "boom" industry of community-oriented corrections. Almost 30 percent of confined juveniles are in privately owned or operated juvenile facilities.[1] Many of those entrepreneurs are now expanding across state borders and operating prisons, jails, and community services almost like a franchise. Such agencies tend to ease the correctional problems by providing (1) alternatives to incarceration in the community, (2) meaningful programs inside the prisons to help prepare inmates for a better life when they are released (see Figure 12.1), and (3) a bridge from incarceration to the free society that will assist in that difficult transition.

SIDEBARS

Privatization of Prison Health Care

Privatization of prison health services is especially appealing to those systems that have difficulty recruiting and retaining qualified health care staff. The management and operation of the health care services then becomes the responsibility of the contractor. The state, however, is still ultimately responsible for ensuring that the health care services provided to inmates are adequate.

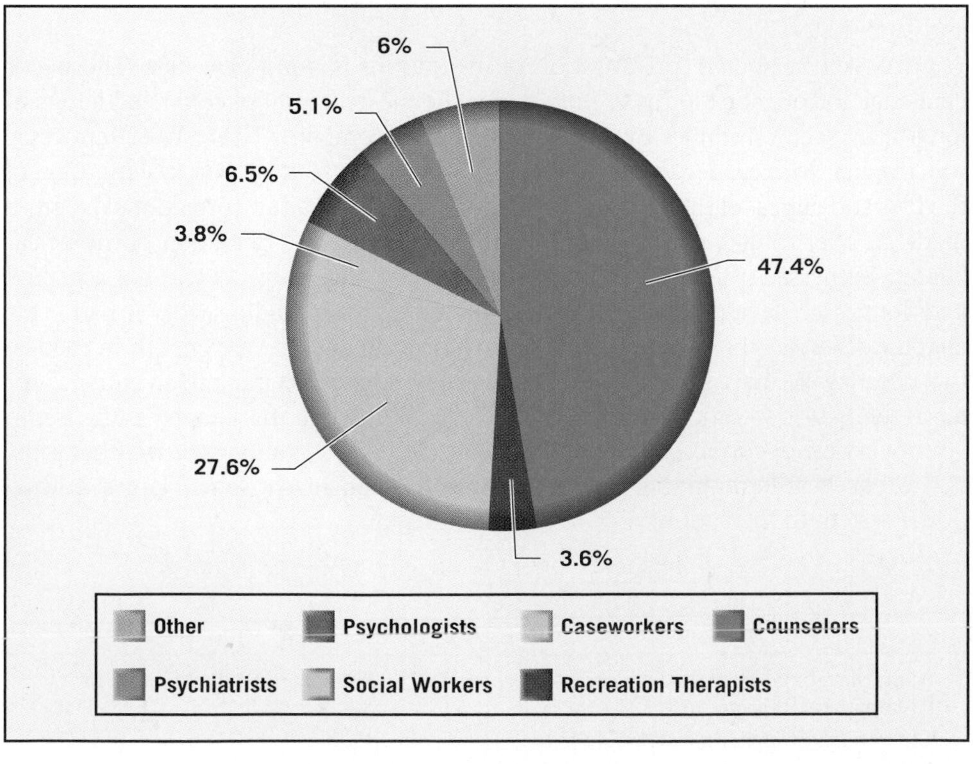

6%
5.1%
6.5%
3.8%
47.4%
27.6%
3.6%
Other
Psychologists
Caseworkers
Counselors
Psychiatrists
Social Workers
Recreation Therapists

FIGURE 12.1

Types of Treatment Staff in Privately Operated Facilities on January 1, 1998 (in Percentages of Total)

SOURCE: C. Camp and G. Camp, *The Corrections Yearbook 1998* (Middletown, CT: Criminal Justice Institute, 1998), p. 404.

The main advantage of private service providers is their ability to expand and contract quickly when needs change. When a government invests in the operation of a community-based program or the building of a major correctional facility, it is often obliged to continue to staff them and operate them even if it is not cost effective to do so.[2] The entrepreneurs of community corrections can choose to modify an existing facility instead of building from the ground up, provide staff on a contract basis, utilize existing community resources for professional services, and close the facility when it is no longer needed and use it for another purpose. The community corrections programs and agencies of the federal courts and prisons house over 3,000 inmates in 330 contracted community correctional centers. Most states also contract for at least some of their community corrections, so this sector of business has continued to burgeon.

One of the major issues for the contractor concerns liability for potential public safety issues. Most government agencies are **self-insured.** This insurance protects them with the resources of the entire government entity—federal, state, county, or municipality. The private sector operator, however, must have some type of liability insurance to cover the same problems. With the incredible growth of litigation in the United States, government agencies have become targets for opportunistic attorneys looking for new markets.[3] This feeding frenzy of litigation has caused insurance rates to skyrocket and has impacted operations in the private sector. The small operators have been put in a squeeze, and the large ones could be hurt as well.

In sum, the private sector is extensively involved in such correctional services as providing food, medical care, and training to facilities and agencies; filling gaps in services governmental agencies cannot or will not address (halfway houses, secure juvenile residential programs); and managing such correctional systems as high-security jails and prisons. Only the latter is the center of heated controversy, not only in light of liability issues, but also over potential use of force situations for which employees might not be adequately trained and competent.

SOME HISTORICAL CONSIDERATIONS

Early History

From a historical perspective, private involvement in corrections during the period from 1870 to 1930 was neither notable nor distinguished. Before this era, some states would lease out their entire prison populations to private bidders who would contract to provide food, custody, and clothing to inmates for a flat fee per inmate annually, in return for the labor of the inmates. Contractors would use the inmates basically to farm or harvest crops, much like the **slaves of the master.** The state would make a profit and could avoid the cost of building additional and adequate facilities, hiring correctional staff, feeding and clothing inmates, and otherwise assuming such care, custody, and provisioning as would have been required. In brief, prisons became attractive "profit centers" for those states willing to lease out their convict populations. Costs incurred by contractors were significantly below those that would have been incurred if free-world labor had been hired or if, in the pre–Civil War era, more slaves had to be bought who would have had to be fed, clothed, housed, and disciplined more attentively than mere criminals.

During the period from 1870 to 1930, when industrialization was running under full steam in this nation, leasing out inmates continued. Inmates were put to work building roads, railroads, and trestles or manufacturing wagons, shoes, boots,

Chain gang working on street.
Photo courtesy of Brown Brothers.

SIDEBARS

Early Prison Labor Efforts

The Walnut Street Jail and the Newgate prisons were established on the premise that work was reformative—and potentially profitable. Piecework and other forms of manufacture were attempted to help finance the operations of these facilities. Those early efforts at prison labor failed, however, both in terms of economics and reformation. Their demise gave way to the Auburn system of silence and labor. These eventually developed into the industrial prisons of America, including the agricultural prisons of the South.

SIDEBARS

The Employer Model of Prison Industry

Of the various models of prison industries, the **employer model** seems to be the most appealing. This model is dominated by small to midsize businesses that employ prisoners directly at a facility on the prison grounds. These businesses sell the prison products on the open market (i.e., cloth products, computer processing, ceramics) and prisoners can be fired if they do not produce. Despite protests from organized labor groups, these ventures are growing and help the inmates learn the value of real work.

and many other consumables easily sold on the open markets. To protect profit margins, contractors often would transport inmates in rolling cages, where they lived without sanitary and bathing facilities and were worked from dawn to dusk under the watchful eye of heavily armed guards ("overseers") who were not afraid to use brute force to achieve production quotas. Inmates attempting to escape were killed or beaten, placed in leg irons, forced to wear ball-and-chain restraints, dressed in distinctive garb, and had shortened life expectancies. Food was abysmal and in short supply, and health care was nonexistent. Seeking redress in court was impossible, and avenues of appeal and protest were closed.[4]

The suffering of inmates under these "chain gang" conditions is common knowledge. What is not as well known is the large percentage of inmates leased out who died under contract arrangements, a figure frequently exceeding 50 percent in a given year. Loss of workers through death, however, had little consequence. Prison administrators were neither criticized nor condemned, and the media rarely covered those events. If a shortage of laborers occurred, prison administrators would lease out newly arrived prisoners who were quickly placed into harness and assigned to labor gangs. Not all states, of course, were this brutal in their approach to prisoners, and perhaps this description best fits only some states in the Deep South after the Civil War, when their prisons were filled with former slaves confined for law-violating behavior.[5] This was one of the most odious chapters in the early history of American corrections, and the residue of feelings and sentiments about leasing inmates through private sector involvement even now colors, even if unfairly, the arguments about privatization of corrections.

More Recent Developments

As noted, **privatization** is by no means a new concept in the field of corrections. Many services provided to state, federal, and local correctional facilities have come from the private sector almost from the beginning and they have persevered. The criminal justice system often appears to be stumbling around like a clumsy giant. It can impose lengthy prison terms, and even execute a few criminals. It can slap offenders on the wrist with fines and suspended sentences. It seems able to do little in between, however, although this condition is changing; but government moves very slowly. In the twentieth century, probation and parole were used as the most frequent options to incarceration. The ability of these two types of sanctions to supervise and control offenders became the standard for the community. We have seen, however, that both of these options came under fire in the 1990s for charges of ineffectiveness.

As discussed in Chapter 8, the development of intermediate sanctions has provided three major options for direct private sector involvement in corrections: (1) treatment programs, (2) supervised release and low-security custody, and (3) **technologies for surveillance** of offenders not incarcerated. These three options provide the greatest area of potential growth opportunity for private contractors, as opposed to the operation of high-security correctional facilities.

PRIVATE SECTOR TREATMENT PROGRAMS

Supervised treatment programs, usually imposed as a condition of probation, include drug and alcohol abuse treatment and job training programs. Virtually nonexistent thirty years ago, such programs are now commonplace components of the criminal justice system. Almost all are private and many are run for profit, deriving both their clients and their incomes from contracts with local governments. Some are designed as long-term residential facilities and others as outpatient clinics. Program philosophies vary widely:

- Some are organized with strict, military-like discipline.
- Others are based on religious beliefs.
- Some are devoted to group therapy.
- Others stress rugged individualism and self-reliance.

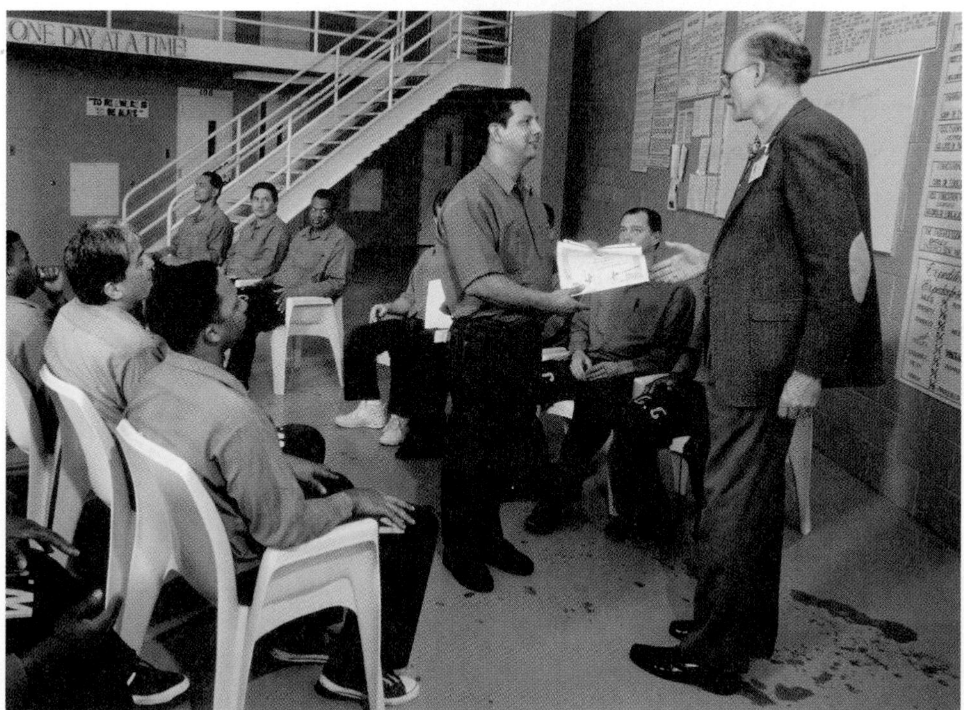

Prisoners at the Kyle New Vision Chemical Dependency Treatment Center receive awards.

Photo courtesy of Wackenhut Corrections Corp.

The growing problem and critical need to respond to the widespread use of drugs creates a demand to treat drug abusers and has rekindled interest in these types of programs, and we can expect their numbers to increase.

Private sector programs handle a large number of criminal offenders. For every offender housed in a privately managed jail or prison, there are hundreds in privately operated noncustodial programs operating under contract with state and local governments. Despite their numbers and importance, these private programs are largely ignored in discussions of the privatization of corrections. This may be because such programs are regarded as merely service providers rather than penal programs, or because their roles as agents of state control are obscured because client participation is primarily voluntary.

Most private operators of prison facilities are for-profit corporations, and are generally listed on stock exchanges as investments. As such, they can be seen as a **growth industry.** Some of the major private operators include Corrections Corporation of America (CCA), The GEO Group, Inc. (formerly Wackenhut Corrections), Cornell Companies, Inc., and Management and Training Corporation. Arguably, the largest is CCA (www.correctionscorp.com/aboutcca.html).

LOW-SECURITY CUSTODY PROGRAMS

Another important development in corrections in recent years has been the growth of low-security custodial facilities.[6] Many of the most innovative types of low-security facilities have been designed and implemented by advocates of privatization and, as such, are operated by private contractors. Today, this form of custody constitutes one of the fastest growing areas of corrections and the most important segment in the business of private, for-profit corrections contractors. See Figure 12.2.

The juvenile justice system, in particular, has come to rely on private contractors to provide such low-security custodial facilities. This in turn has both increased the government's flexibility in dealing with juveniles and expanded its

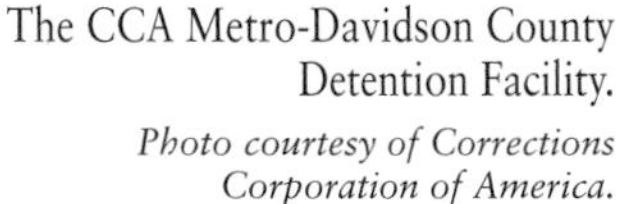

The CCA Metro-Davidson County Detention Facility.
Photo courtesy of Corrections Corporation of America.

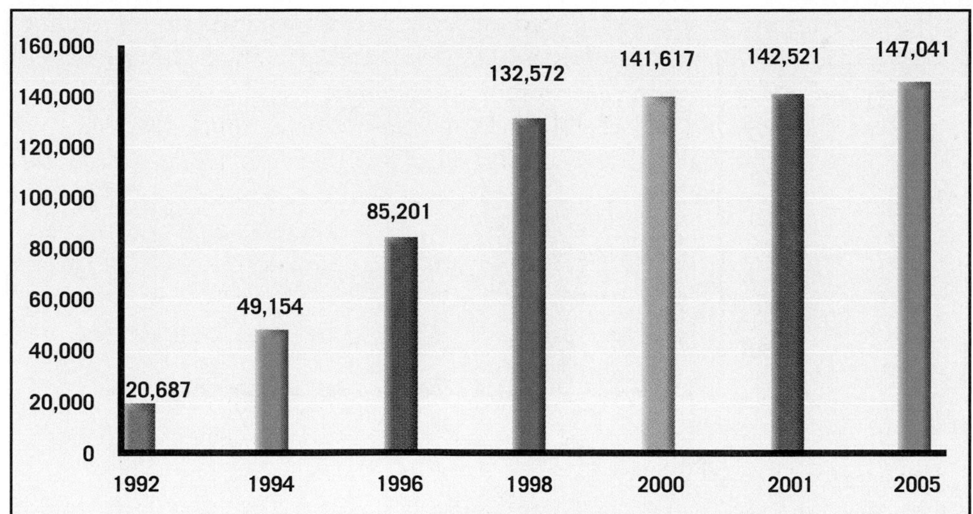

FIGURE 12.2

Growth of Private Sector Capacity (Beds), April 2005

SOURCE: Charles Thomas, "Rated Capacities of Private Facilities by Geographical Location," http://web.crime.ufl.edu/pep/cendus/2002/Chart1.html. Data for 2005 are estimated.

capacity to commit them into custody. California, Florida, Massachusetts, Michigan, Pennsylvania, Rhode Island, and Washington, among others, rely heavily on private contractors to care for their wards. In a number of states, placement in out-of-home settings constitutes a major component of the state's juvenile corrections policy; in some, private placements outnumber placements in public facilities. We should stress that these private custodial placements are not simply more efficient versions of state-run programs. Although these programs have diverted some and provided services to other juveniles who would otherwise have been placed in secure public institutions, they also target groups that once would not have been placed in custody at all. In short, such programs add a new intermediate level of sanctioning to the state's repertoire. See Figure 12.3.

Private contractors have also played a similar role in developing low-security facilities for adult offenders, and there is a growing differentiation between what the private and public sector facilities have to offer. The private sector is developing more facilities at the low end of the spectrum, such as residential treatment facilities, community work release centers, prerelease centers, short-term detention facilities, restitution centers, return-to-custody facilities, and the like. See Figure 12.4. Nonetheless,

SIDEBARS

Legal Liability for Private Correctional Contractors

Legally, the government is ultimately responsible for what happens in a prison or a community corrections facility. The state can contract away the duties, but it cannot contract away responsibility. The government serves as a safety net for private contractors, many of whom could not handle the weight of civil rights and tort suits generated in a correctional environment. Effective monitoring by state and local officials is the answer for both parties.

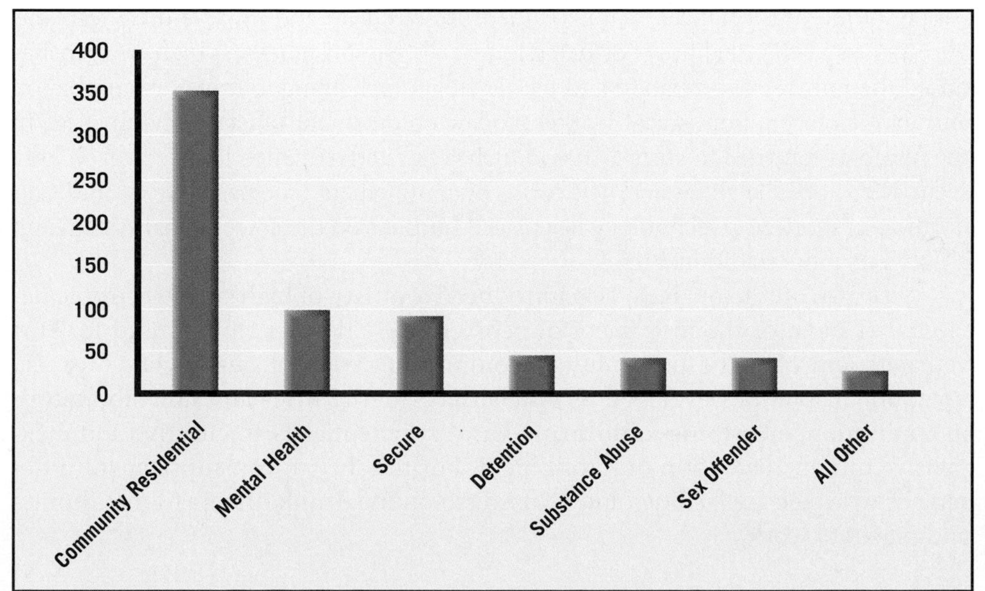

FIGURE 12.3

Privatized Juvenile Facilities

SOURCE: American Correctional Association, *2004 Directory* (Lanham, MD: ACA, 2004), p. 36.

FIGURE 12.4

Privatized Adult Facilities

SOURCE: American Correctional Association, *2004 Directory* (Lanham, MD: ACA, 2004), p. 32.

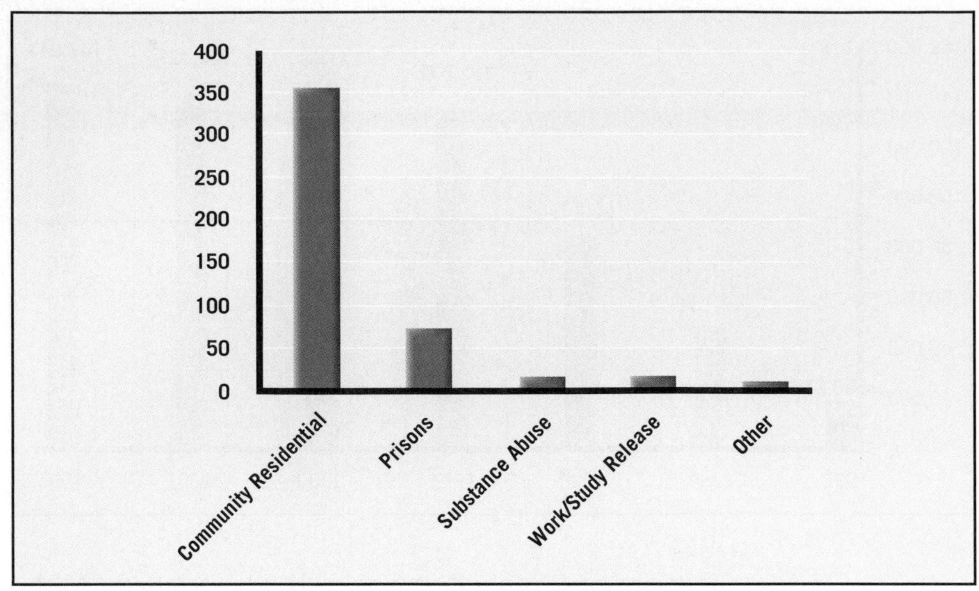

SIDEBARS

Early Privately Operated Facilities for Women

Private "houses of refuge" for women were created throughout the 1800s. They sought to reform prostitutes and other female offenders through religious, educational, sewing, and reading activities. These facilities were oriented more toward reform than punishment and were actually early models of the halfway houses of the twentieth century. Some of the concepts developed in these privately operated facilities were adopted for use later in state reformatories. This early use of the private sector for special-category prisoners was a forerunner of many of today's private sector community correctional operations.

private sector providers also manage and provide services for secure jail and prison institutions.

Private sector involvement in community corrections is increasing, and there are indications that it will continue to grow, especially if prison populations continue to exceed capacity and pressures mount to increase alternatives that are more flexible and less costly. See Figure 12.5. Time will tell if this "net-widening" effect of such expanded services will actually reach enough of the problem clients in the community who would not normally have been served.

SURVEILLANCE AND CONTROL TECHNOLOGIES

New technologies represent yet another area that has emerged in response to the growing concern with crime. Only a few years ago, state laboratories performed chemical testing in a costly and time-consuming manner. Now private drug testing companies across the nation can offer fast, cheap, and reliable tests to detect a large variety of illegal substances. But expanded use of cheap and reliable drug tests has also increased the likelihood of detection of illegal substances, which in turn has raised the number of probation and parole violators, helping to transform probation and parole officers from social workers to law enforcement officers. The upsurge in the numbers returned to custody has in turn generated demands for specialized low-security custodial facilities and new forms of confinement (such as in Texas and California). In short, new technology has placed burdens on the correctional system and affected its more traditional roles.

Private contractors have also introduced a variety of high-tech electronic devices that monitor the movement of people. These devices can be used for surveillance and offer the possibility of confinement without custody, as was also noted in Chapter 8. Developed by specialized security firms and now ubiquitous in application, **electronic monitoring** has vast potential as an effective and inexpensive intermediate form of punishment. For instance, it can supplement if not replace work release facilities and be used to confine drunk drivers to their homes and places of work.

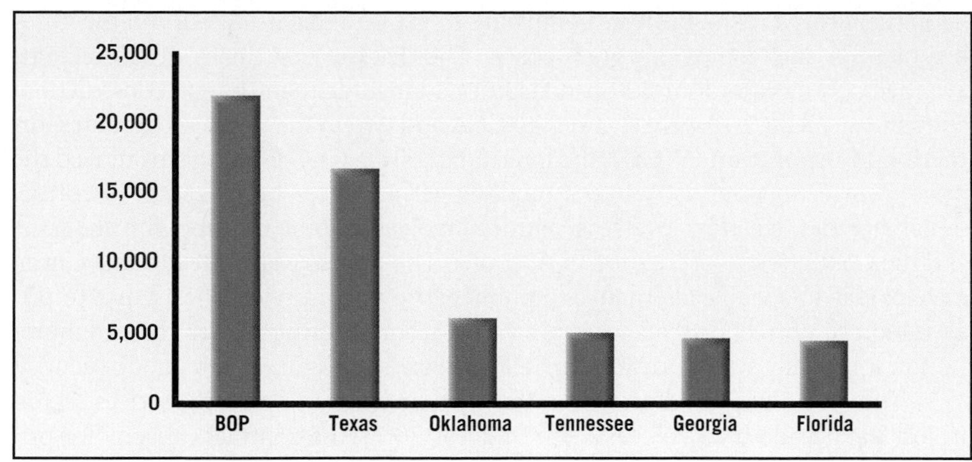

FIGURE 12.5

Number of Prison Inmates in Private Facilities, 2003 Prison inmates total 95,522.

SOURCE: Paige Harrison and Allen Beck, *Prisoners in 2003* (Washington, DC: Bureau of Justice Statistics, 2004), p. 4.

CORRECTIONAL PRIVATIZATION: ISSUES AND EVIDENCE

It is now widely understood that, first, privatization arrangements cast the government and not a private firm as the entity which establishes public priorities and that, second, they involve the efforts to achieve public goals by reliance on private rather than public means. Importantly, one really cannot appreciate the significance of the privatization trends today without having a basic understanding of what is so different today from as little as twenty-five years ago. In 1980, there was not a single privatized jail or prison here or abroad.

The precise moment when this concept of privatization of secure adult facilities was born is the subject of much debate. The foundation was probably laid on or near the date in 1983 when **Corrections Corporation of America (CCA)** was formed in Nashville, Tennessee. The first local contract for a secure county facility was awarded to CCA in 1984. Kentucky awarded the first state-level contract to **U.S. Corrections Corporation (USCC)** in 1985. The first federal-level contract of any size went to CCA from the Immigration and Naturalization Service in 1984.

The lounge area of a privately operated work release facility in Seattle.

Photo by Clifford E. Simonsen, courtesy of Pioneer Human Services.

Soon there was a rush of private companies to get into this new field and the number of beds and companies grew apace. The Texas Department of Corrections awarded contracts for four 500-bed facilities, to include their design, construction, and management. Two were awarded to CCA and two to the new **Wackenhut Corrections Corporation (WCC),** the forerunner of the GEO Group. This moved the private corrections industry into a much larger arena for privatization of correctional facilities. The first overseas venture involved a joint venture with the CCA and the Corrections Corporation of Australia. The industry appeared to move from a novel idea to a viable alternative to publicly provided services. Resistance to privatization by correctional agencies has varied from experimentation to outright rejection, especially when privatization efforts were seen as an attack on job security.

The result was rapid growth in this new niche of the private services sector. In just the decade between 1992 and midyear 2003, the contract capacity for private secure adult correctional facilities across the nation grew from 15,300 to an estimated 147,041, an increase of 800 percent. See Figure 12.6.

Privately managed adult facilities now house diverse prisoner populations in both small and large facilities. The number of jurisdictions electing to hold their prisoners in privately managed facilities has grown nationally at a substantial rate. Critics predicted that no maximum-security facility could be privatized, but CCA opened a privately managed maximum-security facility in Leavenworth, Kansas, in 1992. Numerous other privately managed facilities house significant numbers of maximum-security classified prisoners. The evidence is mixed regarding control problems such as inmate-on-inmate assaults, inmate-on-staff assaults, minor disturbances, riots, and escapes.[7]

At least three of the companies that manage adult correctional facilities (CCA, the GEO Group, and **Esmor Correctional**) have also contracted for youthful offender programs. These programs deal primarily with older juveniles and put less emphasis on treatment, a focus in the typical residential programs that Children Comprehensive Services and Youth Services both operate. The youthful offender programs that are managed by adult corrections companies have lower per diem charges on average (approximately \$65 to \$80 per day), when compared to residential programs run by primarily juvenile service providers (\$85 to \$180 per day). To date, pri-

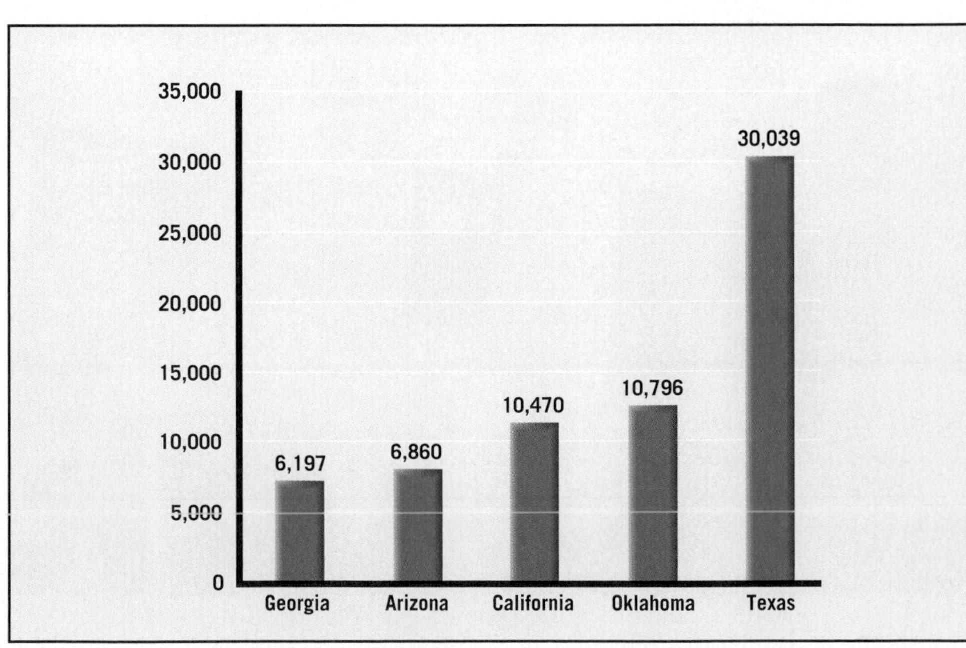

FIGURE 12.6

Rated Capacity of Private Facilities

SOURCE: Charles Thomas, "Ten-Year Growth in Rated Capacity of Secure Adult Correctional Facilities," http://web.crim.ufl.edu/pep/census/2001/figure1.html.

vate corrections companies concentrating on the adult market have chosen not to compete with the companies that concentrate entirely on juvenile programs.

At year-end 2003, privately operated prisons held more than 95,5000 state and federal inmates, over 22,000 on the federal level and almost 74,000 on the state level. These represent almost 13 and 7 percent of their prison populations, respectively.

Correctional systems using private prison providers include thirty-two states, the District of Columbia, and the federal system. Among states, Texas (with 16,570 state inmates housed in private facilities) and Oklahoma (with 6,022) reported the largest number in 2003. Six states had at least 25 percent of their prison population housed in private facilities: New Mexico (44 percent), Montana (29 percent), Alaska (31 percent), and Oklahoma and Wyoming (both at 26 percent). The use of private facilities was concentrated among southern and western states.

SUMMARY

It is difficult at this time to determine if private sector correctional providers, especially of prison facilities, are more effective than public sector providers, if they are cost effective, if they have comparable or better recidivism rates, and if they provide adequate services, particularly in the realm of medical services. The data are just beginning to be amassed and organized, allowing us to see some patterns and directions. This is the first time we have been able to gather enough information to put together a comprehensive chapter on this important topic. The future of privatization seems to be very promising.[8]

Growth in contracting for the management of secure correctional facilities happened far more rapidly in the last decade than virtually everyone expected. Still, it is also true that only slightly more than 6 percent of all prisoners in the United States are presently being housed in private facilities. Although private facilities are now in operation, under contract, or under construction for speculation in many states, and although private facilities presently house prisoners in at least thirty-three states, it is important to note that not all American jurisdictions have awarded local or state-level contracts. Those that have refrained from contracting include numerous states that have both a large prisoner population and significant problems caused by the prisoner populations being above 100 percent of the highest design capacity of their systems (for example, Massachusetts, New York, and Washington).

Most privatization initiatives have involved contract awards that were intended to expand the capacity of correctional systems. Although potential cost savings and performance improvements that could flow from decisions to privatize existing facilities are arguably possible, obvious political considerations reduce the appeal of this kind of contracting. In fact, the Tennessee proposal, mentioned at the beginning of this chapter, was at least in part rejected because the chairperson of the Criminal Justice Committee asked the question of his colleagues: "If these people can do this job cheaper and better, why can't we?" This is an obstacle for privatization proponents. The obstacle could become troublesome as the current general population growth trends continue to moderate.

The appeal of many types of privatization is considerable beyond the boundaries of the United States. However, it remains true that facility management contracts have been awarded in few countries (Australia and the United Kingdom are the largest exceptions). Opposition both to the enactment of legislation authorizing privatization and to exercising existing statutory authority remains strong in many jurisdictions. Corrections managers and administrators, as well as correctional unions, are generally opposed to private sector prison providers.

The arguments have been given here to stimulate the student's interest in this battle during the first decade of the twenty-first century. Perhaps the next decade will see the reinvention of corrections into a model of public and private cooperation to achieve new goals and objectives for the beleaguered system of corrections.

REVIEW QUESTIONS

1. What are the primary reasons for the private sector to become involved in prisons and jails?
2. How many beds are being supplied by the private sector in adult prisons?
3. What are the major arguments against privatization of adult jails and prisons?
4. What are the major arguments in favor of privatization of correctional services?
5. What vested interests are evident in the controversy over privatization of correctional facilities?

ENDNOTES

1. Office of Juvenile Justice and Delinquency Prevention, *Juvenile Offenders and Victims: 1999 National Report* (Washington, DC: OJJDP, 1999), p. 188.
2. Joseph Jacoby, "The Endurance of Failing Correctional Institutions," *The Prison Journal* 82:2 (2002): 168–188.
3. Douglas McDonald, E. Fournier, E. Russell et al., *Private Prisons in the United States* (Cambridge, MA: Abt Associates, 1998).
4. Harry E. Allen and J. Abril, "The New Chain Gang: Corrections in the Next Century," *American Journal of Criminal Justice* 22:1 (1997): 1–12; and Matthew Mancini, *One Dies, Get Another: Convict Leasing in the American South* (Columbia, SC: University of South Carolina Press, 1999). See also Florida Department of Corrections, www.dc.state.fl.us/oth/timeline/1928-1931.html.
5. James Anderson, L. Dyson, and W. Brooks, "Alabama Prison Chain Gangs," *Western Journal of Black Studies* 24:1 (2000): 9–1; and Timothy Dodge, "State Convict Road Gangs in Alabama," *The Alabama Review* 53:4 (2000): 243–270.
6. For example, California has ten contract correctional facilities providing medium to minimum security and treatment. In 2001, nine of these ten units housed more than 4,500 offenders. American Correctional Association, *2001 Directory* (Lanham, MD: ACA, 2001), pp. 99–100.
7. A series of evaluation studies can be found at www.correctionscorp.com/researchfindings.html. None of the authors has any financial interest in any private sector correctional group.
8. Large portions of this chapter were extracted and paraphrased from materials provided by Charles Thomas, former director of the Center for Studies in Criminology and the Law, University of Florida. We are grateful to him for sharing these earlier data and reports.

SUGGESTED READINGS: PART 4

Austin, James. "Prisoner Reentry: Current Trends, Practices, and Issues." *Crime and Delinquency* 47:3 (2001): 335–331.

Bahn, Charles, and J. David. "Day Reporting Centers as an Alternative to Incarceration." *Journal of Offender Rehabilitation* 27:3/4 (1998): 139–150.

Bazemore, Gordon, and L. Walgrave (eds.). *Restorative Juvenile Justice: Repairing the Harm of Youth Crime*. Monsey, NY: Criminal Justice Press, 1999.

Chesney-Lind, Meda, M. Harris, and G. deGroot (eds.). "Female Offenders." *Corrections Today* 60:7 (1998): 66–144.

Feeley, Malcolm. "The Privatization of Prisons in Historical Perspective." *Criminal Justice Research Bulletin* 6:2 (1991): 6–8.

Gagne, Patricia. *Battered Women's Justice: The Movement for Clemency and the Politics of Self-Defense*. New York: Twayne, 1998.

Greenberg, David, and Valerie West. "State Prison Populations and Their Growth, 1971–1991." *Criminology* 39:3 (2001): 615–654.

Hassine, Victor. *Life Without Parole: Living in Prison Today.* Los Angeles: Roxbury, 2002.

Hershberger, Gregory. "The Development of the Federal Prison System." *Federal Probation* 43:3 (1979): 13–23.

Jacoby, Joseph. "The Endurance of Failing Correctional Institutions." *The Prison Journal* 82:2 (2002): 168–188.

Lanza-Kaduce, Lonn, K. Parker, and C. Thomas. "A Comparative Recidivism Analysis of Releasees from Private and Public Prisons." *Crime and Delinquency* 45:1 (1999): 28–47.

Latessa, E. J., and Harry E. Allen. *Corrections in the Community.* Cincinnati, OH: Anderson Publishing, 2003.

Lilly, J. Robert, and M. Deflem. "Profit and Penalty: An Analysis of the Corrections-Commercial Complex." *Crime and Delinquency* 42:1 (1996): 3–20.

Lowenkamp, C., and E. L. Latessa. "Developing Successful Reentry Programs: Lessons Learned from the 'What Works' Research." *Corrections Today* 67:2 (2005): 72–77.

Petersilia, Joan. "Hard Time: Ex-Offenders Returning Home After Prison." *Corrections Today* 67:2 (2005): 66–71, 155.

Sexton, George E. *Work in American Prisons: Joint Ventures with the Private Sector.* Washington, DC: U.S. Department of Justice, 1995.

Thomas, Charles W. *Correctional Privatization: The Issues and Evidence*. Toronto: The Fraser Institute, 1996.

Thomas, Charles W. "Prisoner Rights and Correctional Privatization: A Legal and Ethical Analysis." *Business and Professional Ethics Journal* 10:1 (1991): 3–45.

Western, Bruce, J. Kling, and D. Weinman. "The Labor Market Consequences of Incarceration." *Crime and Delinquency* 47:3 (2001): 410–427.

PART 5 Corrections Functions

THE FOLLOWING CHAPTERS ARE COVERED IN PART 5:

OVERVIEW

Every correctional facility for adults, whether called a prison, reformatory, correctional facility, institution, or correctional hospital, has basic minimal functions that must be performed. These fall into two broad categories: custody and treatment. Both functions are defined as correctional organization components and explained in Part 5, identifying the major problems, challenges, pitfalls, and current solutions as well as the routine of the institution.

CHAPTER 13

Custody Functions

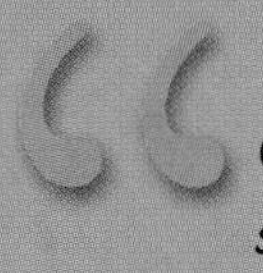

Our endeavors to control violence, in whatever setting, should be shared similarly by what we know about treating violent behavior. . . . Criminal behavior is learned behavior and ignoring its origin is wrong.
—Joseph D. Lehman

KEY WORDS

- bureaucratic control
- custody
- general population
- graduated release
- correctional officers
- "screws"
- unionization
- "blue flu"
- total institution
- prisonization
- lockdowns
- count
- sally port
- prison rules
- contraband
- frisk search
- strip search
- "keester"
- shakedown
- escape
- electrified fence
- paramilitary model
- unit team management

OVERVIEW

The primary mission for any confinement facility, prison, or jail is to "protect the public." That prime directive sometimes has been, and still is, carried to the extreme. Whether from fear, ignorance, apathy, or poor training, custody staffs are defensive of their role and tactics. Emotions in a high-security cell block can run high, with tensions spawning inappropriate behaviors on both sides of the bars. The custody staffs are the front lines of corrections and deserve utmost respect and appreciation for what they do. If the entire staff of an institution cannot work together, they will fail separately.

Custody over another person came into being when the first tribal member was asked to guard a thief until punishment was meted out. The long history of custody far outstrips the short time that "treatment" has been on the correctional scene. Treatment has only been on the agenda of correctional management since the early 1930s in any seriously organized fashion. The long-standing battles between custody and treatment started at the beginning and have continued, sometimes subdued, since that time. Outwardly, although the basic arguments seem to be over one or the other philosophy of corrections, the differences are more often seen in conflict over budgets, manpower, and turf. This chapter and the next examine and compare the various organizational components of corrections to see what they do and how they might do it better. Because custody comprises the largest part of that organizational system, we start with it.

< Prison guard drilling to test new riot-control technology.
Courtesy of AP/Wide World Photos.

INSTITUTIONS: BUREAUCRATIC CONTROL

Despite technological and educational advances, the prevailing management climate for correctional institutions seems to be one of **bureaucratic control,** especially in long-term adult felony institutions. In most major correctional facilities, the inmate population is usually controlled by a combination of coercive rules that are intended to prohibit certain kinds of behavior and punishments that are imposed when the rules are broken. Bureaucratic organizations are insulated by all kinds of documented rules, regulations, and procedures, and violations are quickly punished in the name of equity and control.

SIDEBARS

Misconduct Report

A report written usually by line staff when an inmate is believed to have violated institutional rules ("ticket").

In institutions that house thousands of prisoners, each with his or her own personal problems, the bureaucratic style seems to be the only functional way to maintain order and control; the processes take precedence over the individual, and prisoners become faceless commodities to be housed, moved, worked, fed, secured, and released. This nineteenth-century model stressed warehousing and subjugation of offenders. Any rehabilitation was incidental, a welcome but low-priority by-product, because the bureaucratic style clearly conflicted with any emphasis on rehabilitation. The separate functions of the rigid and formalized organizations create an impoverished climate for behavioral change.[1]

Administration's Problem: Punish, Control, or Rehabilitate?

The lack of coordination articulated for both intersystem and intrasystem activity on corrections, outlined in the previous chapters, suggests some of the reasons correctional administrators are often harried and hampered in their efforts to secure, control, and rehabilitate inmates. Although the public is willing to espouse reformatory goals for corrections, it is seldom willing to provide the support and funding that would make such reform a legislative priority. That inconsistency places dedicated correctional administrators in an awkward position: They can implement only the most meager of programs, and even then they must maintain an overall emphasis on control and punishment. Regardless of the approach to the problem, some aspect of operations will suffer.[2] If improvement requires an increase in the number of security guards, the administrator must obtain the necessary funds by decreasing the support for a treatment or other type of program; and if the administrator tries to amplify the treatment programs, it must usually be done at the expense of the custody staff.

CORRECTIONAL BRIEF

Correctional Managers

Adult correctional agency directors and institutional managers have not been extensively researched in corrections. Some basic facts:

In 2000, the average length of time an agency director had been in office was four years, and directors' average salary was over $98,700 a year. Both the average length of time in office and salary varied by region of the country. The longest term (thirty-three years) was found for a director in the Northeast, but the director of the federal Bureau of Prisons earned the highest ($123,900).

CUSTODY: A TWENTY-FOUR-HOUR IMPACT

Impacts on institutional behavior and the attitudes of incarcerated persons are usually learned by observing and responding to those staff who have direct and continuous contact with them. Administrative and treatment staffs have limited interaction with inmates on a daily basis. Custody staffs, however, are with them twenty-four hours a day. It has been found that, if the whole institutional staff is not working as a team, months of discipline can fall by the wayside as a result of one serious event. Conversely, months of professional counseling can be destroyed by a single custody officer's words or actions. The term **custody** refers to the level of immediate control exercised over offenders within correctional institutions. The levels can range from supermax, to maximum or close, to medium and minimum.

Supermax, maximum, or close custody usually means the inmate is seen as a security risk and cannot be trusted to move from one area to another, in the general prison or in the cell blocks, without being escorted by a correctional officer. It also implies that inmates will not be allowed to have contact visits or to associate with other prisoners freely without supervision. They are also limited in their contacts with other persons in general. The ratio of correctional officers to inmates in most facilities designated as supermax, maximum, or close is usually quite high, as many as one for every three or four inmates. (Death row inmates are usually considered to be in close custody and therefore are expensive to house, especially with their time from conviction to execution running well over twelve years on the average. See Chapter 20.)

Medium and minimum custody levels generally accommodate less risky or dangerous offenders or those closer to the end of their sentences. Generally speaking, the difference between medium and minimum custody is the presence of a high wall or fence and armed guard towers surrounding the former, with reasonably free movement within the facility for both categories. The inmates classified as medium security in an enclosed institution are allowed in what is referred to as **general population** (all prisoners not under special custody control). Staff-to-inmate ratios generally decrease at this level, with one custody staff to every eight or twelve inmates being a common range.

Inmates classified as minimum in a fenced or walled prison are often used on institutional jobs with very little supervision or observation (i.e., groundskeeping, sweeping, and cleanup). Minimum custody offenders are often placed in honor camps or farms, with low levels of supervision for a period of time prior to release, usually three to six months. This is a system that can reimpose a higher level of security, which often serves as both a carrot and a stick—a reward for good behavior and a loss of privileges for misbehavior. Most custody staff see this as a control mechanism and a pathway to **graduated release.** Generally speaking, custody administrators will err on the "side of the angels" and assign a higher level of custody when there is any level of doubt, especially until the inmate becomes established in the institution.

Even though much better trained and educated **correctional officers** have now replaced the old-time prison guards in almost all prisons, many institutions still follow the same oppressive custodial procedures, especially in times of unrest. Until the cause-and-effect relationship between autocratic organizational styles and institutional disturbance is openly acknowledged, the advocates of rigid custodial control will retain their influential role.

WARDENS AND SUPERINTENDENTS

Wardens (sometimes called superintendents) are the chief executive officers of prisons and have management responsibility for attaining mission goals. (See "Facility Mission Statement" in the accompanying sidebar.) The warden's primary responsibility is to manage the operations, supervisory staff, support staff, and inmates. To do this, the warden is usually assisted by several deputy wardens, typically one each for management, custody, programs, and industry. Most wardens are male (see Figure 13.1).

Most wardens are believed to "earn their way up" by serving in subordinate positions in the chain of command within a prison, assuming higher ranks and authority with experience and proven abilities. For many correctional workers, the post of warden is the capstone of a lengthy career, occasionally served within only one institution.

Wardens tend to "face outward" in their daily duties, dealing with politicians, administrators in the central office of corrections, the media, and interest groups. Running the daily affairs of the prison facility is usually delegated to a deputy warden, usually the custody deputy. Few have the time and luxury of overseeing the affairs of the inside of the facility. As Warden Benjamin Cooper said: "The warden's job is made much easier if he follows the MBWA ("Management By Walking Around") principle. You have to tour the facility every day." Information on race/ethnicity of wardens is found in Figure 13.2.

Contemporary wardens are less powerful and exercise less authority than those in office before the period of massive prison litigation began, usually identified as 1970. They defend rehabilitation and reform, face judicial intervention through court orders, deal with inmate grievances, serve as the management representative with unionized correctional officers, deal with the media, and negotiate with directors of corrections as well as the governor. Most go to work each day, leaving behind a partially packed suitcase on the ready in case they trigger a notorious administrative failure.[3]

SIDEBARS

Facility Mission Statement

The Ohio State Penitentiary facility mission is to protect Ohio's citizens, employees, and inmates by confining inmates who pose a threat to staff, other inmates, or institutional security in a controlled setting that is conducive to self-improvement.

SIDEBARS

Unity of Command

A bureaucratic principle that one subordinate reports only to one supervisor.

SIDEBARS

Chain of Command

A bureaucratic principle that authority resides in positions or rank, and a supervisor receives orders from a superior immediately above and issues orders to the one immediately subordinate.

SIDEBARS

Warden or Superintendent

The chief executive officer of a prison or correctional facility.

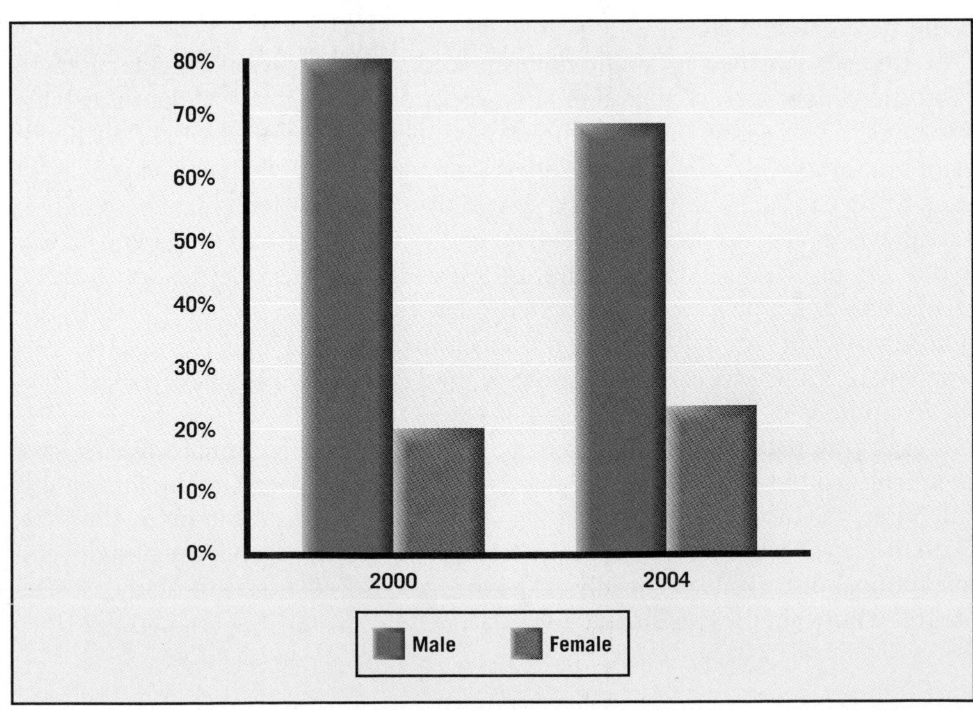

FIGURE 13.1

Gender of Managing Officers, 2004 (in percent)

SOURCE: American Correctional Association, *2004 Directory* (Lanham, MD: ACA, 2004), p. 42.

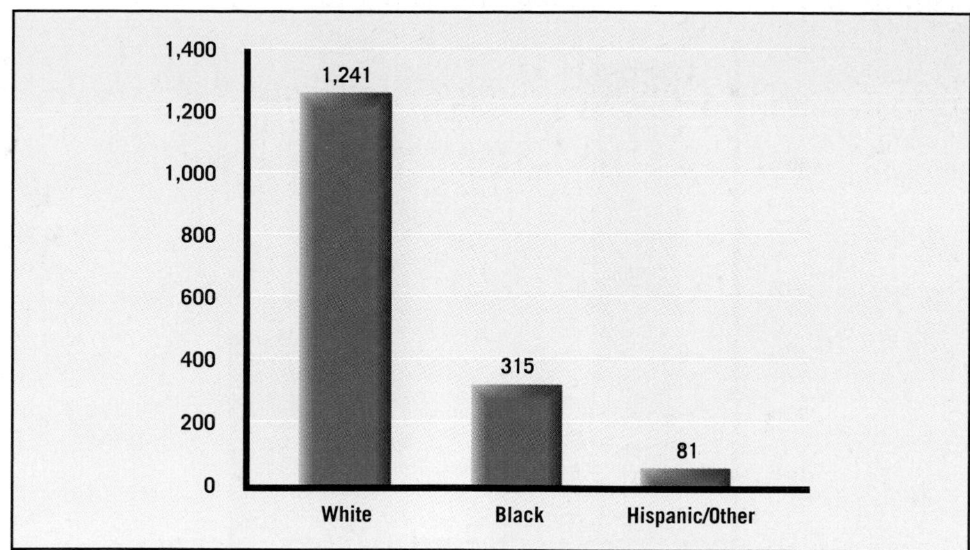

FIGURE 13.2

Wardens and Superintendents of Correctional Facilities, 2004

SOURCE: American Correctional Association, *2004 Directory* (Lanham, MD: ACA, 2004), p. 42.

CORRECTIONAL OFFICERS AND JAILERS: ON THE FRONT LINES

Although custody staff have been called guards, jailers, prison guards, turnkeys, "**screws,**" hacks, detention officers, correctional officers, or security staff, for purposes of this text we choose to use the term *correctional officer.* Regardless of the title used, it refers to those women and men charged with control, movement management, and observation of the inmates in the jails and prisons of America.By 2005, more than 381,000 uniformed custody staff were working in state, federal, and local adult prisons in America.[4] Also, more than 118,000 line officers worked in jails and local detention facilities in 2004, over 70 percent of the total staffing. The proportion of female officers in the prison systems was about 23 percent, with more than 33 percent in local jails and detention facilities. Some 33 percent of prison correctional officers[5] and some 29 percent of jail and local detention officers were nonwhite (see Figures 13.3 and 13.4).

Correctional Officer Attitudes

The last century saw the "get tough on crime" advocates place new and greater demands on correctional officers to do more with less, with little or no recognition. Moreover, prisons can be antagonistic and stressful working environments, as evidenced by the increasing number of assaults on correctional officers by inmates, and by the number of disciplinary actions taken by administrators against correctional officers.

Diminished Control

Correctional officer degradation is a recent phenomenon that has emerged largely as a result of court rulings and an increase in violence and gang membership among inmates. Specifically, some administrators are seen to have adopted a "hands-off" doctrine concerning inmate behavior. Some researchers argue that this doctrine has exposed prison regimes to outside accountability, limited an institution's recourse to coercive sanctions, and provided inmates with a legitimate means of expression with which to challenge the system of social control.

SIDEBARS

Correctional Officers

From the time of the earliest institutions until the late 1940s, the guard forces at prisons were untrained, unprofessional, and received their jobs based on political patronage. Most prisons were in rural settings and the guards were often local farmers, uneducated and unsophisticated. Some prisons, especially in the South, hired few guards and augmented their security force with inmate trustees. The first training facility for guards was opened by the federal Bureau of Prisons in New York City in 1930, but it was well into the 1970s before states developed qualified training academies.

SIDEBARS

Uniformed Staff

All correctional security officers, ranging from majors down to line officers.

SIDEBARS

Line Staff

A security staff member who directly supervises prisoners.

SIDEBARS

Staff Personnel

Employees who provide line personnel with services (such as training officer, clerks, accountants).

FIGURE 13.3

Gender of Correctional Officers, 2004

SOURCE: American Correctional Association, *2004 Directory* (Lanham, MD: ACA, 2004), p. 46; and Camille Camp and George Camp, *The 2000 Corrections Yearbook: Jails* (Middletown, CT: Criminal Justice Institute, 2000), p. 62.

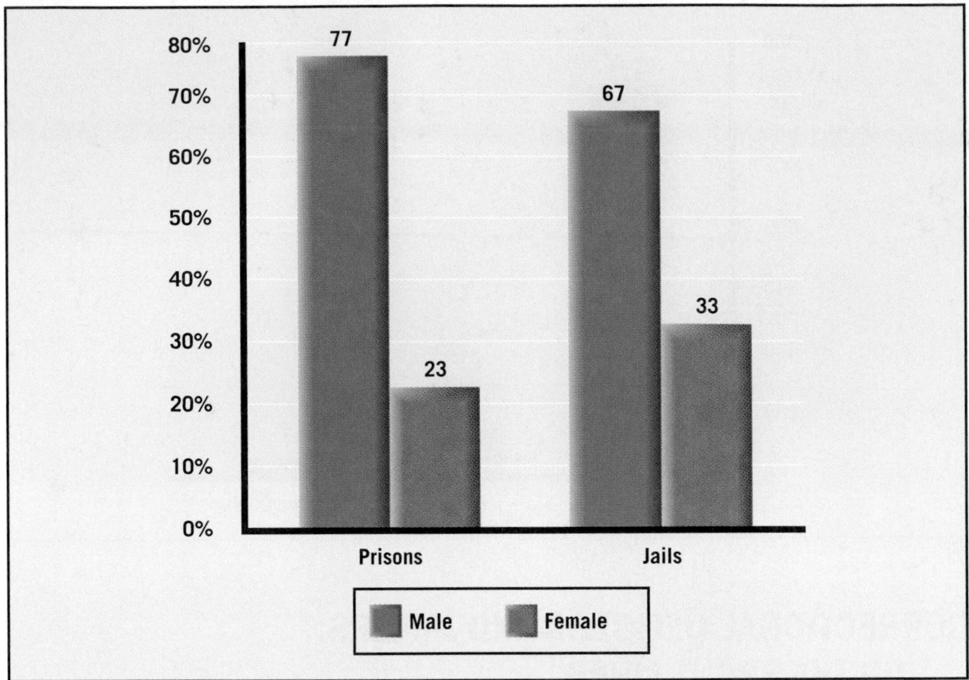

The impact of recent court decisions has been to establish a perceived link between the administrative and inmate control systems. The prison system's typical response to court decisions has been to develop administrative structures to maintain order consistent with the procedural and substantive rights of inmates. However, it appears that the rights of correctional officers might have been neglected while correctional administrators conformed to litigation. For instance, a latent result of court compliance by prison administrators has produced increased bureaucratic regulation and obligation of corrections personnel. This can be accomplished

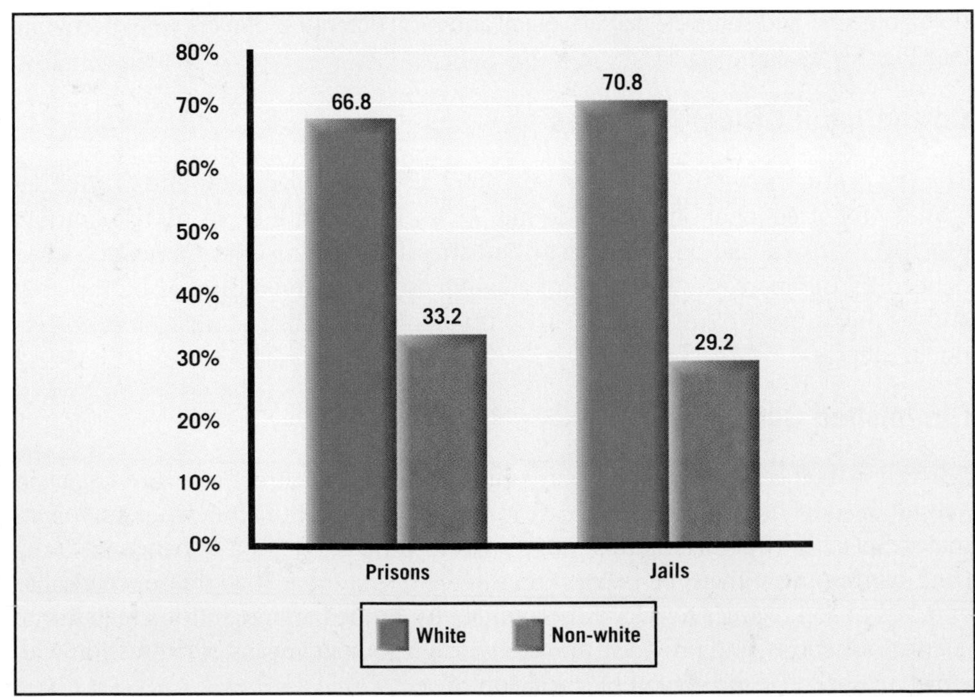

FIGURE 13.4

Uniformed Correctional Staff by Race/Ethnicity, 2004

SOURCES: American Correctional Association, *2004 Directory* (Lanham, MD: ACA, 2004), p. 46; and Camille Camp and George Camp, *The 2000 Corrections Yearbook: Jails* (Middletown, CT: Criminal Justice Institute, 2000), p. 57.

The Ohio State Penitentiary.
Courtesy of Ohio Department of Rehabilitation and Correction.

in a variety of ways, including a drastic increase in the direction and length of a correctional officer's training program. Also, when custody personnel arrive at basic or in-service training classes, correctional instructors should explain the mission of the training, which is to protect the state from further inmate litigation, and they should inform their students that future responsibility for courtroom resolutions rests with corrections personnel.

New legal standards have emerged, burying correctional officers in bureaucratic responsibilities. For instance, when correctional officers use force, they now must complete an official report, with videotapes and other corroborating evidence. This new "bureaucratic-legal order" also forces officers to conform to the letter of the law in the application of force. Some researchers suggest that several prison riots, including the Attica riot of 1971, can be traced to excessive inmate freedoms and the responses of prison systems to court decisions. Thus, inmate rights have produced a variety of bureaucratic regulations that have taken the authority and structure of custody away from the corrections professional.

An increase of violence, due in part to a rise in prison gangs, puts many officers in the trenches of our nation's prisons. Prison violence, crime, and drug trafficking are ways of life for most inmates in high-custody prisons. In fact, some experts say that as gangs and violence increase in high-custody penitentiaries, the less likely an officer is to want to deal directly with inmates; instead, he or she will want to transfer into administrative work.

If the primary concern is to render humane and quality custody service, it appears highly unlikely that alienated officers are motivated toward those ends. A second concern is the need to enhance in-service training at a professional level conducted outside the prison facility. Other recommendations from this study included the idea that administrations should manage through encouraging positive values instead of regulations, and that raises and promotions should be linked to merit, education, and experience.[6]

SIDEBARS

Preservice and In-Service Training

Poorly trained officers with no prior experience are a threat to themselves and others. Yet most new correctional officers (called "ducks" by inmates) have no experience working with prisoners and inmates, and almost none have had any training that applies to the prison setting. The American Correctional Association suggests that all new officers should receive forty hours of preservice training and forty hours of in-service training for every year after hiring.

SIDEBARS

Voluntary Turnover

Turnover is associated with management styles and management effectiveness. Rates of turnover as high as 40 percent a year are recorded in correctional institutions, with an average of about 14 percent for correctional officers nationwide. During good economic times many correctional officers leave voluntarily to seek what they consider "better" jobs. It is the job of management to provide the conditions and leadership that will make them want to stay.

Unionization and the Correctional Officer

Unionization, found in almost every sector of business and industry, has in recent decades spread to the ranks of state and federal employees. The union movement has extended to the "sworn" officers charged with the police, fire, and correctional protection of the public. Police officers and firefighters have established collective bargaining agencies in most urban departments, with improved working conditions and better pay as a result.

Because many jurisdictions forbid government employees from striking, other tactics are employed to create power negotiation in collective bargaining. Correctional officers have resorted to "**blue flu,**" the practice by uniformed personnel of taking sick leave en masse to back up their demands for improved working conditions, salary increments, and other items on their agenda. This method permits negotiating leverage without forcing the employees to strike, an illegal act.

As agents of public protection became more successful in their demands, their counterparts in the correctional institutions took notice. The great move in the late 1960s toward more professionalism and the sharp increases in prisoner populations, community corrections, and other programs pointed up some of the needs of the long-neglected correctional officer. Initial efforts to organize met with disapproval from administrators, often because of limited budgets and already overtaxed custody forces in the crowded prisons. Most administrators wanted the few available funds to be used for new personnel, not pay raises for the officers they already had. In some cases the correctional officers did go on strike, and their duties were assumed by administrative and office personnel.[7]

INMATE ORGANIZATION: THE SOCIAL SYSTEM

Prisons are **total institutions**[8] in which the residents' every moment, activity, movement, and option are carefully regulated by the correctional administrators. Inmates are given little individual responsibility and autonomy, important characteristics of everyday life in a modern achievement-oriented society. The tight regime compounds their personal inadequacies rather than correcting them. Cut off from ordinary social intercourse and their families and friends, then isolated in bastion-like prisons, inmates are quickly taught by the other residents how to exist in that environment. As we described earlier, the process of learning how to exist in prison—the appropriate attitudes and behaviors, the norms of prison life—is called **prisonization.** This process leads to the adoption of the folkways, mores, customs, and general culture of the prison.[9]

Former inmates can import prisonization into prisons if they are reincarcerated. It also occurs spontaneously even in newly opened institutions. The process is handed down from prisoner to prisoner, remaining a strong force that is later transmitted between prisons, working against the rehabilitation goals of even the most enlightened administrator. It impedes rather than facilitates treatment efforts, preventing inmates from acquiring the skills, talents, attitudes, and behavior necessary for successful adjustment in free society. Indeed, the opposite tends to occur: Inmates become more like infants[10] than mature adults.

As part of the process of prisonization, inmates learn codes and roles, and they are subjected to a reward and punishment system that encourages them to act like "good cons." Prison codes emphasize a number of specific behaviors: loyalty to other inmates ("never rat on a con"), maintenance of calm ("keep cool," "don't start feuds"), avoidance of trickery or fraud ("always share with your cellmates," "sell hoarded goods at the going rate"), manliness ("don't complain"), and quick-wittedness in prison dealings ("don't be a sucker," "guards are screws, never to be confided in or trusted").

Leg irons are used in prison.
Courtesy of Smith and Wesson.

Inmates who conform to those expectations become "right guys" or "stand-up guys" who can be trusted and are looked up to by other inmates. They share in the privileges available in prisons, and they can count on support if another inmate attacks them physically. Those who violate the normative structure become outcasts and are referred to by various descriptive and unpleasant names such as rat, snitch, fag, merchant, fink, and punk.

Two recent developments in America's jails and prisons have exacerbated those problems. The first is the rise of gangs in prisons. Most of these gangs have street gang origins and are racial or ethnic in nature, grouping together for power and protection. For example, the four major gangs in California's prisons are two Chicano gangs (ghetto Chicanos or "Nostra Familia" and the Mexican Mafia or "EME"), the Black Brotherhood (often based on gang affiliation such as "Crips" or "Bloods"), and the Aryan Brotherhood (includes most bikers, white supremacists,

Three white male Aryan Supremacist inmates stand together in a recreation room, Maricopa County Jail, Arizona.
Photo by A. Ramey, courtesy of PhotoEdit.

CORRECTIONAL BRIEF

Profiles of Texas: Seven Major Gangs

Texas prisons contend with seven major gangs. Each insists on a lifetime commitment: Once committed to one of these organizations, death is the only way out. Each prison gang is highly structured and operates under a specific "constitution" or set of rules. What follows is a brief description of these gangs and their histories.

- *Texas Syndicate* The Texas Syndicate began in the California Department of Corrections in the mid-1970s. It is mostly comprised of Hispanic inmates who migrated to California from Texas, although a few white inmates have been accepted. Through violent acts, the gang made a reputation for itself as a group to be feared and respected among general population inmates.

  On release from the California Department of Corrections, gang members returned to Texas and continued their illegal activities. Many were subsequently incarcerated in Texas. Since arriving in our agency, the gang has been suspected of involvement in more than forty-eight inmate homicides and numerous other nonfatal assaults on staff and inmates.

  The Texas Syndicate is structured along paramilitary lines and has a set of strictly enforced rules; violations may result in death. The group's members are known to have been incarcerated in California, New Mexico, Arizona, Florida, Illinois, and the federal Bureau of Prisons.
- *Mexikanemi* Mexikanemi, or MM, is the largest and fastest growing prison gang in the Texas Department of Criminal Justice (TDCJ). Mexikanemi is an Aztec term for "free or liberated Mexican." The group originated in Texas prisons in the early 1980s. It initially started as a group of inmates interested in their cultural background, but it rapidly transformed into a prison gang involved in extortion, narcotics trafficking, and assaults on inmates and staff.

  The gang is structured along hierarchical lines, with a president (its founder), a vice president, and three generals, each of whom is responsible for a specific region in the state. Generals can appoint members under them to run activities in specific facilities.

  The gang's constitution states that "in being a criminal organization, we will function in any aspects or criminal interest for the benefit or advancement of the gang. We will traffic in drugs, contracts of assassinations, prostitution, robbery of high magnitude and anything we can imagine."
- *Aryan Brotherhood of Texas* This group, comprised of white racist inmates, originated in the TDCJ in the early 1980s and should not be mistaken with other groups with similar names found across the country.

  The Aryan Brotherhood of Texas has been involved in assaults and murders of inmates in our agency and also conspired to have a state judge assassinated. Operating under a structure resembling a steering committee or a commission, this group has extended its illegal activities to the outside.
- *Texas Mafia* The Texas Mafia is mostly comprised of white inmates, but a few Hispanics have been accepted. The gang has an extensive background in narcotics; many of its members are involved in producing crystal methedrine and have ties with motorcycle gangs. The group is very violent and has been involved in inmate homicides and staff assaults. It has a close working relationship with the Texas Syndicate.
- *Nuestro Carnales* This group has fewer than 100 members. However, they have established a reputation for violence by being involved in several inmate assaults, including one homicide. Formed along a hierarchy structure with one recognized leader, this group is attempting to gain a foothold in the community as well as maintaining its status inside the prison walls. This gang appears to have strong ties with the Texas Syndicate.
- *Hermanos de Pistoleros Latinos* Composed of 174 members within TDCJ, this group has posed security problems for the agency by being involved in numerous illegal activities, including inmate assaults and inmate homicides. An additional 104 members have been released to the community and will have an impact for outside law enforcement agencies. This group appears to have ties with the Texas Syndicate and has been known to discuss joint illegal activities with that group.
- *Raza Unida* This group is the most recent to be identified as a disruptive group with TDCJ. With a membership of only sixty-four members, this group has yet to achieve the status and respect afforded the other prison gangs by the inmate population. However, they are rapidly gaining notoriety due to their recent assaults on inmates at various facilities within the agency. Classification of inmates from one specific region has assisted the group in forming and evolving into a prison gang.

SOURCE: Salvador Buentello, "Texas Turnaround: New Strategies Combat State's Prison Gangs," *Corrections Today* 54:5 (May 1992): 59.

and others like the skinheads). Gangs with many variations on these themes are found in jails and prisons nationwide (see the accompanying Correctional Brief for an example from Texas).

Conflicts between the gangs have led to stabbings, murder outside prison, rape, blackmail, and exploitation of nonaligned prisoners. All prison gangs are organized strictly to take part in only antisocial and criminal behavior. Many administrators have ordered **lockdowns** that confine prisoners to their cells to avoid bloodshed and violence. Such lockdowns have been criticized by legislators and other staff.[11] Jail and prison overcrowding has made matters worse, and many an administrator has resigned because of a sense of hopelessness.

We stress again that the importance of prisonization lies in its negative impact on attempts to provide rehabilitative programs that encourage inmates to engage in legitimate noncriminal activities.

CUSTODY AS A WAY OF LIFE

The "assistant superintendent for custody" or "security programs," also known as the "deputy warden for custody" or the "captain of custody" in jails, is one of the most important figures in any correctional facility. His or her main responsibility is to develop ways of accounting for the whereabouts of all prisoners at all times. Techniques have become more humane and permissive in recent years, but in most institutions the **count** is still the principal method of determining the prisoners' whereabouts, and counts are sometimes conducted as often as every two hours. Preoccupation with counting and recounting prisoners makes it difficult to conduct meaningful programs or permit individualized operations. To some extent, however, outside work details and opportunities for educational and vocational training and furloughs have been included in more streamlined counting methods. Today, counts are often called in to a central office in the prison's control room and tabulated against the daily tally of inmates, in some cases using bar-coded wristbands, access cards with magnetic data stripes, and computers.[12] Although the count is more sensibly administered nowadays, it still remains the most important task for which the custody staff is responsible.

Another function of the custody staff is to establish and maintain security procedures. Security procedures, at a minimum, include the inspection of persons and vehicles passing in and out of the institution, usually at a **sally port** at entry and exit points. The sally port is an area enclosed by a double gate. A vehicle or individual enters through the first gate, which is then closed. Before the second gate is

The control room, from which all doors may be opened and closed. In the event of a riot, officers could oversee all movements from this super-secure room.

Photo by Tony Savino, courtesy of The Image Works.

CORRECTIONAL BRIEF

Technology in Prisons

New technologies will enhance future detection of contraband and other illegal activities. Greatly improved X-ray capabilities will be able to detect weapons, explosives, and particularly controlled substances. Rapid eye scans can be used to detect drug use, and devices in bracelets can monitor vital signs in "real time." Sensitive "air-sniffing" equipment, when placed in prison ventilation systems, can detect drugs and explosives. Night vision goggles may be used to detect suspicious activities in high-security areas at night.

Much of this new technology comes from the security industry and the military development programs. Some of the equipment that was science fiction ten years ago is commonplace today. And we haven't even considered the development of computer hardware and software that is rapidly finding uses in prisons for management and operational use.

opened, the search for forbidden articles (contraband) is made. After the search is completed, the second gate is opened and the individual or vehicle passes through that gate. At no time may both gates be open, and many gate systems are mechanically adjusted so it is impossible to open them both at the same time. Sometimes a visitor feels it is as hard to get into the institution as it is to get out. The fear that inmates and visitors will try to smuggle in contraband or other items to assist escape pervades the maximum-security prison. Searches of vehicles and the requiring of visitors to pass through electronic metal detectors have become standard practices and procedures at major institutions.

Unfortunately, under the assumption that all inmates are alike, similar security practices have also been adopted by medium- and minimum-security prisons. It took over a century before America was prepared to build a prison without massive walls; it may take even longer to convince old-guard custody personnel that less stringent security measures may serve as well to ensure control.[13]

A correctional officer searches an inmate at California State Prison, Sacramento, in Folsom, California. Guards throughout state prisons are being ordered to limit use of deadly force in breaking up inmate fistfights.

Photo by Rich Pedroncelli, courtesy of AP/Wide World Photos.

Discipline and Inmate Traffic Control

Rules and regulations for inmates are usually aimed at strict traffic control. Prisoners' movements are carefully planned and controlled in every detail. In the past, all prisoners were awakened, moved to work, and fed at the same time, always under the eye of custody personnel. That degree of planning has slackened in many institutions; the trend is toward more reasonable controls over inmate traffic within the walls.

The suggestion that when inmates are treated as if they are dangerous they will become dangerous is generally considered valid. One way to avoid that problem is for staff and inmates to maintain meaningful communications. If the custody staff loses contact with inmates, the latter responds only to the inmate subculture. All too often, such limited interaction results in violence among the inmates. The most effective controls over inmate traffic and movement may well be those that guide our behavior in the free community.

The most recently available report on prison rule violators analyzed the characteristics of state prison inmates charged with infractions of institutional rules. Despite an increase of 64 percent in state prison populations from the previous study conducted ten years earlier, some 54 percent of prisoners had infractions charged to them in both studies. Other important aspects of this study are as follows:

- Younger inmates and those with more extensive criminal careers or drug histories were the most likely to have violated **prison rules.**
- Inmates housed in larger prisons or maximum-security prisons had higher percentages of rule violations than prisoners in other types of facilities.
- More than 90 percent of the inmates charged with violating prison rules were found guilty in prison administrative proceedings.
- The 90-and-above rate of guilty decisions occurred for different racial/ethnic, age, and sex categories and did not vary by size or security level of the prison.
- Inmates serving their first sentence in prison had a lower average annual rate of infraction (1.0) than did recidivists (1.6), regardless of how long they had served on their current sentence. A higher percentage of male inmates (53 percent) than female inmates (47 percent) were charged with rule breaking. On an average annual basis, however, women had a higher prison infraction rate than men (2.0 average violations per year versus 1.4 for men).
- Inmates who used drugs prior to admission were more likely to violate prison rules than were nonusers of drugs, 57 percent compared to 37 percent.
- Whites and blacks committed infractions at the same rate—approximately 1.5 violations per inmate per year. White and black rule violators reported nearly identical distributions of punishments received for rule violations. The most common penalties were solitary confinement or segregation and loss of good-time credit.

More recent studies of rule violation behaviors find that the pattern and types of misconduct were the same for males and females in a state prison, although levels of infractions were lower for women. Younger prisoners began their "misconduct careers" sooner.

A second study focused on major and minor ("serious" and "regular") infractions in a medium-security prison and found the ratio to be about 1:3, respectively. Minor infractions include theft of food, horseplay, lying, and use of abusive language to a correctional officer. More serious offenses include homicide, assault, possession of a weapon, and threatening to set a fire. The average processing cost of an infraction is estimated to be about $70 for each infraction charged that results in a finding of guilty. The figures tend to show that the problems with inmate infractions do not seem to have increased any faster than the growing population and that disciplinary actions may deter many other rule infractions. Institutional rules were designed to regulate inmate behavior.

Note, however, that most correctional officers are dedicated and humane persons, and maximizing their potential is an important challenge to concerned administrators. The situation with regard to educating those officers is improving. Prison guards were once hired off the street and trained on the job. Most states now offer extensive preservice training to ensure a minimal level of competence in the officers before they are placed on the job; all states require at least minimal preservice training. The basic course ranges from 40 to 640 hours of preservice training. In-service training is generally 56 hours annually, but many states provide 80 hours.[14] As this trend continues, salaries, the quality of personnel, and working conditions will improve. The tendency to use outdated and counterproductive forms of discipline should decrease accordingly, and the correctional officer, long recognized as the single most important agent for change in institutions, will be able to realize his or her[15] potential contribution to the rehabilitation approach.

Contraband and Shakedowns

In early years of corrections in America's jails and prisons, **contraband** was officially defined as any item that could be used to break an institution's rule or to assist in escape. In practice, the term usually ended up referring to anything the custody staff designated as undesirable for possession by the inmates. Such banning power is unrestricted. It can start with a particular object, such as a knife, and extend to anything that might conceivably be made into a knife—a policy that has placed some relatively innocuous items on contraband lists.

Any item that is not issued or not authorized in the institution is contraband. Control of contraband is necessary for several reasons:

- To control the introduction of articles that can be used for trading and gambling
- To control the collecting of junk and the accumulation of items that make housekeeping difficult
- To identify medications and drugs and items that can be used as weapons and escape implements.

Controlling contraband requires a clear understanding of what contraband is, of regulations that are designed to limit its entry into the institution, and of effective search procedures. The definition of contraband just given is simple and clear. However, this definition can become useless if the facility attempts to supplement it with a long list of approved items. If the institution permits prisoners to have packages, the problem of contraband control will be made difficult, since the list of authorized items may grow long.

Long lists of approved and forbidden items often complicate what appears to be a relatively simple definition. A broad and clear definition, followed by the use of common sense by trained correctional officers, will usually result in better control and less conflict over what is or is not contraband. Prison administrators often see an excessively long contraband list as a challenge to the inmate and an indication of suppression. Such items as guns, however, are clearly dangerous contraband, and prison administrators must continually check packages, visitors, and correctional officers to detect such material. This is usually accomplished using modern metal-detecting and X-ray equipment.

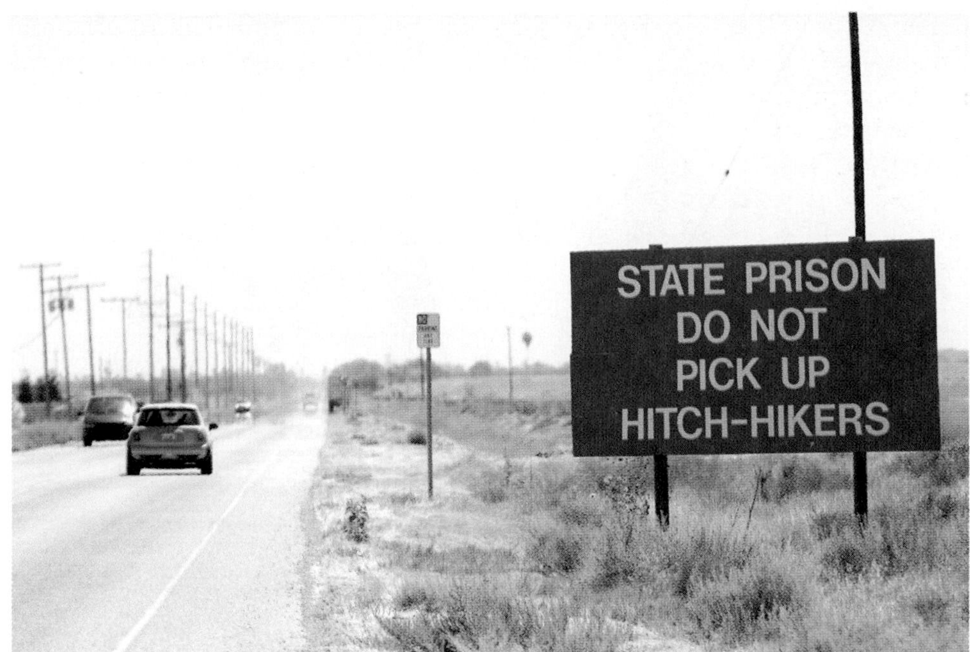

Sign at roadside warns motorists not to pick up hitchhikers near North Kern State Prison vicinity, Delano, California.

Photo by Michael Newman, courtesy of PhotoEdit.

The generally accepted way of defining contraband was to use the affirmative approach. For example, "contraband is any item, or quantity of an item, that is not specifically authorized by the institution rules." This clearly defines what is not contraband and leaves the decision as to what is contraband to the inmate. Contraband is more often found to be the acquisition of excess items that are authorized (e.g., extra blankets, extra books, hoarded food), rather than those items that are dangerous per se. Amassing contraband in this sense is seen as an expression of an inmate's power, plus a way to beat the system and show fellow inmates that the forbidden can be done. That power is used to trade favors or show favoritism to more powerful inmates. Contraband is often used in bartering and as currency (cigarettes and matches, for example) just as we use barter on the outside.

Because the loss of contraband is the loss of power, searches and shakedowns are another source of potential conflict with inmates in security institutions. The most common type of search to prevent contraband entry into and movement within institutions is the **frisk search.** This type of search is used when prisoners enter or leave the institution and when institutional personnel suspect a prisoner may be hiding contraband on his or her person. Figure 13.5 shows the proper procedures for a frisk.

When a prisoner is suspected of having access to drugs, weapons, or other items that can be secreted on the body or in a body cavity, and a frisk reveals nothing, a **strip search** may be conducted. The strip search is ordinarily made in a location where the prisoner will not be observed by other inmates and subjected to ridicule. The basic strip search requires only the visual observation of the entire body and orifices. If a more extensive body cavity search is merited, it must be conducted with the knowledge and permission of the chief administrator of the facility (superintendent, sheriff, etc.). Qualified medical personnel must conduct a body cavity search. Failure to follow those procedures can result in serious lawsuits against the institution.

Plastic capsules or vials inserted in the inmate's rectum are one way to hide ("**keester**" or "keestering") drugs and other small items of contraband, so when there is probable cause, body cavities may need to be examined. The strip search frequently follows visits, usually for every inmate or on a random sample basis. In the past, frequent strips were used to debase and abuse prisoners, a practice that

FIGURE 13.5

The Frisk Search

SOURCE: Nick Pappas, *The Jail: Its Operation and Management* (Lompoc, CA: Federal Prison Industries, 1971), p. 23.

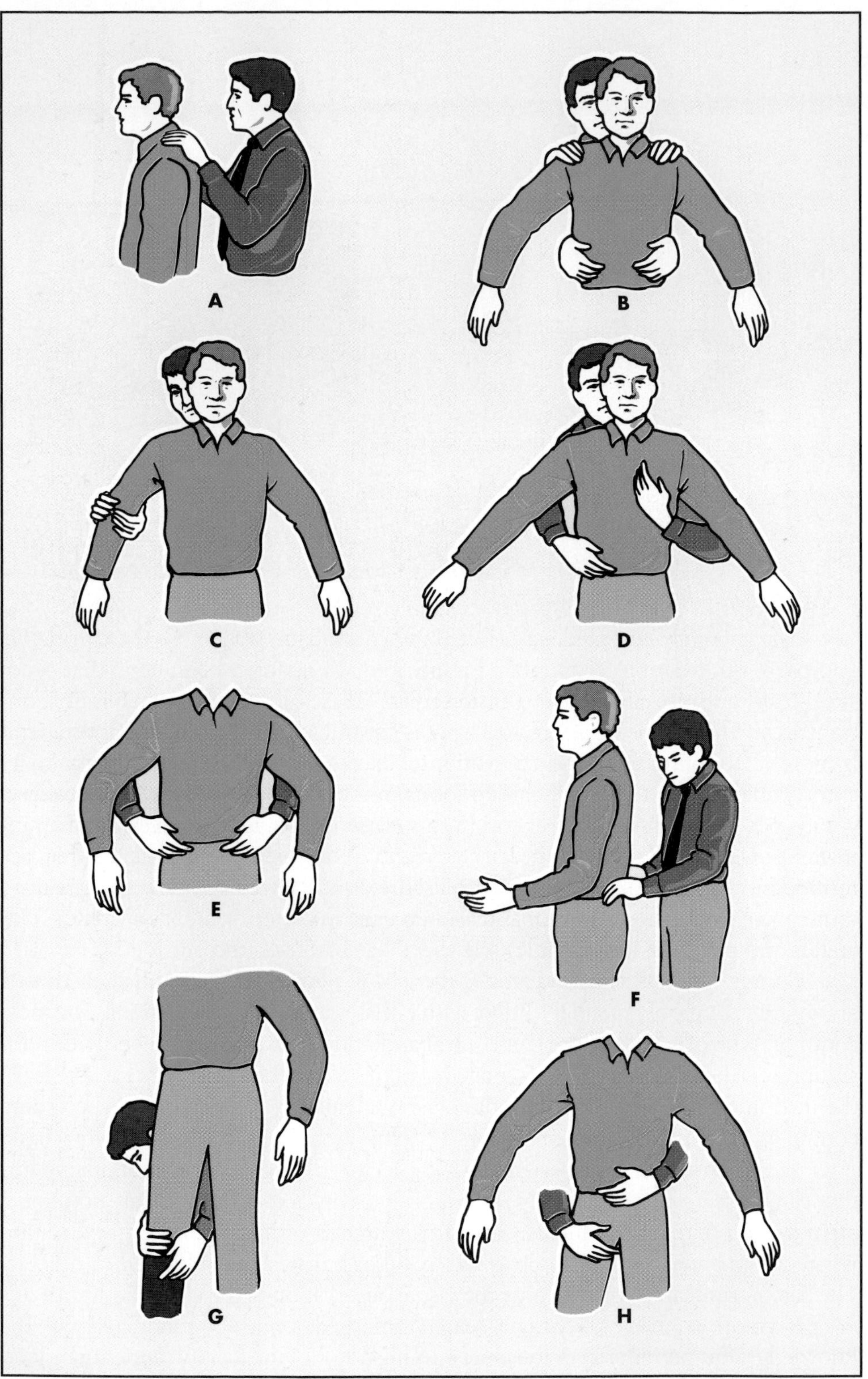

greatly increased prison tension and resulted in many legal actions against offending staff. Frisks are a necessary part of institutional security, but if strip searches become part of an everyday routine, the procedure soon degrades not only the searched but also the searcher.

As rules prohibiting contraband grow more detailed, inmates seek ways to secrete those items in the living area and throughout the institution. There is virtually no limitation to the ingenuity employed in hiding contraband in prisons.

Correctional officer Michael Melo searches a high-security cell at Corcoran State Prison in Corcoran, California. Corcoran has earned a reputation as a repository for the worst prisoners in the state.

Photo by Scott Anger, courtesy of AP/Wide World Photos.

Ironically, the older—and presumably more "secure"—institutions and plants lend themselves best to secret hiding places. The process can almost be seen as a game, with correctional officers periodically searching the same old spots. The need for **shakedowns** (searching of an entire cell or cell block) is reduced when contraband rules are made realistic and humane; prohibiting such items as family pictures and toothpicks creates a needless irritant. The shakedown also has greater effect if used only to locate items that represent a clear and present danger to the institution, not just for the sake of what inmates call "Mickey Mouse" harassment.

PREVENTION OF ESCAPE

Maximum-security jails and adult prisons were built as though they had to contain the most dangerous creature imaginable. "A jail or prison is designed to be as strong as the strongest inmate" is an old correctional chestnut. The high walls, corner towers, and armed guards are external signs of preoccupation with escape. The nature of most jail and prison populations, although changing to harder types, does not seem to justify that model. **Escape** (flight of a confined person from an institution) and riots are serious concerns for administrators, however, and although in 2003 there were at least 3,300 escapes and almost 5,200 returned escapees, most escapees were recaptured quickly.[16] They were mostly walkaways from minimum-security or community programs and represented only a miniscule percentage of the average daily population. When we consider the increasingly dangerous nature of some of the incarcerated inmates, this is actually a very good record (but bad news when they commit serious crimes while on escape status).

Riot

Acts of force or violence against persons or property or resisting the lawful authority of correctional officers under circumstances that produce a clear and present danger of injury to person or property inside penal institutions.

The conception of inmates as highly dangerous, when coupled with the extreme overcrowding of institutions, increases the concern of many correctional officers about the possibility of escape.[17] The issue is complex but revolves around two problems. The first is the philosophy of mass treatment, firmly established since the time when lockstep and silence were required for all prisoner movements.

The second reason is political. Seasoned superintendents know that frequent escapes will be extremely damaging to their records, and so their extreme measures to prevent them are directed toward all prisoners, rather than toward the few who might actually try to escape. In a few prisons, however, administrators have begun to realize that a tax evader and an ax murderer do not have the same potential for escape attempts.

Technology to Prevent Escapes: Electric Fences

The move to replace continuously staffed guard towers with lethal electrified perimeter fences could very well become a national trend because of state governments' urgent need to reduce operating costs. In November 1993, the California Department of Corrections (DOC) activated an electrified fence model at Calipatria State Prison in Imperial County. Since then, another twenty-three have been installed, one is under construction, and more new prisons with electrified fences are being planned. **Electrified fences** have been installed at adult facilities for men and women throughout California's agricultural areas, foothills, deserts, coastal and urban areas, and a few at higher elevations.

At most of the facilities included in the California Statewide Electrified Fence Project, traditional perimeter guard towers are spaced at distances that allow correctional officers to use deadly force to prevent escapes. At newer facilities, as many as ten towers (or 48.3 staff positions over three watches) can be deactivated. Using lethal fences greatly reduces the need for armed tower staff, for they can stop escapes by killing the inmates.[18]

Project Costs and Operational Savings

The construction cost of electrified fences varies depending on the perimeter length and site-specific conditions at each prison. The construction cost typically is within the range of $1 million to $2 million for an individual electrified fence of approximately

The state of California uses electric fences in high-security facilities. *Photo courtesy of State of California Department of Corrections.*

A SWAT team stands watch outside the cafeteria where inmates were holding prison guards hostage at the Broad River Correctional Institution near Columbia, South Carolina. The inmates released the hostages and then surrendered.

Photo by Jamie Francis, courtesy of AP/Wide World Photos.

8,000 lineal feet. The average cost is approximately $1.5 million. The operational cost savings of the electrified fence project result from the reduced staffing of the prison's guard towers and berm positions, minus the operations and maintenance costs of the fence and the additional roving patrol vehicle. Generally, the cost savings range between $400,000 and $2.1 million per year per prison, with an average operational cost savings of $1.38 million per year each. Therefore, the cost of each fence is recouped within the first or second year. For the fences completed or now under construction, the California DOC expects a system-wide reduction of more than 750 positions for a savings of approximately $40 million per year.

The Military Model

The need for an organized and effective custody and control force in jails and prisons has instilled a paramilitary flavor in most security staffs. The adoption of militaristic organizational structures and procedures early in corrections history made it easier to train a force with limited background to do a specific job. The **paramilitary model** is seen in the uniforms, titles, and procedures of custody personnel. Training is directed to the mission of security, and there is little emphasis on interaction with inmates. The model of the aloof but efficient guard has emerged, and the hiring of custody personnel is rarely based on the applicant's ability to work with people. To a great extent, correctional hiring practices inhibit those people who can best fulfill the newer mission of rehabilitation. The seniority system and the growing power of correctional officer unions often discourage the infusion of custody personnel with higher education in the behavioral sciences.

To provide the best entry-level personnel, and to maintain a level of quality and growth in their staff, many jurisdictions have established rigid training standards along the lines recommended by the American Correctional Association. Such requirements will ensure that all staff are eventually exposed to methods that are not simply "more of the same." To reflect the population in institutions, personnel should actively recruit from minority groups, women, young persons, and

CORRECTIONAL BRIEF

Nonlethal Weapons in Prison

As correctional facilities become more crowded, administrators are searching for nonlethal weaponry to run smarter and safer jails and prisons. One approach uses computerized inmate tracking and alarm systems to update the location of every inmate every two seconds. Inmates wear wristwatch-size devices that emit wireless signals that are collected by receivers and fed back along a cable system to display on a control-room computer the exact location of inmates. Lurking inmates are easily detected. Other facilities provide officers with pager-size wireless systems worn on their belts that automatically sound an alarm if the officer falls or is forced into a horizontal position. Assistance can immediately be dispatched.

In addition, various pepper spray devices can be carried on belts, sprayed from fire extinguishers, deployed from water pistols, or used with hoses to douse inmates up to 150 feet away. Pepper spray canisters in inmate dining rooms can be used to quell uprisings, riots, and gang disturbances. Some of these devices are marketed as nonlethal weapons filled with "food-grade pepper with water."

Guns that fire rubber bullets, hard rubber rounds, hard sponge devices, and bean bags are also being adopted as nonlethal armature for prisoner control in close environments, although lawsuits have been filed and are pending that allege excessive force, cruel and unusual punishment, and wanton infliction of unnecessary pain. Does the U.S. Constitution reach behind prison walls?

prospective indigenous workers and see that employment announcements reach those groups and the general public.

It is useful to conduct a task analysis of each correctional position (to be updated periodically) to determine the tasks, skills, and qualities needed. Hands-on testing based solely on relevant features, to ensure that proper qualifications are considered for each position, helps the administrator determine what is needed and can be provided by training. Those procedures will lead to an open system of selection in which any testing device is related to a specific job and is a practical test of a person's ability to perform, at an acceptable standard, the tasks identified for that job. Professionalization of corrections will continue well into this century.

These are a few of the steps that might help span the currently large communication gap between keepers and the kept. Correctional officers and custody staff spend more time with the inmate population than does anyone else in the institution. They should relate well to others because they can be the most positive agents of change in that corrections subsystem. They can also destroy any efforts toward change attempted by a treatment staff that tries to bypass them. A further move away from the military/police image to the correctional image is critical to effective change in the institutional setting.

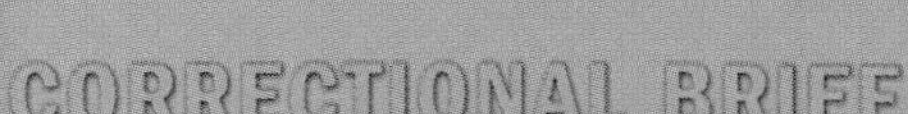

Glass-Topped Cells for Violent Inmates

Surveillance of violent inmates in jails and prisons can be both dangerous and dirty. Even local jails using direct supervision experience frequent officer assault by violent inmates. When confined to their cells, these inmates routinely throw feces, urine, and other bodily fluids at officers.

Some incarceration facilities are considering glass ceilings over special management unit cells for violent offenders, allowing the officers to walk on the glass ceiling, where they can observe and check on every movement of violent inmates, yet not come into direct contact with them.

UNIT TEAM AND OTHER METHODS TO AVOID COMPARTMENTALIZATION

With regard to ongoing conflicts between custody and security, a few final comments seem appropriate to show the student the situation is not hopeless. Many institutions already adhere to these concepts and only the overcrowding and violence are keeping progress in the slow lane.

First, policies should be developed jointly to define the relationships between critical custody and security functions. All staff must be involved in meeting rehabilitative program goals and custody needs for their institutions. The obvious dichotomy between custody and treatment must be erased and greater recognition given to the fact that each is supportive of the other. This kind of activity has been instituted in many institutions as **unit team management**, in which all members of the team of a given cell block, tank, pod, or wing work as a team to provide custody, support, and rehabilitative services in a single coordinated package.

Second, policies and guidelines for institutional rules and regulations should be developed and all present rules and regulations revised to ensure that the demands of security do not negate the objectives of treatment. In policy formation and in specific rules, the principle of clear and present danger should apply; if the regulation is required for the safety of the institutional community, it should be kept. If not, it should be abolished.

Third, in cases where force has been used on an inmate, in addition to an investigation by the institution and/or an outside agency, a report should routinely be submitted to the corrections authority by the prison physician and by the inmate.

Finally, the correctional authority should respond to requests from families that they be permitted to visit and see inmates if they believe excessive force has been used against them. If they desire an outside physician to examine prisoners, their request should be granted without delay, in accordance with rules to be promulgated by the correctional authority. Copies of all "Use of Force" reports should be filed with the correctional authority and be made available for inspection by the inmate's family, attorney, and, with the inmate's written permission, other appropriate people.

UPGRADING CORRECTIONAL PERSONNEL

The most important rehabilitative tool is the impact of one person on another. Thus, a primary goal for the correctional system is the recruitment, training, and retention of employees who are able—physically, emotionally, educationally, and motivationally—to work as a team. In the correctional system, including the nation's prisons and jails, it is hard to hire or keep qualified personnel. There are few reasons for the correctional officer and jailer to complain about salaries in the field. The national average entry-level starting pay of about $23,000 is not bad when one considers that the current minimum qualifications for applicants is usually only a high school diploma or equivalent (GED) and no criminal record.

But even now, in the twenty-first century, some jail and prison jobs go begging. This will make young people interested in possibly seeking jail and prison custody jobs more difficult to hire as they compete in a growing economy. Because of the persistent problem of unfilled slots on most shifts, supervisors ask officers on duty to work another shift (work "doubles"). That situation leads to overtired staff and high overtime budgets, but legislators are seldom willing to increase expenditures for staff. They fear that correctional officers are just padding the rolls, or perhaps are trying to avoid the costs of providing fringe benefits to more employees. Yet the fact is that prisons need a certain number of officers on duty at all times: "minimum critical staffing." Many administrators have tried to implement this concept, but budget needs still seem to override attempts at rationalizing staffing patterns.[19]

Perhaps more important than salary is the custody employees' sense of public rejection, reinforced in some institutions by the belief (whether true or false) that the administrators and professional staff do not consult them, treat them fairly, or care what they think.[20] New channels of communication must be opened between administrators and employees, as well as between employees and inmates. Administrators should meet with staff to discuss employee problems; custodial and treatment staff should also meet together. Those meetings should be regularly scheduled and formally integrated into institutional procedures.

SUMMARY

Even though the official policy of the institution may be humane, the people who are in direct contact with the inmates may have an entirely different view of their role, which sometimes leads to degrading and even brutal treatment of inmates. Recruitment and hiring standards, practices, and procedures have not established sufficiently high educational or personality standards for the position of corrections officer in every state. Salaries authorized by most legislatures for custodial personnel, while improving, are not yet high enough to attract and retain treatment-minded persons with high levels of education. It speaks well for today's correctional personnel that relatively few have been identified as brutal persons and excessive force litigation is rare. The nature of the situation, however, lends itself to individual expressions of punitiveness.

All involved in corrections recognize that custody and security are necessary but are not the only correctional goals. The next chapter deals with management and treatment functions as the other essential components of prison and jail operations.

REVIEW QUESTIONS

1. What is the primary focus of the bureaucratic style of prison management?
2. Where have prison guards been obtained from in the past? How does this situation create problems?
3. Why has the military model been so popular in the prisons?
4. Why do disciplinary and security considerations so greatly affect treatment programs? How can that issue be resolved?
5. What are the effects of imprisonment on inmates? Staff?
6. In what ways have the roles and positions of correctional officers improved during the last two decades?
7. What are the problems with prison gangs? What is their makeup?
8. Give a description of unit team management. How does it work?
9. Discuss the effects of a prison escape.
10. How can management and staff work toward making prison work more rewarding?
11. Does the use of the electric fence around the prison perimeter equate to the death penalty for attempting to escape from prison?

ENDNOTES

1. Clifford English, "The Impact of the Indeterminate Sentence on an Institutional Social System," *Journal of Offender Counseling, Services and Rehabilitation* 8:1/2 (1983): 69–82; and Victor Hassine, *Life Without Parole* (Los Angeles: Roxbury, 2002).

2. Michael Vaughn and C. Morrissey, "Violence in Confinement," *Journal of Offender Rehabilitation* 25:1/2 (1997): 21–42; and Rosemary Gido (ed.), "Evaluation of the Concepts of Correctional Organization and Organizational Change," *Criminal Justice Policy Review* 9:1 (1998): 1–139.
3. Research on prison wardens and superintendents is minimal. The major professional organization is the North American Association of Wardens and Superintendents, C/O Arthur Leonardo, P.O. Box 11037, Albany, NY 12211-0037).
4. Extrapolated from Camille Camp and George Camp, *The Correctional Yearbook 2000: Adult Corrections* (Middletown, CT: Criminal Justice Institute, 2000), p. 140.
5. Camp and Camp, *The Correctional Yearbook 2000,* p. 134.
6. Dennis J. Stevens, "Correctional Officer Attitudes: Job Satisfaction Levels Linked to Length of Employment," *Corrections Compendium* 23:7 (1998): 19–20.
7. Correctional officers have gone on strike in Washington State and in institutions in the Ohio State system. When that happens, administrative personnel or state police are required temporarily to fill the correctional officers' posts. Although police strikes have been found to have a limited impact on the rates of reported crime, little is known about institutional disturbances and rule violations in prison when correctional officers strike.
8. Donald Clemmer, *The Prison Community* (New York: Rinehart, 1940); Anthony Scacco, *Rape in Prison* (Springfield, IL: Chas. C Thomas, 1975); and Hassine, *Life Without Parole.*
9. See David Shichor and Harry Allen, "Correctional Efforts in the Educated Society: The Case of Study Release," *Lambda Alpha Epsilon* 39 (June 1976): 18–24. See also Jon Sorenson, R. Wrinkle, and A. Gutierrez, "Patterns of Rule Violating Behaviors and Adjustments to Incarceration Among Murderers," *Prison Journal* 78:3 (1998): 222–231.
10. Shichor and Allen, "Correctional Efforts," p. 21. See also Judith Clark, "The Impact of Prison Environment on Mothers," *Prison Journal* 75:3 (1995): 306–329.
11. Peter Nacci and Thomas Kane, "Sex and Sexual Aggression in Federal Prisons: Inmate Involvement and Employee Impact," *Federal Probation* 47:4 (1983): 31–36; Florida House of Representatives Committee on Corrections, "Corrections officers: Turnover, security and safety" (Tallahassee, FL: FHRCC, 1996); and "A Lockdown Is in Effect at the Pueblo County Jail," http://certops.com/certops/news/May060501.html (accessed May 8, 2005).
12. Peter Nacci, Kevin Jackson, and Karry Cothorn (eds.), "The Future of Automation and Technology," *Corrections Today* 57:4 (1995): 66–120 (theme issue); and Kevin Jackson, F. Roesel, T. Roy, et al., "Technology and Society," *Corrections Today* 60:4 (1998): 58–96 (theme issue).
13. Michael Reisig, "Rates of Disorder in Higher-Custody State Prisons," *Crime and Delinquency* 44:2 (1998): 229–244.
14. Camp and Camp, *The Corrections Yearbook 2000,* p. 148.
15. Stephen Walters, "Changing the Guard," *Journal of Rehabilitation* 20:1/2 (1993): 46–60; and Mark Pogrebin and E. Poole, "Sex, Gender and Work," in Jeffrey Ulmer (ed.), *Sociology of Crime, Law and Society* (Stamford, CT: JAI Press, 1998), pp. 105–126.
16. American Correctional Association, *2004 Directory* (Lanham, MD: ACA, 2004), p. 58.
17. James Lyons, *Inmate Escape Incidents 1992–1996* (Albany, NY: Department of Correctional Services, 1997); and Centre for Research Evaluation and Social Assessment, *Escape Prisoners: Inside Views of the Reasons for Prison Escapes* (Wellington: New Zealand Ministry of Justice, 1996).
18. Brian Hoffman, Gary Straughn, Jack Richardson, and Allen Randall, "California Electrified Fences: A New Concept in Prison Security," *Corrections Today* 58:4 (1996): 66–68.
19. John Shuiteman, "Playing the Numbers Game: Analysis Can Help Determine Manpower Requirements," *Corrections Today* 49:1 (1987): 40–42. See also Henry Steadman, S. Steadman, and D. Dennis, "A National Survey of Jail Diversion Programs for Mentally Ill Inmates," *Hospital and Community Psychiatry* 45:11 (1994): 1109–1113; and Marcus Nieto, *Health Care for California State Prisoners* (Sacramento: California Research Bureau, California State Library, 1998).
20. Frances Cheek and Marie De Stefano Miller, "Reducing Staff and Inmate Stress," *Corrections Today* 44:5 (1982): 72–76, 78. See also John T. Super, T. H. Blau, B. Charles, et al., "Using Psychological Tests to Discriminate Between 'Best' and 'Least Best' Correctional Officers," *Journal of Criminal Justice* 21:2 (1993): 143–150; and Stevens, "Correctional Officer Attitudes."

CHAPTER 14

Management and Treatment Functions

Recently published evaluative studies [of prison-based therapeutic communities involving drug-abusing inmates] show remarkably consistent reductions in recidivism for offenders who complete the programs.

—Douglas S. Lipton

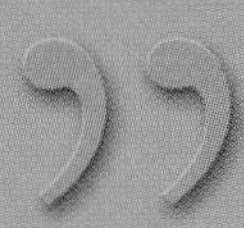

KEY WORDS

- treatment services
- backfilled
- gradualism approach
- isolationism and withdrawal
- sick call
- goldbrickers
- medical services
- hepatitis A and B
- comorbidity
- correctional chaplaincy
- functionally illiterate
- GED
- Project Newgate
- furlough
- vocational training
- cognitive intervention
- cognitive
- anger management
- reintegration model

OVERVIEW

In the last chapter, we focused attention on such custody issues as contraband, security, personnel, custody, and discipline. These issues are, understandably, the dominant concerns of correctional administrators and their management staff, and they consume great amounts of administrative time as well as large fiscal allocations by state or local correctional institutions. That led us to explore the development of management styles in corrections and the application of those styles to the major strategic processes of corrections—custody and treatment. Custody was seen as having a long history of a bureaucratic style of management.

Above all, corrections and correctional institutions are a product of the people's will and legislative action to resolve a perceived problem in society. The early prisons and penitentiaries had no problem with the "lock 'em up" wishes of society. In the twentieth century, however, we have been struggling to determine just what we really want to do with, to, or for our offenders. As noted in Chapter 3, this "model muddle" continues to be a problem for the correctional administrator. As a manager, the correctional leader must contend with staff members who are typically bifurcated into those who are mainly concerned with security and custody and those who are concerned with programs and treatment. As we progress through the first decade of the twenty-first century, we need to understand the problems faced by administrators who are required to accomplish both goals while dealing with overcrowding, budget cuts, a changing clientele, and a myriad other issues. As discussed

< Inmates at Los Angeles County's Peter J. Pitchess Jail in Saugus, California, share the confines of dormitories that house up to 100 men.
Photo by Mark Terrill, courtesy of AP/Wide World Photos.

in Chapter 13, custody's primary role is to protect society. Treatment efforts attempt to return inmates to society prepared to serve it in a humane fashion.

Living within the prisons but seldom part of the management and administrative components are the inmates, who are involuntarily sentenced to prison facilities and, for the most part, eager to be released. In the better prison systems, inmates receive humane treatment and handling designed to prepare them for their eventual return to society. For most inmates, however, the demands of custody and the philosophical orientations of administrators and staff will mean restriction or denial of treatment opportunities. This chapter deals with the current status of treatment programs and policies designed to reduce criminal inclinations and tendencies while strengthening motivations to adopt law-abiding behavior.

SIDEBARS
Managing Time

A major goal of prison management is managing inmates' time. Prisons depend on inmate labor for most of the maintenance and feeding services, but all prison programs serve the essential function of managing time.

SIDEBARS
Prison Program

Any instrumental activity that removes inmates from cells and puts them to work in structured activity.

THE TREATMENT MODEL

Treatment services generally include vocational training, education, counseling, teaching, casework, religious activities, therapeutic communities, peer counseling, and clinical activity, and are believed to play a significant role in offender rehabilitation.[1] In the past, especially in the larger institutions, the allocation of resources and personnel for treatment bore little, if any, relation to that assumed significance. As a national average, the resources allocated for **treatment services** amounted to only about 10 percent of the expenditures of the institutional staffs.

SIDEBARS
Treatment

Any activity designed to make the offender less of a management problem while in prison and/or less active as a criminal when released.

Part of the disproportionate allocation of resources results from a basic difference in nature between treatment and custody operations. Staff on the custody side must work twenty-four hours a day, 7 days a week, 365 days a year. Prisons do not close in observation of national or religious holidays. Furthermore, some inmates are mobile within the correctional facility at all hours of the day or night; inmate-to-inmate violence occurs hourly; and there is never silence in the general population, regardless of the hour.

Treatment staff members, on the other hand, usually work only eight hours a day, five days a week, and have holidays, vacations, and weekends off. When a custody officer is sick or takes vacation, he or she must be replaced (the common term is **backfilled**) by another corrections officer. This often requires someone working overtime, but will be done because minimum critical staffing must be maintained to protect the public. That protection is still the primary mission of corrections. When treatment staff members are sick or take vacation, their position usually goes unfilled until they return to work. Because each twenty-four-hour post requires 5.4 to 5.6 full-time staff, the ratio will always seem heavily weighted toward custody staff.

SIDEBARS
Backfilling

To cover a personnel shortage on the next shift, a correctional officer is asked to stay on duty when his or her shift normally ends. The correctional officer would then work through the next shift (a "double"), in effect working sixteen hours straight (or twenty hours if the agency works on a "four days–ten hours" plan). Union rules ordinarily would require overtime pay, frequently time and one-half for the first four hours and double-time for the remainder. While this can become extremely costly in a short period of time, it is necessary when the post to be filled is part of "minimum critical staffing," which dictates that the post must be filled to maintain a proper level of security. This is the budget planner's worst nightmare.

In the entire corrections system, a very small percentage of institutional personnel are employed in social work or psychological services, and the number of psychiatrists in corrections is infinitesimal. Diagnostic workups and testing processes tend to consume the workday of those involved in these services. Also, some treatment personnel must often spend long hours sitting on disciplinary hearing courts, classification and reclassification committees, and honor placement committees, leaving little time to spend on ongoing treatment with inmates. For example, group psychotherapists in the nation's prisons for men spend about one-third of their time providing individual psychotherapy and less than 30 percent of their time providing group therapy.[2] In addition, correctional administrators and the treatment staff frequently have to contend with the deeply ingrained antagonism of the staff members who are primarily oriented toward custody, security, and maintenance of calm.[3]

Only in recent times has the associate superintendent or deputy warden for treatment been selected from candidates with training in the social sciences, rather than through the promotion of a faithful custody supervisor. This is important, because the typical rank-and-file custody person was usually not someone who had earned the job through training and education, but through experience and staying out of trouble. Thus, a person with a high school education (or less) was often placed over psychiatrists, psychologists, medical doctors and nurses, social workers, and educators who possessed far more academic credentials. Understandably, those roles created many problems as treatment became more important.

PERCEPTIONS AND CORRECTIONAL MANAGEMENT

Three pervasive themes have run through correctional management. First, the goals of restraint and reformation have helped reinforce correctional administrators' perceptions of offenders as morally, psychologically, physically, and educationally inferior human beings who must be upgraded and, in the meantime, controlled. As a result of that perception, correctional administrators focused the resources at their command primarily on the individual offender. Because the offender was the principal target of organizational activity, little effort was made to mobilize and co-opt community resources, a function that is the very essence of the reintegration model of correctional intervention. That management posture has many consequences, such as the division of offenders into caseloads for purposes of treatment and supervision; recruitment of varied specialists (therapists) whose efforts are seldom coordinated; and, as we mentioned earlier, the scarcity of well-conceived efforts to work cooperatively with such community institutions as the schools, employment services, and neighborhood centers.

A second persistent attribute of correctional management has been a **gradualism approach** to program development and change. This approach has been characterized by a somewhat frivolous subscription to "new" ideas (such as boot camps) and generally nonrigorous, nonscientific rules of thumb for determining what to delete from the old system and what to add to it. The predominant conservatism of system managers has militated against deviations from familiar ways, has encouraged the avoidance of risk, and has led to tokenism in the launching of new measures.

Correctional administrators are not so much responsible for that condition as they are victims of two realities: society's uncertainty about the causes of and solutions to the crime problem and, until recently, the inability of social science and research to provide a solid frame of reference for considering alternative courses of action and estimating their consequences.[4] Nevertheless, in any effort to understand how correctional executives might be effective innovators, it is necessary to confront the difficulties and frustration that currently surround the process of change.

It is important to note the numerous examples of change in correctional organization and programming that run counter to the general pattern we have described.[5] Some experimental programs have been firmly supported by theoretical premises and have been evaluated objectively. The use of meta-analysis, a recent development in detecting the effectiveness of programs in reducing recidivism, has provided substantial evidence that demonstrates how certain programs (such as education, anger management, vocational training, and cognitive therapies) reduce criminal reoffending after parole. It is that growing edge of innovation, of improved dissemination of knowledge, and of close connection between discovery and implementation of technique that offers hope for more treatment gains in the near future.

SIDEBARS

Management Tasks and Frustration in Corrections

A prison manager must always deal with many issues over which he or she has little control. Prison facility architecture, the age of the plant, overcrowding, inmate-to-staff ratios, and budget limitations are issues with which prison administrators must deal daily. This has been even more exacerbated by large amounts of litigation, overtime, and backfilling, and constant pressure from the public to do more with less.

SIDEBARS

Prison Management as a Profession

With prison management now recruiting more women and minorities, its profile is now more diverse. Over the years, prison management has become more professional. Managers and staff belong to professional associations, such as the American Correctional Association, and college programs now deal with subjects and degrees directly applicable to corrections. National standards and accreditation programs at jails and prisons contribute to a growing professionalism for prison managers. This has had a "trickle-down" effect on the staff and the whole system.

The third and final theme, which has its roots in the prison culture of the past and still runs through correctional management today, is the syndrome of **isolationism and withdrawal.** That condition has helped conceal from the public the realities of life in institutions and probation and parole agencies, and has thus acted to perpetuate stereotypes and myths. Prisons, after all, were designed and located to keep criminals out of the sight and mind of the larger populace. Prison administrators found it expedient to honor that mandate. When community-based correctional programs gingerly sought to gain a foothold, their managers seemed intuitively to avoid exposure to public scrutiny and judgment. Whereas the police tend to publicize aggressively their views of crime and punishment, the leaders of corrections tend to avoid public debate, particularly debate centering on controversial issues,[6] although former (and even current) prisoners have been more active in this area.

PROFILE

Howard Gill (1890–1989) directed the construction of the Massachusetts Correctional Institution at Norfolk and became its first superintendent in 1927. This radically different facility, for those times, was praised by Edwin Sutherland, the dean of American criminology, as the "most noteworthy achievement in the field of penology in the United States in the last generation." Gill founded the Institute for Correctional Administration at American University, one of the first centers to provide professional training for prison managers.

That tendency has had serious consequences. The correctional field has had little success in developing public understanding and support for needed changes. Simplistic or erroneous conceptions of the nature of crime and its treatment have flourished, partly because of the lack of effective spokespeople for more sophisticated interpretations, especially at times of "opportunity" when conflict or crisis have awakened the interest of an otherwise apathetic public.[7]

Unionized correctional staffs have, in some states, developed effective political action groups whose financial contributions have often influenced politicians into adopting a "hard line" in sentencing and construction of more prisons.

CLASSIFICATION FOR SECURITY AND TREATMENT

SIDEBARS

Classification

A process by which inmates are assigned to levels of custody and to a security level based on potential risk of escape, violence, victimization, or suicide.

Classification is a relatively recent management innovation in corrections and can be found more often in probation and parole supervision situations than in jail and prison facilities. The classification process can frequently intensify the conflict between treatment and custody staff if it is not carefully handled. In most correctional classification processes (either at the individual institution or at a central classification facility), concern lies more with the danger the new inmates might present to the institution than with the possibility that they might respond to treatment. As a result, new inmates are often assigned to higher custody grades than their backgrounds warrant, until they can prove themselves. This security-oriented concept of classification often excludes inmates from participation in programs that could lead to their rehabilitation. Their early treatment, in fact, may be restricted to health care, an essential program because most offenders are in poor physical condition when they enter the institution.

SIDEBARS

Diagnostic and Reception Centers

Diagnostic and reception centers are generally separate facilities or units within a correctional facility or system. Newly admitted inmates are sent there to go through intensive evaluation and classification, orientation, and assignment to the proper facility and level of custody. Modern reception centers differ from earlier models, reflecting new realities as to the types of inmates and viable options in the present day. Most centers are now called "reception and evaluation" (R and E) centers. These new procedures are more receptive to overall system requirements and options.

TREATMENT IN PRISON

The treatment model for corrections is seen in the three basic services first offered to prisoners: religious, medical, and educational. We now examine the development of those services, along with an analysis of some more recent treatment innovations. Much of the public still views any "special programs" for inmates as a form of coddling, and many administrators have responded to this view by rejecting new and promising rehabilitation techniques created by behavioral scientists. Instead, they chose to favor "wars"—against crime, criminals, drugs, ad infinitum—as the easiest way to garner votes from the uninformed and often uncaring public. In fact, the protection of society, not the pampering of offenders, is also the basic reason for treatment and specialized programs in corrections. If at least some of the sources of an individual's criminality can be dealt with before he or she is referred back to the community, or released from aftercare back to the community, corrections should achieve that.

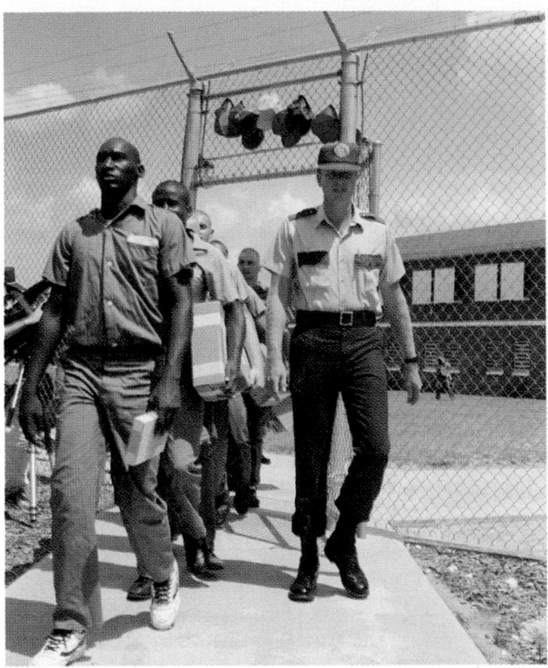

Prison guard walking with inmates at Sumter Correctional Institution, Florida.
Courtesy of Bettmann/Corbis-NY

SIDEBARS

Identifying Suicide Risks

Suicide is one of the leading unnatural causes of death in corrections. The following are the most common signs or risk indicators for potential suicide in prisons and jails:

1. Any pronounced mood or behavioral change
2. Receipt of bad news, such as divorce or death of a loved one
3. A history of mental illness or chemical dependency
4. A terminal illness, such as cancer or AIDS
5. Rape or threats of sexual assault
6. Being incarcerated for the first time and facing a very long sentence
7. A family history of suicide
8. Too much or too little sleep
9. Increase or loss of appetite or weight
10. Talk about death or preoccupation with death or suicide.

The basic services provided by the treatment side of corrections can be combined as health and medical services, religious services, and educational and training programs for inmates. Descriptions of these services and programs follow.

Health and Medical Services

Even in the earliest days of American prisons, certain times were set aside for **sick call.** Of course, the treatment provided was less than one would expect to receive at a clinic in the community. Prisoners often use sick call merely to obtain a brief respite from prison labor or from the dull routine. Time wasted on **goldbrickers** is time the medical staff cannot give to those who really need care. Because the correctional funnel selects out all but the most serious and manipulative offenders, the cream of society does not often end up in prisons; therefore, those who are imprisoned usually have numerous medical and dental needs.

Medical services are often a source of inmates' complaints and frequently become a real headache for administrators. In many areas throughout the country, qualified medical personnel are generally in short supply, and that shortage is felt even more acutely in correctional institutions. To supply the total medical care for which an institution is responsible, it is often necessary to combine the services of full-time medical employees, contractual consultants, and available community resources. Even with all those efforts, inmates and the public often tend to look down on any medically trained person who is willing to become involved with a correctional institution. Any doctor who accepts the prison physician's relatively low income and standard of living, it is thought, must have been a failure in the community. Proper medical care is important to the overall rehabilitation effort. Poor diet, drug abuse, a history of inadequate medical attention, and other debilitating conditions are not uncommon among inmates. Once they have been restored to reasonable health, it is often easier to work on the causes behind their problems.[8]

SIDEBARS

Diet and Food Service

A major part of any prison operation is the daily meals, often the only pleasant activity in an inmate's day. Faced with the diverse tastes and special dietary needs of inmates, the food service manager has a heavy task. The old concept of a gigantic "mess hall" like in the movies of the 1930s has given way to more small areas where food is brought in to a small "pod" and eaten in small groups. The majority of prison riots have historically begun in the dining halls, where large groups gathered to eat. Today's prison fare is nutritious and usually quite palatable, thanks to the hard work of food service managers and prison staff.

Major medical problems now commonly faced by jail and prison inmates are **hepatitis A and B,** HIV infection, mental illness, geriatric issues, prenatal care, rubella (measles), and drug-resistant tuberculosis. Drug-dependent inmates,[9] frequent transfers of inmates among facilities, and overcrowded living conditions are

CORRECTIONAL BRIEF

Smoking in Prison

Among the more controversial issues in prison management today is banning of smoking. Ten state prison systems have a total ban on smoking and thirty-five other states plus the District of Columbia have partial bans, in which, for example, smoking is allowed only in cells or in designated outdoor areas. Motivations for control of smoking range from fitting in with the moral crusade against vice, to providing health and fiscal benefits. "Teaching inmates and staff to take better care of their bodies and health" may be hard to defeat in a debate.

Two important issues are costs to the state and inmate control. While no one knows exactly what health costs are attributable to the adverse effects of tobacco, inmate health-related cost estimates run as high as $100 per inmate per day ($44 billion a year). Obviously, the actual direct and indirect costs are somewhat less.

Few wardens, on the other hand, champion the smoking ban, because smoking is part of the complex system of inmate privileges they use to manage prison populations. Without at least some smoking option, even just allowing smoking only in designated outdoor areas, prison staff have fewer tools and incentives to use with inmates. A total ban increases smuggling, exacerbates the contraband problem, and creates an underground market.

Inmates are less sanguine than the staff. Several state courts have ruled that prisons can be considered private residences and that inmates have a right to smoke in their cells. Other inmate champions are arguing that banning smoking would be cruel and unusual punishment in that it would inflict "needless and unnecessary pain and suffering."

Tobacco companies have acceded that smoking is dangerous and addictive. Health-related costs of smoking in prison are borne by the state. Yet can the state ban freedom of choice in the controlled environment of the prison? These issues will eventually be decided within the federal court system and possibly by the U.S. Supreme Court.

SOURCE: Eric Tischler, "Smoking Bans Have Supporters, Detractors in Prison," *On the Line* 21:1 (1998): 1–3.

conducive to rapid transmission of diseases that could result in epidemics, especially multidrug-resistant tuberculosis. Tuberculosis is easily airborne transmitted, and even dormant carriers can transmit the bacillus. Tuberculosis transmission from inmates to staff has already been documented. And staff could spread the infection to family and friends (tertiary infection), bringing this serious disease into the outside community. Inmates and staff should have tuberculin skin tests on a routine basis,[10] because the incidence of the disease has increased dramatically.[11] Treatment of prisoner health problems is expensive; $1 of every $8 spent on prisoners in Texas is for medical care (see Figure 14.1).

As early as 1988, it was recognized that about 80 percent of all state prison inmates had been serious alcohol and drug abusers. More than three in four state inmates and almost 70 percent of federal prisoners and jail inmates had used drugs regularly in the month preceding arrest. Furthermore, substance-abusing inmates were more likely to be repeatedly reimprisoned. From 1980 until 2003, drug law violators accounted for at least 30 percent of the growth in the number of imprisoned felons, two-thirds of the increase in federal prisoners, and more than 40 percent of the jail populations.

SIDEBARS

Substance Abuse

Use of any chemical substance, including alcohol and drugs, that interferes with the individual's usual living patterns to the extent that disruptions occur in employment, family relations, education, and other social spheres, and may contribute to overt criminal behavior. Of the nation's prisoners, 51 percent reported the use of alcohol or drugs while committing their offense.

In addition to drug and alcohol problems, inmates also have a number of other problems and risk factors that must be addressed. These include lack of employment, bad companions, antisocial attitudes, emotional problems, mental illness, and lack of education.

Drug use has been found to predict subsequent violent behavior among both females and males. When substance abuse occurs among persons with psychopathological problems (**comorbidity**), there is a stronger correlation with subsequent violent behavior among females. One study of probationers undergoing mandatory substance abuse treatment in a residential facility found that 80 percent of the sample had psychopathological problems, more than 70 percent had drug abuse problems, and almost six in ten had concurrent drug abuse and psychopathological problems (comorbidity). Furthermore, prison inmates with both

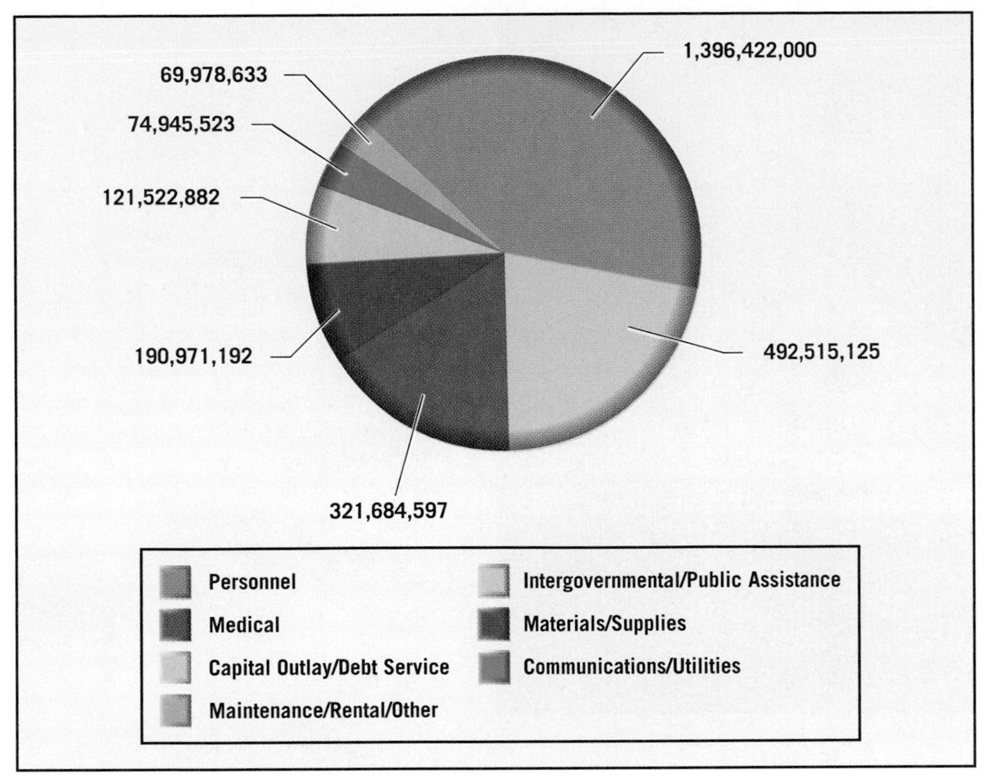

FIGURE 14.1

Total Expenditures by Major Category in Texas for Fiscal Year 1999

SOURCE: Texas Department of Criminal Justice, 2002, www.tdcj.state.tx.us/finances/finops/finop-fipcfundmjrcat-fy00. htm.

drug abuse and psychopathological problems engaged in more frequent preadmission illegal behaviors, had more extensive social impairments, and were found to have *higher* motivation for treatment. Female inmates are even more impacted by co-occurring conditions and higher needs (see Chapter 15).

In 1997, an estimated one-third of state and federal prison inmates reported having a physical impairment or mental condition. More than three in ten state and one in four federal inmates reported having a learning or speech disability, a hearing or vision problem, or a mental or physical condition. About one in five of all in-

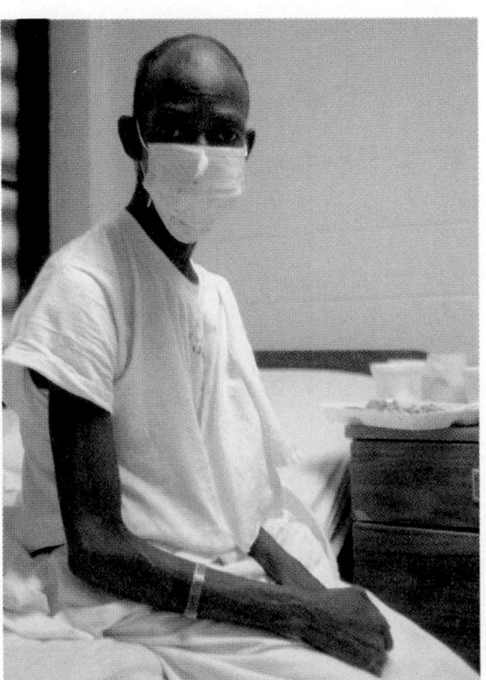

Prisoner with AIDS in isolation room, Hamilton Prison, Alabama.
Photo by A. Ramey, courtesy of PhotoEdit.

Dr. Fernando Hoyas talks with an inmate at the New Jersey State Correctional Facility in Trenton, New Jersey, about a medical problem.

Photo by Charles Rex Arbogast, courtesy of AP/Wide World Photos.

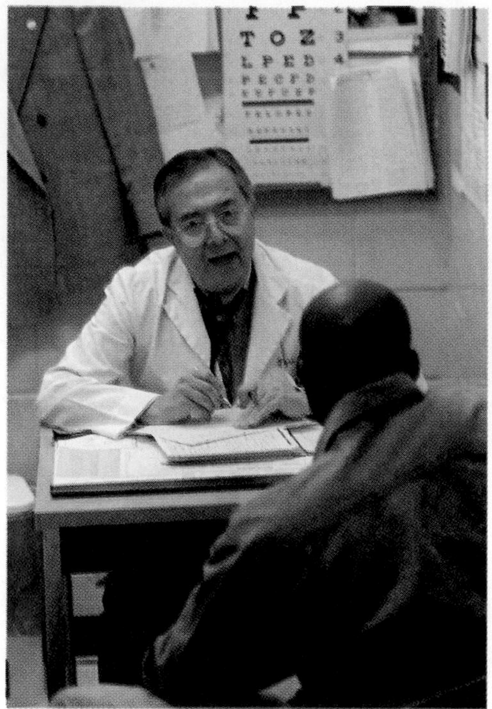

mates said they had been injured in an accident since admission. The longer the period of incarceration, the more likely the inmate was to report an injury.

About one in five inmates reported a medical condition that limits their ability to work. On the federal level, the medical conditions of record were high blood pressure (8 percent), poor mental health (5 percent), asthma and diabetes (4 percent each), heart problems (3 percent), and HIV/AIDS (1 percent). Medical problems were more common among inmates who had used a needle to inject drugs (one in three inmates) and those who were alcohol dependent (38 percent of inmates). Much time and resources are needed to meet the minimal health needs and mandatory medical care.[12] Information on mental health and counseling can be found in Figure 14.2.

FIGURE 14.2

Number and Percentages of Mental Health and Counseling Staff on January 1, 2000

SOURCE: C. Camp and G. Camp, *The Corrections Yearbook 2000: Adult Corrections* (Middletown, CT: Criminal Justice Institute, 2000), p. 158.

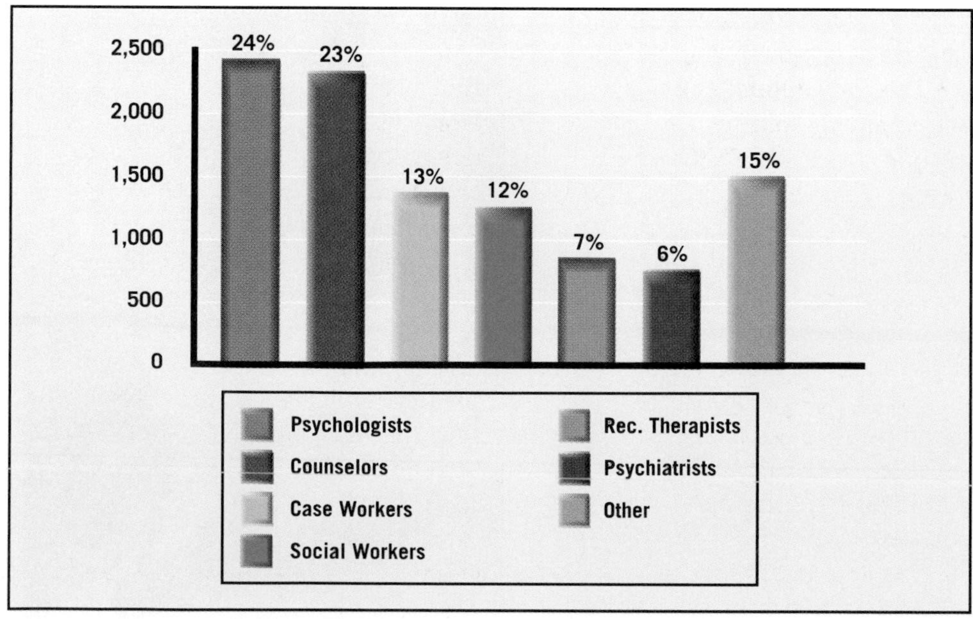

AIDS prisoners conducting their own AIDS-awareness course, Limestone Correctional Facility, Alabama.

Photo courtesy of AP/Wide World Photos.

Another major service for the offender is found in the dental clinic, because most prisoners have very bad teeth. Even in an institution fortunate enough to have good dental care facilities, dental service can take many months because prisoners' teeth have often suffered from long neglect and need extensive work. The effects of dental treatment are similar to those of plastic surgery: Improved appearance enhances the offender's feelings of confidence and well-being, and he or she may be relieved of chronic pain and irritation as well.

Religious Assistance and Services

From 1790 until today, one service that has traditionally been available to the incarcerated felon is religious assistance and guidance. Solitary meditation in the Walnut Street Jail was intended to make offenders realize the error of their sinful ways and make them penitent. Penitence was often encouraged by visits from local ministers and priests. Later, the large institutions of the early 1800s created the need for a full-time chaplain on the premises.

The **correctional chaplaincy** has been and is currently the least sought-after position among ministers, who evidently prefer to serve more conventional congregations. Part of the problem, too, is the remote location of most prisons and a widespread public belief (shared by many administrators) that religion in prisons should be confined to the chaplain's traditional duties. Not well known by the public is the range of services, types of counseling, guidance, and innovation offered by chaplains within prisons.[13] A movement has sprung up to establish a core of clinically oriented clerics, but the correctional field is less attractive to them than are other kinds of institutions. There is a definite need to upgrade the role of the correctional chaplain to attract the best into the institutions. The role of the chief chaplain can be enhanced if it becomes accredited by the Association for Clinical Pastoral Education. With that background, the chaplain can develop programs, recruit and train chaplaincy candidates, and even use seminary students to augment his or her resources.

The new and growing special interest groups inside prisons—those whose religious orientation is toward a particular ethnic group, culture, or subculture—do not

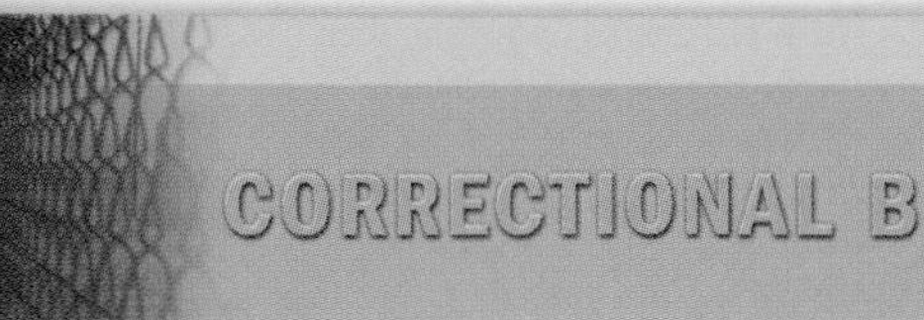

CORRECTIONAL BRIEF

The Contemporary Prison Chaplain

Recent research into the role of prison chaplains found that they perform a diverse range of activities, with the most frequent tasks including counseling inmates, recruiting and supervising volunteers, coordinating and conducting religious programs, and paperwork. They believe their main work is to serve inmates and that their most important duty is counseling inmates. To this end, they offer spiritual hope to the depressed, lost, and forgotten inmates and, as servants of faith, represent humanity and hope behind the bars of prison.

In addition to these more traditional sacred activities, chaplains also serve to control inmates and support institutional needs. They assist inmates as they adjust to prison life, calm inmates down, help correctional officers in emergencies, and may alert custody staff if an inmate is planning a disturbance.

Yet we know little about much of the activities of chaplains. For example, do they act proactively or do custody staff request their assistance in defusing potential disruptive situations? To what extent are chaplains advocates of and supporters of prison inmates? What type of counseling methods do chaplains use, and to what extent is counseling spiritual? Finally, how do various prison environments support or deprecate the spiritual activities expected of the prison chaplain? Much remains to be learned about those dedicated prison servants.

SOURCE: Jody Sundt and F. Cullen, "The Contemporary Prison Chaplain," *The Prison Journal* 78:3 (1998): 271–298.

SIDEBARS

Unit Team Management

This innovative management concept requires that staff assigned to a wing, ward, module, pod, or other residential unit of a prison accept collective responsibility for managing the unit. Correctional officers, for example, may provide counseling when treatment officers are absent from the unit, or treatment personnel may undertake custodial staff functions as necessary. The joint responsibility for managing the unit blurs traditional roles of custody and treatment, provides staff with experience and insight into additional roles and job enrichment, and reduces the social distance between staff and inmates.

accord with the traditional religious outlets. As noted in Chapter 1, their right to pursue their faiths while confined has been firmly established. The traditional correctional institution has provided Protestant, Roman Catholic, and sometimes Jewish chaplains as representatives of the three major religious groups in the United States, because it was not feasible to have a cleric for every religion observed by different inmates. The chaplains attempt to offer ecumenical services and try to provide worship for all prisoners; however, the more vocal members of the smaller sects have protested that arrangement. Sometimes it is difficult to secure a qualified spiritual leader to conduct ceremonies in prison.[14] The number of prisoners of the Islamic faith who are incarcerated has grown considerably. As the need to provide religious services to these Muslims increases, local Imams are beginning to be more active in that ministry.

It is possible, if the chaplain's salary and image can be sufficiently upgraded, that ministers trained in the behavioral sciences will become part of the contemporary prison scene, a far cry from the Walnut Street missionaries whose sole function was to provide Bible reading and prayer. The new chaplains might well play different roles as an integral part of the treatment team in future rehabilitation programs, including unit team management.

Educational and Training Programs for Inmates

In most state correctional systems, education of incarcerated inmates is a legislative mandate. The largest group of treatment personnel is the teachers, who usually far outnumber those in counseling services. Although most institutions have some kind of educational program, there are marked differences in kind and extent. Early efforts were aimed simply at teaching prisoners to read. With 12 million adults in the United States considered to be **functionally illiterate** (cannot read, write, or compute above the third-grade level), it is not too surprising that those considered to be at the bottom of the barrel have literacy problems in even greater measure.

Today, most inmates are able to achieve at least a high school education (or the **GED**, the high school equivalency certificate) through institutional programs, and the more progressive institutions are offering courses at the two-year and four-year college level.[15] It is acknowledged that lack of education is a serious handicap

CORRECTIONAL BRIEF

Inmate Program Involvement

One of the fears of correctional experts when states began to shift to determinate sentences was that, since the best motivator for inmate program participation appeared to be the need to convince releasing authorities of prisoners' reform through completion of prison treatment programs, determinate sentences would render treatment programs underenrolled if not superfluous. After all, if inmates were "playing the reform game" to convince a parole board of their readiness for release, and the parole board's discretion to release was abolished, inmates might very well stop participating in any treatment programs.

This fear has been proven unfounded. The rates of program participation in Illinois, Minnesota, and Connecticut, for example, remained about the same or increased somewhat. How much of the noted participation was voluntary, however, remains in question. Prison administrators need concrete criteria for making decisions about transfers to less secure institutions, institutional job and housing assignments, furlough eligibility, and awarding of meritorious good-time credits based on program participation. The incentives for inmate involvement may have changed, but participation rates and levels appear to be unaffected by the determinate sentence. There is substantial evidence that meaningful job participation can significantly reduce recidivism, particularly for male offenders.

SOURCES: Stephen Anderson, *Evaluation of the Impact of Participation in Ohio Penal Industries on Recidivism* (Columbus: Ohio Department of Rehabilitation and Correction, 1995); and Larry Montiuk and B. Belcourt, "CORCAN Participation and Post-Release Recidivism," *Forum* 8:1 (1996): 15–17.

when inmates return to the free world: Former offenders who cannot get jobs because of insufficient education are likely to return to crime. For that reason, education has long been regarded as a primary rehabilitative tool in the correctional field. The gap between the need for educational services and the provision of adequate educational and vocational training is wide, however.[16]

One of the first barriers to effective educational programs is, once again, the problem of administrative considerations: operational requirements, security needs, shortage of teachers, shortage of educational materials, tight budgets, and a lack of inmate motivation.[17] Inmates and staff are often handicapped by unsuitable or out-of-date textbooks, often below the level of the street sophistication of the average adult prisoner. Inmates who are prevented from attending classes for disciplinary reasons may miss enough to be required to forgo the rest of the term. Denying education as part of disciplinary action devalues its effectiveness as a treatment component and doubles the punishment factor.

The classes held in some institutions are conventional and relatively old fashioned, in contrast with those that use the new learning technologies and innovations available to students at all levels on the outside. Yet educators are making considerable headway with computer technology and rapid change is under way. Most prisoners have had little formal education and probably resisted whatever teaching they were exposed to. Material that bored them as children or truant teenagers is not likely to hold them enthralled as adults. What mature felons neither want nor need are "Dick and Jane" readers or other textbooks designed for children. Inmates may be actually or functionally illiterate, but they are adults in the main, and are in possession of a lot of street smarts. To be given such materials is embarrassing and difficult for them. But because of the low priority and minimal funds assigned to education in most institutions, useless texts are often provided to prisoners, usually by public schools that no longer use them. Small wonder that most prison programs are neither accredited nor enthusiastically supported by inmates. Inmates prefer listening and reading modes for learning.[18] Those with learning disabilities (from 7 to 25 percent of institutional populations) may respond best to tape recorders, television, and computers.[19]

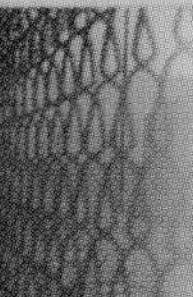

CORRECTIONAL BRIEF

Literacy and Its Impact on Reoffending

The federal prison system established a mandatory literacy program in 1982, requiring sixth-grade reading as the minimum literacy standard. This was changed to eighth-grade reading in 1986, and to a General Education Development (GED) certificate in 1991. The adult basic education program has been very successful when completion rates are compared from 1981 to 1990, which saw an encouraging 724 percent increase in the number of inmates achieving basic literacy.

Eleven studies on the effects of education on reoffending are also encouraging. One investigator reported on three studies by David Fairchild. On the first, there was only a 15 percent reoffending rate for New Mexico inmates who had completed at least one year of college, compared to 68 percent for the general population. Fairchild found zero recidivism for college graduates versus a reoffending rate of 55 percent for the general prison population studied at a California prison. Finally, Fairchild reported that none of the first 200 Indiana reformatory inmates earning a college degree offered by a university extension program returned to the reformatory.

Consistently favorable outcomes have been linked to education in Canada, where three of four prisoner-students remained free of subsequent incarceration for at least three years. Significantly lower relapse and recidivism rates have been found for education and work release in Delaware, and college education in North Carolina and Georgia.

Adult basic education programs show promise for decreasing recidivism, even for inmates with learning disabilities. Technology education (particularly computers) provides inmates with marketing skills. Studies have concluded that the recidivism rate can be as low as 11 percent for inmates who successfully complete training, and as high as 70 percent for those who do not.

SOURCE: Robert Hall and Mark Bannatyne, "Technology Education and the Convicted Felon," *Journal of Correctional Education* 51:4 (2000): 320–323.

PROFILE

George J. Beto (1916–1991)

was known as "Walking George" to the inmates of the Texas Department of Corrections, which he headed from the 1960s to the 1970s. He was the creator of the "control model" of correctional administration and respected for making the Texas system one of the best in the nation under his leadership. He was also jokingly called "the most sued man in Texas." Beto was instrumental in introducing the high school equivalency (GED) program into the Texas system as part of his plan to control and rehabilitate. The Windham School District became the first nongeographic school district to be located in a prison system, offering GEDs, adult basic education, vocational training, and college credits. He was the first to integrate the Texas prison population and to hire the first black correctional officers into that system.

The surprising fact is that some educational services thrive and contribute to the inmates' rehabilitation.[20] Texas has an education district that covers the entire prison system. In Ohio, the Department of Rehabilitation and Correction also established a complete school district composed entirely of the educational programs within the state prison system. In the states of New York and Washington, education programs are contracted with local community colleges and they provide excellent programs, from adult basic education[21] to degree programs in the institutions. **Project Newgate,** a program bringing the first years of college into the prisons, along with instructors and a complete curriculum, was the model for such programs in the 1970s.

Two other education-related programs that have been attempted, with varying results, are work/training release and educational release (sometimes called **furlough**).

Furloughs are release from custody for a discrete and prescribed amount of time for specific reasons, with prior formal authorization by prison authorities. Of the 8,964 furloughs granted in 1999, only 44 inmates failed to return or committed another crime, a 0.005 percent failure rate.[22] In educational release, inmates are allowed to leave the institution to attend college, high school, or vocational-technical schools during the day, though they must return to the institution or an approved site when not at school or at night. The use of educational release became quite widespread in the United States before 1990, but the programs have been somewhat curtailed due to highly visible failures or budget cuts. In the work/training release program, an inmate may be allowed to leave the limits of confinement to secure education and a job; this enables offenders to develop a work history, learn a trade, support dependents, or even make restitution to the victim of their crimes. Forty-two of the fifty states, and both the federal Bureau of Prisons and the District of Columbia have work and education release programs. Of the 44,000 participating prisoners in 1999, few were arrested and reconvicted, although a small number were recalled to prison. This high success rate is partially a function of the process by which eligible inmates are selected, and in part

CORRECTIONAL BRIEF

Windham School District

Established in 1969 by an act of the Texas legislature, Windham School District (WSD) was the first statewide education system operating within a prison. It was created to provide appropriate educational programming and services to meet the needs of the eligible offender population in the Texas Department of Criminal Justice and to reduce recidivism by assisting inmates in becoming responsible and productive members of their communities.

The typical WSD student dropped out of school in the ninth or tenth grade, but functions at the fifth-grade level and registers an IQ of 85. With an average age of thirty-five, the student has a history of academic failure, little confidence in self to find employment, and a limited ability to visualize a productive future.

The student has a defensive and/or negative attitude, low self-esteem, difficulty forming and maintaining relationships, and difficulty in controlling anger. When coupled with impulsive behavior, these students face a tenuous future unless they learn the basics of reading and writing and earn the high school equivalency certificate.

SOURCE: Windham School District, *Annual Performance Report 2000–2001,* www.windhamschooldistrict.org/apr.pdf (accessed September 5, 2002).

a result of the legal status of the participant who remains an inmate, easily returned to prison for nonconformity to rules and regulations.

Education, medical care, and religious practice have served as the basic treatment programs in America's prisons since the days of the Walnut Street Jail. In recent years, this limited three-sided approach to treatment has expanded to include a wide variety of programs aimed at the rehabilitation of incarcerated offenders.

SIDEBARS

Furlough

Temporary authorized and unsupervised prisoner release into the community for the purpose of family visitation, funeral, or for a purpose other than work or study. Formal programs for work or study purposes are usually called release programs.

THE VOCATIONAL-REHABILITATION MODEL

Vocational and technical training in prisons has been available to prisoners ever since the industrial prison was established in the early 1800s. That early training, however, was aimed not at prisoner rehabilitation but at institutional profit. Later, at the Elmira Reformatory, the concept of training for the purpose of teaching a trade to ex-offenders was introduced, and it has slowly taken root over the years. A major setback to adequate **vocational training** came with the passage of restrictive federal laws on the interstate transport of prison industry goods. Those laws, passed during the Depression Era, sounded the death knell for many work programs in state prisons. Only in the past thirty years have institutions begun to reemphasize vocational training programs.

SIDEBARS

Vocational Rehabilitation

Prison programming intended to impart to and improve the vocational and education skills of prisoners and to improve their employability once released.

Inmates ask the teacher a question as they study for the GED examination.

Photo by A. Ramey, courtesy of PhotoEdit.

CORRECTIONAL BRIEF

Prison Release Programs

Work, occupational training, and education are three major objectives for which inmates are allowed to leave the prison. In most states, the legal mechanism for allowing an inmate to leave prison is the furlough program: The legislature extends the limits of confinement to include placement in the community while the prisoner pursues some common and identifiable correctional goal.

Furlough candidates are usually screened carefully and supervised by an agency. Although the extent of recidivism among furlough users is unknown, it is generally believed to be low. One reason for the low recidivism probably is that furloughees in most jurisdictions remain inmates and can be returned to prison easily if they show overt signs of being unable to conform their behavior to community expectations.

Oklahoma has used home furlough (house arrest of inmates) as a mechanism to reduce prison overcrowding, and the recidivism rate is markedly low. In Massachusetts, furlough participation had a pronounced and consistently positive impact on recidivism. More states are exploring the opportunities of increasing furlough programs to extend the limits of confinement for low-risk inmates, and plan to couple house arrest with electronic monitoring, unscheduled drug and alcohol testing, and supervision fees. This approach may become a major prison-release mechanism in the next decade.

Prison industry has continued on a somewhat smaller scope since the restrictive laws were enacted. Prison industry went through several phases, starting at the contract labor level through increasingly more restricted systems. In contract labor, part if not the whole of the prison population was rented to private contractors who used their labor for private gain. Next came the piece-price scheme, in which private contractors provided raw materials and paid a set price to the prison for produced items (such as soccer balls). The next phase was the public account system in which the prison became the manufacturer of a product to be sold on the open market, such as twine, bailing wire, bags ("crooker sacks"), and airplane chocks. These efforts failed for a variety of reasons, including prison corruption, union resistance, excessive cruelty, padded budgets, and inordinate up-front costs. The current prison industry system is the state-use system in which prison labor produces

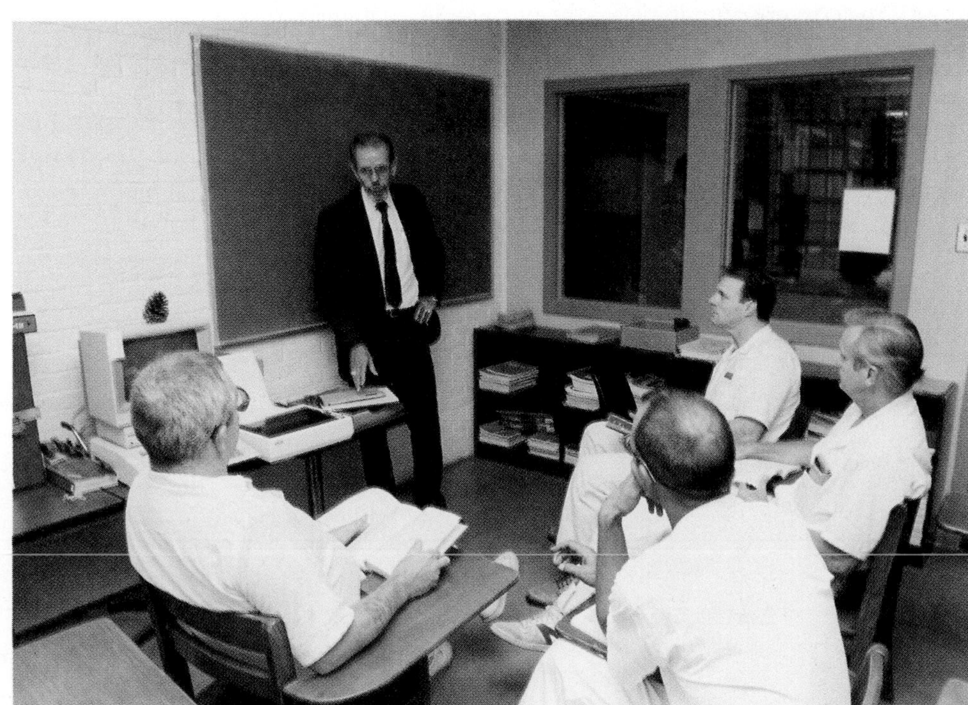

George Trabing, director of the University of Houston–Clear Lake program at the Ramsey I Unit of the Texas Department of Corrections, speaks to inmates taking courses leading to a master's degree. *Photo by EFK, courtesy of AP/Wide World Photos.*

items that do not enter the open market and are instead sold to state-run institutions, facilities, and agencies. This includes the ubiquitous license plate manufacture, tables and chairs used in educational institutions, clothing for inmates and mental patients, soap and eggs, and so on. Critics have raised the question of the usefulness of the limited skills learned in prison industry, and have labeled the work by inmates as exploitation of prisoners.

A common problem with prison industries is their multiple goals, for they sometimes shift and are always ambiguous. The prison administrator may believe the goal of prison industries to be generation of profits; shop managers are convinced it is to train inmates; and inmates believe it is "make work" and that they will receive some wage unrelated to productivity.[23] Leadership in resolving those conflicting goals was exerted by Congress in 1979, when it passed the Prison-Industries Enhancement Act, selectively repealing portions of the federal laws limiting prison industries. Since then, more than twenty states (such as Arizona, Minnesota, Washington, and Kansas) have authorized some form of private sector involvement with state penal industries, such as in the areas of data processing, hotel chain reservations, and manufacturing. Many of those private industry efforts must deal with insurance, initial plant investment costs, and quality control problems. It remains to be seen how effective private industry will be in collaborating with prisons,[24] but such efforts are welcome signs in times of prison overcrowding.

Exciting programs working with companies in South Carolina, California, and Connecticut have formed successful projects with state and local correctional agencies. Some positive features of these collaborations include the following[25]:

1. A cost-competitive, motivated workforce that can continue to work after release from prison
2. The proximity of a prison-based feeder plant to the company's regular facility
3. Financial incentives, including low-cost industrial space and an equipment purchase subsidy, that are offered by correctional officials

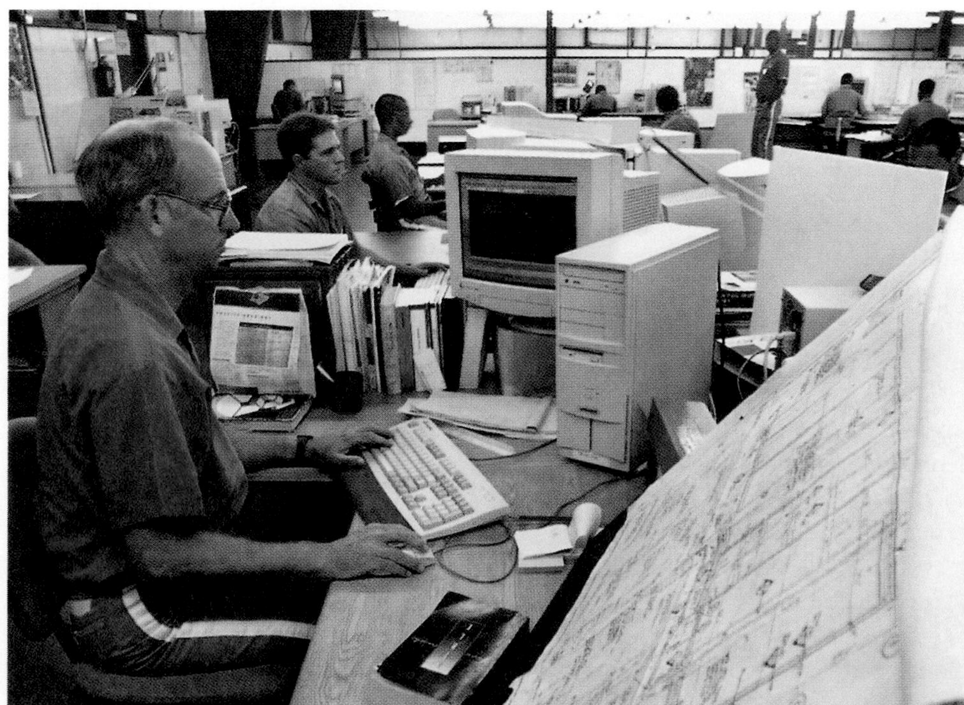

Prisoners at Liberty Correctional Institution work at digitally mapping records of a European utility company as part of PRIDE enterprise's workforce within the state's prison system shown in Bristol, Florida.

Photo by Mark Foley, courtesy of AP/Wide World Photos.

4. Safe work environment due to the presence of security personnel and a metal detector that keeps weapons out of the shop area
5. The partial return to society of inmate earnings to pay state and federal taxes, offset incarceration costs, contribute to the support of the inmate's families, and compensate victims.

THE REINTEGRATION MODEL

The movement toward treatment and corrections in the community has highlighted the need to make programs inside the walls relate to circumstances in the outside world. Crime cannot be controlled by the reformation of prisoners alone. Efforts at reformation and reintegration into the community must continue.

Toward that end, many of the barriers shutting off prisons from their communities have come down in the last decade. The treatment concept has been expanded to include a variety of inmate treatment programs and models usually discussed in correctional treatment courses. We mention five major offender-based institutional models to illustrate the entry of treatment professionals into the prison system.

Perhaps the most effective of therapies is **cognitive intervention,** an approach that focuses on the ways in which offenders think. Thinking includes a wide array of skills and processes, such as problem-solving skills, the ability to empathize with others and victims, the ability to formulate and then achieve plans for the future, and the ability to foresee the consequences of one's own behavior. For example, hitting a correctional officer on the head with a battery wrapped in a sock ("sucker punch") would be perceived by most inmates as a portent of concerted forcible effort to arrest, possibly punish, but certainly isolate the offender in a punitive segregation cell. **Cognitive** also refers to the beliefs, values, attitudes, and stability we impose on our conception of the world around us. Flowing from this approach are techniques that attempt to influence and change the cognitions of offenders. This is done through role-playing, psychodramas, modeling, and changing of irrational beliefs.

One example of program application to prisoners is **anger management.** Without belaboring the theory, it should be noted that many prisoners are clinically depressed, and depression can generate anger expression (assault, verbal abuse, spousal abuse, and even rape). Anger management focuses on preventing the negative behavior that arises from impulsive hostile aggression by teaching self-awareness, self-control, and alternate thinking and behavior. The therapist may intend to reduce aggressive behavior through activating the offender's self-intervention and management skills. The key is to teach the inmate how to lower arousal levels, use relaxation techniques and thinking controls, communicate feelings, recognize anger, and use coping mechanisms (to "cage the rage").

Other interventional programs in use include guided group interaction, therapeutic communities, and reality therapy. Although these programs have major differences, the primary focus (even in therapeutic communities) is on helping the offender change those thoughts, beliefs, attitudes, and actions that create the potential for and actual criminal behavior. These are almost always preparatory to release back into the community, although therapeutic communities increasingly extend from the institution to the community.

Prison treatment also encompasses the efforts of community-based professionals, and community volunteers have begun to give offenders the support and guidance needed to ensure successful reintegration.[26] The main objective of the **reintegration model** is to return the offender to the community as a responsible and productive citizen, rather than as a feared and shunned "ex-con" with little hope for success. Institutions dedicated to that objective have learned to overcome deficits in funding and personnel by using the ingenuity of prison staff and the resources available in the community. Teachers and graduate students are encouraged to offer courses on topics that will help reintegrate the inmate, including such subjects as social problems, mental health, and the use of community resources.[27]

In many institutions, the barriers are coming down for traffic in both directions ("the door swings both ways"). Outside activity by inmates and prison personnel ranges from touring lecture programs to work and educational furloughs. The latter programs serve as a method of graduated release back to the community. The rationale for graduated release has its roots in the problems faced by the newly released inmate. Release is a very stressful time for inmates, especially when they emerge directly from an institution. Inmates know they have failed in the past and fear they will fail again. Without a chance to ease back into society in stages, as is possible with graduated release, the inmate feels vulnerable if he or she has been inside the walls for a long time. The released prisoner needs new social skills and a chance to catch up with a rapidly moving society.

SUMMARY

Corrections has undergone great change in the years since the emphasis shifted from custody to rehabilitation. Public safety demands that the convicted offender emerge from our correctional system a better person, certainly no worse, than when he or she entered it. That high expectation has stimulated the search for more effective ways to handle offenders. One reason for the pressure to create community-based corrections has been the recognition that prisonization can actually aggravate an offender's criminality.

The future of corrections clearly lies in community-based programs. A major obstacle, however, is the prominence of the institutional model, with its physical plants and other programs already in operation, whereas organized community programs have not yet gained widespread acceptance. While most community programs emerged as demonstration projects or individual experiments, rather than as the products of systematic interaction among police, courts, and conventional correctional services, basic changes are under way. The drug court, discussed in Chapter 8, is just one example of integration of formerly separate components of the justice system.

Incarceration clearly is a series of destructive situations for the offender: The custody model intensifies the likelihood of physical danger, deprivation of human values, and loss of self-esteem. It is a basic humanitarian concept that only offenders who pose a threat to society should be subjected to the trauma of incarceration. This last issue demands, of course, a valid system of diagnosis, classification, and evaluation.

The correctional treatment process has many elements. The key to treatment is an organized program designed to prepare the inmate for successful reintegration within the free society. It is obvious how important the cooperation and understanding of the security and custody staff can be in the success of any of the efforts described as "treatment." As the single most influential agent of change, the correctional officer is the keystone to the success or failure of any kind of treatment program. A cooperative effort by custody and treatment staffs, including the blurring of roles, is the essence of an effective institutional program. But treatment cannot end at the prison gate. To ensure maximum success, the treatment must be continued and reinforced in the community. Community programs are discussed in Chapter 21. Chapters 15 through 18 discuss the variety of clients in corrections, and the challenges each poses for the criminal justice system.

REVIEW QUESTIONS

1. Why are there more correctional officers than treatment staff?
2. Is classification more properly a security or a treatment function? Why?
3. Explain why corrections in general has so few spokespersons.
4. What motivates inmates to participate in prison treatment programs?
5. What are five common health problems found in prisons?
6. How are religious services delivered inside prisons?
7. Does education lower recidivism when inmates are paroled?
8. What kinds of inmates are given furloughs?
9. What jobs are available in prisons for staff? Inmates?
10. What can be done to prepare inmates for community reintegration?

ENDNOTES

1. See Don Gibbons, "Review Essay—Changing Lawbreakers: What Have We Learned Since the 1950s?" *Crime and Delinquency* 45:2 (1999): 272–293; Rolf Loeber and D. Farrington (eds.), *Serious and Violent Juvenile Offenders* (Thousand Oaks, CA: Sage, 1998); and Michael Prendergast et al., "Amity Prison-Based Therapeutic Community," *The Prison Journal* 84:1 (2004): 36–60.
2. Robert Morgan, C. Winterowd, and S. Ferrell, "A National Survey of Group Psychotherapy Services in Correctional Facilities," *Professional Psychology Research and Practice* 30:6 (1999): 600–606.
3. See Rob Wilson, "Who Will Care for the 'Mad' and the 'Bad'?" *Corrections Magazine* 6:1 (1980): 5–17. See also Joan Petersilia, "Justice for All? Offenders with Mental Retardation and the California Corrections System," *Prison Journal* 77:4 (1998): 358–380.
4. But see the excellent evaluation of Joan Petersilia, *The Influence of Criminal Justice Research* (Santa Monica, CA: RAND Corporation, 1987); Jeffrey Fagan and M. Forst, "Risk Fixers and Zeal: Implementing Experimental Treatment for Violent Juvenile Offenders," *Prison Journal* 76:1 (1996): 22–59; and Loeber and Farrington, *Serious and Violent Juvenile Offenders.*
5. Francis Cullen and B. Applegate (eds.), *Offender Rehabilitation: Effective Treatment Intervention* (Aldershot, UK: Ashgate, 1997); U.S. Office of Justice Programs Drug Courts Program Office, *Looking at a Decade of Drug Courts* (Washington, DC: U.S. Department of Justice, 1997); and Lorraine Reitzel, "Best Practices in Corrections," *Corrections Today* 67:1 (2005): 42–45, 70.
6. Francis Cullen and K. Gilbert, *Reaffirming Rehabilitation* (Cincinnati, OH: Anderson Publishing, 1982). But see American Correctional Association, *Corrections Issues: Point–Counterpoint* (Lanham, MD: ACA, 1997).
7. See Steve Donziger, *The Real War on Crime* (New York: HarperCollins, 1996), pp. 194–219: John Irwin and J. Austin, *It's About Time,* 2nd ed. (Belmont, CA: Wadsworth, 1997); and Charles Terry, "Managing Prisoners as Problem Populations: The Evolving Nature of Imprisonment: A Convict's Perspective," *Critical Criminology* 12:1 (2003): 43–66.
8. The relationship between ingestion of drugs and crime appears quite strong. See in particular Christopher Mumola, *Substance Abuse and Treatment: State and Federal Prisoners, 1997* (Washington, DC: U.S. Department of Justice, 1999); John Potterat, R. Rothenberg, S. Muth, et al., "Pathways to Prostitution: The Chronology of Sexual and Drug Abuse Milestones," *Journal of Sex Research* 35:4 (998): 330–340; and Craig Rosen, Paige Ouiette, Javaid Sheikh, et al., "Physical and Sexual Abuse History and Addiction Treatment Outcomes," *Journal of Studies on Alcohol* 63:6 (2002): 683–687.
9. Drug abuse is widespread among prison inmates but treatment programs are in short supply. See Donald Dowd, S. Dalzell, and M. Spencer (eds.), "The Sentencing Controversy: Punishment and Policy in the War Against Drugs," *Villanova Law Review* 40:2 (1995): 301–427; and James Marquart, V. Brewer, J. Mullings, et al., "The Implications of Crime Control Policy on HIV/AIDS-Related Risk Among Women Prisoners," *Crime and Delinquency* 45:1 (1999): 82–98.
10. Theodore Hammett, *Public Health and Corrections Collaboration: Prevention and Treatment of HIV/AIDS, STDs, and TB* (Washington, DC: Office of Justice Programs, 1998).
11. U.S. Department of Health and Human Services, *Control of Tuberculosis in Correctional Facilities: A Guide for Health Care Workers* (Washington, DC: USDHHS, 1992). See also Marcus Nieto, *Health Care in California State Prisons* (Sacramento, CA: California Research Bureau, California State Libraries, 1998); and Kenneth Faiver (ed.), *Health Care Management Issues in Corrections* (Lanham, MD: American Correctional Association, 1998).

12. Bureau of Justice Statistics, *Medical Problems of Inmates, 1997* (Washington, DC: BJS, 2001), p. 1, 12; Sophie Davidson and P. Taylor, "Psychological Distress and Severity of Personality Disorder Symptomatology in Prisoners Convicted of Violent and Sexual Offenses," *Psychology, Crime and the Law* 7:3 (2001): 263–272; Kristen Rasmussen, R. Almvik, and S. Levander, "Attention Deficit Hyperactivity Disorder, Reading Disability, and Personality Disorders in a Prison Population," *Journal of the American Academy of Psychology and the Law* 29:2 (2001): 186–193; and Jack Baillergeon, Sandra Black, Charles Leach, et al., "The Infectious Disease Profile of Texas Prison Inmates," *Preventive Medicine* 38:5 (2004): 607–612.
13. But see Jody Spertzel, "Rev. Henry Bouma: Chaplain's Ministry Links Facility with Community," *Corrections Today* 55:3 (1993): 91; and Jody Sundt and F. Cullen, "The Contemporary Prison Chaplain," *The Prison Journal* 78:3 (1998): 271–298.
14. Robert Marsh and V. Cox, "The Practice of Native-American Spirituality in Prison: A Survey," *Justice Professional* 8:2 (1994): 79–95.
15. Dennis Stephens and C. Ward, "College Education and Recidivism: Educating Criminals Is Meritorious," *Journal of Correctional Education* 48:3 (1997): 106–111.
16. Richard Lawrence, "Classroom v. Prison Cells: Funding Priorities for Education and Corrections," *Journal of Crime and Justice* 18:2 (1995): 113–126; and Elliott Currie, *Crime and Punishment in America: Why the Solutions to America's Most Stubborn Social Crisis Have Not Worked—And What Will* (New York: Metropolitan Books, 1998).
17. James Anderson, J. Burns, and L. Dyson, "Could an Increase in AIDS Cases Among Incarcerated Populations Mean More Legal Liabilities for Correctional Administrators?" *Journal of Criminal Justice* 21:1 (1998): 41–52.
18. T. L. Felton, "The Learning Modes of the Incarcerated Population," *Journal of Correctional Education* 4:3 (1994): 118–121; and Theodore Hammett, P. Harmon, and L. Marushak, *1996–1997 Update: HIV/AIDS, STDs, and TB in Correctional Facilities* (Washington, DC: U.S. Department of Justice, 1999), pp. 25–45.
19. Eva Fisher-Bloom, "The Import of Learning Disabilities in Correctional Treatment," *Forum* 7:3 (1995): 20–26; and Barbara Belot and J. Marquart, "The Political Community Model and Prisoner Litigation," *Prison Journal* 78:3 (1998): 299–329.
20. Arnie Nielsen, F. Scarpitti, and J. Inciardi, "Integrating the Therapeutic Community and Work Release for Drug-Abusing Offenders," *Journal of Substance Abuse and Treatment* 13:4 (1996): 349–358. See also Roger Boe, A. Thurber, L. Montiuk, et al. (eds.), "Offender Reintegration," *Forum on Corrections Research* 10:1 (1998): 3–47.
21. See Rick Linden and L. Perry, "The Effectiveness of Prison Educational Programs," *Journal of Offender Counseling, Services and Rehabilitation* 6:1 (1982): 43–57; and Lisa Allen, G. Rondeau, N. Harms, et al. (eds.), "Current Research and Clinical Practice," *Journal of Offender Rehabilitation* 24:3/4 (1997): 101–181.
22. C. Camp and G. Camp, *The Corrections Yearbook 2000: Adult Corrections* (Middletown, CT: Criminal Justice Institute, 2000), pp. 126–129.
23. Neil Singer, *The Value of Inmate Manpower* (Washington, DC: American Bar Association Commission on Correctional Facilities and Manpower, 1973). But see Rose Burton, D. Pens, P. Wright, et al., *The Celling of America: An Inside Look at the U.S. Prison Industry* (Monroe, ME: Common Courage Press, 1998).
24. Larry Mays and T. Gray (eds.), *Privatization and the Provision of Correctional Services* (Cincinnati, OH: Anderson Publishing, 1996).
25. George Sexton, *Work in American Prisons: Joint Ventures with the Private Sector* (Washington, DC: U.S. Department of Justice, 1995), p. 2.
26. Edward Latessa, L. Travis, and H. Allen, "Volunteers and Paraprofessionals in Parole: Current Practices," *Journal of Offender Counseling, Services and Rehabilitation* 8:1/2 (1983): 91–106; and American Probation and Parole Association, *Restoring Hope Through Community Partnerships* (Lexington, KY: APPA, 1996).
27. David Onek, *Pairing College Students with Delinquents: The Minnesota Intensive Case Monitoring Program* (San Francisco: National Council on Crime and Delinquency, 1994); and Pamela Hewitt, E. Moore, and B. Gaulier, "Winning the Battles and the War," *Juvenile and Family Court Journal* 49:1 (1998): 39–49.

SUGGESTED READINGS: PART 5

American Correctional Association. *The Effective Correctional Officer.* Laurel, MD: ACA, 1992.

Anno, B. Jaye. "The Cost of Correctional Health Care: Results of a National Survey." *Journal of Prison & Jail Health* 9:2 (1990): 105–133.

Cullen, Francis T., E. Latessa, and V. Burton, Jr. "The Correctional Orientation of Prison Wardens: Is the Rehabilitative Ideal Supported?" *Criminology* 31:1 (1993): 69–92.

Currie, Elliott. *Crime and Punishment in America: Why the Solutions to America's Most Stubborn Social Crisis Have*

Not Worked—And What Will. New York: Metropolitan Books, 1998.

Di Vito, Robert J. "Survey of Mandatory Education Practices in State Penal Institutions." *Journal of Correctional Education* 42:3 (1991): 126–132.

Durose, Matthew, D. Levin, and P. Langan. *Felony Sentences in State Courts, 1998.* Washington, DC: Bureau of Justice Statistics, 2001.

Franke, Herman. "The Rise and Decline of Solitary Confinement: Social–Historical Explanations of the Long-Term Penal Changes." *British Journal of Criminology* 32:2 (1992): 125–143.

Harris, George A. (ed.). *And Tough Customers: Counseling Unwilling Clients.* Laurel, MD: American Correctional Association, 1991.

Harris, Kay. "Key Differences Among Community Corrections Acts in the United States." *Prison Journal* 76:2 (1996): 129–238.

Hassine, Victor. *Life Without Parole: Living in Prison Today.* Los Angeles: Roxbury, 2004.

Huggins, M. Wayne, E. Reynolds, J. Dare, et al. "Accreditation." *Corrections Today* 54:3 (1992): 40–62.

Langan, Patrick, and David Levin. *Recidivism of Prisoners Released in 1994.* Washington, DC: Bureau of Justice Statistics, 2002.

Lee, David. "Personal Liability Against Corrections Officials and Employees for Failure to Protect the Suicidal Inmate Under 42 U.S.C.§ 1983." *Jail Suicide/Mental Health Update* 11:1 (2002): 1–8.

Light, Stephen C. "Assaults on Prison Officers: Interactional Theme." *Justice Quarterly* 8:2 (1991): 217–242.

Maruschak, Laura. *HIV in Prisons and Jails, 2002.* Washington, DC: Bureau of Justice Statistics, 2004.

Maruschak, Laura, and A. Beck. *Medical Problems of Inmates, 1997.* Washington, DC: Bureau of Justice Statistics, 2001.

McVinney, Donald. "Counseling Incarcerated Individuals with HIV Disease and Chemical Dependency." *Journal of Chemical Dependency Treatment* 4:2 (1991): 105–118.

Morton, Joann B, et al. "Women in Corrections." *Corrections Today* 54:6 (1992): 76–180.

Mumola, Christopher. *Substance Abuse and Treatment, State and Federal Prisoners, 1997.* Washington, DC: Bureau of Justice Statistics, 1999.

Schlossman, Steven, and J. Spillane. *Bright Hopes, Dim Realities: Vocational Innovation in American Correctional Education.* Santa Monica, CA: RAND Corporation, 1992.

Steadman, Henry J., E. Holobean, Jr., and J. Dvoskin. "Estimating Mental Health Needs and Service Utilization Among Prisoner Inmates." *Bulletin of the American Academy of Psychiatry and the Law* 19:3 (1991): 297–307.

Stohr, Mary, and L. Zupan. "Street-Level Bureaucrats and Service Provision in Jail: The Failure of Officers to Identify the Needs of Inmates." *American Journal of Criminal Justice* 16:2 (1992): 75–94.

Sundt, Jody, and F. Cullen. "The Role of the Contemporary Prison Chaplain." *Prison Journal* 78:3 (1998): 271–298.

Super, John T., T. Blau, B. Charles, et al. "Using Psychological Tests to Discriminate Between 'Best' and 'Least Best' Correctional Officers." *Journal of Criminal Justice* 21:2 (1992): 143–150.

Turner, Susan, and J. Petersilia. "Work Release in Washington: Effects on Recidivism and Courtroom Costs." *Prison Journal* 76:2 (1996): 138–164.

Uzoba, Julius. *Managing Older Offenders: Where Do We Stand?* Ottawa: Research Branch, Correctional Service of Canada, 1998.

Van Voorhis, Patricia, F. Cullen, B. Link, et al. "The Impact of Race and Gender on Correctional Officers' Orientation to the Integrated Environment." *Journal of Research in Crime and Delinquency* 28:4 (1991): 472–500.

Wilson, Doris. *Drug Use, Testing and Treatment in Jails.* Washington, DC: Bureau of Justice Statistics, 2000.

Wright, Thomas. "Correctional Employee Turnover: A Longitudinal Study." *Journal of Criminal Justice* 21:2 (1993): 131–142.

PART

6

Institutional Clients

THE FOLLOWING CHAPTERS ARE COVERED IN PART 6:

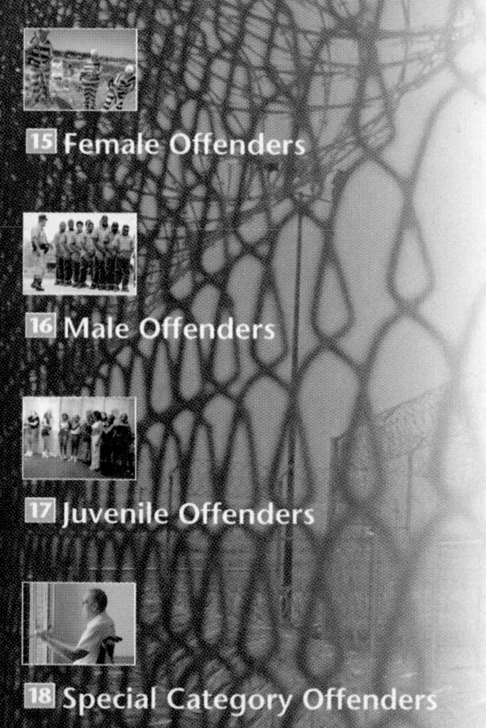

OVERVIEW

Part 4 (Chapters 9 through 12) and Part 5 (Chapters 13 and 14) dealt with correctional systems and correctional functions, respectively. The next four chapters deal with the human beings incarcerated in institutions. In particular, we deal with female offenders (Chapter 15), male inmates (Chapter 16), juvenile inmates (Chapter 17), and special categories of inmates (Chapter 18). Among the latter are groups of inmates with more problems than the other offenders in the mainstream of criminal behavior: the mentally disordered offender, the developmentally challenged offender, the sex offender, HIV-infected inmates, and geriatric inmates. Together, these categories represent the spectrum of the individual offenders under the custody and treatment of correctional administrators.

CHAPTER 15

Female Offenders

Females tend to commit survival crimes, fed by a drug-dependent life, and escape brutalizing conditions and relationships.
—Barbara Owen

KEY WORDS

- arrests by gender
- preferential treatment
- "traditional" female crimes
- "victimless" crimes
- paternalistic attitudes of judges
- women's liberation movement
- abused females
- pregnant inmates
- family cohesion
- single-sex experience
- psychological deprivation
- co-correctional institution

OVERVIEW

Although the male offender will be shown in the following chapter to provide the lion's share of adult prisoners (93 percent), the female inmate population is increasing at a higher rate of growth. In this chapter we examine that phenomenon, as well as those similar processes and conditions with which females must contend. We look at the kinds of women and the crimes that placed them in state, federal, and other adult female prisons and correctional institutions. You will find that many female offenders are moving away from "woman crime" and becoming more mainstream in their criminal behaviors and levels of violence, posing new challenges to old approaches.

To compare the relative levels of incarceration between female and male prisoners, we first examine the crime rates for both categories and look at the differing patterns of conviction and sentencing rates for those crimes. The "steel ceiling" that has traditionally tended to divert females from long-term incarceration in correctional facilities into community mental health and correctional alternatives seems to have cracked somewhat recently; different trends are emerging for female prisoners. The student is presented with information about problems specific to female offenders that may cause them to need special treatment. What happens to female offenders in the prisons of America?

FEMALE CRIME AND INCARCERATION RATES

As shown by Figure 15.1, the number of female prisoners in adult facilities continues to grow rapidly, reaching an all-time high of 103,310 in 2004, excluding the

< Three women on a Maricopa County Jail chain gang cover a casket in a grave with dirt, Phoenix, Arizona.
Photo by A. Ramey, courtesy of PhotoEdit.

approximately 3,600 holdbacks still in jail due to lack of space in state, federal, and other institutions. Although this grand total represents less than 7 percent of the U.S. prison population overall, it is a significant and worrisome trend. Although the total number of male prisoners has grown by more than 26 percent since 1995, the number of female prisoners grew by nearly 32 percent, continuing a long trend of higher rate of growth for female inmates. They constitute more than 12 percent of the jail population on a given day.[1] To get a better understanding of just who these prisoners are and why the rate and numbers are increasing, one has to look closer at the kinds of crimes, regionally and nationally, being committed by females.

The period from 1970 through the 1990s included the years when women's equality and civil rights were asserted, if not established, on almost every front.[2] Yet only recently has there been a movement to push for the rights of female prisoners in corrections. In a way, females still receive differential, sometimes even preferential, treatment at almost every station of the criminal justice system, partly in deference to traditional female gender roles (except in the area of drug arrests).[3] We now examine the more common kinds of Crime Index (see Chapter 4) offenses committed by females, and compare some of the dispositions to institutions for females in a rapidly changing environment.

Although the criminal statistics contained in the FBI's Uniform Crime Reports are somewhat limited and "soft," especially for crimes involving females, they are the best available and can at least be accepted as indicators of trends.[4]

A comparison of total **arrests by gender** in 2003 for the eight major (index) crimes can be found in Table 15.1. Two major conclusions are evident from examination of these data. First, females were arrested for 23 percent of all crimes. Second, they represent a large portion (37 percent) of persons arrested for larceny-theft, which accounts for a whopping 71 percent of all index arrests for females. The eight index crimes do not include drug offenses. As Figure 15.2 illustrates, women are arrested almost three times more frequently for drug offenses than for crimes of violence.[5]

These figures clearly indicate the growing role of the female offender in the entire criminal justice system. As we note later, **preferential treatment** of females seems to be disappearing for those females arrested for nontraditional crimes

SIDEBARS

Female Juvenile Arrests

Since 1987, juvenile female arrests have increased at a faster rate than those of juvenile males. Arrest data indicate that juvenile females make up an expanding proportion of arrests in the total crime category, as well as in the violent crime category. Although the largest percent of juvenile female arrests is for property crimes, data indicate that juvenile females are being arrested in an expanding proportion for violent crimes. The violent crimes arrest rate for the total juvenile population shows an increase of 143 percent from 1967 to 1996, but the rate for females increased 345 percent in that same period. Juvenile male arrest rates for aggravated assault and simple assault fell from the mid-1990s through 2002, while female rates remained near their highest level.

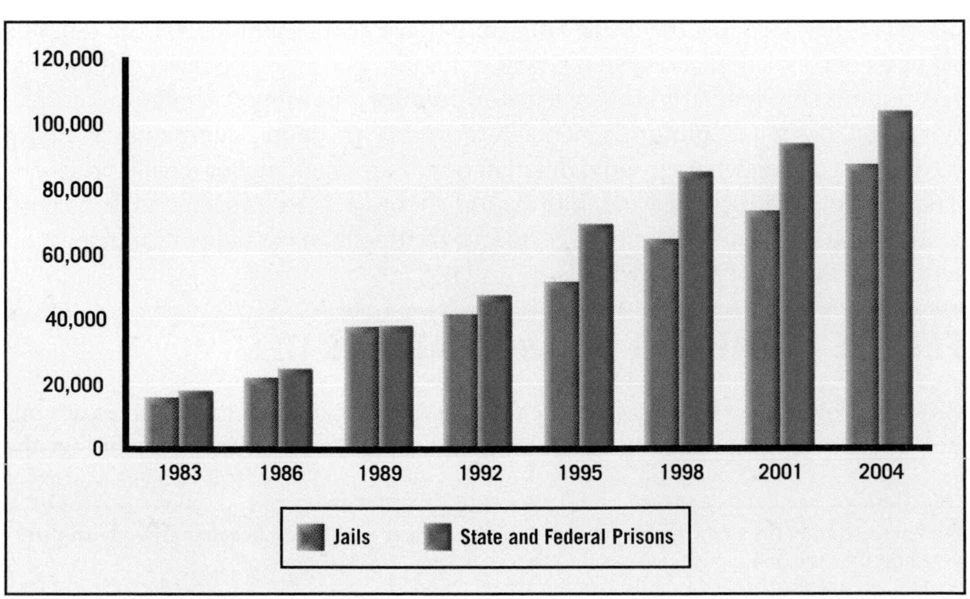

FIGURE 15.1

Female Prisoners in State-Federal Prisons and Local Jails, 1983–2004

SOURCE: Sourcebook of Criminal Justice Statistics Online, *Number of Jail Inmates 1983–2003* (www.albany.edu/sourcebook/ 2004pdf/t620.pdf); *Number of Sentenced Prisoners in State and Federal Prisons 1925–2003* (www.albany.edu/ sourcebook/2004pdf/t627.pdf); and Paige Harrison and Allen Beck, *Prison and Jail Inmates at Midyear 2004* (Washington, DC: Bureau of Justice Statistics, 2005), p. 8.

TABLE 15.1 Arrests of Females by Type of Crime, 2003

	NUMBER OF PERSONS ARRESTED		PERCENTAGE	DISTRIBUTION
OFFENSE CHARGED	TOTAL	FEMALE	FEMALE	FEMALE
Total: All Crimes	9,581,423	2,225,730	23.2%	100.0%
Murder and nonnegligent manslaughter	9,119	941	10.3	0.2
Forcible rape	18,446	247	1.3	0.05
Robbery	75,667	7,849	10.3	1.8
Aggravated assault	315,732	65,492	20.7	15.4
Burglary	204,761	28,043	13.7	6.6
Larceny-theft	817,048	302,958	37.0	71.2
Motor vehicle theft	106,221	17,680	16.6	4.1
Arson	11,330	1,765	15.5	0.4
Violent crime	418,964	74,529	17.7	17.5
Property crime	1,139,360	350,446	30.7	82.5
Crime Index Total	1,558,324	424,975	27.2	NA

SOURCE: Federal Bureau of Investigation, *Crime in the United States 2003* (Washington, DC: U.S. Department of Justice, 2004), p. 23.

(crimes of violence and crimes committed with one or more other female offenders). We may have to take a new look at the **"traditional" female crimes** as we continue to examine the "new" female offender of the twenty-first century.

The general increase in female criminality may also be seen as reflecting the changing patterns of criminal opportunity for females. It is interesting that arrests

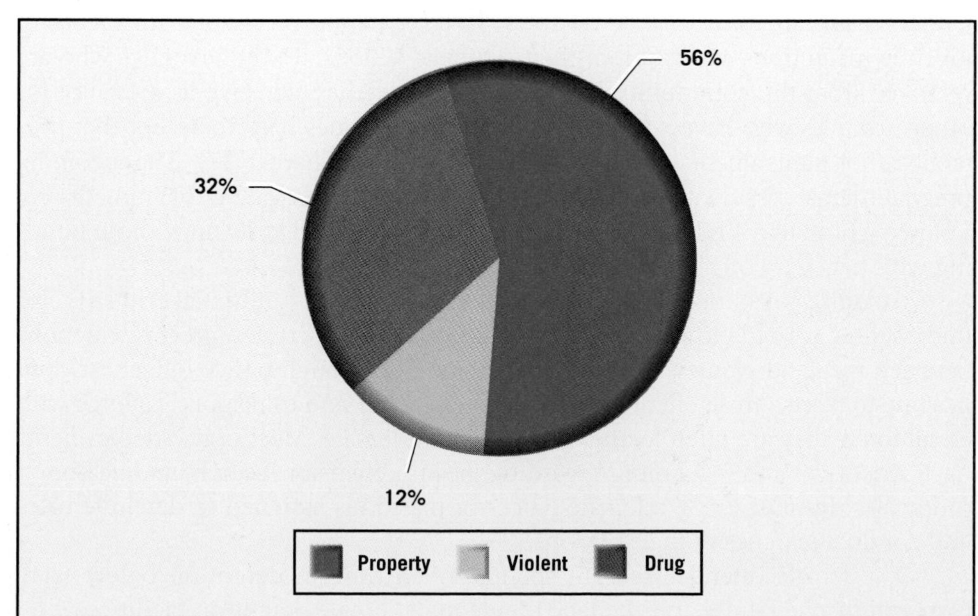

FIGURE 15.2

Arrests of Females by Type of Crime, 2003

SOURCE: Federal Bureau of Investigation, *Uniform Crime Reports: 2003* (Washington, DC: FBI, 2004), p. 275.

for prostitution, the crime Freda Adler calls "the oldest and newest profession,"[6] decreased 21.7 percent between 1994 and 2003.[7] Whether this decrease relates to more jobs and better jobs for females, the growth of AIDS awareness, or a changing moral climate we leave for others to determine.[8]

The arrest figures for prostitution, however, are only the tip of the iceberg. Because prostitution is one of the so-called **"victimless" crimes,**[9] and clients seldom complain because they would be implicating themselves, the number of arrests for prostitution usually reflects only cases of flagrant solicitation, rampant disease, or a local cleanup campaign.[10] Considerable folklore surrounds prostitution, most of it with no basis in fact. Those who profit from prostitution (almost never the prostitutes themselves) are not about to compile statistics or seek publicity. It is a business that thrives on sexual appetite, with the ultimate motive being simple profit.

A DIFFERENTIAL JUSTICE SYSTEM FOR FEMALES?

The previous scarcity of research in the area of female equality in general, and the role of females in the criminal justice system in particular, makes this area the current gold mine for researchers and writers.[11] It is unfortunate that much of the earlier literature was a warmed-over version of the old myths and inaccuracies of the 1940s and 1950s.

The first point at which the female offender comes into contact with the criminal justice system is the point of arrest. Although arrest may be a traumatic experience for the male offender, it has special problems for the female. It is estimated that 80 percent of the female offenders in America have dependent children at home and that a great percentage of those children have no one else to care for them.[12] About 80,000 females in jails and prisons have an estimated 200,000 children under age eighteen.[13] Concern for the children and a tendency among officers to identify female offenders with their own mothers or sisters may cause arresting officers to use more discretion than they might with a male in the same situation. A recognition of the need to provide more pretrial services for female offenders has prompted many communities to develop volunteer programs to assist with the female problems at home. It is important to remember that the children of female offenders often are placed with relatives, foster parents, or become residents of juvenile institutions as a result of their mothers' actions. To the juveniles who are removed from the community and placed in what they perceive as a facility for other juveniles who have committed offenses, it becomes hard to accept that protection, not punishment, is the state's motivation (see Chapter 17). The incoming pregnant female resident whose child is removed from her care at or immediately following birth may find it hard to believe that her child will grow up without bonding with her.

SIDEBARS

Impact on Children

Studies that have focused on the impact of a mother's incarceration on children reveal negative effects. Such children suffer from emotional distress, show poor school performance, and exhibit aggressive behavior. One study of children of incarcerated mothers showed that more than eight in ten had been sexually abused or witnessed violence in their homes.

An officer's traditional reluctance to arrest females for traditional crimes is also the result of age-old customs, mores, and laws that have created great distinctions between men and women under apprehension.[14] Although police officers seldom hesitate to place a male offender "up against the wall" and to respond to force with equal force, they are often loathe to do so with a female. Most police departments have strict rules and regulations regarding the apprehension, search, and detention of females. In most cases, a female officer or matron is assigned to detain females and conduct searches of their persons.

The female offender seldom spends much time in detention before trial. Concern for the family and the lack of adequate female detention facilities or fe-

TABLE 15.2 Types of Sentences Imposed by State Court, Female Felons, 2002

		PERCENT OF FELONS SENTENCED TO:					
		INCARCERATION			NONINCARCERATION		
MOST SERIOUS CONVICTION OFFENSE	TOTAL	TOTAL	PRISON	JAIL	TOTAL	PROBATION	OTHER
All Offenses	100%	56%	25%	31%	44%	40%	3%
Violent Offenses	100%	64%	32%	31%	36%	34%	3%
Murder	100	88	81	7	12	11	1
Sexual assault	100	71	44	27	29	25	4
Robbery	100	74	50	24	26	24	1
Aggravated assault	100	58	23	35	42	39	3
Other violent	100	68	37	31	32	29	3
Property Offenses	100%	53%	22%	31%	47%	44%	3%
Burglary	100	73	30	43	27	25	3
Larceny	100	52	19	33	48	45	3
Fraud	100	49	22	27	51	48	3
Drug Offenses	100%	54%	26%	28%	46%	41%	5%
Possession	100	51	21	30	49	43	6
Trafficking	100	56	29	27	44	40	4
Weapons	100%	60%	27%	33%	40%	35%	5%
Other Offenses	100%	43%	25%	39%	36%	33%	3%

SOURCE: Bureau of Justice Statistics, *State Court Sentencing of Convicted Felons, 2002* (Washington, DC: US Department of Justice, 2003), p. 23.

male personnel in the police department almost demand pretrial release for females.[15] Until quite recently, female offenders also usually committed less serious offenses and could therefore be released on bail or on their own recognizance. Beginning in the 1980s, however, females have been committing more serious crimes and, perhaps owing to the move to equalize punishments for codefendants, have been receiving more severe sentences (see Table 15.2). However, as females are arrested in greater numbers for crimes that have been committed primarily by men in the past, they can expect the **paternalistic attitude of judges**—if such an attitude now exists—to diminish rapidly.[16] As Meda Chesney-Lind notes, the male model of prisons is being superimposed on female prisoners in the rush to vengeful equity.[17]

The differential treatment accorded to females in many cases does not automatically mean better treatment or consideration. Moreover, as an alternative to differential treatment, the model of the male prison is sometimes copied, even to the point of ignoring the female inmates' obvious physical differences.[18]

For those and other reasons, female offenders had traditionally received discretionary treatment by police and prosecutors. Females brought to court now are still apt to receive consideration for probation, fines, and suspended sentences more often than are men who commit comparable crimes. Of course,

First Prison for Women

The first prison exclusively for women was the Indiana Reformatory Institute for Women. It was opened in 1873 and followed Zebulon Brockway's methods.

SIDEBARS

First Federal Institution for Women

The first institution in the Federal Bureau of Prisons exclusively for women was the Federal Correctional Institution at Alderson, West Virginia, in 1925.

FIGURE 15.3

Increase in the Number of Females in State Prison Between 1990 and 2005 by Type of Offense (in number and percent)

SOURCE: Paige Harrison and Allen Beck, *Prison and Jail Inmates at Midyear 2003* (Washington, DC: Bureau of Justice Statistics, 2004), p. 9. Data for 2005 are extrapolated.

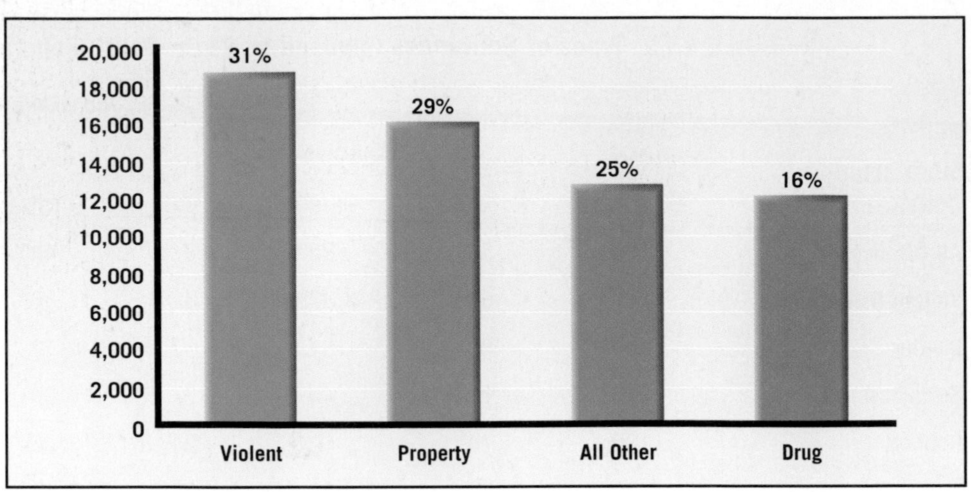

SIDEBARS

First Female Warden

The first female to hold the position of warden was Mary Belle Harris at the Federal Correctional Institution at Alderson, West Virginia, in 1925.

female offenders are less likely to have long criminal offense records and to commit violent crimes.

Statistics on the growth of female prisoners in state prisons and their offenses between 1990 and 2003 can be found in Figure 15.3.[19] It appears that the greatest change has been in the area of females committed for violent and property offenses. With regard to violent crime, the numbers are still significantly lower than for males. The War on Drugs has become a war on females and has materially contributed to the exploding growth of female prisoners. Yet they are not the "major players" in the drug trade; at least one-third are jailed for drug possession. In one sense, they can be seen as "prisoners" of the War on Drugs; in the federal prison system, drug offenders approach 60 percent of the prison population.

Why has the female prison population increased so sharply? No one knows for certain, but some of the reasons given are that females have more opportunities to commit crime than ever before, they are committing more serious crimes, and they are being sentenced more severely by judges. Many state drug statutes mandate imprisonment and restrict the sentencing discretion of the judge. Other theories are that presentence investigators and the judiciary, influenced by the **women's liberation movement,** are less likely to give favorable sentencing considerations than they were in the past, that parole boards are using uniform sentencing guidelines that force female inmates to serve more time, and that females are getting their "just deserts" under the conservative backlash to treat all offenders more severely. Others argue that the War on Drugs has sent many more female drug addicts into prisons than in the past, and that excessively long sentences for possession of controlled substances to which the offender is addicted (a medical problem) may violate the U.S. Constitution prohibition against "cruel and unusual punishment." There are many theories, but not much data to support any one theory in particular.

The plight of the woman behind jail or prison bars is often a difficult one. In terms of institutions, the male-oriented criminal justice system may totally ignore the special requirements of the female offender.[20] The nature of punishment for female offenders has come a long way from the time when they were thrown into the gaols as diversions for the incarcerated male felons, but more needs to be done before treatment of the female offender can be said to be an integrated part of corrections.[21]

CORRECTIONAL BRIEF

Characteristics of Drug-Abusing Female Offenders

To gain a picture of the special needs of drug-abusing women offenders, information was taken from several sources covering women arrestees, women incarcerated in jails and prisons, women offenders diverted into community-based treatment instead of incarceration or as a condition of probation or parole, and women in publicly supported drug and treatment programs. Provided below are characteristics of these women:

- *Health problems.* Many drug-abusing women are physically or mentally ill. All drug users, and cocaine users in particular, are at increased risk for extreme weight loss, dehydration, digestive disorders, skin problems, dental problems, gynecological and venereal infections, tuberculosis, hepatitis B, hypertension, seizures, respiratory arrest, and cardiac failure.
- *Educational/vocational background.* Most of the women are unemployed or work at low-paying jobs. Most have not completed high school, have inadequate vocational skills, and lack many of the skills and knowledge needed to function productively in society.
- *Psychosocial problems.* Drug-addicted women tend to come from families with a high incidence of mental illness, suicide, alcohol or drug dependence, or violence, or are victims of incest, rape, or physical or sexual abuse.
- *Responsibility for parenting.* Most drug-abusing women offenders are of childbearing age, already have children, and are single mothers. Many of them receive little or no help from the children's father(s), lack supportive family and social networks, and have limited or no financial resources. Often their children become drug abusers themselves, thereby perpetuating both drug abuse and dysfunctional parenting across generations.
- *Drug use and treatment.* Most drug-abusing women offenders started abusing drugs and alcohol at an early age, and many used drugs, especially cocaine, on a daily basis prior to incarceration. In one survey of women in prison, 46 percent of respondents reported they had used drugs and/or alcohol at the time of their offense. Approximately 25 percent of adult women offenders have spent some time in a drug/alcohol treatment program, which, however, has most likely been of limited duration and intensity.
- *Criminal justice and child protective services involvement.* A large percentage of drug-abusing women who seek treatment have had some involvement with the criminal justice system or with child protective services. One study reported that an estimated 60 to 80 percent of child abuse and neglect cases were from substance-abusing families.

Although these characteristics have been found to typify the population of drug-abusing women offenders, they have different implications for programs. Individual women will differ in the manifestations and severity of these characteristics and attendant problems. Such diversity calls for an assessment of specific clients' needs and the provision of services designed to meet those needs. If a program lacks a well-developed assessment procedure, clients are less likely to receive appropriate services, such as treatment in a style matched to cultural identity and cognitive level and of adequate intensity and duration.

SOURCE: Jean Wellisch, Michael Prendergast, and Douglas Anglin, *Drug-Abusing Women Offenders: Results of a National Survey* (Washington, DC: National Institute of Justice, 1994).

FEMALES IN JAIL

Females have never been a large portion of the inmates of jails in the nation, but the War on Drugs has contributed significantly to the number arrested and placed in jails and detention centers and has also increased the proportion of all inmates who are female. The number of females held in America's jails has increased dramatically during the past 15 years and is up over 130 percent since 1990.[22]

The characteristics of female jail inmates are generally the same, except for drug-related crime increases, as those found in an earlier survey of jails. More than 80 percent had used drugs in their lives, and more than half of the convicted inmates had used drugs in the month prior to the current offense that brought them to jail; almost 40 percent had used drugs daily. Some 24 percent of the female jail inmates had used cocaine or crack in the month before their current offense. About one in six convicted females in jail reported they had committed their current offense for money to buy drugs. Better than one in three convicted female inmates reported being under the influence of alcohol at the time of their offense.

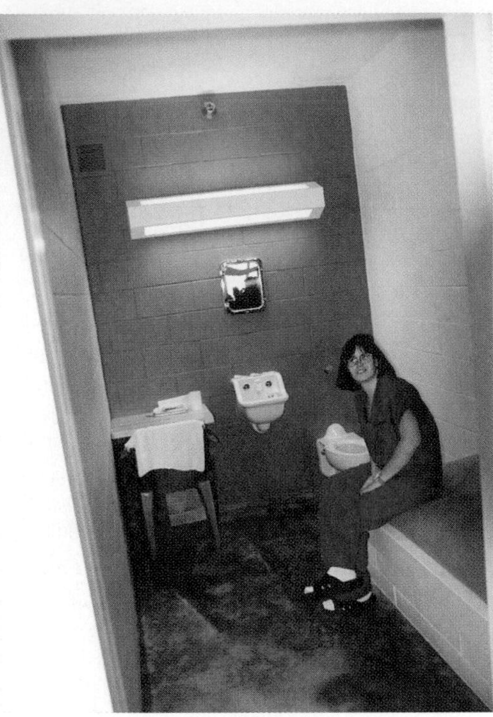

A typical female detention cell.
Photo by Clifford E. Simonsen, courtesy of King County Department of Adult Detention, Washington.

A profile of jail inmates from 2002 illustrates other important demographic and criminal characteristics of females in jails, including the following[23]:

- About 17 percent of the female inmates were in jail for a violent offense.
- Female jail inmates were more likely than males to be drug offenders, 29 percent versus 24 percent.
- More than 49 percent of the females were first-time offenders, compared to 37 percent for men.
- Female jail inmates were less likely to be employed in the month prior to their arrest than males; 40 percent versus 60 percent.
- Around 16 percent of female jail inmates had sustained an injury following an assault.
- More than 55 percent of females reported they had been sexually abused in their past, up from 47.5 percent in 1996. Of these, more than 20 percent reported the abuse had occurred prior to age eighteen. Women were also more likely to have been abused by an intimate partner (68 percent) than men (11 percent), and 26 percent said they had been abused by a parent or guardian, and 34 percent by a friend.
- More than 46 percent were using drugs or alcohol at the time of their offense, and more than 55 percent admitted to drinking regularly.
- Low income was typical of almost all inmates.

A recent study of women in jail found high rates of lifetime trauma exposure (98 percent), current mental health disorders (36 percent), and drug and alcohol problems (almost three out of four). Most were deficient in parenting skills.[24]

This brief overview of female jail inmates suggests that they generally are not drawn from mainstream America, come from deprived and unstable backgrounds,

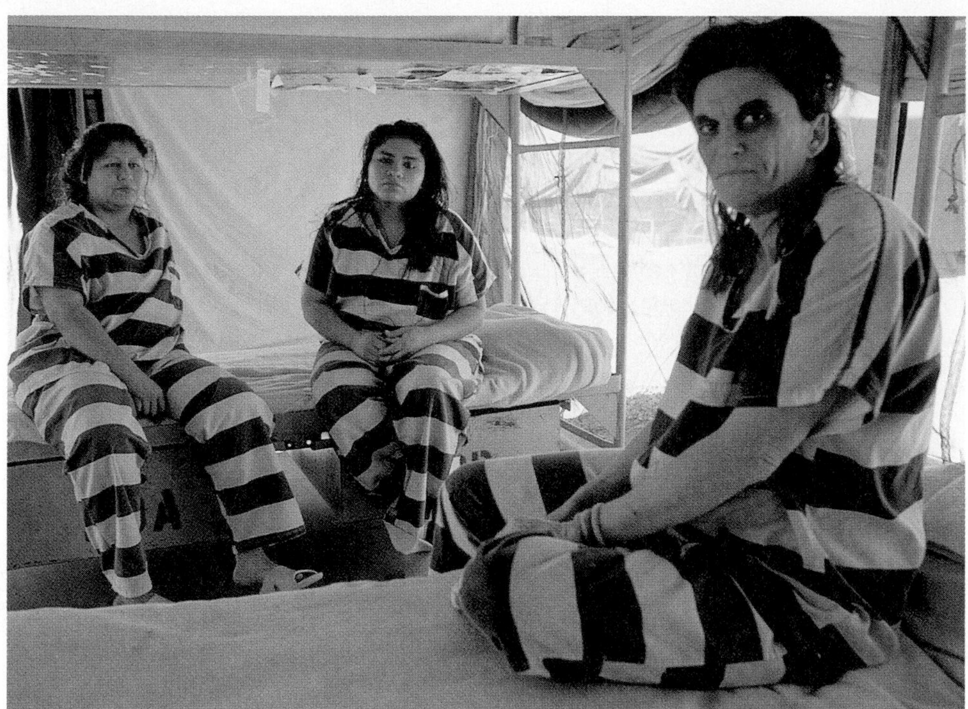

Female inmates relax on bunk beds in Tent City at Maricopa County Jail in Arizona.

Photo by A. Ramey, courtesy of PhotoEdit.

have been extensively abused over time, and face significant employment, financial, psychological, emotional, and social barriers in their efforts to live in and seek reintegration into their local communities.[25] Most of these jail inmates are not dangerous but need assistance in existence and living. Incarceration in jail or prison may achieve punishment; societal goals would probably be better achieved if these high-problem female offenders were sentenced to community alternatives and received extensive treatment and service delivery. This is particularly true of abused females who enter the correctional system.[26]

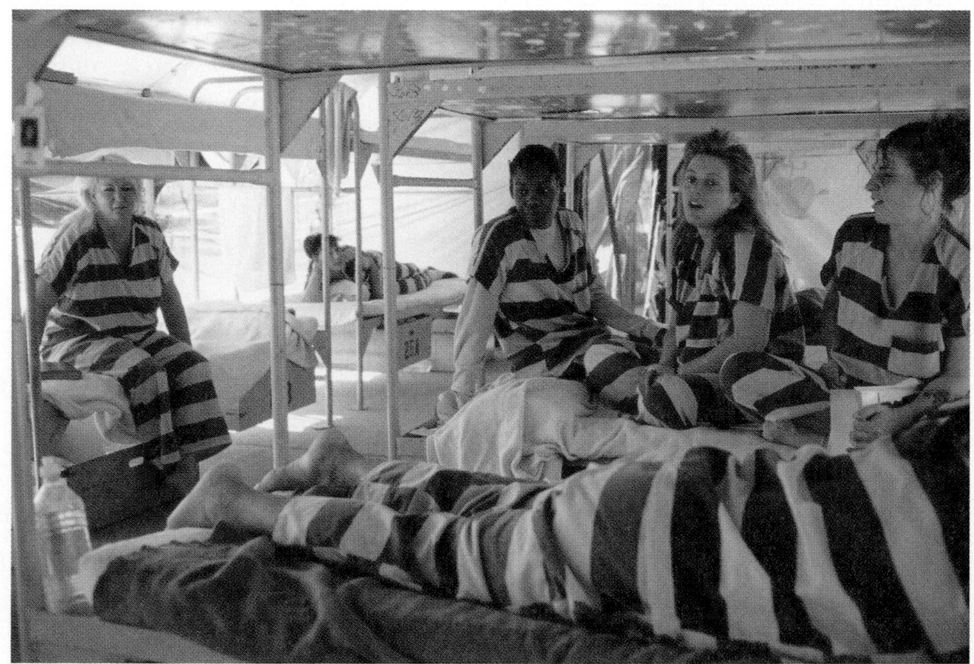

Female prisoners in stripes take a break from work in a tent detention center in Arizona.

Photo by A. Ramey, courtesy of PhotoEdit.

FEMALES IN PRISON

As noted earlier, despite the earlier preferential treatment of female offenders, the number of incarcerated females in the United States started to rise sharply in the 1980s. Today, California, Texas, Florida, and the federal system hold four out of every ten female inmates, while Oklahoma leads the country in the incarceration rate for females at 130 per 100,000.[27]

Overall, the rate of growth for female prison inmates exceeded that for males for each of the last ten years. From 1995 to 2003, the male population increased an average of 3.4 percent per year, and the female population increased by 5.2 percent. Although the rate of incarceration for females is still considerably lower than that of males (61 per 100,000 females in the nation versus 914 per 100,000 for males), the gap is narrowing.[28] Not all groups of females are incarcerated at the same rate in America. As with males, blacks are incarcerated at a rate eight times that of white females; Hispanics are overrepresented by a ratio of three to one to white females.

The typical female prisoner is black, non-Hispanic, age twenty-five to thirty-four, never married, with some high school education and not employed at the time of arrest. She has likely been sentenced for a nonviolent crime (see Figure 15.4), and is a recidivist (either been sentenced to probation or previously incarcerated as a juvenile or adult). A third of all female inmates reported they were under the influence of a drug at the time of their offenses. Overall, just over half of the females in prison had been using drugs or alcohol or both at the time the imprisonment offense occurred. An estimated 84 percent of the females in state prisons had used drugs at some time in their lives prior to admission, fairly close to 80 percent of the men. Some 40 percent of the female inmates had participated in a drug treatment program at some point in their lives.[29]

Prior abuse by spouse, family member, parent, and significant other (boyfriend or girlfriend) creates consequences for the abused.[30] (See Table 15.3.) Childhood and adult victimization of females is frequently a precursor to female criminality. Many **abused females** are left with emotional scars and diminished self-confidence. More than 75 percent of the female prisoners were mothers, and two in three had children under age eighteen. Female prisoners reported that more than 80 percent of their children under age eighteen were living with a relative, usually the maternal grandmother. For male prison inmates, almost 90 percent of their children under age eighteen are living with the children's mothers. This is an important difference that we discuss later.

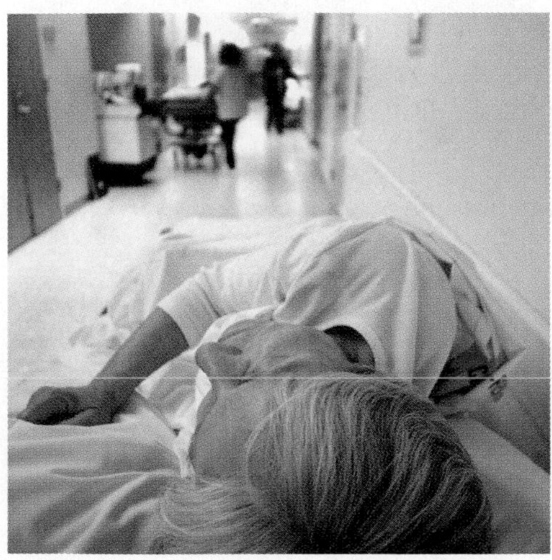

The health care needs of incarcerated women are inadequately addressed by many jails and prisons.
Photo by Spencer Grant, courtesy of PhotoEdit.

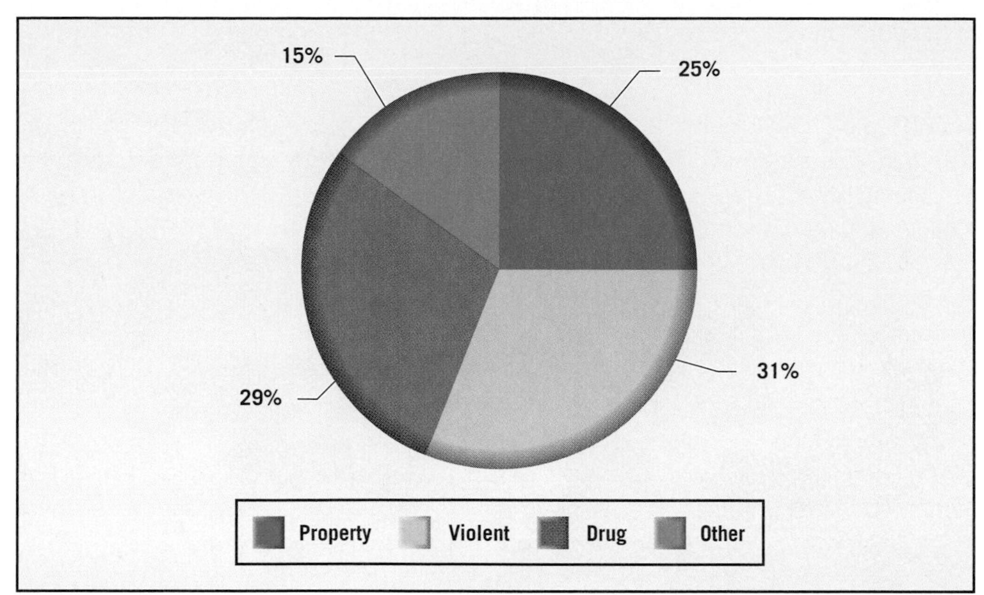

FIGURE 15.4

Most Serious Crime Committed by Female Prisoners, 2005

SOURCE: D. K. Gilliard and A. J. Beck, *Prisoners in 1997* (Washington, DC: Bureau of Justice Statistics, 1998), p. 11; and A. J. Beck and P. M. Harrison, *Prisoners in 2000* (Washington, DC: Bureau of Justice Statistics, 2001), p. 11. Data extrapolated to 2005.

Female inmates are housed in a variety of facilities. About half of these facilities are penal institutions, known by a variety of names: prisons, reformatories, penitentiaries, correctional facilities, and prison camps. Most are housed in minimum- to low-security units (see Figure 15.5).

This profile of the imprisoned female inmate hardly reflects a dangerous offender for whom incarceration in prison is required. Instead, many such offenders could probably be handled more effectively,[31] less expensively, and more humanely in alternatives to prison. Unfortunately, this situation most likely reflects probable national practice throughout the country.

FEMALE INSTITUTIONS

Only 51 training schools and centers, 291 coed programs for female juvenile delinquents, 100 institutions for women, and 61 coeducational facilities were listed in the 2004 American Correctional Association's *Corrections Compendium* survey. Texas led the way with 11 institutions for females and 4 coed facilities.[32] The picture with regard to the administration of these female prisons has changed greatly in recent years. In 1966, female correctional administrators headed only ten of the nation's institutions. The 2005 ACA directory showed that 971 of the 3,467 correctional administrators of adult and juvenile institutions were females.[33] Female correctional administrators tend to be managing male as well as female and co-correctional institutions, or community and minimum custody facilities. As a matter of fact, the

TABLE 15.3 Prior Abuse Reported by State Inmates and Probationers, 1997

ABUSED	TOTAL	MALE	FEMALE
Ever abused	19%	16%	57%
Physically abused	15	13	47
Sexually abused	8	6	39

SOURCE: Caroline Wolf Harlow, *Prior Abuse Reported by Inmates and Probationers* (Washington, DC: U.S. Department of Justice, 1999), p. 1.

Part of a group of 21 women waiting for mercy while serving life sentences for killing men who they say abused them.

Photo by Chris Martinez, courtesy of AP/Wide World Photos.

PROFILE

Elizabeth Gurney Fry (1780–1845)

established in the early 1800s a program in London of lay visitors who visited and aided female inmates who were generally considered depraved and fallen. One of the first to care about female criminals, this British Quaker led the way for many others to follow.

SIDEBARS

Female Presidents of the ACA

The six distinguished female presidents of the American Correctional Association:

Blanche LaDu	1935
Martha Wheeler	1972
Su Cunningham	1986–1988
Helen Corruthers	1990–1992
Bobbie Huskey	1994–1996
Betty Adams Green	2000–2002

president of the American Correctional Association from 2000 to 2002 was Betty Adams Green, the sixth female president of that prestigious organization.[34] Other women of note in contemporary corrections include Kathleen Hawk, who served as the director of the Federal Bureau of Prisons from 1992 to 2003, and Lucie McClung, until recently, commissioner of Correctional Services of Canada.

Because conditions in female institutions vary greatly, it would be fruitless to attempt to describe them individually. They are not all horror stories; it is sufficient to state that the best and the worst aspects of the male institution are also in evidence in the female prison, the only major differences being the variations based on the traits unique to each gender and the varied training and education programs available to males. Figure 15.6 lists programs that were available to female prisoners at the end of 2003.

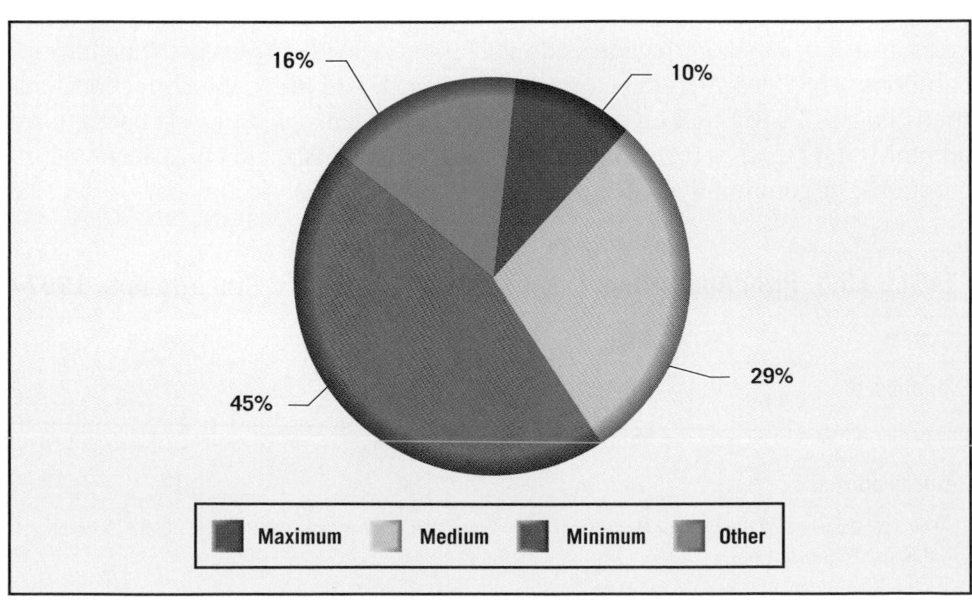

FIGURE 15.5

Female Prison Inmates, by Classification, 2005

SOURCE: American Correctional Association, *2005 Directory* (Lanham, MD: ACA, 2005), p. 56.

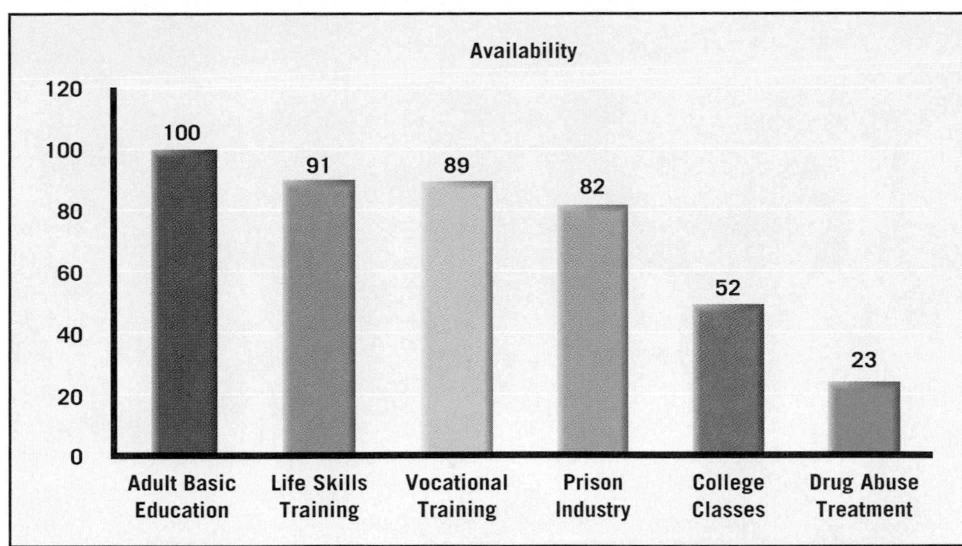

FIGURE 15.6

Vocational Training Programs for Female Prisoners, 1998 (in percent)

SOURCE: Editors, "Female Offenders," *Corrections Compendium* 23:3 (1998): 9.

One notable difference between prisons for males and females lies in the fact that many states only have one major facility for females compared to many prisons for males. As a result, a state's female prison will often house every classification level: high, close, medium, and minimum all within one compound. Unlike the male prison where one or two levels may be present, the range of classification levels within female institutions poses unique management issues.

SPECIAL PROBLEMS FOR INCARCERATED FEMALES

Among the many problems female inmates face when in prison are pregnancy, loss of family ties, and aging behind the walls. We start this discussion with the pregnant inmate entering prison. Earlier studies suggest that some one in four adult females entering prison either were pregnant or had given birth to an infant within the last twelve months.[35] In 2003, more than 2,100 pregnant females

Female inmates learn useful skills in modern prisons.

Photo by Drew Crawford, courtesy of The Image Works.

Female inmates relaxing at Julia Tutwiler Prison, Alabama.
Photo by A. Ramey, courtesy of PhotoEdit.

were imprisoned and more than 1,400 babies were born in prison.[36] Medical care, resources, and programs, while varying across institutions, are thought to be inadequate for such inmates. A primary explanation for the lack of programs has been the relatively small size of the female offender population and the expense involved in special programming for the small segment of prisoners that female inmates represent. The size argument, however valid in past decades, does not hold in current correctional scenes. Although female inmates remain a small portion of the total prison populations, their numbers have increased to the point that new policies are needed.

Pregnant inmates need special diets, lighter work assignments, supportive programs, and a less stressful environment. Programs and resources are needed for miscarriages, premature birth, and deliveries. Until recently,[37] the major options were abortion, placing children with relatives, putting the children up for adoption, or foster care. Not only do such forced separation policy options pose severe emotional anguish and problems for mothers, separation of the newborn child from the mother can create severe emotional and developmental problems for the infant.[38] Many prisons are now starting to provide family services as well as classes in child development and parenting, parental functioning, and stress management. Some female prisons have even started programs that allow young infants to remain with their mothers. For example, Washington State has a nursery program at its female prison in Gig Harbor that includes an Early Head Start component. Inmate mothers are accountable for the twenty-four-hour care of their children while living in a supervised environment.[39] The accompanying Correctional Brief describes California's Community Prisoner Mother Program, which is operated by its Department of Corrections.[40] Unfortunately, while such programs have been introduced in a number of prisons across the country, the percentage of inmates that can participate is still relatively low.

In addition, research on female inmates documents that females are more family oriented than male inmates and that as many as 80 percent of imprisoned females are mothers.[41] Evidence of the significance children play in the life of female inmates can be seen in pictures displayed on desks or taped behind prison identification badges, articles in prison newspapers, the frequency with which children are dis-

CORRECTIONAL BRIEF

California Community Prisoner Mother Program

In seven small, community-based facilities throughout California, inmate mothers live with their young children. The Community Prisoner Mother Program (CPMP) is designed to build better parenting relationships and brighter futures while the inmates serve their time.

While in the program, mothers reestablish bonds with their children and prepare to return to the community as working, productive members. The homelike facilities provide a stable, caregiving environment. At the same time, mothers learn valuable skills. In preemployment training, they gain practical information and tips about applying for, landing, and keeping a job.

In specialized parenting classes, they learn how to talk and relate to their children and how to discipline effectively. Both mothers and children also may receive counseling.

Because the majority of the mothers have had some sort of chemical dependency in the past, they also attend drug education classes geared to keep them from returning to their old habits, make them aware of the dangers of drug addiction, and show them how drugs impair both their lives and the lives of their children.

cussed, and general concern about the well-being of their individual children. Many females feel their families and friends have abandoned them when they are sent to prison, just when their needs for support and friendship are highest and inmates are at the lowest point of their lives: ashamed, incarcerated, lonely, depressed, guilt ridden, acutely worried about their children, scared, and with tarnished self-esteem. Family members are particularly central at this time, since they can care for the inmate's children and bring them to visit, send money and special foods, write and call, guard their property, and take up their cause if mistreated by institutional staff. Thus, visiting is of crucial importance to female inmates who sense—if not know—that their role as mother is weak and their incarceration and absence can lead to a child's behavioral problems (obsessive crying, deterioration in relations with peers and school work, withdrawal from relatives and reality, and so on).

"Sally" with her son "Bob" in a California Community Prisoner Mother Program facility.

Courtesy of State of California Department of Corrections.

Andrea Yates, accused of killing her five children.

Photo by Reuters NewMedia, Inc., courtesy of Corbis/Bettmann.

Although failure of relatives to visit is a great hardship for most incarcerated mothers, often it results more from physical and institutional barriers than lack of care and concern on the part of relatives. Many institutions are located far away from the urban centers from which most female inmates originate, and travel and related expenses are hurdles to be overcome. Many relatives do not own cars and must depend on the kindness of neighbors for travel. Other discouraging factors include having to submit to searches before visiting, being too poor to afford overnight accommodations, or having work schedules too tight to permit frequent or lengthy visits. Some institutions are not "visitor friendly," with visits limited in frequency to once a month, provision of only one large room for visitations of all families, having no children's toys or a playground, and presenting an unfriendly and hostile setting. Better managed institutions (such as in Nebraska and New York) have children's nurseries, play areas, and equipment; allow conjugal and family visits; and provide accommodations for mothers to plan, cook for, and feed their children in separate visiting rooms and trailers. Weekend passes, home visits, home furloughs, halfway house placements, and frequent visiting privileges not only ease parenting problems but also lessen the probability that the children will become innocent victims. Clearly there is a need for institutions to establish policies that encourage **family cohesion** and strengthen ties for the mother when she is eventually released. Figure 15.7 lists the types of visitation privileges available to female inmates.

The third major problem is aging in prison. The graying of America is reflected in prison populations, as seen in Table 15.4. This is particularly a problem with the older female inmates undergoing social, psychological, emotional, and physical changes within the institutional walls.[42] Females in America tend to live longer than men (about seven or eight years), and make up about 60 percent of older Americans. In prison, they are "forgotten" inmates and have been little studied or recognized. Incarceration encourages dependency and passivity, factors that tend to shorten life expectancy under any circumstance. Visual, physical, and muscular impairments pose particular problems for elderly female inmates. Not only will staff have to be specifically trained and programs individualized, but gerontology consultants and medical programs also will be

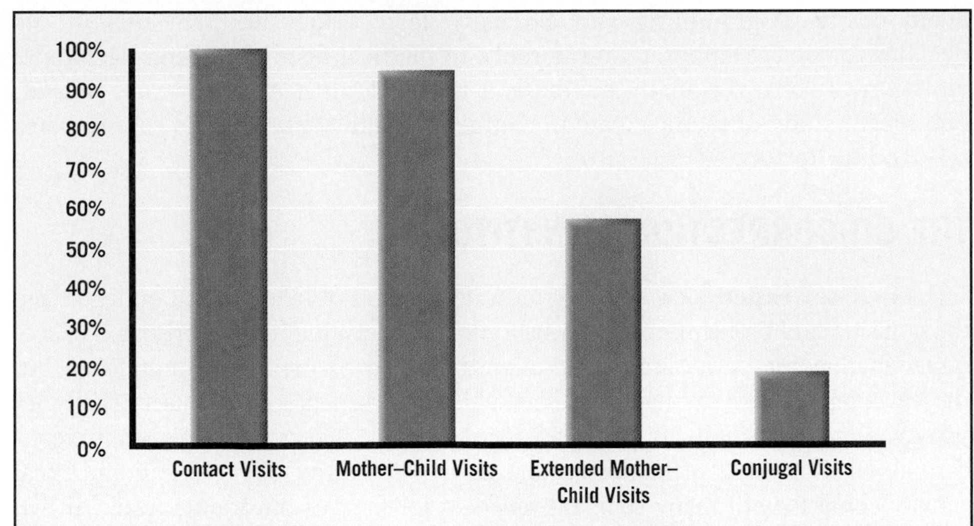

FIGURE 15.7

Jurisdictions with Visiting Privileges for Female Prisoners, 2003 (in percent)

SOURCE: Editors, "Female Offenders," *Corrections Compendium* 29:3 (2003): 22–24. No data for five jurisdictions.

required that address issues such as dealing with menopause, breast cancer, hysterectomies, eye cataracts, and hip, spine, and back impairments. As the numbers of elderly female inmates swell, physical plants will need to be retrofitted, including color coding of floors and buildings, adding wall handrails and wheelchair ramps, widening door frames and entries, providing rest areas for more challenged inmates, and revamping space to include nursing and convalescent rooms and services. Special diets, medications, nursing patterns, and physical therapy will need to be initiated and expanded. It is clear a correctional crisis is in the making and that prisons are not conducive to caring for the elderly (age sixty-five and over), aged (age seventy-five plus), or very old (age eighty-five and over). Alternative sentencing, timely and compassionate release, and community correctional centers are more realistic options for those who pose no threat to the community or self. Correctional action now may

TABLE 15.4 Inmate Population over Age Fifty-Five, 1988–2004 Inmates

COMPARISON	MALES	FEMALES
1988	13,955	511
1990	17,244	709
1992	21,564	875
1994	25,832	1,141
1998	43,258	2,043
2000	38,200	1,900
2004	71,038	3,792
Change	+409%	+642%

SOURCE: American Correctional Association, *ACA Directory, 1999* (Lanham, MD: ACA, 1999), and American Correctional Association, *2005 Directory* (Lanham, MD: ACA, 2005), p. 54.

avoid costly programming and extensive legal issues and lawsuits in the decades to come. Deliberate indifference to medical needs has been declared a violation of constitutionally guaranteed rights (Eighth Amendment). Indeed, one recent study of medical care in a large jail facility likened the care inmates received to "torture."[43]

THE CO-CORRECTIONAL INSTITUTION

The **single-sex experience** and long-term deprivation of heterosexual outlets create the same kinds of problems in female institutions as are found in male prisons. The recommendations for coeducational institutions may seem extreme to the uninitiated, but the leavening effect of a system that allows at least nonsexual social contact in daily activity with members of the opposite sex is considerable. Excessive administrative concern about overt signs of friendship that may be indicative of possible homosexual activity conflicts with many standard practices for females outside the walls. If two males were observed holding hands as they walked down the street, they would be suspected of being gay. That same behavior, though not considered at all strange for females (and particularly girls) on the outside, is viewed with great suspicion inside the walls, for girls and adult females alike. An inmate graphically describes the situation:

> *It's tough to be natural. The thing that most of us are trying to accomplish here, we're trying to get our minds at a point to where we can handle whatever comes our way, to get our emotions balanced, to maybe straighten up our way of thinking. You know, it just makes it hard when you're trying to be a natural person—to react to things normally—when the staff won't let you be normal—when you do a normal thing that being a woman makes it normal, and then have them say no, you can't do that because if you do, that's personal contact and that's homosexuality. So there's our mental hassle.*
>
> *I know that when females are thrown together without men or without the companionship of men it makes it pretty rough on them—females being the emotional people that they are. They have to have a certain amount of affection and close companionship. You know, a woman, if she's with a man she'll put her hand on him or maybe she'll reach up and touch him. This is something that a woman does naturally without thinking, and so if a woman has a good friend, or an affair, she does the same thing because this is her nature. The thing of it is—like I have a friend at the cottage—neither one of us have ever played. We're never gonna play. And if somebody tried to force us into it, we couldn't, wouldn't, or what have you. But being a woman and after being here for quite a while, we put our arms around each other, we don't think there's anything the matter with it, because there's nothing there—it's a friendship. We're walking down the hall, our records are both spotless, she's a council girl, I'm Minimum A [minimum custody classification]. I've never had anything on my record that was bad and my god, the supervisor comes out and says, "Now, now girls, you know we don't allow that sort of thing here." And we look at her and say, "What sort of thing?" "This personal contact." And yet this same supervisor, we saw her up at the corner putting her arm around another supervisor the same way we were doing. So this is where part of our mental hassle comes in.*[44]

The redefinition of the natural acts just described into something considered evil and proscribed is another reason that institutionalization is so crippling to the long-term female prisoner. As inmates, male or female, learn that simple signs of friendship are prohibited, they learn to repress their impulses toward interpersonal warmth when they get out. The kind of behavior that makes them acceptable on the inside makes them appear hard case (unfeeling, unresponsive) on the outside. In the male this kind of coldness can be viewed as "tough" or "macho," but is sometimes considered unattractive.

Until recently, very few studies have been conducted on the homosexuality of female prisoners. Much conjecture is found in the literature, but true scientific research is rare. Even the monumental effort to compile statistics on female offenders in Sheldon and Eleanor Glueck's *500 Delinquent Women*[45] did not consider homosexuality, but gender and sex role research is increasing.[46]

The demands of institutional management make it difficult to prevent homosexual activity. There are never enough personnel to watch all of the inmates, so lovers get together despite the staff's efforts. In many institutions the staff adopts the attitude of "looking the other way" with regard to the female inmates' sexual activity. (The same is true in many men's institutions[47]; see Chapter 16.) It is possible that homosexuality and homosociality are even more prevalent in female institutions than in men's, because a high percentage of the inmates have been so misused by men[48] that they have already turned to other females to fulfill their emotional needs on the outside. In addition, prisons for females are generally less secure and less compartmentalized, making it easier for women to interact. It is also quite possible that the impact of imprisonment is significantly different for females, tending to encourage a homosexual response. Females appear more likely to view arrest, jailing, the court trial, and commitment to prison in highly personal terms. This personalized reaction could harden antisocial attitudes and lead to further illegal behavior. One study has identified three **psychological deprivations** that might contribute to homosexual behavior[49]:

1. Affection starvation and need for understanding
2. Isolation from previous symbiotic interpersonal relations
3. Need for continued intimate relationships with a person.

It is hard to imagine an incarcerated felon (male or female) who does not suffer those deprivations to some degree.

The co-correctional, or coeducational, prison is a new development in corrections. Two were opened in 1971 in the federal Bureau of Prisons system. Since that time there have been many coed adult state and federal facilities; eighty-four coed facilities existed in 1998.[50] John Smykla and J. Williams defined adult cocorrections as adult institutions, the major purpose of which is the institutional confinement of felons. Each is managed by one institutional administration and has regular programs or areas in which female and male inmates have daily opportunities for interaction.[51] The general concept of **co-correctional institutions** is as follows[52]:

1. To reduce the dehumanizing and destructive aspects of confinement by allowing continuity or resumption of heterosexual relationships
2. To reduce the institutional control problems through the weakening of disruptive homosexual systems, reduction of predatory homosexual activity, lessening of assaultive behavior, and the diversion of inmate interests and activities

SIDEBARS

Co-Correctional Programs

A co-correctional program is a management program for adult prisons, the major purpose of which is confining felons, that has a single institutional administrator and regular programs or areas in which both male and female inmates have daily opportunities for interaction. The coeducational institution reduces levels of tension in the prison and violent homosexual behaviors between males. Female homosexuality is infrequent. Inmates have positive feelings about serving their time, feel they are safe from violence, and benefit from a less controlled atmosphere. Some sexual behavior has resulted, but correctional administrators are more concerned with public image and potential criticism of their management approach than they are with emotionally laden sexual relations.

3. To protect inmates likely to be involved in "trouble" were they in a same-sex institution
4. To provide an additional tool for creating a more normal, less institutionalized atmosphere
5. To cushion the shock of adjustment for releasees, by reducing the number and intensity of adjustments to be made
6. To realize economies of scale in terms of more efficient utilization of available space, staff, and programs
7. To provide relief of immediate or anticipated overcrowding, sometimes of emergency proportions
8. To reduce the need for civilian labor, by provision of both light and heavy inmate workforces
9. To increase diversification and flexibility of program offerings, and equal access for males and females
10. To expand treatment potentials for working with inmates having "sexual problems," and development of positive heterosexual relationships and coping skills
11. To provide relief from immediate or anticipated legal pressures to provide equal access to programs and services to both sexes
12. To expand career opportunities for females, previously often "boxed into" the single state female institutions, as co-correctional staff.

The question of whether these objectives have been met cannot yet be answered, primarily because evaluations of their effectiveness continue to be weak at best.[53]

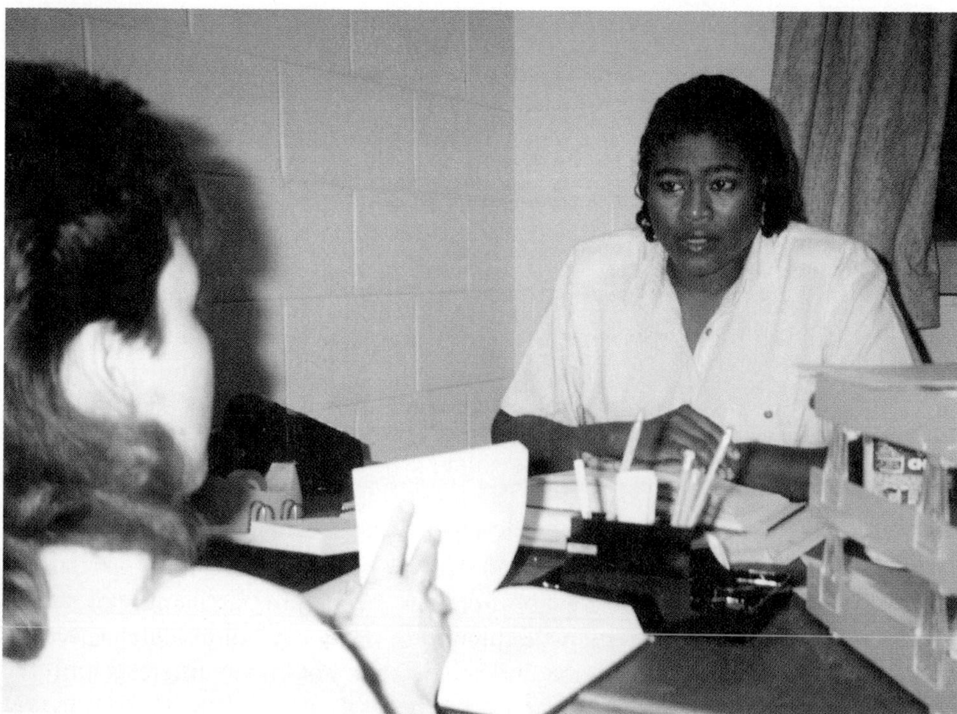

One-on-one counseling works well in a female facility.
Courtesy of New York Department of Corrections.

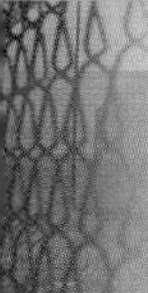

CORRECTIONAL BRIEF

Girl Scouts Beyond Bars

Children of prison inmates are the hidden victims of their parents' crimes. Like children of divorced or deceased parents, they often show signs of distress caused by the lack of a stable home life and parental separation, such as depression, aggression, poor school performance, and truancy. Many times they also follow their parents' criminal behavior patterns. To keep mothers and daughters connected and to enhance parenting skills, Girl Scouts Beyond Bars involves mothers in their daughters' lives through a unique partnership between a youth services organization and state and local corrections departments.

Girl Scouts Beyond Bars programs have been implemented in the following states:

- *Maryland* In 1992 the pilot program began at the Maryland Correctional Institution for Women. More than thirty girls now visit their mothers two Saturdays each month. On alternate Saturdays, they attend meetings at a community church, just as girls in other troops would. Before the Girl Scout program started, many of these girls rarely visited their incarcerated mothers.
- *Florida* Florida's first program started at the Jefferson Correctional Institution near Tallahassee in early 1994, and a second program soon followed in Fort Lauderdale. The Florida Department of Corrections hopes to expand the program to correctional facilities throughout the state. The program includes formal parenting instruction and transitional services for the mothers and monitoring of the children's school performance, and collaboration with mental health care providers.
- *Ohio* The Seal of Ohio Girl Scout Council launched the first program in a prerelease center, the Franklin Pre-Release Center in Columbus. When the Girl Scout council expanded the program to the Ohio Reformatory for Women in 1994, Ohio became the first to connect the in-prison program with the transition to home.
- *Arizona* Maricopa County (Phoenix) is the first jail site in the country to form a Girl Scouts Beyond Bars partnership. Parents Anonymous and Big Brothers/Big Sisters have also joined the effort.

Girl Scout councils in four other states have also begun Girl Scouts Beyond Bars programs with their corrections partners. While the partnership has demonstrated its ability to increase mother-daughter visitation time, the long-term effect of breaking the cycle of criminal behavior will require a more comprehensive approach on the part of the correctional institution, the Girl Scout council, and the mothers involved.

The program, however, can be used as a model to involve more youth service organizations in crime prevention. Partnerships should include many community service organizations that can provide the range of support services for incarcerated parents and their children to stop negative social behaviors and to break intergenerational cycles of involvement in crime.

SOURCE: Marilyn C. Moses. "Keeping Incarcerated Mothers and Their Daughters Together: Girl Scouts Beyond Bars," *Program Focus* (Washington, DC: National Institute of Justice, 1994), p. 2.

COMMUNITY CORRECTIONS AND FEMALE OFFENDERS

Our review of the problems posed by female offenders as well as problems female inmates face due to incarceration has suggested that most female offenders pose little danger to public safety, that substance abuse underlies much of their criminal behavior, and that much damage to inmates and their families may be done through incarcerating those whose basic problem is alcohol and/or drug abuse.

Institutions for females are not known for the long-term effectiveness of their "inside the walls" treatment programs, which tend to be limited in number and occur in an artificial environment, thus reducing their effectiveness.[54] What is needed are more reasonable risk reduction programs that speak to the underlying problems that have led to criminal behavior and incarceration. Those are, of course, generally found in the community, and include halfway houses, group homes, residential treatment facilities, mental health and substance abuse programs, probation, and other intermediate sanctions as discussed in more detail in the chapters on probation, parole, and reentry. Such programs have long been recommended for nonviolent offenders, and were reiterated by the Alliance of Non-Governmental Organizations on Crime Prevention and Criminal Justice in 1987.[55]

CORRECTIONAL BRIEF

Females and Crime Fighting

One of the more overlooked facts about the criminal justice system is that women suffer significantly from the failings of crime-fighting policy. Though men dominate prison populations in raw numbers, women are the fastest growing category of prisoners nationwide. In the 1980s, taxpayers financed the construction of thirty-four prisons for women, compared to only seven in the 1960s. In a 1990 survey, the American Correctional Association found that nearly half of the jurisdictions nationwide were planning to build additional jails for women. Women offenders have been affected harshly by changes in sentencing laws, by the impact of the War on Drugs, and by laws that allow for the termination of child custody if parents are imprisoned.

The imbalances of our crime-fighting policies are even more critical to women. None of our current strategies have stemmed the single greatest threat to the safety of women: domestic violence. The federal Centers for Disease Control and Prevention reports that more women seek treatment in hospitals for injuries from domestic violence than from all muggings, car accidents, and rapes combined.

SOURCE: Steven R. Donziger (ed.), *The Real War on Crime* (New York: HarperCollins, 1996), p. 146.

There are now more than 906,600 females on probation (23 percent of adult probationers, up from 21 percent in 1990), and an additional 108,200 on parole (14 percent of all parolees, up from 12 percent in 2000).[56] Unfortunately, gender-specific programs are often lacking, and residential programs specifically designated for females are often found only in the largest urban areas.

Because female offenders seldom pose much threat to public safety and are seldom violent, managing them in a community-wide, coordinated correctional system with graduated degrees of supervision in the community is a viable option for this correctional population.

For those females who are incarcerated, it is equally important to develop and expand family-based programming to allow them to maintain contact with their children.

SUMMARY

This review of the expanding role of the female offender on the correctional scene reveals the overuse of imprisonment as a correctional alternative in sentencing. This policy does not reflect contemporary correctional thought or recommended practice.

The philosophy of the reintegration model is to handle as many causes of criminal behavior as possible in the environment in which it arises—that is, in the local community. Sentencing low-danger/risk female offenders to prisons run by state authorities does little to deal with the causes that have contributed to the criminal events that bring the female offender before a sentencing court. Indeed, imprisonment itself is likely to lessen the ability of the female offender to function when released on parole, because imprisonment ruptures familial, economic, social, and parental ties. Separation from children due to incarceration is a major problem faced by returning mothers.

Local communities and counties, working in conjunction with volunteer and professional organizations (such as the International Community Corrections Association, the National Council on Crime and Delinquency, the John Howard Society, and the National Center on Institutions and Alternatives), continue to develop and maintain correctional programs that allow the female offender to remain in the local community and support the process of reintegrating offenders by involvement with local agencies. Reintegration is clearly the direction of the future for female offenders.

Now that we have examined the female clients who are sent on different paths from the jail environment, we move on to an even larger problem—male inmates and what to do with them in a society that has grown alarmed over and hardened to the violence on the street that makes headlines. How we have dealt, are dealing, and should deal with male offenders are questions for the next chapter.

REVIEW QUESTIONS

1. What are the major crimes for which females are convicted? Explain why.
2. Why have females been treated so differently in the correctional system?
3. What impact does incarceration have on "mothering" of children?
4. Develop a model for handling the female offender that would have differing degrees of social control and offer female criminals an opportunity to stop criminal activity.
5. Describe the typical female inmate.
6. Identify three groups of special-problem female offenders and their specific needs.
7. How has the War on Drugs impacted corrections and specifically female offenders?
8. What should be done with the pregnant female prison inmate? With her baby?
9. What special problems do female offenders who have been victims of prior abuse face when they are imprisoned?

ENDNOTES

1. Paige Harrison and Allen Beck, *Prison and Jail Inmates at Midyear 2004* (Washington, DC: Bureau of Justice Statistics, 2005), p. 8.
2. Michael Tonry, "Why Are U.S. Incarceration Rates So High?" *Overcrowded Times* 10:3 (1999): 1, 8–16. See particularly p. 8.
3. Most apprehended drug couriers ("mules") are female. If arrested in New York City's John F. Kennedy Airport, they could be sentenced under New York statutes for a minimum penalty of three years to life imprisonment, but the sentence may be reduced to lifetime probation if the mule provides "material assistance" leading to the arrest of a drug dealer or higher placed drug entrepreneur. Few mules can offer "material assistance" of any prosecutorial value because they are so marginally involved (if at all) with the ongoing criminal enterprise. In 1996, U.S. district courts granted almost 8,000 "substantial assistance reductions," almost two-thirds of which were granted to drug offenders. Few were granted to females. William Sobol, *Time Served in Prison by Federal Offenders: 1996–97* (Washington, DC: U.S. Department of Justice, 1999), p. 5.
4. Federal Bureau of Investigation, *Crime in the United States 2003* (Washington, DC: U.S. Department of Justice, 2004).
5. Ibid.
6. Freda Adler, *Sisters in Crime* (New York: McGraw-Hill, 1975). See also Bernard Schissel and K. Fedec, "The Selling of Innocence," *Canadian Journal of Criminology* 41:1 (1994): 33–56.
7. Federal Bureau of Investigation, *Crime in the United States 2003.* See also Jacqueline Boles and K. Elifson, "Sexual Identity and HIV: The Male Prostitute," *Journal of Sex Research* 31:1 (1994): 39–46; Thomas Calhoun and G. Weaver, "Rational Decision-Making Among Male Street Prostitutes," *Deviant Behavior* 17:2 (1996): 209–227; and Leon Pettiway, *Honey, Honey Miss Thang: Being Black, Gay and On the Streets* (Philadelphia: Temple University Press, 1996).
8. Studies of lifetime prevalence of intimate partner abuse suggest that at least four in ten females will be physically and sexually abused during their lifetimes. There is some evidence that physical and sexual abuse may be highest for females age eighteen to thirty-nine, with monthly income of less than $1,000, children under age eighteen being at home, and those ending a relationship within the last twelve months. Stephen Dearwater, J. Coben, J. Campbell, et al., "Prevalence of Intimate Partner Abuse in Women Treated at Community Hospital Emergency Departments," *Journal of the American Medical Association* 280:5 (1998): 433–438.
9. Robert Meier and G. Geis, *Victimless Crime? Prostitution, Drugs, Homosexuality and Abortion* (Los Angeles: Roxbury Publishing, 1997); Barrie Flowers, *The Prostitution of Women and Girls* (Jefferson, NC: McFarland, 1998); and Karen Stout and B. McPhail, *Confronting Sexism and Violence Against Women: A Challenge for Social Work* (New York: Longman, 1998).
10. See Ira Sommers, D. Baskin, and J. Fagan, "The Structural Relationship Between Drug Use, Drug Dealing and Other Income Support Activities Among Women Drug Users," *Journal of Drug Issues* 26:4 (1996): 975–1006; John Potterat, R. Rothenberg, S. Muth, et al., "Pathways to Prostitution," *Journal of Sex Research* 35:4 (1998): 333–340; and Tove P. Tiby, "The Production and Reproduction of Prostitutions," *Journal of Scandinavian Studies in Crime and Crime Prevention* 3:2 (2003): 154–172.
11. Joanne Belknap, *The Invisible Woman: Gender, Crime and Justice* (Belmont, CA: Wadsworth, 1996).
12. Cynthia Seymour (ed.), "Children with Parents in Prison," *Child Welfare* 77:5 (1998): 469–639; James Boudouris, *Parents in Prison* (Lanham, MD: American

Correctional Association, 1996); and Bonnie Green, J. Miranda, A. Daroowalla, and J. Siddique, "Trauma, Mental Health Functioning, and Program Needs of Women in Jail," *Crime and Delinquency* 51:1 (2005): 131–151.
13. Amnesty International, *"Mothers Behind Bars,"* www.amnesty-usa.org/_ rightsforall/women/ report-101.html (accessed August 9, 1999).
14. As early as 1984, Candace Kruttschnitt and D. Green were debunking the chivalry assumptions in their "The Sex-Sanctioning Issue: Is It History?" *American Sociological Review* 49:4 (1984): 541–551. See also Ellen Steury and F. Nancy, "Gender Bias and Pretrial Release: More Pieces of the Puzzle," *Journal of Criminal Justice* 18:5 (1990): 417–432; and Randall Shelden, "Confronting the Ghost of Mary Ann Crouse: Gender Bias in the Juvenile Justice System," *Juvenile and Family Court Journal* 49:1 (1998): 11–26.
15. Mark Pogrebin and E. Poole, "Sex, Gender and Work: The Case of Women Jail Officers," in Jeffrey Ulmer (ed.), *Sociology of Crime, Law and Deviance* (Stamford, CT: JAI Press, 1998), pp. 105–126.
16. B. Farnsworth and R. Teske, "Gender Differences in Felony Court Processing," *Women and Criminal Justice* 6:2 (1995): 23–44.
17. Meda Chesney-Lind, "Women in Prison: From Partial Justice to Vengeful Equity," *Corrections Today* 60:7 (1998): 66–73.
18. Susan Crawford and R. Williams, "Critical Issues in Managing Female Offenders," *Corrections Today* 60:7 (1998): 130–134.
19. Bureau of Justice Statistics, *Prison and Jail Inmates at Midyear 2002* (Washington, DC: BJS, 2003).
20. Louise Bill, "The Victimization and Revictimization of Female Offenders," *Corrections Today* 60:7 (1998): 106–112.
21. Donna Kerr, "Substance Abuse Among Female Offenders," *Corrections Today* 60:7 (1998): 114–120.
22. Bureau of Justice Statistics, Prison and Jail Inmates at Midyear 2003 (Washington, DC: BJS, 2004).
23. Doris J. James, *Profile of Jail Inmates, 2002,* (Washington, DC: Bureau of Justice Statistics, 2004). Also see Tracy Snell, *Women in Jail 1989* (Washington, DC: U.S. Department of Justice, 1992), pp. 1–11.
24. Green, Miranda, Daroowalla, and Siddique, "Trauma, Mental Health Functioning."
25. Virginia McCoy, J. Inciardi, and L. Metch, "Women, Crack and Crime," *Contemporary Drug Issues* 22:3 (1995): 435–451; and Meda Chesney-Lind, *The Female Offender: Girls, Women and Crime* (Thousand Oaks, CA: Sage, 1997). See also the theme issue "Female Offenders," *Corrections Today* 60:7 (1998).
26. Boot camps, with their requirements of absolute obedience to authority, may be harmful to female offenders who have been in abusive relationships. See Doris MacKenzie, L. Ellis, S. Simpson, et al., *Female Offenders in Boot Camp* (College Park, MD: University of Maryland, 1994).
27. Bureau of Justice Statistics, *Prison and Jail Inmates at Midyear 2003.*
28. Ibid.
29. L.I.S., Inc., *Profiles of Correctional Substance Abuse Treatment Programs* (Langmont, CO: National Institute of Corrections, 1994); and Christopher Mumola, *Substance Abuse and Treatment, State and Federal Prisoners, 1997* (Washington, DC: U.S. Department of Justice, 1999), p. 13.
30. Caroline Wolf Harlow, *Prior Abuse Reported by Inmates and Probationers* (Washington, DC: U.S. Department of Justice, 1999). For data on abuse across the nation, see Patricia Tjaden and M. Thoennes, *Prevalence, Incidence and Consequences of Violence Against Women* (Washington, DC: U.S. Department of Justice, 1998).
31. Natalie Pearl, "Use of Community-Based Social Services to Reduce Recidivism in Female Parolees," *Women and Criminal Justice* 10:1 (1998): 27–52.
32. Corrections Compendium Survey Summary Female Offenders, Vol. 29(3), 2004: 10–28. Also see American Correctional Association, *Directory* (Lanham, MD: ACA, 1999), p. xxii. Twelve states did not report the number of their facilities and programs for adults.
33. American Correctional Association, *Directory,* p. xlvi. Ten states did not report on wardens and superintendents in adult institutions.
34. Excellent chronicles of female correctional managers can be found in *Women and Criminal Justice.* See in particular Mary Hawkes, "Edna Mahan: Sustaining the Reformatory Tradition," *Women and Criminal Justice* 9:3 (1998): 1–21; and Joann Morton, "Martha E. Wheeler: Redefining Women in Corrections," *Women and Criminal Justice* 5:2 (1994): 3–20. See also Joann Morton (ed.), "Women in Corrections," *Corrections Today* 54:6 (1992): 76–180; and the theme issues on "Best in the Business," *Corrections Today* (yearly).
35. George Church, "The View from Behind Bars," *Time* (September 22, 1990): 20–22.
36. Corrections Compendium Survey Summary Female Offenders. There are no national data, and your authors know of no data on babies born to jail inmates.
37. John Wooldredge and K. Masters, "Confronting Problems Faced by Pregnant Inmates in State Prisons," *Crime and Delinquency* 39:3 (1993): 195–203; and Jessica Pearson and N. Thoennes, "What Happens to Pregnant Substance Abusers and Their Babies?" *Juvenile and Family Court Journal* 47:2 (1996): 15–28.
38. Joann Morton and D. Williams, "Mother/Child Bonding," *Corrections Today* 60:7 (1998): 98–105; and Paula Dressel, J. Porterfield, and S. Barnhill,

"Mothers Behind Bars," *Corrections Today* 60:7 (1998): 90–94.

39. Washington Correctional Center for Women, Washington Department of Corrections, www.wa.gov/doc.
40. Community Prisoner Mother Program (CPMP) California Department of Corrections, www.cdc.state.ca
41. Joann Morton and D. Williams, "Mother/Child Bonding", and Dressel et al., "Mothers Behind Bars."
42. See also Phyllis Ross and J. Lawrence, "Health Care for Women Offenders," *Corrections Today* 60:7 (1998): 122–129; Susan Crawford and R. Williams, "Critical Issues in Managing Female Offenders," *Corrections Today* 60:7 (1998): 130–134.
43. *Estelle v. Gamble,* 97 S. Ct. 285 (1976). See also Michael Vaughn and L. Carroll, "Separate But Unequal: Prison Versus Free-World Medical Care," *Justice Quarterly* 15:1 (1998): 3–40; Kristine Shields and C. de Moya, "Correctional Health Care Nurses' Attitudes Toward Inmates," *Journal of Correctional Health Care* 4:1 (1997): 37–59. See also Michael S. Vaughn and Linda G. Smith, "Practicing Penal Harm Medicine in the United States: Prisoners' Voices from Jail," *Justice Quarterly* 16 (1999): 175–232; Michael Vaughn and Sue Collins, "Medical Malpractice in Correctional Facilities," *The Prison Journal* 84:4 (2004): 505–534; and Paul von Zielbauer, "Private Health Care in Jails Can Be a Death Sentence," *New York Times* (February 27, 2005): A7.
44. David Ward and Gene Kassenbaum, "Sexual Tension in a Woman's Prison," in M. Wolfgang and L. Savitz (eds.), *The Criminal in Confinement* (New York: Basic Books, 1971), pp. 149–150; Candace Kruttschnitt, "Race Relations and the Female Inmate," *Crime and Delinquency* 29:4 (1983): 577–592.
45. Sheldon Glueck and Eleanor Glueck, *500 Delinquent Women* (New York: Knopf, 1934).
46. John Smykla, *Co-Corrections: A Case Study of a Co-Ed Federal Prison* (Washington, DC: University Press of America, 1979). See also Christopher Uggen and C. Kruttsnitt, "Crime in the Breaking: Gender Differences in Desistance," *Law and Society Review* 33:2 (1998): 339–366.
47. Victor Hassine, *Life Without Parole: Living in Prison Today* (Los Angeles: Roxbury, 2002); Robert Johnson and H. Toch, *Crime and Punishment: Inside Views* (Los Angeles: Roxbury, 2000); and Christopher Hensley and Richard Tewksbury, "Warden's Perceptions of Prison Sex," *The Prison Journal* 85:2 (2005): 127–144.
48. Patricia Tjaden and M. Thoennes, *Prevalence, Incidence, and Consequences of Violence Against Women* (Washington, DC: U.S. Department of Justice, 1998); and Bonita Versey, K. de Cou, and L. Prescott, "Effective Management of Female Jail Detainees with Histories of Physical and Sexual Abuse," *American Jails* 16:2 (1998): 50–54.
49. Leslie Acoca and J. Austin, *The Crisis: The Women Offender Sentencing Study and Alternative Sentencing* (Washington, DC: National Council on Crime and Delinquency, 1996).
50. American Correctional Association, *Directory,* p. xxxii.
51. John Smykla and J. Williams, "Co-Corrections in the United States of America, 1970–1990: Two Decades of Disadvantages for Women Prisoners," *Women and Criminal Justice* 8:1 (1996): 61–76.
52. Pamela Schram, "Stereotypes About Vocational Programming for Female Inmates," *The Prison Journal* 78:3 (1998): 255–270.
53. Smykla and Williams, "Co-Corrections in the United States."
54. Paul Gendreau, Shelia A. French, and Angela Taylor, *What Works (What Doesn't Work): The Principles of Effective Correctional Treatment.* International Community Corrections Association Monograph Series (LaCrosse, WI: ICCA, 2002).
55. Alliance of Non-Governmental Organizations on Crime Prevention and Criminal Justice, *Children with Their Mothers* (New York: ANOCOCJ, 1987).
56. Bureau of Justice Statistics, *Prisoners in 2001.*

CHAPTER 16

Male Offenders

We know how hard it is to help prisoners become better men, and many penal authorities have given up too easily on that task. But whatever prisons do, they must not make men needlessly worse.
—John P. Conrad

KEY WORDS

- racial and ethnic groupings
- institutional threat groups
- "designer" drugs
- functionally illiterate
- institutional work assignment
- commitment lag
- population at risk
- age at risk
- prisonization
- homosexual attacks
- family (conjugal) visits
- elderly inmates
- geriatric centers

OVERVIEW

In the last chapter we acquired an understanding of the variety of female offenders who are dealt with as "clients" of the jail and prison systems of America. As we saw in Part 1, until very recently, earlier incarceration practices were not intended to "correct" the behavior of inmates. Consequently, the young and the old, the sick and the well, the women and the men, and the dangerous and the helpless were housed and placed indiscriminately in a single, all-inclusive facility. As the concepts of penitence and corrections were developed, men and women were segregated into separate institutions. Later, institutions became further specialized, with different kinds of institutions for the younger inmates, who were separated from the more hardened felons (though these groups are still sometimes hard to tell apart), and a separate system was created for juveniles (see Chapter 17).

In this chapter we examine the processes used with and conditions of men who have been convicted and sentenced to the adult prisons of America, and probably placed there following some length of exposure to the conditions of jail life. If corrections and prisons can be considered businesses, we continue our analogy by considering adult male inmate groups as clients with different needs, problems, and demands than other types of clients. Using a business analogy, we can describe corrections in all areas as a growth industry. As this chapter unfolds, you will see the crimes for which inmates are committed, problems inmates pose to staff and correctional officers, the inmate culture into which they settle, the realities of danger and death in prison, and the challenges of the aged prisoner. Inmates face widespread boredom, lack of contact with the outside world, dulling routine, and bland and frequently repetitive food. Most institutions are loud, cheerless, and (sometimes) fraught with dangers that range from sexual assault to unwarranted punishment from

New prisoners arrive in chains at the South Florida Reception Center to begin their sentences.
Photo by Daniel Portnoy, courtesy of AP/Wide World Photos.

A lot of "doing time" results in dead time.
Photo by Lew Lause, courtesy of SuperStock, Inc.

correctional officers to gangs, "crazies," and foes. This is the environment into which most inmates step when they are sent to prison.

This chapter deals with several questions. Who are the male prison inmates? What are their needs, and what programs should be devised to address those needs? What should we know about their backgrounds? What happens to the men in the prisons of America?

PRISON POPULATIONS CONTINUE TO SOAR

Keeping track of the rapidly fluctuating adult male prison population is like trying to paint a moving bus. The number of male offenders housed in America's prisons is rising at an alarming rate, along with the total prison population. The population rose from 883,500 in 1993 to the staggering figure of 1,390,906 in the middle of 2004. See Figure 16.1. This does not include more than 60,000 males sentenced to state prisons by the courts but who were, at the time, "holdbacks," that is, inmates being held in county jail facilities because of prison overcrowding.

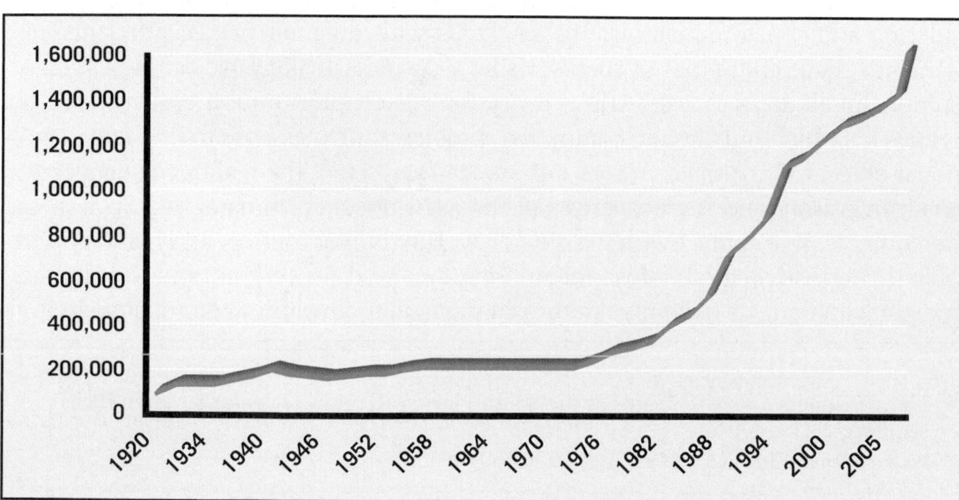

FIGURE 16.1

Sentenced Male Prisoners in State and Federal Institutions in the United States, 1920–2005

SOURCES: *Sourcebook of Criminal Justice Statistics* (2000), "Sentenced Prisoners Under Jurisdiction of State and Federal Correctional Authorities on December 31," www.albany.edu/sourcebook, p. 505; and Paige Harrison and A. Beck, *Prison and Jail Inmates at Midyear 2004* (Washington, DC: Bureau of Justice Statistics, 2005), p. 2.

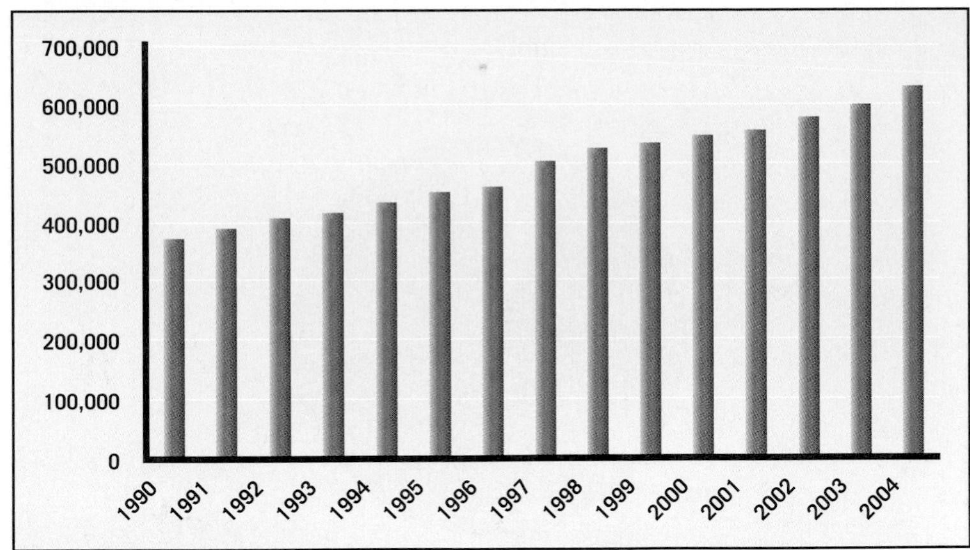

FIGURE 16.2

Number of Male Jail Inmates, 1990–2004

SOURCE: Bureau of Justice Statistics, *Jail Populations by Age and Gender, 1900–2000,* www.ojp.usdoj.gov/bjs/glance/tables/jailagtab.htm; and Doris James, *Profile of Jail Inmates, 2002* (Washington, DC: Bureau of Justice Statistics, 2004), p. 2.

Ninety percent of male inmates were incarcerated in state prisons and slightly more than 10 percent were in federal prisons. Another 33,000 inmates were being held in other adult long-term institutions (for example, the Cook County Department of Corrections, the New York City Department of Corrections, and the Philadelphia Prison System). In total, there are approximately 923 male inmates in adult prisons for every 100,000 male residents in the country. Said differently, almost 1 percent of the adult males in the nation were in prison on a given day in 2004. (Another 433 out of 100,000 adult males are in jail on any given day, and almost nine out of every ten jail inmates are males.) See Figure 16.2.

PRISONER POPULATION

Criminal History

Male prisoners have committed a broad range of criminal acts, and at least eight in ten are recidivists. Violent offenses account for almost half (47 percent) of the crimes for which males were sentenced to prison, and these include homicide, manslaughter, rape, robbery, aggravated assault, sexual assault, and rape. Drug law violations (possession, possession for sale, and trafficking) accounted for one in five sentences being served by males in state correctional facilities. All other crimes, ranging from forgery, fraud, embezzlement, theft, and motor vehicle theft to public order offenses, accounted for one in three male inmates. See Figure 16.3.

We must remember that those sentenced and actually incarcerated in adult prisons are at the bottom of the correctional filter. As a group, men in prisons are undereducated and underemployed, primarily because of their social class and lack of opportunity. Those men are often beset with medical and psychological problems, particularly depression (see Correctional Brief, "Characteristics of Jail Inmates"). Two-thirds are from minority **racial and ethnic groupings,** are poor, and have been unable to cope with the complexities of urban life. Almost one-third or more black men were in jails and prison in 2000 than were enrolled in all college and universities.[1] This sharply reverses the pre-1980 pattern in which black men in colleges and universities outnumbered incarcerated black men by a ratio of three to one. The number in confinement in 2000 was 791,600; the number in institutions of higher education was 603,032. Explanations of this vast disparity include law enforcement bias, selective incapacitation, saturation policing

FIGURE 16.3

Offenses of Male Prisoners in States, 2001

SOURCE: Allen Beck and P. Harrison, *Prisoners in 2001* (Washington, DC: Bureau of Justice Statistics, 2002).

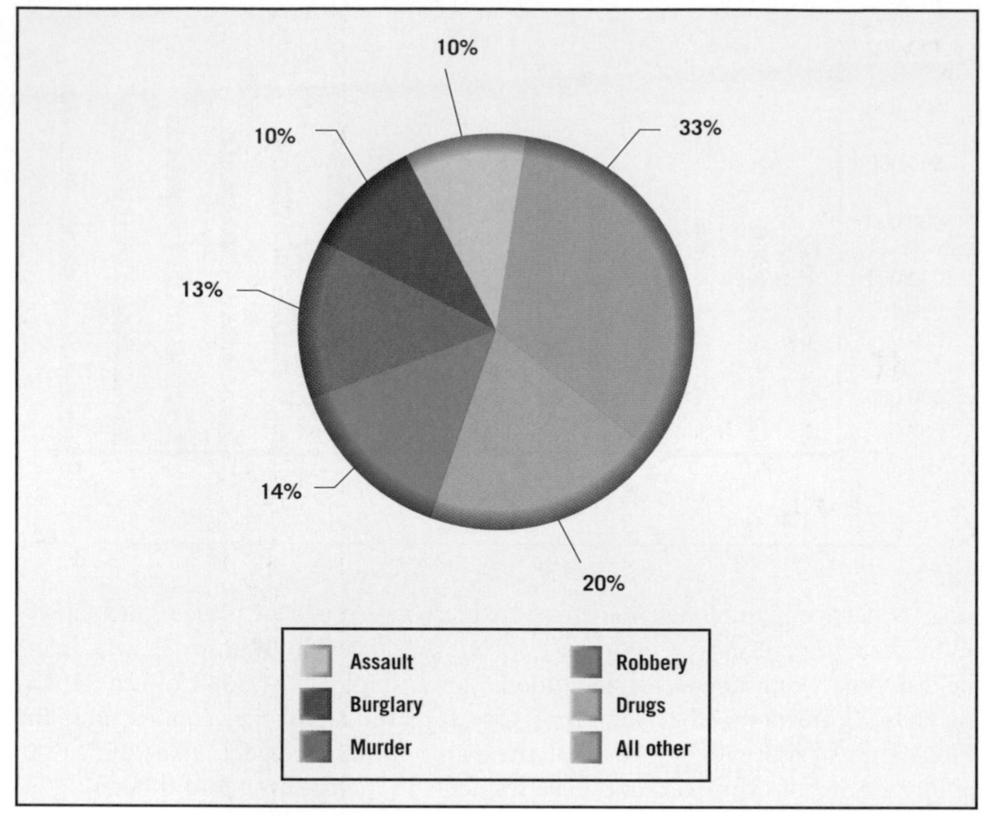

of black neighborhoods, lack of social services and employment opportunities, zero tolerance policies, and law enforcement focusing on crack (rather than cocaine) sales. Crack (primarily for cost factors) is the drug of choice for lower income persons, including blacks; cocaine is most frequently trafficked and used by wealthier whites. But police find that crack sales occur on the streets and public places, are easy to videotape, and can be more readily done with marked bills. In addition, surveillance and arresting officers generally have a clear line

Dead time is also a problem in jail.
Photo by Dennis MacDonald, courtesy of PhotoEdit.

CORRECTIONAL BRIEF

Characteristics of Jail Inmates

There were more than 626,400 male jail inmates at midyear 2004, a majority of whom were black (40 percent) or Hispanic (19 percent) and almost 55 percent of whom had not been convicted. Almost half of jail inmates in 2002 were under correctional or court supervision at the time of their most recent arrest, almost a third on probation, an eighth on parole, and 7 percent on bail or bond. More than seven out of ten male inmates had prior sentences to probation or incarceration; over four in ten had served at least three sentences, and almost one in three were violent recidivists.

More than six in ten convicted male inmates reported they consumed alcohol (beer, wine, or liquor) regularly, and one in three said they had used alcohol at the time of their instant offense. When drug use and alcohol use are combined, half of the convicted male inmates were using drugs or alcohol (or both) at the time of the offense. In 1996, they reported life experiences they had after using alcohol and drugs, and about half said that, through use of alcohol or drugs, they had threatened their own or others' lives, had damaged relationships with other people, or had marred their personal and work histories. Nearly two-thirds confessed to driving a motor vehicle after drinking or drug use, including almost one in five who had been in a subsequent accident. Almost half had been in a physical fight after substance consumption. More than one in five had lost a job because of substance abuse. In 1998, ten percent of sampled jail inmates were positive for one or more drugs consumed while in jail.

More than one-third of male inmates reported they had a physical, mental, or emotional condition, or difficulty seeing, learning, hearing, or speaking. Over their lifetime, more than four in ten had developed an illness, injury, or medical condition that needed professional medical attention. A third had a medical problem in jail (like a cold or the flu). One in twenty had been injured in a fight or assault after admission to jail. Some one in four had at least once received treatment for a mental or emotional problem other than drug or alcohol abuse. In 1998, one in six men was defined as mentally ill; a third of the mentally ill jail inmates were alcohol dependent; and more than one in four will receive mental health services while in jail.

The picture that emerges from the characteristics of men in jail suggests a group of "problemed" men in need of a variety of remedial and interventional programs designed to lessen their criminal activities and proclivities. They appear to be particularly in need of drug and alcohol treatment programs, including self-help groups (such as Alcoholics Anonymous and Narcotics Anonymous), drug resistance training, counseling, residential treatment programs, detoxification, antabuse treatment, or related programming. Despite widespread cynicism about enforced substance abuse treatment, there is accelerating evidence that such treatment works.

Many of these unconvicted defendants will later be committed to prison, where they will receive mostly inadequate or insufficient treatment for their underlying conditions.

SOURCES: Darrell Gilliard, *Prison and Jail Inmates 1998* (Washington, DC: U.S. Department of Justice, 1999); Caroline Wolf Harlow, *Profile of Jail Inmates 1996* (Washington, DC: U.S. Department of Justice, 1998); Paula Ditton, *Mental Health and Treatment of Inmates and Probationers* (Washington, DC: U.S. Department of Justice, 1999); Doris Wilson, *Drug Use, Testing and Treatment in Jails* (Washington, DC: U.S. Department of Justice, 2000); and Doris James, *Profile of Jail Inmates, 2002* (Washington, DC: Bureau of Justice Statistics, 2004).

of sight necessary for successful prosecution on the evidence. These latter factors contribute to building prosecutable and convictable offenses. Approximately 16 percent of black males age twenty to twenty-nine were in prisons in 2004.[2] It is also interesting to note that according to the Government Accounting Office, in 2004, more than 49,000 foreigners were incarcerated in state prisons, the majority from Mexico.

Recent arrivals often have limited job skills and do not know how to use available social services in the community. Many come from broken homes with low annual incomes, frequently have other family members who have been convicted and incarcerated in jails and prisons, and a large number are drug and alcohol abusers. Those characteristics suggest the number of treatment challenges faced by correctional administrators whose mandate is to provide reasonable and effective reintegration services while protecting society from the offenders. The problems in meeting this mission are exacerbated by a hardening of public attitudes toward the male felon.[3]

Dangerousness

Adult male prisons (and almost all other detention facilities) are overcrowded to the danger point,[4] and it is obvious that the present systems will be unable to meet the increasing demands. Some male offenders are extremely dangerous and must be isolated from others. In the 1970s, it was estimated that only some 15 to 25 percent of the male population in prison fell into this category. That situation, however, has changed; overcrowding and citizen alarm about violence in the community have tended to force correctional administrators to find ways to release those men considered least dangerous back into the community. This has left an increasingly greater percentage of violent offenders smoldering in the potential tinderbox of the maximum-security prison, as well as the creation of the supermax prison. In some states, the number of violent offenders in maximum-security prisons who committed crimes against the person is closer to 62 percent and growing, as property offenders are given alternatives to incarceration. The presence of prison gangs (**institutional threat groups**) heightens anxiety, triggers lawsuits, and poses potential personal threat to other inmates.[5]

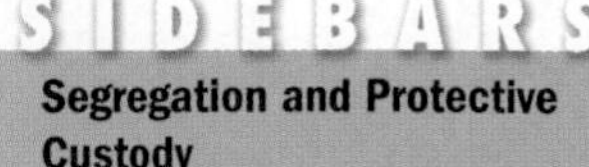

Segregation and Protective Custody

Almost 4 percent of the nation's prison inmates were being held in administrative or disciplinary segregation or in protective custody in 1998.

Drugs and Alcohol

As stated earlier, male offenders tend to be heavy users of alcohol and drugs. In 1997, for example, almost one-third of the men in prison had been drinking at the time of their current offense and more than one-third were under the influence of drugs. That pattern has changed only in the acquisition of a broader catalog of ever more powerful **"designer" drugs**, such as methamphetamine and Ecstasy, many of which can induce violent behavior.

Tests of inmates at male adult prisons and correctional facilities continue to find ongoing drug use. Of all inmates tested, at least 1 percent tested positive for cocaine and heroin. Another 2 percent were positive for methamphetamines, and almost 6 percent were positive for marijuana. These statistics indicate that drug and alcohol abuses are serious problems that continue to contribute negatively to the offenders' behavior, both in the community and in the institutions. In California, some 35 percent of incoming male inmates were convicted of drug law violations. Drug and alcohol treatment programs both in and out of prison are no longer a luxury—they are a necessity.[6]

Drug Treatment

More than 100,000 inmates were in drug treatment programs on January 1, 2002, most in drug addiction groups. This represents only a small percentage of those inmates in need of such treatment.

CORRECTIONAL BRIEF

Suicide in Confinement Facilities

The number of suicides in California's jails increased dramatically in 2001 to a record high of 38, or a rate of 52 per 100,000 jail inmates. Most died of strangulation by using socks, shoelaces, or jail bedding. The California state prison rate was much lower: 21 per 100,000 prisoners.

This jail suicide rate was the highest since 1983, before wrongful death and liability suits led to jail reforms and prevention programs for potentially suicidal inmates. This may be a reflection of the number of mentally ill inmates in jail. The number of mentally ill jail inmates receiving treatment has more than doubled in the last five years.

Many first-time prisoners may become unstable in a confinement environment. The public has increasingly become intolerant of quality-of-life crimes such as aggressive panhandling ("unarmed robbery") and public drunkenness. At the same time, the number of community mental health services and treatment facilities has been drastically reduced, leaving no alternative to jail detention and punishment.

Nationally, there are between 400 and 600 jail suicides each year, about nine in ten by hanging. Suicide is the leading cause of deaths in most jails. The rate (per 100,00 inmates) is four times greater than in the community. There are almost 200 prison suicides each year, a rate that is close to that in the community.

SOURCE: "In California's County Jails, Suicides Are Up Sharply," *The Bakersfield Californian* www.bakersfield.com/24hour/healthscience/v-print/story/436652p-3494415c.html (accessed July 16, 2002); and Lindsay Hayes, "Scope of a National Public Health Problem," *Preventing Suicide* 2:4 (2002): 3.

Education and Work

Education is an important factor in American society; it is viewed by many as an essential prerequisite for economic stability and success. In a high-tech society such as that of the United States, education is crucial for getting a job and earning an adequate income. Despite this need for education, the most recent national survey found that one in five Americans can be considered **functionally illiterate.**[7] As a group, male state prison inmates are less educated than their counterparts in the civilian population. Sixty-three percent of the inmates have not received a high school diploma, in contrast with 36 percent of the general population eighteen years of age or older. This sad situation may become worse if youths pass through our public school systems without being properly prepared to function with developed problem-solving skills in an urban environment. It is not too surprising that crime is often chosen as one alternative for survival under those circumstances. It is not enough that many inmates are now given a chance to earn a high school education in prison; the nation as a whole must insist that the education provided by our public school systems supply the skills needed to keep these men out of prison.

Finally, almost one in four imprisoned men are eligible to be furloughed into an early release procedure, but fewer than half of those eligible are given the opportunity to take such a furlough. Most inmates (69 percent) have some kind of **institutional work assignment**, but the average pay is less than $1 per hour for their work. It is hard to motivate an incarcerated man to make a serious effort to learn a trade while he is working in prison for such low wages, when the same man has made up to $500 a day illegally in his community—and knows it can be done again.

SIDEBARS

Prison Industry Pay

Inmates are paid from 21 cents per hour to $36 a day for work in institutional prison industries (average is a low of $2.63 and a high of $7.64), whereas private prison industries, contracting for work done in prison facilities while using inmate labor, pay from $1.16 per hour to $92 per day (range is between $21.43 and $36.50).

Reasons for the Soaring Prison Populations

As discussed in Chapter 15, the increase in female inmates in prison has been heavily impacted by the War on Drugs and violence. This is true also of male inmates. This

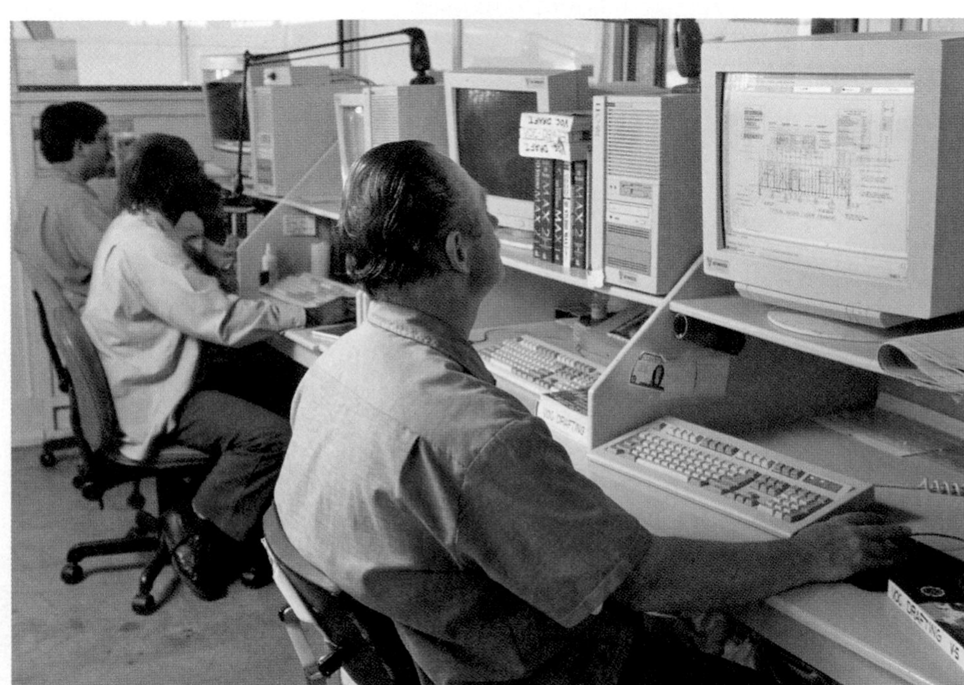

Inmates learn drafting at Deuel Vocational Institution, California.
Photo by Frank Pedrick, courtesy of the ImageWorks.

factor was discussed in Chapter 3, in terms of a pendulum swing toward strong enforcement and the opening up of the floodgates into adult male prisons. Violent offenses accounted for 54 percent of the prison population increase from 1990 to 2004; drug offenses were the second largest category.[8] More than one in five male state prison inmates, and almost six of ten federal prison inmates, are serving time for a drug law violation or drug-related crime. A decline in the prison release rate (down from 37 to 31 per 100 state prisoners) and an increase in the number of parole violators returned to prison account for most of the rest of the portion of the prison population growth.

As discussed, prison populations have sharply increased, much to the dismay of both prisoner advocates and concerned correctional administrators. There is little agreement on the exact reasons for the population boom, although some correctional personnel are quick to note that the police and courts may have become more efficient more quickly than the correctional subsystem did. Not only did law enforcement increase in efficiency, but expanded use of plea bargaining by prosecutors led to more commitments to prison. Court administration procedures were enhanced by using computers and other technology, further feeding the growth of prison populations.

Others have identified the hardening of public opinion as a factor, pointing out that judges are perceiving considerable local pressure to commit offenders rather than use other alternatives. It could be that the reaction to crime in America has exceeded the threshold of fear[9] and reached panic proportions, with widespread public clamor for commitments contributing to prison overpopulation. This is particularly probable in the drug abuse area.[10]

It is more likely, however, that one cause is the increase in the **population at risk,**[11] those males in the age range of eighteen to twenty-nine. Inasmuch as crime is a young person's occupation and considering the fact that the number of persons in the high crime rate ages doubled between 1965 and 1985, one would expect the factor of age to contribute heavily to the overpopulation of American prisons. The **age at risk** problem was made worse by a population shift over the last fifteen years,

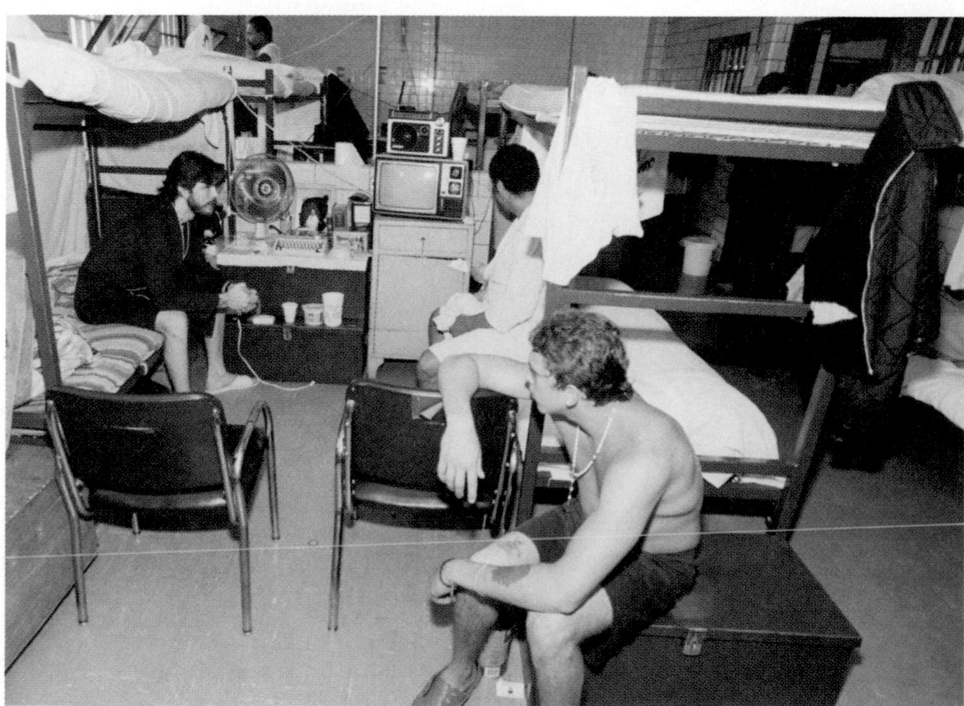

Inmates begin the day in a crowded dormitory at a prison in the Northeast.
Photo by Jim Shea, courtesy of AP/Wide World Photos.

CORRECTIONAL BRIEF

Effect of the Baby Boom

After World War II, returning soldiers tended to marry young and begin families. The result was a large number of offspring born between 1945 and 1964, some 200 percent larger than would have been expected had the war not created delays in family formation and childbearing.

These large numbers of children worked their way through the school system, and the children matured, creating overcrowding first in grade school and then in high school populations. Many baby boomers entered college, creating another service-delivery crisis.

The significance of the baby boom for corrections lay in the high crime rate years of ages nineteen to twenty-nine, when offenders were most likely to commit crime. Thus, the baby boom struck the correctional system from about 1970 to 1985. Because there is a **commitment lag** (generally ten years) between early onset of criminal behavior and being sent to prison, correctional overcrowding in the late 1980s can be seen as caused in part by World War II.

Baby boomers have themselves begun families, and there is an "echo boom" in the offing that will continue to affect the criminal justice system and corrections in the first decade of the twenty-first century.

during which families with young sons moved to urban areas from rural environments. The rural settings had provided more control and more wholesome outlets for young men. Historically, such population shifts—regardless of the population group in motion—meant that the second generation engaged in more frequent criminal behavior. In that case, recent population shifts coincided with an increase in the population at risk, and we can therefore expect the committed population to rise for several more years.

Three other factors have contributed to the growth in male prison populations, although the amount of effect is not yet precisely known. First, sentence enhancements were enacted by many states and include lengthening of prison sentences, enactment of three-strikes legislation (in some states mandating twenty years to be served in prison before possibility of parole release), and "prior imprisonment" statutes, mandating prison terms for any subsequent felony conviction, even if the first disposition was not incarceration.

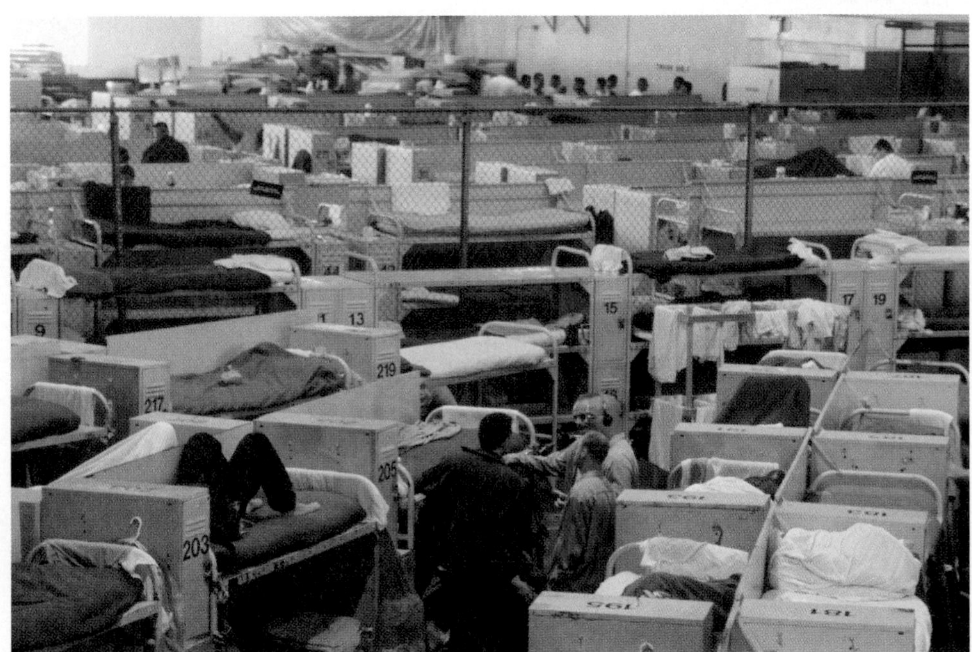

An auditorium converted into a dormitory to house prisoners at Deuel Vocational Institution, California.

Photo by Frank Pedrick, courtesy of The ImageWorks.

Second, Congress enacted a "truth-in-sentencing" program that provides funds for states to construct new prisons, provided the state enacts legislation requiring inmates to serve 85 percent of the imposed sentence. Male offenders are serving greater portions of their sentences, thus slowing the "turnover" rate.

Finally, prosecutors appear determined to focus on crimes of violence in their communities, seeking imprisonment as a sentencing outcome and stiffening plea negotiations by raising the minimum period of incarceration recommended to sentencing judges. A collateral consequence of such a strategy is that a subsequent second felony conviction, in some states, imposes a mandatory sentence of imprisonment that would be twice as long as if the offender had never been convicted.

America seems determined to resolve its crime problems with a "lock 'em up and throw away the key" philosophy.[12] Although incapacitation may be an effective way to prevent crime temporarily, helping offenders expand their opportunities and enter the mainstream of American society might be a more permanent way of lowering crime rates and the collateral national costs of incarceration.[13]

PRISONIZATION PLAYS A ROLE

Every venture intended to elevate humanity (or at least to encourage improvement) has as many unplanned and unwanted effects as it has desired effects. Efforts to give male offenders a setting in which to do penance and be "reformed" have resulted in a number of unwanted side effects, ranging from the mental and physical deterioration caused by extreme solitary confinement at Sing Sing to a more contemporary unwanted phenomenon called **prisonization** (see Chapter 9 sidebar titled, "Prisonization"). The originator of the term, Donald Clemmer, described this process as "the taking on in greater or less degree of the folkways, mores, customs, and general culture of the penitentiary."[14] Clemmer observed that acculturation into the prison community subjects the inmate to certain influences that either breed or deepen criminal behaviors, causing the prisoner to learn the criminal ideology of the prison, that is, to become "prisonized." Prisonization is a process that includes accepting the subordinate role into which one is thrust as an inmate; developing new habits of sleeping, dressing, eating, and working; undergoing status degradation; adopting a new language; and learning that one is dependent on others (including one's fellow inmates) for the scarce pleasures found in incarceration, including food, work assignment, freedom from assault, and privileges. Students of prisonization believe this process not only leads the inmate to further identify with criminal codes, goals, and behaviors, but also serves to undercut reintegration programs and to lessen the offender's ability to adjust to society after release.[15]

Many inmates have come to develop a set of social beliefs, attitudes, and conception of destiny from experiences in their younger and formative years, as well as hearing such negative comments and orientations from peers and, to some extent, parents. They believe, for example, that a victim of theft has insurance and will not be harmed, thus devaluing and dehumanizing the victim; and that most of the people they assault were about to assault them first or owed them money and the only way to secure it was the use of physical force. Others think life owes them a living, since they never got any "breaks" when growing up. They also learn quickly to deny responsibility for their behavior, assigning responsibility to the "stupid person who tried to jack me up" and who "failed to show respect." Such offenders have poor self-control, are often self-centered, and possess distorted perceptions of the world. Most have almost no skills in management of aggression and lack appropriate assertiveness. They have low victim empathy, little impulse control, and undertake behavior that sets themselves up in a high-risk situation. These

Inmate Slang

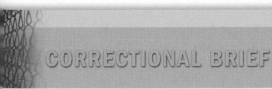

Male prisons are a society unto themselves, separated almost totally from the free society. Under these conditions prison slang, a form of dialect, is developed. Slang has emerged partly as an expression of community for the inmates, and also as an effort to confuse the correctional staff. We include some examples of inmate slang terminology, which may or may not be in use in every institution:

- The barn: a large open dorm
- Box: radio
- Brown shirt: correctional officer
- Dead man walking: inmate on way to execution
- Fire in the hole: correctional officer approaching
- Hack: guard
- Duck: a new guard
- Fish: a new inmate
- Home boy: someone from the same city
- One time: stash the drugs, guard on floor
- The man: usually the warden, can be a captain
- Pack the rabbit: secrete object in rectum
- Shank: homemade knife
- Snitch: informant
- Stinger: homemade electric apparatus for heating water
- Tailor-mades: factory-made cigarettes
- Thump: to fight
- Keester it: hide object in rectum
- Pruno: homemade alcohol
- Range queen: inmate who takes woman's role

are cognitive beliefs that assure the offender that criminal behavior makes sense. In some ways, no amount of boot camp programming will remove this socially disruptive behavior or dissolve this negative approach, address cognitive defects, or erase poor parenting. This treatment approach (cognitive skill building) has been repeatedly shown to significantly reduce criminal reoffending. The point here is that prisonization is an ubiquitous process and mechanism of reinforcing antisocial patterns of reasoning.

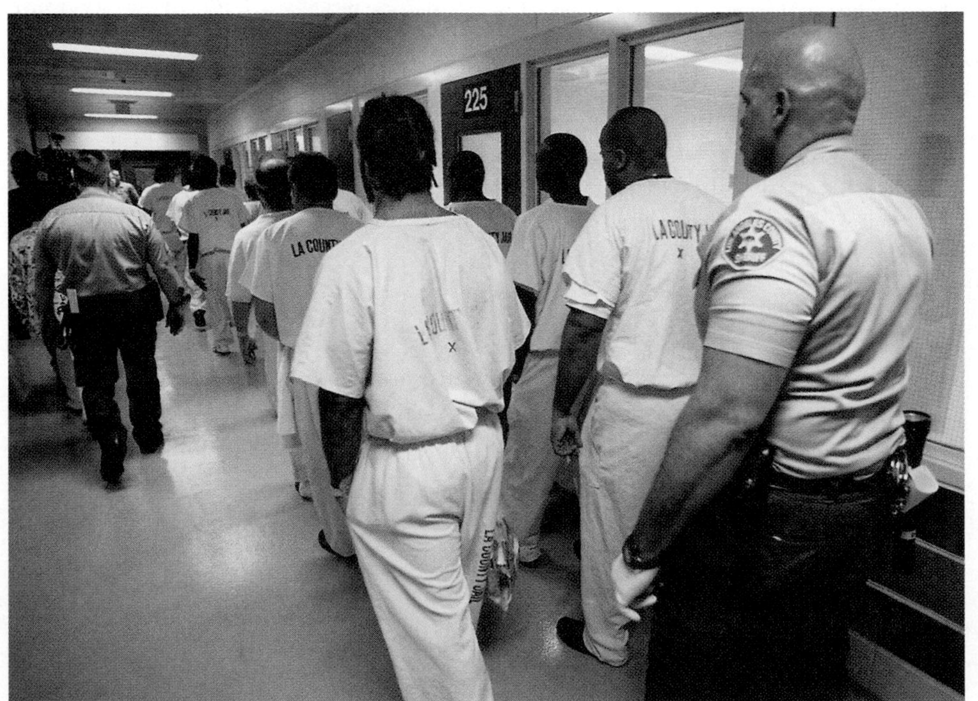

Los Angeles sheriff's deputies escort mentally ill patients to a new facility.

Photo by Chris Pizzello, courtesy of AP/Wide World Photos.

The phenomenon of prisonization appears to exist in all prisons, not just the large gothic bastions that testify to archaic prison philosophies. Former inmates can bring it into the prison, but even in new prisons that receive first-time offenders, the inmates' pains of imprisonment can generate the prisonization process.

Because prisonization occurs in every institution, although to varying degrees, it is necessary to understand the benefits that accrue to the men who adhere to the inmate codes. The future correctional administrator must also understand the pains of imprisonment that encourage socialization into the inmate subculture. Those pains are status deprivation, sexual deprivation, material deprivation, and enforced intimacy with other and more dangerous offenders.

If the institutional administrator and staff emphasize individual and group treatment rather than custody and discipline, if a pattern of cooperation can be developed between informal inmate leaders and institutional authorities, if a medium or minimum custody level can be achieved, and if violators of rules governing the use of force by the correctional staff are consistently reprimanded, then the prison culture and the prisonization process can be markedly reduced. Some researchers have suggested that shorter prison terms tend to undercut the power of the prison culture, because inmates can and do participate in "anticipatory socialization" as they near the end of their prison sentences and begin to prepare for their participation in the activities of the free world. It thus is reasonable to assume that short fixed periods of incarceration would help reduce the negative effects of prisonization.

Rape in All-Male Institutions

In 2003, President Bush signed the Prison Rape Elimination Act, the first U.S. government law passed to deal with sexual assault behind bars. The law calls for the gathering of national statistics about the problem; the development of guidelines for states about how to address prisoner rape; the creation of a review panel to hold annual hearings; and the provision of grants to states to combat the problem. Estimates are that one in five men in prison has been sexually abused, often by other inmates. Rates for women, who are most likely to be abused by male staff, reach as high as one in four in some facilities.

In a detailed study of aggression among men behind prison walls, Anthony Scacco boasted that sex is a vehicle for exploitation rather than an expression of pathological personality or situational frustration.[16] The sexual assaults that occur within prisons and jails cannot be categorized solely as **homosexual attacks**[17]; rather they are often assaults made by heterosexually oriented males for political reasons—that is, to show power and dominance over other human beings. It is a depressing fact that victimization, degradation, racism, and humiliation of victims are the foremost reasons that sexual assaults are perpetrated on men in this setting. As Victor Hassine, himself an inmate, notes:

> *Gang bangers often rely on rape in prison to generate fear and to maintain power over the general population. While street gangs use gunplay and murder to gain power, prison gangs use the threat of rape to dominate inmates and to ensure the repayment of even small debts. Some prison gangs require new inmates to commit rape as a gang initiation ritual. The act of raping another inmate is viewed as a way for gang members to demonstrate courage, strength, and cunning.*[18]

In institutions for only male felons, homosexual behavior between consenting adults has been a recurrent phenomenon, as in other such unisexual settings as naval ships and religious monasteries. It is unreasonable to expect inmates to abandon sexual behavior in prison, particularly when they face increasingly long sentences. As Peter Buffum noted,

> *[The present pattern of homosexuality in prisons] means that as long as the prison is an environment, which is largely devoid of situations where legitimate affectional ties can be established, there will be a tendency for the formation of homosexual relationships, especially among those persons serving long sentences who have concomitantly lost contact with meaningful persons in the free community. If in addition the prison does not allow legitimate attempts of the inmates to control their own lives and does not give an opportunity for expressions of masculinity and self-assertion that are meaningful among men at this social level, there will be homosexual relationships created to fulfill this need.*[19]

Especially among younger inmates and those who accept passive roles, homosexual behaviors and relationships could impair future commitments to heterosexuality as well as create exploitative situations. When such relationships create jealousy among inmates, the potential for serious violence and administrative problems increases. If a third inmate becomes involved in a dyadic relationship or there is a transfer of affection, extreme violence can occur. The once frequent pattern of transferring the passive partner to another institution is no longer an adequate or constitutional response by prison management. Segregating passive partners may cause the active inmates to coerce others into sexual behavior, as well as to raise legal issues of inmate rights and to create the potential for lawsuits arising from such isolation.

Prison administrators will need to consider and implement home visits at known intervals for those under long sentences, as well as provide activities and programs that will attack the real problems. At the beginning of 2005, however, only six states reported permitting inmates to have **family (conjugal) visits.** This allowed inmates to have some control over their own lives and maintain affectionate relationships and stable interpersonal interaction. Encouraging correspondence with and visits from relatives and family helps reduce the pains of imprisonment and help family reunification.

SIDEBARS

AIDS in State Prisons

In 2002 some 2 percent, about 22,300, of state prisoners were infected with the human immunodeficiency virus (HIV), which can result in AIDS. New York, Florida, Texas, Georgia, and California had the largest number of HIV-positive inmates. More than 8 percent of New York prison inmates are HIV positive. All state systems had recorded some HIV cases. HIV was the single largest cause of death in state prisons in 1997. About one in eleven deaths in state prison is due to AIDS-related illnesses. Treatment for prisoners with AIDS in prison is extremely expensive. California estimates the cost per year to house inmates with AIDS at about $87,000 per case.

SIDEBARS

Conjugal Visits

Conjugal, or so-called "family," visits were allowed in only six states in 2003: California, Connecticut, Mississippi, New Mexico, New York, and Washington.

THE GRAYING OF AMERICA'S MALE PRISONERS

The proportion of prisoners in the nation's institutions who are elderly is rapidly increasing, in part due to the tougher long-term sentences inherent in the current "get tough on crime" stance, but also in part due to the aging of the general population in America. It has been estimated that by the year 2010, at least one in ten (about 125,000 inmates) will be age fifty or over. There were more than 71,000 prisoners ages fifty-five and older in all prison institutions in the nation in 2004.

The growth rate of "geriatric inmates" (age fifty or above) in Florida already exceeds the growth rate of younger offenders; in California, almost 7,500 men are serving sentences of twenty-five years to life for conviction of a "third-strike" felony.[20]

Elderly inmates are *more* likely than other prisoners to have committed crimes such as homicide and manslaughter, as well as sexual offenses. They are *less likely* than other inmates to be imprisoned for robbery and burglary. Because of their significantly longer sentences, elderly inmates may be concentrated in prisons well beyond their proportions in the civilian population, which will pose problems for them as well as prison administrators.

First, they will have health care concerns and need preventive health care programs that, if not provided, could be a source of considerable and, for correctional administrators, substantial litigation costs. At the least, they will suffer from depression and differing nutritional needs (less protein, fewer calories, and more soft food and fiber). Because taste sensations decline with aging, the elderly will request

A geriatric unit in Estelle Prison, Texas.
Photo by Andrew Lichtenstein, courtesy of The ImageWorks.

SIDEBARS

Charges for Inmate Medical Service

Thirty-two states charge inmates for routine health care, from $2 to $5 per service. Some charge $5 for a sick call and up to a $5 copay for prescriptions.

food richer in seasonings and will have a decrease in gastric acid and increase in gas production and constipation.

In addition, growing old in prison will mean having to avoid exploitation and violence by younger inmates,[21] having to adjust new personal needs to prison life, and not having suitable programs (recreational, educational, or housing). Vulnerability to victimization, frailty, and isolation from outside relatives and friends will take their toll, as will fear of death, hopelessness, and being unable to cope when released.

Health care costs will increase significantly as a result of treatment for hypertension, diabetes, stroke, cancer, and emphysema. Glasses, dentures, kidney dialysis, and heart surgery will be required. In 2001 the medical costs for prisoners exceeded $3.3 billion, and it has been estimated that by the year 2005, health care costs for elderly inmates will increase fourteenfold.[22] Many prisons will become

A psychiatrist begins his day at the Pelican Bay Supermax Prison in northwest California.
Photo by Bob Galbraith, courtesy of AP/Wide World Photos.

geriatric centers,[23] and special staff and staff training will be necessary to treat this special problem segment of the nation's offenders. Perhaps a nation that can explore outer space can find the necessary compassion to care for that small but increasing group during this decade of the new century. Executive clemency, including pardons, may once again become a frequent act as government struggles with the problems of elderly inmates.

SUMMARY

Male offenders in prison are increasing in number as well as age. It is evident that such changes will continue to have significant impacts on prison management, programs, and costs. Corrections will be tasked with doing more, but with fewer resources than are needed. This will in turn pose management issues for correctional administrators.

It is likely that the next decade will see efforts to expand custody technology within maximum-security institutions, as well as lower the potential for assault on staff and inmates. Rape of male inmates by other men will continue to be a challenge, probably due to court decisions on liabilities of correctional managers for inattention to sexual aggression.

Another challenge corrections will face is the development of geriatric programs if not centers within a state's correctional facilities. Some states may opt to aggregate elderly inmates into one or more facilities or cellblocks. Others may decide to implement humanitarian release by extending the limits of confinement to include placement of geriatric inmates in community corrections. Many of these policy changes will be driven in part by consideration of expenses associated with incarcerating large numbers of offenders in general, and geriatric offenders in particular.

Male offenders will continue to crowd existing prisons that will be overcrowded to the extreme. Much remains to be done to resolve the underlying issues and problems.

REVIEW QUESTIONS

1. Why have prison populations increased recently? What short-term effects will result from that increase?
2. What is meant by the "population at risk"? How does it contribute to the population problem in male prisons?
3. Explain the dynamics of rape in a male prison.
4. What factors contribute to prisonization?
5. What can be done to reduce homosexuality in prisons?
6. How should male inmates be sentenced?
7. Why are so many prisoners members of minority groups?
8. What problems do elderly inmates pose or face?
9. How can corrections address the problems of elderly offenders?
10. What impacts do street and prison gangs have on prison management?
11. Debate: Offenders should be released to community control when they reach age seventy.

ENDNOTES

1. Fox Butterfield, "More Black Men Are in Jail than in College," *Cincinnati Inquirer* (August 28, 2002): A4. See also Marc Mauer and Ryan King, *Schools and Prisons Fifty Years after* Brown v. Board of Education (Washington, DC: The Sentencing Project, 2004).
2. Paige Harrison and Allen Beck, *Prisoners in 2003* (Washington, DC: Bureau of Justice Statistics, 2004), p. 2.
3. Timothy Hart, "Causes and Consequences of Crime and Violence," *American Journal of Criminal Justice* 23:1 (1998): 131–143; and Tomislav Kovandzic, "The Impact of Florida's Habitual Offender Law on Crime," *Criminology* 39:1 (2001): 179–203.
4. Prison administrators argue that reserve capacity is needed to operate a prison effectively. Prison dormitories and cells need to be repaired and maintained periodically. Additional space may be needed for emergencies. Special housing (such as protective custody and punitive segregation) and administrative

units (such as prison recreation, intake, and program space) are required. The federal prison system is running at 139 percent of capacity, and thirty-two states are over at least their lowest capacity, some (such as Alabama) by as much as 209 percent of capacity. Harrison and Beck, *Prisoners in 2003,* p. 7.

5. Dan Eckhart, "Civil Actions Related to Prison Gangs," *Corrections Management Quarterly* 5:1 (2001): 9–64.
6. Caroline Wolf Beck, *Drug Enforcement and Treatment in Prison, 1990* (Washington, DC: U.S. Department of Justice, 1992). See also Henry Wexler, "The Success of Therapeutic Communities for Substance Abuse in American Prisons," *The Prison Journal* 75:1 (1995): 57–66; Dorothy Lockwood, J. McCorkle, and J. Inciardi, "Developing Comprehensive Prison-Based Therapeutic Community Treatment for Women," *Drugs and Society* 13:1/2 (1998): 193–212; and Michael Pendergast et al., "Reducing Substance Abuse in Prisons," *The Prison Journal* 84:2 (2004): 265–280.
7. Charles Bailey, "Prison Populations Surging, and Not Just Because of the Nation's Economic Slowdown," *Corrections Digest* 7:2 (1976): 9. See also Miriam Williford, *A Contradiction in Terms?* (Phoenix, AZ: Oryx Press, 1994); and Elliott Currie, *Crime and Punishment in America: Why the Solutions to America's Most Stubborn Social Crisis Have Not Worked—And What Will* (New York: Metropolitan Books, 1998).
8. Harrison and Beck, *Prisoners in 2003,* p. 12.
9. Ron Akers et al., "Fear of Crime and Victimization Among the Elderly in Different Types of Communities," *Criminology* 25:4 (1987): 487–505. See also Ronet Bachman, *Elderly Victims* (Washington, DC: U.S. Department of Justice, 1992); Steven Donziger, *The Real War on Crime* (New York: HarperCollins, 1996); and Matthew Yeger, "Ideology and Dangerousness: The Case of Lisa Colleen Neve," *Critical Criminology* 9:1/2 (2000): 9–21.
10. Donziger, *The Real War,* pp. 99–129; and Richard McCorkle and T. Miethe, "The Political and Organizational Response to Gangs: An Evaluation of a 'Moral Panic' in Nevada," *Justice Quarterly* 15:1 (1998): 41–64; and Scott Paguting, Greg Noble, and Paul Tabar, "Middle Eastern Appearances: Ethnic Group, Moral Panic and Media Framing," *Australian and New Zealand Journal of Criminology* 34:1 (2001): 67–90.
11. Rob Wilson, "U.S. Prison Population Sets Another Record," *Corrections Magazine* 4:2 (1980): 5; Currie, *Crime and Punishment.* But see Grant Stitt, Donia Giascopassi, and Mark Nichols, "The Effect of Casino Gambling on Crime in New Casino Jurisdictions," *Journal of Crime and Justice* 23:1 (2000): 1–23.
12. A term developed in the 1930s. See also Joan Petersilia, "California's Prison Policy: Causes, Costs, and Consequences," *The Prison Journal* 72:1/2 (1992): 8–36; and Theodore Sasson, *Crime Talk: How Citizens Construct a Social Problem* (Hawthorne, NY: Aldine, 1995).
13. See Curie, *Crime and Punishment;* and John Donahue and P. Siegelman, "Allocating Resources Among Prisons and Social Programs in the Battle Against Crime," *Journal of Legal Studies* 27:1 (1998): 1–43.
14. Donald Clemmer, *The Prison Community* (New York: Rinehart, 1940), p. 8. See also Barbara Peat and T. Winfree, "Reducing the Intra-Institutional Effects of 'Prisonization': A Study of a Therapeutic Community for Drug-Using Inmates," *Criminal Justice Behavior* 19:2 (1992): 206–225; Hans Toch, "Inmate Involvement in Prison Governance," *Federal Probation* 59:2 (1995): 34–39; and Darren Lawson, C. Segrin, and T. Ward, "The Relationship Between Prisonization and Social Skills Among Prison Inmates," *The Prison Journal* 76:3 (1996): 293–301.
15. Kenneth Adams, "Adjusting to Prison Life," in Michael Tonry (ed.), *Crime and Justice: A Review of Research* (Chicago: University of Chicago Press, 1993), pp. 275–359; and Paula Faulkner and W. Faulkner, "Effects of Organizational Change on Inmate Status and the Inmate Code of Conduct," *Journal of Crime and Justice* 20:1 (1997): 55–72.
16. Anthony Scacco, *Rape in Prison* (Springfield, IL: Chas. C. Thomas, 1975); Michael Scarce, *Male on Male Rape* (New York: Plenum, 1997); Thomas Fagan, D. Wennerstrom, and J. Miller, "Sexual Assault of Male Inmates," *Journal of Correctional Health Care* 3:1 (1996): 49–65; and Christine Saum, H. Surratt, and J. Inciardi, "Sex in Prison: Exploring the Myth and Realities," *The Prison Journal* 75:4 (1995): 413–430. But see Richard Tewksbury, "Measures of Sexual Behavior in an Ohio Prison," *Sociology and Social Research* 74:1 (1989): 34–39; Richard Tewksbury and Elizabeth Mustaine," Lifestyle Factors Associated with the Sexual Assault of Men," *Journal of Men's Studies* 9:2 (2001): 23–42; and Christopher Hensley and Richard Tewksbury, "Wardens' Perceptions of Inmate Fear of Sexual Assault," *The Prison Journal* 85:2 (2005): 198–203.
17. Helen Eigenberg, "Homosexuality in Male Prisons: Demonstrating the Need for a Social Constructionist Approach," *Criminal Justice Review* 17:2 (1992): 219–234.
18. Victor Hassine, *Life Without Parole* (Los Angeles, CA: Roxbury Publishing Company, 2004), p. 138.
19. Peter Buffum, *Homosexuality in Prisons* (Washington, DC: U.S. Government Printing Office, 1972), p. 28. See also James Stephan, *Prison Rule Violators* (Washington, DC: Bureau of Justice Statistics, 1989); David Hallpren, "Sexual Assault of New South Wales Prisoners," *Current Issues in Criminal Justice* 6:3 (1995): 327–334; and Saum et al., "Sex in Prison."
20. Harry E. Allen and Bruce S. Ponder, "Three Strikes Legislation and Racial Disparity in California: 1994–2001." Paper presented at the Annual Meeting of the Academy of Criminal Justice Sciences,

Anaheim, CA, March 8, 2002; and California Department of Corrections, *Second and Third Strikers in the Institution Population* www.corr.ca.gov/OffenderInfoServices/Reports/Quarterly/Strike1/STRIKE1do412,pdf (updated March 2005).

21. Richard Dagger, "The Graying of America's Prisons," *Corrections Today* 50:3 (1988): 26–34; and Ronald Day, "Golden Years Behind Bars," *Federal Probation* 58:2 (1994): 47–54.
22. American Correctional Association, *2005 Directory* (Lanham, MD: ACA, 2005), p. 22. See also Sarah Bradley, "Graying of Inmate Population Spurs Corrections Challenges," *On the Line* 13:2 (March 1990): 5. The average costs for imprisoning elderly inmates is high because they suffer from an average of three chronic illnesses during their incarceration. In New York, these costs range from $50,00 to $75,000 a year. Rozann Greco, *The Future of Aging in New York State* http://aging.state.ny.us/explore/project2015/briefs04.htm (accessed February 16, 2005).
23. Gennaro Vito and D. Wilson, "Forgotten People: Elderly Inmates," *Federal Probation* 49:2 (1985): 18–24; Deborah Wilson and G. Vito, "Long-Term Inmates: Special Need and Management Considerations," *Federal Probation* 52:3 (1988): 21–26. At least 22 states already have special geriatric prison wings or housing units for their older inmates. See also Todd Edwards, *The Aging Inmate Population* (Atlanta, GA: Council of State Governments, 1998); and Project for Older Prisoners, California Department of Corrections, *A Look at Other States' Program for Older Inmates,* www.sfgate.com/cgi-bin/article.cgi?file=/news/archive/2003/02/25/state2034EST0156.DTL (accessed December 16, 2004).

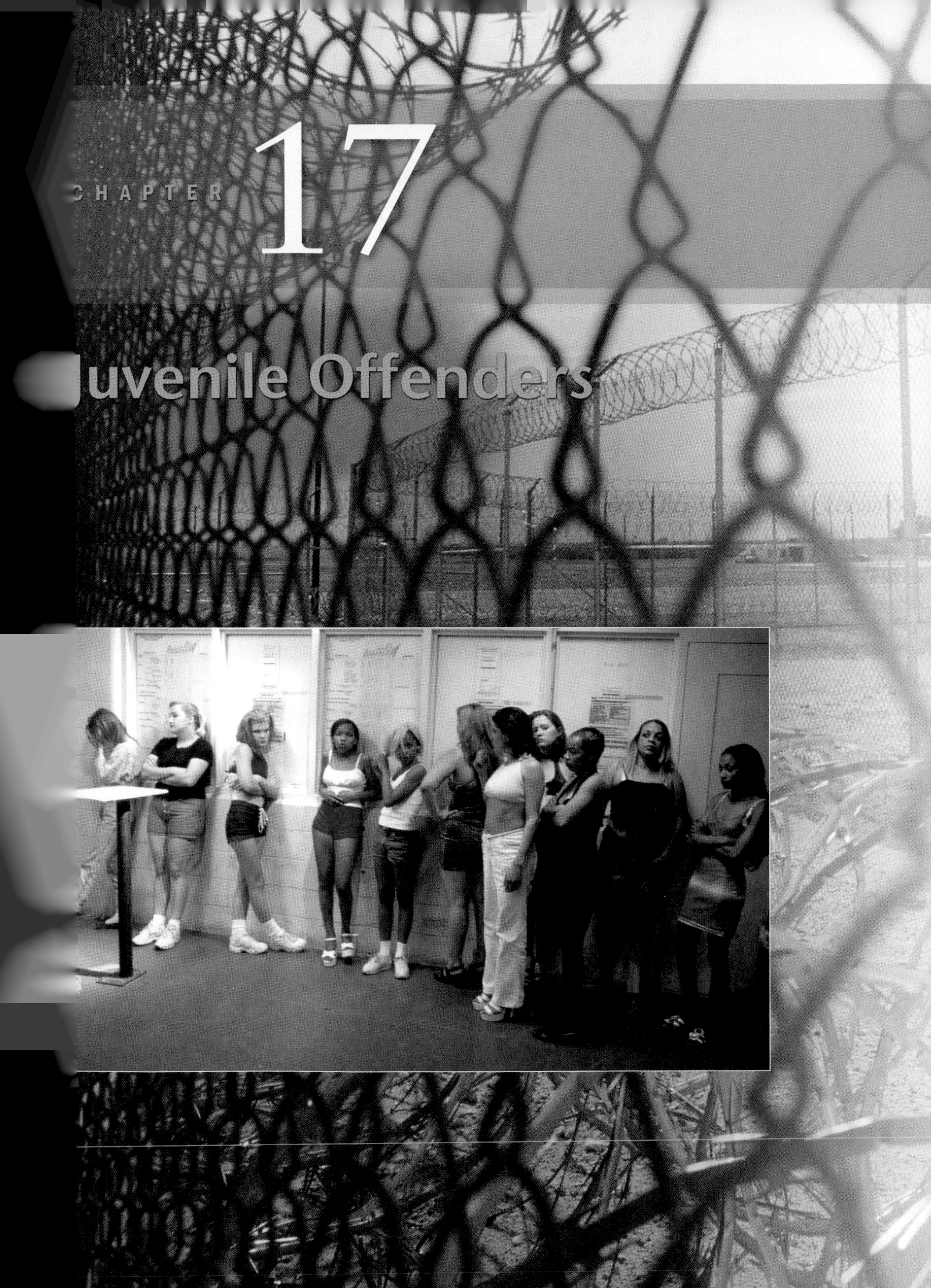

CHAPTER 17

Juvenile Offenders

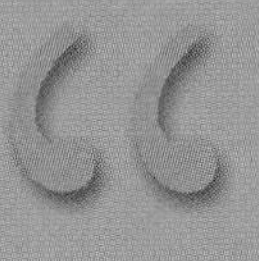

The call for a national "crackdown on juvenile offenders" and the fear of a "new generation of super predators" is, I believe, an overreaction to one of our weakest emotions—fear.

—James A. Gondles, Jr., Executive Director, American Correctional Association

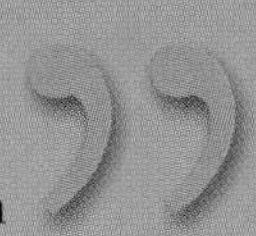

KEY WORDS

- common law
- *parens patriae*
- ward
- chancery court
- dependent
- neglected
- delinquent juveniles
- status offenders
- incorrigible (unruly) juveniles
- *Kent v. United States*
- *In re Gault*
- Juvenile Justice and Delinquency Prevention Act
- diversion
- decriminalization
- deinstitutionalization
- decarceration
- custody philosophy
- super predator
- statutory exclusion
- juvenile waiver
- direct filing
- RECLAIM
- U.S. Office of Juvenile Justice and Delinquency Prevention (OJJDP)
- youth gangs
- crack cocaine

OVERVIEW

The last two chapters, and the one that follows, describe the variety of "clients" that usually are formed into separate groups for sentencing and incarceration following arrest and detention. In the early history of American justice, the distinctions of sex, age, or personal infirmities were given little thought, and "offenders" were lumped into a single category—prisoners. Institutional inmates needed only be classified as convicted, and even that distinction was often overlooked in society's haste to punish actual or alleged miscreants. Over the decades, many different paths were developed for various categories of offenders; jails were separated into male and female sections and those convicted were sent to different, specialized kinds of institutions to serve out their sentences and meet their special needs. But what about those offenders classified, by age, as juveniles? What became of them in the adult systems?

This chapter digresses somewhat from the general pattern, because the process of handling juvenile offenders has grown into an entirely separate system of justice. Therefore, we develop the history of juvenile justice in more detail than was covered earlier in the text to show how juvenile procedures have developed almost independently from adult justice and are designed to assist wayward youth. The juvenile justice system has now grown into an entirely separate "industry." This is especially timely as we follow the activities of street gangs, children who murder

< Female teen prostitutes wait in line in a booking area at Maricopa County Jail, Arizona. *Photo by A. Ramey, courtesy of PhotoEdit.*

Members of the Culver City street gang use hand signs to communicate membership.
Photo by Alon Reininger, courtesy of Contact Press Images, Inc.

other children, and all the punitive and neoclassical efforts to again try juveniles in adult courts as "super predators."[1] We hope to provide the student, in this single chapter, with a basic understanding of juvenile justice in relationship to the other clients of corrections. Other texts and other courses have been written and presented on this single offender group. This is not meant to be an exhaustive or complete treatise on juvenile justice or juvenile offenders, but simply a base on which to build an understanding of the origins and current practices in this separate and unique system.

WHERE DOES THE JUVENILE FIT IN?

SIDEBARS

Parens Patriae

A legal philosophy by which the state would assume the role of the parent of a juvenile. The term literally means "the parent is the state." It derives from the time when the king was considered to be the father of the country.

How did we go from wayward youth to super predators in such a short time? Like most of America's criminal justice system, our juvenile justice system derives from the **common law** of England, as brought to the United States by our forefathers. With regard to criminal responsibility, the English common law made three assumptions concerning age and criminal responsibility:

1. Children under the age of seven were presumed to be incapable of holding criminal intent.
2. From the ages of seven to fourteen, offenders were not held responsible unless the state could prove they could clearly distinguish between right and wrong.
3. If offenders were fourteen or older, they were assumed to be responsible for their acts and therefore deserving of punishment. Here, the burden was on the defendants to prove they were not responsible.

The king was considered the father of his country (***parens patriae***), who assumed responsibility for protecting all dependent children. In England that responsibility was fulfilled by the chancery court[2] in which the needful child became a **ward** of the state under the protection of parens patriae. The **chancery court** was designed to act more flexibly than the more rigid criminal courts. The main concern was for the welfare of the child; legal procedures that might hamper the court in its beneficial actions were either circumvented or ignored. Thus, there were two concepts under the common law: that children under certain ages were not responsible for their actions and that a certain category of children was in need of protection by the state. It was not until the ages of possible responsibility were raised to sixteen and eighteen that those two concepts merged into the concept of juvenile delinquency.

CRIMINAL BEHAVIOR DECLINES WITH AGING

Data on the relationship between crime and age indicate that crime is a young person's game. It seems to peak at age seventeen, before beginning to drop. Younger people may be more likely to be arrested because of inexperience and ineptness in crime. Young people also commit crimes that more easily result in arrest, such as shoplifting, purse snatching, and drug selling. Also, youths tend to commit crimes in groups, and the resolution of a single crime (such as a car theft) may result in several arrests. The decline by age could also be an artifact of incapacitating repeat offenders by imposing longer sentences; such offenders then grow older in prison. Habitual offenders also seem to become less likely to be caught and arrested. Therefore, older prisoners who do return to crime tend to have longer periods before rearrest ("survival periods") and enjoy longer periods of freedom between incarcerations.

Although the juvenile crime rate has been declining during the past several years, this could be a result of the shrinking of the population at risk (twelve- to eighteen-year-old youths), or it could mean that real progress is being made in the juvenile justice system. But, as we will show, juveniles contribute to a significant and alarming portion of the crime problem.

Because a very large percentage of incarcerated felons were first incarcerated as juveniles in training institutions and schools for delinquents,[3] we look briefly at the development and function of the juvenile court and the juvenile justice system, starting with the philosophy that produced them.

Despite concern for their children's welfare, most communities have a tolerance point for juveniles' disruptive behavior. When children go beyond that point, they can be taken into custody and recorded as delinquents. The mixing of juvenile offenders and adult felons was a practice that had existed for centuries, but in America's early history was looked on as repugnant. In 1899 children in trouble, dependent children, and (finally) delinquent juveniles began to receive differential attention in the courts. The first juvenile court was established in that year in Chicago, and the delinquent joined the dependent and neglected child as a ward of the state. Serious delinquents were the last category to come to the attention of the juvenile court. When the juvenile delinquent was thus placed under the cloak of *parens patriae*, he or she was removed entirely from the formal criminal justice system. The general procedures for the handling of juvenile offenders today are shown in Figure 17.1, where the correctional funnel for juveniles can be seen at work. Table 17.1 shows the similarities and differences between the adult and juvenile processing systems.

SIDEBARS

Juvenile

A person subject to juvenile court proceedings because a statutorily defined event was alleged to have occurred while his or her age was below the statutorily specified limit of original jurisdiction of a juvenile court. A juvenile delinquent, then, has been adjudicated by an officer of a juvenile court for law violations that would be crimes if an adult had committed them.

CATEGORIES OF JUVENILE OFFENDERS

Essentially three kinds of children come into contact with the juvenile court system—a significant event in their lives. The children in two of those categories have committed no offense; they are either **dependent** (without family or support) or **neglected** (having a family situation that is harmful to them). The only category that involves an offense is the **delinquent juvenile.**

FIGURE 17.1

The Stages of Delinquency Case Processing in the Juvenile Justice System

NOTE: This chart gives a simplified view of case flow through the juvenile justice system. Procedures vary among jurisdictions. The weights of the lines are not intended to show the actual size of caseloads.

SOURCE: Howard Snyder et al., *Juvenile Offenders and Victims: 1996 Update on Violence* (Washington, DC: U.S. Department of Justice, 1996), p. 76.

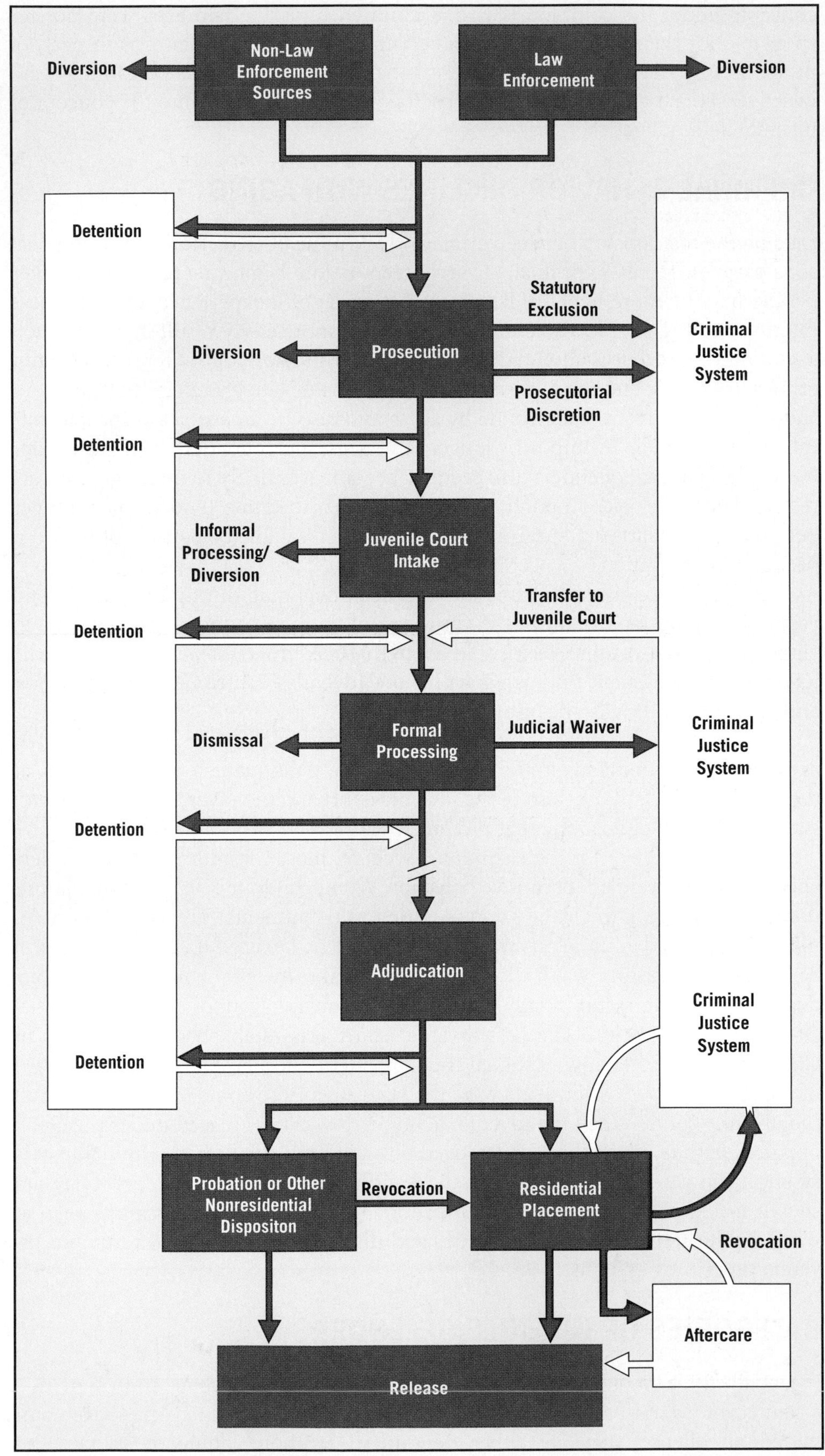

TABLE 17.1 Similarities and Differences between the Juvenile and Criminal Justice System in the Handling of Offenders

JUVENILE JUSTICE SYSTEM	COMMON GROUND	CRIMINAL JUSTICE SYSTEM
	Operating Assumptions	
■ Youth behavior is malleable ■ Rehabilitation is usually a viable goal ■ Youth are in families and not independent	■ Community protection is a primary goal ■ Law violators must be held accountable ■ Constitutional rights apply	■ Sanctions proportional to the offense ■ General deterrence works ■ Rehabilitation is not a primary goal
	Prevention	
■ Many specific delinquency prevention activities (e.g., school, church, recreation) ■ Prevention intended to change individual behavior—often family focused	■ Educational approaches to specific behaviors (drunk driving, drug use)	■ Generalized prevention activities aimed at deterrence (e.g., a Crime Watch)
	Law Enforcement	
■ Specialized "juvenile" units ■ Some additional behaviors prohibited (truancy, running away, curfew violations) ■ Limitations on public access to information	■ Jurisdiction involves full range of criminal behaviors ■ Constitutional and procedural safeguards exist ■ Both reactive and proactive (targeted at offense types, neighborhoods, etc.)	■ Open public access to all information
Diversion A significant number of youth are diverted away from the juvenile justice system—often *into* alternative programs		**Discretion** Law enforcement exercises discretion to divert offenders out of the criminal justice system
	Intake—Prosecution	
■ In many instances, juvenile court intake, not the prosecutor, decides what cases to file ■ Decision to file a petition for court action is based on both social and legal factors ■ A significant portion of cases are diverted from formal case processing	■ Probable cause must be established ■ Prosecutor acts on behalf of the state	■ Plea bargaining is common ■ Prosecution decision based largely on legal facts ■ Prosecution is valuable in building history for subsequent offenses 
Diversion Intake diverts cases from formal processing to services operated by the juvenile court or outside agencies		**Discretion** Prosecution exercises discretion to withhold charges or divert offenders out of the criminal justice system
	Detention—Jail/Lockup	
■ Juveniles may be detained for their own or the community's protection ■ Juveniles may not be confined with adults without "sight and sound separation"	■ Accused offenders may be held in custody to ensure their appearance in court	■ Rights to apply for bond

(Continued)

TABLE 17.1 Similarities and Differences Between the Juvenile and Criminal Justice System in the Handling of Offenders (*continued*)

JUVENILE JUSTICE SYSTEM	COMMON GROUND	CRIMINAL JUSTICE SYSTEM
	Adjudication—Conviction	
■ Juvenile court proceedings are "quasi-civil"—not criminal—may be confidential ■ If guilt is established, the youth is adjudicated delinquent regardless of offense. ■ Right to jury trial not afforded in all states	■ Standard of "proof beyond a reasonable doubt" is required ■ Rights to a defense attorney, confrontation of witnesses, remain silent are afforded ■ Appeals to a higher court are allowed	■ Constitutional right to a jury trial is afforded ■ Guilt must be established on individual offenses charged for conviction ■ All proceedings are open
	Disposition—Sentencing	
■ Disposition decisions are based on individual and social factors, offense severity, and youths' offense history ■ Dispositional philosophy includes a significant rehabilitation component ■ Many dispositional alternatives are operated by the juvenile court ■ Dispositions cover a wide range of community-based and residential services ■ Disposition orders may be directed to people other than the offender (e.g., parents) ■ Disposition may be indeterminate—based on progress	■ Decision is influenced by current offense, offending history, and social factors ■ Decision made to hold offender accountable ■ Victim considered for restitution and "no contact" orders ■ Decision may not be cruel or unusual	■ Sentencing decision is primarily bound by the severity of the current offense and offender's criminal history ■ Sentencing philosophy is based largely on proportionality and punishment ■ Sentence is often between determinate based on offense
	Aftercare—Parole	
■ A function that combines surveillance and reintegration activities (e.g., family, school, work)	■ A system of monitoring behavior upon release from a correctional setting ■ Violation of conditions can result in reincarceration	■ Primarily a surveillance and reporting function to monitor illicit behavior

SOURCE: Editors, *Juvenile Offenders and Victims: A National Report* (Washington, DC: Office of Juvenile Justice and Delinquency Prevention, 1995), pp. 74–75.

SIDEBARS

Status Offender

A "status offender" is generally accepted as a juvenile who has come into contact with the juvenile authorities based on conduct that is an offense only when committed by a juvenile. A status offense is conduct that would not be defined as a criminal act when committed by an adult.

The care of neglected and dependent children is important, of course, but the juvenile courts were established primarily to handle delinquent juveniles. For judicial purposes, delinquents are divided into three categories:

1. Children who have allegedly committed an offense that would be a crime if an adult had committed it. This group now comprises more than 75 percent of the population of the state institutions for delinquent juveniles.
2. **Status offenders** who have allegedly violated regulations that apply only to juveniles: curfew restrictions, required school attendance, and similar rules and ordinances.
3. **Incorrigible (unruly) juveniles** who have been declared unmanageable by their parents and the court. The second and third groups are often referred to as persons in need of supervision (PINS) or minors in need of supervision (MINS).

CORRECTIONAL BRIEF

Terms Used in Juvenile Proceedings

The principal features that distinguish current juvenile delinquency proceedings from adult criminal proceedings can be summarized as follows:

1. *Absence of legal guilt.* Legally, juveniles are not found guilty of crimes but are "found to be delinquent." Juveniles are not held legally responsible for their acts. Juvenile status, like insanity, is a defense against criminal responsibility. It is not, however, an absolute defense because of the possibility of waiver to criminal court.
2. *Treatment rather than punishment.* Whatever action the court takes following a finding of delinquency is done in the name of treatment or community protection, not punishment, as is the case for adult felony offenders.
3. *Absence of public scrutiny.* Juvenile proceedings and records are generally closed to the public. What goes on in court is presumed to be the business only of juveniles and their families. This position clearly has its roots in the early child-saving mission of the court. Hearings for serious juvenile offenders are now being opened to the public.
4. *Importance of a juvenile's background.* Juveniles' needs and amenability to treatment can, it is widely presumed, be deduced from their social history, prior behavior, and clinical diagnosis. This presumption is used to justify the wide discretionary powers granted to probation officers in screening petitions, to the court in deciding fitness and making dispositions, and to youth correction agencies in deciding when a ward should be released.
5. *No long-term incarceration.* Terms of confinement for juveniles are considerably shorter than those for adults.
6. *Separateness.* The juvenile system is kept separate from the adult criminal justice system at every point, from detention at arrest to the identities of the officials who handle the case in court, and in subsequent placements as well.
7. *Speed and flexibility.* Delinquency cases are disposed of more quickly than comparable adult criminal cases, and the juvenile court judge has a broader range of disposition alternatives.

Thanks to federal intervention, status offenders have been removed from the facilities designed primarily for the first category of delinquent juveniles.[4]

A juvenile institution is intended to provide specialized programs for children who must be under some form of restraint to be treated. Accordingly, it normally houses the more hardened, unstable, or nontreatable youths who fail to meet even the liberal standards for juvenile probation. The institution program attempts to prepare the youth for return to the community.

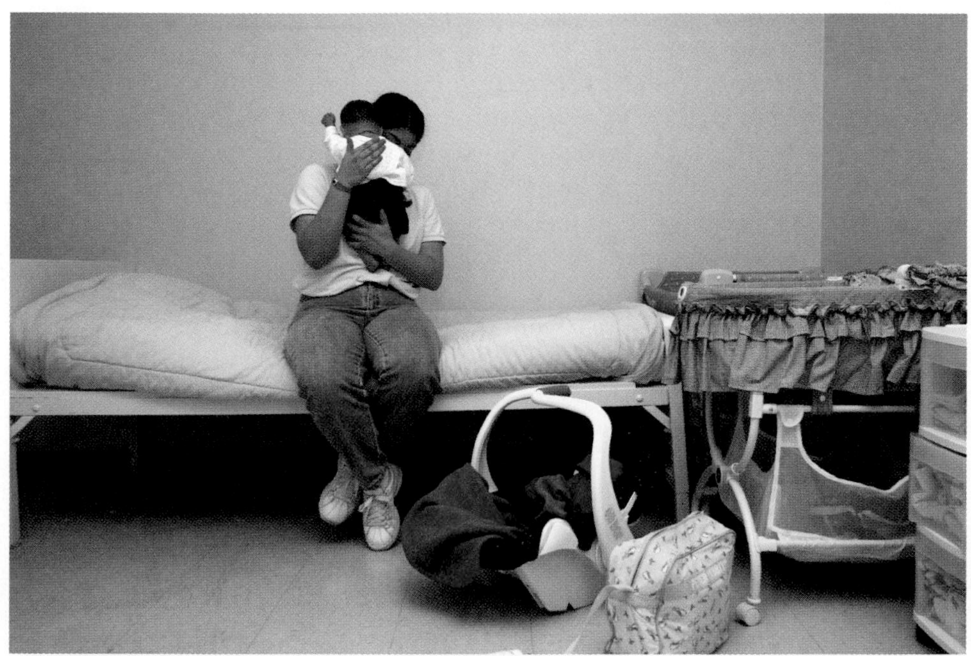

Parenting skills are learned with a mechanical baby in the "Baby, Think Twice" program.

Photo by Spencer Grant, courtesy of PhotoEdit.

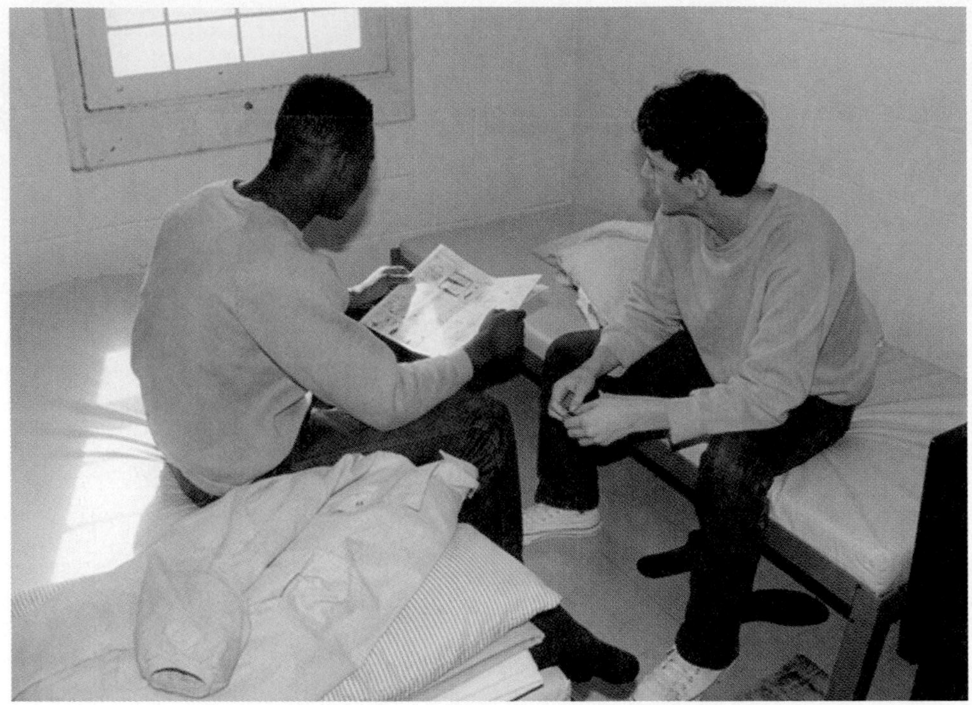

A typical room in a juvenile detention center.
Courtesy of Ohio Department of Youth Services.

Despite the vast expansion and growth of community-based facilities, there has been no major decline in the use of juvenile institutions. Spending months or years in confinement away from family, friends, and familiar circumstances, however, is an odious prospect for a person of any age. For a young person, the prospect is especially frightening. Compared to the juvenile court's other disposition options, institutional placement of a juvenile in a residential facility is the court's ultimate disposition power. It is the court's most severe and only really feared disposition.

JUVENILE RIGHTS: THE LANDMARK CASES

Figure 17.2 displays an excellent schematic and brief explanation of the landmark Supreme Court cases that established many juvenile rights. In the landmark opinions ***Kent v. United States,*** 383 U.S. 541 (1966), and ***In re Gault,*** 387 U.S. 1 (1967), the Supreme Court at long last evaluated juvenile court proceedings and children's constitutionally guaranteed rights. In *Kent v. United States,* the Court noted that the child involved in certain juvenile court proceedings was deprived of constitutional rights and at the same time not given the rehabilitation promised under earlier juvenile court philosophy and statutes. It pointed out "there may be grounds for concern that the child receives the worst of both worlds."[5] On May 15, 1967, the Supreme Court rendered its first decision in the area of juvenile delinquency procedure. In the decision, the U.S. Supreme Court ruled that a child alleged to be a juvenile delinquent had at least the following rights:

- Right to notice of the charges in time to prepare for trial
- Right to counsel
- Right to confrontation and cross-examination of his or her accusers
- Privilege against self-incrimination, at least in court.

FIGURE 17.2

A Series of U.S. Supreme Court Decisions Made Juvenile Courts More Like Criminal Courts but Maintained Some Important Differences

1965

1966 — ***Kent v. United States***
Courts must provide the "essentials of due process" in transferring juveniles to the adult system.

1967 — ***In re Gault***
Juveniles have four basic constitutional rights in hearings that could result in commitment to an institution.

1970 — ***In re Winship***
In delinquency matters the state must prove its case beyond a reasonable doubt.

1971 — ***McKeiver v. Pennsylvania***
Jury trials are not constitutionally required in juvenile court hearings.

1975 — ***Breed v. Jones***
Waiver of a juvenile to criminal court following adjudication in juvenile court constitutes double jeopardy.

1977 — ***Oklahoma Publishing Co. v. District Court***
1979 — ***Smith v. Daily Mail Publishing Co.***
The press may report juvenile court proceedings under certain circumstances.

1982 — ***Eddings v. Oklahoma***
Defendant's youthful age should be considered a mitigating factor in deciding whether to apply the death penalty.

1984 — ***Schall v. Martin***
Preventive "pretrial" detention of juveniles is allowable under certain circumstances.

1988 — ***Thompson v. Oklahoma***
1989 — ***Stanford v. Kentucky***
Minimum death penalty age set at sixteen.

2004 — ***Roper v. Simmons***
Execution of killers under age 18 is prohibited.

The *Gault* decision ended the presumption that the juvenile courts were beyond the scope or purview of due process protection. With *In re Winship,* 397 U.S. 358 (1970), the Supreme Court held that to justify a court finding of delinquency against a juvenile, the proof must be beyond a reasonable doubt that the juvenile committed the alleged delinquent act. *McKeiver v. Pennsylvania,* 403 U.S. 528 (1971), implied that the due process standard of "fundamental fairness" applied; the Court rejected the concept of trial by jury for juveniles. The Court contended that the "juvenile proceeding has not yet been held to be a 'criminal prosecution' within the meaning and reach of the Sixth Amendment."[6] The cases shown in Figure 17.2 following *McKeiver* have slowly added more and more rights to the juvenile process, while still trying to keep it separate.[7]

The Supreme Court has not been the only source of change in the area of juvenile rights, however. Federal acts and legislation have also played an important role. Until the Uniform Juvenile Court Act of 1968, police or others could still take a child into custody in a situation in which the Fourth Amendment would have exempted an adult. In 1974, the U.S. Congress passed the **Juvenile Justice and Delinquency Prevention Act** (Public Law 93–415). This act required a comprehensive assessment regarding the effectiveness of the existing juvenile justice system. The intent of the act was to clearly identify those youth who are victimized or otherwise troubled but have not committed criminal offenses and to divert such youth from institutionalization. Simultaneously the act was intended to promote the utilization of resources within the juvenile justice system to more effectively deal with youthful criminal offenders.

Thus far, the procedural rights guaranteed to a juvenile in court proceedings are as follows:

1. The right to adequate notice of charges against him or her
2. The right to counsel and to have counsel provided if the child is indigent
3. The right to confrontation and cross-examination of witnesses
4. The right to refuse to do anything that would be self-incriminatory
5. The right to due process, prior to the transfer of a juvenile to an adult court[8]
6. The right to be considered innocent until proven guilty beyond a reasonable doubt.

Decisions of the U.S. Supreme Court have led to four major trends in the handling of juveniles: diversion, decriminalization, deinstitutionalization of status offenders, and decarceration.

Diversion is the official halting or suspension, at any legally prescribed processing point after a recorded justice system entry, of formal juvenile (or criminal) proceedings against an alleged offender, and referral of that person to a treatment or care program administered by a nonjustice agency or private agency. Sometimes

A non-profit–operated youth development center that treats troubled juveniles.
Courtesy of Eckerd Youth Alternatives, Inc.

no referral is given. Diversion programs function to divert juveniles out of the juvenile justice system, encourage the use of existing private correctional agencies and facilities for such youths, and avoid formal contact with the juvenile court. Those programs include remedial education programs, foster homes, group homes, and local counseling facilities and centers. The effectiveness of such programs has not yet been demonstrated, but they are being closely evaluated.

Decriminalization does just what it sounds like it does—it makes the act not criminal anymore. The principal aim in the juvenile and criminal justice systems is to remove from the scope of law and social control certain types of currently proscribed behaviors that pose little perceived danger to society. Those behaviors are frequently seen as "deviant" rather than illegal and thus "not the law's business."[9] The decriminalization movement, then, would delete deviant behavior from juvenile laws and proceedings and leave to social agencies the task of providing assistance if and when requested.

One category of juveniles that falls under the aegis of the juvenile court is the status offender. These youths commit offenses that are based only on the offender's status as a juvenile. These offenses include ungovernability, running away, unruliness, school truancy, disregard for or abuse of lawful parental authority, and repeated use of alcoholic beverages. The nation has moved away from putting status offenders into secure institutional settings **(deinstitutionalization)**.[10]

Decarceration removes as many juveniles from custody as possible and treats them in an open environment. This option, given the violent nature of juveniles incarcerated, seems to still be waiting for its time to come. These recommendations reflect the earlier intent of the Juvenile Justice and Delinquency Prevention Act to divert status offenders to shelter facilities rather than juvenile detention centers or jails, as well as not to detain or confine status offenders in any institution in which they would have regular contact with adult offenders.

PROFILE

Jerome Miller (1928–)

served as the commissioner of Massachusetts' Department of Youth Services, a pioneer in deinstitutionalization, and in that post convinced the governor to approve the closing of all but one juvenile correctional institution (the Shirley Training School, which served a few remaining girls) and placing all other adjudicated juveniles into community-based programs. This bold move, supported by the media and politicians, has been copied in many states since that time and proved that the large majority of adjudicated juveniles could be better dealt with in the community.

JUVENILES HELD IN INSTITUTIONAL ENVIRONMENTS

In the landmark *Gault* decision, the U.S. Supreme Court emphasized the reality of institutionalization for a juvenile:

> *Ultimately, however, we confront the reality. . . . A boy is charged with misconduct. The boy is committed to an institution where he may be restrained of liberty for years. It is of no constitutional consequence . . . and of limited practical meaning . . . that the institution to which he is committed is called an Industrial School. The fact of the matter is that, however euphemistic the title, a "receiving home" or an "industrial school" for juveniles is an institution of confinement in which the child is incarcerated for a greater or lesser time. His world becomes "a building with whitewashed walls, regimented routine and institutional hours. . . ." Instead of mother and father and sisters and brothers and friends and classmates, guards, custodians, state employees people his world, and delinquents confined with him for anything from waywardness to rape and homicide.*[11]

An estimated 132,700 juveniles were in correctional institutions and other residential programs at year-end 2005, a 20 percent increase from 1999.[12] Figure 17.3 shows the disposition of juvenile offenders between 1990 and 2000.

Facilities designated exclusively for juvenile detention are usually not the best examples of how an ideal juvenile correctional facility should be designed and operated. Most of the structures were originally built for some other purpose and converted to their present use with as little expense as possible. Most are overcrowded before they reach their rated capacities. In the adult institutions the emphasis is on

FIGURE 17.3

Adjudicated Delinquency Cases by Disposition, 1990–2000

SOURCE: Adapted from C. Puzzanchera, A. Stahl, T. Finnegan, and N. Tierney, *Juvenile Court Statistics 1999* (Washington, DC: Office of Juvenile Justice and Delinquency Prevention, 2002).

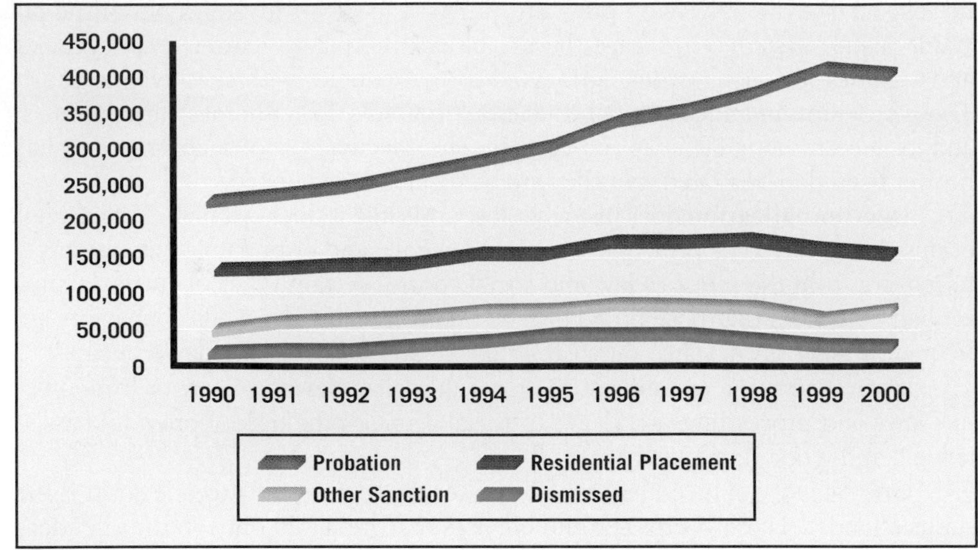

custody, and the same preoccupation with security shapes the programs and general environment in the juvenile facilities. Most are located in urban areas and are virtually sealed off from the community by their physical structure and other security measures. The youths are placed in dormitory-style housing, or single cells in some cases, often with the fixed furniture and dreary interiors that are typical of adult institutions. Most juvenile detention centers lack services and programs that might improve the residents' chances of staying away from crime. The average cost for juvenile institutional confinement is more than $100 per resident per day, although the cost of small and highly specialized state facilities can easily exceed $200 per resident per day.

One example of an initiative that has successfully reduced the number of youth held in institutions is **RECLAIM** Ohio (Reasoned and Equitable Community and Local Alternatives to the Incarceration of Minors). One of the purposes of RE-

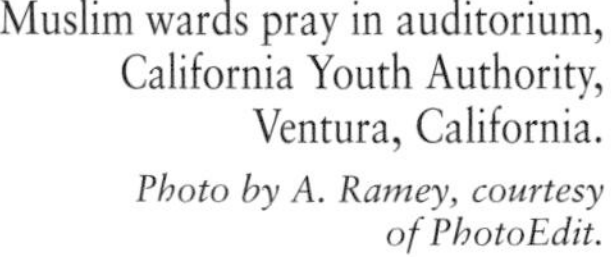

Muslim wards pray in auditorium, California Youth Authority, Ventura, California.

Photo by A. Ramey, courtesy of PhotoEdit.

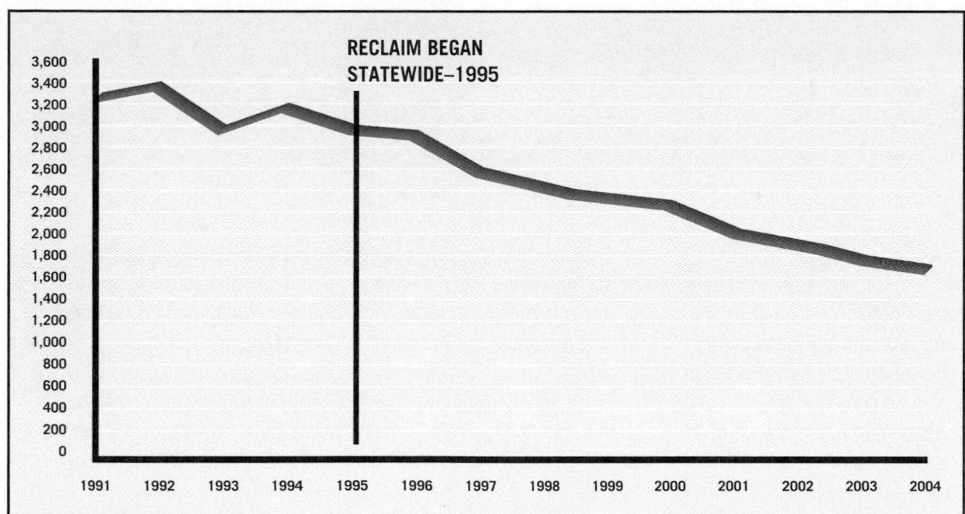

FIGURE 17.4

Ohio Department of Youth Services Admissions, 1991–2004

SOURCE: Ohio Department of Youth Services.

CLAIM was to provide funding to local jurisdictions to develop community programming so that fewer youth would be sentenced to state facilities. Since 1995 when RECLAIM went statewide, well over $300 million have been distributed, and the effects on admissions to state institutions have been significant. Figure 17.4 shows the impact of this innovative policy shift on admissions. Recently, Illinois began REDEPLOY Illinois, modeled after Ohio's program. Only time will tell if it has an impact on that state's juvenile offender population.

Institutions are the most expensive and least successful method of handling juvenile offenders, but until the services needed for supervision and treatment in the community are forthcoming, judges often have no other choice but to commit offenders. The junior prisons are not all bad, but the **custody philosophy** is the prevailing model, which creates the same problems as those at the adult level.

The New Breed: Dispelling the Myth of the Super Predator

In the past, many of the juveniles in the system were not considered hardened criminals, but simply wayward youngsters who had strayed from the right path. Today, buzzwords such as **super predator** are used increasingly in the press and by politicians to describe the new type of youthful offender, ruthless young men and women who see crime as a way of life and who are unconcerned about the consequences of their actions, more likely to engage in crime and violence, and less likely to be deterred by the threat of harsh punishment.

Television news splatters images of heinous crimes perpetrated by youthful offenders. Politicians, eager to look tough on crime, issue promises that they will cure America of this disease by severely cracking down on juvenile delinquency. Although the attacks win political points, not everyone is convinced of their merit. Juvenile justice experts say these attacks can be destructive. But instead of blaming the youth, the media and politicians need to look at the root causes of juvenile delinquency—in particular, the breakdown of the family, child abuse, poverty, and the ready availability of guns. The atmosphere of blame has pressured juvenile justice departments in many states to ignore the causes and concentrate mainly on the crimes. As a result, more youths are being tried in criminal courts and sent to adult prisons. This is a departure from the way juveniles were handled in the past. Indeed, the prediction of large numbers of juvenile super predators has not proven true. In fact, juvenile crime, including violent crime, has been declining steadily during the past few years.

CORRECTIONAL BRIEF

A View from a Practitioner

A little human touch can go a long way toward improving the behavior of troubled youth. Or so believes Carl Oliver, the retired superintendent (1950–1998) of a juvenile detention center just outside Washington, D.C. He tells the story of one youth under his care who, with some encouragement, became the institution's artist-in-residence. The boy had refused to pay attention in class, and was ordered to stay behind each day to make up for the time he had wasted. To alleviate his boredom, the boy doodled in his notebook. Oliver saw creativity in the drawings and encouraged him to continue. It wasn't long before the boy was commissioned to decorate the school's walls. He also stopped acting up in class and became a better student. "Kids need recognition and new experiences," says Oliver. "Get them in a situation where there is understanding, and changes can take place."

Since the 1950s, many changes have taken place at juvenile detention centers. The cottage-type facilities where Oliver worked during the 1950s have given way to the more institutional-type settings common today.

PROFILE

Edwin H. Sutherland (1883–1950)

was the developer of the best-known theory aimed at explaining delinquent behavior. It is called "differential association" and it first appeared in 1939 in the third edition of his *Principles of Criminology.* Basically, it says that criminal behavior is learned in interaction with others. Sutherland's theory has been heavily criticized but it still acts as a cornerstone for many others. The highest award of the American Society of Criminology is named in his honor.

Today's Challenges

Adaptations and new programs continue to be developed today. In the 1990s we saw a rise in the number of military-style boot camps designed to drill discipline and coax self-worth into juveniles. Although boot camps were popular with the public and politicians, research on their effectiveness has generally found that they are not effective in reducing recidivism. In fact, there is some evidence that juvenile boot camps actually lead to higher failure rates. Some believe this is because the social learning in most boot camps actually teaches and models aggressive behavior.

Fortunately, much research has demonstrated that well-designed treatment programs for youth can be effective in reducing delinquent behavior. See the accompanying Correctional Brief for a discussion of the more effective treatment models for youth. Research on effective programs for youth has found that the most effective approaches are behavioral interventions, where offenders learn to replace their delinquent behavior through prosocial modeling and reinforcement. A recent

Members of Asian "Tiny Rascals" gang holding weapon and flashing gang signs, Long Beach, California. *Photo by A. Ramey, courtesy of PhotoEdit.*

Juvenile offenders in Los Angeles, California, work with children with severe disabilities at the El Camino School as part of their jail time and rehabilitation program.

Photo by Tony Savino, courtesy of The Image Works.

study commissioned by the National Institute of Justice found that some of the more widely used programs are not effective. These are also listed in the Correctional Brief.

Although the number of violent juveniles arrested in a given year is still quite small (estimates are 0.5 percent of youth), the perception of the dangerous youth remains. This accounts for the pressure to punish juveniles for their crimes by waiving them to criminal courts. People have been looking for a silver-bullet answer to juvenile crime, and the current focus is more on locking them up than on treatment.

Many experts in juvenile justice stress the need to work with families and communities to diffuse problems before they get out of hand.

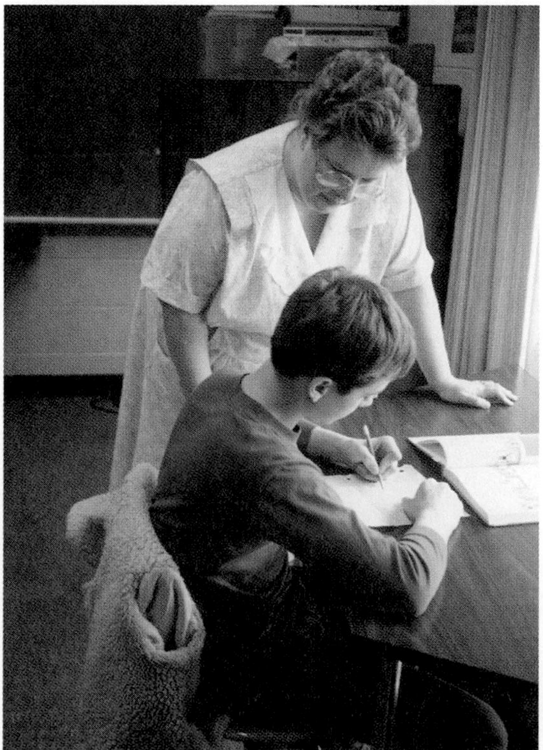

A patient teacher works with a very young offender.

Courtesy of Ohio Department of Youth Services.

CORRECTIONAL BRIEF

What Works with Youthful Offenders?

Two national assessments of the effectiveness of literally hundreds of intervention programs for treating and handling juvenile offenders found interesting and surprising results.

The most effective approaches are behavioral in nature and include the following types of interventions:

- Structured social learning programs that teach new skills (how to interact with the opposite sex, problem-solving skills, etc.) and reinforce behavior and attitudes
- Cognitive behavioral programs that target attitudes, values, peers, substance abuse, anger, etc.
- Family-based interventions that train family on appropriate behavioral techniques.

Perhaps the most important results dealt with what does not work with youthful offenders:

- Drug prevention classes focused on fear and other emotional appeals (DARE)
- Drug education programs
- Talking cures
- Nondirective interventions
- Self-help programs
- Increasing cohesion of criminal groups
- Targeting non-crime-producing factors
- Fostering self-regard (self-esteem)
- Radical nonintervention (doing nothing)
- Targeting low-risk offenders
- Correctional boot camps using traditional military basic training
- School-based leisure-time enrichment programs
- "Scared Straight" programs in which juvenile offenders visit adult prisons
- Home detention with electronic monitoring
- Rehabilitation programs using vague, unstructured counseling
- Residential programs for juvenile offenders using challenging experiences in rural settings.

SOURCES: National Institute of Corrections, *Promoting Public Safety Using Effective Interventions with Offenders,* www.nicic.org, (accessed 2001); and Lawrence Sherman et al., *Preventing Crime: What Works, What Doesn't, What's Promising* (Washington, DC: National Institute of Justice, 1998).

Before we put all this money into jails, we must look at education and strengthening the family. Just getting tough and locking juveniles up for long periods will not solve the problem. When values are not being taught and when juveniles have low self-concepts, you are going to get attention one way or another. And attention from the press, politicians and the public is what juvenile delinquents are getting. Many see "Get Tough" as the way to deal with young offenders. They want more jails built and tougher sentences enforced. But many of those who work with juvenile delinquents want more emphasis put on treatment programs so that the interned youth have an opportunity to be rehabilitated. Oliver recounts the tale of a boy who so badly wanted to return to the facility after he was released that he stole a bike and rode back. These stories recounted tenfold over the years beg the question: Do juvenile facilities protect society from the youths under their care, or do they protect delinquent youths from society? Perhaps a bit of both, juvenile experts agree.[13]

WHO IS A JUVENILE TODAY?

The "upper age of jurisdiction" is the key factor in this first decade of the twenty-first century. It is the oldest age at which a juvenile court has original jurisdiction over an individual for law-violating behavior. State statutes define which youth are under the original jurisdiction of the juvenile court. These definitions are based primarily on age criteria. In most states, the juvenile court has original ju-

Juvenile offenders entering boot camp, Los Angeles Youth Authority.
Photo by A. Ramey, courtesy of PhotoEdit.

risdiction over all youth charged with a criminal law violation who were below the age of eighteen at the time of the offense, arrest, or referral to court. Many states have higher upper ages of juvenile court jurisdiction in status offense, abuse, neglect, or dependency matters, often through age twenty. Today, as shown in Table 17.2, twenty-three states plus the District of Columbia have at least one provision for transferring juveniles to the criminal court for which no minimum age is specified. Many states have statutory exceptions to basic age criteria. The exceptions, related to the youth's age, alleged offense, and/or prior

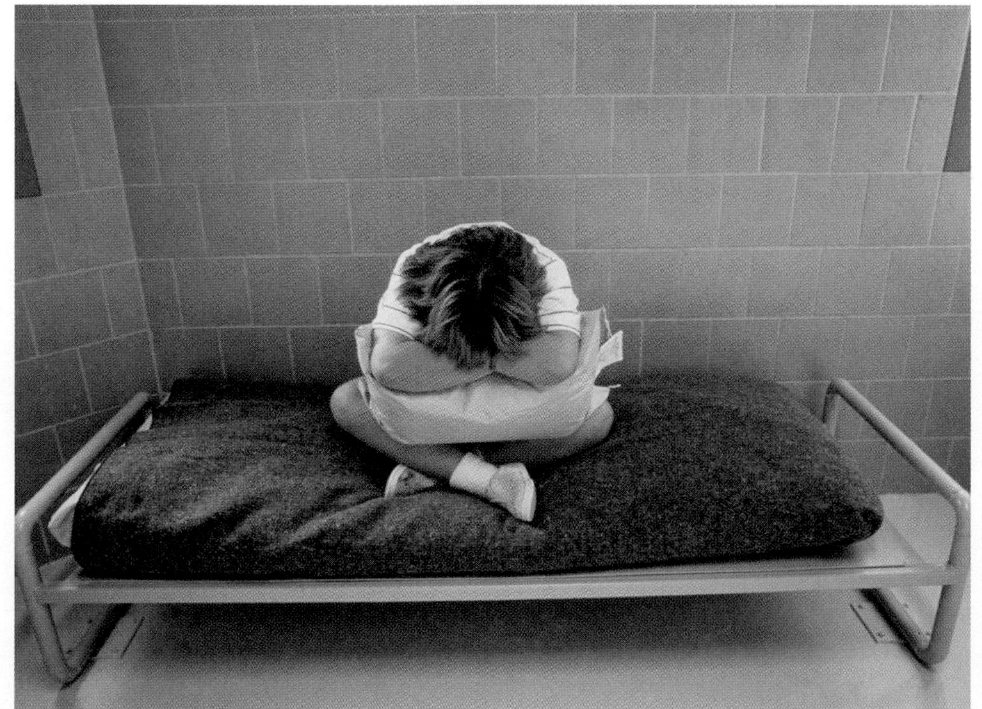

Anglo teen in cell, Texas.
Photo by Bob Daemmrich, courtesy of The Image Works.

TABLE 17.2 Minimum Transfer Age Specified in Statute, 1999

AGE	STATE
10	Kansas, Vermont
12	Colorado, Missouri
13	Illinois, Mississippi, New Hampshire, New York, North Carolina, Wyoming
14	Alabama, Arkansas, California, Connecticut, Iowa, Kentucky, Louisiana, Massachusetts, Michigan, Minnesota, Nevada, New Jersey, North Dakota, Ohio, Utah, Virginia
15	New Mexico
No minimum age specified	Alaska, Arizona, Delaware, District of Columbia, Florida, Georgia, Hawaii, Idaho, Indiana, Maine, Maryland, Montana, Nebraska, Oklahoma, Oregon, Pennsylvania, Rhode Island, South Carolina, South Dakota, Tennessee, Texas, Washington, West Virginia, Wisconsin

SOURCE: Office of Juvenile Justice and Delinquency Prevention, *OJJDP Statistical Briefing Book*, http://ojjdp.ncjrs.org/ojstatbb/html/qa089.html (accessed April 12, 2002).

court history, place certain youth under the original jurisdiction of the criminal court, known as **statutory exclusion.** In some states, a combination of the youth's age, offense, and prior record places the youth under the original jurisdiction of both the juvenile and criminal courts. In these situations where the courts have concurrent jurisdiction, the prosecutor is given the authority to decide which court will initially handle the case. This is known as concurrent jurisdiction, prosecutor discretion, **juvenile waiver,** certification to adult criminal court, or **direct filing.**[14] As shown in Figure 17.5, the number of delinquency cases judicially waived to criminal court grew 46 percent between 1990 and 1994 and then declined 36 percent through 1999. Notice that the trend does vary across offense categories.

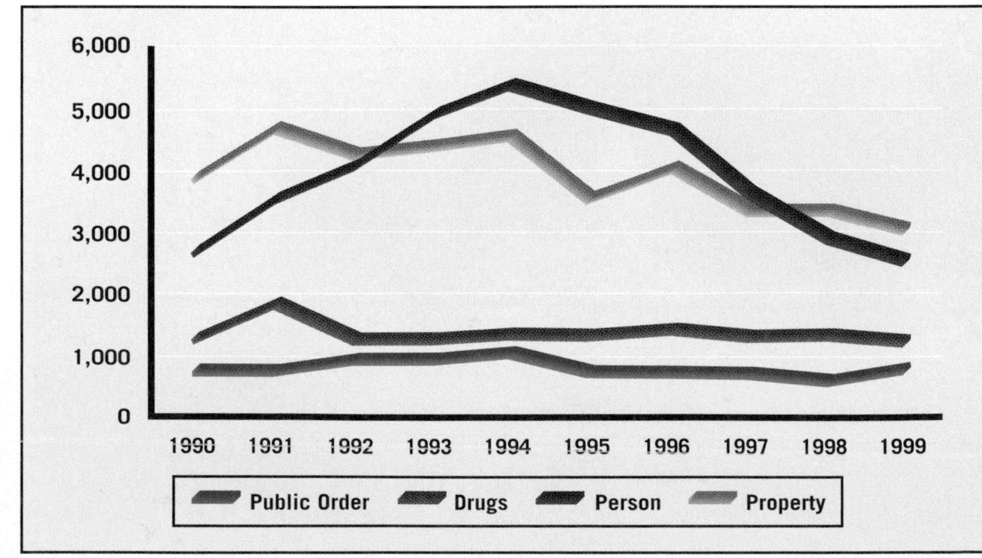

FIGURE 17.5

Delinquency Cases Judicially Waived to Criminal Court

SOURCE: Adapted from C. Puzzanchera et al., *Juvenile Court Statistics 1999* (Washington, DC: Office of Juvenile Justice and Delinquency Prevention, 2002).

THE JUVENILE CRIME PROBLEM

It has been estimated that approximately one of every six boys and one of every twelve girls in the United States will be referred to a juvenile court before their eighteenth birthday. The rise in juvenile crime has been considered the most serious aspect of the crime problem in the nation. In 2002, approximately 2.2 million arrests were made of persons under the age of eighteen. As shown in Table 17.3, juvenile arrests have been declining during the past few years, and in 2002 juvenile arrests for property crimes were at the lowest levels since at least the 1960s.

Law enforcement agencies in 2002 made 1,360 arrests of juveniles for murder and nonnegligent manslaughter; 24,470 arrests of persons under eighteen for robbery; 61,610 arrests for aggravated assault; and 4,700 for rape as reported in the Violent Crime Index (see Table 17.3 and Figure 17.6). These figures were down from the previous decade. Male juveniles were arrested in 90 percent of the juvenile murder cases and a whopping 90 percent were under the age of fifteen.[15]

JUVENILE VIOLENCE IN DECLINE

We can now see that, across the nation, the amount of violent crime involving juveniles as offenders or victims is on a decline. This is good news, since from about the time of the emergence of crack cocaine in the mid-1980s, the use of violence has become a part of juvenile gang culture, and these crimes seem to have also

TABLE 17.3 Most Serious Offense for Which Juveniles Were Arrested, 1993–2002

	2002	PERCENT OF TOTAL JUVENILE ARRESTS		PERCENT CHANGE	
MOST SERIOUS OFFENSE	NUMBER OF JUVENILE ARRESTS	FEMALE	UNDER AGE 15	1993–2002	1998–2002
Total	2,261,000	29%	31%	−11%	−19%
Violent Crime Index	92,160	18	32	−29	−17
Murder and nonnegligent manslaughter	1,360	10	10	−64	−36
Forcible rape	4,720	3	37	−27	−14
Robbery	24,470	9	24	−38	−21
Aggravated assault	61,610	24	36	−23	−5
Property Crime Index	481,600	32	37	−34	−23
Burglary	86,500	11	36	−39	−26
Larceny-theft	341,700	39	38	−30	−23
Motor vehicle theft	45,200	17	25	−50	−15
Arson	8,200	11	64	−23	−11

SOURCE: Office of Juvenile Justice and Delinquency Prevention, *Number of Juvenile Arrests, 2002,* http://ojjdp.ncjrs.org/ojstatbb/html/qa250.html, (accessed 2004).

FIGURE 17.6

Percent of Arrests Involving Juveniles

SOURCE: Howard Snyder, *Juvenile Arrests 2000* (Washington, DC: Office of Juvenile Justice and Delinquency Prevention, 2002), p. 2.

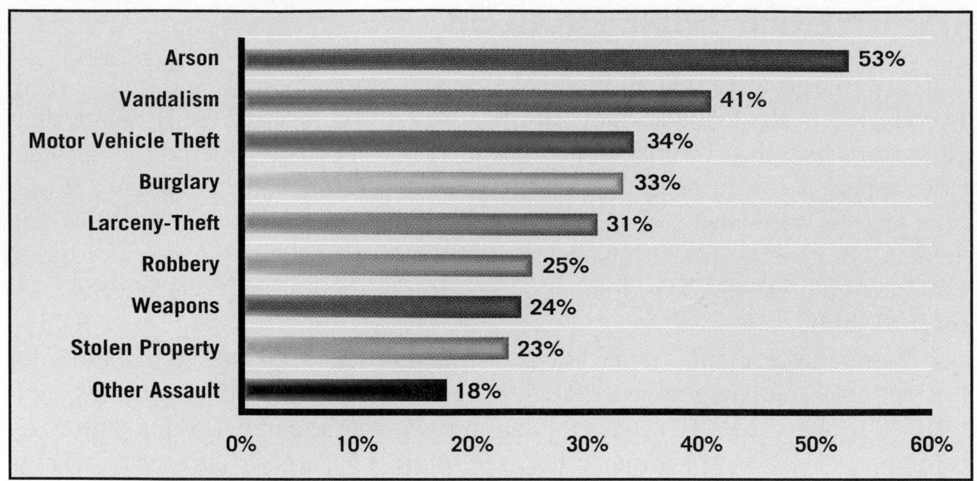

spread to many youths who are not gang members. Table 17.3 shows that between 1998 and 2002 violent crime for juvenile offenders dropped nearly 17 percent. Unfortunately, despite the reduction in juvenile crime, the increase in the 1980s and early 1990s, combined with some high-profile cases, has caused society as a whole, and the juvenile courts as well, to develop a "get tough" attitude toward violent crime by juveniles. Despite the drops, juveniles still account for a significant number of the arrests made in the United States. Juveniles accounted for 17 percent of all arrests in 2002, more than 15 percent of all violent crimes, and 30 percent of the property crimes (see Table 17.4). Furthermore, while the murder rate has fallen more than 72 percent since 1993, 9 percent of all murder arrests in 2002 involved a juvenile under age eighteen.[16]

TABLE 17.4 Juvenile Contribution to the Crime Problem

	2002 JUVENILE PROPORTION OF CRIME ARRESTS	
MOST SERIOUS OFFENSE	ARRESTS	CRIMES CLEARED
Violent Crime Index	15%	12%
Murder	10	5
Forcible rape	17	12
Robbery	23	14
Aggravated assault	13	12
Property Crime Index	30	20
Burglary	30	17
Larceny-theft	29	21
Motor vehicle theft	30	18
Arson	49	43

SOURCE: Howard Snyder, *Juvenile Arrests: 2002. Juvenile Justice Bulletin* (Washington, DC: Office of Juvenile Justice and Delinquency Prevention, 2004), p. 2.

JUVENILE VICTIMS OF VIOLENCE

Contrary to popular perceptions of the risk of violent crime, teenagers are victimized at higher rates than adults. The following shows some of the findings concerning victimization:

- Between 1980 and 2000, nearly 41,000 juveniles were murdered in the United States.
- Schools with gangs had higher victimization rates. Eighteen percent of the students reporting gangs at school were victimized compared with 11 percent of those who reported no gang presence.
- Until their teenage years, boys and girls are equally likely to be murdered.
- Between 1980 and 2000, most murdered children younger than age six were killed by a family member, while an acquaintance or stranger killed most older juveniles.
- One in four reported murders of juveniles in 2001 occurred in just five of the nation's more than 3,000 counties (cities in these counties were New York, Los Angeles, Detroit, Chicago, and Philadelphia).
- In one-third of all sexual assaults reported to law enforcement, the victim was younger than age twelve.
- Fewer than 50 percent of teenage homicide victims were shot to death. The overwhelming majority of youth homicide victims in the ten to seventeen year age range were male (77 percent).
- The annual number of juveniles killed with a firearm increased substantially between 1987 and 2001, while the other types of homicides remained constant.[17]

It is important to note that the juveniles who are charged with violent crimes represent 15 percent of the total crimes committed by juveniles. Despite these relatively small numbers, such crimes of violence as drive-by shootings, casual murder, and senseless abuse of other children create a hard-line attitude in the American public. The courts recognize this perception and are responding with more severe dispositions, including referring those who commit such violent crimes to stand trial as adults (through waiver to adult court).

Violent crime has been and will remain a problem well into this new century. Evidence continues to mount that a small proportion of offenders commits most of the serious and violent juvenile crimes. Decades of research[18] on delinquent careers and prevention have identified the following risk factors as contributing to serious, violent, and chronic juvenile crime:

- Weak family attachments
- Lack of consistent discipline
- Physical abuse and neglect
- Poor school performance
- Delinquent peer groups
- High-crime neighborhoods.

The **U.S. Office of Juvenile Justice and Delinquency Prevention (OJJDP)** proposed six strategies for preventing and reducing at-risk behavior and juvenile delinquency[19]:

1. Strengthen families in their role of providing guidance, discipline, and strong values as their children's first teacher.

2. Support core social institutions, including schools, churches, and other community-based organizations, to alleviate risk factors and help children develop to their full potential.
3. Promote prevention strategies that reduce the impact of negative risk factors and enhance protective factors.
4. Intervene immediately when delinquent behavior first occurs.
5. Establish a broad range of graduated sanctions that provides both accountability and a continuum of services to respond appropriately to the needs of each delinquent offender.
6. Identify and control the small percentage of juvenile offenders who are serious, violent, and chronic offenders.

The offending of juveniles is not the only concern. Young people are disproportionately the victims of violence as well. Violence impacts the quality of life for these children in their developing years.

JUVENILE GANGS

It is estimated that in 2002 **youth gangs** were active in more than 2,300 cities with a population over 2,500. It is also estimated that approximately 731,500 gang members and 21,500 gangs were active in the United States in 2002. As alarming as these figures are, the good news is that between 1996 and 2002 the number of gangs decreased by 14 percent.[20]

The presence of youth gangs and gang problems must be recognized before anything meaningful can be done to address the gang problem. Identifying the manifest and underlying factors contributing to the problem is also important. Promising approaches include the following:

1. Targeting, arresting, and incarcerating gang leaders and repeat gang offenders
2. Referring fringe members ("wannabees") and their parents to youth services for counseling and guidance
3. Providing preventive services for youths who are clearly at risk
4. Crisis intervention or mediation of gang fights
5. Patrols of community "hot spots"
6. Close supervision of gang offenders by criminal justice and community-based agencies
7. Remedial education for targeted youth gang members, especially in middle school
8. Job orientation, training, placement, and monitoring for older youth gang members
9. Safe zones around schools
10. Vertical prosecution, close supervision, and enhanced sentences for hard-core youth gang members. (Vertical or hard-core prosecution puts the same prosecutor in charge of all aspects of a case from charging to sentencing.)[21]

Not until the underlying reasons for belonging to a gang are found will appropriate solutions be developed. Gangs have been part of the urban scene for decades, but it took the advent of cocaine, especially **crack cocaine,** to create gangs whose only real motivation is money.

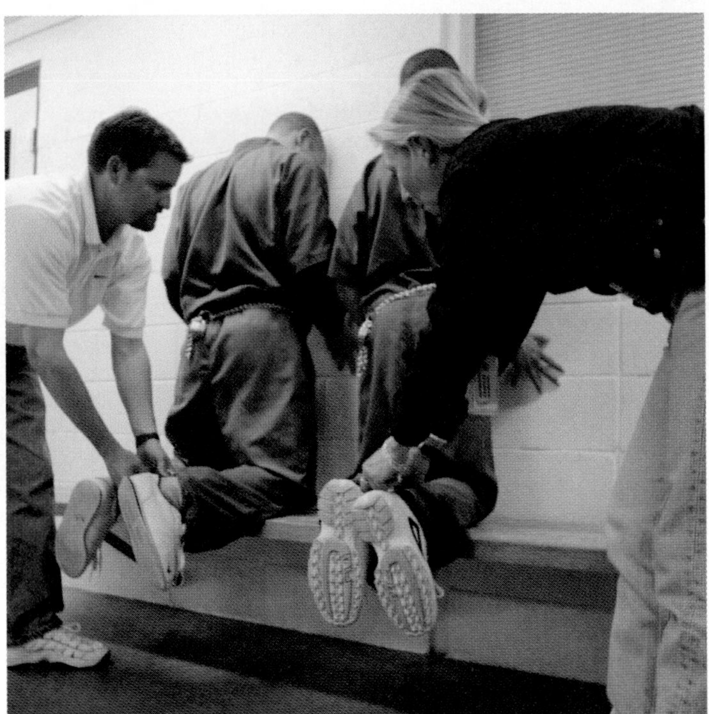

Prison guards remove shackles from ankles of juvenile offenders at a juvenile hall in California.

Photo by Spencer Grant, courtesy of PhotoEdit.

TODAY'S APPROACH TO JUVENILE INSTITUTIONS

Directors of early juvenile institutions were concerned chiefly with the protection of society. Youths confined within institutional walls were judged enemies of society, and their custody was looked on as a disciplinary measure. How far have things advanced since then? Has there been measurable progress in the search for an answer to the problem of juvenile delinquency? For the past several decades, juvenile institutions have been subscribing, at least superficially, to

Hispanic male inmate inside cell at Venture School V, California Youth Authority.

Photo by A. Ramey, courtesy of PhotoEdit.

FIGURE 17.7

Forty-Six States and the District of Columbia Have Statutes Allowing Judicial Waiver

SOURCE: Melissa Sickmund, "States with Judicial Waiver, 1996." Adapted from M. Sickmund, H. Snyder, and E. Poe-Yamagata, *Juvenile Offenders and Victims: 1997 Update on Violence* (Washington, DC: Office of Juvenile Justice and Delinquency Prevention, 1997); *OJJDP Statistical Briefing Book*, http://ojjdp.njrs.org/ ojstatbb/qa062.html, (accessed June 20, 2005).

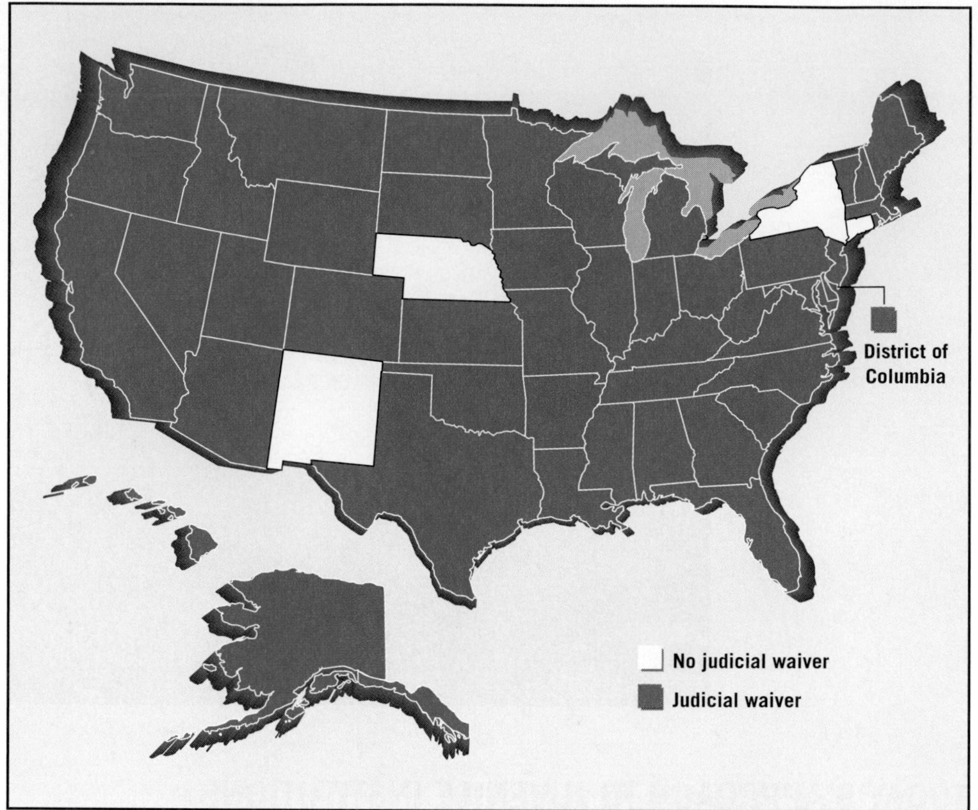

a philosophy of social responsibility for the rehabilitation of deviant youth. As a consequence, today's institutions call for greater emphasis on education, vocational training, and personality training, and on the inculcation of socially accepted living habits.

Society has a way of placing its concerns in an order of priority, concerns that are social and technological. One often hears the inquiry, "If we can put a man on the moon, why can't something be done about crime?" In the meantime, the public wants something done about juvenile crime, many urban public schools are barely functioning, and organized and armed youth gangs have emerged as a deadly menace in communities nationwide. A return to the extensive use of incarceration, which stigmatizes youthful criminals as the enemies of society, has not proven effective in solving the juvenile crime problem. Likewise, the trend of treating juveniles like adult offenders has increased, with little evidence that trying juveniles in adult courts has much promise.[22] (See Figure 17.7.)

INSTITUTIONAL TREATMENT AND REHABILITATION

Nearly thirty years ago, the Commission on Criminal Justice Standards and Goals offered extensive guidelines and standards to assist the juvenile institutions in their reexamination of educational and vocational training programs. Unfortunately, in spite of those standards and guidelines, actual experience has shown that many youths committed to juvenile institutions are just "doing time."[23] Instead of being a constructive and maturing experience, incarceration

A sixteen-year-old displays the ankle bracelet that restricts her to a 100-foot range from her home.
Photo by John M. Discher, courtesy of AP/Wide World Photos.

in a juvenile institution is likely to be harmful for the juvenile. All juvenile institutions require youth to attend school; but beyond that, the treatment and services offered youth vary considerably from state to state and facility to facility.

One example of a state that is trying to improve the treatment and services offered incarcerated youth is West Virginia. There, a pilot program funded by a federal grant has teachers and juvenile correctional staff joining together to improve the treatment of youth in their care. Youth are assessed using a standardized and objective risk/need assessment tool designed to identify those areas of the youth's life that should be targeted for change. Youth then receive a range of programs and services including school, vocational training, anger management, cognitive behavioral interventions, substance abuse treatment, and mental health services. While other states are also working to improve the treatment and services offered incarcerated youth, much remains to be done.

SUMMARY

It is reasonable to consider that the relatively high proportion of adult felons who were processed through the juvenile treatment delivery systems and training institutions as youths might decrease sharply as alternatives to formal processing, institutionalization, and labeling are developed for juveniles. Unfortunately, those youth who are left to go through the ever-hardening juvenile institutions are being labeled more like their adult counterparts, and are being referred directly to the adult justice system.[24]

Although there are many examples of programs for our youth that seem to be breaking the patterns of delinquent and criminal behavior,[25] the public seems to have little patience with wayward youth. Gangs and violent acts reinforce that attitude. The number of community-based beds for juvenile programs is shrinking. It is essential that the impacts of poor programming and systems that punish instead of treat our children become known to the general public. Only with informed public support can the patterns of "crime schools" and neglect be broken, so that juveniles will be able to escape the further impact of the adult system. The public seems to be responding to that kind of logic by making attempts to lower the age of responsibility for criminal remand to adult courts.

It seems that juvenile justice in America will continue at least to give lip service to the ideals of *parens patriae,* but with the Supreme Court watching closely to see that the rights of young citizens are not abused. If we abandon our young people and begin to assume their behavior is adult because it is repugnant or violent, then the jails and prisons of the current century will continue to be overcrowded to the extreme and places where it is difficult to provide high-quality programs and services.

REVIEW QUESTIONS

1. Explain the concept of *parens patriae.* How does it apply today?
2. Describe and differentiate between the three kinds of children who come into contact with the juvenile courts.
3. What were the major findings in the case of *In re Gault?*
4. What are the major trends in the juvenile justice system?
5. Explain the effect of diversion on the correctional funnel for juveniles.
6. Explain the significance of Edwin Sutherland and Jerome Miller.
7. What are five promising approaches to dealing with youth gangs?
8. Debate: Super predator juveniles should be bound over to the adult courts to be tried as adults.
9. What are the most effective treatment models? The least effective?

ENDNOTES

1. Only about 6 percent of juvenile gang members in adult and juvenile institutions meet the basic criteria of "super predator." See George Knox, J. Harris, T. McCurrie, et al., *The Facts About Gang Life in America Today* (Chicago: National Gang Crime Research Center, 1997).
2. Chancery courts date back to England's feudal era. They traditionally had broad power over the welfare of children, but exercised that authority almost exclusively on behalf of minors whose property rights were in jeopardy. In America, this authority was extended to minors in danger of both personal and property attacks.
3. Evidence suggests that taking juveniles to juvenile court at first referral may reduce the likelihood of going to prison later in adult life. Wain Brown, T. Miller, and R. Jenkins, "The Human Costs of 'Giving the Kid Another Chance,'" *International Journal of Offender Therapy and Comparative Criminology* 34:5 (1991): 296–302. In addition, about 40 percent of court referrals in South Carolina were found to have gone on to adult probation and/or prison systems over an eleven-year follow-up period. Jan Rivers and T. Trotti, *South Carolina Delinquent Males* (Columbia: South Carolina Department of Corrections, 1995).
4. Irving Spergel, R. Chance, K. Ehrensaft, et al., *Gang Suppression and Intervention: Community Models* (Washington, DC: Department of Justice, 1994), pp. 3–4.
5. *In re Gault,* 387 U.S. 1, 27 (1967).
6. *McKeiver v. Pennsylvania,* 403 U.S. 541 (1971).
7. See Christopher Manfredi, *The Supreme Court and Juvenile Justice* (Lawrence: University Press of Kansas, 1998).
8. Lamar Empey, "The Social Construction of Childhood, Delinquency and Social Reform," in Malcolm Klein (ed.), *The Juvenile Justice System* (Beverly Hills, CA: Sage, 1976), pp. 27–54. See also Ralph Weisheit and Katherine Johnson, "Exploring the Dimensions of Support for Decriminalizing Drugs," *Journal of Drug Issues* 22:1 (1992): 53–73; and Barry Feld, "Juvenile and Criminal Justice Systems' Responses to Youth Violence," in Michael Tonry and M. Moore (eds.), *Youth Violence* (Chicago: University of Chicago Press, 1998), pp. 189–261.
9. Robert Meier and G. Geis, *Victimless Crime?* (Los Angeles: Roxbury Publishing, 1997).
10. Philip Secret and J. Johnston, "The Effect of Race in Juvenile Justice Decision-Making in Nebraska," *Justice Quarterly* 14:3 (1997): 445–478.
11. *In re Gault.*
12. Melissa Sickmund, *Juvenile Residential Facility Census, 2000* (Washington, DC: Office of Juvenile Justice and Delinquency Prevention, 2002), p. 1.
13. Stephen Gluck, "Wayward Youth, Super Predator: An Evolutionary Tale of Juvenile Delinquency from the 1950s to the Present," *Corrections Today* 59:3 (1997): 62–66.

14. Melissa Sickmund, "Upper Age of Original Juvenile Court Jurisdiction, 1996," adapted from M. Sickmund, H. Snyder, and E. Poe-Yamagata, *Juvenile Offenders and Victims: 1997 Update on Violence* (Washington, DC: Office of Juvenile Justice and Delinquency Prevention, 1997).
15. Howard Synder, *Juvenile Offenders and Victims: National Report Series, Law Enforcement and Juvenile Crime* (Washington, DC: Office of Justice Programs, 2001).
16. Following are excellent Web sites provided by the government: Bureau of Justice Statistics (www.ojp.usdoj.gov/bjs/ijs.html); Justice Information Center (www.ncjrs.org/); OJJDP home page (http://ojjdp.ncjrs.org/); OJJDP Statistical Briefing Book (http://ojjdp.ncjrs.org/ojstatbb/index.html); and the BJS Corrections Statistics (www.ojp.usdoj.gov/bjs/correct.html).
17. Carl McCurley and Howard N. Snyder, "Victims of Violent Juvenile Crime," *Juvenile Justice Bulletin* (July 2004); Paul Harms and Howard Snyder, "Trends in the Murder of Juveniles: 1980–2000," *Juvenile Justice Bulletin* (September 2004); and *Juvenile Offenders and Victims: 1995. National Report* (Washington, DC: Office of Juvenile Justice Delinquency and Prevention, 1995).
18. See the excellent review by David Farrington, "Predictors, Causes and Correlates of Male Youth Violence," in Tonry and Moore (eds.), *Youth Violence,* pp. 421–475.
19. Jeffrey Butts and D. Conners, *The Juvenile Court's Response to Violent Offenders: 1985–1989* (Washington, DC: U.S. Department of Justice, 1993), pp. 14–15.
20. Arlen Egley and Aline Major, *Highlights of the 2002 National Youth Gang Survey,* OJJDP Fact Sheet. (Washington, DC: Office of Juvenile Justice and Delinquency Prevention, 2004).
21. Barbara Allen-Hagen and M. Sickmund, *Juveniles and Violence: Juvenile Offending and Victimization* (Washington, DC: U.S. Department of Justice, 1993), p. 4.
22. Stephen Feiler and J. Sheley, "Legal and Racial Elements of Public Willingness to Transfer Juvenile Offenders to Adult Court," *Journal of Criminal Justice* 27:1 (1999): 55–64.
23. But see Michael Hagan, M. Cho, J. Jensen, et al., "An Assessment of the Effectiveness of an Intensive Treatment Program for Severely Mentally Disturbed Juvenile Offenders," *International Journal of Offender Therapy and Comparative Criminology* 41:4 (1997): 340–350.
24. Michael Tonry (ed.), *The Handbook of Crime and Punishment* (New York: Oxford University Press, 1998). See also Don Gibbons, "Review Essay: Changing Lawbreakers: What Have We Learned Since the 1950s?" *Crime and Delinquency* 45:2 (1999): 272–293; and Sharon Levrant, F. Cullen, B. Fulton, and J. Wozniak, "Reconsidering Restorative Justice: Adolescence and Early Childhood," *Crime and Delinquency* 45:3 (1999): 3–27.
25. Steven Donziger, *The Real War on Crime* (New York: HarperCollins, 1996), pp. 134–140.

CHAPTER 18

Special Category Offenders

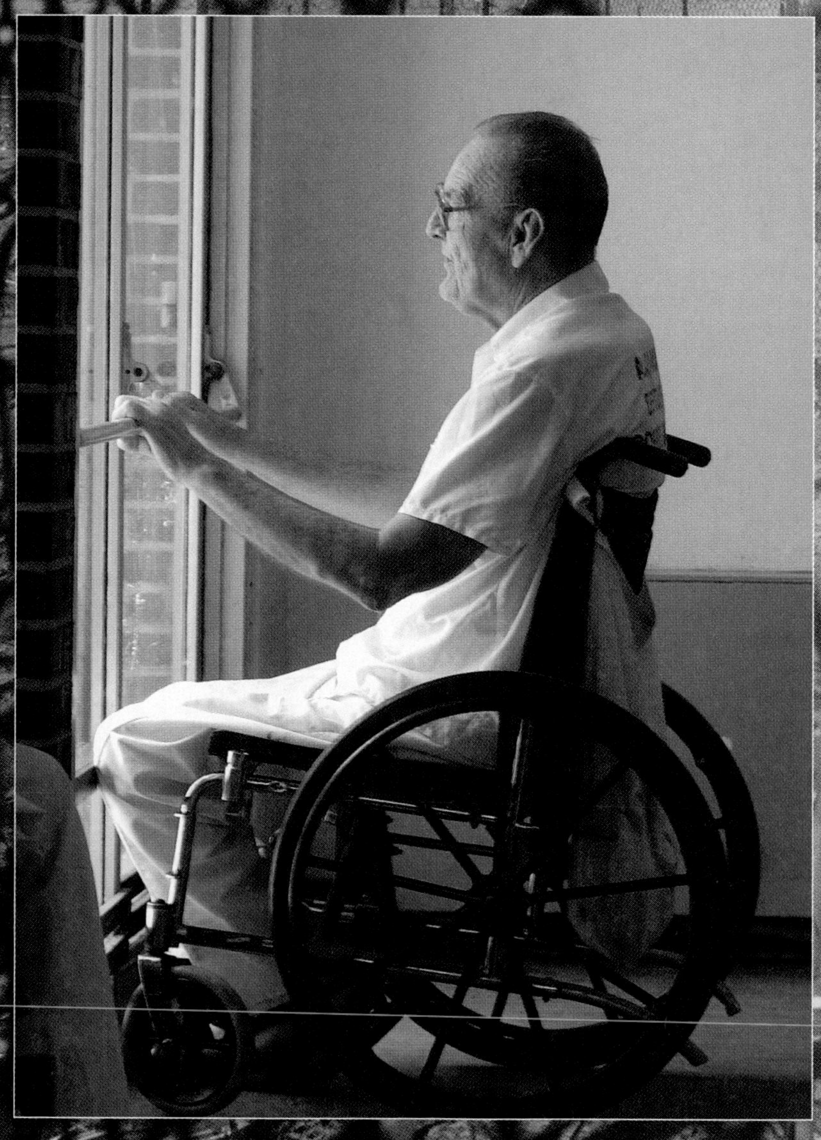

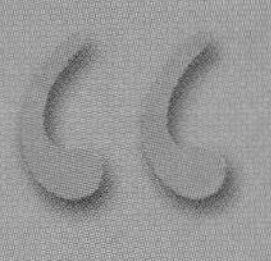

The United States currently has more mentally ill men and women in jails and prisons than in all state hospitals combined.
—Chris Sigurdson

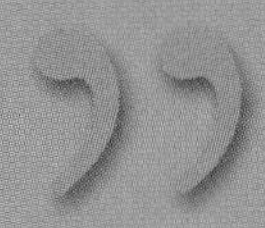

KEY WORDS

- transincarceration
- mentally disturbed
- asylum
- transinstitutionalization
- not guilty by reason of insanity (NGRI)
- incompetent to stand trial
- criminally insane
- guilty but mentally ill (GBMI)
- predict potential dangerousness
- developmentally challenged (mentally retarded)
- *Ruiz v. Estelle*
- sodomy
- child abusers
- child molester
- sex offenses
- fornication
- adultery
- male homosexual conduct
- AIDS
- HIV infection
- antiviral drugs
- elderly inmates
- geriatric prisoner

OVERVIEW

Now we come to the chapter that deals with those offenders who have many more problems than other offenders in the mainstream of criminal behavior. We examine some of the so-called "rejects" of society who are too often found in America's jails and correctional facilities.[1] Many of those individuals are handicapped by their mental processes, and others are labeled by their specific problems, extreme behavior, or personal background.

Of the many categories that could be examined, we have chosen to discuss the mentally disordered offender, the developmentally challenged (retarded) offender, the sex offender, HIV-infected inmates, and geriatric inmates. Although these categories do not constitute an exhaustive list of the possible types of special category offenders, we feel they are a fair spectrum of the problems faced by correctional administrators and the individual offenders who are in their custody and treatment. We first delve a little into the history and development of categories of mentally disordered (mentally ill) offenders to provide a proper framework for examination of these special people.

Since 1970, the closing of 90 percent of the mental health facilities and centers in local counties and their state-funded counterparts has diverted the mentally disordered into correctional facilities (jails and prisons), a process called **transincarceration.** The increasing and unrestrained overcrowding continues to

< A mentally ill inmate looks out the window in the Los Angeles County Jail.
Photo courtesy of AP/Wide World Photos.

place these stigmatized offenders into the correctional bureaucratic system, where their special needs are more often ignored than met. What their needs are and how they are met are discussed in this chapter. We also assess the growing numbers of these special category offenders and how our systems are coping with this problem. The student has now been exposed to most of the clients found in the criminal justice and juvenile justice systems. In Part 7 we delve into the rights of all of these offenders, in or out of the confinement facilities in America, as well as their right to life itself.

THE MENTALLY DISORDERED OFFENDER

What kind of illness would civilized people find so repulsive that they would reject the sufferers in the most barbaric fashion and brand them with a stigma that would remain with them for a lifetime, even if a cure were achieved? Those unfortunates, persons with mental disability (mentally disturbed and disordered), were once scorned, banished, and even burned as evil. But, in more enlightened times, we built backwoods fortresses for them, presumably to protect ourselves from contagion. They have been executed as witches, subjected to exorcisms, chained, or thrown into gatehouses and prisons to furnish a horrible diversion for the other prisoners.[2]

Before the Middle Ages, persons with a mental illness (**mentally disturbed**) were generally tolerated and usually cared for locally by members of their own family, tribal system, or primitive society. However, the advent of widespread poverty, disease, and religious fanaticism seemed to trigger intolerance for any unexplainable deviation from the norm. People who were mentally disturbed were thought to be possessed by devils and demons and were punished harshly because of it. As mentioned in Chapter 1, they were subjected to having "the Devil beaten out of them." At that time, the insane were driven out of society, but later they were confined in asylums, another form of isolation from society.

The first insane **asylum** was constructed in Europe in 1408.[3] From that date until recently, the asylum was a dumping ground for all the mentally disordered people that could be neither understood nor cured. In the United States, one after another of the individual states responded to that compelling method of ridding society of misfits by building numerous institutions during the mid-1800s. The inflated claims of cures for mental illness could not stand up against the process of institutionalization, however, and long-term commitments, often for a lifetime, not cures, became the rule of the day.

SIDEBARS

Deinstitutionalization

This concept contains the transfer of the mentally ill to confinement facilities for criminal actions (rather than underlying mental health problems). Prison overcrowding, an acute shortage of funds for treatment services, the deleterious effects of confinement, and lengthier sentences to prison have meant that prison mental health services are generally found to be inadequate.

Asylums became yet another "invisible empire" in America, with the punitive excesses and lack of care or caring ignored by society. "Out of sight, out of mind" was the catch phrase for these unfortunates. With the discovery of tranquilizing drugs, these "snake pits" became places where patients were put into a controllable stupor, until the "magic bullet," a cure for mental illness, could be found. Longer and longer periods of institutionalization, often ordered at the request of family members, finally got the attention of the courts.

In the 1960s, the rights of all citizens, including the mentally ill and convicts, were being reexamined at every level. The abuses in the back wards of the asylums were brought to light and the counterreaction was extreme. In the early 1970s, state after state adopted policies under the Community Mental Health Act that swept the country. The essential goal was to release (deinstitutionalize) all inmates of the asylums who were not a "clear and present danger" to themselves and society.

Although benign in their intents, these acts flooded the central cities of America with tens of thousands of street people with mental impairments and created poorhouses. The response by most jurisdictions has been to transfer the problem to the criminal justice system, filling the jails and correctional institutions of America, a process known as **transinstitutionalization.**[4] In the early 1980s in Seattle, Randy Revelle, the former King County executive, was fond of saying that the King County Jail was the "third largest mental health facility in the state. The first being the Western State Hospital, the second the section of I-5 [freeway] between the jail and the hospital."[5]

Mentally Ill Inmates

From the 1960s to the 1980s, the deinstitutionalization movement demanded that people with mental illnesses be treated in the community, using new drug therapies that appeared to control even the most extreme behaviors of people with mental illnesses. People with mental illnesses suffer from one or more brain dysfunctions that include depression, schizophrenia, and anxiety disorders, which are often successfully treated with such medications as Prozac and Zoloft. This liberation of psychiatric patients was reinforced by court decisions that awarded certain legal rights to people who were emotionally ill. But few community-based programs were developed to treat psychiatric patients effectively. Released to the community without adequate support and treatment services, people with mental illnesses gravitated to criminal confinement facilities for offenders, particularly to jails, but also to the prisons of the United States.

It is estimated that about 15 percent of offenders imprisoned at any time have severe or acute mental illnesses, such as schizophrenia, manic-depression illness, and depression. Approximately 10 to 15 percent of persons with these three illnesses die by suicide. Yet current treatment is extremely effective, if given.[6]

Prisoners tend to be in poor mental health and about 80 percent of male prisoners (and 80 percent of female jail inmates) will, over their lifetime, have at least one psychiatric disorder. The greater the level of disability while in prison, the more likely the inmate is to receive mental health services. In practice, proportionately more female prisoners use mental health services than do males, and whites are more likely to seek or secure prison mental health services than others. At least half of the inmates who need such treatment go without it.

While the U.S. Supreme Court has not found that inmates have a constitutional right to treatment, it has ruled an inmate's constitutional right to medical treatment includes the right to treatment for serious emotional illness. The corrections system is caught in the middle. Institutions are not required to provide services simply because their clients are criminals, and thus have shifted critical funds to other uses (such as increased security staffing). On the other hand, the threat of potential litigation has meant that some revision and provision of mental health services for seriously ill inmates is necessary.[7]

As people with mental illnesses became a larger segment of the population in jails and prisons, professionals in the mental health field became essential to the correctional administrators. Although the ratio of mental health practitioners to inmates remains much too low, there has been some progress. Because many institutions must deal with mental health issues on a priority basis, few to no services are provided for the majority who do not exhibit violent or bizarre behavior. It is a practical fact that in corrections "the squeaky wheel gets the grease."[8]

It appears that the relationship between crime and mental disorder (at least in *groups,* as shown in one study) has no real causal effect.[9] It is essential for society to learn more about distinguishing between different kinds of mental illness and their impacts on safe and secure administration of correctional institutions. It is important to remember that the real link to look for is one that indicates the potential for harm to the mentally ill person and others. It may be a long time before

CORRECTIONAL BRIEF

Mental Illness and Corrections

Most persons familiar with the justice system will understand that the courts are concerned with the three major types of pleas that could be entered in the preadjudication phases: "incompetent to stand trial," "not guilty by reason of insanity," and "guilty but mentally ill." The special issues in determining guilt are described in this chapter. In addition, there are two categories of postadjudication offenders whose special psychological needs pose problems for institutional corrections: inmates whose mental health deteriorates to episodic crises and those sentenced to death who become mentally disturbed.

For some inmates, the impacts of prison life overwhelm their usual coping patterns. Some factors that lead to "prison psychosis" include the routine of the prison, fear of other inmates, forced homosexual behavior, assault and fear of assault, deterioration in affairs and circumstances of family on the outside of prison, and depression. When the psychological crisis comes, correctional administrators frequently transfer affected inmates to prison infirmaries or psychological treatment wards, or initiate inmate transfer to a mental health system. Long-term and intensive psychotherapy for "mentally ill" inmates, however, is believed to be rare. Treatment for episodic mental crisis tends to remain at the first aid level in many states.

Death rows do not usually contain a large proportion of a prison's population but subsume a disproportionate share of the per inmate cost due to the demands of observing, caring, and maintaining death row. That includes a lower staff-to-inmate ratio, mail processing, deathwatch officer workload, and closer custody during recreational periods. Some inmates on death row become mentally ill and, as such, cannot be executed (*Ford v. Wainright,* 106 S. Ct. 2595, 1986). The state has an additional burden of determining if the death row inmate is insane, establishing some procedure to restore the inmate to sanity, and then certifying the sanity of the patient-inmate. Because this would be tantamount to a "death sentence" and thus not a favor for the inmate, it is unlikely mental health physicians would undertake that process alone or with great enthusiasm. It remains for the states to develop procedures for identifying, diagnosing, treating, and certifying the sanity of death row inmates who claim to be insane.

For the extreme behavior cases, there are special units for more intensive treatment, such as the one in Washington State. That unit is a model of how to deal with extreme mentally and behaviorally disordered prisoners. Unfortunately, that fine facility can handle only 144 inmates. Though commendable, the figure is only about one-tenth of the commonly recognized population of inmates who could use more intensive mental health services. One quickly finds that only the really severe cases are able to be referred to the Special Offender Center.

Is the mentally disordered person more prone to criminal behavior? Or does the criminal justice system respond to such misfits in a legal manner only because the mental health system has been rendered helpless to deal with most of them? Steadman and Monahan have studied that relationship and have made some rather interesting discoveries:

- The correlates of crime among the mentally disordered appear to be the same as the correlates of crime among any other group: age, gender, race, social class, and prior criminality.
- Likewise, the correlates of mental disorder among criminal offenders appear to be the same as those in other populations: age, social class, and previous disorder. Populations characterized by the correlates of both crime and mental disorder (e.g., low social class) can be expected to show high rates of both, and they do.

SOURCE: Henry J. Steadman and John Monahan, *Crime and Mental Disorder* (Washington, DC: U.S. Department of Justice, 1984), p. 5.

such options are available to the already overcrowded corrections systems in the United States.

Two Ways to Escape Criminal Responsibility

There are two justifications that defendants can invoke in an attempt to relieve themselves of criminal responsibility for a criminal act. The first is **not guilty by reason of insanity (NGRI)**; the second is **incompetent to stand trial.** In the first instance, offenders do not deny the commission of the act, but assert they lacked the capacity to understand the nature of the act or that it was wrong. The second instance is based on the common law criterion that defendants must be able to understand the charges against them and to cooperate with their counsel in the preparation of their own defense. The procedures for determining competency vary considerably among jurisdictions, but most make it a court decision based on psychiatric testimony. If defendants are found incompetent to stand trial, then they are usually committed to a mental institution until declared competent.

A unit for mentally disturbed inmates at the Los Angeles County jail, built in 1998.

Photo courtesy of Pennsylvania Department of Corrections.

The Criminally Insane

With the advent of legal insanity and legal incompetence as defenses against criminal conviction came the development of special asylums for the **criminally insane**, in most cases just another form of prison without due process protections. A visiting student from Italy once remarked to the authors, when visiting a hospital for the criminally insane, "How can a person be criminally insane? If you are criminally responsible you cannot be insane, if you are insane you cannot be criminally responsible?" That question is difficult to answer directly; such institutions are usually reserved for the following categories of offenders[10]:

1. Persons adjudicated incompetent to enter a plea or stand trial
2. Defendants found not guilty by reason of insanity
3. Persons adjudicated under special statutes (e.g., "sexually dangerous persons," "defective delinquents," or "sexual psychopaths")
4. Convicted and sentenced offenders who have become mentally disturbed while serving a prison sentence and have been transferred to a mental health facility
5. Other potentially hazardous mentally ill persons requiring special security during the course of their evaluation and treatment

In more recent years, those claiming to be NGRI have been the subjects of considerable debate.[11] President Nixon sought to have the NGRI defense abolished. More informed criminologists point to such problems with the insanity defense as excessive media coverage, suspicion of malingering by the defendant, and conflicting and suspicious testimony by mental health professionals testifying for either the defense or the prosecution.

The insanity defense is used in less than 1 percent of all felony cases and, of those, only one in four are found to be NGRI. One study found only the most emotionally and behaviorally disturbed defendants to be successful in their plea and that the successful petitioners had committed more serious offenses. The decision to acquit is more frequently made in court by prosecutors, defense attorneys, and the judge, and less frequently by jury members. Persons acquitted by NGRI are generally found less likely than their cohort of convicted offenders to commit crimes after release.[12]

Prosecutors often hope that those accused offenders acquitted through the plea of NGRI will be institutionalized for a period sufficient to reduce their dangerousness, and to provide both public safety and some retribution. The debate continues. Perhaps the most reasonable solution would be to determine guilt first and then shift the issue of diminished capacity (insanity, in this case) to the sentencing or case disposition stage. The American Psychiatric Association, following the attack by John Hinckley on the life of President Reagan, recognized that position.

As a response, by 1986, twelve states abolished the insanity defense entirely, then created **guilty but mentally ill (GBMI)** statutes in its place.[13] Under those statutes, an offender's mental illness is acknowledged but not seen as sufficient reason to allow him or her to escape criminal responsibility. If convicted, offenders are committed to prison. Some states will provide mental health treatment in the prison setting, but others may transfer the offender to a mental health facility for treatment. In Georgia, defendants who entered insanity pleas but were determined GBMI received harsher sentences than their counterparts, whose guilt was determined in trial, suggesting increased punishment for the disturbed offender.[14]

The position of the American Psychiatric Association is that significant changes in the legislation should be made to deal with the disposition of violent persons acquitted by NGRI[15]:

1. Special legislation should be designed for those persons charged with violent offenses who have been found not guilty by reason of insanity.
2. Confinement and release decisions should be made by a board including both psychiatrists and other professionals representing the criminal justice system and akin to a parole board.
3. Release should be conditional on having a treatment supervision plan in place, with the necessary resources available to implement it.
4. The board having jurisdiction over the released insanity acquittees should also have the authority to reconfine them.
5. When psychiatric treatment in a hospital setting has obtained the maximal treatment benefit possible, but the board believes that for other reasons confinement is still necessary, the insanity acquittee should be transferred to the most appropriate nonhospital facility (prison).

While the public remains upset by a seemingly gaping loophole in the net of justice, the courts continue to seek equitable ways to deal with the offender who has diminished mental capacity.

The Problems of Prediction

It is unfortunate that the long indeterminate sentences often given to mentally disordered offenders reflect a fear that those committed might be a problem in the future. It is the expectation that someone is capable of predicting criminal inclination that makes so questionable the programs for treating those who are mentally disordered.

Who can **predict potential dangerousness** with any degree of accuracy? The noted psychiatrist Bernard Rubin stated, "The belief in the psychiatrist's ability to predict the likely dangerousness of a patient's future behavior is almost universally held, yet it lacks empirical support." He added, "Labeling of deviancy as mental illness or predicting dangerousness is just a convention to get someone to treatment. Once in treatment the concept of dangerousness is forgotten."[16]

So we see the paradox of requiring psychiatrists to predict behavior and to attach a label to offenders, when that might result in an indefinite, or even lifelong, commitment to a mental institution for someone who is not really dangerous (a false-positive prediction). Further, the individual is then labeled for custody and treatment in a special area within that institution. When we consider the wealth of folklore surrounding mental institutions, it becomes clear that a dreadful lifelong stigma accompanies the label of "criminally insane."

THE DEVELOPMENTALLY CHALLENGED OFFENDER

Within the correctional system are offenders who, though considered legally sane and competent to stand trial, are **developmentally challenged (mentally retarded).** (An IQ score of 69 or below on a standardized test is the generally accepted measure for identifying the developmentally challenged, with exceptions.) Their intellectual level and social adaptability measure well below average, yet they are adjudged legally responsible for their actions. Some 4 to 9 percent of the prison population is composed of developmentally challenged inmates.

In addition to the developmentally challenged, prisons contain an unknown but larger number of lower functioning inmates with fewer intellectual abilities (compared to the general prison population) and IQs that may approach 70, but who are not technically retarded. They have diminished intellectual abilities but a diagnosis of mental retardation is not warranted. Unlike mental illnesses the developmentally challenged and lower functioning inmates are not treated with medication, but may learn both skills and coping mechanisms that would allow them to lead more satisfactory and productive lives.

In their guidelines for incarcerated developmentally challenged offenders, Santamour and West address the problems encountered[17]:

1. In prison, the retarded [developmentally challenged] offender is slower to adjust to routine, has more difficulty in learning regulations, and accumulates more rule infractions, which, in turn, affect housing, parole, and other related matters.
2. Retarded [developmentally challenged] inmates rarely take part in rehabilitation programs because of their desire to mask their deficiencies.
3. They often suffer the brunt of practical jokes and sexual harassment.
4. Such inmates are more often denied parole, serving on the average two or three years longer than other prisoners for the same offense.

Administrators from both fields (corrections and mental health) have a tendency to regard the developmentally challenged offender as a misfit in their system of services. (People with developmental challenges tend to have higher rates of involvement in violent incidents in prison.)[18] Well-meaning administrators from both systems look to one another to assume responsibility for programming and funding. Because of the few resources available to each system and even more pressing concerns, the result is often very limited programming.

CORRECTIONAL BRIEF

Developmentally Disabled Prisoners: Findings

Few jails or prisons have sufficient facilities and programs to handle the special needs of developmentally disabled offenders, and hospitals and other health facilities are seldom capable of administering correctional programs with sufficient security to protect society's rights. Without alternatives, judges are left with no other choice than to sentence those individuals to prison.

- Some mentally retarded offenders require incarceration because of the seriousness of their crimes or their records as repeat offenders, but most other mentally retarded offenders could be diverted from prison to community treatment programs while still ensuring the safety of the community.
- There is tremendous variation in estimates of the number of mentally retarded persons incarcerated in prison: Earlier research indicates that the percentage of those offenders is higher than the percentage within the general population, while the most recent studies place the percentage at about the same level as that within the general population.
- Mentally retarded offenders are often used by their peers, reflecting their great need for approval and acceptance. They have no long-term perspective and little ability to think in a causal way to understand the consequences of their actions.
- Retarded persons are often victimized or abused by other inmates.
- Identifying the offenders who have special needs is essential for planning individualized programs. Due process and functional diagnosis and evaluation performed by specially trained staff utilizing sophisticated assessment tools and procedures are essential.
- Because developmentally challenged people are usually undetected, violation of the legal rights of such persons is frequent.
- Criminal justice and corrections personnel are not presently trained to handle the special problems and needs of such offenders.
- Matters of competency relating to diminished mental capacity should be considered at the first point of contact with the criminal justice system and at each decision point in the continuum.
- Developmentally disabled offenders should be assigned to programs that meet their individual needs: Some may be mixed in with the regular prison population; some need a segregated environment; some would benefit most from a community setting; and others might be placed in a regular group home or guardianship arrangement.
- A survey of local jurisdictions revealed the need for training about developmentally challenged people for criminal justice personnel who normally do not distinguish between the developmentally challenged and mental illness; the need for early identification of such persons once they come in contact with the criminal justice system; and the need for more community resources, particularly residential programs, to serve this category of offenders.

The special needs of the developmentally challenged offender are unique, and the program models are few. Those models that do exist are limited primarily to special education programs geared more to the needs of the individual with learning disabilities other than those of the developmentally challenged person. One promising model concerned with these offenders on a county level focuses on substance abuse, psychological needs, and both vocational and educational improvement.[19]

A Historic Perspective

In reviewing historical and philosophical trends in the study of the developmentally challenged offender, it is noteworthy that before the late nineteenth century, little attempt was made to differentiate between the developmentally challenged individual and anyone who commits a crime.

Currently there is less reluctance to associate "retardation" directly with delinquency. Much of the revived interest from the 1960s to date has been generated by the legal community and not by criminologists. Such a phenomenon stems from a growing awareness that the preponderance of developmentally challenged individuals in the criminal justice system may be more an administrative and legal artifact than evidence for a causal relationship between the developmentally challenged and criminality.

The landmark ***Ruiz v. Estelle*** decision has also set the tone for judicial consideration of the developmentally challenged inmate.[20] This class action suit

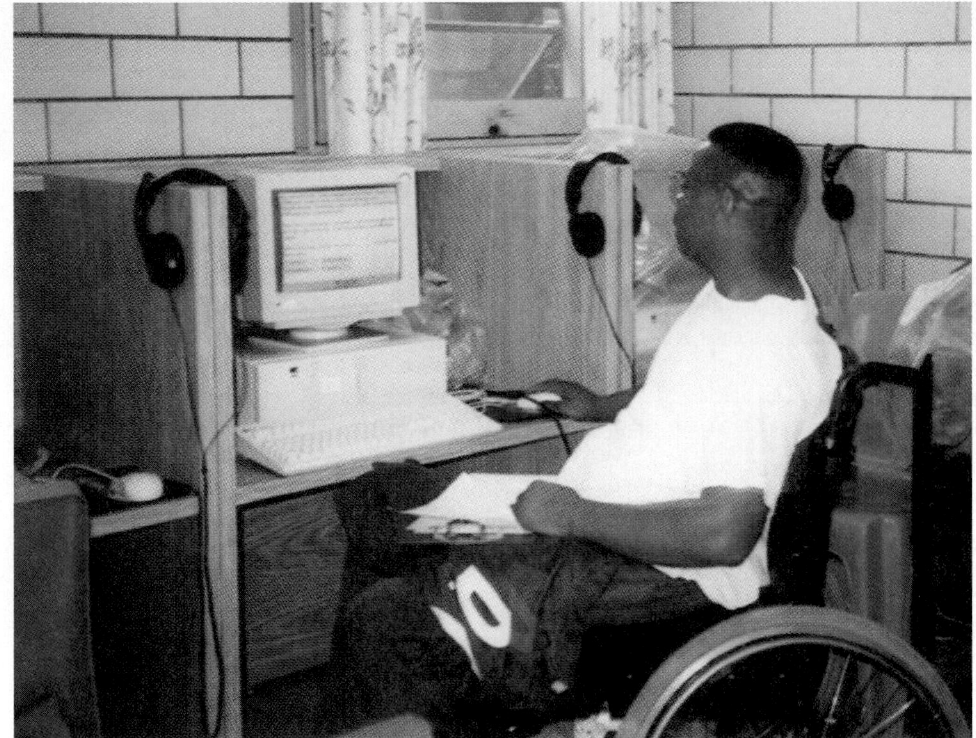

Prisoner with learning disabilities working with a computer.
Courtesy of AP/Wide World Photos.

involved issues of overcrowding, medical care, inmate trustees as guards, and other conditions; the federal court declared the Texas prison system to be unconstitutional. Judge Justice found that between 10 and 15 percent of the Texas Department of Corrections inmates were developmentally challenged and that they were distributed throughout the system. The judge echoed Santamour and West concerning the developmentally challenged inmates' special problems and added the following:

1. They are abnormally prone to injuries, many of which are job related.
2. They are decidedly disadvantaged when appearing before a disciplinary committee.

This raises basic problems of fairness and the special need for assistance.[21] It seems obvious that the issue of the developmentally challenged inmate is slowly coming to the forefront, led by the efforts of the courts.

Recent litigation has determined emerging rights of the developmentally challenged inmate. In 1981, *Green v. Johnson* (512 F. Supp. 965) established that mentally retarded inmates under age twenty two have a right to receive special education. In *Atkins v. Virginia* (536 U.S. 304, 2002), the U.S. Supreme Court ruled that mentally retarded inmates cannot be executed. The Americans with Disabilities Act requires all correctional agencies to establish procedures to screen for developmentally challenged inmates and provide rehabilitation programs specifically designed for them.

Developmentally challenged offenders are often individuals who have never been accepted by society at large. Becoming a part of the "society of captives" is often their first experience of acceptance and thus has a pervasive impact. At Bridgewater State Hospital and Prison in Massachusetts, personnel commenting on the strengths of the association between developmentally challenged inmates and the prison culture noted that only the developmentally challenged inmates returned to prison for social visits. Are developmentally challenged offenders in need of special consideration in regard to criminal responsibility? As noted by Richard C. Allen,

CORRECTIONAL BRIEF

Texas Has Recommendations

All criminal justice personnel should receive basic training in regard to the developmentally challenged ("mentally retarded") inmate.

Every effort should be made to identify offenders who are mentally retarded at each stage of the criminal justice process, especially in the earlier stages.

Funding should be increased, both for adult probation and for parole, for the purchase of community services for the mentally retarded probationer and parolee.

In all appropriate cases the mentally retarded offender should be diverted to community programs.

For those mentally retarded offenders who are sentenced to prison, great care should be taken to protect them from abuse and manipulation by other inmates, and special program activities should be provided that take into consideration their handicap of mental retardation.

Experts in the field of mental retardation in Texas should direct some of their efforts to development of prevention programs to keep mentally retarded persons from becoming offenders.

Mentally retarded offenders should be accepted by all programs designed for mentally retarded persons.

The Texas Code of Criminal Procedures should be amended to allow for the transfer of mentally retarded offenders from the Texas Department of Corrections to an appropriate Texas Department of Mental Health and Mental Retardation (TDMHMR) program where the prisoner may, in fact, serve out the full prison term.

The question of competency should be considered at the first possible stage in the criminal justice system.

Mental retardation should be considered in the law as a mitigating circumstance and therefore be taken into consideration at the time of sentencing if, in fact, the offender has been found competent but mentally retarded.

The standards of the Texas Commission on Jail Standards should include specific references to mentally retarded inmates and their needs.

Ultimately, the TDMHMR should provide services to all mentally retarded adult offenders.

In Texas IQ tests should be developed that are less culturally biased against blacks and minorities.

SOURCE: Texas Correctional Office on Offenders with Medical and Mental Impairments, *Biennial Report* (www.tdej.state.tx.us/publications/tcomi/TCOMI-Biennial-Report-2005-final.pdf, August 20, 2005).

> *Historically, society has pursued three alternative courses with the developmentally challenged offender: we have ignored his limitations and special needs; or we have sought to tailor traditional criminal law processes to fit them; we have grouped him with psychopaths, sociopaths, and sex deviates in a kind of conventicle of the outcast and hopeless.*[22]

One way to accomplish such consideration would be with a special court, similar to a juvenile court, where the developmentally challenged offenders are handled both for the crime and for their condition.

SEX OFFENDERS

Common Sex Offenses

Any analysis of sex offenses is complicated because state legislatures are often too inhibited to describe specifically the acts they are seeking to punish. Thus, punishment may be decreed for "lewd and lascivious conduct," "acts against nature," "carnal knowledge," "imperiling the morals of a minor," and so on. Almost any sexual activity can be prosecuted under one or another of those vague and overly broad rubrics. The same term, moreover, means different things in different states. Thus, **sodomy,** which in many states would refer primarily to male homosexual acts, might also be applied to heterosexual oral or anal intercourse or to sexual contacts with animals.

Highly misleading terms may be used, such as *statutory rape* for an offense that is not rape at all, but sexual intercourse with a fully consenting female who has not yet reached the age of legal consent (eighteen in some states). Discussions of **sex**

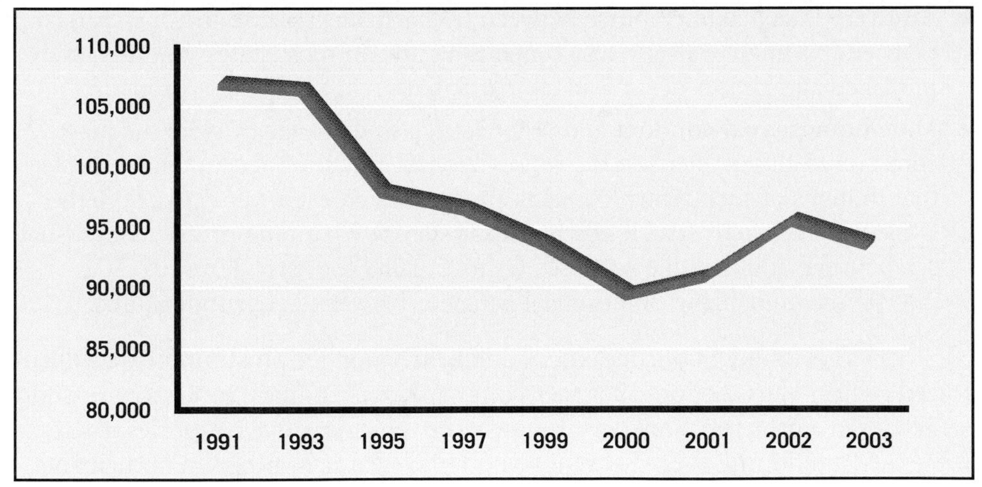

FIGURE 18.1

Number of Reported Female Rapes, 1991–2003

SOURCE: Federal Bureau of Investigation, *Uniform Crime Reports 1991–2003* (Washington, DC: U.S. Department of Justice, 1992–2003).

offenses are further complicated by the fact that a man charged with a serious offense such as rape may be permitted, in the course of plea bargaining, to plead guilty to a lesser offense; hence, men who are in fact rapists may be lodged in correctional institutions for such apparently nonsexual offenses as breaking and entering or assault. In the following discussion we consider the actual offenses committed, rather than the vague legal terminology often used or the lesser offenses to which an offender may plead. Trends in reported rape can be found in Figure 18.1.

Until the past few years, the term *sex offense* commonly called to mind a lust-murder of the most irrational and heinous type. More recently, the intense and proper concern of the women's movement with rape and related crimes, such as assault with intent to commit rape, has tended to make rape the predominant sex offense in the minds of many people. Data on forcible female rape can be found in Figure 18.2. Many experts believe that heterosexual rape, in its more violent forms, is not a sex crime at all but a crime of power and dominance over women.[23]

By far the most common sex offenses, however, are three that are rarely prosecuted: fornication, adultery, and male homosexual contact:

- **Fornication** is sexual intercourse between persons not married to each other; it remains a crime in most states but is generally ignored by the law enforcement and criminal justice systems.

SIDEBARS

Child Abusers and Molesters

Child abuse is any act of commission or omission that endangers or impairs a child's physical or emotional health and development. The major forms are physical (such as neglect), emotional (deprivation and abandonment), and sexual. ***Child abusers*** are found among all ethnic, racial, class, and religious groups. A child abuser is typically a person closely related by blood, kinship, or marriage, such as a parent, stepparent, guardian, other relative, or even a neighbor engaged in a repeated pattern of abuse.

A ***child molester*** is one who injures or has questionable sexual relations or dealings with a person under the age of puberty or legal age. Victims may be subject to rape, fondling, indecent exposure, sodomy, or murder.

In correctional facilities, child abusers and molesters rank low in the social system and are themselves frequently targets of prejudicial or lethal acts by other inmates.

SOURCE: George Bush, *The Dictionary of Criminal Justice* (Guilford, CT: Dushkin, 1991), p. 44.

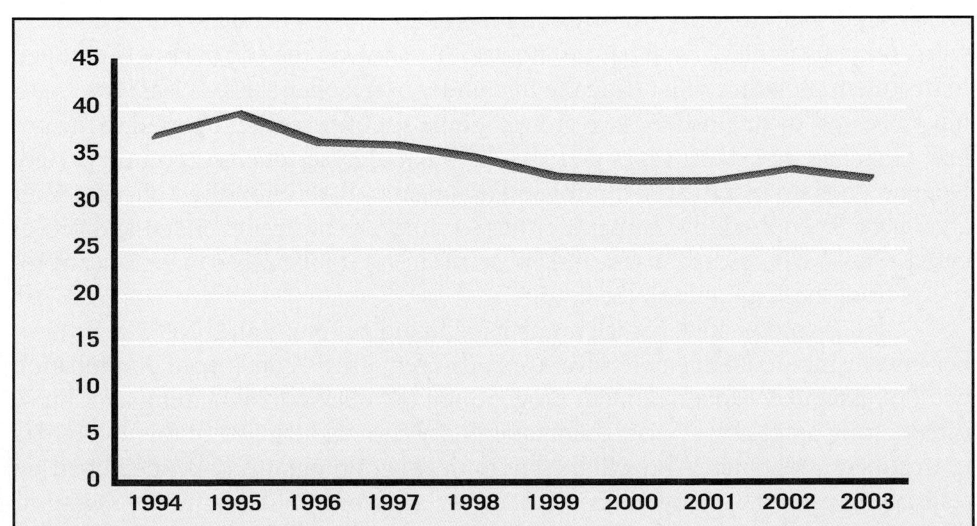

FIGURE 18.2

Forcible Female Rape, 1991–2003

SOURCE: Federal Bureau of Investigation, *Uniform Crime Reports 1991–2003* (Washington, DC: U.S. Department of Justice, 1992–2003).

- **Adultery** is sexual intercourse between two persons, at least one of whom is married to someone else. It also remains a crime in most states, but it is rarely punished and almost never leads to participation in a treatment program.
- **Male homosexual conduct** and other acts classed as *sodomy* were the most common of all sex offenses; the Kinsey reports and more recent data indicate that millions of such sexual contacts are committed each week. In 2003, the U.S. Supreme Court struck down a Texas state law banning private consensual sex between adults of the same sex (*Lawrence and Garner v. Texas,* 02-102, 2003), decriminalizing homosexual behavior between consenting adults.[24]

Laws governing public indecency and solicitation for prostitution are still enforced in many jurisdictions. But they commonly lead to fines, probation, or short sentences in local correctional institutions. The remaining five categories of sex offenses account for the overwhelming majority of treatment program participants:

1. Rape, attempted rape, assault with intent to rape, and the like[25]
2. Child molestation[26]
3. Incest[27]
4. Exhibitionism and voyeurism
5. Miscellaneous offenses (breaking and entering, arson, and the like) in cases involving a sexual motivation.

The majority of sex offenders currently participating in treatment programs are predominantly heterosexual and are there for heterosexual offenses, though some of them, like some heterosexual nonoffenders, have had occasional or incidental homosexual contacts. Most homosexual participants in treatment programs are there for sexual contacts, rarely violent, with children or adolescents. Some are homosexual incest offenders. A few have committed homosexual rape or rape-related offenses.

Almost all sex offenses *prosecuted* in the United States today (except for prostitution-related offenses and offenses involving indecent public performances) are committed by men. The only significant exceptions are the rare cases of child molestation in which a woman is prosecuted along with a man, often her husband, as an accessory, or in child pornography. As a rough estimate, 200 or 300 males are prosecuted for sex offenses for every female prosecuted. It is probable, of course, that the ratio of offenses committed by females is much higher than the ratio of prosecutions.

Most sex offenders in treatment programs are eighteen to thirty-five years of age. A significant minority (mostly child molesters, those offenders whose contacts with children are of a sexual nature) is past fifty. How do the sex offenders enrolled in treatment programs differ from the remainder of sex offenders? At least five "sorting processes" distinguish the two groups. Some sex offenses are reported to the police; others are not. Most rapes and a wide range of lesser offenses go unreported. No man ends up in a treatment program as a result of an unreported offense. After an offense is reported, the perpetrator may or may not be apprehended and prosecuted. Those who escape arrest and prosecution no doubt differ in significant respects from those who reach the courts.

Of those prosecuted, a small number are found not guilty and a very large number (mostly minor offenders) receive suspended sentences or are placed on probation without assignment to a treatment program. Of the offenders remaining after those three sorting processes, some are sent to ordinary correctional institutions and others to treatment programs. Who will be sent to treatment programs depends in part on state law, in part on the judge, and in part on the availability of a treatment program.[28]

Finally, most treatment programs can (and do) reject or transfer to other institutions those offenders they deem unsuitable for treatment. The net effect of these five sorting processes is a population of program participants from which most of the very serious offenders and most of the very minor offenders have been screened.

Sex Offenders and Probation

Probation officers are generally underprepared or undertrained to work with sex offenders because such preparatory efforts are complex, expensive, and time intensive. Most officers lack specific training in the required interpersonal and professional skills. Often caseload size inhibits effective supervision; probation linkages with other social service agencies and providers are not optimal. Often female officers feel concerned about their own safety, and most sex offenders are "high-need" cases.

Probation officers, to control sex offenders, increasingly use enhanced probation services, through specialized caseload and electronic monitoring, and intensive supervision. Probation and parole agencies also contract with privately run community correctional centers to provide treatment programs for sex offenders as an adjunct to community control (see Chapter 21). As these strategies are more widely implemented across the nation, a smaller proportion of treatable sex offenders will be committed to prison facilities.

It is possible, of course, that tomorrow an alumnus of one of those treatment programs may commit a heinous lust-murder; however, an alumnus of a local high school or a member of a church choir could do the same. Treatment programs are specifically designed to minimize the likelihood that an offender will commit any sex offense following release, either a crime of the grossly offensive type or a lesser offense like the ones the offender committed in the past.

Sex Offenders in Prison

Attitudes toward sex offenders widely held by the public[29] as well as by legislators,[30] judges,[31] corrections officers,[32] and others in positions of power are largely influenced by traditional beliefs, and continue to change. The number of sex offenders who are prisoners in state corrections systems continues to climb.

In correctional facilities providing more comprehensive treatment services to sex offender populations, treatment program elements (modalities) are usually combined. Such modalities can include sex education, human sexuality, stress and anger management, social skills, substance abuse programs, how to identify and avoid high-risk situations, relapse prevention, and coping skills.

Long-term programs generally provide intensive and highly structured programs of at least two years, aftercare (up to a year), and follow-up services. Clients can be returned for refresher treatment ("tune-ups"), if necessary. Treatment with the so-called castration drug (Depo Provera) provides the same effect as castration, without the need for surgery. Although its use is not common, it might be used as an adjunct to supervision.

Initial studies of the effectiveness of combined treatment are favorable. California reports rearrest follow-up rates (for sexual or other offenses) of 6 to 8 percent. Texas, using Depo Provera as an adjunct to individual and group treatment, showed relapse rates for Depo Provera–treated subjects to be one-third that for comparison offenders not treated, and about 40 percent less than comparison cases after the drug was withdrawn. The Texas evaluation concludes that maintenance-level Depo Provera drug treatment is beneficial for the compulsive sex offender.[33]

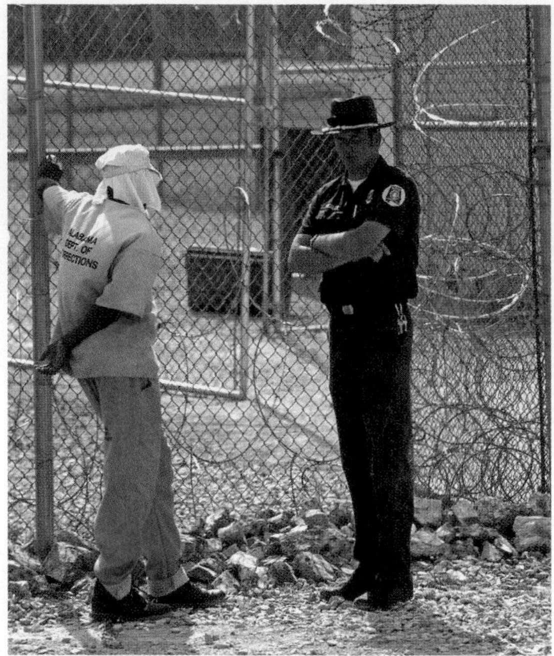

Security guard talks to a "pink-garbed" sex offender at the Limestone Facility, Capshaw, Alabama.

Photo by A. Ramey, courtesy of PhotoEdit.

One outstanding example of a sensible and apparently successful program for the treatment of the sex offender is the 180 Degrees, Inc., program at a halfway house in Minneapolis. This program involves all prospective members in a men's sexuality group. There seems to be some hope in this program:

> *After several years of operation, the program's long-term impact on its participants is not clear. Short-term statistics, however, are encouraging. Of the men who have participated in the sexuality group and who are no longer residents of the 180 Degrees, almost 75 percent successfully completed their stay at the halfway house, 7 percent absconded from the program, and 18 percent were terminated administratively.*[34]

The attitude toward the child molester, particularly those who use ritual child abuse and mutilation in cults,[35] has activated many states to legislate extreme increases in the range of punishment for such offenses. The attitudes are reinforced by continued recidivism reported almost daily with regard to these "headline" offenders. The history of the success with sexual offenders was initially poor, and the future is bleak if additional new approaches to this age-old problem are not developed, tested, and tried.

AIDS IN PRISONS

The AIDS pandemic growing in the United States has of course reached prisons, particularly through offenders with histories of injecting drugs, sharing needles, and engaging in unprotected sexual activities. Estimates of the extent of infection vary across states and institutions, but by 2002, almost 24,000 inmates had been diagnosed HIV positive, almost 2.0 percent of the custody population. Almost 24 percent of HIV-positive inmates had AIDS. The proportions of inmates carrying the virus that causes AIDS ranged from nearly zero in some prisons to over 7 percent in New York prisons. The overall rate of confirmed AIDS among the nation's prison population was 0.48 percent, more than 3 times the rate in the U.S. population of 0.14 percent. At year-end 2002, 2.9 percent of all female state prison inmates were

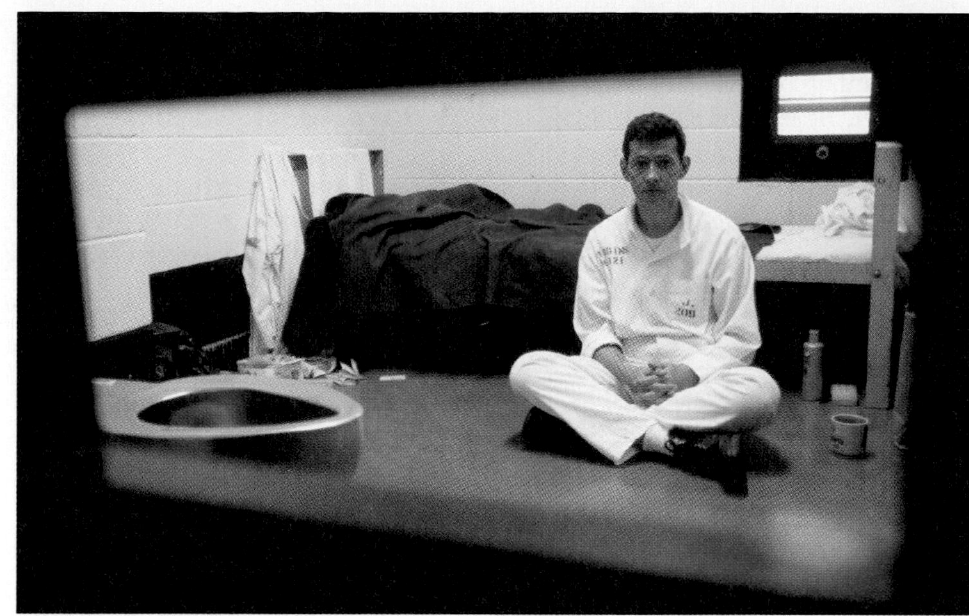

Prisoner with AIDS sits on the floor of his cell, Hamilton Prison, Alabama.

Photo by A. Ramey, courtesy of PhotoEdit.

HIV positive, compared to 1.9 percent of male state prisoners, a rate 1.5 times higher than the male infection rate. Prisoner-to-prisoner (intraprisoner) transmission is also a factor, but the rate appears to be low.[36]

AIDS infection has become increasingly problematic for correctional administrators for many reasons. **AIDS** is a medical term describing terminal phases of **HIV infection.** It indicates an acquired immune system in which the human body is progressively unable to ward off common diseases and illnesses that others would quickly overcome. First, the War on Drugs has serious implications for concentration of HIV-positive cases in prisons. As the National Commission on AIDS pointed out, "By choosing mass imprisonment as the federal and state governments' response to the use of drugs, we have created a de facto policy of incarcerating more and more individuals with HIV infection." That trend is shown in Figure 18.3.[37]

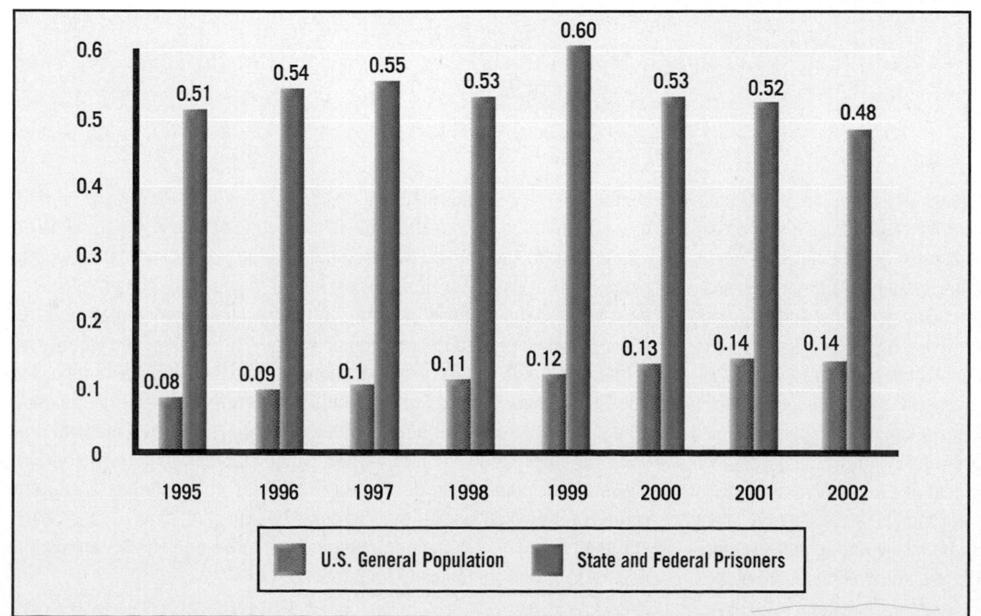

FIGURE 18.3

Population with Confirmed AIDS, 1995–2002 (in percent)

SOURCE: Laura Maruschak, *HIV in Prisons and Jails, 2002* (Washington, DC: Bureau of Justice Statistics, 2004), p. 1.

HIV-Positive Prison Inmates, by Offense and Prior Drug Use

The percentage of state and federal prison inmates reporting that they were HIV positive varied by level of prior drug use. By type of drug use practice, the following percentages of state prison inmates reported being HIV positive: never using drugs, 1.7 percent HIV positive; ever used drugs, 2.3 percent; used drugs in the month before their current offense, 2.7 percent; used a needle to inject drugs, 4.6 percent; and shared a needle, 7.7 percent HIV positive. Like state inmates, federal inmates who used a needle and shared a needle had a higher rate of HIV infection than those inmates who reported ever using drugs or using drugs in the month before their current offense (1.3 and 2.1 percent compared to 0.7 and 0.3 percent). Unlike state inmates, federal inmates using drugs in the month prior to their current offense reported a lower rate of HIV infection (0.3 percent) than inmates who reported ever using drugs (0.7 percent).[38]

HIV infection and resulting AIDS cases pose particular problems for corrections in terms of staff and inmates. Staff have been alarmed by the introduction of AIDS into prison, and initially little was done through education or training to reduce levels of irrational fear. Institutional policies need to be developed and reconsidered in the areas of diagnosing, managing, and treating HIV infection.[39] Additional policy development and implementation are necessary in the areas of staff training and education, inmate counseling, pretest and post-test counseling, voluntary (versus mandatory) testing, medical parole, and discharge and aftercare services (for parole and community supervision). Infection control policies are necessary for dentists, nurses, physicians, security staff, and treatment personnel. HIV transmission and risk factors and precautionary and preventive measures are as follows:

- High-risk behaviors for HIV transmission—sex, drug use, sharing of injection materials, and tattooing—occur in correctional facilities.
- HIV transmission among correctional inmates has been shown to occur.

CORRECTIONAL BRIEF

Needle Sharing and Condoms

Correctional administrators and investigators usually agree that major problems in prisons include the availability of illicit injectable drugs inside prison, and frequent voluntary and involuntary homosexual activity, including homosexual rape. Despite the clear evidence of the spread of AIDS through sharing dirty needles and anal intercourse, correctional personnel and managers are unreasonably resistant to providing prophylactics and bleach to inmates.

Men in prison who wish to engage in anal intercourse are usually sufficiently capable of bringing that act to a successful completion. If the act is forcible intercourse with a passive male coerced into receiving an unwanted intrusion and the HIV is spread, the matter of liability might mean considerable financial loss for the state, managing officer, and lowest level correctional employee. Providing condoms to prisoners will soon be a constitutional right.

Dirty needles shared by prisoners can be easily and effectively sterilized by double rinsing of syringe and needle in common household bleach. Institutions with substantial availability of injectable illicit drugs should make distribution of household bleach a routine sanitary procedure. To do less is to invite liability and eventual punitive and exemplary damages that place them at risk, as well as to discourage prevention. Almost all states have some forms of these programs, but not all have written materials, reinforced by videotaped information on HIV and safer living, and verbal presentations made by an informed health professional, with a following question/answer period. Some institutions have English-only documents; others do not provide periodic updates or ongoing access to medical professionals steeped in HIV information. Some states have prerelease training sessions; others have developed extensive community-based support groups of HIV-positive volunteers to ease the transition of AIDS cases back into the community. These components should be unified into an institutional policy and periodically updated.

- Comprehensive and intensive education and prevention programs represent the best response to these facts, although the precise content of such programs is controversial.
- Rape and coerced sexual activity also occur in correctional facilities but require a different response, one based on inmate classification, housing, and supervision.
- The implementation of "standard precautions" represents the heart of a correctional infection-control program and the first line of defense against the occupational transmission of HIV.
- Condom distribution and other harm-reduction strategies have not been widely adopted in American correctional systems.
- Experience with harm reduction in correctional facilities in Europe and elsewhere may warrant the attention of U.S. correctional administrators.[40]

AIDS and Custody Staff

Craig identified five communicable diseases frequently found in correctional facilities: hepatitis A and B, HIV, Rubella and tuberculosis. She presented procedures thought necessary to address HIV infection.[41] These include the following:

- Avoid blind pocket searches and reaching into blind crevices to lessen the possibility of needle-sticks and other puncture wounds; instead, use flashlights, mirrors, and other visual aids.
- Protective equipment should be provided and used, including latex gloves, masks, protective eye goggles, and gowns for invasive therapy by dentists or at autopsies, and one-way valve masks for emergency CPR equipment and procedures.
- Handwashing should be required after every contact with potentially infectious materials, and both sinks and disinfectants should be available.
- Infectious waste policies should be implemented that cover bodily wastes, particularly blood or bodily fluids, including used tampons.
- Exposure reporting procedures should be developed to document possible infection incidents and reduce chains of transmissions of bloodborne and airborne infectious agents (including hepatitis B, HIV, tuberculosis, rubella, and hepatitis A). Such procedures should include after-contact counseling, medical tests of possible contaminant sources, serial blood tests of exposed staff members, and appropriate medical intervention (such as the hepatitis B immune globulin).
- Comprehensive infection control plans should be implemented, updated, monitored, and revised to maintain a healthy working environment, avoid litigation, and encourage officers to practice universal medical procedures.

Adopting these policies will go a long way toward easing staff anxiety and tension in prison settings.

AIDS and Inmates

Perhaps the best single program for managing HIV infections revolves around educational programs to inform inmates of behaviors. Consensus on appropriate medical treatment within prison settings is that prisons should adopt existing community treatment as the standard of care.[42] At a minimum, special infirmaries

TABLE 18.1 AIDS-Related Deaths in State Prisons, 1991–2002

YEAR	NUMBER	RATE PER 100,000 STATE INMATES
1991	520	71
1992	648	83
1993	761	89
1994	955	104
1995	1010	100
1996	907	90
1997	538	48
1998	350	30
1999	242	20
2002	215	17

SOURCE: Laura Maruschak, *HIV in Prisons and Jails, 2002* (Washington, DC: Bureau of Justice Statistics, 2004), p. 2.

should be established to prevent AIDS patients from becoming further victims of airborne infections.[43] Infirmaries[44] should also have drug treatment protocols that specify **antiviral drugs** (such as AZT and protease inhibitors) and drug therapy for such opportunistic infections as tuberculosis and pneumonia. The AIDS death rate is dropping in prisons (see Table 18.1).

Correctional administrators should propose and encourage a medical-parole mechanism for AIDS patients who are no longer a threat to the public safety, for early release back into the community by paroling authorities. Prerelease counseling[45] well in advance of the proposed release date would help inmates identify resources and service providers in the communities to which they will be released. Ideally, each institution should identify a community-based support group of HIV-positive volunteers for inmate referral and ease of transition.

The cost of HIV and AIDS treatment in prison is unknown, but California approximates its costs as $86,000 per inmate per year. Existing Social Security and related medical insurance coverage would pay most of these costs if the offender were in a community setting. By managing medical care, corrections could develop an efficient health care system in prison, lessen stigma, reduce paranoia and staff–inmate tensions, and sharply curtail the potential for costly litigation.[46] Figure 18.4 charts inmate deaths by type, including from AIDS. Corrections faces a medical challenge unparalleled in American history. Innovation and leadership are required to overcome these problems.

GERIATRIC INMATES: THE GRAYING OF AMERICAN PRISONS

As was mentioned in Chapter 16, the proportion of prisoners in the nation's institutions who are elderly is rapidly increasing, in part due to the tougher long-term sentences inherent in the current "get tough on crime" stance, but also because of the aging of the general population in America. In 2004, a total of 71,463 male inmates housed in state and federal institutions were over fifty-five years of age.[47] This trend,

FIGURE 18.4

Inmate Deaths in State Prisons, 1995–2002

SOURCE: Laura Maruschak, *HIV in Prisons and Jails, 2002* (Washington, DC: Bureau of Justice Statistics, 2004), p. 5.

	Number of Deaths			Rate of Deaths per 100,000 Inmates		
Cause of Death	1995	1999	2002	1995	1999	2002
Total	3,133	2,933	3,105	311	240	246
Natural Causes other than AIDS	1,569	2,179	2,405	156	178	190
AIDS	1,010	242	215	100	20	17
Suicide	160	169	166	16	14	13
Accident	48	44	41	5	4	3
Execution	56	98	70	6	8	6
By Another Person	86	56	53	9	5	4
Other/Unspecified	204	145	155	20	12	12

which appears likely to continue, will have a significant impact on correctional administration and budgets in this new century. We estimate that by 2010, at least one in ten (over 160,000 inmates) will be age fifty or over. The number of older inmates (age fifty-five or above) in Florida is now one-third that of prisoners aged eighteen to twenty-four.

Elderly inmates are more likely than other prisoners to have committed crimes such as homicide and manslaughter, as well as sexual offenses. They are less

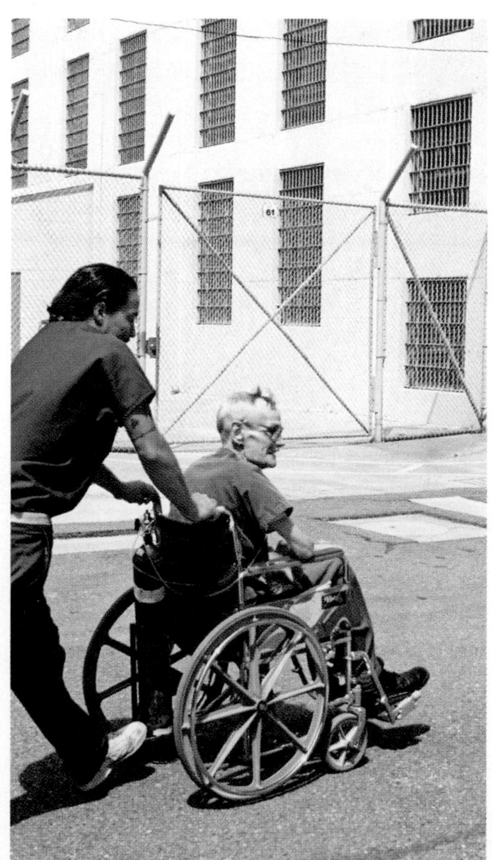

Robert Lee Lilley, a convicted sex-offender, is wheeled into the yard at Territorial Prison (Colorado). The 70-year-old Lilley, who has numerous health problems, requires an inmate attendant. Lilley has been denied parole twice and will likely die in prison. His case highlights the public health costs associated with elderly prisoners throughout the country.

Photo by Sean Cayton, courtesy of The Image Works.

likely than younger inmates to be imprisoned for robbery and burglary. Because of their significantly longer sentences, elderly inmates may be concentrated in prisons well beyond their proportions in the civilian population, which will pose problems for them as well as prison administrators. First, they will have health care problem concerns and need preventive health care programs that, if not provided, could be a source of considerable and, for correctional administrators, substantial litigation costs. At the least, they will suffer from depression and differing nutritional needs (less protein, fewer calories, and more soft food and fiber). Because taste sensations decline with aging, the elderly will request food richer in seasonings and will have a decrease in gastric acid and increase in gas production and constipation. Special diets will be needed.

In addition, growing old in prison will mean having to avoid exploitation and violence by younger inmates, having to adjust new personal needs to prison life, and not having suitable programs (recreational, educational, or housing). Vulnerability to victimization, frailty, and isolation from outside relatives and friends will take their toll, as will fear of death, hopelessness, and being unable to cope when released.

Health care costs will increase significantly for hypertension, diabetes, stroke, cancer, and emphysema. Glasses, dentures, kidney dialysis, and heart surgery will be required. It has been estimated that in two years, health care costs for elderly inmates will increase by fourteenfold.[48] Many smaller prisons will become geriatric centers, or special centers for elderly inmates will be built, and special staff as well as staff training will be necessary to treat this special category of the nation's offenders. Perhaps a nation that can explore space can find the necessary compassion to care for this small but increasing group as we delve into this new century. Executive clemency, including pardons, may become a frequent act, if for nothing else than to save money on prisoners who are probably no longer a danger to society.

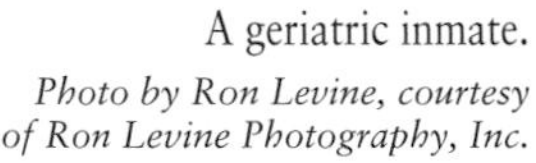

A geriatric inmate.
Photo by Ron Levine, courtesy of Ron Levine Photography, Inc.

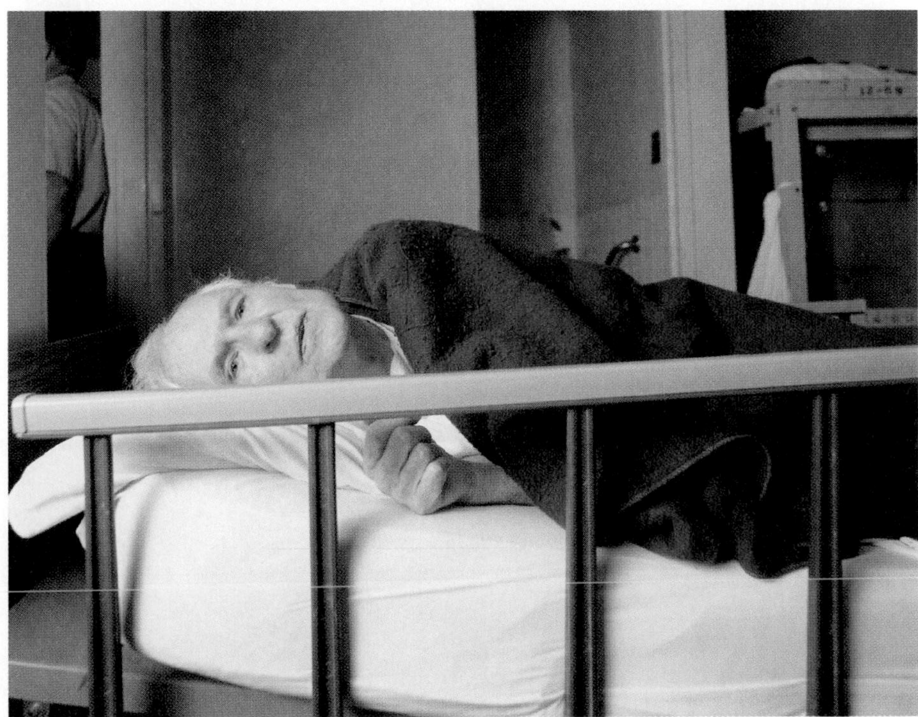

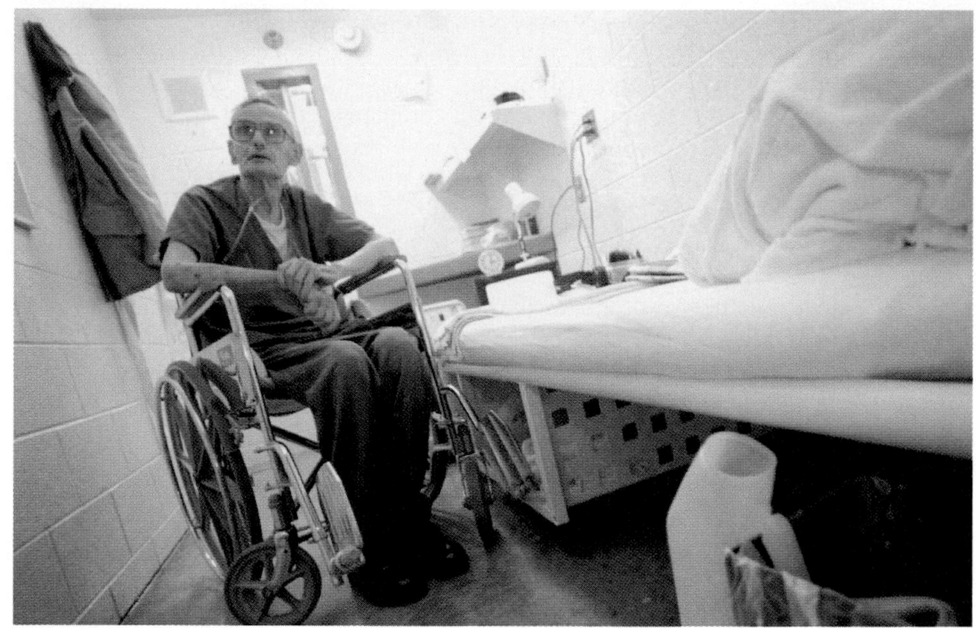

An elderly prisoner in his room.
Photo by Sean Cayton, courtesy of The Image Works.

State prison expenditure for calendar year 2001 (the last year for which national data were available) totaled $29.5 billion. The Federal Bureau of the Prisons expended $3.8 billion. The average cost of imprisoning a state inmate was $22,650. This translates to a nationwide average operating expenditure of $100 per person. States spent some $3.3 billion for medical care of inmates, averaging $2,625 per inmate. The State of Maine spent the most for medical services for each inmate ($5,600) and Louisiana spent the least ($860). These amount to 12 and 4 percent, respectively, of their total prison budgets for 2001. The national average percentage for medical care was 12 percent of operating expenditures.[49]

The **geriatric prisoner,** sentenced to life without hope of parole, could live many years in the prisons of America—long after his or her dangerousness has passed. The courts of the land will be checking carefully to ensure that the person's rights are not violated, and it is certain that imprisonment costs will soar. Geriatric prisoners are "special people" and must be considered such when considering sentences that are too long (beyond what is cost effective).

SUMMARY

The process of labeling is strong and pervasive in our society. Once labeled as mentally disordered, developmentally challenged, a sex fiend, or just old, a special category person's lot is rough indeed. Add to those heavy labels the term *offender* and the problems multiply geometrically. Although mental illness is the nation's largest health problem, affecting one of ten citizens, it is still frequently regarded with the snake pit philosophy of the Middle Ages, especially if some criminal act has been linked to the condition. The developmentally challenged citizen is in a real dilemma if placed in a treatment program that requires measurable improvement as a condition of release. This concept led to laws in the 1930s that essentially gave developmentally challenged persons de facto life sentences if they were placed in an institution until they "improved."

The sex offender is involved in a situation in which society's sexual mores are in transition. Some behaviors that put many in prison just a few years ago are no longer considered criminal. That change has not removed the stigma of the label sex offender, however, and the tolerance of the outside world is low for those so labeled.

Inmates with AIDS and those who are aging in the prisons also cause problems with special handling procedures and huge medical bills. Both of these categories are unable to avoid transitioning from an HIV positive situation to AIDS or to continue to stay young forever. Those problems, along with the "right to treatment," seem at constant odds with one another. When treatment programs fail, blame is often placed on the attendant, the overworked and undertrained staff, the legislators, and the courts. In the final analysis, however, it is up to society to decide whether it wants to spend the time and money to provide care and treatment for its bottom-line "losers" and then to attempt to remove the labels and reintegrate those individuals into the mainstream. Without a firm commitment for change, the castoffs of society will continue to return to institutions and then be released to the public, either with no change or with a decided change for the worse.

We now move on to discuss some of the rights that prisoners, as human beings and American citizens, are entitled to receive both in confinement and as ex-offenders back in the community. We will also visit the ultimate right—the right to live—where we will examine the ongoing controversy around the death penalty.

REVIEW QUESTIONS

1. What spurred the growth of asylums in America?
2. How can one avoid criminal responsibility?
3. What are the most common sex offenses?
4. What would the American Psychiatric Association do with insanity acquittees?
5. What problems do developmentally challenged offenders pose for correctional administrators?
6. What former sex offense has been decriminalized?
7. What recommendations have been offered for correctional processing of developmentally challenged offenders?
8. Can sex offenders be treated?
9. What can be done to reduce staff fear of AIDS?
10. What should be done with geriatric prisoners?
11. What can be done to reduce AIDS in prison?
12. Why does inmate health care cost more than that of the general public?
13. Debate: Inmates over age seventy should be released to community supervision.
14. Why are there so many mentally disordered offenders in prison?
15. What problems does the prison pose for developmentally challenged inmates?
16. Has the GBMI statute approach solved the dilemma of protecting society while providing treatment to disturbed offenders?

ENDNOTES

1. Kenneth Adams, "Who Are the Clients? Characteristics of Inmates Referred for Mental Health Treatment," *The Prison Journal* 72:1/2 (1992): 120–141. See also Richard Bembo, H. Cervenka, B. Hunter, et al., "Engaging High-Risk Families in Community-Based Intervention Services," *Aggression and Violent Behavior* 4:1 (1999): 41–58.
2. G. Ives, *A History of Penal Methods* (London: S. Paul, 1914). Exploitation of incarcerated developmentally challenged offenders by more aggressive and stronger inmates remains a problem in all facilities: mental institutions, juvenile centers, nursing homes, jails, and prisons. In 1980, Congress passed the Civil Rights of Institutionalized Persons Act, authorizing the attorney general to intervene in correctional settings if violations of inmates' civil rights are suspected. For an example of juvenile victimization, see C. Bartollas, S. Miller, and S. Dinitz, *Juvenile Victimization: The Institutional Paradox* (New York: Holsted Press, 1976), pp. 53–76. See also Freda Briggs, *From Victim to Offender: How Child Sexual Abuse Victims Become Offenders* (St. Leonards, Australia: Allen and Unwin, 1995). For a study of missed opportunity, see Luke Birmingham, D. Mason, and D. Grubin, "A Follow-Up Study of Mentally Disordered Men Remanded to Prison," *Criminal Behavior and Mental Health* 8:3 (1998): 202–213.
3. J. Wilpers, "Animal, Vegetable or Human Being?" *Government Executive* (May 1973): 3. See also Terry Kupers, "Trauma and Its Sequelae in Male Prisoners: Effects of Confinement, Overcrowding and Diminished Services," *American Journal of Orthopsychiatry* 66:2 (1996): 189–196.
4. Bruce Arrigo, "Transcarceration: A Constructive Ethnology of Mentally-Ill 'Offenders,'" *The Prison Journal* 81:2 (2002): 162–186.

5. Randy Revelle, former King County executive, while accepting the National Association of Counties award for the "6 East" project for mentally ill inmates at the King County Jail, 1982.
6. Chris Sigurdson, "The Mad, the Bad and the Abandoned: The Mentally Ill in Prisons and Jails," *Corrections Today* 62:7 (2001): 162–186.
7. Henry Steadman et al., "Estimating Mental Health Needs and Service Utilization Among Prison Inmates," *Bulletin of the American Academy of Psychiatry and the Law* 19:3 (1991): 297–307. Canadian data from Laurence Motiuk and Frank Porporino, *The Prevalence, Nature and Severity of Mental Health Problems Among Federal Inmates in Canadian Penitentiaries* (Ontario: Correctional Service Canada, 1992). See also Margaret Severson, "Mental Health Needs and Mental Health Care in Jails," *American Jails* 18:3 (2004): 9–18; and Jerrod Steffan and R. D. Morgan, "Meeting the Needs of Mentally Ill Offenders," *Corrections Today* 67:1 (2005): 38–41.
8. In 1999, Los Angles County had to appropriate more than $8 million as a supplemental allocation to improve mental health care in its jail. Chris Sigurdson, "The Mad, The Bad and the Abandoned," p. 72.
9. This is a hotly debated point. First see S. Wessely and P. J. Taylor, "Madness and Crime: Criminology Versus Psychiatry," *Criminal Justice and Mental Health* 1:3 (1991): 193–228. See also Mary Ann Finn, "Prison Misconduct Among Developmentally Challenged Inmates," *Criminal Justice and Mental Health* 2:3 (1992): 287–299; Lynette Feder, "A Comparison of the Community Adjustment of Mentally Ill Offenders with Those from the General Prison Population," *Law and Human Behavior* 15:5 (1991): 477–493; and Bruce Link, Howard Andrews, and Francis Cullen, "The Violent and Illegal Behavior of Mental Patients Reconsidered," *American Sociological Review* 57:2 (1992): 275–292. But see Barry Wright, I. McKenzie, J. Stace, et al. (eds.), "Adult Criminality in Previously Hospitalized Child Psychiatric Patients," *Criminal Behavior and Mental Health* 8:1 (1998): 19–38.
10. National Institute of Mental Health, *Directory of Institutions for the Mentally Disordered Offenders* (Washington, DC: U.S. Government Printing Office, 1972); and Anthony Walsh, *Correctional Assessment, Casework and Counseling* (Lanham, MD: American Correctional Association, 1997).
11. Valerie Hans, "An Analysis of Public Attitudes Toward the Insanity Defense," *Criminology* 24:3 (1986): 393–413. Among her more interesting findings were that the public wants insane lawbreakers punished, believes that insanity defense procedures fail to protect the general public, and wildly overestimates the use and effectiveness of the insanity defense. See also Bruce Arrigo, *The Contours of Psychiatric Justice* (New York: Garland, 1996); and Caton Roberts and S. Golding, "The Social Construction of Criminal Responsibility and Insanity," *Law and Human Behavior* 15:4 (1991): 349–376.
12. Marnie Rice, Grant Harris, and Carol Lang, "Recidivism Among Male Insanity Acquitees," *Journal of Psychiatry and the Law* 18:3/4 (1990): 379–403; and Richard Pasework, B. Parnell, and J. Rock, "Insanity Defense: Shifting the Burden of Proof," *Journal of Police Science and Criminal Psychology* 10:1 (1994): 1–4.
13. John Klofas and Ralph Weisheit, "Guilty But Mentally Ill: Reform of the Insanity Defense in Illinois," Justice Quarterly 4:1 (1987): 40–50. The effects of the GBMI statutes are discussed in Kurt Bumby, "Reviewing the Guilty But Mentally Ill Alternatives," *Journal of Psychiatry and the Law* 21:2 (1993): 191–220.
14. Lisa Callahan, Margaret McGreevy, Carmen Cirincione, et al., "Measuring the Effects of the Guilty But Mentally Ill (GBMI) Verdict: Georgia's 1982 GBMI Reform," *Law and Human Behavior* 16:4 (1992): 447–462; Carmen Cirincione, H. Steadman, and M. McGreevy, "Rates of Insanity Acquittals and the Factors Associated with Successful Insanity Pleas," *Bulletin of the American Academy of Psychiatry and the Law* 23:2 (1995): 339–409.
15. American Psychiatric Association, *Standards for Psychiatric Facilities* (Washington, DC: APA, 1981), pp. 17–18. But see Washington State Department of Corrections, *Mentally Ill Offenders: Community Release Outcome Study* (Olympia, WA: WSDOC, 1997).
16. Bernard Rubin, "Prediction of Dangerousness in Mentally Ill Criminals," *Archives of General Psychiatry* 27:1 (September 1972): 397–407; Robert Prentky, A. Lee, R. Knight, et al. (eds.), "Recidivism Rates Among Child Molesters and Rapists," *Law and Human Behavior* 21:6 (1998): 635–659; and Michael Ross, "Reflections from Death Row," in Robert Johnson and H. Toch (eds.), *Crime and Punishment: Inside Views* (Los Angeles: Roxbury, 2000).
17. Miles Santamour and Bernadette West, *Sourcebook on the Mentally Disordered Prisoner* (Washington, DC: U.S. Department of Justice, 1985), p. 70. Petersilia estimates the mentally retarded offender in California as 2 percent of all probationers and 4 percent of all incarcerated persons. Joan Petersilia, "Justice for All? Offenders with Mental Retardation and the California Corrections System," *The Prison Journal* 77:4 (1997): 358–380.
18. Finn, "Prison Misconduct," p. 296.

19. Severson identifies ten basic services necessary for inmate mental health. Margaret Severson, "Refining the Boundaries of Mental Health Services: A Holistic Approach to Inmate Mental Health," *Federal Probation* 56:3 (1992): 57–63; Rudolph Alexander, "Incarcerated Juvenile Offenders' Right to Rehabilitation," *Criminal Justice Policy Review* 7:2 (1995): 202–213.
20. *Ruiz v. Estelle,* 503 F. Supp. 1265 (S. D. Tex. 1980), *aff'd in part,* 679 F. 2d 1115 (5th Cir. 1982), *cert. denied,* 103 S. Ct. 1438 (1983) at 1344. See Rolando Del Carmen, B. Witt, W. Hume, et al., *Texas Jails: Law and Practice* (Huntsville, TX: Sam Houston Press, 1990); and John Sharp, *Behind the Walls: The Price and Performance of the Texas Department of Criminal Justice* (Austin: Texas Comptroller of Public Accounts, 1994).
21. Joan Petersilia, *Doing Justice: Criminal Offenders with Development Disabilities* (Berkeley: University of California, 2000).
22. Richard C. Allen, "Reaction to S. Fox: The Criminal Reform Movement," in M. Kindred (ed.), *The Developmentally Challenged Citizen and the Law* (Washington, DC: U.S. Government Printing Office, 1976), p. 645. See also Mark Nichols, L. Bench, E. Morlok and K. Liston, "Analysis of Mentally Retarded and Lower-Functioning Offender Correctional Programs," *Corrections Today* 65:2 (2003): 119–121.
23. The relationship between offender and victim is under intense study, particularly for stranger and serial rapists. See James LeBeau, "Patterns of Stranger and Serial Rape Offending: Factors Distinguishing Apprehended and At-Large Offenders," *Journal of Criminal Law and Criminology* 78:2 (1987): 309–326. See also Kate Painter, *Wife Rape, Marriage and the Law* (Manchester, U.K.: University of Manchester, 1991); and Gregory Matoesian, "'You Were Interested in Him as a Person?' Rhythms of Domination in the Kennedy Smith Rape Trial," *Law and Social Inquiry* 22:1 (1997): 55–93.
24. David O'Connor, "Hawaii Moves Closer to Legalizing Gay Marriages," *Bay Area Reporter* 22:29 (July 22, 1993): 12; United Press International, "Florida Lesbians Sue for the Right to Marry," *Bay Area Reporter* 22:9 (July 22, 1993): 13; and Robert Meier and G. Geis, *Victimless Crime? Prostitution, Drugs, Homosexuality and Abortion* (Los Angeles: Roxbury, 1997).
25. See Patricia Cluss et al., "The Rape Victim: Psychological Correlates of Participation in the Legal Process," *Criminal Justice and Behavior* 10:3 (1983): 342–357; and Patricia Mahoney and L. Williams, "Sexual Assault on Marriage: Wife Rape," in Jana Jasinski and L. Williams (eds.), *Partner Violence* (Thousand Oaks, CA: Sage, 1998), pp. 113–162.
26. David Finkelor, "Removing the Child—Prosecuting the Offender in Cases of Sexual Abuse: Evidence from the National Reporting System for Child Abuse and Neglect," *Child Abuse and Neglect* 7:2 (1983): 195–205. But see Philip Jenkins, *Moral Panic: Changing Concepts of the Child Molester in Modern America* (New Haven, CT: Yale University Press, 1998).
27. Jean Goodwin et al., *Sexual Abuse: Incest Victims and Their Families* (Boston: John Wright, 1982). See also Katherine Beckett, "Culture and the Politics of Signification: The Case of Child Abuse," *Social Problems* 43:1 (1996): 57–76; and Joann Brown and G. Brown, "Characteristics and Treatment of Incest Offenders," *Journal of Aggression Maltreatment and Trauma* 1:1 (1997): 335–354.
28. Karl Hanson, B. Cox, and C. Woszczyna, "Assessing Treatment Outcomes for Sexual Offenders," *Annals of Sex Research* 4:3/4 (1991): 177–208; Fay Honey Knopp, R. Freeman-Longo, and W. Ferree, *Nationwide Survey of Juvenile and Adult Sex Offender Treatment Programs and Models* (Orwell, CT: Safer Society Program, 1992); and Ross Cheit, R. Freeman-Longo, M. Greenberg, et al., "Symposium on the Treatment of Sex Offenders," *New England Journal of Criminal and Civil Confinement* 23:2 (1997): 267–462.
29. Richard McCorkle, "Research Note: Punish or Rehabilitate: Public Attitudes Toward Six Common Crimes," *Crime and Delinquency* 39:2 (1993): 250–252; and Joel Rudin, "Megan's Law: Can It Stop Sexual Predators?" *Criminal Justice* 11:3 (1996): 2–10, 60–63.
30. Timothy Flanagan, P. Brennan, and D. Cohen, "Conservatism and Capital Punishment in the State Capitol: Lawmakers and the Death Penalty," *The Prison Journal* 72:1/2 (1992): 37–56.
31. Anthony Walsh, "Placebo Justice: Victim Recommendations and Offender Sentences in Sexual Assault Cases," *Journal of Criminal Law and Criminology* 77:4 (1986): 1126–1141; and Federal Bureau of Investigation, *Crime in the United States 1994* (Washington, DC: U.S. Department of Justice, 1995), p. 225.
32. John Weeks, G. Pelletier, and D. Beaulette, "Correctional Officers: How Do They Perceive Sex Offenders?" *International Journal of Offender Therapy and Comparative Criminology* 35:1 (1995): 55–61; and American Correctional Association, *Point/Counterpoint* (Lanham, MD: ACA, 1997).
33. E. Brecher, *Treatment Programs for Sex Offenders,* prepared for the National Institute of Law Enforcement and Criminal Justice (Washington, DC: U.S. Government Printing Office, 1978), pp. 1–12. The material for this section has been extracted from this document and reflects the current literature on the subject. See also Walter Meyer, C. Cole, and D. Lipton, "Links Between Biology and Crime," *Journal of Offender Rehabilitation* 25:3/4 (1997): 1–34.
34. John Driggs and T. Zoet, "Breaking the Cycle—Sex Offenders on Parole," *Corrections Today* 49:3 (1987):

124. See also Brian Dixon, "Sex Offender Treatment Services in Australia and New Zealand," *Psychiatry, Psychology and the Law* 3:2 (1996): 179–188.

35. Steven Glass, "An Overview of Satanism and Ritualized Child Abuse," *Journal of Police and Criminal Psychology* 7:2 (1991): 43–50; Ben Crouch and K. Damphouse, "Newspapers and the Antisatanism Movement: A Content Analysis," *Sociological Spectrum* 12:1 (1992): 1–20; and William Bernet and C. Chang, "The Differential Diagnosis of Ritual Abuse Allegations," *Journal of Forensic Sciences* 42:1 (1997): 32–38.

36. Harry E. Allen, "HIV Transmission Issues in Correctional Facilities," *National Social Sciences Journal* 2:1 (1992): 32–37. See also Clyde McCoy and J. Inciardi, *Sex, Drugs and the Continuing Spread of AIDS* (Los Angeles: Roxbury, 1995).

37. National Commission on Acquired Immune Deficiency Syndrome, *Report: HIV Disease in Correctional Facilities* (Washington, DC: U.S. Department of Justice, 1992), p. 5. See also James Marquart, V. Brewer, J. Mullins, et al., "The Implication of Crime Control Policy on HIV/AIDS-Related Risk Among Women Prisoners," *Crime and Delinquency* 45:1 (1999): 82–98.

38. Theodore Hammett, P. Marmon, and L. Maruschak, *1996–1997 Update: HIV/AIDS, STDs, and TB in Correctional Facilities* (Washington, DC: Bureau of Justice Statistics, 1998), p. xiv; and Laura Maruschak, *HIV in Prisons and Jails, 2002* (Washington, DC: Bureau of Justice Statistics, 2004).

39. Caroline Wolf Harlow, *Drug Enforcement and Treatment in Prisons, 1990* (Washington, DC: U.S. Department of Justice, 1992), p. 1. See also Myer et al., "Links Between Biology and Crime."

40. There are no confirmed cases of a correctional officer whose workplace exposure resulted in HIV infection. Jeanne Flavin, "Police and HIV/AIDS: The Risk, The Reality, The Response," *American Journal of Criminal Justice* 23:1 (1998): 33–58.

41. Rebecca Craig, "Six Steps to Stop the Spread of Communicable Diseases," *Corrections Today* 54:7 (1992): 104–109. See also Mary Coplin, "Managing the Challenge of HIV," *Corrections Today* 54:8 (1992): 104–107.

42. Robert Reeves, "Approaching 2000: Finding Solutions to the Most Pressing Issues Facing the Corrections Community," *Corrections Today* 54:3 (1998): 74, 76–79.

43. Mary Campbell, "Managing Exposure to Communicable Diseases," *Corrections Today* 54:3 (1992): 68–83; H. Parker Eales, "MDR Tuberculosis: Correction's Newest Communicable Danger," *Corrections Today* 54:3 (1992): 64–67; H. Parker Eales, "TB, HIV, and MDR-TB—A Tragic Combination," in *The State of Corrections: Proceedings of the 1992 Annual Conferences* (Laurel, MD: American Correctional Association, 1993), pp. 48–50.

44. Joseph Paris, "Why an AIDS Unit?" in *The State of Corrections: Proceedings of the 1991 Annual Conferences* (Laurel, MD: American Correctional Association, 1992), pp. 3–56.

45. Donald McVinney, "Counseling Incarcerated Individuals with HIV Disease and Chemical Dependency," *Journal of Chemical Dependency Treatment* 4:2 (1991): 105–118.

46. Patricia Satterfield, "A Strategy for Controlling Health Care Costs," *Corrections Today* 54:2 (1992): 190–194. But see Margaret Norris and M. May, "Screening for Malingering in a Correctional Setting," *Law and Human Behavior* 22:3 (1998): 315–323.

47. American Correctional Association, *2001 Directory* (Lanham, MD: ACA, 2001), p. 42.

48. Sarah Bradley, "Graying of Inmate Population Spurs Corrections Challenges," *On the Line* 13 (March 1990): 5; and Ronald Aday, "Golden Years Behind Bars," *Federal Probation* 58:2 (1994): 47–54.

49. James Stephan, *State Prison Expenditures, 2001* (Washington, DC: Bureau of Justice Statistics, 2004).

SUGGESTED READINGS: PART 6

American Jail Association. *American Jails.* Quarterly publication of the American Jail Association.

Bazemore, Gordon, and Lode Walgrave (eds.). *Restorative Juvenile Justice: Repairing the Harm of Youth Crime.* Monsey, NY: Criminal Justice Press, 1999.

Donziger, Steven. *The Real War on Crime.* New York: HarperCollins, 1996.

Harrison, Paige, and Allen Beck, *Prisoners in 2003* (Washington, DC: Bureau of Justice Statistics, 2004).

Harrison, Paige, and Allen Beck, *Prison and Jail Inmates at Midyear 2004* (Washington, DC: Bureau of Justice Statistic, 2005).

Harlow, Caroline Wolf. *Prior Abuse Reported by Inmates and Probationers.* Washington, DC: U.S. Department of Justice, 1999.

Hassine, Victor. *Life Without Parole: Living in Prison Today.* Los Angeles: Roxbury, 2002.

Hayes, Lindsay, and Eric Blaauw (eds.). "Prison Suicide." Special issue of *Crisis* 18:4 (1997): 146–189.

Heidi, Kathleen. *Young Killers: The Challenge of Juvenile Homicide*. Thousand Oaks, CA: Sage, 1999.

James, Doris. *Profile of Jail Inmates, 2002* (Washington, DC: Bureau of Justice Statistics, 2004).

Johnson, Robert, and Hans Toch. *Crime and Punishment: Inside Views*. Los Angeles: Roxbury, 2000.

Immarigeon, Russ, and Meda Chesney-Lind. *Women's Prisons: Overcrowded and Underused*. San Francisco: National Council on Crime and Delinquency, 1992.

Maruschak, Laura. *HIV in Prisons and Jails, 2002* (Washington, DC: Bureau of Justice Statistics, 2004).

Mauer, Marc. "Americans Behind Bars." *Criminal Justice* 6:4 (1992): 12–18, 38–39; and "The International Use of Incarceration." *The Prison Journal* 75:1 (1995): 113–123.

McCoy, Clyde, and James Inciardi. *Sex, Drugs, and the Continuing Spread of AIDS*. Los Angeles: Roxbury, 1995.

Nichols, Mark, L. Bench, E. Morlok, and K. Liston. "Analysis of Mentally Retarded and Lower-Functioning Offender Correctional Programs." *Corrections Today* 65:2 (2003): 119–121.

Sickmund, Melissa. *Juveniles in Corrections* (Washington, DC: Office of Justice Programs, 2004).

Snyder, Howard. *Juvenile Arrests 2002*. Washington, DC: U.S. Department of Justice, 2004.

Stephan, James. *State Prison Expenditures, 2001*. Washington, DC: U.S. Department of Justice, 2004.

Tjaden, Patricia, and Nancy Thoennes. *Prevalence, Incidence, and Consequences of Violence Against Women*. Washington, DC: U.S. Department of Justice, 1998.

Uzoaba, Julius. *Managing Older Offenders: Where Do We Stand?* Ottawa: Correctional Service of Canada, 1998.

Zimring, Franklin. "Toward a Jurisprudence of Youth Violence," in Michael Tonry and M. Moore (eds.). *Youth Violence*. Chicago: University of Chicago Press, 1998, pp. 477–501.

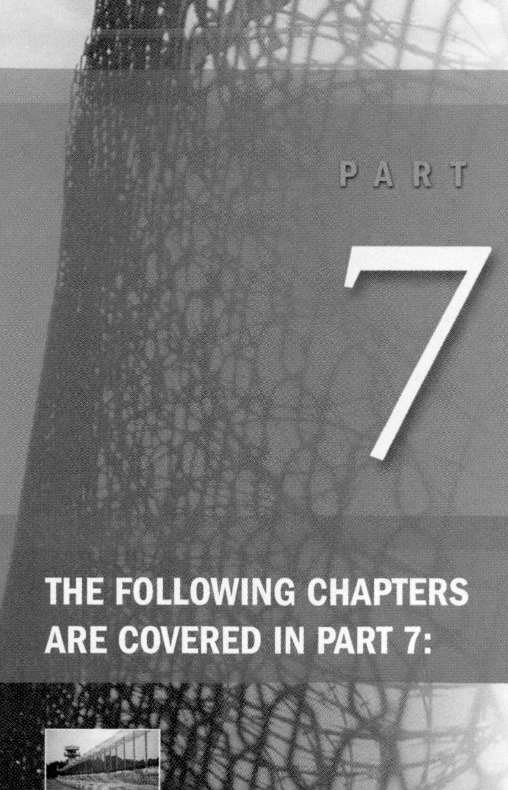

PART

7

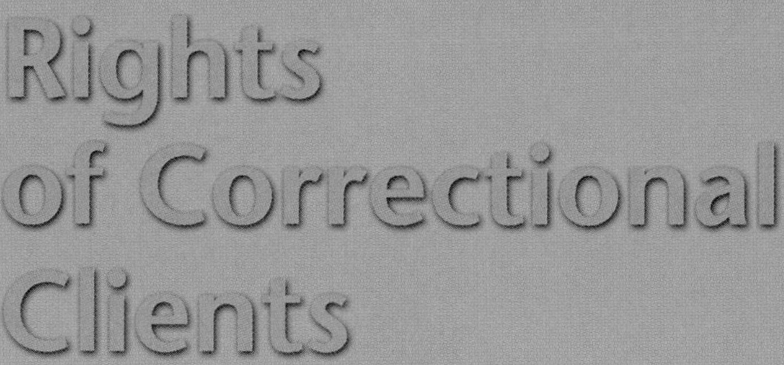

Rights of Correctional Clients

THE FOLLOWING CHAPTERS ARE COVERED IN PART 7:

OVERVIEW

Even though convicted of crimes, offenders retain certain rights guaranteed all citizens under state and federal constitutions, except for those expressly denied due to their legal status as probationers, inmates, or parolees. Part 7 examines inmate and ex-offender rights, as well as the ultimate right inherent in the death penalty: the right to life.

CHAPTER 19

Inmate and Ex-Offender Rights

> *Young, unskilled, poorly educated, the typical offender has few marketable capabilities to offer potential employers. Unable to find or keep a job upon his release from prison, the offender often returns to crime—the only "business" he knows. Breaking the cycle of recidivism is a difficult task, involving many complex contributing factors. One of these is employment potential. Effective programs for building relevant job skills do ease the offender's reentry into society.*
>
> —Gerald M. Caplan, Former Director, Law Enforcement Assistance Administration

KEY WORDS

- convicted offender
- civil death
- clear and present danger
- Black Muslims
- jailhouse lawyer
- *Estelle v. Gamble*
- deliberate indifference
- Section 1983
- grievance board
- inmate grievance
- ombudsman
- mediators
- court master
- ex-con
- collateral consequences
- social stigma
- self-efficacy
- transitional period
- occupational disability
- firearms disability
- employment restrictions
- registration of criminals
- "yellow card"
- sex offender file
- Community Protection Act
- Megan's Law
- expungement
- pardon

OVERVIEW

Ask the average person on the street what "rights" prisoners have coming to them when in confinement—or eventually when released after their sentence has been served. After a few seconds of a blank stare, most would answer, "What do you mean rights? They don't have any." In Part 7 we present in some detail the misunderstood world of those rights that apply to inmates and ex-offenders. The incredible amount of litigation in institutions, the long battles for the lives of what appear to be heinous animals who deserve to die, and the problems with the ex-prisoner trying to deal with society and carrying a heavy record for life cause us to wonder how this all came about.

The rights of inmates and offenders are important and the courts and rights advocates carefully monitor them. When those persons have finally done their time and now find themselves back in their former neighborhood—burdened by a record and a stigma that are hard to overcome—they still have rights as well. Literally millions of citizens on the streets of America have been convicted of a crime and placed under correctional supervision at some point in their lives. (More than 7 million inmates and ex-offenders are under active correctional supervision, from probation to incarceration to parole.) This chapter deals with the sometimes gray area of the offender and the problems offenders face while incarcerated and while trying to reintegrate into society. This task is one that has many bumps in the road back to being a productive and useful citizen, but many more make that trip and succeed than we often acknowledge. This chapter considers the restrictions on inmates and ex-offenders

< Easterling Correctional Facility where nineteen prisoners were hospitalized after a fight.
Courtesy of AP/Wide World Photos.

CORRECTIONAL BRIEF

Individual Rights Guaranteed by the "Bill of Rights"

A Right Against Unreasonable Searches of Person and Place of Residence

A Right Against Arrest Without Probable Cause

A Right Against Unreasonable Seizures of Personal Property

A Right Against Self-Incrimination

A Right to Fair Questioning by the Police

A Right to Protection from Physical Harm Throughout the Justice Process

A Right to an Attorney

A Right to Trial by Jury

A Right to Know the Charges

A Right to Cross-Examine Prosecution Witnesses

A Right to Speak and Present Witnesses

A Right Not to Be Tried Twice for the Same Crime

A Right Against Cruel or Unusual Punishment

A Right to Due Process

A Right to a Speedy Trial

A Right Against Excessive Bail

A Right Against Excessive Fines

A Right to Be Treated the Same as Others, Regardless of Race, Sex, Religious Preference, and Other Personal Attributes

A Right to Be Assumed Innocent Until Proven Guilty

SOURCE: Frank Schmalleger, *Criminal Justice Today,* 5th ed. (Upper Saddle River, NJ: Prentice Hall, 2001).

and the current status of efforts to provide additional rights. We start with some of the myths and legends about these efforts.

THE STATUS OF THE CONVICTED OFFENDER

When defendants have gone through the whole criminal justice process, including all appeals, and their sentences have been upheld, they officially acquire the status of **convicted offender.** They may already have spent a long time in jail or prison as their appeals made their tedious way through the courts. But with the final guilty verdict in, the offender's relationship to the correctional system undergoes a significant change. In this section we examine the offender's new status and his or her rights during and after incarceration. Over the years, a body of folklore has grown up about the rights of prisoners and ex-prisoners. We hope this chapter will dispel some of those myths and clarify recent developments.

With almost 7 million people[1] subject to the control of some kind of correctional authority in America each day, the status of those convicted offenders poses a significant problem. Correctional officials have been slow to draw up internal policies and procedures to guide their administrators in protecting the offenders' rights. Under the "hands-off" policy mentioned in Chapter 5, the courts were reluctant to criticize decisions and procedures developed by correctional administrators. That policy was abandoned in the mid-1960s, opening the door to case after case regarding prisoners' rights, with no end in sight. Let us start with the basic rights of the confined inmate.

BASIC INMATE RIGHTS

Visiting and Community Ties

You should recall from Chapter 1 that penal punishments included **civil death,** which meant that the offender's property was confiscated in the name of the state and his wife declared a widow, eligible to remarry. To society, the offender was, in effect, dead. The vestiges of civil death are probably most visible in correctional practices that pertain to the privilege of having visitors. Debate continues about whether having visitors is actually a privilege or is in fact a right. The practice of having visitors is not new. Occasional visitors were allowed even as early as 1790 in the Walnut Street Jail. If a prisoner was diligent and good, a visit was allowed from a close family member—but only once every three months, for fifteen minutes, through two grills, and under the scrutiny of a keeper.[2] This procedure may seem absurdly strict, but is not too far from the current practice in some high-security correctional institutions. The overriding security focus at most prisons dictates that visits be limited, subject to highly regimented conditions, and likely to discourage close physical or emotional contact. The dehumanizing rules and procedures for visiting do not accord with modern goals of rehabilitation and correction. Although security is important in maximum-security prisons, it could be tempered with humanity in such a personal thing as a visit from a friend or family member.

Limitations on visiting hours, restricted visitor lists,[3] overcrowded visiting rooms, and the overwhelming presence of guards contribute to the inmate's difficulty in maintaining ties with family and the outside world.[4] Most institutions are located far from large urban centers (where most inmates' families live), requiring long hours of travel and expense for visitors. Not only family ties but also friendships wither quickly under such conditions. This alienation creates serious problems for both the inmate and the institution. Typically, an inmate is allowed to receive a visitor once a week (in some places as seldom as once a month), usually a member of his or her immediate family. This is hardly representative of social life in contemporary America.

For the married inmate, family ties are inevitably weakened by long separation. With divorce frequent, the social consequences to the family, community, and institution are incalculable; imprisonment itself is grounds for divorce in some jurisdictions.[5] Institution officials often face severe problems caused by the deterioration of an inmate's family situation. When, for example, a wife does not write, or the inmate hears through the grapevine that she has a lover, violence can and often

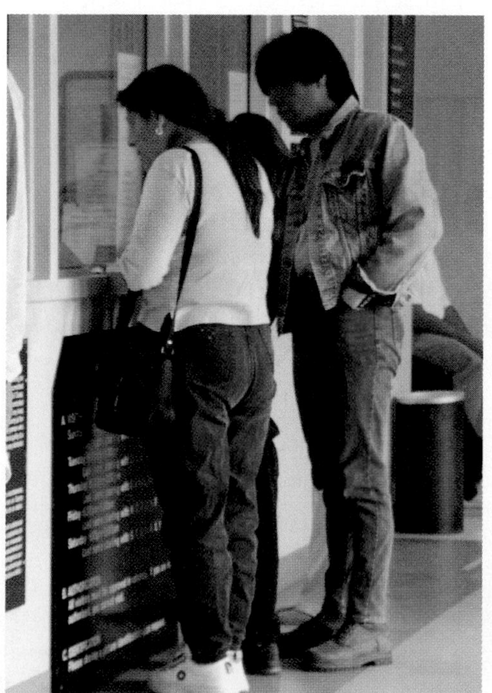

Couple checking in at a window to visit relatives at juvenile hall annex, Santa Ana, California.

Photo by Spencer Grant, courtesy of PhotoEdit.

does result—expressed in attacks against prison personnel,[6] another prisoner,[7] or attempts to escape.

Deprived of even a semblance of normal relations with the outside, the inmate turns to the other inmates and the inmate subculture for solace. It seems ironic that inmates are cut off from both friends and relatives and must depend almost entirely on the company of criminals. Yet when finally released on parole, some parole rules forbid the parolee to associate with known ex-offenders. Such paradoxical situations seem to run counter to the basic premises of American corrections. There is no better way to combat the inmate social system and prepare an inmate for freedom than by strengthening his or her ties with the outside world through visitations, family or conjugal visits,[8] home furloughs, telephone access, and mail.

Use of Mail

The mail system is closely tied to visitation as another way to maintain essential contact with the outside world. As in the case of visits, stated reasons for the limitation and censorship of mail are tied either to security or to the prison's orderly administration. Although the use of the mail system is a right, case law has established that correctional administrators can place reasonable restrictions on prisoners in the exercise of that right if there is a "clear and present danger" or compelling state need. As with most situations behind the walls, in the past, mail rules were systematically stiffened to facilitate the institutions' smooth operation. If it became too great an administrative burden to read all the incoming and outgoing mail, the number of letters or the list of correspondents was reduced. Eventually, a small maximum of allowed letters and very restrictive lists of correspondents became the standard. As long as the prisoners could not turn to the courts, this practice did not create a stir. When the attorneys appointed to help prisoners began to see the unjustness of restrictions concerning mail and other so-called privileges, they began to question the rules and reestablish those privileges as rights.

How much mail should a prisoner receive? Administrators have usually restricted it to an amount that can readily be censored. During personnel shortages (in wars, for example), the amount of mail was often limited to one letter a month. Outgoing mail was similarly restricted. Communications with an attorney could be opened and read, but not censored unless the correspondence referred to plans for illegal activity or contained contraband. More recently, court decisions have found that most censorship of

CORRECTIONAL BRIEF

Family/Conjugal Visiting

During a conjugal, or what is most commonly called a "family visit," inmate, spouse, and children are allowed to spend time together on the prison campus, unsupervised and alone in private quarters, trailers, houses, and rooms. During this time, the couple may or may not engage in sexual intercourse.

European and Latin American countries have been the leaders in permitting conjugal visiting, but some states (e.g., California and Mississippi) have formal programs of conjugal visiting. Others (like Montana) permit the program without granting formal approval.

Advantages cited in some studies include lessening forced and voluntary homosexual acts within prison, maintaining a more normal prison environment, lowering tension levels, lessening attacks on correctional officers, reinforcing gender-appropriate roles, helping to preserve marriages, and (from the perspective of the prison administration) encouraging appropriate behavior by inmates hoping to earn a conjugal visitation pass. Opponents argue that it puts too much emphasis on the physical aspects of marriage, is unfair to the unmarried resident, raises welfare costs through increased family size, and decreases the intensity of punishment to offenders.

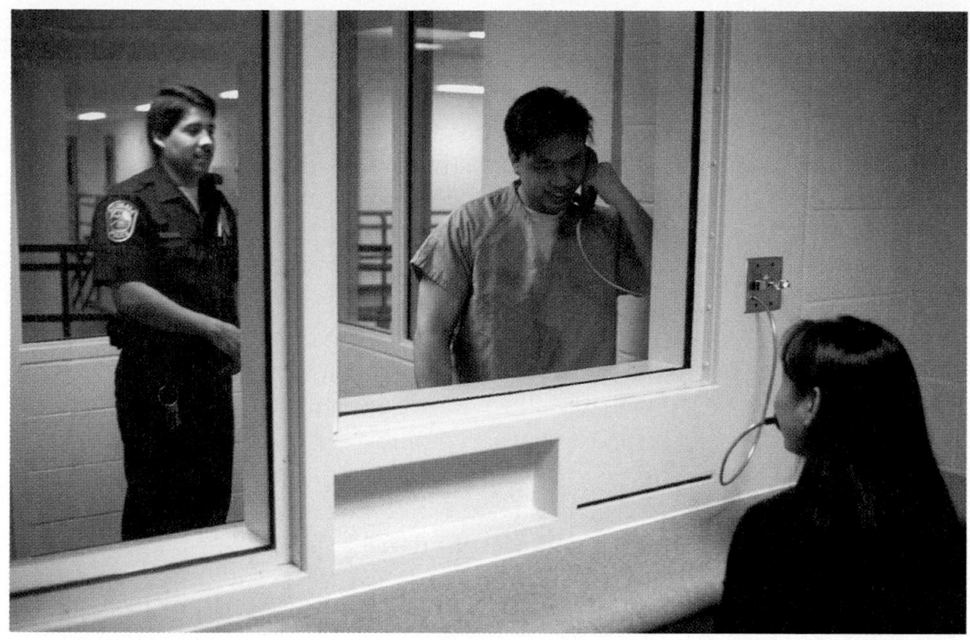

Asian couple visit by telephone in jail, separated by a glass partition.

Photo by Spencer Grant, courtesy of PhotoEdit.

communications between inmates and their lawyers is unconstitutional[9]; this direction also appears in decisions regarding communications with the news media.[10]

Death row inmates frequently receive only photocopies of correspondence sent to them from persons other than attorneys. There is a clear and present danger of poisoning from chemicals sprayed on stationery at the inmate's request. Stamps can also be affixed to envelopes with a liquid poison or drugs. Finally, lethal poison can also be suspended in ink. Ironically, death row inmates cannot be allowed to kill themselves before their execution, although many do commit suicide.[11]

Contraband and Mail

In the past, contraband was commonly described as "any material that might be used for an escape or used to take advantage of other prisoners." Such items as matches,

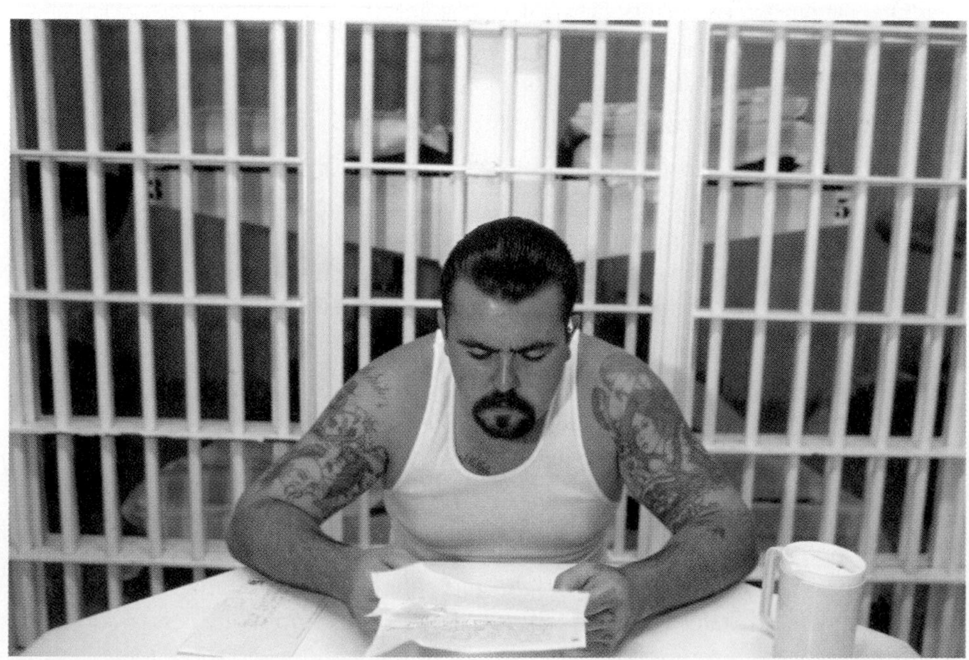

A heavily-tattooed inmate reads a letter inside his cell at Seal Beach Detention Facility in California.

Photo by A. Ramey, courtesy of PhotoEdit.

money, pornographic pictures, guns, knives, lubricants, drugs, and tools are generally considered contraband. Any item could have been placed on the contraband list if it was seen as a threat to the prison's orderly operation.

The more recent definition of contraband is any item found on the prisoner or in his or her cell that is not specifically authorized by the administration in written rules. This helps simplify the process and eliminate any controversy as to what is, or is not, contraband. (For example, if written rules state that a prisoner is authorized two blankets, and three are found in a cell inspection, the third blanket is, by definition, contraband and subject to removal.)

When an inmate wishes to communicate with a second inmate, either a friend or jailhouse lawyer who is incarcerated at another institution, the courts have stuck to a hands-off policy, leaving that problem to the discretion of the correctional administrators. The general policy has been to prohibit the passage of any correspondence between inmates. This policy continues to be under attack, however, and has been rejected by some states.[12] In most court cases, the test for permissibility of mail and literature has been the **clear and present danger** standard:

> *We accept the premise that certain literature may pose such a clear and present danger to the security of a prison, or to the rehabilitation of prisoners, that it should be censored. To take an extreme example, if there were mailed to a prisoner a brochure demonstrating in detail how to saw prison bars with utensils used in the mess hall, how to make a bomb, or how to provoke a prison riot, it would properly be screened. A magazine detailing for incarcerated drug addicts how they might obtain a euphoric "high," comparable to that experienced from heroin, by sniffing aerosol or glue available for other purposes within the prison walls, would likewise be censored as restraining effective rehabilitation. Furthermore, it is undoubtedly true that in the volatile atmosphere of a prison, where a large number of men, many with criminal tendencies, live in close proximity to each other, violence can be fomented by the printed word much more easily than in the outside world. Some censorship or prior restraint on inflammatory literature sent into prisons is, therefore, necessary to prevent such literature from being used to cause disruption or violence within the prison. It may well be that in some prisons where the prisoners' flash-point is low, articles regarding bombing, prison riots, or the like, which would be harmless when sold on the corner newsstand, would be too dangerous for release to the prison population. The courts have also upheld restrictions on incoming newspapers and magazines that would permit receipt of such mail if "only the publisher" is the sender.*[13]

Ohio took the lead in the reform of mail censorship, eliminating all of it in Ohio's prisons on August 3, 1973.[14] Under the Ohio system, both incoming and outgoing mail is merely inspected for contraband and delivered unread. Each inmate may write and receive an unlimited number of items of mail. The adoption of those standards has caused few if any problems. Most states, however, still inspect, electronically, incoming packages and open letters to look for contraband.

Religious Rights in Prison

SIDEBARS

Right to Religious Freedom

Cooper v. Pate, a case dealing with freedom of religion, used Section 1983 of the Civil Rights Act. That strategy made the case a landmark decision in inmates' rights.

The idea underlying the penitentiary was drawn from religious precepts. It thus seems ironic that there would be any conflict in providing freedom of religion in prisons, but this has indeed been the case. The early efforts to restore the criminal through penitence and prayer were conducted in small homogeneous communities. As immigration to America expanded, it became the most heterogeneous nation in the world. Because the United States was founded on a belief that freedom of worship could not be infringed by the government, the First Amendment addressed those issues: "Congress shall make no law respecting an establishment of religion, or prohibiting the free exercise thereof. . . . " It is the conflict between what constitutes an established religion and the individual's right to exercise it that has caused grief in the nation's prisons.

A clear example of this problem was the **Black Muslim** decision, which has dominated case law for more than two decades. After a long string of cases,[15] the courts finally held that the Black Muslim faith did constitute an established religion and that the Black Muslims were therefore entitled to follow the practices the religion prescribed.[16] The resolution of the Black Muslim issue meant the standards applied there can be applied to any duly recognized religion.[17] This puts a strain on the prison administrator, who must allow equal protection for all inmates. The question of whether the state really grants each inmate "free exercise" simply by ensuring access to a minister of his or her particular faith is still unsettled.

SIDEBARS

The Black Muslim Decision

In what has become titled "the Black Muslim decision," the court of appeals held that prison officials were not required to make available to prisoners Black Muslim publications that urged defiance of prison authorities and thus threatened prison security, unless properly interpreted by a trained Muslim minister. The resolution of the Black Muslim issue meant the standards applied there can be applied to any duly recognized religion.

Access to Court and Counsel

Access to the federal courts was not established as a constitutional right for inmates until 1940, in a case called *Ex parte Hull.* In that decision, the U.S. Supreme Court established that "the state and its officers may not abridge or impair a petitioner's right to apply to a federal court for a writ of habeas corpus." Despite that clear ruling, the courts still maintained a strict hands-off policy in this regard until the 1964 case of *Cooper v. Pate.*[18]

Once the prisoners' right to use jailhouse lawyers was established in *Johnson v. Avery,*[19] inmates needed to be assured of an adequate supply of legal research materials; in 1971, the case of *Younger v. Gilmore*[20] guaranteed the inmate writ writers such assistance. But the extent of provided materials has varied considerably, from complete law libraries[21] in the state prisons to the bare essentials elsewhere.[22] Meanwhile, other states allow law students to run legal clinics inside institutions, under the supervision of a law school faculty member qualified to practice in that jurisdiction. It seems the courts must continue to require that correctional administrations offer adequate legal counsel to inmates, or they will have to live with the continued use of jailhouse lawyers and the problems that result.

The right to consult with counsel has been clearly established.[23] The problem, before *Gideon* and the cases it generated, was that most inmates could not afford a

SIDEBARS

Right to Legal Assistance

Through a writ of *certiorari,* a court of appeals decision was reversed in favor of an inmate who had been disciplined for violating a prison regulation that prohibited inmates from assisting other prisoners in preparing writs. The court of appeals had reversed a district court decision that voided the regulation because it had the effect of barring illiterate prisoners from access to general habeas corpus. This decision established the "jailhouse lawyer" as a part of the modern correctional scene.

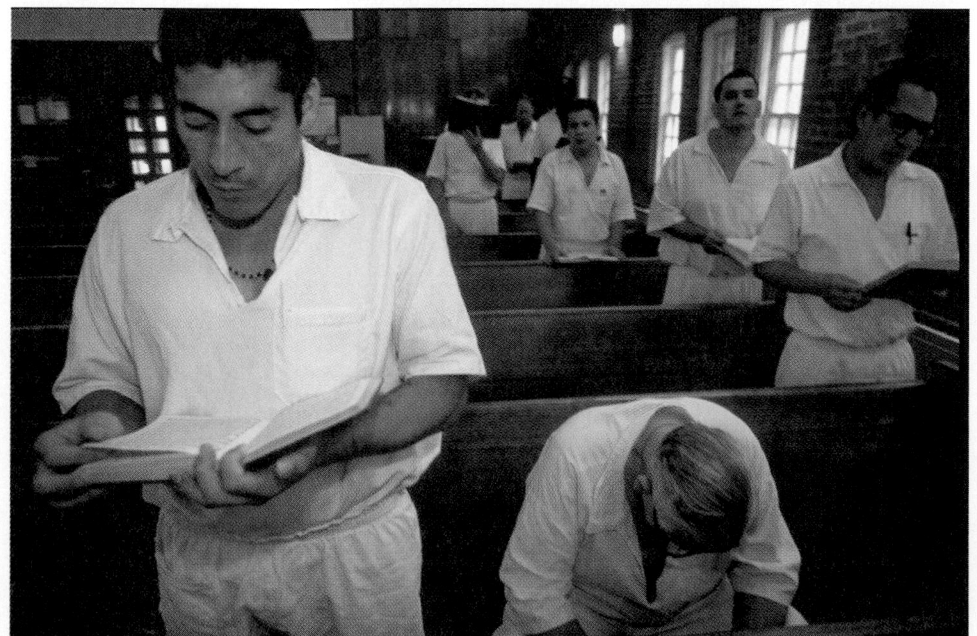

Inmates partake in a prison church service at the Walls, Huntsville, Texas.

Photo by Andrew Lichtenstein, courtesy of Corbis/Sygma.

SIDEBARS

Sovereign Immunity

Sovereign immunity is a judicial doctrine that precludes bringing suit against the government without its consent. Founded on the ancient principle that "the king can do no wrong," it bars holding the government or its political subdivisions liable for the torts of its officers or agents unless such immunity is expressly waived by statute or necessary inference from legislative enactment. The federal government has generally waived its nontort action immunity in the Tucker Act, 28 U.S.C.A. 1346(a)(2), 1491, and its tort immunity in the Federal Court Claims Act, 28 U.S.C.A. 1346(b), 2674. Most states have also waived immunity in various degrees at both the state and local government levels.

The immunity from certain suits in federal court was granted to states by the Eleventh Amendment to the United States Constitution.

SIDEBARS

Writ of *Certiorari*

A writ of *certiorari* is applied for at a superior appeal court to call up the records of an inferior court to determine if the person to whom the appeal applies has merit for further examination of the record by the higher court. Most people associate this with the Supreme Court of the United States.

lawyer to defend them or prepare later appeals.[24] Early prison rules restricted the use of **jailhouse lawyers**, those inmates who learn something about the law and use their skills to assist other inmates to file suits against correctional administrators and facilities. Restricting jailhouse lawyers from helping other inmates meant that few prisoners were able to file writs in the federal courts. After the courts established the right to counsel in *Gideon, Johnson v. Avery* covered those administrative agencies that could not or would not comply. Though not all jurisdictions have been able to provide counsel for all inmates, the remedies incorporated in the court decisions have helped fill the void—while incidentally creating a flood of writs that have washed over the civil and appeals courts. During the past two decades, the petitions filed in the U.S. district courts by federal prisoners increased 64 percent and by state prisoners increased 238 percent. The latter's civil rights suits increased by a whopping 389 percent. As a result of this steep increase, Congress enacted two legislative initiatives that sought to limit prisoners' ability to file petition in federal courts: the Prison Litigation Reform Act and the Antiterrorism and Effective Death Penalty Act. Together, these initiatives have sharply reduced inmate civil rights petitions (see Figure 5.2).

The Right to Medical Treatment and Care

The issue of adequate medical care in our prisons has finally prompted a decision from the U.S. Supreme Court. Only when a constitutionally guaranteed right has been violated has the Court become involved in the provision of medical care. Because both medical programs and the backgrounds of prison medical personnel are extremely diversified, the quality of medical aid varies among institutions. Ironically, a nation that demands adequate medical care for all inmates is, at this writing, still struggling with providing adequate medical care for all of its citizens.

The U.S. Supreme Court has taken the position that inmates in state prisons should seek remedy in the state courts. In the 1976 case of ***Estelle v. Gamble,***[25] that position was made even clearer. Although suits in the past have shown that prisoners' rights to proper diagnosis and medical treatment of illness have been violated on a grand scale, the courts have moved slowly in that area. In *Estelle,* however, the Court stated, "We therefore conclude that *deliberate indifference* [emphasis added] to serious medical needs of prisoners constitutes the unnecessary and wanton infliction of pain proscribed by the Eighth Amendment. This is true whether the indifference is manifested by prison doctors in their response to the prisoner's needs or by prison guards in intentionally denying or delaying access to medical care or intentionally interfering with the treatment once prescribed."[26] This was a giant step forward in the provision of medical treatment, but it still falls short of the individual remedies provided by decisions in other areas. For example, the U.S. First Circuit Court of Appeals has ruled that inmates must receive "adequate medical care" but do not necessarily deserve "the most sophisticated care that money can buy."[27] Medical care in prison in relationship to the AIDS problem has been described as "a national disgrace."[28]

Estelle stated a position of sympathy for complaints about the system-wide failure to provide adequate and humane medical care. The test of **deliberate indifference**, however, a requirement for evoking the Eighth Amendment, seems to be a major hurdle for most who choose to use *Estelle* as a basis for action. Mere negligence or malpractice leaves the prisoner with remedy only in a state civil case. Total deprivation of medical service seems to be the current standard for application of constitutional prohibitions.

One recent example of state failure to provide adequate health care services is seen in the state of California. In 2002, a federal judge determined that the California Department of Corrections system that provided health care to roughly 164,000

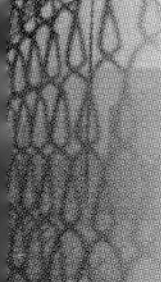

CORRECTIONAL BRIEF

Deliberate Indifference

Deliberate Indifference Standard, *Farmer v. Brennan* For a claim to be presented, the inmate must show that he or she was incarcerated under conditions posing a substantial risk of serious harm. See *Helling v. McKinney,* 509 U.S. 25, 30, 113 S. Ct. 2475, 125 L. Ed. 2d 22 (1993). This is the objective test, the *Rhodes* test: "Was the deprivation sufficiently serious?" If a plaintiff is able to establish a sufficiently serious deprivation, he must next satisfy the *Farmer* test, the "deliberate indifference" test: "Did the officials act with a sufficiently culpable state of mind?" *Farmer v. Brennan,* 511 U.S. 825, 114 S. Ct. 1970 (1994).

Before the 1994 *Farmer* case, courts looked to an objective standard to determine if a prison official violated a prisoner's rights. The *Farmer* decision of 1994 set entirely different and personally responsible standards: "For a claim . . . based on a failure to prevent harm, [Plaintiff] must show that [the inmate] [was] incarcerated under conditions posing a substantial risk of serious harm." Id. 511 U.S. at 834, 114 S. Ct. at 1976. [The objective test] The state of mind requirement follows from the several Supreme Court holdings that only the unnecessary and wanton infliction of pain implicates the Eighth Amendment. To violate the Cruel and Unusual Punishments Clause, a prison official must have a sufficiently culpable state of mind. [The subjective test] The subjective component is the equivalent of criminal recklessness, much more than negligence or even malice. It is not similar to; it is criminal conduct that is required to be proven.

"Subjective recklessness" as used in the criminal law is a familiar and workable standard that is consistent with the Cruel and Unusual Punishments Clause as interpreted in our cases, and we adopt it as the test for "deliberate indifference" under the Eighth Amendment. *Farmer,* 511 U.S. at 838, 114 S. Ct. at 1980.

SOURCE: Personal communications with Deputy Attorney General Martin Basiszla, Office of the Attorney General, State of Hawaii, Honolulu, 1999.

inmates was unconstitutional. He ordered major medical reforms, but the state failed to comply. As many as 64 preventable deaths of inmates a year (and injury to many others) due to medical malfeasance led to the Court's 2005 decision to order a receiver to take control of California's prison health care system.[29]

Because of the relative ineffectiveness of using state and tort courts to remedy inadequate medical services and treatment in institutions, inmates have more recently begun to sue correctional administrators through **Section 1983** of the U.S. Code. This section, passed in 1871 to protect the civil rights of recently freed slaves,

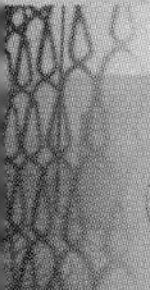

CORRECTIONAL BRIEF

Court Masters in Corrections

Both federal and state courts in which litigation over correctional issues has been filed may appoint a servant of the court, or **court master,** a functional adjunct whose task is to assist the court in whatever manner the court directs. Typically, the master oversees the day-to-day compliance of the institution to the decree of the court or the consent decree. A decree of the court implies that the defendant (correctional unit) lost the case and the court has issued orders that are to be implemented. A consent decree occurs where the complainants (inmates) or defendants agree to a set of actions that both would find acceptable.

Generally, masters monitor the lawsuit, report to the court, investigate complaints by inmates, have access to prisoners and their files, hold hearings, and write reports that inform the appointing judge about progress in the settlement of the orders. They also advise the court (through their special expertise in corrections, in particular) and help arrange compromises between the extremes of the demands of the inmates and the realities of prison administration.

When a master is appointed, correctional administrators tend to resist the intrusion of the master into the routine affairs of the institution. Some masters have their own reform agenda or fail to represent the correctional unit in securing compromise. Finally, the defendant (correctional system) must pay for the master and any staff, and there usually is little disincentive to the master's office running up long hours of work at high rates of compensation. Currently, masters are seen as providing correctional expertise to a court that has no competence in correctional administration. Future correctional administrators will need to develop positive working relationships with the court and negotiate with all parties to define clearly the powers, role, and scope of the master, to minimize any negative fallout from the appointment of an intervention agent.

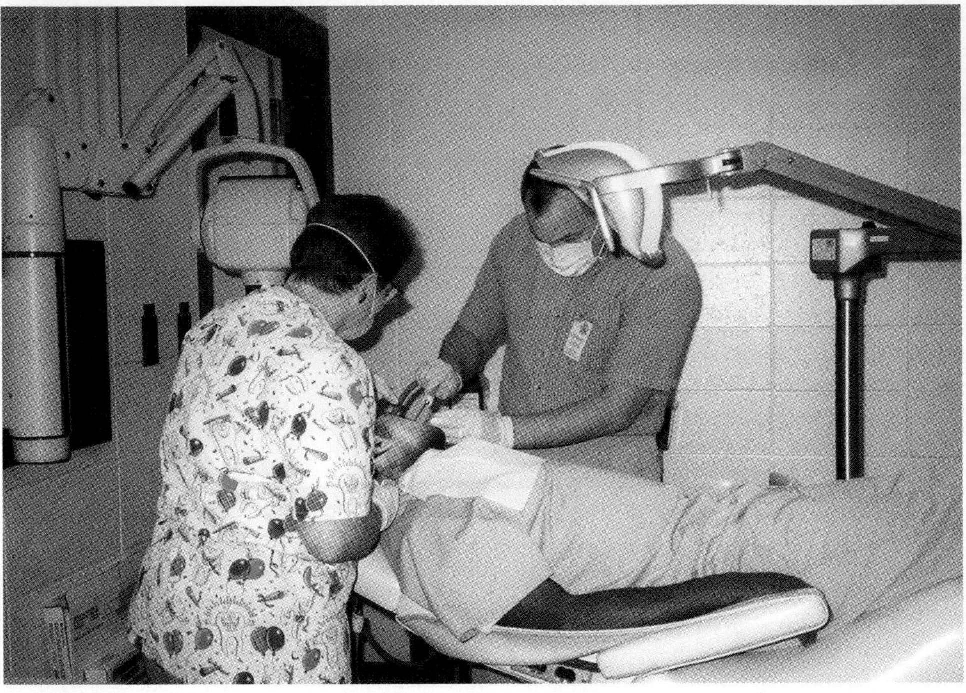

An inmate receives dental care from the jail's dental care professionals. *Photo by American Jails, courtesy of HBP, Inc.*

allows petitioners to sue in a federal court without having first exhausted all existing state courts' remedies. The federal district and circuit courts are currently deciding a number of important cases, and some of those will eventually come before the U.S. Supreme Court.

CORRECTIONAL BRIEF

Alternatives to Litigation

Civil litigation abounds over correctional issues such as prison overcrowding, compensation for lost personal property, need for a special diet, and restoration of good-time credits, increasing every year at great expense and time consumed by institutional managers. Further, court litigation is not a speedy technique for resolving inmate needs. Finally, correctional administrators have become increasingly concerned with the impact of lawsuits on the institution, including the reluctance of correctional staff to take actions, decline in staff morale, officer stress, and general reluctance to comply with discretionary duties. In the search for alternatives to litigation, four basic approaches have been proposed: grievance boards, inmate grievance procedures, ombudsman, and mediators.

The **grievance board** is usually staffed by institutional employees, or an occasional concerned citizen, to accept and investigate inmate complaints and then propose solutions, as relevant, to correctional administrators.

The **inmate grievance** procedure is similar to the grievance board, except that inmates are selected to serve as part of the grievance committee, a procedure many correctional managers find unacceptable, because it might strengthen the influence of inmate grievance committee members over staff and other inmates.

The third alternative is the **ombudsman,** a public official who investigates complaints against correctional personnel, practices, policies, and customs and who is empowered to recommend corrective solutions and measures. Empowered to investigate, the ombudsman has access to files, inmates, records, and staff. The ombudsman (and office staff) tends to be impartial, have special expertise, and be independent of the correctional administrator. Reports are filed not only with the institutional manager, but also with the correctional department director and funding agent for the office of the ombudsman. At least seventeen correctional systems in the nation operate with the ombudsman to protect inmates.

Mediators are relatively new on the correctional scene and represent a third party skilled in correctional work who agrees to hear differences and to render a decision to remedy the condition that would be binding on both parties. Maryland, Rhode Island, Arkansas, and South Carolina have experimented with this approach.

An inmate might file a lawsuit in conjunction with any of these alternatives. The methods are seen as promising ways to avoid litigation over correctional issues.

TORT SUITS

A tort is a civil wrong. In corrections, the term typically means that the plaintiff alleges the defendant failed to perform a duty required by the defendant's position or owed to the plaintiff. The objective of the suit is usually financial compensation for damages. A tort case alleges the defendant was negligent, grossly negligent, or deliberately negligent. The same objectives are seen in medical malpractice suits brought by inmates against the facility and, in cases where others have attacked the inmate, for negligence in not protecting the inmate from attack.[30]

Tort cases are handled in state courts, and are very time consuming. If the state should lose the suit, the court may award damages and attorneys' fees. Inmates are successful in lawsuits in less than 2 percent of the cases that go to trial.

CIVIL RIGHTS ACT "1983" SUITS

Title 42, Section 1983, of the U.S. Code, commonly known as the Civil Rights Act, reads as follows:

> *Every person who, under color of any statute, ordinance, regulation, custom, or usage, or any state, or territory, subjects or causes to be subjected, any citizen of the United States or other person within the jurisdiction thereof to the deprivation of any rights, privileges, or immunities secured by the Constitution and laws, shall be liable to the party injured in an action at law, suit in equity, or other proper proceedings for redress.*

One example of the use of Section 1983 to redress medical malpractice and mistreatment can be seen in *Tucker v. Hutto,*[31] a Virginia case in which Tucker's arms and legs became permanently paralyzed as a result of improper use of antipsychotic drugs while he was a patient at the Virginia State Penitentiary Hospital. The suit was initiated by the National Prison Project[32] and settled out of court for $518,000. Section 1983 suits can be an effective, although usually unwelcome, avenue for defining and improving prisoner rights while under confinement.

Many times the federal courts have been forced to overlook the issue of constitutional rights in order to correct situations involving a flagrant disregard of the need for adequate medical service. That disregard has often produced prison riots in the past, and it will continue to be a factor in right-to-treatment cases during the 2000s. Right to treatment is covered in detail in Chapter 18.

REMEDIES FOR VIOLATIONS OF RIGHTS

The first steps to remedy the almost standard practice of depriving convicted offenders of all rights have been taken, starting with the recognition that the Constitution does entitle those individuals to retain a substantial portion of their rights, even while incarcerated. The push for that recognition has come from the offenders themselves, often with the assistance of jailhouse lawyers, and has resulted in active and sympathetic judicial intervention.[33] The writ of habeas corpus, designed as a tool for prisoners to test the legality of their confinement, has been the main weapon in the battle for prisoner rights.[34] In 2002, the U.S. Supreme Court struck down Alabama's hitching post restraints as cruel and unusual punishment [*Hope v. Pelzer,* 536 U.S. 730 (2002)]. The battle continues today, especially with regard to increased maintenance of community ties and the abolition of the death penalty.

The role of the federal courts in responding to inmate complaints is significant. The number of complaints filed in state and federal courts over jail and prison conditions, violations of inmate civil rights, due process violations, mistreatment, and lack of treatment of inmates has increased every year for the last two decades. Clearly, the rights of prisoners have become a driving factor in planning by administrators, legislators, and jurists in regard to operations and conditions in America's jails and prisons. Next we examine the plight of the ex-offender and the problems faced with a record that may result in a number of rights either being taken away or restored.

THE LEGEND OF THE EX-CON

The highly stylized version of the **ex-con** presented in the movies and on television usually depicts a tough, streetwise, scar-faced thug who is able to survive on wits and muscle, with a good-looking, submissive, and willing woman not too far in the background. The ex-con is often depicted as a person to be feared and never trusted. With a granite jaw and shifty eyes, he talks out of the corner of his mouth and prefers a life of crime. The real-life ex-offender, of course, is something quite different from our legendary ex-con of movie and mystery novel fame. Newly released ex-offenders found in most cities are young, with little life experience outside prison walls; they are male or female, poor, with only the funds they managed to acquire while in prison; uneducated, generally with less than a high school diploma; former illicit drug users; and frightened, most having spent several years away from a rapidly changing world. After release from prison, these individuals must start a new life and make it in the free world while being watched by the correctional authorities, local police, employers, friends, and family. They often return to the same social and environmental conditions that gave rise to their trouble in the first place. The wonder is not that so many ex-offenders recidivate—but that more do not do so. If we add to this already heavy burden the legal and administrative restrictions placed on ex-offenders, it becomes evident that the happy-go-lucky ex-con is indeed a legend invented for the reading and viewing public.[35]

CONSEQUENCES OF A CONVICTION

Conviction for an offense carries with it the punishment imposed by statute. In addition, the convicted offender must carry several other disabilities and disqualifications that result from the conviction per se. Many state and federal statutes restrict some of the rights and privileges ordinarily available to law-abiding citizens in the nation. They include the rights to vote, to hold offices of private and public trust, to assist in parenting, to be on jury duty, to own firearms, to remain married, and to have privacy. Those and other rights may be lost upon conviction. They are collectively called **collateral consequences** of criminal conviction. Just how many citizens face collateral consequences is unknown, but a conservative estimate is that there are at least 50 million persons living in our societies who have been arrested for some offense in the nation, and at least 14 million of them have been convicted of a felony.

Even after offenders have served their sentences, these secondary handicaps continue to plague them in the form of **social stigma**, loss of civil rights, and administrative and legislative restrictions. Each of those areas interacts with the others, and their overall effect is to prevent the successful reintegration of ex-offenders into the free community. The greatest dilemma faced by the ex-offender in search of a job is obvious.

Stigma

The stigma of a prison record is to ex-offenders like a millstone to be worn around their necks until death. Though we pride ourselves that we have advanced beyond the eye-for-an-eye mentality of the past, we do not show it in the treatment of our offenders who have allegedly paid their debt to society. Aaron Nussbaum pointed out some of the problems of stigma for the discharged prisoner:

> *It is a grim fact that total punishment for crime never ends with the courts or jails. None can deny that a criminal record is a life-long handicap, and its subject a "marked man" in our society. No matter how genuine the reformation, nor how sincere and complete the inner resolution to revert to lawful behavior, the criminal offender is and remains a prisoner of his past record long after the crime is expiated by the punishment fixed under the criminal codes.*
>
> *This traditional prejudice and distrust stalks him at every turn no matter what crime he may have committed or the nature of the punishment meted out to him. It strikes at the first offender as ruthlessly, and with as deadly effect, as upon the inveterate repeater or the professional criminal. It pursues those alike who have served time in imprisonment, of long or short duration, and those who have been merely cloaked with a criminal record in the form of a suspended sentence, a discharge on probation, or even a fine.*[36]

Stigma

A stigma is a mark of dishonor or shame attached to a person based on how deviant the crime or criminal status and behavior is. Stigma lessens self-esteem, social acceptance, and support and can contribute toward additional criminal behavior by the person stigmatized.

One needs **self-efficacy** to survive in the competitive atmosphere of the free world. Thus, the diminished self-efficacy of the offender makes it difficult to bridge the gap between institutional life and the community.[37] It is the search for self-efficacy and status that leads many ex-offenders back to the circle of acquaintances that first led them afoul of the law. The personal disintegration encouraged by the fortress prisons of America makes many a discharged offender both a social and an economic cripple. We can only hope that the new techniques in corrections, designed to strengthen competencies and produce reasonable readjustment in the community, will help offset that effect, as will increased use of community corrections and intermediate punishments.

The Transition Period

Many ex-inmates, particularly those having served long sentences, face a difficult **transitional period** when released back into the communities of America, regardless of whether they are under parole supervision. Not only do they have breaks in their employment histories that are difficult to explain to potential employers, but also many are taken aback by the cost of food and services on the outside, especially when inflation may have doubled the cost of housing, food, and other basic commodities during a long incarceration. Because of those problems, many ex-offenders need intensive assistance from reintegration services, such as community residential centers and halfway houses.[38] In the federal Bureau of Prisons and many state systems, a large portion of prerelease inmates in fact spend their last six months in halfway houses, where they receive training in how to fill out employment applications, how to get and hold a job, how to deal with family problems and crises, where to secure services available in their communities, how to manage money, and so on. Such services will be even more important as states decrease or eliminate parole services, while even more inmates are incarcerated and sentences are extended. The concept of charging ex-offenders fees for parole services may even further aggravate the situation.[39] It seems obvious that few will be eager to or able to pay for their own parole.

Loss of Civil Rights

Though most people recognize that released prisoners do not automatically regain all of their civil rights that were lost in prison, there is widespread confusion as to which rights are permanently lost and which suspended, and what machinery is available to regain them. Sol Rubin, a lawyer and writer on penology, discussed the offender's loss of the rights to vote and engage in certain kinds of employment:

> *[W]hen a convicted defendant is not sentenced to commitment, but is placed on probation, and receives a suspended sentence, he should lose no civil rights. This is a recommendation of the Standard Probation and Parole Act published as long ago as 1955. It is a contradiction of the purposes of probation and parole that this view does not prevail. A California case cites the following instruction to a new parolee: "Your civil rights have been suspended. Therefore, you may not enter into any contract, marry, engage in business, or execute a contract without the restoration of such civil rights by the Adult Authority." A look at the rights restored by the Adult Authority at the time of release on parole is just as sad, hardly more than that on release he may be at large. He may rent a habitation, he is told, buy food, clothing, and transportation, and tools for a job; and he is advised that he has the benefit of rights under Workman's Compensation, Unemployment Insurance, etc.*
>
> *When the sentence is commitment, the principle of* Coffin v. Reichard *ought to apply, that a prisoner retains (or should retain) all rights of an ordinary citizen except those expressly or by necessary implication taken away by law.*[40]

The issue of restoring the rights of disenfranchised felony offenders in the nation is hotly debated, led in part by the Sentencing Project (www.sentencingproject.org/issues_03.cfm).

Legal Consequences of a Felony Conviction

Under federal law and the laws of many states, conviction of a felony has consequences that may continue long after a sentence has been served. For example, convicted felons may lose essential rights of citizenship, such as the rights to vote and to hold public office, and may be restricted in their ability to obtain occupational or professional licenses. Under the federal gun control laws, and under the laws of virtually all states, felons lose their firearms privileges. These and other "collateral" consequences of a felony conviction are burdens that follow from conviction, in addition to any prison sentence, probation, or fine imposed by a court. Restoration of one or more of these rights frequently can be achieved, either automatically by the passage of time or the occurrence of an event, such as completion of sentence, or through some affirmative executive or judicial act, which may be based on evidence of rehabilitation.

Although it may come as a surprise to many, state rather than federal law imposes a number of significant disabilities on conviction, even when the conviction is for a federal rather than state offense. The losses of the rights to vote, to hold state office, and to sit on a state jury are chief examples of such disabilities. Just as state law imposes a disability on a federal felon, so too a federal felon may be able to employ a state procedure to remove the disability, instead of employing the only presently available federal restoration mechanism, presidential pardon.

The Office of the Pardon Attorney in the U.S. Department of Justice conducted research on federal statutes and the principal laws of all fifty states and the

District of Columbia that deal with the effect of a felony conviction on the rights to vote, to hold office, to sit as a juror, and to possess firearms. It revealed that the laws governing the same rights and privileges vary widely from state to state, making something of a national crazy-quilt of disqualifications and restoration procedures. It also showed that there were disagreements among agencies about how the law in a particular jurisdiction should be interpreted and applied. More importantly, the uncertain state of the law in various jurisdictions raises questions about a convicted felon's ability to determine his legal rights and responsibilities, which obviously can have serious consequences for affected individuals, particularly in connection with some felons' legal ability under federal law to possess firearms.

Not all states have paid consistent attention to the place of federal offenders in the state's scheme for loss and restoration of civil rights. While some state statutes expressly address federal offenses, both as to the loss of rights and as to the availability of restoration procedures, many do not. The disabilities imposed on felons under state law generally are assumed to apply with the same force whether the conviction is a state or federal one; in only a few states have particular disabilities been held not to apply to federal offenders. Similarly, state laws dealing with restoration of rights do not always address how federal felons' rights may be regained, particularly when state-law disabilities for state offenders can be removed only by a state pardon. In at least sixteen states, federal offenders cannot avail themselves of the state procedure for restoring one or more of their civil rights, either because state law restores that right to state offenders only through a pardon and federal offenders are ineligible for a state pardon, or because a state procedure to restore rights to state offenders is unavailable to federal offenders.

There is considerable variation among the states as to whether loss or denial of a license or permit based on a conviction is mandatory or discretionary. Under some **occupational disability** statutes, revocation and/or denial of a license or permit are mandatory for certain offenses and/or for certain occupations. For example, revocation and denial of a teaching certificate may be mandatory for someone convicted of a drug offense or of a sex offense involving children. Nearly all states have enacted statutes requiring the registration of sex offenders.

The federal **firearms disability** on convicted felons raises particularly complex issues for state offenders because the applicability of the federal disability turns on the extent to which the state felon's "civil rights have been restored" under state law and the extent to which the restoration "expressly provides that the person may not ship, transport, possess, or receive firearms." Although federal firearms laws seem to assume that restoration of civil rights is a monolithic concept with a specific meaning, that premise is belied by practice. Federal courts have grappled with whether and to what extent the federal firearms disability applies to state felons who lost no civil rights under state law as a result of their conviction, compared to state felons who lost civil rights on conviction but who had them automatically restored by operation of state law. State felons, despite restoration of their political rights and certain firearms privileges, are still prohibited by state law from exercising other firearms privileges.

RIGHT TO WORK VERSUS NEED TO WORK

Ex-offenders are often faced with the cruel paradox that they must have employment to remain free, even though the system denies them employment because they have a record.[41] Many studies have shown that opportunity for employment is one of the most important factors in the successful reintegration of ex-offenders into the

A skill—the ultimate rehabilitation.
Courtesy of Federal Bureau of Prisons.

community. In the past, ex-offenders could move on to new territory and establish a new identity, thus escaping the stigmatization that goes with a prison record. On the advancing frontiers of early America, the new settlers asked few questions and judged individuals on their present actions rather than past records. But today, computers record every aspect of our lives, and privacy has become less a right than a very rare privilege. To many people, the informational expansion is a boon. To ex-offenders, it often represents a mystery and potential catastrophe. Even citizens who find themselves involved in an arrest that does not result in conviction may suffer the worst consequences of a record, including the failure to obtain a job—or loss of a current one.

There appear to be two levels where action is necessary to alleviate this crushing burden for the ex-offender. At the community level, barriers to employment that work against the poor and uneducated must be overcome; that is, more realistic educational requirements for jobs must be negotiated. (Degrees and diplomas are often used as screening devices for jobs that do not require them in order to keep out most ex-offenders.) A structural framework must be created in which the community has jobs to fill, training to give, and a willingness to offer both to inmates and ex-offenders. Those conditions can be met only by basic changes in society, not by programs for the individual. The use of ex-offenders as parole officer agents by some states is an example of such a favorable development.

At the individual level, the offender must overcome any personal handicaps. Many recent programs are aimed at the employability of the inmate and the ex-offender, often the young, the unemployed, and the unskilled (frequently also members of minority groups), who comprise the bulk of official U.S. arrest statistics. In community-based programs to help in the employment of inmates and ex-offenders, it must be assumed that the person has the capability for regular employment but is unfamiliar with and inexperienced in certain of the required be-

Barber training program in jail.
Courtesy of American Jail Association.

havioral skills. In other words, behavioral training, rather than therapy, is needed. It must also be assumed that if inmates learn to handle themselves in the community while under correctional control, they will be able to do so when those controls have been lifted. In planning employment assistance for inmates and ex-offenders who may need it, program planners are faced with the following questions:

- Should supportive services be provided in-house or be contracted?
- How good a job should be sought ("dead end," having job mobility, on a career ladder, etc.)?
- Who should be trained, and what kind of training should be offered?
- What kind of and how much training should be provided in the institutions? When?

To answer these questions, a comprehensive service program should include the following:

- Assessment of the client's skills and abilities
- Training in job hunting and job readiness skills and in acquiring acceptable work attitudes
- Job training and basic education, if necessary
- Job development and job placement
- Follow up with employee and employer after placement
- Other supportive services, as required (medical or legal aid).

RESTRICTED TRADES: BARRIERS TO EMPLOYMENT

Although barriers to employment still exist in general for ex-offenders, today's standards are more likely to apply to the individual and his or her offense. Ex-offenders as an identified class (or minority) are appealing more to the courts. The 1990s continued to work toward improvements in that area, especially in the removal of **employment restrictions** for ex-offenders based simply on their being ex-offenders.[42] It is only the general unemployment picture that most severely affects the ex-offender. When work is scarce for all, the ex-offender finds it more difficult to find any kind of employment. This tends to highlight the overall problem in all aspects of society that results from a criminal record. The fast-growing economy at the start of the new millennium, combined with slowly decreasing levels of crime and incarceration, has brightened the picture for the present.

The National Alliance for Business and the Probation Division of the Administrative Office of the U.S. Courts operate a partnership venture designed to test a delivery system for ex-offender training services and employment. The model is designed to use existing resources, which are coordinated to attain the model's objectives. The alliance provides technical assistance to localities attempting to implement the model, and it is proving to be a promising operation.[43]

THE PROBLEM WITH A RECORD

As we have seen, the person with a record of conviction is at a major disadvantage when trying to reintegrate into the community. The deprivation of rights and bars to employment are related to that record, and so it is vital to know what having a record means in the age of information. It seems that a record, even a record of mere contact with the criminal justice system, is extremely difficult to shed once it has been acquired. This record becomes the basis for special attention by the police and difficulty with credit agencies. Once the record has been placed in the computers, it can be retrieved when requested by an authorized agency and, inevitably, by some unauthorized agencies.

The problem with having a criminal record in this country is especially critical when an arrest does not result in a conviction. In most foreign countries, an arrest with no conviction cannot be used against the person in later actions. In the United States, in most jurisdictions, employment applications can include questions about an arrest, regardless of whether a conviction followed. Even a pardon, exonerating the suspect from guilt, does not remove the incident from the record. Not surprisingly, current attacks on this perpetual record is based on the cruel and unusual punishment clause of the Eighth Amendment.[44] Another legal approach is reflected in recent suits claiming that prisoners and ex-offenders are being discriminated against as a class, instead of being treated on the basis of individual merit: It is a truism that we find hard to accept that the protections of the Bill of Rights against police and other official abuse are for all of the criminals, the noncriminals, and us. But when we consider that perhaps as many as 50 million people have a record of arrest, it is clear that the civil rights of those who are in conflict with the law are, indeed, in the most pragmatic way, the interest of all. We are in an era of struggle for civil rights—for blacks, for Latinos, for women, for those with mental illnesses, for the young, even the delinquent young. We are well into a period of civil rights for homosexuals and others whose sexual practices are unreasonably subject to legal condemnation.

It is timely, indeed, that we awake to the excesses in punishing those in conflict with the law. It is a field of great discrimination, and must be remedied, just as much as other discriminations must be remedied. Not all people with a criminal record are vicious or degraded to begin with or, if their crime was vicious, doomed to remain as they were—unless, of course, we strive by discrimination and rejection to make them so.[45] Too often the way the public deals with ex-offenders is like driving a car by looking in the rearview mirror—eventually there will be a serious crash.

Registration of Criminals

Registration of criminals has been a practice ever since society started imprisoning individuals. In ancient times, registration was used to identify prisoners in penal servitude: Prisoners were branded or marked to decrease their already minimal chances of escape. Because penal slaves had no hope of ever being free, the markings were a sign of their permanent status. The "**yellow card**" was later used in European countries to identify former prisoners who were lucky enough to have lived through their sentences.[46] The registration of felons has also been a widespread practice in America, especially at the local level. A problem with local registration is that it tends to single out offenders for special attention from authorities to which they would not otherwise be subject. Most of those requirements are obsolete today. As information on offenders and arrested persons is placed into computer data banks, a public official can easily query the computer to check the status of almost anyone.

Registration of Ex-Offenders

The most common form of local registration concerns sex-related offenses. The **sex offender file** is used to check out former offenders in the event of similar crimes. Such a file is no doubt an asset to law enforcement, but it becomes a real problem for the ex-offender who is seriously trying to reform. Such inquiries are legitimate for law enforcement personnel; however, the discretion with which they are conducted can make a great difference to the ex-offender.

This problem was recently highlighted in the state of Washington, where legislation allows for community notification when a predatory sex criminal is about to be released and considered to be still dangerous under the state's **Community Protection Act**, passed and implemented in 1990. The release of Joseph Gallardo, a convicted sex offender, with police notification to the community under the act and the citizen anger it engendered apparently resulted in the arson of the ex-offender's home and his being badgered out of the state and, subsequently, out of a second state. No matter how one might feel about the crimes committed by such offenders, it seems clear that the practices used to notify (and often inflame) communities will almost certainly end up being challenged in the Supreme Court before this kind of behavior is ultimately approved or banned.

The practice of registering felons seems to be matter of interest again, mainly because of the mobility of our present American society, and is now in force in all jurisdictions. The furor around the Washington State law will surely raise the issue to a level of prominence again. Registration may be much more subtle than the practice of branding with a scarlet letter,[47] but it also has the potential to become a permanent stigma.

In 1994, Megan Kanka was killed in New Jersey by a paroled sex offender who had twice been committed to prison for sex offending. His criminal history was unknown to the local community before he killed the child. Her mother led a movement to enact a sex offender and community notification law that, in conjunction with federal statutes, coalesced into a national movement to require registration of predatory sex offenders. All fifty states have now passed such laws (**Megan's Law**, named after the slain girl), and at least forty-seven of the states have included community notification components. Whether such laws will lead to increased public safety and whether identified offenders will be displaced to other communities are not known, and these assumptions should be continuously assessed.

Expungement as a Response

Clearly the debilitating effect of a criminal conviction is often heightened, rather than reduced, when the ex-offender returns to the free society. Some states have recognized that fact and attempted to develop **expungement** statutes, which erase the history of criminal conviction and completely restore the ex-offender's rights, thus removing the stigma of a criminal record. This idea was first developed in 1956, at the National Conference on Parole:

> *The expunging of a criminal record should be authorized on a discretionary basis. The court of disposition should be empowered to expunge the record of conviction and disposition through an order by which the individual shall be deemed not to have been convicted. Such action may be taken at the point of discharge from suspended sentence, probation, or the institution upon expiration of a term of commitment. When such action is taken the civil and political rights of the offender are restored.*[48]

SIDEBARS

Expungement

This is the process by which a record of crime conviction is destroyed or sealed after expiration of a statutorily required period of time. It also is the act of physically destroying information—including criminal records—in files, computers, or other depositories. A related process is "erasure of record" of juveniles, a procedure by which a person's criminal record may be sealed or destroyed if certain conditions (as may be set forth in the jurisdiction) are met. This is commonly provided for by statute for juvenile records.

Note that not all states restore rights at expungement; in others (such as Louisiana), a pardon remains necessary for full restoration of rights. Almost three decades ago, the American Bar Association Project on Standards for Criminal Justice made the following points regarding the need to remove the record stigma. These statements are still valid, but their general adoption has been agonizingly slow.

> *Every jurisdiction should have a method by which the collateral effects of a criminal record can be avoided or mitigated following the successful completion of a term on probation and during its service.*
>
> *The Advisory Committee is not as concerned with the form which such attitudes take as it is with the principle that flexibility should be built into the system and that effective ways should be devised to mitigate the scarlet letter effect of a conviction once the offender has satisfactorily adjusted.*
>
> *Clearly, there is growing support for the principle that ex-offenders (especially those who have demonstrated they are in fact reformed) should be given a means of eliminating the brand of the felon. Though expungement is not the only answer to the problem of the burden and consequences of a criminal record, a sensible approach to the method is sorely needed.*[49]

SIDEBARS

Annulment

An annulment is a judicial proceeding that nullifies, abolishes, cancels, and abrogates a judgment or former judicial proceeding. An annulment results in a legal statement that the arrest and conviction never existed, and deprives the former judgment of all force currently or in the future.

RESTORING OFFENDER'S RIGHTS

Some states restore civil rights when parole is granted; others do so when the offender is released from parole. In still others, it is necessary for a governor to restore all rights, usually through a **pardon.**[50] California's procedures for pardon illustrate the latter. What is required for a pardon in California?

Pardons can be full or conditional; the former generally applies to both the punishment and the guilt of the offender, and blots out the existence of guilt in the eyes of the law. It also removes an offender's disabilities and restores civil rights. The conditional pardon usually falls short of the remedies available in the full par-

CORRECTIONAL BRIEF

California Pardon Procedures

California's procedures illustrate some of the steps required for a pardon. Generally, the offender must have led a crime-free existence for ten years following release from parole. The offender must initiate a petition for pardon in a superior court (also called a court of common pleas in other jurisdictions). A formal hearing is held, and the presiding judge solicits opinions from the local district attorney and chief law enforcement officer in the jurisdiction. A computer search is made for any arrests and convictions. The local probation department prepares a prepardon hearing report.

If the preponderance of evidence is favorable and no arrest or conviction record is found, the petition is approved by the superior court and is forwarded to the governor's office. The governor may then order the equivalent of a parole board (Board of Prison Terms) to prepare an investigation that would contain a recommendation for pardon. If the report is favorable, the governor may pardon the petitioner, thereby restoring to him or her all of the rights and immunities of an ordinary citizen. It is evident that most ex-offenders, though no doubt preferring a pardon, may favor even more having the crime and conviction put as far behind them as possible. They may also not have the perseverance to endure such an involved and expensive procedure. Finally, statistics show that almost all ex-offenders are rearrested within the ten-year time period, even if there is no further action by criminal justice system officials. No wonder so few ex-offenders seek and receive pardons!

don, is an expression of guilt, and does not obliterate the conviction but may restore civil rights.

The U.S. Supreme Court decisions on pardons and their effects are directly contradictory, and thus state laws usually govern pardons. While pardons are not frequent in the nation at this time, it is reasonable to expect they may become more frequent as prison overcrowding becomes more critical. In 2003, Illinois Governor George Ryan pardoned four inmates he was convinced had been tortured into confessing to murder. President George W. Bush pardoned no one in 2002. The Office of the Pardon Attorney has not issued a report on presidential pardons since that date.

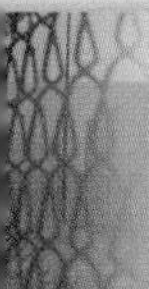

CORRECTIONAL BRIEF

Clemency and the President

The U.S. Constitution (Article II, Section 2) authorizes the president to grant executive clemency for federal offenses. Petitions are received and reviewed by a pardons attorney who makes recommendations. Clemency may be a reprieve, revision of a fine or penalty, commutation of a sentence, or a full pardon. A pardon, which is generally considered only after the completion of a sentence, restores all basic civil rights and may aid in the restoration of professional credentials and licenses that were lost due to the conviction. A commutation is a significant reduction in the sentence. Outcomes for clemency applications are listed on the right for the years shown.

Executive Clemency Granted/Denied

Year	Pardons	Commutation	Denied
1980	155	11	500
1985	32	3	279
1990	0	0	289
1994	0	0	785
1998	21	0	378
2000	59	3	601
2002	0	0	1,985

SOURCE: K. Maguire and A. Pastore, *Sourcebook of Criminal Justice Statistics 2002* (Washington, DC: U.S. Department of Justice, 2005), p. 468.

SUMMARY

Laws that deprive ex-offenders of civil rights are vestiges from distant times and contradict both the principles of reintegration and the purposes of correction. It seems sensible and fair that all laws depriving ex-offenders of civil rights should be abolished until and unless it is proved that the public's safety and protection require them. Doing so would advance the goals of corrections and reintegration and is more defensible than is the continuing disenfranchisement of current law-abiding persons.

Many organizations contend that when convicted felons have paid their debt to society, they should have a chance to start over with a clean record. This belief has been translated into statutes that provide for the annulment and expungement of criminal records in a number of states, but many of them lack adequate mechanisms to implement the provisions. These efforts seem to get derailed today by extremely violent crimes, especially those involving predatory sex offenders, that have frightened the public and inflamed them to press for tougher measures to control those who return to society with this stigma. This group of ex-offenders is small, but has a great impact on the public and the criminal justice system. The vast majority of ex-offenders (living today in almost every community in America) need to have a way to deal with the problems of never-ending stigma. Only when the general public has fully accepted the idea of a fresh start for the ex-offender will our legislators pass the revisions necessary to make the statutes fully effective.

REVIEW QUESTIONS

1. Discuss the collateral consequences of a conviction.
2. How could expungement improve the reintegration process for ex-offenders?
3. Why does registration of criminals have such a drastic effect on the ex-offender? What are the alternatives?
4. What will be the outcome of registration of predatory sex offenders? How do you feel about this practice?
5. Why is it important for offenders to retain their ties with the community?
6. What are the advantages and disadvantages of having a court master?
7. Explain Megan's Law.
8. What is the name of the writ that tests the legality of confinement?
9. How have the courts developed offender rights?
10. What are four alternatives to litigation that inmates might use to secure their rights?
11. What have been the impacts of the more conservative courts on the definition of inmate rights?

ENDNOTES

1. Lauren Glazer and Sera Palla, *Probation and Parole in the United States 2003* (Washington, DC: Bureau of Justice Statistics, 2004), p. 1.
2. Harry Barnes and N. Teeters, *New Horizons in Criminology,* 3rd ed. (Englewood Cliffs, NJ: Prentice Hall, 1959), p. 505.
3. Visiting lists may be restricted, and persons who have violated visiting regulations may be removed from the lists. See *Patterson v. Walters,* 363 F. Supp. 486 (W.D. Pa. 1973). In addition, any person who previously attempted to help an inmate escape may be required to visit via noncontact means. See *In re Bell,* 168 Cal. Rptr. 100 (App. 1980).
4. But see the evaluation of the New York Family Reunion Program in Bonnie Carlson and Neil Cervera, *Inmates and Their Wives: Incarceration and Family Life* (Westport, CT: Greenwood, 1992); Sara Unnutia, "Words Travel," *Corrections Today* 66:2 (2004): 80–83; and Taylor Dueker, "Video Visitation: A Boon at Omaha," *American Jails* 18:5 (2004): 65–67.
5. Velmer Burton, Francis Cullen, and Lawrence Travis, "The Collateral Consequences of a Felony Conviction: A National Study of State Statutes," *Federal Probation* 51 (1987): 52–60.
6. James Stephan, *Prison Rule Violators* (Washington, DC: U.S. Department of Justice, 1989); and Andrea Toepell and L. Greaves, "Experience of Abuse Among Women Visiting Incarcerated Partners," *Violence Against Women* 7:1 (2001): 80–109.
7. R. W. Dumond, "The Sexual Assault of Many Inmates in Incarcerated Settings," *International Journal of the Sociology of Law* 20:2 (1992): 135–158; Victor Hassine, *Life Without Parole* (Los Angeles: Roxbury, 1996), pp. 71–76; and Stephen Donaldson, "The Rape Crisis Behind Bars," *The New York Times* (December 29, 1993): A13.
8. George Kiser, "Female Inmates and Their Families," *Federal Probation* 55:3 (1991): 56–63; and Peter Breen, "Bridging the Barriers," *Corrections Today* 57:7 (1995): 98–99.

9. *Palmigiano v. Travisono,* 317 F. Supp. 776 (D.R.I. 1970).
10. William Gilbertson, "Irked by Focus on Inmates, California Bans Interviews," *The New York Times* (December 29, 1995): A-8.
11. See the special death penalty theme issue of *Corrections Today* 55:4 (1993): 56–98; Kevin Correia, "Suicide Assessment in a Prison Environment," *Criminal Justice and Behavior* 27:5 (2000): 581–599: and Elizabeth Gillespie, "Suicide Prevention in Jails," *American Jails* 19:1 (2005): 17–21.
12. Some courts have upheld the restriction of communications between inmates at different institutions for security reasons. *Schlobohm v. U.S. Attorney General,* 479 F. Supp. 401 (M.D. Pa. 1979).
13. *Guajardo v. Estelle,* 580 F. 2d 748 (5th Cir. 1978). See also Joseph Bouchard and A. Winnicki, "'You Found What in a Book?' Contraband Control in a Prison Library," *Library and Archival Security* 17:1 (2002): 9–16.
14. Executive Order Number 814 for incoming mail, 814A for outgoing mail. Office of the Governor, State of Ohio, August 3, 1973.
15. *Sewell v. Pegelow,* 304 F. 2d 670 (4th Cir. 1962); *Banks v. Havener,* 234 F. Supp. 27 (E.D. Va. 1964); and *Knuckles v. Prasse,* 435 F. 2d 1255 (3rd Cir. 1970). These three cases dealt with the right of Black Muslim inmates to freedom of religion. In *Knuckles v. Prasse,* the court of appeals held that prison officials were not required to make available to prisoners Black Muslim publications that urged defiance of prison authorities and thus threatened prison security, unless properly interpreted by a trained Muslim minister. In the *Sewell* decision, a clear instance of discrimination against a Black Muslim prisoner was brought before the court of appeals, which dismissed the case on the grounds that it properly came under the jurisdiction of the district court. In *Banks v. Havener,* responding to a petition under the Civil Rights Act by Black Muslim prisoners, the district court held that the antipathy of inmates and staff occasioned by the Black Muslims' belief in black supremacy was alone not sufficient to justify suppression of the practice of the Black Muslim religion. See also *Hasan Jamal Abdul Majid v. Henderson,* 533 F. Supp. 1257 (N.D. N.Y., March 11, 1982).
16. Although correctional personnel originally feared them, the Black Muslims are paradoxically now viewed as a source of stability among inmates. See Keith Butler, "The Muslims Are No Longer an Unknown Quality," *Corrections Magazine* 4 (June 1978): 55–65.
17. Access to a minister is a constitutional right. See *Cruz v. Beto,* 405 U.S. 319 (1972).
18. *Cooper v. Pate.* See also Rudolph Alexander, "Slamming the Federal Courthouse Door on Inmates," *Journal of Criminal Justice* 21:2 (1993): 103–116.
19. *Johnson v. Avery,* 393 U.S. 483, 484 (1969). Through a writ of *certiorari,* a court of appeals decision was reversed in favor of an inmate who had been disciplined for violating a prison regulation that prohibited inmates from assisting other prisoners in preparing writs. The court of appeals had reversed a district court decision that voided the regulation because it had the effect of barring illiterate prisoners from access to general habeas corpus.
20. *Younger v. Gilmore,* 92 S. Ct. 250 (1971).
21. Alexander Parker and Dana Schwertfeger, "A College Library and Research Center in a Correctional Facility," *Journal of Offender Rehabilitation* 17:1/2 (1991): 167–179.
22. Gene Teirelbaum, *Inspecting a Prison Law Library* (New Albany, IN: W. Homer Press, 1989), and American Association of Law Libraries, *Correctional Facility Law Libraries: An A to Z Resource Guide* (Laurel, MD: American Correctional Association, 1991).
23. The U.S. Supreme Court has determined that death row inmates wishing to challenge their convictions and sentences have no constitutional right to a court-appointed counsel. See Michael Mello, "Is There a Federal Constitutional Right to Counsel in Capital Post-Conviction Proceedings?" *Journal of Criminal Law and Criminology* 79 (1990): 1065–1104, for arguments in favor of such a right. The other side is addressed by Donald Zeithaml, "Sixth and Fourteenth Amendments—Constitutional Right to State Capital Collateral Appeal: The Due Process of Executing a Convict Without Attorney Representation" *Journal of Criminal Law and Criminology* 80 (Winter 1990): 1123–1144. The case is *Murray v. Giarranto,* 109 S. Ct. 2675 (1989).
24. Jennifer Gararda Brown, "Posner, Prisoners and Pragmatism," *Tulane Law Review* 66:5 (1992): 1117–1178.
25. *Estelle v. Gamble,* 97 S. Ct. 285 (1976). The standard for judging the adequacy of medical treatment is the level of care offered to free people in the same locality. The prison must furnish comparable services, and inmates may collect damages for inadequate medical treatment. See *Newman v. Alabama,* 559 F. 2d. 283 (1977). Medical treatment in jails is generally less adequate than that in prisons. See also American College of Physicians; National Commission on Correctional Care, "The Crisis in Correctional Health Care: The Impact of the National Drug Control Strategy on Correctional Health Services," *Annals of Internal Medicine* 117:1 (1992): 71–77. Also see Kipnis Kenneth et al., "Correctional Health Care—In Critical Condition," *Corrections Today* 54:7 (1992): 92–120. Also see B. Jayne Anno, *Prison Health Care: Guidelines for the Management of an Adequate Delivery System* (Washington, DC: U.S. National Institute of Corrections, 1991).

26. Ibid. In 1995, the U.S. district court in San Francisco ruled that the California Pelican Bay Prison inflicts unconstitutional cruel and unusual punishment on prisoners. See Bill Wallace, "Pelican Bay Prison Ruled Too Harsh," *San Francisco Chronicle* (January 12, 1995): A7.
27. *United States v. DeColegro,* 821 F. 2d, 1st Circ., 1987.
28. Frederick Millen, "AIDS in Prison—A National Disgrace," *San Francisco Sentinel* (March 8, 1990): 7. See also Howard Messing, "AIDS in Jail," *Northern Illinois University Law Review* 11:2/3 (1991): 297–317. Especially useful is John R. Austin and Rebecca S. Trammell, "AIDS and the Criminal Justice System," *Northern Illinois University Law Review* 11:2/3 (1991): 481–527. See also Susan Jacobs, "AIDS in Correctional Facilities: Current Status of Legal Issues Critical to Policy Development," *Journal of Criminal Justice* 23:2 (1995): 209–221.
29. James Sterngold, "Judge Orders Takeover of State's Prison Health Care System," *San Francisco Chronicle* (June 30, 2005), p. 1. See also James Sterngold, "U.S. Seizes State Prison Health Care; Judge Cites Preventable Deaths, 'Depravity of System,'" http://sfgate.com/cgi-bin/article.cgi?f=/c/a/2005/07/01/MNGOCDHPP71.DTL&hw=prison+medicine&sn=001&sc=1000 (accessed July 1, 2005).
30. See *Farmer v. Brennan,* 114 S. Ct. 1970 (1994), and *Wilson v. Seiter,* 111 S. Ct. 2321 (1991); also Michael Vaughn and Rolando del Carmen, "Civil Liability Against Prison Officials for Inmate-on-Inmate Assault," *The Prison Journal* 75:1 (1995): 69–89.
31. In *Tucker v. Hutto,* entered as a civil case under 78–0161-R, Eastern District of Virginia, the trial judge approved the out-of-court settlement on January 5, 1979, just five days before the trial was to open. See also R. Allinson, "Inmate Receives $518,000 Damage Award," *Criminal Justice Newsletter* 10 (January 15, 1979): 7.
32. The National Prison Project, American Civil Liberties Union Foundation, 1346 Connecticut Avenue, N.W., Washington, DC 20036.
33. Office of Legal Policy, *Report to the Attorney General: Federal Habeas Corpus Review of State Judgments* (Washington, DC: U.S. Department of Justice, 1988).
34. Sue Davis and Donald Songer, "The Changing Role of the United States Court of Appeals: The Flow of Litigation Revisited," *Justice System Journal* 13 (1989): 323–340.
35. Dennis Massey, *Doing Time in American Prisons: A Study of Modern Novels* (Westport, CT: Greenwood Press, 1989). See also Hassine, *Life Without Parole.*
36. As cited in Barnes and Teeters, *New Horizons in Criminology,* p. 544.
37. Michael Braswell, "Correctional Treatment and the Human Spirit: A Focus on Relationship," *Federal Probation* 53:2 (1989): 49–60. See also Michael T. French and Gary A. Zarkin, "Effects of Drug Abuse on Legal and Illegal Earnings," *Contemporary Policy Issues* 10:2 (1992): 98–110 (compares the impact of length of time in drug treatment and post-treatment legal and illegal earnings).
38. Ann Yurkanin, "Meeting Offenders Halfway: An Interview with J. Brian Riley," *Corrections Today* 51 (April 1989): 16–20.
39. For a parallel discussion of fees in probation, see Christopher Baird, Douglas Holien, and Audrey Bakke, *Fees for Probation Services* (Madison, WI: National Council on Crime and Delinquency, 1986); and Gordon Bazemore, "New Concepts and Alternate Practice in Community Supervision of Juvenile Offenders Rediscovering Work Experience and Competency Development," *Journal of Crime and Justice* 14:1 (1991): 27–52. See also American Probation and Parole Association, "Supervision Fees," www.appa-net.org/about%20appa/supervis.htm (accessed July 4, 2005).
40. Sol Rubin, "The Man with a Record: A Civil Rights Problem," *Federal Probation* (September 1971): 4.
41. Kathleen Dean Moore, *Pardons: Justice, Mercy, and the Public Interest* (New York: Oxford University Press, 1989).
42. There is a potential liability in disclosing a parolee's background to a prospective employer if it results in the client not getting the job. See Rolando del Carmen and Eve Trook-White, *Liability Issues in Community Service Sanctions* (Washington, DC: U.S. Department of Justice, l986), pp. 19–21. See also Davis E. Barlow, Melissa Hickman Barlow, and Theodore G. Chiricos, "Long Economic Cycles and the Criminal Justice System," *Crime, Law, and Social Change* 19:2 (1993): 143–169 (examines the relationship between long cycles of capitalist activity and formation of public policy on criminal justice).
43. For a discouraging note on the impact of fiscal constraints on ex-offender programs, see Danesh Yousef, "Baton Rouge Ex-Offenders' Clearinghouse: A Casualty of Misguided Savings," *International Journal of Offender Therapy and Comparative Criminology* 33 (1989): 207–214. See also Ted Chiricos, "Unemployment and Punishment: An Empirical Assessment," *Judicature* 75:3 (1991): 154–160 (an attempt to explain the relationship between unemployment and imprisonment).
44. "Excessive bail shall not be required, nor excessive fines imposed, nor cruel and unusual punishment inflicted."
45. Rubin, *The Man with a Record,* pp. 6–7.

46. Most European countries have required residents to carry identification cards for population control purposes. A "yellow card" (identification card of yellow color) was, in many countries, a sign of an ex-offender.
47. The scarlet letter was a scarlet "A" that the Puritans required known female adulterers to wear around the neck as a punitive mark. The practice is fully described in Nathaniel Hawthorne's novel *The Scarlet Letter.*
48. Georgetown University Law School, *The Closed Door: The Effect of a Criminal Record on Employment with State and Local Public Agencies* (Springfield, VA: National Technical Information Service, 1972), p. v.
49. American Bar Association, *Laws, Licenses and the Offender's Right to Work* (Washington, DC: ABA, 1973), p. 7.
50. For a discussion of executive clemency, see Center for Policy Research and Analysis, *Guide to Executive Clemency Among American States* (Washington, DC: National Governors' Association, 1988).

CHAPTER 20

The Death Penalty—The Ultimate Right

I am not convinced that capital punishment, in and of itself, is a deterrent to crime because most people do not think about the death penalty before they commit a violent or capital crime.

—Willie L. Williams

KEY WORDS

- capital punishment
- execution
- *Gregg v. Georgia*
- capital crimes
- *Furman v. Georgia*
- arbitrary
- intent to kill
- malice aforethought
- death penalty
- cruel and unusual punishment
- gatekeeper function
- deterrent
- life certain
- equability
- retentionist
- revenge
- just deserts argument
- societal protection argument

OVERVIEW

Perhaps no subject in the field of corrections has had as much controversy at the individual, judge, church, or the administrator levels than **capital punishment.** The arguments rage on, ranging from the aspects of morality, through to the fringes of justice, to the core of retribution and revenge. Is it right to kill someone in the name of the state for killing someone? We change the methods of execution to somehow make the act more acceptable to the general public. Popular films such as *Dead Man Walking*[1] attempt to show both sides of this controversial ultimate punishment.

This chapter explores the history, methods, nature of crimes, application, and operation of the death penalty. Whether a person is for or against capital punishment often depends on who the offender is and who the victim(s) may be. The student must keep an open mind about the death penalty and realize it has been around as long as societies have existed. Is it time to abolish the death penalty—or make it more efficient, less gruesome, and more certain? We cover all the bases in this chapter, exploring a unique facet of American justice and a problem for corrections.

SIDEBARS

Fifth Amendment to the U.S. Constitution

No person shall be held to answer for a capital, or otherwise infamous crime, unless on a presentment or indictment of a Grand Jury, except in cases arising in the land or naval forces, or in the Militia, when in actual service in time of War or public danger; nor shall any person be subject for the same offense to be twice put into jeopardy of life or limb; nor shall be compelled in any criminal case to be a witness against himself, nor be deprived of life, liberty, or property without due process of law; nor shall private property be taken for public use, without just compensation.

ORIGINS OF THE DEATH PENALTY

In earlier chapters, we made brief references to some of the issues regarding capital punishment, or the death penalty. The frequency with which the topic comes up demonstrates how intertwined it is with the other aspects of criminal justice. The

< Death row inmate Thomas Provenzano talks with his attorney about his claim that electrocution is cruel. He was executed in 2000.
Courtesy of AP/Wide World Photos.

SIDEBARS

Sixth Amendment to the U.S. Constitution

In all criminal prosecutions, the accused shall enjoy the right to a speedy and public trial, by an impartial jury of the State and district wherein the crime shall have been committed, which district shall have been previously ascertained by law, and to be informed of the nature and cause of the accusation; to be confronted with the witnesses against him; to have compulsory process for obtaining witnesses in his favor, and to have the Assistance of Counsel for his defense.

SIDEBARS

Eighth Amendment to the U.S. Constitution

Excessive bail shall not be required, nor excessive fines imposed, nor cruel and unusual punishments inflicted.

SIDEBARS

Fourteenth Amendment to the U.S. Constitution

No State shall make or enforce any law which shall abridge the privileges of immunities of citizens of the United States; nor shall any State deprive any person of life, liberty, or property, without due process of law; nor deny to any person within its jurisdiction the equal protection of the laws.

term *capital punishment* generally refers to the **execution**, in the name of the state, of a person convicted of certain crimes. The crimes for which this punishment has been imposed have varied over the centuries, but treason, murder, and rape have been the most common. In some states in the nation, death-eligible offenses also include train-wrecking, treason, perjury causing execution, drug trafficking, aircraft piracy, and contract murder.[2] The U.S. military, the federal government, and most states have the death penalty except Alaska, the District of Columbia, Hawaii, Iowa, Maine, Massachusetts, Michigan, Minnesota, North Dakota, Rhode Island, Vermont, West Virginia, and Wisconsin.

The methods by which the punishment has been carried out have been even more varied, and include being hanged, burned, boiled in oil, impaled, shot, strangled, beheaded, drawn and quartered, electrocuted, gassed, and now injected with lethal drugs. In the United States, contemporary techniques include the firing squad, hanging, the gas chamber, electrocution, and lethal injection. Lethal injection appears to be the most frequent and humane technique, although debate continues as to whether execution should be humane.[3]

In the nation's earliest history, executions were almost always administered as a public spectacle, in the hope they would serve as a warning and a deterrent to others. It could be argued that the human desire to obtain retribution for crimes was transferred from the individual to the state in a way that finally became repugnant to many enlightened societies. Still, long after the elimination of the more bloody forms of capital vengeance, controversy still centers on the possible deterrent value of the death penalty. The arguments for and against the death penalty concern the issues of deterrence, excessive cruelty (Eighth Amendment arguments), equability (Sixth and Fourteenth Amendment considerations), and attitudes toward capital punishment.[4]

BETTER WAYS TO DIE?

Probably America's most innovative contribution to the various methods of execution was the invention of the electric chair. Although this invention was extolled as a more humanitarian way to kill the offender than the then current ways (hanging and firing squad, for example), many considered it merely a promotional scheme of the New York electrical company that developed it. The first electrocution was conducted at the Auburn Penitentiary in New York on August 6, 1890. The first person to die in this highly touted new device was William Kemmler, a convicted murderer from Buffalo, New York.

Opponents of the electric chair, including Thomas Edison, claimed that it must be excessively painful (a claim vehemently denied by prison administrators who used it).[5] The opposition advocated lethal gas as the most humane execution method. The first person to die in America in a prison gas chamber was a Chinese immigrant worker named Gee Jon. The crude system, gaining favor after a series of incredibly gruesome executions by electric chair, used cyanide gas. On February 8, 1924, in Nevada, Gee died in just six minutes.

In an effort to make the execution of condemned criminals easier and cleaner still, lethal injection gained favor in the 1970s and 1980s. It seems that many states thought they could reinstate the death penalty more easily if it was seen to be less cruel and unusual. Charles Brooks, a co-defendant in a murder, was the first prisoner to die in this manner, executed December 6, 1982, in Texas.

It is interesting to note that thirty-eight states (some states authorize more than one method) and the federal government have passed legislation to use a lethal injection of chemicals as the latest, "most humane" form of execution as the primary or secondary option.[6] Physicians' associations are expressing concern that their members, whose profession it is to save lives, may be asked by the state to take lives and create a conflict with their Hippocratic oath. It seems we are still seeking a way to make more humane the process, if not the practice, of execution.

The physical pain of the execution is probably the smallest concern of the offenders during their prolonged wait in the death house, a wait that averages almost eleven years.[7] The longest time from being sentenced to death and execution appears to be twenty-five years. The mental anguish the condemned must endure, which that long wait can only intensify, has been a primary focus of the recent widespread controversy surrounding the death penalty, as the more industrialized societies have moved to abolish it.[8] The use of the death penalty in the United States peaked in the crime-laden 1930s, when a total of 1,513 prisoners were executed, an average of about fourteen per month. The increased number of appeals and rising opposition to the death penalty peaked in the turbulent 1960s, and in 1972 the U.S. Supreme Court placed a moratorium on the death penalty while states considered legislation that could meet strict constitutional guidelines.[9] That moratorium was dissolved by the decision of ***Gregg v. Georgia*** in 1976, and executions began anew in 1977 with convicted murderer Gary Gilmore's cry of "Let's do it!" before being voluntarily executed before a firing squad in Utah.

ARBITRARY AND INFREQUENT PUNISHMENT

To better understand the magnitude of the death penalty issue, we must examine the somewhat incomplete records on the subject. The total number of executions between 1976 and midyear 2005 was 972. As mentioned earlier, the death penalty has most often been prescribed for murder and rape. One thus would reasonably expect a fairly high correlation between the number of such offenses and the number of executions. In the 1930s, the earliest period for which relatively reliable statistics are available, the average number of executions was about 165 per year. The number of murders and rapes reported per year during the 1930s averaged 3,500 and 3,800, respectively, a ratio of about one execution to every forty-four **capital crimes** reported.[10]

Also significant is the number of executions in different states and regions. Most executions have taken place in the South. Two-thirds of the 972 executions between 1976 and midyear 2005 took place in the five states of Texas (345), Virginia (94), Oklahoma (77), Missouri (64), and Florida (60). Industrial states that extend from Illinois to New York accounted for only about 4 percent of the executions. It is worth noting that 58 percent of those executed between 1976 and midyear 2005 were black, 6 percent Hispanic, and 2 percent Native Americans and Asians.[11]

The number of executions per year dropped to only eleven in 1998 (see Figure 20.1). The pace since then has fluctuated, with ninety-eight in 1999, down to fifty-nine in 2004. When we consider the thousands of murders and rapes reported during that period, we must consider the comments of Justice William Brennan:

> *When a country of over 200 million people inflicts an unusually severe punishment no more than fifty times a year, the inference is strong that the*

FIGURE 20.1

Executions, 1976–2004 (Total 948)

SOURCES: Thomas Bonczar and Tracy Snell, *Capital Punishment, 2003* (Washington, DC: Bureau of Justice Statistics, 2004), p. 3 (does not include 28 executions in the first half of 2005); Death Penalty Information Center, *Facts About the Death Penalty* www.deathpenaltyinfo.org (accessed June 26, 2005).

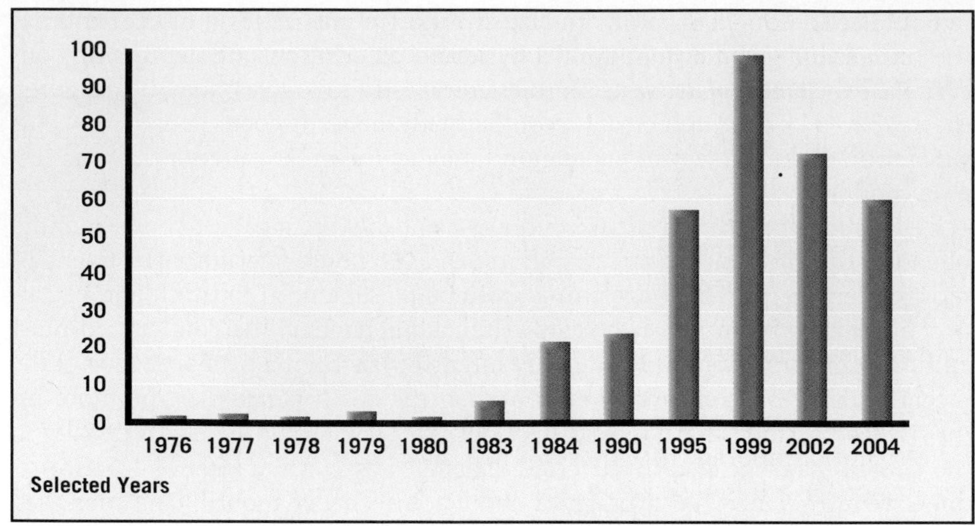

> *punishment is not being regularly and fairly applied. To dispel it would indeed require a clear showing of non-arbitrary infliction.*[12]

Even if one agrees that the number of murders and rapes does not necessarily reflect the number for which the death penalty might have been imposed, the difference is still staggering. As Justice Potter Stewart explained in ***Furman v. Georgia,*** the death penalty is "freakishly" or "spectacularly" rare in its occurrence. In an argument in Furman, Justice Brennan in 1972 summed up the **arbitrary** nature of the death penalty:

> *When the punishment of death is inflicted in a trivial number of cases in which it is legally available, the conclusion is virtually inescapable that it is being inflicted arbitrarily. Indeed, it smacks of little more than a lottery system. The states claim, however, that this rarity is evidence not of arbitrariness, but of informed selectivity: Death is inflicted, they say, only in "extreme" cases.*
>
> *Informed selectivity, of course, is a value not to be denigrated. Yet presumably the states could make precisely the same claim if there were ten executions per year, or five, or even if there were but one. That there may be as many as fifty per year does not strengthen the claim. When the rate of infliction is at this low level, it is highly implausible that only the worst criminals or the criminals who commit the worst crimes are selected for this punishment. No one has yet suggested a rational basis that could differentiate in those terms the few who die from the many who go to prison. Crimes and criminals simply do not admit of a distinction that can be drawn so finely as to explain, on that ground, the execution of such a tiny sample of those eligible. Certainly the laws that provide for this punishment do not attempt to draw that distinction; all cases to which the laws apply are necessarily "extreme." Nor is the distinction credible in fact. If, for example, petitioner Furman or his crime illustrates the "extreme," then nearly all murderers and their murders are also "extreme." Furthermore, our procedures in death cases, rather than punishment, actually sanction an arbitrary selection. For this Court held [that] juries may, as they do, make the decision whether to impose a death sentence wholly unguided by standards governing that decision,* McGautha v. California 402

U.S. 183, 196–208 (1971). In other words, our procedures are not constructed to guard against the totally capricious selection of criminals for the punishment of death.[13]

This argument is further reinforced by the fact that the two crimes of murder and rape have accounted for nearly 99 percent of the executions in the United States since 1930, with 87 percent of the total for murder alone.

It appears that the original practice of *mandating* the death penalty for murder has become repugnant to American society as a whole. This is demonstrated by the reluctance of juries to convict in such cases, despite the earlier efforts of state legislators to pass laws that call for mandatory executions for certain types of murder.

The concept of **intent to kill** or **malice aforethought**,[14] usually an essential element of proof in the capital murder statutes, provided a rationale for juries to opt for a lesser penalty. Legislatures finally recognized that juries were using this concept to avoid the death penalty and passed statutes that attempted to differentiate between the degrees of various capital crimes (for example, first- and second-degree murder, and first- and second-degree rape), thus trying to restrict mandatory execution to the first offenses. In response, juries simply refused to convict in cases in which they felt—arbitrarily—that the death penalty was inappropriate. The further refinement of the distinction between capital and noncapital cases was abandoned by legislation in many jurisdictions, and juries were given legal discretion to continue the practice they had already established in fact. The sentence of death is now discretionary in every jurisdiction in which it is still used, and it is the jury that must determine to impose death rather than another sentence.

In those states with capital punishment, the prosecutor must decide to seek the **death penalty**, using the vast discretion inherent in that office. If the decision is not to pursue a death-eligible charge, then the jury is usually prevented from imposing the sentence of death. Consistent (but not unchallenged) evidence suggests that race of the victim colors the prosecutor's decisions: Victim-based discrimination has been found to be an important determinant in Texas,[15] the Chattahoochee Judicial District (Georgia),[16] and Kentucky,[17] but not in California.[18] Evaluations of prosecutorial discretion are ongoing.[19] We discuss the role of the prosecutor in more detail later.

Ted Bundy

was a man of many faces. He hid his murderous "hobby" from all those who knew and loved him. He was a law student, a crisis counselor, a governor's campaign worker, a rapist, a murderer, and a necrophiliac. His method of operations (MO) included luring young women to his aid with a fake cast, posing as a police officer or security guard, or just introducing himself to women who were interested in handsome, charming men. After thirty-three innocent women were murdered, Bundy was imprisoned until January 24, 1989, the day he was executed.

THE EIGHTH AMENDMENT AND THE DEATH PENALTY

American jurisprudence has borrowed much from the English law. The ban against **cruel and unusual punishment** embodied in the Eighth Amendment was lifted from the English Bill of Rights of 1689. As Justice Thurgood Marshall indicated in *Furman v. Georgia:*

Perhaps the most important principle in analyzing "cruel and unusual" punishment questions is one that is reiterated again and again in the prior opinions of the Court: i.e., the cruel and unusual language "must draw its meaning from the evolving standards of decency that mark the progress of a maturing society." Thus, a penalty, which was permissible at one time in our nation's history, is not necessarily permissible today. The fact, therefore, that the Court, or individual justices, may have in the past expressed an opinion that the death penalty is constitutional is not now binding on us.[20]

The reference to unusual punishment helps clarify the relationship between this particular amendment and the customs and practices of any given period. The death penalty was surely not an unusual punishment in the early nineteenth century, and there appears to be no national consensus that it is in the first decade of the twenty-first century.[21] In *Furman,* the U.S. Supreme Court found that Georgia's death penalty gave the sentencer (judge or jury) complete and unguided discretion to impose the death penalty, and ruled that the Georgia death penalty had been imposed arbitrarily and discriminatorily against minorities. In the later *Gregg v. Georgia* opinion, the U.S. Supreme Court mandated a bifurcated trial, the first part to determine guilt and the second trial to determine the penalty.

Cruelty was examined by the Supreme Court in 1878 in *Wilkerson v. Utah.*[22] It was Utah's practice to punish premeditated murderers by shooting them at a public execution. This case examined the concepts of the developing frontier and the execution practices being used in other areas around the world. The Court did not stick to the doctrine of traditional practice, but examined contemporary thought on the matter of cruel punishment. It found that the case against Utah was not cruel in the context of the times, but it left open the door for future Court examinations of the cruelty issue:

Three ways to carry out a sentence.

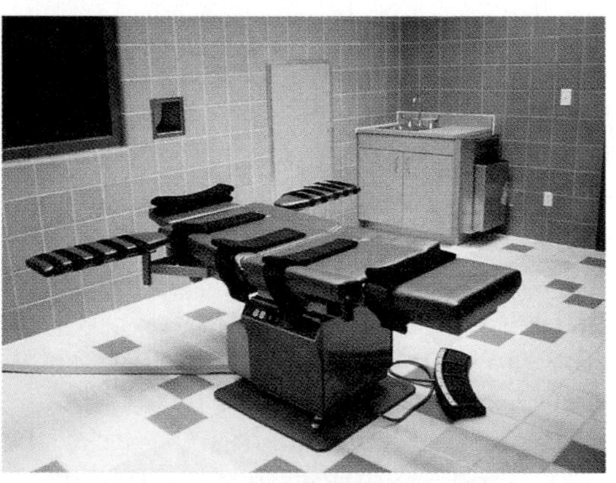

a. Lethal injection.
Courtesy of AP/Wide World Photos.

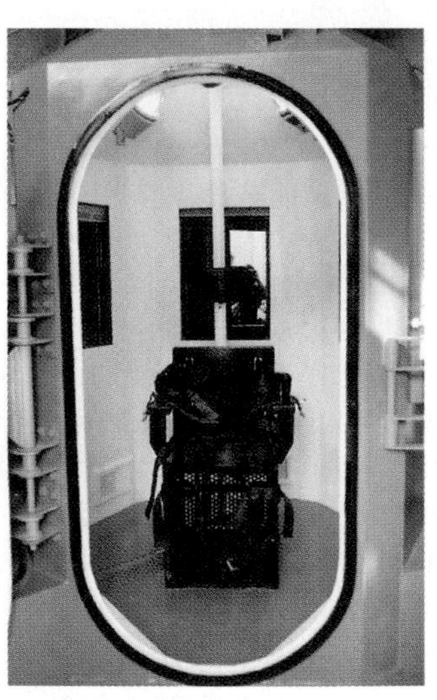

c. Gas chamber.
Courtesy of AP/Wide World Photos.

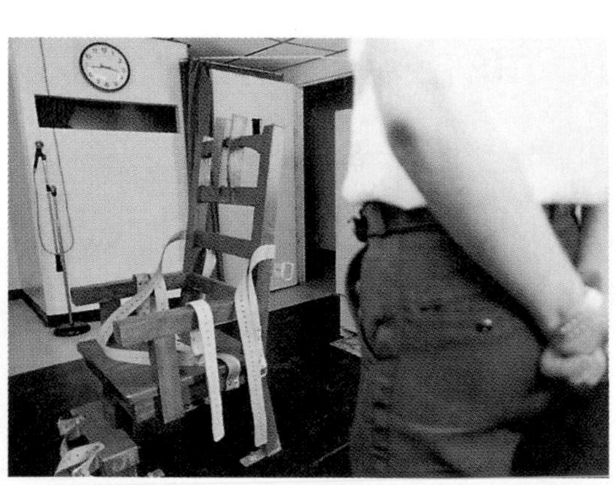

b. Electric chair.
Courtesy of AP/Wide World Photos.

Difficulty would attend the effort to define with exactness the extent of the constitutional provision which provides that cruel and unusual punishments shall not be inflicted: but it is safe to affirm that punishments of torture . . . and all others in the same line of unnecessary cruelty, are forbidden by that amendment to the Constitution.[23]

Only with the introduction of the electric chair in New York was the issue of cruel and unusual punishment raised again. The 1890 case of *In re Kemmler* challenged the use of that new form of execution as cruel and unusual punishment, but the Court was unanimous in its decision that electrocution was not unconstitutional just because it was unusual. It also came very close to employing the Due Process clause of the Fourteenth Amendment in the case, giving early warning that it might do so at a later, more substantial hearing. In the 1892 case of *O'Neil v. Vermont,* the court again affirmed that the Eighth Amendment did not apply to the states, but with three strong dissenting opinions. One of the dissenting justices wrote the following:

That designation [cruel and unusual], it is true, is usually applied to punishments which inflict torture, such as the rack, the thumbscrew, the iron boot, the stretching of limbs and the like, which are attended with acute pain and suffering. . . . The inhibition is directed not only against punishments of the character mentioned, but against all punishments which by their excessive length or severity are greatly disproportionate to the offenses charged. The whole inhibition is against that which is excessive.[24]

This logic, though a minority attitude at the time, prevailed to dominate the 1910 landmark case of *Weems v. United States,*[25] the first time the Court invalidated a penalty because they found it excessive. Clearly, excessive punishment had become as objectionable to the Court as what was inherently cruel. Not until 1947 did the Court decide another significant case on the issue of whether the Eighth Amendment applied to the states. In the case of *Louisiana ex rel. Francis v. Resweber,*[26] the Court was virtually unanimous in its agreement that the infliction of unnecessary pain is forbidden by traditional Anglo-American legal practice. This unusual case involved a convicted murderer (Francis) who was sentenced to die in the electric chair. The electrical system malfunctioned at the execution, so Francis was not killed the first time the current passed through his body.[27] Pleading that a second attempt at electrocution would be cruel and unusual punishment, Francis took his case to the Supreme Court. Although the case brought out many of the crucial Eighth Amendment issues, the Court stopped short of enforcing that amendment on the states, and Francis lost his appeal on a five-to-four split. He thus was finally executed, but his case paved the way for several that came in the 1960s.

The next significant case we note is the landmark 1972 case on capital punishment, *Furman v. Georgia.* The Court's decision was five to four in favor of a ban on using capital punishment as it was currently being practiced. Indeed, the justices were so widely divided on the issue that each wrote a separate opinion. Only two of the justices (Brennan and Marshall) held that the death penalty was cruel and unusual punishment under all circumstances. The due process clause of the Fourteenth Amendment was evoked, leaving the states with the problem of passing legislation that met the Court's requirements, as described in the opinion of Chief Justice Warren Burger:

The legislatures are free to eliminate capital punishment for specific crimes or to carve out limited exceptions to a general abolition of the penalty, without

> *adherence to the conceptual strictures of the Eighth Amendment. The legislatures can and should make an assessment of the deterrent influence of capital punishment, both generally and as affecting the commission of specific types of crimes. If legislatures come to doubt the efficacy of capital punishment, they can abolish it either completely or on a selective basis. If new evidence persuades them that they acted unwisely, they can reverse their field and reinstate the penalty to the extent it is thought warranted. An Eighth Amendment ruling by judges cannot be made with such flexibility or discriminating precision.*[28]

Although the minority opinion seemed to feel the Court had overstepped its jurisdiction, the tenor of the dissenting remarks made it clear they were willing to hear a new appeal when the findings in *Furman* were challenged. The high level of legislative activity in the states, seeking to reinstate the death penalty under the Court's new guidelines, suggested there would be a challenge in the near future. Though *Furman* gave a new lease on life[29] to the 600 plus men who had been sitting on death row,[30] new death sentences continue to be handed down, awaiting final resolution of the issue.

PROSECUTOR'S DISCRETION

As yet unresolved is the controversial role of discretion in the decision to seek the death penalty. The prosecutor must enter a formal charge and may or may not seek the death penalty. One factor that affects the decision to seek the death penalty is the race of the victim. In South Carolina, for example, studies show that if the victim is white and the offender black, then the black offender is eight times as likely to face a death sentence as that same offender would face if the victim were black.[31] Keil and Vito found that, in Kentucky, blacks who killed whites, as compared to other homicide offenders, had more than an average chance of being charged with a death-eligible crime (by the prosecutor) and sentenced to die (by the jury). They also found thirteen cases in their study's time frame in which whites murdered blacks and prosecutors failed to seek the death penalty even once. Prosecutors have a **gatekeeper function** in the judicial system: If they choose not to seek the death penalty, then the jury cannot impose it. Keil and Vito suggest the following:

> *It may be to the prosecutor's political and career advantage to treat murders in which the black kills a white more seriously than murders involving other racial combinations, even when such murders have the same legal attributes of seriousness. Juries may find it socially expedient to act in the same way in sentencing offenders to death.*[32]

Radelet reaches a similar conclusion using status attributes (race, social class, economic status) in his study of executions since 1608.[33]

The effect of offender's race in light of the race of the victim suggested racism at work in the pre-*Furman* years. The death row population has since shifted from a majority black population to a more diverse population in which blacks are only about one-third of the offenders on death row. Yet the race of the victim continues to play a major role. More than 80 percent of the murder victims whose cases resulted in an execution were white; nationally, about half of the murder victims generally were white. Does racism jaundice the decisions of law enforcement, prosecutors, judges and juries? The debate continues.

DETERRENCE OF THE DEATH PENALTY

While there are substantial claims that the death penalty may act as a **deterrent** to others, depending on the ideological position of the debater, one should realize that if the death penalty were a deterrent, no crime would occur. Those who favor the death penalty ("retentionists") point out that a lighthouse sits beside a dangerous rock-strewn coastline to warn ships away. The fact that a few ill-fated ships run afoul of the dangers the lighthouse proclaims is no reason to tear the lighthouse down—or to abolish capital punishment. For those ships the lighthouse warns away, there is no evidence of deterrence, although deterrence has no doubt been in effect. Only the ones that ignore to their peril the lighthouse's warning will show up as "failures" of the deterrent effect.

Public Opinion and the Death Penalty

The American public's attitude toward the death penalty has fluctuated wildly, as reflected in public opinion polls. Although most polls show strong support for the death penalty in the abstract (that is, if no alternative is considered)—with a 66 percent approval in a 2004 Gallup, poll—several opinions are somewhat softened when the public is given viable alternatives. As shown by Figure 20.2, support for the death penalty falls to only 41 percent when the alternative is no parole ever plus restitution. However, this fact seems to have as little impact on death penalty legislation as public opinion has on gun control. Those who advocate the death penalty claim there is no viable alternative that provides equal protection for society. They would also argue that the seriousness of the crime requires the maximum penalty.[34] The 1993 study shows that many would be supportive of the alternatives, however.

Many who oppose the life sentence as a replacement for the death penalty observe that the parole laws in many states make it possible for a "lifer" to get out in a relatively brief time.[35] Usually, those who receive life sentences become eligible for parole in thirteen years, but the national average served under a life sentence is currently less than eighteen years. The proposed answer to this argument is to remove the hope of parole from a prisoner given a life sentence (**life certain**), but that action would constitute an admission that certain prisoners could not be rehabilitated and would destroy the offenders' possible incentive to

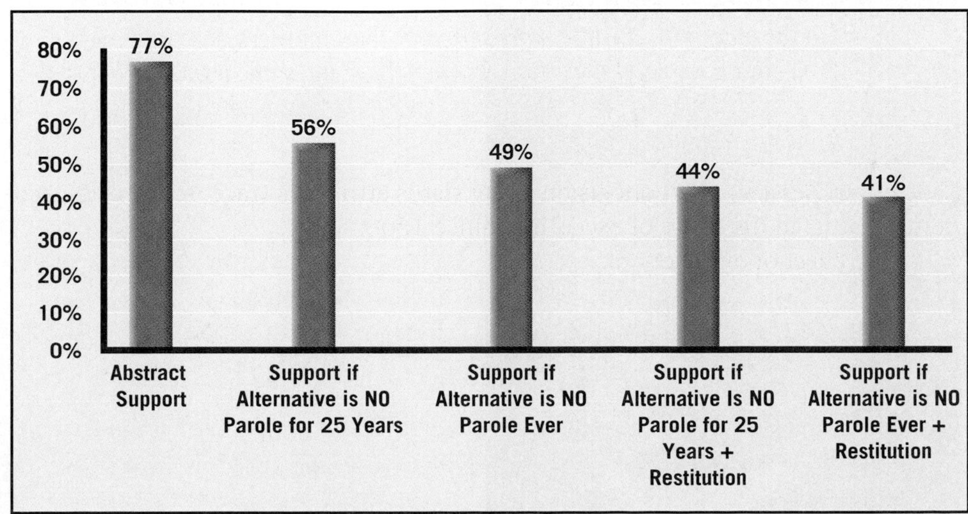

FIGURE 20.2

Support for the Death Penalty When Alternatives Are Presented

SOURCE: Richard D. Dieter, *Sentencing for Life: Americans Embrace Alternatives to the Death Penalty* (Washington, DC: Death Penalty Information Center, April 1993), p. 5.

FIGURE 20.3

Death Row Exonerations by Year (Total Through 2004: 119)

SOURCE: Death Penalty Information Center, *Facts About the Death Penalty,* www.deathpenaltyinfo.org/innoc.html#Year (accessed June 26, 2005).

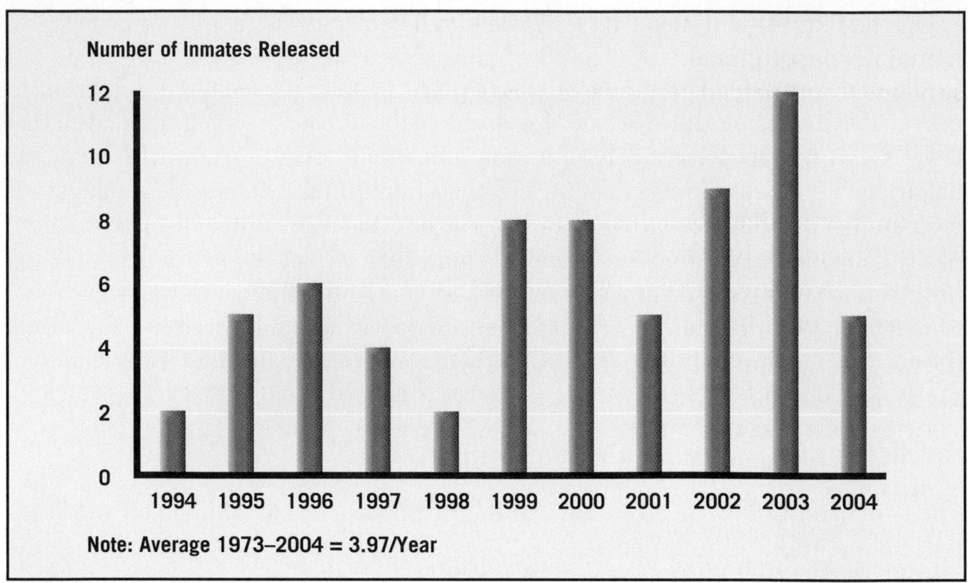

change their behavior patterns. The chance that an innocent person might be convicted also detracts from the acceptability of the irreversible death penalty.[36] See Figure 20.3.

The Controversy Continues

Many death row inmates profess their innocence, and recently developed scientific techniques (such as DNA testing) have established the factual innocence of at least a dozen inmates on death row, some of whom were within days of executions and all of whom have subsequently been released.

In 2002, Justice Jed Rakoff, United States District Judge in the Southern District of New York, addressed the problem of executing the innocent before they might establish their innocence. He concluded that this would deprive them of their opportunity to prove their innocence, and thus would be a violation of rights

Earl Washington came within nine days of execution before being cleared by DNA tests. He spent almost ten years in prison for a crime he did not commit.
Photo by Alexa Welch Edlund, courtesy of Reuters/CORBIS-NY.

under the Fifth Amendment. Judge Rakoff then declared the federal death penalty statute unconstitutional.[37] A U.S. court of appeals reversed the decision; the U.S. Supreme Court denied certiorari (124 S. Ct. 807, 2003).

THE ISSUE OF EQUABILITY

The heart of the question of **equability** is whether the punishment is applied evenhandedly across a jurisdiction. Are judges imposing similar sentences on offenders who have committed similar crimes? Another related question involves the issue of whether the punishment fits the crime. This question arises in the case of a single court staffed by eleven judges, all of whom sentence offenders accused of driving under the influence of alcohol. One judge may routinely impose fines of $100 on all offenders to be sentenced; another sentencing judge may impose thirty days in jail plus thirty hours of community service. The other nine judges may place their offenders on probation, one condition of which may be compulsory attendance at meetings of Alcoholics Anonymous. Which, if any, of these punishments best fits the crime: a fine, jail time plus community service, or probation with mandatory attendance in an alcohol-avoidance program?

In terms of the death penalty, perhaps the question could best be phrased like this: "Are blacks who kill white victims more likely to receive a death sentence than white killers who murder black victims?" As noted earlier, the answer is most certainly yes. Retentionists might argue that such selectivity is immaterial.

Behavioral science may not provide the most adequate basis for arguments against the equitable application of the death penalty for juveniles or adults, but available evidence suggests that the death penalty is not evenly applied and may be wanton and freakish in its imposition. That conclusion, in more tentative form, can be found in the 1990 report by the General Accounting Office,[38] as well as in the work of Keil and Vito, cited previously.

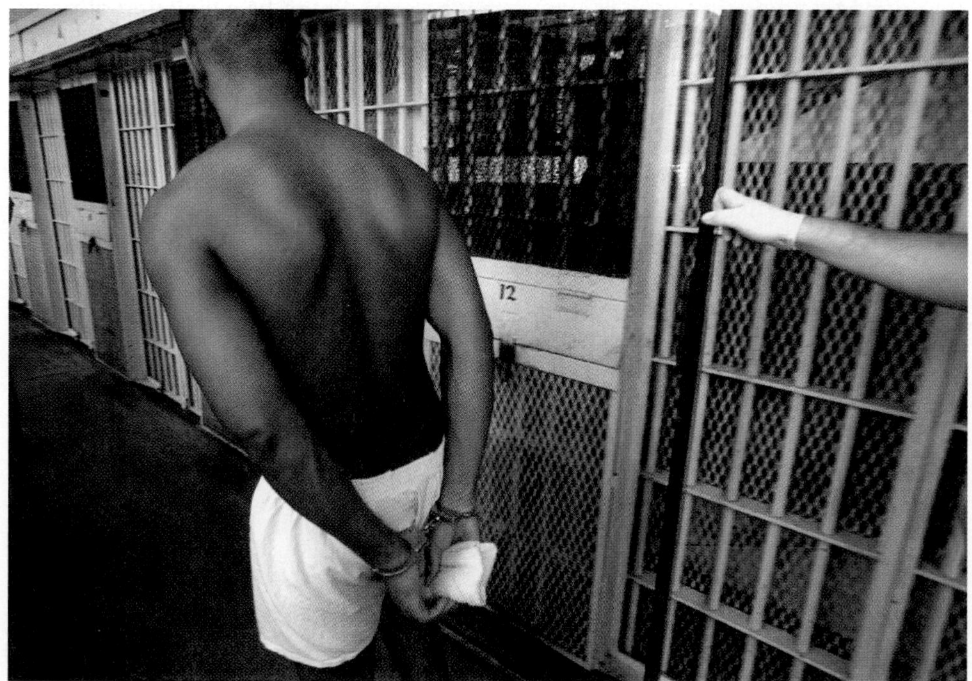

Kerry Duns, on death row in Texas, being escorted to the shower while officer slides Plexiglas shield to prevent attacks on Duns by other inmates.

Photo by David Lesson/Dallas Morning News, courtesy of The ImageWorks.

CORRECTIONAL BRIEF

The Execution Process Today

In Florida, when the governor signs a death warrant, the prison superintendent reads the warrant to the condemned inmate. The inmate then is taken from the death row cell to the death watch cell. Final preparation for the execution begins five days prior to the week of the scheduled execution. At this time, the condemned inmate and the administrative staff review the inmate's wishes for disposal of personal property, visits, last meal, and disposition of the body.

Executions are usually scheduled for 7 A.M. so as not to disrupt the institution's routine and to ensure the availability of the [Department of Corrections] secretary and the governor's staff before regular office hours.

The morning of the execution, the inmate is served a final meal and is showered. [Death row inmates may choose between lethal injection and electrocution. If electrocution is selected,] . . . staff must shave the inmate's head and leg. The inmate is allowed a chaplain visit before being led down the hall to the execution chamber.

The assistant superintendent for operations and the chief correctional officer escort the inmate to the chamber. The superintendent leads the inmate into the chamber, where the maintenance superintendent and an electrician secure the straps around the head, chest, arm, and leg. The inmate is given an opportunity to make a final statement or read a prepared one before having the head gear put on.

The prison superintendent indicates to the executioner that the execution is to proceed. The executioner, an anonymous citizen hired by the Department of Corrections, is paid $150 per execution. He or she pulls a switch to activate the electrical equipment. The electrocution cycle lasts two minutes or less. A physician then verifies the inmate's death.

Twelve volunteer citizen witnesses and twelve media representatives are present in the viewing room at the execution. They are escorted into the room by two correctional officers, and a public information officer is available to assist them. The superintendent and assistant superintendent are also available to respond to reporters' inquiries.

Media representatives are selected from a pool of credentialed reporters and are required to provide information to all media representatives who are not able to attend.

In addition to the media attention, a contingent of supporters and opponents of the death penalty usually gathers across the street to demonstrate and hold vigils before and during the execution. Local law enforcement are on hand to maintain order.

SOURCE: Kerry Flock, "In Florida: Day-to-Day Death Row Operations," *Corrections Today* 55:4 (1993): 78.

WOMEN AND THE DEATH PENALTY

In general, both the sentencing to death rate and the death row population remain very small for women in comparison to that for men. Actual execution of female offenders is quite rare, with only 564 documented instances beginning with the first in 1632. These 564 female executions constitute less than 3 percent of the total of 19,510 confirmed executions in the United States since 1608. Only ten female offenders have been executed since 1976, the most recent in October 2002 (Aileen Wournos).

Death sentences and actual executions for female offenders are also rare in comparison to such events for male offenders. In fact, women are more likely to be dropped out of the system the further the capital punishment system progresses. Following in summary outline form are the data indicating this screening out effect:

- Women account for about 1 in 10 (10 percent) murder arrests.
- Women account for only 1 in 50 (2.0 percent) death sentences imposed at the trial level.
- Women account for only 1 in 71 (1.4 percent) persons presently on death row.
- Women account for only 1 in 92 (1.1 percent) persons actually executed since *Furman*.[39]

Homicides by women are less likely to involve the felony murders and other specific circumstances that are more likely to result in death sentences.

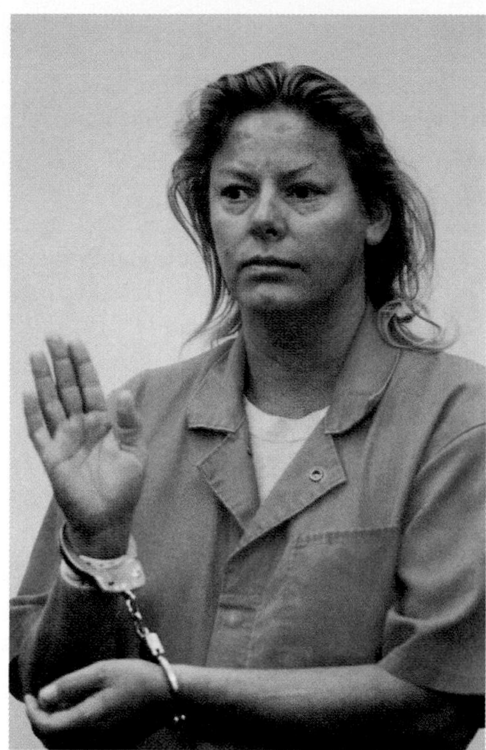

Serial killer and prostitute Aileen Wuornos taking oath during a murder trial. She was convicted of killing six men and was executed in 2002.

Photo by Daytona Beach News Journal, courtesy of CORBIS-NY.

Women usually kill friends and relatives, for which they are unlikely to get death. Of the about 3,400 inmates on death row at the start of 2004, only 50 offenders (or 1 of every 71 of the condemned on death row) were women, even though about 1 of 10 arrestees for murder is a woman. This unequal ratio of sentences to death for women who commit murder seems to be a harbinger for a more tough and "equitable" push for the death penalty for women in the future.[40]

JUVENILES AND THE DEATH PENALTY

The United States still endorses capital punishment as a response to crime, particularly homicide. Fluctuating but substantial public support remains for the death penalty, particularly for homicide. In a 2004 Gallup poll, as noted earlier, some 66 percent of respondents endorsed the death penalty in general. There is apparently less support for the death penalty for juveniles; 69 percent of the respondents in one 2002 survey opposed capital punishment for juvenile offenders, although other national and state surveys found mixed to supportive public attitudes toward putting juveniles to death.

The U.S. Supreme Court ruled in 1988 that a death penalty for a person committing a crime while age fifteen or under was "cruel and unusual punishment" and thus a violation of the Eighth Amendment.[41] A year later, the Court decided the death penalty was not cruel and unusual if imposed on sixteen-year-old offenders.[42] In 2004, the Court held that the Eighth and Fourteenth Amendments forbid the execution of offenders who were under the age of eighteen when their crime was committed.[43]

Justifications

Nowhere else in the correctional system can the justifications for capital punishment be seen so clearly than in the area of the murderer. Three major justifications for the death penalty are collectively referred to as the **retentionist** position, and include revenge, just deserts, and protection. Those advocating **revenge** as a justification argue that victims, survivors, and the state are entitled to "closure." Only after the execution can psychological, emotional, and social wounds begin to heal. Executing the offender permits that closure. This argument is sometimes referred to as "life for a life."

Other proponents argue that some persons are beyond rehabilitation, and their acts are so grievous an affront to societal standards and humanity that the only adequate response is the penalty of death. This is sometimes referred to as the **just deserts argument.**

Finally is the **societal protection argument.** Once executed, the dead cannot continue their violent and frequently murderous life-course. They can commit no further crime. In this sense, social defense is strengthened when the offender is permanently disabled through execution. Many members of society believe that all three arguments form a sufficient basis for retaining and imposing the death penalty, even on mentally retarded, mentally ill, and (previously) juvenile offenders. (In June 2002, the Supreme Court declared execution of persons with mental retardation unconstitutional.[44])

Other persons favoring the death penalty argue that capital punishment has a deterrent effect, and increasing the probabilities of being executed tends to *reduce* the crime rate.[45] Some retentionists argue that Christian scriptures mandate the death penalty[46]; others argue that society has a *duty* to impose the death penalty for heinous crimes, because any other punishment would denigrate both the values that crime violates and the victim.

Finally, some retentionists argue that there are killers on death row who, if not executed but eventually released, would continue to kill other victims. Case studies of certain offenders whose death sentences were commuted to life in prison and were subsequently paroled only to kill again are used as examples that prove their dangerousness. This position is sometimes called the "*mad dog*" argument in favor of the death penalty.[47] The debate continues.

THE DEATH PENALTY AND TERRORISM

The federal government and the U.S Code of Military Justice have death penalty statutes that permit capital punishment for designated offenses. The accused would be tried in either a federal court or military tribunal, depending on the jurisdiction. If tried in federal court, the panoply of rights, immunities, and protections afforded under the U.S. Constitution would apply, including rules of procedure and evidence. The U.S. Code of Military Justice restricts many of the rights otherwise available to civilians. At the time of this writing, it is unclear which, if either, jurisdiction would be appropriate for terrorists.

By midyear 2005, a number of captured Taliban and al-Qaeda prisoners had been taken to military detention camp "X-ray" at Guantanamo Bay, Cuba. Detainees are believed to pose a threat to the United States or have intelligence value. Exactly how many detainees and their identities are unknown, although plans are to build 2,000 cells on this site and a permanent 200-bed military prison. Detainees may face a military trial, a trial in U.S. courts, prosecution in their homelands if returned, or trial in an international court. The first two of those options could result in the death penalty.

Prisoners being held at the Abu Ghraib Prison in Iraq by the U.S. military.

Photo by Ed. Kashi, courtesy of CORBIS-NY.

The nation's policy toward this special group of offenders challenges national and international law, as the government attempts to redefine criminal actions to avoid Articles of War and rights guaranteed under the Geneva Convention. If defendants are punished with limited or no due process, would there be secret trials? How could the accused call witnesses to offer evidence to refute the prosecutor's evidence? How could exculpatory evidence be offered? Will appeals be permitted? It is challenges such as these that not only sharpen the contrast between a government and citizenry under law, but also validate the necessity of adhering firmly to rights, liberties, and freedom.

COMMITMENTS TO DEATH ROW CONTINUE

With more than 3,500 prisoners on death rows across the nation (see Figure 20.4) and the number of executions still high, what will be the public's reaction if an unprecedented number of executions occur in the next few years? Administrators,

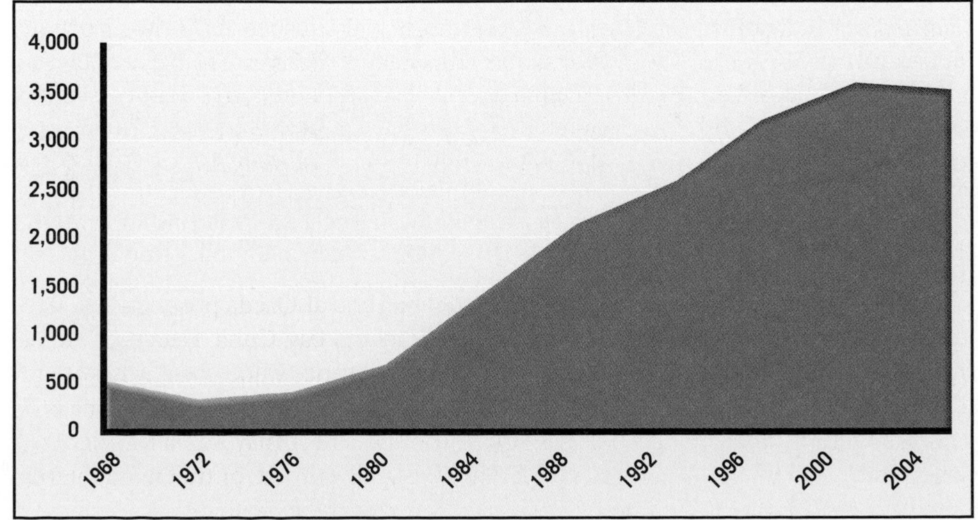

FIGURE 20.4

Size of Death Row, 1968–2004

SOURCE: Death Penalty Information Center, *Death Row Population by Year,* www.deathpenaltyinfo.org/article.php?scid=9&did=188#year (accessed June 16, 2005).

politicians, legislators, and the public wrestle with what to do about the backlog of incarcerated evil.

SUMMARY

At midyear 2005, 972 men and women had died by state execution since the day Gary Gilmore was shot through the heart in 1977. The U.S. Supreme Court has streamlined and expedited its procedures for appellate review and seems to have tackled the issue of capital punishment head-on. However, the death rows in thirty-eight states are packed, with over 3,500 convicted persons sentenced to die by hanging, electrocution, lethal injection, gas, or the firing squad.

After it showed clearly what provisions it was willing to accept with regard to the death penalty in *Gregg*, the Supreme Court has been relatively supportive of the states' implementing them. It is clear, however, that the limited circumstances acceptable for the ultimate punishment must be administered on a scrupulously equitable basis or the Supreme Court may hold that even such limited application of the sanction of death is unconstitutional. The matter of equity is the one that must be watched during the next few years, as the number of admissions to death row continues.

Finally, while the death penalty is a large chalkboard on which the basic rights of citizens are charted, only a small percentage of imprisoned offenders are on death row. Most will serve their sentences and be released to reenter society. We now turn to parole and inmate reentry.

REVIEW QUESTIONS

1. Explain the guidelines that came out of *Furman v. Georgia* and its related decisions.
2. Prepare an argument for the retention of the death penalty, and then prepare an argument against it.
3. How does the race of the victim affect being charged with a capital crime?
4. Why might the number of executions increase sharply in the 2000s?
5. Who were the first to die in America by electrocution, by the gas chamber, by the use of lethal injection? What are your reactions to each form?
6. Debate: The death penalty should be abolished.
7. Defend the death penalty.

ENDNOTES

1. Tim Robbins, director, *Dead Man Walking* (Hollywood, CA: Grammercy/Polygram Film Productions, 1995). This film was nominated for a number of Academy Awards. Susan Sarandon played the nun who tried to help save a condemned man's soul by counseling him to admit to the crimes, and she won the best actress Oscar for 1995.
2. Death Penalty Information Center, *Crime Punishable by the Death Penalty,* www.deathpenaltyinfo.org/capitaloffenses.html (accessed February 12, 2003).
3. See Chris Little, "Bible Supports the Death Penalty," http://i2i.org/Publications/Op-Eds/Other/op971029.htm (accessed February 12, 2003). See also "Death Penalty Debate," www.lexingtonprosecutor.com/death_penalty_debate.htm; "Seventeen Arguments for the Death Penalty," http://yesdeathpenalty.com/argument_1.htm; and www.prodeathpenalty.com (accessed June 26, 2005).
4. The most readable discussion of these issues can be found in P. Lewis et al., "A Post-*Furman* Profile of Florida's Condemned—A Question of Discrimination in Terms of the Race of the Victim and a Comment on *Spinkellink v. Wainwright,*" *Stetson Law Review* 9:4 (Fall 1979): 1–45. The general public strongly supports the death penalty. A 2004 Gallup poll reports 66 percent of adults nationwide support the death penalty (www.deathpenaltyinfo.org/Polls.html#Gallup-8/04). See also John Arthur, "Racial Attitudes About Capital Punishment," *International Journal of Comparative and Applied Criminal Justice* 22:1 (1998): 131–144.

5. Personnel required to participate in an execution are an ignored component of capital punishment. See Robert Johnson, *Death Work: A Study on the Modern Execution Process* (Belmont, CA: Wadsworth, 1998).
6. Nebraska is the only state that requires electrocution.
7. Harry Barnes and Negley Teeters, *New Horizons in Criminology* (New York: Prentice Hall, 1948) p. 309. In 1988, the average wait from conviction to execution was 6 years and 8 months, but by 2003, had increased to 131 months, almost 11 years. John Bonczar and Tracy Snell, *Capital Punishment 2003,* www.ojp.usdoj.gov/bjs/pub/pdf/cp03.pdf, p. 12.
8. For a good reference to this controversy, see Ernest van den Haag and J. Conrad, *The Death Penalty: A Debate* (New York: Plenum, 1983). See Roger Hood, "Capital Punishment—A Global Perspective," *Punishment and Society* 3:3 (2001): 331–354.
9. *Furman v. Georgia,* 408 U.S. 238 (1972).
10. J. Edgar Hoover, *Crime in the United States* (Washington, DC: US Government Printing Office, 1931–1939). A rough average of such crimes known to the police is presented.
11. Death Penalty Information Center, *Race of Defendants Executed Since 1976,* www.deathpenaltyinfo.org/dpicrace.html (accessed February 12, 2003).
12. Justice William J. Brennan, *Furman v. Georgia,* 408 U.S. 238 (1976).
13. Brennan, *Furman v. Georgia.* See also Susan Cho, "Capital Confusion: The Effect of Jury Instructions on the Decision to Impose Death," *Criminology* 36:3 (1998): 711–733.
14. Malice aforethought means malice in fact or implied malice in the intent of one who has had time to premeditate an act that is unlawful or harmful. This issue is wrapped around the plea of not guilty by reason of insanity. See William Schabas, "International Norms on Execution of the Insane and the Mentally Retarded," *Criminal Law Forum* 4:1 (1993): 95–117; and James Aker, R. Bohm, and S. Lanier (eds.), *America's Experiments with Capital Punishment* (Durham: North Carolina University Press, 1998).
15. Paige Ralph, J. Sorensen, and J. Marquart, "A Comparison of Death-Sentenced and Incarcerated Murderers in Pre-*Furman* Texas," *Justice Quarterly* 9:2 (1992): 185–209.
16. Death Penalty Information Center, *Chattahoochee Judicial District: Buckle on the Death Belt: The Death Penalty in Microcosm* (Washington, DC: DPIC, 1992); see also Death Penalty Information Center, *Killing Justice: Government Misconduct and the Death Penalty* (Washington, DC: DPIC, 1992).
17. Gennaro Vito and T. Keil, "Capital Sentencing in Kentucky: An Analysis of Factors Influencing Decision Making in the Post-*Gregg* Period," *Journal of Criminal Law and Criminology* 79:2 (1988): 483–508. See also Thomas Keil and G. Vito, "The Effects of the *Furman* and *Gregg* Decisions on Black–White Execution Ratios in the South," *Journal of Criminal Justice* 20:3 (1992): 217–226; and Richard Deiter, *The Death Penalty in Black and White* (Washington, DC: DPIC, 1998).
18. Stephen Klein and J. Ralph, "Relationship of Offender and Victim Race to the Death Penalty in California," *Jurimetrics Journal* 32:3 (1991): 33–48. But see Steven Shatz and N. Rivkind, "The California Death Penalty Scheme," *New York University Law Review* 72:6 (1997): 1283–1343.
19. Franklin Zimring, A. Sarat, R. Emerson, et al., "Symposium: Research on the Death Penalty," *Law and Society Review* 27:1 (1993): 9–175; Mark Small, "A Review of Death Penalty Caselaw: Future Directions for Program Evaluation," *Criminal Justice Policy Review* 5:2 (1991): 114–120; Thomas Keil and J. Vito, "Race and the Death Penalty in Kentucky Murder Trials: 1976–1991," *American Journal of Criminal Justice* 20:1 (1995): 17–35; and John Whitehead, " 'Good Ol' Boys' and the Chair," *Crime and Delinquency* 44:2 (1998): 245–256. On the possible impact of racial stereotyping and death eligibility, see Sara Steen, Rodney Enger, and Randy Gainey, "Images of Danger and Culpability: Racial Stereotyping, Case Processing and Criminal Sentencing," *Criminology* 45:2 (2005): 405–468.
20. Justice Thurgood Marshall, *Furman v. Georgia.* Actually, the U.S. Supreme Court shifted from the earlier standard (concerned only with historical techniques for imposing punishment) to the "emerging standards" doctrine in 1910 (*Weems v. United States,* 217 U.S. 349). See also Southern Center for Human Rights, *Capital Punishment on the 25th Anniversary of* Furman v. Georgia (Atlanta: SCHR, 1997).
21. *Atkins v. Virgina,* 536 U.S. #304 (2002).
22. *Wilkerson v. Utah,* 99 U.S. 130 (1878). The State Supreme Court of Utah upheld a lower court decision sentencing a prisoner convicted of murder in the first degree to be shot publicly. See also Kay Gillespie, *The Unforgiven: Utah's Executed Men* (Salt Lake City, UT: Signature Books, 1991).
23. Justice Nathan Clifford, *Wilkerson v. Utah,* 99 U.S. 130 (1878). See also William Schabas, *The Death Penalty as Cruel and Unusual Torture* (Boston: Northeastern University Press, 1996).
24. Justice Stephen Field, *O'Neil v. Vermont,* 1944 U.S. 323 (1892). See also Faith Lutze and D. Brody, "Mental Abuse as Cruel and Unusual Punishment," *Crime and Delinquency* 45:2 (1999): 242–255.
25. *Weems v. United States,* 217 U.S. 349 (1910). This decision represented a broad interpretation of the Eighth Amendment, asserting that "cruel and unusual punishment" could apply to prison sentences of a length disproportionate to the offense.

26. *Louisiana ex rel. Francis v. Resweber,* 329 U.S. 459 (1947). The Louisiana State Supreme Court denied a writ of habeas corpus against a second attempt to execute a prisoner convicted of murder, the first attempt at electrocution having failed because of mechanical difficulty.
27. See Death Penalty Information Center, *Post*-Furman *Botched Executions,* www.deathpenaltyinfo.org/botched.html (accessed 2002).
28. Burger, *Furman v. Georgia.*
29. Gennaro Vito and D. Wilson, "Back From the Dead: Tracking the Progress of Kentucky's *Furman*-Commuted Death Row Populations," *Justice Quarterly* 5:1 (1988): 101–111.
30. They included such notable figures as Sirhan Sirhan, the convicted killer of Senator Robert Kennedy, and Charles Manson, leader of the group of mass killers in California known as the "Family."
31. Raymond Paternoster and A. Kazyaka, "The Administration of the Death Penalty in South Carolina: Experience over the First Few Years," *South Carolina Law Review* 39:2 (1988): 245–411; and Aker et al., America's Experiments.
32. Thomas Keil and G. Vito, "Race and the Death Penalty in Kentucky Murder Trials: An Analysis of Post-*Gregg* Outcomes," *Justice Quarterly* 7:1 (1990): 189–207. See also Amy Phillips, "Thou Shalt Not Kill Any Nice People," *American Criminal Law Review* 35:1 (1997): 93–118.
33. Michael Radelet, "Executions of Whites for Crimes Against Blacks: Exceptions to the Rule?" *Sociological Quarterly* 30:4 (1989): 529–544. A more recent study was conducted; see Keil and Vito, "The Effects of the *Furman* and *Gregg* Decisions." But see John DiIulio, "My Black Crime Problem, and Ours," *The City Journal* 6:2 (1996): 14–28.
34. In a telephone survey of respondents in Ohio, Skrovon et al. found disapproval of the death penalty being used on juveniles. Sandra Skovron, J. Scott, and F. Cullen, "The Death Penalty for Juveniles: An Assessment of Public Support," *Crime and Delinquency* 35:4 (1989): 546–561. William Carlsen reports that Californians solidly support the death penalty for adults (82 percent favor versus 14 percent opposed), but life in prison without the possibility of parole as an alternative to capital punishment is favored by 67 percent of the respondents. William Carlsen, "Support for the Death Penalty—Sometimes," *San Francisco Chronicle* (March 28, 1990): A9. The war against drugs has been spread to the death penalty. See Charles Williams, "The Death Penalty for Drug-Related Killings," *Criminal Law Bulletin* 27:5 (1991): 387–415.
35. Richard Deiter (1993), Sentencing for Life: Americans Embrace Alternatives to the Death Penalty, www.deathpenaltyinfo.org/article.php?scid-45&did-481 (accessed September 5, 2005). For the average time to be served, see Paula Dixon, *Truth in Sentencing in State Courts* (Washington, DC: U.S. Department of Justice, 1999), p. 7.
36. H. Bedeau and M. Radelet, "Miscarriages of Justice in Potentially Capital Cases," *Stanford Law Review* 40:1 (1987): 21–179. See also Elizabeth Rapaport, "The Death Penalty and Gender Discrimination," *Law and Society Review* 25:2 (1991): 367–383; Michael Radelet, H. Bedeau, and C. Putnam, *In Spite of Innocence: The Ordeal of 400 Americans Wrongly Convicted of Crimes Punishable by Death* (Boston: Northeastern University Press, 1992); and Michael Weinstock and G. Schwartz, "Executing the Innocent: Preventing the Ultimate Injustice," *Criminal Law Bulletin* 34:4 (1998): 328–347.
37. *United States of America v. Alan Quinones* (2002 U.S. Dist. Lexis 7320).
38. *Death Penalty Sentencing: Research Indicates Pattern of Racial Disparities* (Washington, DC: General Accounting Office, 1990).
39. Death Penalty Information Center, *Women and the Death Penalty,* www.deathpenaltyinfo.org/ (accessed June 26, 2005).
40. Darrell Steffensmeier, J. Schwartz, H. Zhong, and J. Ackerman, "An Assessment of Recent Trends in Girls' Violence Using Diverse Longitudinal Sources: Is the Gender Gap Closing?" *Criminology* 43:2 (2005): 255–405.
41. *Thompson v. Oklahoma,* 487 U.S. 815 (1988).
42. *Stanford v. Kentucky,* 492 U.S. 361 (1989).
43. *Roper v. Simons,* 03-633 (2004).

Atkins v. Virginia, 536 U.S. 304 (2002).

44. Hashem Dezhbakhsh, Paul Rubin, and Joanna Mehlhop Shepherd, "Does Capital Punishment Have a Deterrent Effect?" www.ipta.net/pubs/emory.edu (accessed June 26, 2005).
45. Dudley Sharp, "Death Penalty and Sentencing Information," (www.prodeathpenalty.com/DP.html, accessed September 5, 2005).
46. Dudley Sharp, "Death Penalty and Sentencing Information," www.prodeathpenalty.com/DP.html#F.Christianity (accessed June 26, 2005).
47. Clark County Prosecutor, "Robert Lee Massie," www.clarkprosecutor.org/html/death/US/massie703.htm (accessed June 26, 2005).

SUGGESTED READINGS: PART 7

Adams, Devon. *Summary of State Sex Offender Registry Dissemination Procedures.* Washington, DC: U.S. Department of Justice, 1999.

Amnesty International. *On the Wrong Side of History: Children and the Death Penalty.* New York: Amnesty International, 1998.

Bailey, William. "Deterrence, Brutalization and the Death Penalty: Another Examination of Oklahoma's Return to Capital Punishment." *Criminology* 36:4 (1998): 711–733.

Bureau of Justice Statistics. *Capital Punishment 2003.* Washington, DC: U.S. Department of Justice, 2004, www.ojp.usdoj.gov/bjs/pub/pdf/cp00.pdf.

Bureau of Justice Statistics. *Prisoners Executed in the United States: 1930–1999,* www.ojp.usdoj.gov/bjs.

Death Penalty Information Center, www.deathpenalty info.org.

English, Kim, S. Pullen, and L. Jones. *Managing Adult Sex Offenders in the Community: A Containment Approach.* Washington, DC: U.S. Department of Justice, 1997.

Finn, Peter. *Chicago's Safer Foundation: A Road Back for Ex-Offenders.* Washington, DC: U.S. Department of Justice, 1998.

———. *Successful Job Placement for Ex-Offenders.* Washington, DC: U.S. Department of Justice, 1998.

Hassine, Victor. *Life Without Parole.* Los Angeles: Roxbury, 2004.

Johnson, Robert. *Death Work: A Study of the Modern Execution Process.* Belmont, CA: Wadsworth, 1998.

Johnson, Robert, and H. Toch. *Crime and Punishment: Inside Views.* Los Angeles: Roxbury, 2000.

Kilpatrick, D., D. Beatty, and S. Howley. *The Rights of Crime Victims.* Washington, DC: U.S. Department of Justice, 1998.

Lutze, Faith, and D. Brody, "Mental Abuse as Cruel and Unusual Punishment," *Crime and Delinquency* 45:2 (1999): 242–255.

Office of the Pardon Attorney. *Civil Disabilities of Convicted Felons.* Washington, DC: U.S. Department of Justice, 1996.

Petrosino, Anthony, and C. Petrosino. "The Public Safety Potential of Megan's Law in Massachusetts." *Crime and Delinquency* 45:1 (1999): 122–139.

Scalia, John. *Prisoner Petitions filed in U.S. District Courts, 2000.* Washington, DC: Bureau of Justice Statistics, 2004, www.ojp.usdoj.gov/bjs/pub/pdf/ppfusd00.pdf.

Sorensen, Jon, and D. Wallace, "Prosecutorial Discretion in Seeking Death." *Justice Quarterly* 16:3 (1999): 559–578.

Vaughn, Michael, and Sue Carter Collins, "Medical Malpractice in Correctional Facilities: State Tort Remedies for Inappropriate and Inadequate Health Care Administered to Prisoners," *The Prison Journal* 84:4 (2004): 505–534.

PART

8

Reintegration Systems

THE FOLLOWING CHAPTER IS COVERED IN PART 8:

OVERVIEW

Up to now, the student has been able to learn about the history and operations of the correctional concepts, practices, and systems used to deal with, punish, and take away from society those whom the law and the justice system have found deserving of such action. What about the 95 percent of such persons who will serve their time and eventually return to society? What will become of these stigmatized individuals whom we have labeled as "ex-offenders"?

Part 8 will introduce the student to the issue of reentry and the parole systems that often deal with those on the far end of the correctional process. The reintegration of offenders back into society is a critical issue. For some offenders, parole is the mechanism that releases them, while others are mandatory releasees placed under community control. For some, parole provides support and assistance in the reintegration process, while others find it difficult to deal with the changes in society after a long term of confinement or are unable to abide by the conditions imposed on them.

CHAPTER 21

Parole and Reentry

We must develop and maintain the capacity to forgive. He who is devoid of the power to forgive is devoid of the power to love.
— Martin Luther King, Jr.

KEY WORDS

- Alexander Maconochie
- Irish system
- Sir Walter Crofton
- good time
- released on parole
- truth in sentencing movement
- discretionary release
- mandatory release
- "max out"
- executive clemency
- pardon
- amnesty
- reprieve
- commutation
- parole
- parole board
- "flopped"
- parole agreement
- technical violation
- *Morrissey v. Brewer*
- procedures for pardon
- work release
- furlough
- reintegration
- halfway house
- community residential center

OVERVIEW

The correctional process as described so far has followed offenders as they were filtered through the correctional system. We have seen how those who wind up in prison face both challenges and opportunities as they serve out their sentences and descend the classification ladder until they reach their minimum status and ultimate release date. This chapter now brings our focus to parole, traditionally the most often used method for leaving prison and reentering society in a graduated manner. Parole (or earned early release) is a correctional process that has often found itself under attack as a method for inmates to easily gain early release from their stated sentence. The attitude that has swept the nation in the past couple of decades, as prison populations continued to soar, is to make sentencing even harsher and to make the inmates serve as much of their sentence in a prison as possible.[1] The student needs to understand the fact that many other issues underlie the process of parole in today's environment and to reexamine the use of this longtime-tested tool. We begin with a brief history of parole.

THE DEVELOPMENT OF PAROLE

Parole is a correctional option that often evokes strong feelings. Some people argue that it should be abolished entirely, whereas others believe it provides men and women with an opportunity to demonstrate that they can reenter society and lead law-abiding and productive lives. Regardless of one's position, parole is an important

< A parole board holds inmate reviews with an inmate in Texas while they videoconference from Massachusetts.
Courtesy of AP/Wide World Photos.

part of the American correctional scene. Because more than 492,000 inmates were released to the community in 2003, many of whom are under some form of correctional supervision, it is important that we understand the roots of parole and how it is granted.

The Roots of American Parole

Parole from prison, like the prison itself, is primarily an American innovation.[2] It emerged from a philosophical revolution and a resulting tradition of penal reform established in the late eighteenth century in the newly formed United States. As with many other new ideas that emerged in early America, parole had its roots in the practices of English and European penal systems.

In England, orders of transportation were thought to be a severe punishment. In the eighteenth century, banishment, a common penalty for the aristocracy or nobility for centuries, was imposed on the common offender for the first time. The judge would order the common offender transported to the colonies rather than to the gallows or pillory. The criminal would be allowed to go at liberty in the new land, sometimes for a period of indenture,[3] on the condition of not returning to England for a specified time period (such as ten years), if at all.[4]

Criminologists commonly accept punishment by transportation as the principal forerunner of parole.[5] They argue that transportation was an organized, uniform process by which thousands of convicts were punished in a manner short of execution or corporal punishment, because it was a system wherein offenders eventually obtained their freedom.

PROFILE

Alexander Maconochie (1787–1860),

the head of the British penal colony on Norfolk Island close to Australia, established an early form of parole in 1840. The "mark" system allowed inmates to earn credits toward a conditional release called a ticket-of-leave. He believed that punishment should be geared toward reform. On his return to England, Maconochie was dismissed as governor of the Birmingham Borough for being too lenient in 1851.

Early Practices in Other Nations

The governor of a prison in Spain started the first operational system of conditional release in 1835. Up to one-third of a prison sentence could be reduced by good behavior and a demonstrated desire to do better. A similar system was enacted in Bavaria in 1837, and many prison reformers in France in the 1840s advocated the adoption of similar conditional release systems. In fact, the term *parole* comes from the French *parole d'honneur,* or "word of honor," which characterized the French efforts to establish parole release. Prisoners would be released after showing good behavior and industry in the prison,[6] and on their word of honor that they would obey the law.

Despite the fact that these efforts predate those of **Alexander Maconochie**, it is he who is usually given credit as being the father of parole. In 1840, Captain Maconochie was put in charge of the English penal colony in New South Wales at Norfolk Island, about 1,000 miles off the coast of Australia. To this colony were sent the criminals who were "twice condemned." They had been shipped from England to Australia, and then from Australia to Norfolk. Conditions were allegedly so bad at Norfolk Island that men reprieved from the death penalty wept and those who were to die thanked God.[7]

SIDEBARS

Parole

Release of an inmate from confinement prior to expiration of sentence on condition of good behavior and supervision in the community. This is also referred to as *postincarceration supervision* or *aftercare.*

It was under these conditions that Maconochie devised an elaborate method of granted conditional release.[8] Under his plan, prisoners were awarded marks and moved through stages of custody until finally earning release. Although Maconochie was soon removed from his position, the ideas he had formulated spread to Ireland, and eventually the United States. The **Irish system** as designed by **Sir Walter Crofton** permitted inmates to work their way into lower security settings, earn a ticket-of-leave, and work and live outside the prison.

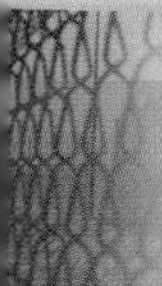

CORRECTIONAL BRIEF

Good-Time Laws

The term **good time** does not refer to having fun within prison walls. Instead, it involves taking days off an offender's sentence as a result of conduct and behavior in accordance with the institutional rules. In 1817, New York was the first state to pass a good-time statute. The rules throughout the nation were firm and fairly straightforward, even though they varied from state to state. New York's statute enabled the correctional administrator to reduce by one-fourth the time of any prisoner sentenced to imprisonment for not less than five years, upon certificate of the principal keeper and other satisfactory evidence that such prisoner had behaved well and had acquired, on the whole, the net sum of $15 or more per annum. Every state in the union and the District of Columbia had passed some kind of good-time law by 1916. California began awarding good time in 1990 at a "1 for 2" ratio: one day of reduction for every two days of good time.

Parole Comes to the United States

In 1870, the first meeting of the American Prison Association was held in Cincinnati, Ohio. Reform was the battle cry of the day, and the meeting took on an almost evangelical fervor.[9] Both Sir Walter Crofton and American warden F. B. Sanborn advocated the Irish system.[10]

Armed with the success of the meeting, the focus of prison reformers shifted from incarceration as the answer to crime to a concentrated movement to return offenders to society. Prisons remained central, but they were now seen almost as a necessary evil, not as an end. Prison reformers everywhere began to advocate adoption and expansion of good-time laws, assistance to released prisoners, the adoption of the ticket-of-leave system, and parole. In 1869, the New York State legislature passed an act creating the Elmira Reformatory and an indeterminate sentence ". . . until reformation, not exceeding five years."

With the passage of this law, parole in the United States became a reality. It soon spread to other jurisdictions, and by 1944, every jurisdiction in the nation had a parole authority.[11]

Sir Walter Crofton (1815–1897),

director of the Irish prison system in 1846, improved on the ticket-of-leave system developed by Alexander Maconochie. Crofton included revocation of the ticket-of-leave if previously established conditions were violated. His system also had provisions for supervision by police officials, the first parole officers.

PARDON AND PAROLE: TWO OF THE WAYS OUT OF PRISON

Most offenders who enter the prisons of America eventually end up back on the streets of the old neighborhoods. Unless prisoners die in prison (from natural or other causes), almost all will be released back into society someday. The cruelly long sentences of the nineteenth century usually meant that the few offenders who did leave the prisons were bitter, broken, or both. Today, many offenders leave prison on parole, sometimes long before the expiration of their maximum sentences. In recent years, the number and percentage of prisoners **released on parole** have declined steadily. In 1966, prisoners released on discretionary parole numbered 61 percent of the total, but that figure declined to 39 percent in 1990. Since the **truth in sentencing movement**[12] (explained in Chapter 4), the percentage has declined even more; down to an estimated 29 percent in 2003. Although the use of discretionary parole release before sentence expiration has declined, many offenders whose sentences expire are now required to have a period of parole supervision (sometimes called *postrelease control*). As a result, the U.S. total of persons under parole supervision

FIGURE 21.1

Release of State Inmates, 1980–2003

SOURCE: Timothy Hughes, Doris Wilson, and Allen Beck, *Trends in State Parole, 1990–2000* (Washington, DC: Bureau of Justice Statistics, 2001). Data for 2003 are extrapolated.

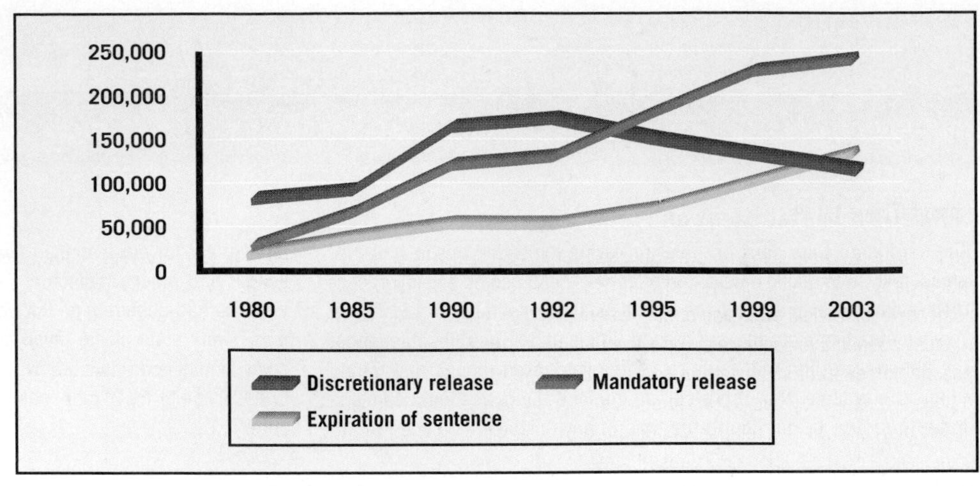

increased from about 531,000 in 1990 to more than 774,000 by the beginning of 2004, over 11 percent of the total of those placed under correctional supervision.[13] The significance of parole is clear when we recognize that the only alternatives are clemency, commutation, completion of sentence, death, escape, or some form of shock probation. Information on avenues by which inmates leave prison is given in Figure 21.1. As can be seen in these data, conditional **discretionary release,** which is traditional parole release with supervision, has declined steadily since 1992. Conditional **mandatory release** is when an offender is released prior to expiration of sentence (usually triggered after a set portion of the sentence has been served), with supervision in the community. This mechanism for release has steadily increased due primarily to determinate sentencing. Unconditional release is when the sentence has expired ("expiration of sentence") and the offender is released without conditions or supervision.

SIDEBARS

Discretionary Release

Parole of an inmate from prison prior to the expiration of maximum sentence, according to the boundaries set by the sentence and the legislature. Discretionary release usually functions under the indeterminate sentence and implies the inmate is ready to undergo community treatment and supervision.

In the days of frequent capital punishment and life certain sentences, death in prison was always a strong possibility. The prisoner might die as a result of natural causes, an accident, suicide, or homicide inside the walls. Another way out, sometimes not much better from the offender's viewpoint, is to be forced to serve the entire maximum sentence before release (to "**max out**" a sentence). Infinitely better, but rare, is **executive clemency,** in the form of a pardon or similar action by the governor. A full **pardon** usually means complete exoneration of blame for the offense and relieves the prisoner of the stigma of guilt. One version of the pardon is **amnesty,** which may be granted to a group or class of offenders. For example, the United States has a long tradition of granting amnesty to soldiers who deserted or avoided service in major wars. In countries where it is customary to imprison political dissidents, the government also may use mass amnesty to gain public favor. Executive power can also be used to grant a **reprieve,** usually in the case of the death penalty (a well-used plot line in grade B movies of the 1930s and 1940s, in which the star is granted a last-minute reprieve while being strapped into the electric chair). A reprieve does not usually result in a release, but merely a reduction in the severity of the punishment or a delay in its imposition. Punishment can also be lessened by **commutation,** shortening of the sentence by executive order. Usually the commutation is based on time already spent in jail and prison and results in almost immediate release of the petitioner. Another form of release, discussed in Chapter 5, results from some sort of appellate review action. These procedures, along with parole (and, of course, escape or natural death), cover the major ways a prisoner can expect to leave prison.

SIDEBARS

Mandatory Release

The required release of an inmate from incarceration because the statutes mandate the release of any inmate having served the equivalent of the maximum term. Mandatory release means the parole board refused to release the inmate prior to attainment of the equivalent of the maximum time imposed by the court. Mandatory release reflects the impacts of good-time, jail-time, and program-time credits on the actual length of time an offender can be held on a sentence of incarceration. More than 50 percent of prison releases are a result of mandatory release.

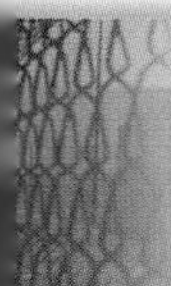

CORRECTIONAL BRIEF

APPA Position Statement on Parole

The purpose of parole is to improve public safety by reducing the incidence and impact of crime committed by parolees. Parole is not leniency or clemency but a logical extension of the sentence to provide the opportunity to return offenders to society as productive and law-abiding citizens after a reasonable period of incarceration and at a time when they are assessed to have the capability and desire to succeed and live up to the responsibilities inherent in such a release. Conditions of parole and supervision services provided to conditionally released offenders are means by which the parole authority can assist the offender to successfully reintegrate into the community while providing a continuing measure of protection to society. The core services of parole are to provide investigation and reports to the parole authority, to help offenders develop appropriate release plans and to supervise those persons released on parole. Parole authorities and supporting correctional agencies, in addition to fulfilling these responsibilities, may provide a wide variety of supporting pre-release and post-release programs and services, such as employment and life skills counseling, halfway house accommodation, counseling services, specialized community work programs and family services.

Parole is premised on the following beliefs:

- The majority of incarcerated offenders can benefit from a period of transition into the community prior to completion of their sentence.
- The protection of society is a primary objective of conditional release.
- Not all offenders have the same potential and motivation to benefit from conditional release. Each offender must be judged on his or her own merits.
- Community services available to all citizens should be utilized wherever possible, but specialized services for some offenders are necessary to meet special needs.
- Society benefits from a successful parole program. Most incarcerated offenders eventually complete their sentence and return to the community.

SOURCE: American Probation and Parole Association, *APPA Position Statement on Parole,* www.appanet.org/ (accessed April 21, 2005).

WHAT IS PAROLE?

The classic definition of **parole** is "release of an offender from a penal or correctional institution, after he has served a portion of his sentence, under the continued custody of the state and under conditions that permit his reincarceration in the event of misbehavior."[14] The definition by the American Probation and Parole Association (APPA) can be found in the accompanying Correctional Brief. Parole has two major elements: the release of an offender from prison under some guidelines, and the supervision of the offender in the community.

Today, all but two states have some system of parole supervision for released offenders, even though some sixteen states and the federal government have eliminated parole board release ("discretionary parole"), and another four have abolished parole board authority for releasing certain violent offenders. In 1999, Wisconsin became the most recent state to abolish parole board release.[15]

SIDEBARS

Jamming Time

This term refers to the early sentencing practice of a definite release date, with no time off for any reason. Today, it also refers to inmates whose conduct in incarceration is such that they do every day of their sentence because they have lost all good time and are eventually released only on their mandatory sentence completion date.

PAROLE ADMINISTRATION

If prisoners want to be released on parole, they must be recommended for it and their records reviewed by some procedure that will select them for that option. For this reason, how parole is administered and by whom is of vital concern to the prison population, as well as to the rest of society.

Parole is a complex procedure and has many functions and processes that differ from one jurisdiction to another. Traditionally, parole includes five basic functions:

1. Selecting and placing prisoners on parole
2. Establishing conditions of supervision

3. Aiding, supervising, assisting, and controlling parolees in the community
4. Returning parolees to prison if the conditions of parole are not met
5. Discharging parolees when supervision is no longer necessary or when sentence is completed.

The executive branch of government administers parole, unlike probation, which is a judicial function. As such, its form and operation vary from state to state.

SIDEBARS

Parole Board

Any correctional person, authority, or board that has the authority to release on parole those adults (or juveniles) committed to confinement facilities, to set conditions for behavior, to revoke from parole, and to discharge from parole.

THE PAROLE BOARD

Just who are the people who make so many inmate release decisions?

When parole selection procedures were first instituted, many states had a single commissioner of parole, appointed by the governor. That kind of political patronage soon led to corruption and controversy and was generally abandoned after World War II. Today most states have a **parole board** that serves the function formerly held by one person. Today, parole boards across the country vary greatly by size, operating procedures, independence, and selection. For example, New York has nineteen members on the board, whereas three states have only three members.[16] In some states, parole board members are closely linked to, or actually part of, the correctional system staff; in other states, parole board members are appointed by the governor and are independent of correctional institutions and the administrators of the system. It is important to remember that even states that have abolished parole release will operate parole boards long into the future in order to hear cases that were sentenced under previous sentencing laws.

Although an independent board may well be more objective than the correctional bureaucracy in making parole recommendations, it does not provide the perfect system. The argument is sometimes made that independent systems tend to place on parole boards persons who have little training or experience in corrections, which in turn causes unnecessary conflict between prison authorities and the boards.

SIDEBARS

Parole Board Members

Governors appoint parole board members in forty-one jurisdictions, most often with the advice and consent of the state legislature. The most frequent term of service is four years, and forty-one states have staggered terms of office for members, thus ensuring continuity of parole boards regardless of changes in the governor's mansion. There are no statutory qualifications for being a parole board member in twenty-nine jurisdictions, and the other twenty-two jurisdictions have qualifications that speak to length of time and experience in corrections (or a related field). In addition, seven jurisdictions have an education requirement of at least a bachelor's degree.

PAROLE RELEASE

How is an offender selected for parole? This question is important, not only for the inmate being considered, but also for the public.

Parole selection guidelines differ widely from state to state. The U.S. Supreme Court has consistently held parole to be a privilege and, consequently, held that a full complement of due process rights does not need to be afforded at parole-granting hearings.[17] As a result, the states have been given the opportunity to establish whatever inmate privileges they believe appropriate at parole-granting hearings.

Most states have established regulations as to the amount of time an inmate is required to serve prior to parole eligibility. In sixteen states, eligibility is obtained on completion of the minimum sentence. In ten states, eligibility is achieved on completion of one-third of the maximum sentence. Other states use the number of prior felony convictions and length of prior sentences to calculate eligibility rules. Even in the states that use the same eligibility guidelines, wide variation exists in the length of the minimum and maximum prison terms handed down for the same offense. In reality, there are literally as many variations in eligibility as there are parole jurisdictions.[18] In addition to time factors, some states restrict the use of parole for those convicted of various serious personal offenses, such as first-degree mur-

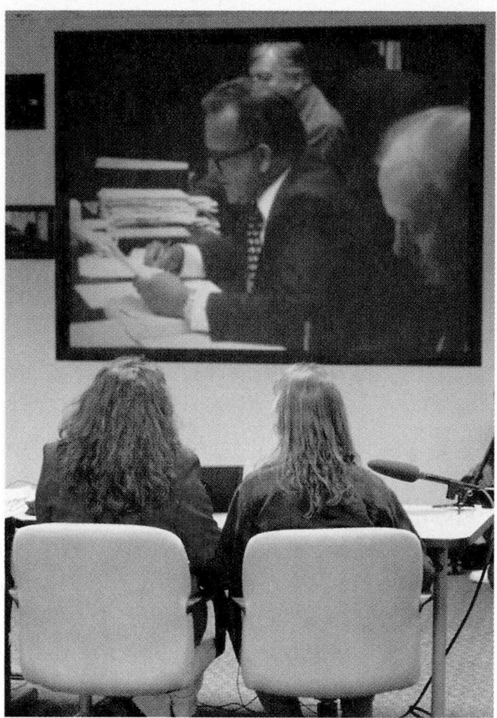

Victims participate in a parole board meeting in California via videoconferencing for the first time. *Courtesy of AP/Wide World Photos.*

der, kidnapping, and aggravated rape.[19] Many states now advise victims of pending parole hearings, especially if the inmate has been convicted of a violent crime. Victims are permitted to submit written commentary and attend (or send a representative to) the parole board hearing. Videoconferencing allows victims to participate without being threatened by their assailant. Evidence suggests that parole boards are heavily influenced by such communications.[20]

If inmates do not meet the standards the board has established for parole, their sentences are continued and they are **"flopped."** But if accepted, they are prepared for turnover to the parole authority for a period of supervision determined by the parole board.

PAROLE RELEASE GUIDELINES

Critics of the parole process have commented on the release decision, characterizing it as arbitrary, capricious, prejudiced, lawless, and offering no meaningful future directions for inmates who have not been released. One response to those criticisms has been the development of parole guidelines. Today, thirty states have structured parole guidelines.[21]

The most common guideline system will factor in the seriousness of the crime, and the traits and previous criminal behaviors the inmate brings to the current offense (that is, substance abuse history, prior record, work history), to construct a matrix that specifies the amount of time (within narrow bounds) an inmate would have to serve before release. Good-time and earned-time credits can reduce the anticipated prison sentence. Such an approach permits the offender to know immediately how long the sentence will be and what must be done to shorten it. This approach also reduces the anxiety and hostility of the on-the-spot decision-making process frequently found in other jurisdictions. Generally, guidelines attempt to structure discretion, not eliminate it, and while parole boards can deviate

SIDEBARS

Flopped

Inmate slang for failing to meet parole board standards for release. A flop usually means the inmate will not be eligible to be considered anew by the board until another six months or more of incarceration, treatment, or observation in the institution.

SIDEBARS

Misplaced Memo

In 1965, David Brown pled guilty to a murder charge on condition of release in fifteen years (1980). The seven-page written deal disappeared and, for an additional nineteen years, David Brown kept telling authorities that he had done his time and was not supposed to be locked up. No one could find the deal; his original lawyer had died, and the prosecutor could not recall any deal.

In 1999, David Brown's current public defender lawyer found the lost paperwork in a folder for one of Brown's codefendants who had been released in 1980 as per the original deal. It had been used in the co-defendant's case and then filed in that inmate's folder. David Brown was released in September 1999, his parole delayed by nineteen years.

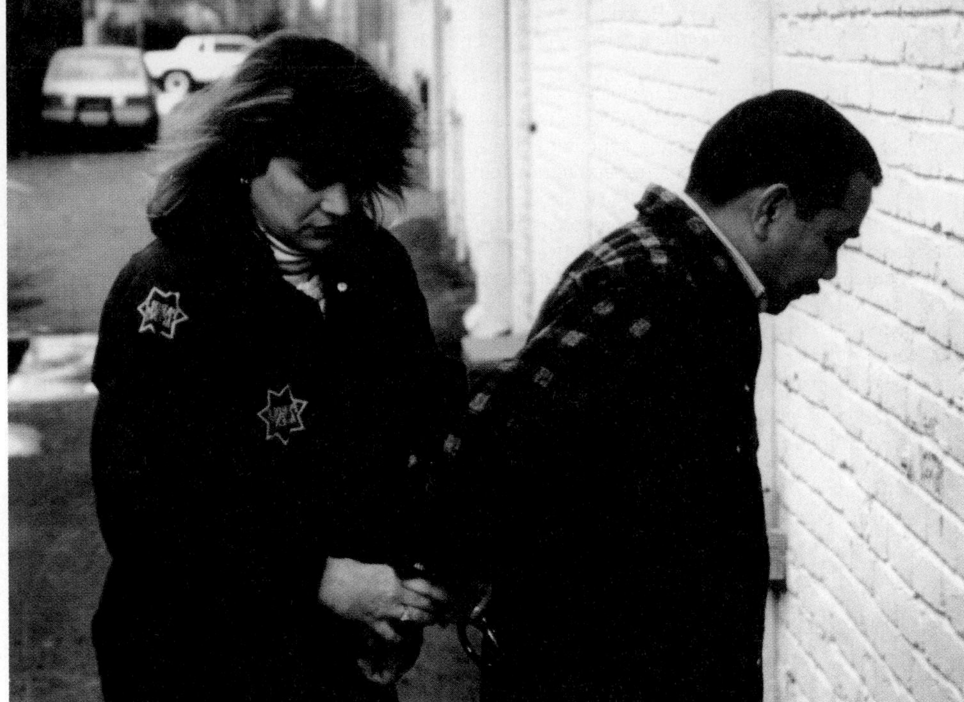

If necessary, parole agents can arrest parolees who violate their parole conditions.
Courtesy of State of California Department of Corrections.

SIDEBARS
Parole Violation

A parolee can be returned to prison for committing a new criminal act or failing to conform to the conditions of parole. The latter is frequently known as a technical parole violation: a rule violation that is not a criminal act but is prohibited by the conditions of the parole agreement. The latter might include persistent consumption of alcohol, failure to observe curfew, refusal to make victim restitution, and failure to file required reports. Approximately 38 percent of offenders on parole in 2003 were returned to custody for parole violation.

SIDEBARS
California Parole Violators

In 1978, approximately 8 percent of offenders admitted to California prisons were parole violators. By 2002, that figure had increased to 54 percent! California now leads the nation in the number of parole violations.

California was second in the nation for the use of urine testing for parolees. Drug use accounts for almost 90 percent of the violations. Parole officials have few intermediate punishments to use. Prison treatment programs are generally insufficient, and community resistance to implementing community treatment centers is considerable. A promising change is diverting drug-abusing parole violators into privately run facilities providing drug abuse treatment.

from the recommendations of the guidelines, they usually have to provide a rationale in writing.

PAROLE CONDITIONS

Parole is in essence a contract between the state and the offender. If the offender is able to abide by the terms of the contract, freedom is maintained. If a violation of these conditions occurs, or if a parolee is charged with a new crime, the parole board may revoke parole and return the offender to prison. The offender must abide by the contract, and stay under parole supervision for the period of time outlined by the parole board. Although every state has its own policies and procedures, parole usually lasts more than two but usually less than seven years. Some states may permit discharge from parole after a very short time, as long as the offender has diligently adhered to the prerelease contract. Although the exact content of the contracts varies among states and individuals, Figure 21.2 shows a simple and commonsense **parole agreement.**

PAROLE REVOCATION

Parolees who violate the conditions of their release can be returned to prison for a **technical violation.** Because of arbitrary procedures used in earlier parole revocation hearings, the U.S. Supreme Court in 1971 defined the basic rights of parolees at a parole revocation hearing in ***Morrissey v. Brewer,*** 408 U.S. 271. Parolees must be notified in writing of the charges they face, at least twenty-four hours before the preliminary hearing ("probable cause"). Revocation candidates have a right to hear the evidence against them, to cross-examine, and to refute the testimony. Furthermore, they can present their own evidence, and they have the right to a written report from the hearing that must be held before a neutral third party. Some states mandate legal

The Members of the Parole Board have agreed that you have earned the opportunity of parole and eventually a final release from your present conviction. The Parole Board is therefore ordering a Parole Release in your case.

Parole Status has a two-fold meaning: One is a trust status in which the Parole Board accepts your word you will do your best to abide by the Conditions of Parole that are set down in your case; the other, by state law, means the Adult Parole Authority has the legal duty to enforce the Conditions of Parole even to the extent of arrest and return to the institution should that become necessary.

1. Upon release from the institution, report as instructed to your Parole Officer (or any other person designated) and thereafter report as often as directed.
2. Secure written permission of the Adult Parole Authority before leaving the [said] state.
3. Obey all municipal ordinances, state and federal laws, and at all times conduct yourself as a responsible law-abiding citizen.
4. Never purchase, own, possess, use or have under your control, a deadly weapon or firearm.
5. Follow all instructions given you by your Parole Officer or other officials of the Adult Parole Authority and abide by any special conditions imposed by the Adult Authority.
6. If you feel any of the Conditions or instructions are causing problems, you may request a meeting with your Parole Officer's supervisor. The request stating your reasons for the conference should be in writing when possible.
7. Special Conditions: (as determined). I have read, or have had read to me, the foregoing Conditions of my Parole. I fully understand them and I agree to observe and abide by my Parole Conditions.

Witness ______________________ Parole Candidate ______________________

Date ______________________

FIGURE 21.2

Statement of Parole Agreement

SOURCE: State of Ohio, Department of Rehabilitation and Correction, Adult Parole Authority, *Statement of Parole Agreement APA. 271* (Columbus: State of Ohio).

counsel at this stage. At the second hearing, usually before a representative or member(s) of a parole board, the same rights are continued. Figure 21.3 shows the outcome of state parole discharges in 2003. As shown, parole revocations are major issues facing corrections.

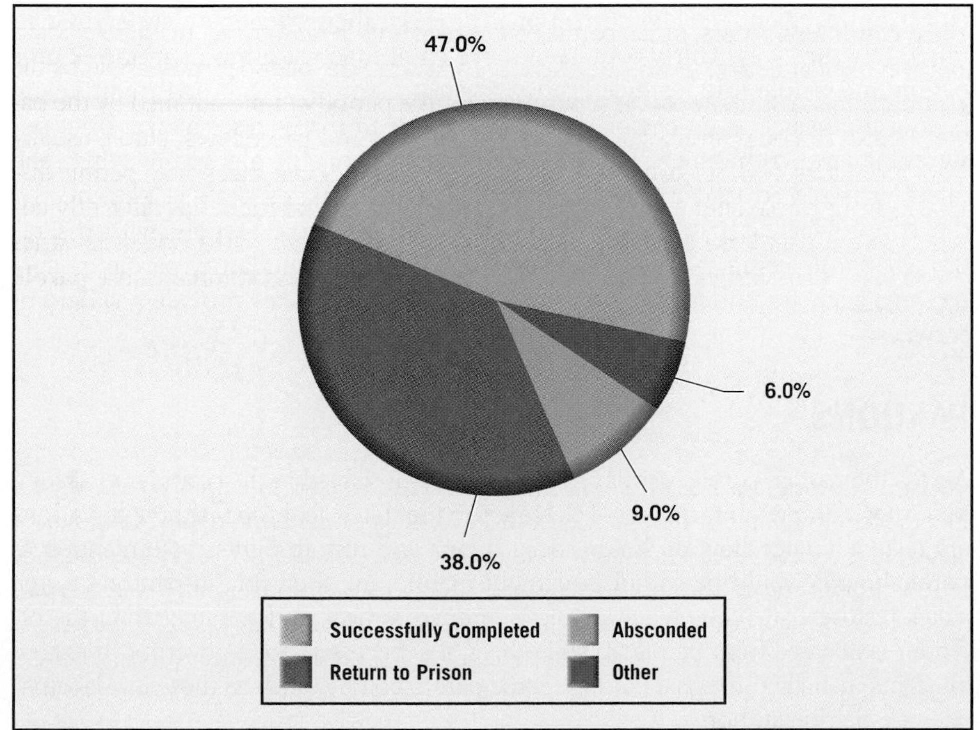

FIGURE 21.3

Outcomes of State Parole Board Discharges, 2003

SOURCE: Bureau of Justice Statistics, *Probation and Parole in the United States, 2003* (Washington, DC: BJS 2004).

CORRECTIONAL BRIEF

Shock Incarceration and Parole

Shock incarceration facilities, or boot camp prisons for young female adults, have been developed in city, county, and state jurisdictions. These include the New York State Program for youthful female offenders. A typical case is discussed below. Rita is an example of the type of offender who often ends up in a boot camp program. Her case is described to indicate how boot camps interface with parole.

Women in Shock Incarceration Rita finishes fifty sit-ups and springs to her feet. At 6 A.M. her platoon begins a five-mile run, the last portion of this morning's physical training. After five months in New York's Lakeview Shock Incarceration Correctional Facility, the morning workout is easy. Rita even enjoys it, taking pride in her physical conditioning.

When Rita graduates and returns to New York City, she will face six months of intensive supervision before moving to regular parole. More than two-fifths of Rita's platoon did not make it this far; some withdrew voluntarily, and the rest were removed for misconduct or failure to participate satisfactorily. By completing shock incarceration, she will enter parole eleven months before her minimum release date. The requirements for completing shock incarceration are the same for male and female inmates. The women live in a separate housing area of Lakeview. Otherwise, men and women participate in the same education, physical training, drill and ceremony, drug education, and counseling programs. Men and women are assigned to separate work details and attend "Network" group meetings held in inmates' living units.

PAROLE REMAINS A MAJOR SEGMENT OF CORRECTIONS

Despite growing pressures for the determinate sentence and the elimination of supervision on release, parole is still a growing segment of community corrections and a critical element in the correctional system. Although many prisoners are now released unconditionally back to the community, many are still released to community supervision. In some states, the title of parole officer has been changed to community control officer, to reflect a custodial leaning, but the inmates remain under essentially the same controls as before.

Both parole and probation have a similar history and, even though they occur at opposite ends of the correctional process, their clients are supervised in much the same way. Thirty-four states have combined the administration of probation and parole into a single agency. Even probation, which had traditionally been a preincarceration option, now takes place in many cases after a brief period of jail or prison time. The main difference remains the method by which the offender is placed under either option. Probation remains a direct sentence by the court, whereas parole is a function of the executive branch, with discretionary parole being granted by the parole board and mandatory parole by corrections agencies under the governor. These parole agencies provide a variety of services.

PARDONS

Across the nation, parole boards are often directly involved in the consideration for a pardon, recommending this act of clemency to the state's governor. Although pardons are relatively rare, they can lessen social stigma and restore rights.[22] No mention of parole boards would be complete without mentioning their role in pardons. Some states restore civil rights when parole is granted; others do the same when the offender is released from parole. In still others, it is necessary for a governor to restore all rights, usually through a pardon. Some parole boards (such as those in Alabama) exercise pardon authority.

CORRECTIONAL BRIEF

Pardon

An act of executive clemency that absolves the party in part or in full from the legal consequences of the crime and conviction. For the accused, pardon stops further criminal justice proceedings. Pardons can be full or conditional; the former generally applies to both the punishment and the guilt of the offender and blots out the existence of guilt in the eyes of the law. It also removes an offender's disabilities and restores civil rights. The conditional pardon usually falls short of the remedies available in the full pardon, is an expression of guilt, may restrict some freedoms, and does not obliterate the conviction but may restore civil rights.

Perhaps the most famous pardon was granted to former President Richard Nixon by President Gerald Ford. Many believe that this decision cost Ford the 1976 election. More recently, President Bill Clinton was widely criticized for his end-of-term pardons.

California's **procedures for pardon** illustrate the latter. What is required for a pardon in California? Generally, the offender must have led a crime-free existence for ten years following release from parole. The offender must initiate a petition for pardon in a superior court (also called a court of common pleas in other jurisdictions). A formal hearing is held, and the presiding judge solicits opinions from the local district attorney and chief law enforcement officer in the jurisdiction. A computer search is made for any arrests and convictions. The local probation department prepares a pre-pardon hearing report. If the preponderance of evidence were favorable and no arrest or conviction record were found, the petition would be approved by the superior court and forwarded to the governor's office. The governor may then order the equivalent of a parole board (Board of Prison Terms) to prepare an investigation that would contain a recommendation for pardon. If the report is favorable, the governor may pardon the petitioner, thereby restoring to him or her all of the rights and immunities of an ordinary citizen. It is evident that most ex-offenders, though no doubt preferring a pardon, may favor even more having the crime and conviction put as far behind them as possible. They may also not have the perseverance to endure such an involved and expensive procedure. Finally, statistics show that most ex-offenders are rearrested within the ten-year time period, even without further action by criminal justice system officials. No wonder so few ex-offenders seek and receive pardons.

REENTRY: THE NEW CHALLENGE

The large number of incarcerated offenders in the United States has led to the inevitable result—numerous offenders will reenter society each year. In fact, reentry has become the new buzzword used by policy makers to describe the process by which offenders come back into the community. Some have argued that parole is essential to this process,[23] while others[24] believe that since a high percentage of offenders pose minimal risk to public safety, parole supervision should be eliminated or shortened to about six months. Given estimates that a significant percentage of offenders who will be returning to the community have a number of important needs,[25] little doubt remains that services and treatment in the community should be an important part of the reentry process. Indeed, several states have already created reentry programs designed to coordinate efforts and services between the institution, parole, and community correctional programs and treatment providers.

SIDEBARS

Early Release

Release from confinement before the sentence has been completed, usually through parole, time off for good behavior or work performed, or modification of sentence by the court. In the last case, confinement may be followed by a term of probation.

Recently, the federal government committed funds to states to assist with the reentry process and to help ensure that offenders receive the services and treatment necessary to help them remain crime free. Discussed next are some of the programs that have been traditionally used for offender reentry into the community from the institution.

SIDEBARS

Work Release Programs

More than 87,000 offenders were in work release programs at the end of 2001. Work release is any program in which inmates of jails or prisons are allowed to work in the community with minimal restriction, are compensated at the prevailing minimum wage, and must serve their nonworking hours in a secure facility. This program was first used in 1906. Local sheriffs in Vermont issued day passes to inmates, allowing them to work all day without correctional supervision in the local community. The first state-sanctioned work release program was in Wisconsin in 1913.

Work Release Programs

One of the earliest programs for releasing prisoners before their full sentences expired was the result of the first **work release** legislation. The use of offenders for community work programs had its origins in ancient Rome, where prisoners aided in the construction of massive public works. Those workers, however, had no hope for release; their work was just another form of slave labor, but with a new label. This has been the fate of many new efforts by penologists over the history of correctional efforts. The work release philosophy, which permits inmates to work on their own in the free community, dates back to a 1913 Wisconsin statute that allowed misdemeanants to continue to work at their jobs while serving short sentences in jail. North Carolina applied the principles of the Wisconsin statute to felony offenders in 1957, under limited conditions; Michigan and Maryland soon followed suit with similar acts. In 1965, Congress passed the Federal Prisoner Rehabilitation Act, which provided for work release, furloughs, and community treatment centers for federal prisoners. This act, an excerpt of which is found in an accompanying sidebar, served as a model for many states.

Institutional work release is not intended to be a substitute for parole, but it can be a valuable tool for the correctional administrator and the parole officer who must eventually supervise an individual who has participated in work release. The work release program is not really an alternative to incarceration. Rather, it is a chance for offenders to develop and test their work skills, job discipline, and personal control over their behavior in the community—and it allows them to spend the major part of the day away from the institution. Because of-

Work release facilities provide a place to grow, and even have a meaningful job on parole.
Courtesy of Ohio Department of Rehabilitation and Correction.

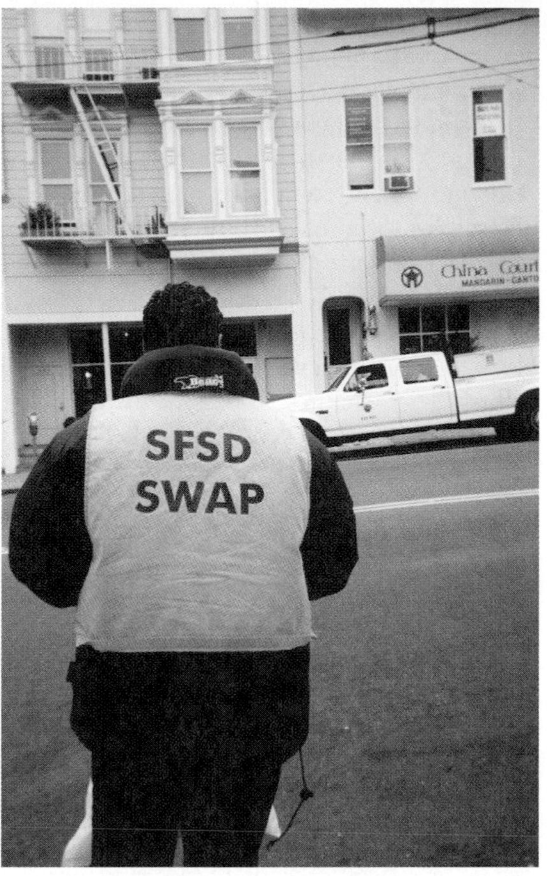

Participant in the San Francisco Sheriff Department's SWAP program, released from jail to perform community service.
Photo by Harry E. Allen.

fenders must still return to the institution, the work release program may be considered only a partial alternative that gives limited relief from the negative pressures of incarceration.

Work release has other benefits besides allowing inmates to be outside the walls for a period of time each day. The income derived from the work can be used in a number of ways: If the inmates have families, the earnings can be used to keep them off welfare rolls or to augment the assistance they might be receiving; inmates can reimburse victims for their loss, if the judge has required it[26]; or they may be able to build a nest egg for the time when they will be released. In many cases, the inmates can contribute toward their cost of housing and sustenance as well. This teaches them valuable budgeting and money management skills. One of the main fringe benefits is that their community becomes aware of their ability to maintain a job without creating problems for themselves or others. Also, their association with stable coworkers in the free world may give them support and guidance[27] that they could not find inside the walls. In the American tradition, the ability to do a good day's work both heightens the offenders' self-esteem and commands respect from others. Scandinavian prisons have some kind of work facility attached to them, allowing inmates to work at real-world jobs for pay equal to that earned by a similarly skilled outside worker.

Furlough Programs

Another form of partial incarceration is the **furlough.** Both work release and furlough extend the limits of confinement to include unsupervised absences from the institution. Furloughs and home visits have been allowed for many years on an informal basis. The

SIDEBARS

Federal Prisoner Rehabilitation Act

The Attorney General may extend the limits of the place of confinement of a prisoner as to whom there is reasonable cause to believe he will honor this trust, by authorizing him, under prescribed conditions, to:

1. Visit a specifically designated place or places for a period not to exceed thirty days and return to the same or another institution or facility. An extension of limits may be granted only to permit a visit to a dying relative, attendance at the funeral of a relative, the obtaining of medical services not otherwise available, the contacting of prospective employers, or for any other compelling reason consistent with the public interest; or
2. Work at paid employment or participate in a training program in the community on a voluntary basis while continuing as a prisoner of the institution or facility to which he is committed. . . .

The willful failure of a prisoner to remain within the extended limits of his confinement, or to return within the time prescribed, to an institution or facility designated by the Attorney General, shall be deemed an escape from the custody of the Attorney General.

SOURCE: American Academy of Political and Social Science, The Future of Corrections: The Annals *(Washington, DC: AAPSS, 1969), p. 65.*

death of a family member or some other crisis situation at home ("emergency furlough") was the most common reason for the home furlough. As states have passed legislation making furloughs a legal correctional tool, furloughs have been used for a number of purposes, including a home visit during holidays or just before release ("meritorious furlough"), so the return to the free world is a graduated process and includes **reintegration.** Education has been another reason for extensive use of the furlough; it often allows the inmate to be in residence at the school during the week; he or she then returns to the correctional institution on the weekend. One benefit of home furloughs, obviously, is decreased sexual tension in institutions. More uses for furloughs are being explored as correctional administrators gain experience with them.[28] A major roadblock to progress in such programs has been a few highly publicized and sensational failures. Those failures,[29] combined with the generally increasing numbers of violent and dangerous inmates coming out of the prisons, made it difficult to promote any kind of furlough program.[30]

SIDEBARS

Furlough

A prison release program permitting the inmate to pursue education, vocational training, or employment in the community. Another purpose is to achieve closer surveillance of the offender by requiring a transitional period of up to 120 days in a community residential center (CRC). The Bureau of Prisons requires almost every offender nearing release from confinement to reside in a CRC as prerelease furloughers. In most jurisdictions, furloughers are legally inmates and can be more easily returned to confinement than parolees if they commit technical violations or a new offense.

Halfway Houses

The search for ways to assist offenders transitioning from prison has pumped new life into an old option: the **halfway house.**[31] The interest in the halfway house as an important part of the reentry process has grown in the past few decades. Although earlier halfway houses served as residences for homeless men and women released from prison, they have since been used for a variety of purposes. Small residences offering shelter have been managed by prison aid societies since the early 1800s. In recent years, more attention has been given to halfway houses as the possible nuclei of community-based networks of residential treatment centers, drug-free and alcohol-free living spaces, or as prerelease guidance centers.[32]

SIDEBARS

Reintegration

Rehabilitation of the offender within the community, based on the beliefs that the causes of crime lie within the community and the manner in which the offender functions, criminal behavior results from an absence of legitimate opportunity to succeed, and legitimate opportunities must be provided. It also assumes that the offender will be returning to the community from a period of incarceration in a jail or prison.

There are different patterns of referral to halfway house programs, the most frequent of which occurs when an inmate is granted a conditional release (such as parole, shock parole, or shock probation) and is required to enter a halfway house during at least the initial period following release. This provides services to and surveillance of parolees who need support during this period. Time of residency may be specified before referral, but usually is a shared decision to be made collaboratively by the supervision officer, client, and house staff. This decision is frequently based on such factors as resident's readiness to leave the house, employment, fine and restitution payments, savings, and alternative residential plan. The offender generally continues on supervision after leaving the halfway house.

Another source of residents are those inmates whose release plans call for placement in a halfway house as the initial phase of their release procedure. Unlike the first option, however, halfway house residency occurs prior to formal granting of parole and subsequent supervision as a releasee or parolee. These inmates typically have a definite release date before they move from the prison to the halfway house. Note that these clients remain inmates who will serve the remainder of their sentences while residing in a halfway house. For these residents, halfway houses provide needed and significant assistance and direction in the transition from prison to community.[33] Additional benefits include continuation of jurisdiction by the referring correctional agency,[34] ability to return the inmate to incarceration without formal violation of parole, development of a more positive attitude toward the halfway house by the resident, lessening of loneliness and sense of isolation,[35] and less expensive aftercare service that can be more legitimately compared to imprisonment, rather than the costs of parole.[36] The U.S. Bureau of Prisons was a leader in initiating this model for using halfway houses, and continues to use this model on a prerelease basis.

SIDEBARS

Community Correctional Center

A small group-living facility for offenders, particularly those who are failing on probation, who have recently been released from prison, or who have been transferred as a prisoner to serve a short period of their final sentence under community supervision.

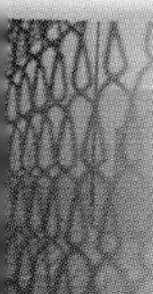

CORRECTIONAL BRIEF

Turning Point Program

The Turning Point Program is part of the Talbert House, Inc., a nonprofit multiservice agency than consists of thirty-five programs in four areas: victim assistance, chemical dependency, mental health, and criminal corrections. The Turning Point program consists of a 40-bed, 28-day chemical dependency treatment program for men and women serving sentences for multiple DUI offenses.

After a thirty-day jail incarceration, select offenders are relocated to the program site, a community residential confining program that permits visits but not leaves. The program is a comprehensive treatment regimen focused on drug and alcohol addiction and includes Individualized alcohol treatment, family counselling, and educational services. AA (Alcoholics Anonymous) and NA (Narcotics Anonymous) are required. Turning Point participants were less likely after treatment to be arrested than comparison groups; the comprehensive treatment reduced DUI behavior.

SOURCE: Robert Langworthy and Edward Latessa, "Treatment of Chronic Drunk Drivers: The Turning Point Project," *Journal of Criminal Justice* 21:3 (1992): 265–276.

The third avenue for residents to enter a halfway house differs by time of placement into the program; most offenders under probation and parole supervision do not initially reside in a halfway house. However, if such clients revert to criminal behavior or encounter unanticipated problems that could be resolved by program services or by a period of residency in a halfway house, the supervising agency may remand the offender to short-term residency in such a community corrections program. For example, in one study of halfway houses it was found that parole violators who were placed in a halfway house had a 12 percent lower recidivism rate than those returned to prison.[37]

At the federal level, the U.S. Bureau of Prisons established prerelease guidance centers in major metropolitan areas during 1961. The offender is sent to

PMI residents talk about their day while eating supper. PMI is a halfway house funded primarily by the Missouri Department of Corrections and has been operating in Columbia since 1983.
Courtesy of AP/Wide World Photos.

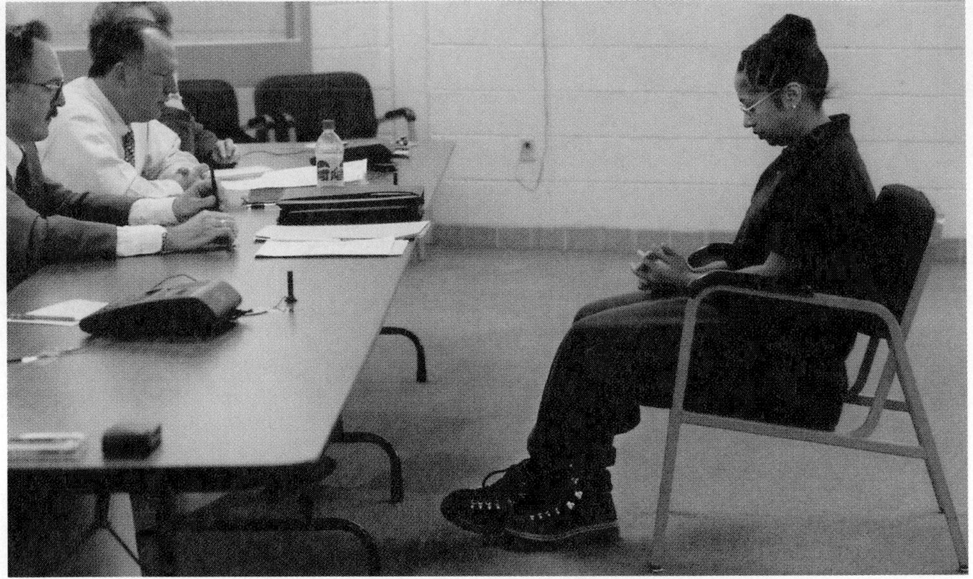

A drug lifer offender pleads for parole in the community under a relaxed lifer law in Plymouth, Michigan.
Courtesy of AP/Wide World Photos.

those centers from a correctional institution several months before he or she is eligible for parole. The offender is allowed to work and attend school in the community without supervision, and he or she participates in a number of programs in the halfway house itself. This approach has been copied by many states and appears to be a viable program when properly staffed and supervised. As possible uses for the halfway house are explored and outcomes are verified,[38] such units will offer not only short-term residency before the prisoner's placement on parole but also noninstitutional residence facilities[39] for a number of different categories of offenders.[40] At that point, **community residential centers** will constitute the first real alternative to institutional incarceration that works well in the community.

IS PAROLE EFFECTIVE?

The most critical questioned asked of parole and other post-releases programs is whether or not they are effective. Outcome measures can include cost, humaneness, employment, and family reunification just to name a few; however, the most important measure is public safety. Public safety is usually operationalized in corrections as recidivism, which, while it has some inherent limitations, is the ultimate indicator of a correctional program's success. The indicators used to measure recidivism, such has how it is defined (i.e., arrest, conviction, incarceration), the lengths of follow-up, and the source of data (official, self-report), are all factors that can affect reported recidivism rates. Indeed, the best way to ensure a low recidivism rate may be to define it very narrowly (e.g., incarceration in a state penal institution) and to utilize a very short follow-up period. Despite these challenges, recidivism remains the most important outcome of a correctional sanction.

Despite its widespread use, little is actually known about whether parole reduces recidivism. We do know that fewer than half of parole discharges successfully complete parole. Figure 21.4 shows that, among state parole discharges in 1999, over half of discretionary parolees successfully completed their term of supervision compared to a third of mandatory parolees, but this

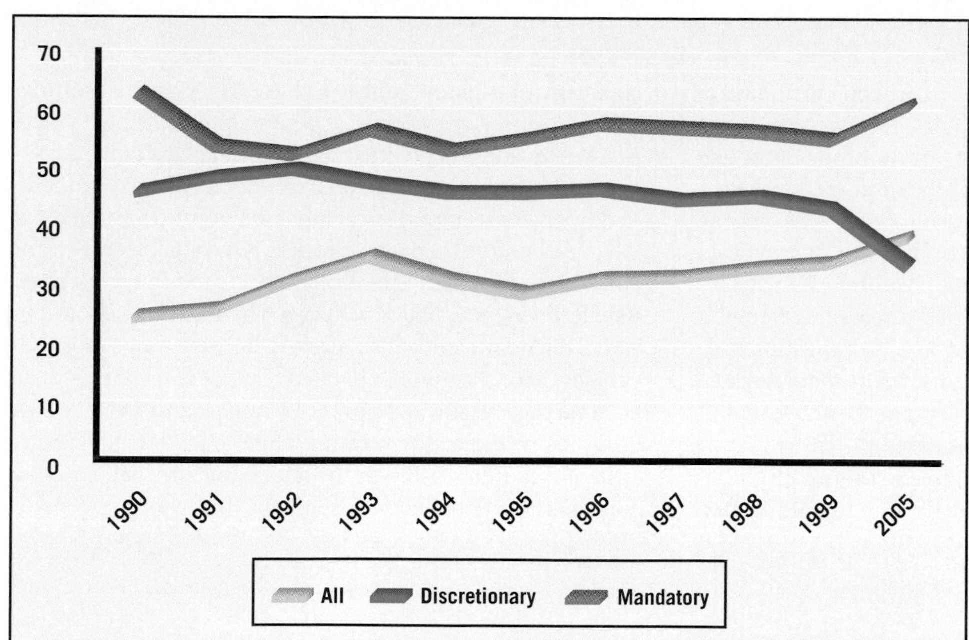

FIGURE 21.4

Successful Parolees by Method of Release, 1990–2005

SOURCE: Timothy Hughes, Doris Wilson, and Allen Beck, *Trends in State Parole, 1999–2000* (Washington, DC: Bureau of Justice Statistics, 2001), p. 11. Data for 2005 are extrapolated.

actually tells us little about the effectiveness of parole. In a 2005 study of parole, the Urban Institute concluded that parole supervision has little effect on rearrest rates of released prisoners.[41] However, using the same data, Lowenkamp and Latessa came to very different conclusions.[42] Figure 21.5 shows the adjusted probabilities of rearrest within two years of release. This figure indicates that discretionary parolees outperformed both mandatory parolees and unconditional releasees. Furthermore, overall, parolees had a lower rearrest rate than those who were not supervised. The debate about the effectiveness of parole will certainly continue into the future, and only more research will answer this important question.

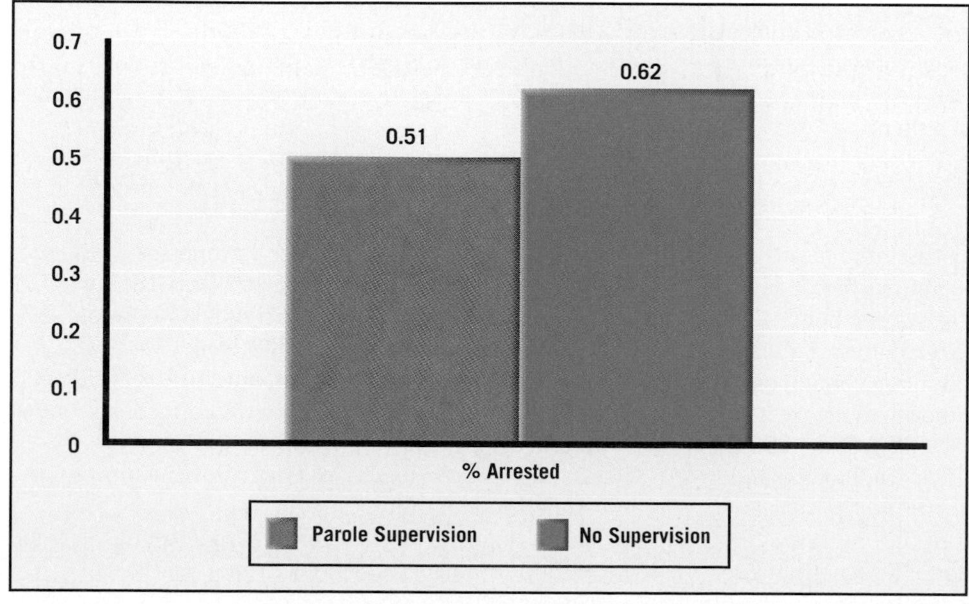

FIGURE 21.5

Probabilities of Rearrest within Two Years of Release for Parolees

SOURCE: C. T. Lowenkamp and E. J. Latessa. *Does Parole Work? A Reanalysis of the Urban Institute Study* (Cincinnati, OH: University of Cincinnati, 2005).

SUMMARY

We have seen that nearly every offender who enters prison is eventually released in some fashion. The question is not when will the offender be released, but how; and although the number of offenders released through discretionary parole has dropped, the number released to some other type of supervision continues to grow. Two functions are involved in parole: the surveillance function, ensuring adequate supervision and control (in the form of a parole officer) to prevent future criminal activity; and the helping function, marshaling community resources to support the parolee in establishing noncriminal behavior patterns.

The parole process is a series of steps that frequently includes an appearance before a parole authority, establishment of a set of conditions to be met by the parolee, the assignment to a parole officer followed by regular meetings with the officer, appearance at a revocation hearing if parole is violated, and the eventual release from conditional supervision. That process has sometimes been changed or modified by the heat of public opinion and court decisions.

Although the parole process is a valuable aid to the corrections system, it is far from perfect, and the research on its effectiveness is not conclusive. The issue of how to improve offender reentry has recently become a hot topic, especially since the number of offenders being released is at an all-time high. Halfway houses, furloughs, and work release are three of the major ways in which offenders are reintegrated back into society. In the last chapter we will consider some of these issues as we discuss the future for corrections.

REVIEW QUESTIONS

1. What are the main models of parole boards?
2. What are the main differences between parole and probation?
3. Why should parole boards be independent of institutions? Why not?
4. How much time do offenders spend in prison? For how long are they under correctional control? How do you feel about this?
5. What are parole guidelines and how do they structure discretion?
6. Should parole supervision be abolished?
7. Why has the number of offenders released on discretionary parole declined?
8. What is your evaluation of the qualifications for parole board members?
9. Why is graduated release so beneficial to both the community and the offender?
10. How can the effectiveness of a correctional program be measured?

ENDNOTES

1. Restrictions on early release from prison and other reforms to reduce the discrepancy between sentence imposed and actual sentence served in prison have come to be known as "truth in sentencing." See Thomas Bonczar and L. Glaze, *Probation and Parole in the United States, 1998* (Washington, DC: U.S. Department of Justice, 1999), p. 6.
2. Various forms of conditional release from incarceration were developed in other countries before an American state adopted a parole system; however, the core elements of a parole system administrative board making release decisions and granting conditional, supervised release with the authority to revoke it were first created by legislation in New York State (1869).
3. A. Pisciotta, "Saving the Children: The Promise and Practice of Parens Patria, 1838–1898," *Crime and Delinquency,* 28:3 (1982): 410–425.
4. K. O. Hawkins, "Parole Selection: The American Experience," unpublished doctoral dissertation (Cambridge, England: University of Cambridge, 1971).
5. Ibid.
6. R. M. Carter, R. A. McGee, and K. E. Nelson, *Corrections in America* (Philadelphia: J. B. Lippincott, 1975).
7. See Ellen Chayet, "Correctional Good Time As a Means of Early Release," *Criminal Justice Abstracts,* 26:3 (1994): 521–538.
8. J. V. Barry, "Captain Alexander Maconochie," *Victorian Historical Magazine* 27:1 (June 1957): 1–18. For a history of the American Correctional Association, see A. Travisono and M. Hawkes, *Building a Voice: The American Correctional Association, 125 Years of History* (Landham, MD: ACA, 1995), www.corrections.com/aca/history/html.
9. D. Fogel, *We Are the Living Proof . . .* (Cincinnati, OH: Anderson Publishing Co., 1975).
10. John Langbein, "The Historical Origins of the Sanction of Imprisonment for Serious Crime," *Journal of Legal Studies 5* (1976): 35–60.
11. Hawkins, "Parole Selection: The American Experience."

12. Probation and Parole Statistics, *Summary Findings* (Washington, DC: Bureau of Justice Statistics, U.S. Department of Justice, 2002).
13. *Probation and Parole in the United States, 2003* (Washington, DC: U.S. Department of Justice, 2004), www.ojp.usdoj.gov/bjs/pardp.htm.
14. Wayne Morse, *The Attorney General's Survey of Release Procedures* (Washington, DC: U.S. Government Printing Office, 1939), p. 23.
15. Paula Ditton and Doris Wilson, *Truth in Sentencing in State Prisons* (Washington, DC: Bureau of Justice Statistics, 2004), p. 3.
16. Camille Camp and G. Camp, *The Corrections Yearbook, Adult Corrections 2002* (South Salem, NY: Criminal Justice Institute, 2002).
17. *Greenholtz v. Inmates of the Nebraska Penal and Correctional Complex*, 99 S. Ct. 2100, 1979.
18. No presidential pardon was awarded from 1994 to 1998, but twelve conditional pardons were awarded in 1999.
19. U.S. Office of the Pardon Attorney, *Civil Disabilities of Convicted Felons: A State-by-State Survey* (Washington, DC: USOPA, 1996).
20. Brent Smith, E. Watkins, and K. Morgan, "The Effect of Victim Participation on Parole Decisions," *Criminal Justice Policy Review* 8:1 (1997): 57–74.
21. J. Runda, E. Rhine, and R. Wetter, *The Practice of Parole Boards* (Lexington, KY: Council of State Governments, 1994).
22. U.S. Office of the Pardon Attorney, *Civil Disabilities.*
23. J. Travis and J. Petersilia, "Reentry Reconsidered: A New Look at an Old Problem," *Crime and Delinquency* 47 (2001): 291–313.
24. J. Austin, "Prisoner Reentry: Current Trends, Practices, and Issues," *Crime and Delinquency* 47 (2001): 314–334.
25. A. J. Lurigio, "Effective Services for Parolees with Mental Illnesses," *Crime and Delinquency* 47 (2001): 446–461.
26. Cece Hill, "Inmate Fee-for-Service Programs," *Corrections Compendium* 23:8 (1998): 7–16.
27. The longer a work release participant remains employed in the same work release job after earning parole status, the greater the potential for parole success. Kyu Man Lee, *The Wichita Work Release Center: An Evaluative Study* (Ann Arbor, MI: University Microfilms International, 1983). See also Richard Jones (ed.), "Conditions of Confinement," *Journal of Contemporary Criminal Justice* 13:1 (1997): 3–72.
28. James Ryan, "Who Gets Revoked? A Comparison of Intensive Supervision Successes and Failures in Vermont," *Crime and Delinquency* 43:1 (1997): 104–118.
29. David Anderson, *Crime and the Politics of Hysteria: How the Willie Horton Story Changed American Justice* (New York: Random House, 1995); and Tali Mendelberg. "Executing Horizons: Racial Crime in the 1988 Presidential Campaign," *Public Opinion Quarterly* 61:1 (1997): 134–157.
30. The failure rate (both new crimes and failure to return) in furlough programs is remarkably low: about 1 percent. Camp and Camp, *The Corrections Yearbook, Adult Corrections 2000,* p. 148.
31. James Bonta and L. Motiuk, "The Diversion of Incarcerated Offenders to Correctional Halfway Houses," *Journal of Research in Crime and Delinquency* 24:3 (1987): 302–323; Edward Latessa and L. Travis, "Residential Community Correctional Programs," in James Byrne and A. Lurigio (eds.), *Smart Sentencing? An Examination of the Emergence of Intermediate Sanctions* (Beverly Hills, CA: Sage, 1991); and Sarah Twill, L. Nackerud, E. Risler, et al., "Changes in Measured Loneliness, Control and Social Support Among Parolees in a Halfway House," *Journal of Offender Rehabilitation* 27:3/4 (1998): 77–92.
32. Additional information may be obtained from the International Community Corrections Association, P.O. Box 1987, La Crosse, Wisconsin 54602; (608)785-0200.
33. Carolyn Tucker, K. Herman, B. Brady, et al., "Operation Positive Expression: A Behavioral Change Program for Adolescent Halfway House Residents," *Residential Treatment for Children and Youth* 13:2 (1995): 67–80.
34. Brian Grant, L. Montiuk, L. Brunet, et al., *Day Parole Program Review* (Ottawa: Correctional Service of Canada, 1996).
35. Twill et al., "Changes in Measured Loneliness."
36. Camp and Camp report that the cost per resident for private halfway house providers is 14 percent less than that provided by state departments of corrections. Camp and Camp, *The Corrections Yearbook 1998* (Middletown, CT: Criminal Justice Institute), p. 123.
37. C. T. Lowenkamp and E. J. Latessa E. J. 2002. *Evaluation of Ohio's Halfway Houses and Community-Based Correctional Facilities* (Cincinnati, OH: University of Cincinnati, 2002).
38. Marc Levinson, "In South Carolina, Community Corrections Means the Alston Wilkes Society," *Corrections Magazine* 9:1 (1983): 41–46. See also Bobbie Huskey and A. Lurigio, "An Examination of Privately-Operated Intermediate Punishments in the United States," *Corrections Compendium* 17:12 (1992): 1, 3–8; and Joseph Callahan and K. Koenning, "The Comprehensive Sanctions Center in the Northern District of Ohio," *Federal Probation* 59:3 (1995): 52–57.
39. Daniel Glaser, "Supervising Offenders Outside Prisons," in James Wilson (ed.), *Crime and Public Policy* (San Francisco: Institute for Contemporary Studies, 1983), p. 212.
40. James Beck, "An Evaluation of Federal Community Treatment Centers," *Federal Probation* 43:5 (1979):

36–41; and Paul Gendreau, M. Shilton, and P. Clark, "Intermediate Sanctions: Making the Right Move," *Corrections Today* 57:1 (1995): 28–65.

41. A. L. Solomon, V. Kachnowski, and B. Avinash, *Does Parole Work?* (Washington, DC: Urban Institute, 2005).

42. C. T. Lowenkamp, and E. J. Latessa, *Does Parole Work? A Reanalysis of the Urban Institute Study* (Cincinnati, OH: University of Cincinnati 2005).

SUGGESTED READINGS: PART 8

American Correctional Association, Reentry. Special theme issue, *Corrections Today* 67:2 (2005).

Burke, Peggy, *Abolishing Parole: Why the Emperor Has No Clothes.* Lexington, KY: American Probation and Parole Association, 1995.

Council of State Governments, *Report of the Re-Entry Policy Committee.* Lexington, KY: Council of State Governments, 2004.

Ditton, Paula, *Mental Health and Treatment of Inmates and Probationers.* Washington, DC: Bureau of Justice Statistics, 1999.

Glaze, Lauren, and Seri Palla, *Probation and Parole in the United States 2003.* Washington, DC: Bureau of Justice Statistics, 2004.

Hanrahan, Kate, John Gibbs, and Sherwood Zimmerman, "Parole and Revocation." *The Prison Journal* 85:3 (2005): 251–269.

Hughes, Timothy, and Doris Wilson, *Reentry Trends in the United States.* Washington, DC: Bureau of Justice Statistics, 2005. Also at www.ojp.usdoj.gov/bjs/reentry/reentry.htm.

Latessa, Edward, and Harry Allen, *Corrections in the Community.* Cincinnati, OH: Anderson, 2003.

Lowenkamp, C. T., and Edward Latessa, *Does Parole Work: A Reanalysis of the Urban Institute Study* (Cincinnati, OH: University of Cincinnati, 2005).

Wilkinson, Reginald, and Edward Rhine, "Confronting Recidivism," *Corrections Today* 67:5 (2005): 54–57.

PART

9

A Link to the Future

THE FOLLOWING CHAPTER IS COVERED IN PART 9:

OVERVIEW

Chapter 22 identifies current trends in corrections and projections for the future, as well as major new approaches to handling offenders in the community and organizing the community to address those factors that contribute to the causes of crime. We identify promising new developments and paradigms for the environment of corrections.

CHAPTER 22

The Futures of Corrections

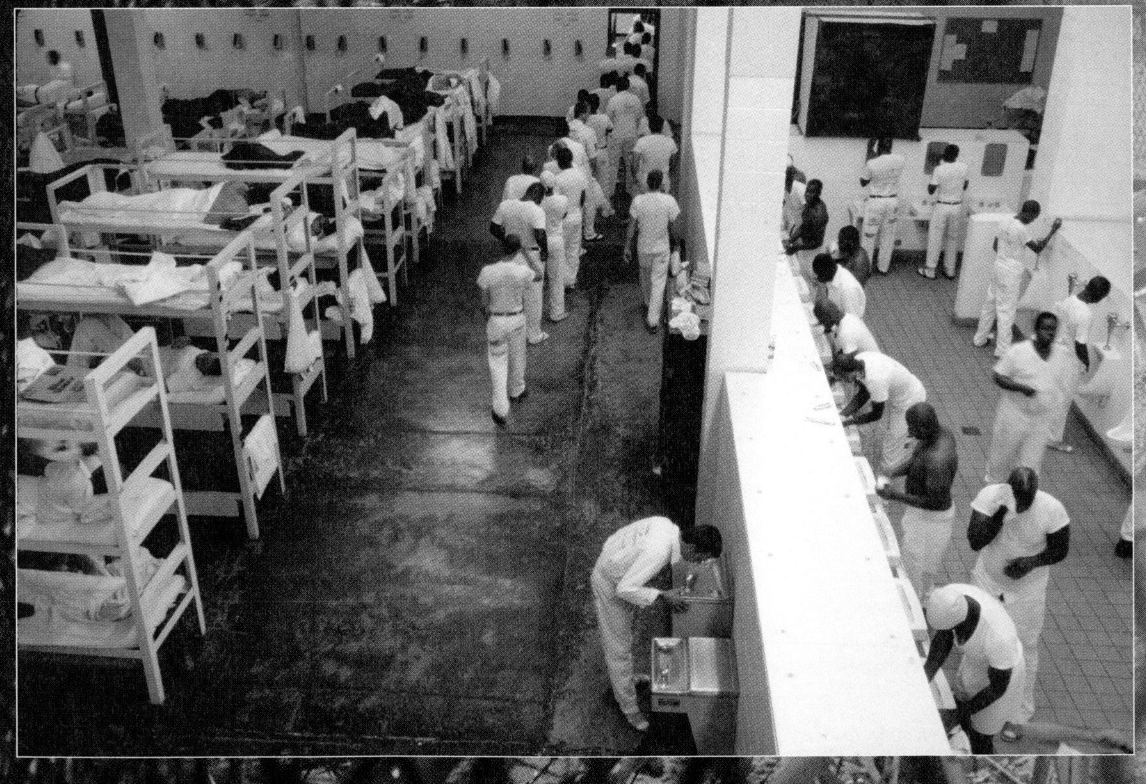

Chain gangs debase and humiliate offenders, make for effective bumper sticker politics, and lead to the re-election of politicians who stress retributive justice. The public may even cheer the practice. Chain gangs will certainly not reduce crime but will lead to inmate bitterness, frustration and aggression, enhancing recidivism.

—Harry E. Allen

OVERVIEW

Since the nation has now entered the twenty-first century, it is instructive to ask ourselves what corrections might look like a decade from now, and what changes might occur. These are legitimate questions and provide closure on corrections. We call this chapter "The Futures of Corrections" because several possible scenarios come to the fore, any one or more of which might happen. We start by examining once again the major trends and current status of corrections *now.*

Data on the current status of corrections can be found in Table 22.1. At the start of 2004, more than 7 million adults were under correctional control in America, approximately one of every thirty-two adult Americans. About 58 percent were on probation and another 11 percent were on parole; that is, 69 percent of all offenders were under community supervision. The remaining 31 percent were in correctional facilities: 10 percent in jail and 21 percent in prisons.[1]

Altogether, we incarcerate more adult residents in this country (726 per 100,000 residents) than any other major Western country, including the Russian Republic (548).[2] Men are incarcerated at a rate of 923 per 100,000 residents. The incarceration rate of African American males is eight times that of the Russian Republic's entire adult rate (4,848 to 548).[3] Remember that the Russian Republic

TABLE 22.1 Correctional Populations Past and Future

CORRECTIONAL PROGRAM	1990	2000	2010*
Probation	2,670,234	4,074,000	5,164,248
Jail	403,019	713,990	1,049,448
Prison	743,382	1,494,216	3,190,228
Parole	531,407	774,000	1,139,133
Totals	4,348,042	7,056,206	10,543,057

*Straight-line projections from current trends.

SOURCE: Bureau of Justice Statistics, *Probation and Parole in the United States 2004* and *Prison and Jail Inmates at Midyear 2004* (Washington, DC: Bureau of Justice Statistics).

< Inmates preparing to start the day get out of bed and wash up, Limestone Correctional Facility, Capshaw, Alabama.
Photo by A. Ramey, courtesy of PhotoEdit.

was formerly a totalitarian country that now is struggling toward democratization amid chaos and upheaval. The United States has now taken the lead as the most aggressive imprisoner.

The use of imprisonment varies across racial groups. Although African Americans comprise only about 12 percent of the total population of the nation, they represent well over 40 percent of those in jails and prisons. This turns out to approximate one in twelve of African American men between the ages of fourteen and fifty-four. More African American males are in jail and prison than are enrolled in all colleges and universities throughout the nation.[4] The racial disparity in imprisonment rates in 2004 was about seven times that of whites.

Roughly 13 million Americans (representing 7 percent of the adult population and almost 12 percent of the men) have been found guilty of a felony. Approximately one in five black men has been incarcerated at some point in his life, and one in three has been convicted of a felony.[5]

Apologists for the differential impact of incarceration argue that the higher rate reflects the differential rate of involvement of African Americans in violent crimes and effects of the "get tough on crime" policy and the War on Drugs. Cullen and his colleagues have described the latter as a "crass attempt to purchase the votes of affluent white Americans."[6] The War on Drugs is continuing and its differential impact on African Americans will further increase their concentration in the nation's jails and prisons.

CURRENT TRENDS

Data on the future of corrections are not difficult to project, given the dramatic increases during the past twenty plus years. The good news is that some states have actually experienced a decline in prison populations, including Alabama, Connecticut, Ohio, and New York. Unfortunately, most recent figures indicate that the federal system has experienced a more than 25 percent increase in the inmate population.[7]

We estimate that future correctional populations will total more than 10.5 million offenders, or about one in twenty-eight adult residents in America in 2010. As before, the largest proportion of offenders will be handled in community corrections, on probation or parole. The incarcerated population will swell to 4.2 million, with the largest part of those offenders located in prisons. The steady increase in incarcerated offenders will continue well into the new century.

As noted in previous chapters, the typical offenders who go to prison are disadvantaged in many ways. In contrast to the general population, they are more likely to be poor and poorly educated, have a sorry employment history, be drug or alcohol abusers, be mentally ill, and be members of a minority group (particularly black and Hispanic). Many—if not most—are functionally illiterate, and have few prospects for employment when released from incarceration.

Most will find it difficult to secure employment, and some two-thirds will be rearrested for a new offense, almost half will be reconvicted of a new crime, and better than half will be back in prison within three years. Released prisoners with the highest rearrest rates are motor vehicle thieves (79 percent), those previously convicted for possessing or selling stolen property (77 percent), and those formerly in prison for possessing, using, or selling illegal weapons (70 percent) or robbery (70 percent).[8]

Where the resources might come from to manage this level of correctional crisis is not yet clear. In previous chapters, we detailed the sometimes dramatic changes taking place in the crime rates and patterns in the nation. Overall, both the incidence and rates of crime were dropping as we left the twentieth century, yet the reach of the criminal justice system has been expanding at a rapid rate. Our arguments have been that the increased volumes of offenders being swept up into the system are primarily the result of political decisions to handle major social problems, particularly drug abuse and violence, through a reactive criminal justice system. In the past, our search for a quick fix for crime (programs such as Scared Straight, electronic monitoring, mandatory prison sentences for gun use, three strikes laws, Megan's Law, and boot camps) has led us into the current quagmire of an ever-increasing correctional system. It is abundantly clear that there is no quick fix or low-cost solution to the crime problem.

ALTERNATIVES

Certain alternatives can address crime prevention and crime control, many of which have been suggested by the crime prevention and criminological disciplines. Some of these are still in their infancy, while others are widely accepted crime prevention strategies. Following are examples of effective intervention and prevention strategies:

- Programs such as prenatal and early childhood nurse home visitation efforts[9]
- Treatment for mental health and substance abuse problems of juveniles[10]
- Early intervention programs for at-risk youth, including children of incarcerated parents
- Mandatory residential treatment programs for habitual drunk driving offenders[11]
- Increased use of therapeutic courts (i.e., mental health, drug, domestic violence)
- Effective family strengthening interventions[12]
- Mandatory substance abuse programs for prisoners (particularly female inmates)[13]
- Aggressive and mandatory interventions in domestic violence.[14]

CORRECTIONAL BRIEF

U.S. Dream Academy

The U.S. Dream Academy was founded in 1998 by Dr. Wintley Phipps to provide educational services to youth whose parents are incarcerated. The mission of the Dream Academy is to empower at-risk children and youth to maximize their potential by providing them with academic, social and values enrichment through supportive mentoring and the use of technology.

Through aggressive and innovative academic enrichment and mentoring, the U.S. Dream Academy is working to build the dreams of the children of prisoners and those failing in school, and to provide the tools that they need to achieve their dreams. The U.S. Dream Academy recognizes that the "digital divide" that exists in many of the nation's disadvantaged communities further divides the haves and have-nots. Development of computer skills and access to the Internet are central elements of the U.S. Dream Academy's service delivery. The target population is comprised of:

1. Children ages 7 to 11 and grades 3, 4, and 5 with a family history of incarceration who have a high risk of underachievement and perpetuating a legacy of criminal behavior and are in need of remedial education and supportive adults who are critical to breaking this pattern
2. Those from disadvantaged backgrounds that are falling behind in school who need academic training and positive lifestyle reinforcement beyond what is available in their immediate environments
3. Parents and custodial caretakers who may need additional resources in order to do as much as possible to maximize their child's opportunities or who do not have the support necessary to afford an investment in their children's future.

In recent years we have seen a dramatic increase in the use of alternative courts to handle offenders who are clearly in need of treatment. Led by drug courts, which appear to be effective in compelling treatment for drug-abusing offenders, these alternatives have changed the nature of court involvement from adversarial to supportive. In the juvenile area, multisystemic therapy and functional family therapy have been found to significantly reduce further delinquent behavior by using the family unit (not just the juvenile) as the focus of treatment.[15] These are a few examples of alternative and proactive responses to the challenge of crime in a free society.

Other trends and developments are also under way that might significantly improve both the reintegration of offenders and enhancement of public safety. For example, many states are now focusing considerable resources toward the successful reentry of offenders back into the community. In addition to court and correctional change, it is probably far better to implement more fundamental structural changes in underclass communities that contribute disproportionately to the commitment rates to prison, as well as those locked out from participation in the American dream.[16] Addressing racism, discrimination, economic disparities, and injustice[17] is crucial to finding a more permanent solution to the crime problem.[18]

PROMISING CHANGES

Three bright spots on the correctional horizon are the increasing evidence of the effectiveness of rehabilitation as documented by evaluation research, a dawning realization of elected officials that parolees face reentry problems, and a burgeoning segment of middle America who have rethought their formerly favorable opinions that supported the War on Drugs.

Thus, we conclude that the future of change in corrections in this century will lie in developing, implementing, and expanding intermediate sanctions through "transformative rationality," the sustaining over time of broad policy principles while simultaneously adapting those policies to state and local circumstances.[19]

CORRECTIONAL BRIEF

Reentry in Ohio

In February 2001, the Ohio Department of Rehabilitation and Correction (ODRC) began examining prisoner reentry in Ohio and developing recommendations to move the department toward a more holistic and systematic approach to helping inmates successfully reintegrate into their communities. Rather than starting the reentry process at the very end of an inmate's prison term, the ODRC is working to establish a system in which the concept of reentry underlies the assessments, programming, and services that a prisoner receives during incarceration as well as after release from prison. Ohio's reentry strategy centers around interdisciplinary teams that develop a "reentry accountability plan" (RAP) for both before and after release. Moreover, the reentry strategy acknowledges and prioritizes the role of family, citizens, victims, community institutions, and faith-based organizations, in addition to justice system and medical/mental health professionals.

SOURCE: Adapted from Nancy G. La Vigne and Gillian L. Thompson, with Christy Visher, Vera Kachnowski, and Jeremy Travis, *A Portrait of Prisoner Reentry in Ohio* (Washington, DC: Urban Institute Justice Policy Center, 2003).

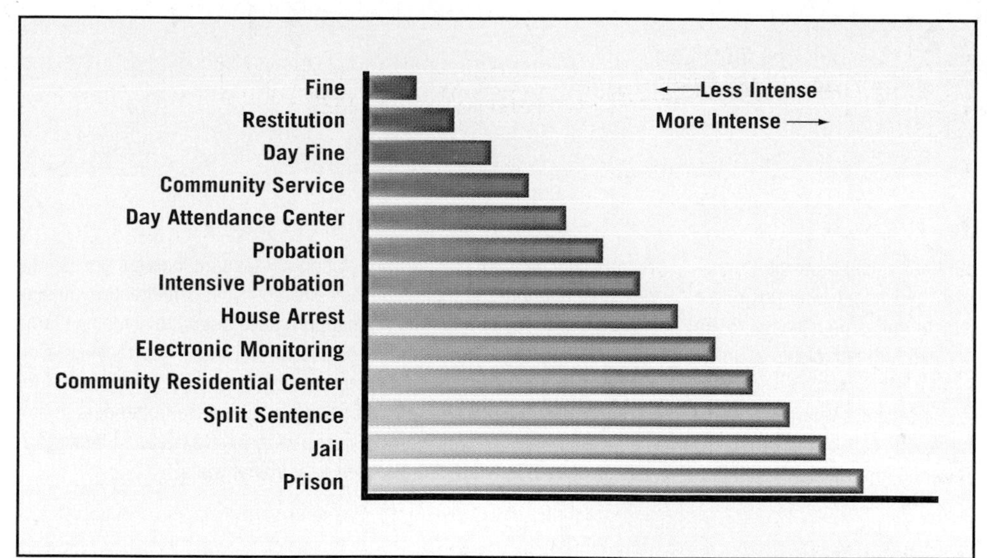

FIGURE 22.1

Sentencing Options Ranked by Level of Punishment

SOURCE: Adapted from James Byrne, "The Future of Intensive Probation Service," *Crime and Delinquency* 36:1 (1990): 29.

INTERMEDIATE SANCTIONS

The student should now be familiar with intermediate sanctions, which we explored in Chapters 7, 8, and 21, and recall that these are correctional intervention programs falling somewhere between fines and prison.[20] Their primary advantages are that they permit increased surveillance of and control over the offender; they also enhance the goals of avoiding institutional crowding and offender reintegration.

Intermediate sanctions are ranked in Figure 22.1 and combine to provide thirteen distinct sanctions programs, each of which increases punishment and control.[21] Some of these programs, of course, are composed of various technologies, and many permit effective treatment and lowered recidivism. Using "tourniquet sentencing," the court can combine intermediate sanctions to achieve correctional objectives. In the immediate future, sentencing courts may become responsible for correctional reentry of the offenders they formerly sentenced to incarceration, providing community correctional services under local control.

CREATING CHANGE

The use of prisons, we believe, will continue to play a vital role in corrections in the future years. The prison system will increasingly expand to meet the challenges of overcrowding and new demands as the prison population ages. Some of these challenges have been and will continue to be met with temporary efforts, such as tent-city prisons and release of low-risk elderly inmates. Other challenges will demand shifts in architecture and technology. Building of prisons will probably continue, but at a less hectic pace, especially in those states with sentence enhancement, three strikes laws, and mandatory sentencing statutes, or in states that opt for federal prison construction funds that require their prison inmates to serve at least 85 percent of the sentence imposed by the court. Other states with differing approaches will build prisons more judiciously, if at all.

Preventing or slowing the increasing reliance on prisons will require an agenda for change, the most effective approach of which would be to encourage local jurisdictions to find better ways to manage crime and criminals in their own communities. Of course, such an approach would demand that leadership at the

CORRECTIONAL BRIEF

Releasing Low-Risk Elderly Inmates

When should elderly inmates be released? What social protection benefits accrue to locking up geriatric inmates in bad health who pose little danger to society? Can these low-risk geriatric inmates be released to the community under supervised release or, for medium-risk oldsters, under electronic monitoring?

It is well established that prisoners become progressively less dangerous as they age. It is also well recognized that health care costs rise rapidly as inmates go gray. Yet they occupy cells designed for more dangerous offenders. Recognizing that this population of stagnant inmates poses little risk of reoffending and that prisons are costly and ineffective nursing homes, some states (such as Washington) have begun to screen geriatric inmates (over age sixty-five) for release to community corrections. One program (Project for Older Prisoners or POPS) that screens oldsters for community supervision found that none of the released offenders recidivated. Many POPS prisoners simply pass away in a few years. Should low-risk geriatric inmates be imprisoned in their final years?

state government level change the existing legal environment to sentence "smarter," not just more harshly. It seems doubtful, however, that there are many politicians in today's political scene who believe that taking a "soft on crime" approach will help in winning an election. What is needed is not the artificial "softer or harsher" approach but a recognition that what is needed is a philosophy for organizing corrections.[22] No better creation for such reorganization exists than the original court that sentenced the offender to incarceration.

SUMMARY AND CONCLUSION

Your authors find it is hard to stop writing about this fascinating area of corrections but reluctantly we must close, with the hope that students' interest in corrections has been piqued and they will now become dedicated to pursuing a career in corrections further. Many colleges and universities offer courses in community corrections, the prison, or even the jail. We encourage every student to take advantage of these offerings to explore their interests further.

One final note: The nation's corrections system continues to drain local and state treasuries, and it is abundantly clear that we cannot possibly build ourselves out of the current prison and jail population explosion. Yet states and county jurisdictions can control and manage not only the prison populations but also the integrity and costs of the justice system that deals with juvenile and adult law violators. This can be done by first developing a logical set of correctional objectives and sentencing policies that have not only clear goals but also a wide range of intermediate sanctions and options. In addition, an aggressive public information and documentation effort is in order, led by correctional administrators and their "natural friends," corrections scholars. Public acceptance will require information and accountability. Not only must offenders be held accountable for their behaviors, but correctional managers and politicians also must be held accountable to the public for their behaviors and actions. This is the era of accountability.

We are confident that the leaders in the corrections field will rise to the occasion, and we base this confidence on our knowledge of the professionals who already work in or who will enter the field. These dedicated leaders brighten the future of corrections and will hasten the moment when a coherent and safe system for handling criminal offenders is a reality. We are confident that this will happen although we are acutely aware that change is not easy and sometimes is glacially slow in coming. Yet partners in change are present, and corrections has a bright future.

ENDNOTES

1. Bureau of Justice Statistics, *Prison and Jail Inmates at Midyear 2004; Probation and Parole in the United States, 2004* (Washington, DC: BJS 2004).
2. Bureau of Justice Statistics, *Prisoners in 2001* (Washington, DC: BJS, 2002), p. 1; and Editors, "Prisons and Beyond: A Stigma That Never Fades," *The Economist* (August 10, 2002): 2–27.
3. BJS, *Prison and Jail Inmates at Midyear 2004.*
4. Fox Butterfield, "More Black Men Are in Jail Than in College," *Cincinnati Inquirer* (August 28, 2002): A4.
5. Jerome Miller, *Hobbling a Generation: Young African-Americans in D.C.'s Criminal Justice System* (Alexandria, VA: National Center on Institutions and Alternatives, 1992).
6. Francis Cullen, P. Van Voorhis, and J. Sundt, "Prisons in Crisis: The American Experience," in Roger Matthews and P. Francis (eds.), *Prisons 2000* (London, UK: Macmillan, 1996).
7. BJS, *Prison and Jail Inmates at Midyear 2004.*
8. Bureau of Justice Statistics, *Recidivism of Prisoners Released in 1994* (Washington, DC: BJS, 2003).
9. David Olds, P. Hill, and E. Rumsey, *Prenatal and Early Childhood Nurse Home Visitation* (Washington, DC: U.S. Department of Justice, 1998).
10. Shay Bilchik, *Mental Health Disorders and Substance Abuse Problems Among Juveniles* (Washington, DC: U.S. Department of Justice, 1998).
11. Robert Langworthy and E. Latessa, "Treatment of Chronic Drunk Drivers," *Journal of Criminal Justice* 24:3 (1996): 273–281.
12. Karol Kumpfer and R. Alvarado, *Effective Family Strengthening Interventions* (Washington, DC: U.S. Department of Justice, 1998).
13. Christopher Mumola and T. Bonczar, *Substance Abuse and Treatment of Adults on Probation, 1995* (Washington, DC: U.S. Department of Justice, 1995).
14. Daniel Brookoff, *Drugs, Alcohol, and Domestic Violence in Memphis* (Washington, DC: U.S. Department of Justice, 1997).
15. Scott Henggler, "Effective Family-Based Treatments for Juvenile Offenders: Multisystemic Therapy and Functional Family Therapy." Paper presented at the annual conference of the International Community Corrections Association, Cincinnati, OH, September 26, 1999.
16. Harry Allen, "The American Dream and Crime in the Twenty-First Century," *Justice Quarterly* 12:3 (1995): 427–445.
17. Christopher Stone, "Race, Crime, and the Administration of Justice," *National Institute of Corrections Journal* (April 1999): 26–32.
18. Elliott Currie, *Crime and Punishment in America: Why the Solutions to America's Most Stubborn Social Crisis Have Not Worked—And What Will* (New York: Metropolitan Books, 1998).
19. Michael Musheno, D. Palumbo, S. Maynard-Moody, and J. Levine, "Community Corrections as an Organizational Innovation: What Works and Why," *Journal of Research in Crime and Delinquency* 26:2 (1989): 136–167.
20. Joan Petersilia, "Diverting Nonviolent Prisoners to Intermediate Sanctions," *Corrections Management Quarterly* 1:1 (1997): 1–15; and Christopher Lowenkamp and Edward Latessa, "Developing Successful Reentry Programs" *Corrections Today* 67:2 (2005): 72–77.
21. But see Joan Petersilia and E. Deschenes, "Perceptions of Punishment: Inmates and Staff Rank the Severity of Prison Versus Intermediate Sanctions," *The Prison Journal* 74:2 (1994): 306–328; and David May and Peter Wood, "What Influences Offenders' Willingness to Serve Alternative Sanctions?" *The Prison Journal* 85:2 (2005): 145–167.
22. Bobbie Huskey, "The New Mission: Corrections Professionals Can and Must Shape the Debate," *Corrections Today* 58:5 (1996): 33.

SUGGESTED READINGS: PART 9

Andrews, Don. "Recidivism Is Predictable and Can Be Influenced: Using Risk Assessments to Reduce Recidivism." *Forum on Correctional Research* 1:2 (1989): 11–17.

Black, Leonard, and R. Clasby. "When Government and the Private Sector Work Together, Everyone Wins." *Corrections Today* 62:1 (2000): 46–51.

Byrne, James. "Reintegrating the Concept of Community into Community-Based Corrections." *Crime and Delinquency* 35:3 (1989): 471–499.

Center for Civic Innovation. *"Broken Windows" Probation: The Next Step in Fighting Crime.* New York: The Manhattan Institute, 1999.

Dickey, Walter, and M. Smith. *Rethinking Probation: Community Supervision, Community Safety.* Washington, DC: U.S. Department of Justice, 1998.

Gendreau, Paul, T. Little, and C. Goggin. "A Meta-Analysis of the Predictors of Adult Offender Recidivism: What Works?" *Criminology* 34:4 (1996): 575–607.

Kurki, Leena. *Incorporating Restorative and Community Justice into American Sentencing and Corrections.* Washington, DC: U.S. Department of Justice, 1999.

Lehman, Joseph. "The Leadership Challenge: Back to the Future." *Corrections Management Quarterly* 3:1 (1999): 19–23.

Petersilia, Joan. "Hard Time: Ex-Offenders Returning Home After Prison." *Corrections Today* 67:2 (2005): 66–71, 155.

Rhine, Edward, and M. Paparozzi. "Reinventing Probation and Parole: A Matter of Consequence." *Corrections Management Quarterly* 3:2 (1999): 47–52.

Smith, Michael, and W. Dickey. *Reforming Sentencing and Corrections for Just Punishment and Public Safety.* Washington, DC: U.S. Department of Justice, 1999.

———. "What If Corrections Were Serious About Public Safety?" *Corrections Management Quarterly* 2:3 (1998): 12–30.

Tonry, Michael. *The Fragmentation of Sentencing and Corrections in America.* Washington, DC: U.S. Department of Justice, 1999.

———. *Reconsidering Indeterminate and Structured Sentencing.* Washington, DC: U.S. Department of Justice, 1999.

GLOSSARY

The authors are grateful to the Law Enforcement Assistance Administration for the publication of the *Dictionary of Criminal Justice Data Terminology*, from which many of the following terms and definitions have been extracted. It is in the spirit of that effort to standardize criminal justice terminology that we have decided to include this section. We hope that students, especially those who are new to the field, will take the time to read and absorb the meanings of these tools of the trade. To obtain more detailed information about the terms in this glossary, the student should write to U.S. Department of Justice, National Criminal Reference Service, Washington, DC 20531.

Abscond (corrections) ■ To depart from a geographical area or jurisdiction prescribed by the conditions of one's probation or parole, without authorization.

Abscond (court) ■ To intentionally absent or conceal oneself unlawfully to avoid a legal process.

Acquittal ■ A judgment of a court, based either on the verdict of a jury or a judicial officer, that the defendant is not guilty of the offense(s) for which he or she has been tried.

Adjudicated ■ Having been the subject of completed criminal or juvenile proceedings.

Adjudication (criminal) ■ The judicial decision terminating a criminal proceeding by a judgment of conviction, acquittal, or dismissal of the case or, if juvenile, adjudicated a delinquent, status offender, or dependent.

Adjudication (juvenile) ■ The juvenile court decision, terminating an adjudicatory hearing, that the juvenile is a delinquent, status offender, dependent, or that the allegations in the petition are not sustained.

Adjudicatory hearing ■ In juvenile proceedings, the fact-finding process wherein the juvenile court determines whether sufficient evidence exists to sustain the allegations in a petition.

Adult ■ A person who is within the original jurisdiction of a criminal, rather than juvenile, court because his or her age at the time of an alleged criminal act was above a statutorily specified limit.

Alternative facility ■ A place of limited confinement that may be an option for certain kinds of offenders. Such facilities may include treatment settings for drug-dependent offenders, minimum-security facilities in the community that provide treatment and services as needed, work/study release centers, and halfway houses or shelter-type facilities. These settings are less secure than the traditional jail, but offer a more stimulating environment for the individual.

Appeal ■ A request by either the defense or the prosecution that a case be removed from a lower court to a higher court in order for a completed trial to be reviewed by the higher court.

Appearance ■ The act of coming into a court and submitting to the authority of that court.

Appearance, first (initial appearance) ■ The first appearance of a juvenile or adult in the court that has jurisdiction over his or her case.

Appellant ■ A person who initiates an appeal.

Arraignment ■ The appearance of a person before a court during which the court informs the individual of the accusation(s) against him or her and during which he or she enters a plea.

Arrest ■ Taking a person into custody by authority of law for the purpose of charging him or her with a criminal offense or initiating juvenile proceedings, terminating with the recording of a specific offense.

Assigned counsel ■ An attorney, not regularly employed by a government agency, assigned by the court to represent a particular person(s) in a particular criminal proceeding.

Attorney/lawyer/counsel ■ A person trained in the law, admitted to practice before the bar of a given jurisdiction, and authorized to advise, represent, and act for other persons in legal proceedings.

Backlog ■ The number of pending cases that exceeds the court's capacity, in that they cannot be acted on because the court is occupied in acting on other cases.

Bombing incident ■ The detonation or attempted detonation of an explosive or incendiary device with the willful disregard of risk to the person or property of another, or for a criminal purpose.

Bondsman-secured bail ■ Security service purchased by the defendant from a bail bondsman. The fee for this service ranges upward from 10 percent and is not refundable. The bail bondsman system, which permits a private entrepreneur to share with the court the decision on pretrial release, has been criticized for many years and is becoming obsolete in more progressive jurisdictions.

Camp/ranch/farm ■ Any of several types of similar low-security confinement facilities, usually in a rural location, that contain adults or juveniles committed after adjudication.

Case ■ At the level of police or prosecutorial investigation, a set of circumstances under investigation involving one or more persons; at subsequent steps in criminal proceedings, a charging document alleging the commission of one or more crimes; a single defendant; in juvenile or correctional proceedings, a person who is the object of agency action.

Case (court) ■ A single charging document under the jurisdiction of a court; a single defendant.

Caseload (corrections) ■ The total number of clients registered with a correctional agency or agent during a specified time period, often divided into active and inactive or supervised and unsupervised, thus distinguishing between clients with whom the agency or agent maintains contact and those with whom it does not.

Caseload (court) ■ The total number of cases filed in a given court or before a given judicial officer during a given period of time.

Caseload, pending ■ The number of cases at any given time that have been filed in a given court, or are before a given judicial officer, but have not reached disposition.

Cash bail ■ A cash payment for situations in which the charge is not serious and the scheduled bail is low. The defendant obtains release by paying in cash the full amount, which is recoverable after the required court appearances are made.

CCH ■ Computerized criminal history.

Charge ■ A formal allegation that a specific person(s) has/have committed a specific offense(s).

Charging document ■ A formal written accusation, filed in a court, alleging that a specified person(s) has/have committed a specific offense(s).

Child abuse ■ Willful action or actions by a person causing physical harm to a child.

Child neglect ■ Willful failure by the person(s) responsible for a child's well-being to provide for adequate safety, food, clothing, shelter, education, and supervision.

Citation (to appear) ■ A written order issued by a law enforcement officer directing an alleged offender to appear in a specific court at a specified time in order to answer a criminal charge.

Citizen dispute settlement ■ The settlement of interpersonal disputes by a third party or the courts. Charges arising from interpersonal disputes are mediated by a third party in an attempt to avoid prosecution. If an agreement between the parties cannot be reached and the complainant wishes to proceed with criminal processing, the case may be referred to court for settlement.

Commitment ■ The action of a judicial officer ordering that an adjudicated and sentenced adult, or adjudicated delinquent or status offender who has been the subject of a juvenile court disposition hearing, be admitted into a correctional facility.

Community facility (nonconfinement facility, adult or juvenile) ■ A correctional facility from which residents are regularly permitted to depart, unaccompanied by an official, to use daily community resources such as schools or treatment programs, or to seek or hold employment.

Community service ■ A period of service to the community as a substitute for, or in partial satisfaction of, a fine. This disposition is generally a condition of a suspended or partially suspended sentence or of probation. The offender volunteers his or her services to a community agency for a certain number of hours per week over a specified period of time. The total number of hours, often assessed at the legal minimum wage, is determined by the amount of the fine that would have been imposed or that portion of the fine that is suspended.

Complaint ■ A formal written accusation made by any person, often a prosecutor, and filed in a court, alleging that a specified person(s) has/have committed a specific offense(s).

Complaint denied ■ The decision by a prosecutor to decline a request that he or she seek an indictment or file an information or complaint against a specified person(s) for a specific offense(s).

Complaint granted ■ The decision by a prosecutor to grant a request that he or she seek an indictment or file an information or complaint against a specified person(s) for a specific offense(s).

Conditional diversion ■ At the pretrial stage, suspension of prosecution while specific conditions are met. If conditions are not satisfied during a specified time period, the case is referred for continued prosecution.

Conditional release ■ The release of a defendant who agrees to meet specified conditions in addition to appearing in court. Such conditions may include remaining in a defined geographical area, maintaining steady employment, avoiding contact with the victim or with associates in the alleged crime, avoiding certain activities or places, participating in treatment, or accepting services. Conditional release is often used in conjunction with third-party or supervised release.

Confinement facility ■ A correctional facility from which the inmates are not regularly permitted to depart each day unaccompanied.

Convict ■ An adult who has been found guilty of a felony and who is confined in a federal or state confinement facility.

Conviction ■ A judgment of a court, based either on the verdict of a jury or a judicial officer or on the guilty pleas of the defendant, that the defendant is guilty of the offense(s) for which he or she has been tried.

Correctional agency ■ A federal, state, or local criminal justice agency, under a single administrative authority, of which the principal functions are the investigation, intake screening, supervision, custody, confinement, or treatment of alleged or adjudicated adult offenders, delinquents, or status offenders.

Correctional day program ■ A publicly financed and operated nonresidential educational or treatment program for persons required, by a judicial officer, to participate.

Correctional facility ■ A building or part thereof, set of buildings, or area enclosing a set of buildings or structures operated and administrated by a government agency for the custody and/or treatment of adjudicated and committed persons, or persons subject to criminal or juvenile justice proceedings.

Correctional institution ■ A generic name proposed in this terminology for those long-term adult confinement facilities often called prisons, "federal or state correctional facilities," or "penitentiaries," and juvenile confinement facilities called "training schools," "reformatories," "boys ranches," and the like.

Correctional institution, adult ■ A confinement facility having custodial authority over adults sentenced to confinement for more than a year.

Correctional institution, juvenile ■ A confinement facility having custodial authority over delinquents and status offenders committed to confinement after a juvenile disposition hearing.

Corrections ■ A generic term that includes all government agencies, facilities, programs, procedures, personnel, and techniques concerned with the investigation, intake, custody, confinement, supervision, or treatment of alleged or adjudicated adult offenders, delinquents, or status offenders.

Count ■ Each separate offense, attributed to one or more persons, as listed in a complaint, information, or indictment.

Count, institutional ■ A specific time in the day at which all inmates are counted physically, or are accounted for by documentation.

Court ■ An agency of the judicial branch of government, authorized or established by statute or constitution, and consisting of one or more judicial officers, which has the authority to decide on controversies in law and disputed matters of fact brought before it.

Court of appellate jurisdiction ■ A court that does not try criminal cases but that hears appeals.

Court of general jurisdiction ■ Of criminal courts, a court that has jurisdiction to try all criminal offenses, including all felonies, and that may or may not hear appeals.

Court of limited jurisdiction ■ Of criminal courts, a court of which the trial jurisdiction either includes no felonies or is limited to less than all felonies and which may or may not hear appeals.

Crime (criminal offense) ■ An act committed or omitted in violation of a law forbidding or commanding it for which an adult can be punished, upon conviction, by incarceration and other penalties, or for which a corporation can be penalized, or for which a juvenile can be brought under the jurisdiction of a juvenile court and adjudicated a delinquent or transferred to adult court.

Crime Index offenses (index crimes) ■ A Uniform Crime Reports (UCR) classification that includes all Part I offenses with the exception of involuntary (negligent) manslaughter.

Crimes of violence (violent crime) ■ A summary term used by UCR and the National Crime Panel, but with different meanings:

As a subset of UCR Index Crimes
Murder
Nonnegligent (voluntary) manslaughter
Forcible rape
Robbery
Aggravated assault

As a subset of National Crime Panel crimes against persons
Forcible rape
Robbery (against persons)
Aggravated assault
Simple assault

Criminal history record information ■ Information collected by criminal justice agencies on individuals, consisting of identifiable descriptions and notations of arrests, detentions, indictments, informations, or other formal criminal charges, and any disposition(s) arising therefrom, including sentencing, correctional supervision, and release.

Criminal justice agency ■ Any court with criminal jurisdiction and any other government agency or subunit that defends indigents, or of which the principal functions or activities consist of the prevention, detection, and investigation of crime; the apprehension, detention, and prosecution of alleged offenders; the confinement or official correctional supervision of accused or convicted persons; or the administrative or technical support of the above functions.

Criminal proceedings ■ Proceedings in a court of law undertaken to determine the guilt or innocence of an adult accused of a crime.

Culpability ■ The state of mind of one who has committed an act that makes him or her liable to prosecution for that act.

De novo ■ Anew, afresh, as if there had been no earlier decision.

Defendant ■ A person against whom a criminal proceeding is pending.

Defense attorney ■ An attorney, hired by the defendant or appointed by the court, who represents the defendant in a legal proceeding.

Delinquency ■ Juvenile actions or conduct in violation of criminal law and, in some contexts, status offenses.

Delinquent ■ A juvenile who has been adjudicated by a judicial officer of a juvenile court as having committed a delinquent act, which is an act for which an adult could be prosecuted in a criminal court.

Delinquent act ■ An act committed by a juvenile for which an adult could be prosecuted in a criminal court but for which a juvenile can be adjudicated in a juvenile court or prosecuted in a criminal court if the juvenile court transfers jurisdiction.

Dependency ■ The legal status of a juvenile over whom a juvenile court has assumed jurisdiction because the court has found his or her care by parent, guardian, or custodian to fall short of a legal standard of proper care.

Dependent ■ A juvenile over whom a juvenile court has assumed jurisdiction because the court found his or her care by parent, guardian, or custodian to fall short of a legal standard of proper care.

Detention ■ The legally authorized holding in confinement of a person subject to criminal or juvenile court proceedings until the point of commitment to a correctional facility or release.

Detention center ■ A government facility that provides temporary care in a physically restricting environment for juveniles in custody pending court disposition.

Detention facility ■ A generic name proposed in this terminology as a cover term for those facilities that hold adults or juveniles in confinement pending adjudication, adults sentenced for a year or less of confinement, and in some instances postadjudicated juveniles, including facilities called "jails," "county farms," "honor farms," "work camps," "road camps," "detention centers," "shelters," "juvenile halls," and the like.

Detention facility, adult ■ A confinement facility of which the custodial authority is forty-eight hours or more and in which adults can be confined before adjudication or for sentences of a year or less.

Detention facility, juvenile ■ A confinement facility having custodial authority over juveniles confined pending, and after, adjudication.

Detention hearing ■ In juvenile proceedings, a hearing by a judicial officer of a juvenile court to determine whether a juvenile is to be detained, to continue to be detained, or to be released, while juvenile proceedings are pending in his or her case.

Diagnosis or classification center ■ A functional unit within a correctional institution, or a separate facility, that evaluates persons held in custody to determine to which correctional facility or program they should be committed.

Dismissal ■ A decision by a judicial officer to terminate a case without a determination of guilt or innocence.

Disposition ■ The action by a criminal or juvenile justice agency that signifies that a portion of the justice process is complete and jurisdiction is relinquished or transferred to another agency or that signifies that a decision has been reached on one aspect of a case and a different aspect comes under consideration, requiring a different kind of decision.

Disposition, court ■ The final judicial decision, which terminates a criminal proceeding by a judgment of acquittal or dismissal, or which states the specific sentence in the case of a conviction.

Disposition hearing ■ A hearing in juvenile court, conducted after an adjudicatory hearing and subsequent receipt of the report of any predisposition investigation, to determine the most appropriate disposition of a juvenile who has been adjudicated a delinquent, a status offender, or a dependent.

Disposition, juvenile court ■ The decision of a juvenile court, concluding a disposition hearing, that a juvenile be committed to a correctional facility, placed in a care or treatment program, required to meet certain standards of conduct, or released.

Diversion ■ The official halting or suspension, at any legally prescribed processing point after a recorded justice system entry, of formal criminal or juvenile justice proceedings against an alleged offender, and referral of that person to a treatment or care program administered by a nonjustice agency or a private agency, or no referral.

Driving under the influence of alcohol (drunk driving) ■ The operation of any vehicle after having consumed a quantity of alcohol sufficient to potentially interfere with the ability to maintain safe operation. This is usually determined by a blood alcohol reading high enough to ascertain the status of being legally drunk in that jurisdiction.

Driving under the influence of drugs ■ The operation of any vehicle while attention or ability is impaired through the intake of a narcotic or an incapacitating quantity of another drug.

Drug law violation ■ The unlawful sale, transport, manufacture, cultivation, possession, or use of a controlled or prohibited drug.

Early release ■ Release from confinement before the sentence has been completed. Early release to supervision means less jail time and, with more rapid turnover, lower jail populations and capacity requirements. Early release may come about through parole, time off for good behavior or work performed, or modification of the sentence by the court. The last procedure is usually associated with sentences to jail with a period of probation to follow. Although there are some objections to its use, "probation with jail" is a common disposition in some jurisdictions. More often than not, these sentences are in lieu of a state prison term.

Escape ■ The unlawful departure of a lawfully confined person from a confinement facility or from custody while being transported.

Expunge ■ The sealing or purging of arrest, criminal, or juvenile record information.

Felony ■ A criminal offense punishable by death or by incarceration in a state or federal confinement facility for a period of which the lower limit is prescribed by statute in a given jurisdiction, typically one year or more.

Field citation ■ Citation and release in the field by police as an alternative to booking and pretrial detention. This practice reduces law enforcement costs as well as jail costs.

Filing ■ The commencement of criminal proceedings by entering a charging document into a court's official record.

Finding ■ The official determination of a judicial officer or administrative body regarding a disputed matter of fact or law.

Fine ■ The penalty imposed on a convicted person by a court requiring that he or she pay a specified sum of money. The fine is a cash payment of a dollar amount assessed by the judge in an individual case or determined by a published schedule of penalties. Fines may be paid in installments in many jurisdictions.

Fugitive ■ A person who has concealed himself or herself or fled a given jurisdiction to avoid prosecution or confinement.

Group home ■ A nonconfining residential facility for adjudicated adults or juveniles or those subject to criminal or juvenile proceedings, intended to reproduce as closely as possible the circumstances of family life and at the minimum, providing access to community activities and resources.

Halfway house ■ A nonconfining residential facility for adjudicated adults or juveniles or those subject to criminal or juvenile proceedings, intended as an alternative to confinement for persons not suited for probation or needing a period of readjustment to the community after confinement.

Hearing ■ A proceeding in which arguments, evidence, or witnesses are heard by a judicial officer or administrative body.

Hearing, probable cause ■ A proceeding before a judicial officer in which arguments, evidence, or witnesses are presented and in which it is determined whether there is sufficient cause to hold the accused for trial or whether the case should be dismissed.

Indictment ■ A formal written accusation made by a grand jury and filed in a court, alleging that a specified person(s) has/have committed a specific offense(s).

Information ■ A written formal accusation, filed in a court by a prosecutor, that alleges a specific person has committed a specific offense.

Infraction ■ An offense punishable by fine or other penalty, but not by incarceration.

Inmate ■ A person in custody in a jail or correctional institution.

Institutional capacity ■ The officially stated number of inmates or residents that a correctional facility is designed to house, exclusive of extraordinary arrangements to accommodate overcrowded conditions.

Intake ■ The process during which a juvenile referral is received and a decision is made by an intake unit to file a petition in juvenile court, to release the juvenile, to place the juvenile under supervision, or to refer the juvenile elsewhere.

Intake unit ■ A government agency or agency subunit that receives juvenile referrals from police, other government agencies, private agencies, or persons and screens them, resulting in closing of the case, referral to care or supervision, or filing of a petition in juvenile court.

Jail ■ A confinement facility, usually administered by a local law enforcement agency, intended for adults but sometimes also containing juveniles, that holds persons detained pending adjudication and/or persons committed after adjudication for sentences of a year or less.

Jail (sentence) ■ The penalty of commitment ot the jurisdiction of a confinement facility system for adults, of which the custodial authority is generally limited to persons sentenced to a year or less of confinement.

Judge ■ A judicial officer who has been elected or appointed to preside over a court of law, whose position has been created by statute or by constitution and whose decisions in criminal and juvenile cases may only be reviewed by a judge or a higher court and may not be reviewed de novo.

Judgment ■ The statement of the decision of a court that the defendant is convicted or acquitted of the offense(s) charged.

Judicial officer ■ Any person exercising judicial powers in a court of law.

Jurisdiction ■ The territory, subject matter, or person over which lawful authority may be exercised.

Jurisdiction, original ■ The lawful authority of a court or an administrative agency to hear or act upon a case from its beginning and to pass judgment on it.

Jury, grand ■ A body of persons who have been selected and sworn to investigate criminal activity and the conduct of public officials and to hear the evidence against an accused person(s) to determine whether there is sufficient evidence to bring that person(s) to trial.

Jury, trial (jury, petit; jury) ■ A statutorily defined number of persons selected according to law and sworn to determine certain matters of fact in a criminal action and to render a verdict of guilty or not guilty.

Juvenile ■ A person subject to juvenile court proceedings because a statutorily defined event was alleged to have occurred while his or her age was below the statutorily specified limit of original jurisdiction of a juvenile court. See *youthful offender.*

Juvenile court ■ A cover term for courts that have original jurisdiction over persons statutorily defined as juveniles and alleged to be delinquents, status offenders, or dependents.

Juvenile justice agency ■ A government agency, or subunit thereof, of which the functions are the investigation, supervision, adjudication, care, or confinement of juveniles whose conduct or condition has brought or could bring them within the jurisdiction of a juvenile court.

Juvenile record ■ An official record containing, at a minimum, summary information pertaining to an identified juvenile concerning juvenile court proceedings and, if applicable, detention and correctional processes.

Misdemeanor ■ An offense usually punishable by incarceration in a local confinement facility for a period of which the upper limit is prescribed by statute in a given jurisdiction, typically limited to a year or less.

Model Penal Code ■ A generalized modern codification of that which is considered basic to criminal law, published by the American Law Institute in 1962.

Monitored release ■ Recognizance release with the addition of minimal supervision of service; that is, the defendant may be required to keep a pretrial services agency informed of his or her whereabouts, and the agency reminds the defendant of court dates and verifies the defendant's appearance.

Motion ■ An oral or written request made by a party to an action, before, during, or after a trial, that a court issue a rule or order.

Nolo contendere ■ A defendant's formal answer in court to the charges in a complaint, information, or indictment in which the defendant states that he or she does not contest the charges and which, though not an admission of guilt, subjects the defendant to the same legal consequences as does a plea of guilty.

Offender (alleged) ■ A person who has been charged with a specific criminal offense(s) by a law enforcement agency or court but has not been convicted.

Offender (criminal) ■ An adult who has been convicted of a criminal offense.

Offense ■ An act committed or omitted in violation of a law forbidding or commanding it.

Pardon ■ An act of executive clemency that obsolves the party in part or in full from the legal consequences of the crime and conviction.
Annotation
Pardons can be full or conditional. The former generally applies to both the punishment and the guilt of the offender and blots out the existence of guilt in the eyes of the law. It also removes his or her disabilities and restores civil rights. The con-

ditional pardon generally falls short of the remedies of the full pardon, is an expression of guilt, and does not obliterate the conviction. (U.S. Supreme Court decisions on pardons and their effects are directly contradictory, and thus state laws usually govern pardons.)

Parole ■ The status of an offender conditionally released from a confinement facility, prior to the expiration of his or her sentence, and placed under the supervision of a parole agency.

Parole agency ■ A correctional agency, which may or may not include a parole authority and of which the principal function is the supervision of adults or juveniles placed on parole.

Parole authority ■ A person or a correctional agency that has the authority to release on parole those adults or juveniles committed to confinement facilities, to revoke parole, and to discharge from parole.

Parole violation ■ A parolee's act or a failure to act that does not conform to the conditions of his or her parole.

Parolee ■ A person who has been conditionally released from a correctional institution before the expiration of his or her sentence and who has been placed under the supervision of a parole agency.

Partial confinement ■ An alternative to the traditional jail sentence, consisting of "weekend" sentences, that permit offenders to spend the workweek in the community, with their families, and at their jobs; furloughs, which enable offenders to leave the jail for a period of a few hours to a few days for specified purposes—to seek employment, take care of personal materials or family obligations, or engage in community service; or work/study release, under which offenders work or attend school during the day and return to the detention facility at night and on weekends.

Penalty ■ The punishment annexed by law or judicial decision to the commission of a particular offense, which may be death, imprisonment, fine, or loss of civil privileges.

Percentage bail ■ A publicly managed bail service arrangement that requires the defendant to deposit a percentage (typically 10 percent) of the amount of bail with the court clerk. The deposit is returned to the defendant after scheduled court appearances are made, although a charge (usually 1 percent) may be deducted to help defray program costs.

Personally secured bail ■ Security that is put up by the defendant or the defendant's family. This arrangement is generally out of reach of the less affluent defendant.

Petition (juvenile) ■ A document filed in juvenile court alleging that a juvenile is a delinquent, a status offender, or a dependent and asking that the court assume jurisdiction over the juvenile or that the juvenile be transferred to a criminal court for prosecution as an adult.

Petition not sustained ■ The finding by a juvenile court in an adjudicatory hearing that there is not sufficient evidence to sustain an allegation that a juvenile is a delinquent, status offender, or dependent.

Plea ■ A defendant's formal answer in court to the charges brought against him or her in a complaint, information, or indictment.

Plea bargaining ■ The exchange of prosecutorial and/or judicial concessions, commonly a lesser charge, the dismissal of other pending charges, a recommendation by the prosecutor for a reduced sentence or a combination thereof, in return for a plea of guilty.

Plea, final ■ The last plea to a given charge, entered in a court record by or for a defendant.

Plea, guilty ■ A defendant's formal answer in court to the charges in a complaint, information, or indictment, in which the defendant states that the charges are true and that he or she has committed the offense as charged.

Plea, initial ■ The first plea to a given charge, entered in a court record by or for a defendant.

Plea, not guilty ■ A defendant's formal answer in court to the charges in a complaint, information, or indictment, in which the defendant states that he or she is not guilty.

Police department ■ A local law enforcement agency directed by a chief of police or a commissioner.

Police officer ■ A local law enforcement officer employed by a police department.

Population movement ■ Entries and exits of adjudicated persons, or persons subject to judicial proceedings, into or from correctional facilities or programs.

Predisposition report ■ The document resulting from an investigation by a probation agency or other designated authority, which has been requested by a juvenile court, into the past behavior, family background, and personality of a juvenile who has been adjudicated a delinquent, a status offender, or a dependent, to assist the court in determining the most appropriate disposition.

Presentence report ■ The document resulting from an investigation undertaken by a probation agency or other designated authority, at the request of a criminal court, into the past behavior, family circumstances, and personality of an adult who has been convicted of a crime, to assist the court in determining the most appropriate sentence.

Prior record ■ Criminal history record information concerning any law enforcement, court, or correctional proceedings that have occurred before the current investigation of, or proceedings against, a person; or statistical descriptions of the criminal histories of a set of persons.

Prison ■ A confinement facility having custodial authority over adults sentenced to confinement for more than a year.

Prison (sentence) ■ The penalty of commitment to the jurisdiction of a confinement facility system for adults, whose custodial authority extends to persons sentenced to more than a year of confinement.

Prisoner ■ A person in custody in a confinement facility or in the personal custody of a criminal justice official while being transported to or between confinement facilities.

Privately secured bail ■ An arrangement similar to the bail bondsman system except that bail is provided without cost to the defendant. A private organization provides bail for indigent arresters who meet its eligibility requirements.

Pro se (in propria persona) ■ Acting as one's own defense attorney in criminal proceedings; representing oneself.

Probable cause ■ A set of facts and circumstances that would induce a reasonably intelligent and prudent person to believe that an accused person had committed a specific crime.

Probation ■ The conditional freedom granted by a judicial officer to an alleged offender, or adjudicated adult or juvenile, as long as the person meets certain conditions of behavior. One requirement is to report to a designated person or agency over some specified period of time. Probation may contain special conditions, as discussed in the definition of suspended sentence. Probation often includes a suspended sentence but may be used in association with the suspension of a final judgment or a deferral of sentencing.

Probation (sentence) ■ A court requirement that a person fulfill certain conditions of behavior and accept the supervision of a probation agency, usually in lieu of a sentence to confinement but sometimes including a jail sentence.

Porbation agency (probation department) ■ A correctional agency of which the principal functions are juvenile intake, the supervision of adults and juveniles placed on probation status, and the investigation of adults or juveniles for the purpose of preparing presentence of predisposition reports to assist the court in determining the proper sentence or juvenile court disposition.

Probation officer ■ An employee of a probation agency whose primary duties include one or more of the probation agency functions.

Probation violation ■ An act or a failure to act by a probationer who doès not conform to the conditions of his or her probation.

Probationer ■ A person required by a court or probation agency to meet certain conditions of behavior and who may or may not be placed under the supervision of a probation agency.

Prosecutor ■ An attorney employed by a government agency or subunit whose official duty is to initiate and maintain criminal proceedings on behalf of the government against persons accused of committing criminal offenses.

Prosecutorial agency ■ A federal, state, or local criminal justice agency whose principal function is the prosecution of alleged offenders.

Public defender ■ An attorney employed by a government agency or subdivision, whose official duty is to represent defendants unable to hire private counsel.

Public defender's office ■ A federal, state, or local criminal justice agency or subunit of which the principal function is to represent defendants unable to hire private counsel.

Purge (record) ■ The complete removal of arrest, criminal, or juvenile record information from a given records system.

Recidivism ■ The repetition of criminal behavior; habitual criminality.

Referral to intake ■ In juvenile proceedings, a request by the police, parents, or other agency or person that a juvenile intake unit take appropriate action concerning a juvenile alleged to have committed a delinquent act or status offense or to be dependent.

Release, pretrial ■ A procedure whereby an accused person who has been taken into custody is allowed to be free before and during his or her trial.

Release from detention ■ The authorized exit from detention of a person subject to criminal or juvenile justice proceedings.

Release from prison ■ A cover term for all lawful exits from federal or state confinement facilities primarily intended for adults serving sentences of more than a year, including all conditional and unconditional releases, deaths, and transfers to other jurisdictions, excluding escapes.

Transfer of jurisdiction
Release on parole
Conditional release
Release while still under jurisdiction of correctional agency, before expiration of sentence

Discretionary
Release date determined by parole authority

Mandatory
Release date determined by statute
Discharge from prison
Release ending all agency jurisdiction
Unconditional release

Discretionary
Pardon, commutation of sentence

Mandatory
Expiration of sentence
Temporary release
Authorized, unaccompanied temporary departure for educational, employment, or other authorized purposes
Transfer of jurisdiction

In some systems release on "parole" represents only discretionary conditional release. It is recommended that mandatory conditional releases be included, because both types describe conditional releases with subsequent parole status.

Release on bail ■ The release by a judicial officer of an accused person who has been taken into custody, upon the accused's promise to pay a certain sum of money or property if he or she fails to appear in court as required, a promise that may be secured by the deposit of an actual sum of money or property.

Release on own recognizance ■ The release, by a judicial officer, of an accused person who has been taken into custody, upon the accused's promise to appear in court as required for criminal proceedings.

Release to third party ■ The release, by a judicial officer, of an accused person who has been taken into custody, to a third party who promises to return the accused to court for criminal proceedings.

Residential treatment center ■ A government facility that serves juveniles whose behavior does not necessitate the strict confinement of a training school, often allowing them greater contact with the community.

Restitution ■ Usually a cash payment by the offender to the victim of an amount considered to offset the loss incurred by the victim or the community. The amount of the payment may be scaled down to the offender's earning capacity, and/or payments may be made in installments. Sometimes services directly or indirectly benefiting the victim may be substituted for cash payment.

Retained counsel ■ An attorney, not employed or compensated by a government agency or subunit or assigned by the court, who is privately hired to represent a person(s) in a criminal proceeding.

Revocation ■ An administrative act performed by a parole authority removing a person from parole, or a judicial order by a court removing a person from parole or probation, in response to a violation by the parolee or probationer.

Revocation hearing ■ An administrative and/or judicial hearing on the question of whether a person's probation or parole status should be revoked.

Rights of defendant ■ Those powers and privileges that are constitutionally guaranteed to every defendant.

Runaway ■ A juvenile who has been adjudicated by a judicial officer of a juvenile court as having committed the status offense of leaving the custody and home of his or her parents, guardians, or custodians without permission and failing to return within a reasonable length of time.

Seal (record) ■ The removal, for the benefit of the subject, of arrest, criminal, or juvenile record information from routinely available status to a status requiring special procedures for access.

Security ■ The degree of restriction of inmate movement within a correctional facility, usually divided into maximum, medium, and minimum levels.

Security and privacy standards ■ A set of principles and procedures developed to ensure the security and confidentiality of criminal or juvenile record information to protect the privacy of the persons identified in such records.

Sentence ■ The penalty imposed by a court on a convicted person, or the court decision to suspend imposition or execution of the penalty.

Sentence, indeterminate ■ A statutory provision for a type of sentence to imprisonment in which, after the court has determined that the convicted person shall be imprisoned, the exact length of imprisonment and parole supervision is afterward fixed within statutory limits by a parole authority.

Sentence, mandatory ■ A statutory requirement that a certain penalty shall be imposed and executed on certain convicted offenders.

Sentence, suspended ■ The court decision postponing the pronouncement of sentence on a convicted person or postponing the execution of a sentence that has been pronounced by the court.

Sentence, suspended execution ■ The court decision setting a penalty but postponing its execution.

Sentence, suspended imposition ■ The court decision postponing the setting of a penalty.

Shelter ■ A confinement or community facility for the care of juveniles, usually those held pending adjudication.

Speedy trial ■ The right of the defendant to have a prompt trial.

Stationhouse citation ■ An alternative to pretrial detention, whereby the arrestee is escorted to the precinct police station or headquarters rather than the pretrial detention facility. Release, which may occur before or after booking, is contingent on the defendant's written promise to appear in court as specified on the release form.

Status offender ■ A juvenile who has been adjudicated by a judicial officer of a juvenile court as having committed a status offense, which is an act or conduct that is an offense only when committed or engaged in by a juvenile.

Status offense ■ An act or conduct that is declared by statute to be an offense, but only when committed or engaged in by a juvenile, and that can be adjudicated only by a juvenile court.

Subjudicial officer ■ A judicial officer who is invested with certain judicial powers and functions but whose decisions in criminal and juvenile cases are subject to de novo review by a judge.

Subpoena ■ A written order issued by a judicial officer requiring a specified person to appear in a designated court at a specified time to serve as a witness in a case under the jurisdiction of that court or to bring material to that court.

Summons ■ A written order issued by a judicial officer requiring a person accused of a criminal offense to appear in a designated court at a specified time to answer the charge(s). The summons is a request or instruction to appear in court to face an accusation. As an alternative to the arrest warrant, it is used in cases for which complaints are registered with the magistrate or prosecutor's office.

Supervised release ■ A type of release requiring more frequent contact than monitored release does. Typically, various conditions are imposed and supervision is aimed at enforcing these conditions and providing services as needed. Some form of monetary bail also may be attached as a condition of supervised release, especially in higher risk cases.

Suspect ■ A person, adult or juvenile, considered by a criminal justice agency to be one who may have committed a specific criminal offense but who has not been arrested or charged.

Suspended sentence ■ Essentially a threat to take more drastic action if the offender again commits a crime during some specified time period. When no special conditions are attached, it is assumed that the ends of justice have been satisfied by conviction and no further action is required, as long as the offender refrains from involvement in new offenses. Suspended sentences may be conditioned on various limitations as to mobility, associates, or activities or on requirements to make reparations or participate in some rehabilitation program.

Suspicion ■ Belief that a person has committed a criminal offense, based on facts and circumstances that are not sufficient to constitute probable cause.

Third-party release ■ A release extending to another person the responsibility for ensuring the defendant's appearance in court. This may be a person known to the defendant or a designated volunteer. Third-party release may be a condition of unsecured bail, with the third party as a cosigner.

Time served ■ The total time spent in confinement by a convicted adult before and after sentencing, or only the time spent in confinement after a sentence of commitment to a confinement facility.

Training school ■ A correctional institution for juveniles adjudicated to be delinquents or status offenders and committed to confinement by a judicial officer.

Transfer hearing ■ A preadjudicatory hearing in juvenile court to determine whether juvenile court jurisdiction should be retained or waived for a juvenile alleged to have committed a delinquent act(s) and whether he or she should be transferred to criminal court for prosecution as an adult ("bound over").

Transfer to adult court ■ The decision by a juvenile court, resulting from a transfer hearing, that jurisdiction over an alleged delinquent will be waived and that he or she should be prosecuted as an adult in a criminal court.

Trial ■ The examination of issues of fact and law in a case or controversy, beginning when the jury has been selected in a jury trial, the first witness is sworn, or the first evidence is introduced in a court trial and concluding when a verdict is reached or the case is dismissed.

Trial, court (trial, judge) ■ A trial in which there is no jury and a judicial officer determines the issues of fact and law in a case.

Trial, jury ■ A trial in which a jury determines the issues of fact in a case.

UCR ■ An abbreviation for the Federal Bureau of Investigation's Uniform Crime Reports program, published each year and based on voluntary reports from law enforcement agencies nationwide.

Unconditional discharge ■ As a post-trial disposition, essentially the same as unconditional diversion. No savings are obtained in criminal justice processing costs, but jail populations may be reduced; conditions of release are imposed for an offense in which the defendant's involvement has been established.

Unconditional diversion ■ The cessation of criminal processing at any point short of adjudication with no continuing threat of prosecution. This type of diversion may be a voluntary referral to a social service agency or program dealing with a problem underlying the offense.

Unsecured bail ■ A form of release differing from release on recognizance only in that the defendant is subject to paying the amount of bail if he or she defaults. Unsecured bail permits release without a deposit or purchase of a bondsman's services.

Venue ■ The geographical area from which the jury is drawn and in which trial is held in a criminal action.

Verdict ■ In criminal proceedings, the decision made by a jury or judicial officer in a court trial that a defendant is either guilty or not guilty of the offense(s) for which he or she has been tried.

Verdict, guilty ■ In criminal proceedings, the decision made by a jury in a jury trial, or by a judicial officer in a court trial, that the defendant is guilty of the offense(s) for which he or she has been tried.

Verdict, not guilty ■ In criminal proceedings, the decision made by a jury in a jury trial, or by a judicial officer in a court trial, that the defendant is not guilty of the offense(s) for which he or she has been tried.

Victim ■ A person who has suffered death, physical or mental suffering, or loss of property as the result of an actual or attempted criminal offense committed by another person.

Warrant, arrest ■ A document issued by a judicial officer that directs a law enforcement officer to arrest a person who has been accused of an offense.

Warrant, bench ■ A document issued by a judicial officer directing that a person who has failed to obey an order or notice to appear be brought before the court.

Warrant, search ■ A document issued by a judicial officer that directs a law enforcement officer to conduct a search for specified property or persons at a specific location, to seize the property or persons, if found, and to account for the results of the search to the issuing judicial officer.

Witness ■ A person who directly perceives an event or thing or who has expert knowledge relevant to a case.

Youthful offender ■ A person, adjudicated in criminal court, who may be above the statutory age limit for juveniles but who is below a specified upper age limit, for whom special correctional commitments and special record sealing procedures are made available by statute.

AUTHOR INDEX

A

B

D

E

F

G

K

L

M

N

O

P

T

U

V

W

Y

Z

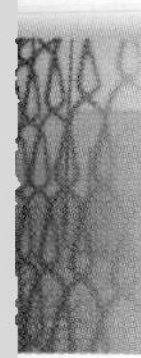

SUBJECT INDEX

D

G

J

K

L

Q

R

S

T

U

V

W

Y

Pearson Education, Inc.

YOU SHOULD CAREFULLY READ THE TERMS AND CONDITIONS BEFORE USING THE CD-ROM PACKAGE. USING THIS CD-ROM PACKAGE INDICATES YOUR ACCEPTANCE OF THESE TERMS AND CONDITIONS.

Pearson Education, Inc. provides this program and licenses its use. You assume responsibility for the selection of the program to achieve your intended results, and for the installation, use, and results obtained from the program. This license extends only to use of the program in the United States or countries in which the program is marketed by authorized distributors.

LICENSE GRANT

You hereby accept a nonexclusive, nontransferable, permanent license to install and use the program ON A SINGLE COMPUTER at any given time. You may copy the program solely for backup or archival purposes in support of your use of the program on the single computer. You may not modify, translate, disassemble, decompile, or reverse engineer the program, in whole or in part.

TERM

The License is effective until terminated. Pearson Education, Inc. reserves the right to terminate this License automatically if any provision of the License is violated. You may terminate the License at any time. To terminate this License, you must return the program, including documentation, along with a written warranty stating that all copies in your possession have been returned or destroyed.

LIMITED WARRANTY

THE PROGRAM IS PROVIDED "AS IS" WITHOUT WARRANTY OF ANY KIND, EITHER EXPRESSED OR IMPLIED, INCLUDING, BUT NOT LIMITED TO, THE IMPLIED WARRANTIES OR MERCHANTABILITY AND FITNESS FOR A PARTICULAR PURPOSE. THE ENTIRE RISK AS TO THE QUALITY AND PERFORMANCE OF THE PROGRAM IS WITH YOU. SHOULD THE PROGRAM PROVE DEFECTIVE, YOU (AND NOT PRENTICE-HALL, INC. OR ANY AUTHORIZED DEALER) ASSUME THE ENTIRE COST OF ALL NECESSARY SERVICING, REPAIR, OR CORRECTION. NO ORAL OR WRITTEN INFORMATION OR ADVICE GIVEN BY PRENTICE-HALL, INC., ITS DEALERS, DISTRIBUTORS, OR AGENTS SHALL CREATE A WARRANTY OR INCREASE THE SCOPE OF THIS WARRANTY.

SOME STATES DO NOT ALLOW THE EXCLUSION OF IMPLIED WARRANTIES, SO THE ABOVE EXCLUSION MAY NOT APPLY TO YOU. THIS WARRANTY GIVES YOU SPECIFIC LEGAL RIGHTS AND YOU MAY ALSO HAVE OTHER LEGAL RIGHTS THAT VARY FROM STATE TO STATE.

Pearson Education, Inc. does not warrant that the functions contained in the program will meet your requirements or that the operation of the program will be uninterrupted or error-free.

However, Pearson Education, Inc. warrants the diskette(s) or CD-ROM(s) on which the program is furnished to be free from defects in material and workmanship under normal use for a period of ninety (90) days from the date of delivery to you as evidenced by a copy of your receipt.

The program should not be relied on as the sole basis to solve a problem whose incorrect solution could result in injury to person or property. If the program is employed in such a manner, it is at the user's own risk and Pearson Education, Inc. explicitly disclaims all liability for such misuse.

LIMITATION OF REMEDIES

Pearson Education, Inc.'s entire liability and your exclusive remedy shall be:

1. the replacement of any diskette(s) or CD-ROM(s) not meeting Pearson Education, Inc.'s "LIMITED WARRANTY" and that is returned to Pearson Education, or
2. if Pearson Education is unable to deliver a replacement diskette(s) or CD-ROM(s) that is free of defects in materials or workmanship, you may terminate this agreement by returning the program.

IN NO EVENT WILL PRENTICE-HALL, INC. BE LIABLE TO YOU FOR ANY DAMAGES, INCLUDING ANY LOST PROFITS, LOST SAVINGS, OR OTHER INCIDENTAL OR CONSEQUENTIAL DAMAGES ARISING OUT OF THE USE OR INABILITY TO USE SUCH PROGRAM EVEN IF PRENTICE-HALL, INC. OR AN AUTHORIZED DISTRIBUTOR HAS BEEN ADVISED OF THE POSSIBILITY OF SUCH DAMAGES, OR FOR ANY CLAIM BY ANY OTHER PARTY.

SOME STATES DO NOT ALLOW FOR THE LIMITATION OR EXCLUSION OF LIABILITY FOR INCIDENTAL OR CONSEQUENTIAL DAMAGES, SO THE ABOVE LIMITATION OR EXCLUSION MAY NOT APPLY TO YOU.

GENERAL

You may not sublicense, assign, or transfer the license of the program. Any attempt to sublicense, assign or transfer any of the rights, duties, or obligations hereunder is void.

This Agreement will be governed by the laws of the State of New York.

Should you have any questions concerning this Agreement, you may contact Pearson Education, Inc. by writing to:

Director of New Media
Higher Education Division
Pearson Education, Inc.
One Lake Street
Upper Saddle River, NJ 07458

Should you have any questions concerning technical support, you may contact:

Product Support Department: Monday–Friday 8:00 A.M.–8:00 P.M. and Sunday 5:00 P.M.-12:00 A.M. (All times listed are Eastern). 1-800-677-6337

You can also get support by filling out the web form located at http://247.prenhall.com

YOU ACKNOWLEDGE THAT YOU HAVE READ THIS AGREEMENT, UNDERSTAND IT, AND AGREE TO BE BOUND BY ITS TERMS AND CONDITIONS. YOU FURTHER AGREE THAT IT IS THE COMPLETE AND EXCLUSIVE STATEMENT OF THE AGREEMENT BETWEEN US THAT SUPERSEDES ANY PROPOSAL OR PRIOR AGREEMENT, ORAL OR WRITTEN, AND ANY OTHER COMMUNICATIONS BETWEEN US RELATING TO THE SUBJECT MATTER OF THIS AGREEMENT.